Swami Lokeswarananda's
Eternal Wisdom of India

Swami Lokeswarananda's
Eternal Wisdom of India

Compiled by
Swami Chidrupananda

Rupa & Co

Copyright © Swami Chidrupananda 2010

Published 2010 by
Rupa Publications India Pvt. Ltd.
7/16, Ansari Road, Daryaganj
New Delhi 110 002

Sales Centres:
Allahabad Bengaluru Chandigarh
Chennai Hyderabad Jaipur Kathmandu
Kolkata Mumbai

All rights reserved.
No part of this publication may be reproduced, stored in a retrieval system, or transmitted, in any form or by any means, electronic, mechanical, photocopying, recording or otherwise, without the prior permission of the publishers.

The author asserts the moral right to be identified
as the author of this work.

Typeset by
Mindways Design
1410 Chiranjiv Tower
43 Nehru Place
New Delhi 110 019

Printed in India by
Nutech Photolithographers
B-240, Okhla Industrial Area, Phase-I,
New Delhi 110 020, India

*Published on the occasion of
Swami Lokeswarananda's Birth Centenary Year,
this volume
is dedicated
to all his admirers*

Contents

Preface	xi
Introduction	xiii

I. INDIA: PHILOSOPHY, CULTURE AND CIVILISATION — 1

The Message of India	3
Outlines of The Upanishads	10
The Brahma Sutras: A Brief Sketch	19
The Bhagavad Gita: An Introduction	26
The Ganga: Élan-vital and Soul of India	39
Some Special Features of Indian Civilisation	44
The Essence of Indian Culture	62
India and Democracy	71

II. Religion and Spirituality — 81

The Necessity of Prayer	83
The Effect of Meditation	89
Self-surrender	96
Philosophy of Peace	101
The Role of Religion in a Modern Secular State	106
Religion and Social Tension	115
Religious Harmony: An Impossible Dream?	119
Religion: Ends and Means	125
Religion: Man's Quest for Freedom	134
Science and Religion	155

III. Hinduism—The Eternal Religion — 167
What is Hinduism? — 169
Mantra: Its Meaning and Significance — 176
Mother Kali — 179
Mother Durga — 182
Durga Puja: Past and Present — 185
Kumari Puja — 190
Krishna — 195

IV. Buddhism—Fulfilment of Hinduism — 199
Are you a Buddhist? — 201
Re-reading Buddha in the Light of Swami Vivekananda — 206
Buddhism and Vedanta — 215
Buddham Saranam Gachhami — 248

V. Medieval Saints of India — 251
Jnaneswar — 253
Namadeva — 261
Ekanatha — 267
Dadu — 273
Mirabai — 282
Chaitanya — 287

VI. Sri Ramakrishna—The Soul of India — 295
Sri Ramakrishna — 297
Sri Ramakrishna's Earliest Appraiser: Srinivas — 306
Sri Ramakrishna as Portrayed in Brahmo Journals — 315
Sri Ramakrishna: Householder or Sannyasin? — 322
Sri Ramakrishna the Complete Teacher — 326
Sri Ramakrishna—Lived in and with God — 331
The Religion of Sri Ramakrishna — 341

VII.	SARADA DEVI—MOTHERHOOD EMBODIED	359
	Sarada Devi	361
	Sarada Devi—a Unique Personality	364
	Sarada Devi: The Highest Ideal of Womanhood	373
	Sarada Devi—The Universal Mother	382
	Sarada Devi: The Last of an Old Order or The Beginning of a New?	391
VIII.	SWAMI VIVEKANANDA—AS CONDENSED INDIA	403
	Swami Vivekananda and Indian Renaissance	405
	Swami Vivekananda and India's Spiritual Heritage	410
	Swami Vivekananda's Philosophy and Religion	443
	Swami Vivekananda's Approach to Social Work	451
	Swami Vlvekananda's Vision of a New Social Order	457
IX.	SISTER NIVEDITA AND INDIAN ART	465
	Sister Nivedita	467
	Nivedita and the Revival of Indian Art	470
	Nivedita's Contribution to the Development of Indian Art	482
X.	Men I Have Seen	495
	Swami Sivananda: A Direct Disciple of Sri Ramakrishna	497
	Swami Visuddhananda: An Apostle of God-awareness	508
	A Real Gentleman: Swami Madhavananda	517
	Gandhi, the Great Experimenter	534
	Netaji Subhas Bose in the Light of Swami Vivekananda	540
XI.	National Education and its Values	549
	Crisis in Education	551
	Education: Theories and Practice	559
	Ideals and Methods of National Education	587

Human Rights and Community Education ... 599
Learning Sanskrit ... 605

XII Monastic Order with a New Vision ... 607
The Sri Ramakrishna Movement ... 609
Monasticism with a New Vision ... 619
The Ideal of Service: In the Institutions of the Ramakrishna Mission ... 633

XIII Appendix ... 639
Swami Lokeswarananda: A Life Dedicated to Humanity ... 641

Preface

MUCH HAS ALREADY BEEN WRITTEN ABOUT INDIA AND HER RICH cultural heritage, and much more will be written in the future. But compilation of this particular volume is an effort to represent all facets of the eternal truth of India essentially through the prism of the lives of Sri Sri Ramakrishna Paramhansa Dev, the Holy Mother Sarada Devi and Swami Vivekananda, loved and revered by people all over the world for whom they were even more than what they said. Max Muller called Sri Ramakrishna 'not only a high-souled man, a real Mahatma, but a man of original thought'. Tolstoy declared Sri Ramakrishna 'a remarkable sage' while Christopher Isherwood believed he was a 'phenomenon'. Romain Rolland described him as 'the symphony of India'. As for Swami Vivekananda, when Romain Rolland wanted to learn more about India, Rabindranath Tagore reportedly told him, 'If you want to know India, study Vivekananda. In him everything is positive and nothing negative.' On the other hand, Sarada Devi represents the real motherhood of India. Sister Nivedita says, 'Sarada Devi, our Holy Mother as we call her, is only a simple Hindu woman, and yet, as I think, the greatest woman in the world today . . . the most wonderful thing of God—She is Sri Ramakrishna's own chalice of His Love for the world . . .'

Apart from these three great lives, this volume tries to represent India and her wisdom through her rich philosophy, civilisation, art, culture, education, religion, spirituality, monasticism, and biography of different saints and notable personalities.

Swami Lokeswarananda was an eminent monk of the Ramakrishna Mission and a brilliant spiritual leader of his time. A scholar, philosopher, educationist, writer, orator, art and music lover, he was, above all, a selfless seer who dedicated his life to the service of humanity. He was also the founder of the reputed Ramakrishna Mission Ashrama, Narendrapur, and spent the last twenty-five years of his life as the head of the renowned Ramakrishna Mission Institute of Culture in Calcutta.

As an authority on education and an able exponent of Indian philosophy and the philosophy of Sri Ramakrishna and Swami Vivekananda, Swami Lokeswarananda was invited by various Universities and other learned bodies within the country and abroad to speak on these subjects. His weekly lectures and discourses at the Institute of Culture on various subjects, mainly on Indian philosophy, drew large appreciative audiences.

He thus spread the message of Indian philosophy to the United States, Canada, Russia, Lithuania, Latvia, England, France, Germany, Switzerland, Italy, the Vatican, Japan, Malaysia, Thailand, Singapore, Mauritius, Sri Lanka, Bangladesh, and delivered lectures at the Vatican Radio and the Universities of Oxford, Cambridge, Berlin, and Moscow, to name a few.

The present volume has been compiled from his lectures as well as selected articles originally published in various Bengali and English periodicals. We hope that this volume will help in spreading the message of Swami Lokeswarananda in India and the world outside.

We gratefully acknowledge Ms Susan Walter's assistance during the initial stages of this project. We also owe much gratitude to all those who have helped, both directly and indirectly, to source material from different journals, transcribe from voice recorded data, and translated the Bengali lectures and articles (marked*) into English.

Swami Chidrupananda

Introduction

A COUNTRY IS CONSIDERED GREAT NEITHER BY THE NUMBER OF people living in it nor by the wealth it has, but by the character of its people. Swami Vivekananda used to say 'Man-making is my mission', which was all about moulding men of honesty, integrity and a sense of oneness with others. Character is built based on these basic eternal principles.

The sages of ancient India proclaimed two major ideals. The first was *Tat-tvam-asi*—'you are That' or 'you are that infinite Atman', i.e. the Supreme Divinity is within you and it is present everywhere and in all beings. The second was *Vasudhaiva kutumbakam*—'treat the whole world as your own.' This is the message of India and the collective message of eternal Vedanta philosophy. The idea of Vedanta is oneness, that we are all one. The Vedanta says that the goal of life is to realise that divinity is within oneself, i.e. that God is not up there in heaven, but here within us. The Vedanta shows us the way to realise that divinity lying hidden in us and apply it in our day-to-day lives through the path of Yoga, meditation and prayer.

Our ancient Indian scriptures exhort us to enjoy our wealth, health, beauty, power and family but not to be a slave to these things nor let these things enjoy us. They say, 'be in the world but not of the world.' This is what is meant by non-attachment. The Bhagavad Gita says, be in the world like a lotus leaf which floats on water but it does not itself get wet. Instead of saying 'I', let us learn to say 'You', i.e. referring to God. I belong to You. Everything here belongs to You. It is the 'You' that is permanent in this world while all else remains impermanent in this perishable world. Sri Ramakrishna always said, 'Turn your mind to God, only God.' Therefore, we say, 'God, this property is yours. I only look after it and take good care of it. This is the spirit with which we have to live in this world. Whatever I do, I do as a token of my love and my devotion to God. Indeed, work is worship and that should be our motto.

Always treat your body as the temple of God. He is right here in our hearts. Within us is the temple, the church, the holiest place. God is here. I can see Him. I can feel His presence. I worship Him. I love Him. I talk to Him. We make distinctions between the spiritual and the secular, but our scriptures say everything is spiritual. Everything I do, say and think is spiritual, provided I dedicate my action, my speech, my thought to God. Always feel that you are with God, in God, on God, God within, God without, God onward. God is with me all the time. You belong to God. He is your guardian, protector, friend, master, father, mother—in short, your everything.

However, every individual has to discover for himself the best way to approach God. To us, it is a matter of great fortune that there have been so many great souls down the ages who have shown us the path. The life of Sri Ramakrishna is especially relevant to our age and time. He says people are safe if they just depend upon God, if they love God, if they are able to think that God is their own. His message is nothing but to love God. I may be in the world but my mind should be with God. God is my dearest, my nearest. I will love you whether you love me or not. Swami Vivekananda used to talk of 'selfless love'—love for love's sake that declares I do not want anything in return; I love you because I love you. This is how we have to live in this world.

This volume is divided into twelve chapters, with an appendix briefly sketching the life and times of Swami Lokeswarananda. The first chapter begins with the message of India with its eternal Vedanta philosophy, culture, civilisation and democracy. The message of India is nothing but oneness. Every individual soul is nothing but Brahman. You are Brahman. You are God whether you are aware of it or not. You may not be aware of it but at least try to think that God exists, everything is God, that God is everywhere. This concept is established by the three pillars of Vedanta—the Upanishads, the Brahma Sutras, and the Bhagavad Gita, also known as the *prasthana traya* or the 'three paths' of Vedanta. The Upanishads (*Sruti prasthana*) are based on the scriptures, the Brahma Sutras (*Nyaya prasthana*) on logic, and the Bhagavad Gita (*Smriti prasthana*) on the *Smriti* or subsidiary scriptures. These scriptures teach us about self-knowledge.

The second chapter describes the ends and means of religion and spirituality. It tells us how to live with God, i.e. through prayer, meditation and selfless service. There is no distinction between secular and spiritual. Everything is spiritual. What does religion do? It helps man manifest this infinite power, this infinite purity. It transforms him, makes sinner a saint, man a superman. It tells man, 'Look, there is your goal, follow that goal, go on and on till you get there.' It tells him that he must be his own true self. It lends meaning to life. The real goal of life is freedom to its fullest. All religions promise this freedom, although they describe it differently. It is embodiment of this freedom which is called God. The goal of life is communion with the Supreme. It is a life of realisation, gnosis and an inner intuitive vision of God when man achieves absolute freedom and escapes from the blind servitude to ordinary experience.

The third chapter briefly outlines Hinduism, known as *sanatana dharma* or eternal religion because it does not derive from a single teacher but from many teachers, most of whom are nameless. Nothing, in fact, is known about those teachers except that they were very extraordinary persons, judging from the nature of their thought and experiences. The most important characteristic of those great souls was that they taught only that which they themselves had experienced, not in their day-to-day careworn existence, but in a state of superconsciousness they attained through many years of struggle. They did not guess at the truth, or speak about it from second-hand information or from what they had learnt through study and reasoning; they spoke about it only when they had known and verified it from their personal and direct experience. It is the direct, personal experience of many teachers over many hundreds of years which form the corpus of what is known as Veda. The knowledge which the Veda represents is accepted as valid because it is verified and verifiable through personal experience. It explains that the goal of life is to penetrate this veil of ignorance and realise that we all are one and the same, differing only in name and form, but not in substance; the goal of life is also to realise that however weak we may appear now, we are essentially one with Brahman and thus, divine and infinitely powerful. The body is subject to decay and death, but not the soul, which is beyond the pale of birth and death, joy and sorrow, being one with that Supreme Soul called Brahman.

But how do we overcome our ignorance and recognise our true nature—that we are all one and that we are one with Brahman? By both physical and mental disciplines, in other words, by practising Yogas. Hinduism preaches four Yogas, viz., *Karma* (work, selfless work), *Bhakti* (devotion), *Jnana* (knowledge, discrimination, etc.) and *Raja* Yoga, i.e. control of breath and such other methods of physical discipline by which perfect control of the mind is obtained.

The fourth chapter is a brief history of Buddhism as the fulfilment of Hinduism. Swami Vivekananda famously said that the Buddha was a rebel child of Hinduism. He says '*Shakya Muni* himself was a monk, and it was his glory that he had the large-heartedness to bring out the truths from the hidden Vedas and broadcast them all over the world.' Buddha was also the first 'missionary' in the history of religion, but he did not claim to preach anything new. He said he was preaching the Aryan Path, the eternal Dharma, only because Vedanta, with its literature mostly in Sanskrit, was a closed book to the common man. What Buddha taught was essentially a practical Vedanta that people would understand, independent of dogma, priesthood and sacrament. He presented Vedanta in a new garb, stripped of vague phrases, laying the greatest stress on reason and experience and taking care not to quote from the scriptures in order not to confuse and confound people.

The fifth chapter illustrates the teachings of some of the medieval saints of India, viz., Jnanesvara, Namadeva, Ekanatha, Saint Dadu, Mirabai and Chaitanya, which show us that the goal of life is realisation of God and that Truth is our religion and our God, that indeed, there is no alternative to truth and honesty.

The sixth chapter defines the religion of Sri Ramakrishna. Though he was born a Hindu, he practised other religions as well. It is important to note that Sri Ramakrishna's attitude towards other religions was not one of 'tolerance'. Sri Ramakrishna would say, 'Not tolerance, but acceptance; you have to accept. This is also a path leading to the goal; it may not be your path. Never mind, allow that man to follow his own path and respect him.' Sri Ramakrishna said that religion is not creed or dogma; what is important is not just worship or knowledge, but practice. Practice is important; being and becoming is the core of religion. You have to become aware of your inner divinity and manifest it in your daily life, in your conduct. That is what Sri Ramakrishna taught; that was his religion. And, he himself was its best exemplar.

The seventh chapter illustrates the unique and simple life of the Holy Mother Sarada Devi who is, in Sister Nivedita's words, 'the greatest ideal of Indian womanhood.' Sri Ramakrishna and Sarada Devi did not propagate any new religious doctrine; rather they showed everyone the basic principle of religion by living example, through their own lives and conduct.

The eighth chapter describes the philosophy of Swami Vivekananda. As an individual, he embraced the whole world, rising above all racial or geographical limitations. He taught three truths—

oneness of the world, divinity of man and harmony of religions. He used to say that the whole world is my home, I belong to the world. India and Truth were one and the same to him. He spoke at the Parliament of Religions at Chicago for the regeneration of India. Once, he declared, 'I am condensed India.' He wrote, 'May I be born again and again, and suffer thousands of miseries so that I may worship the only God that exists, the only God I believe in, the sum total of all souls; and above all, my God the wicked, my God the miserable, my God the poor of all races, of all species, is the special object of my worship.' He spoke about history, philosophy, religion, literature, and science, but the gist of whatever he taught was his supreme love and concern for man.

The ninth chapter details the contribution of Sister Nivedita (Miss Margaret Elizabeth Nobel) who gave herself wholeheartedly to India because she saw in India the personification of the universal Truth that is valid for all countries, all religions, all times. The supreme goal of life is to manifest that oneness in all our thoughts, words, and deeds. In adopting India as her own country, she was in fact adopting the whole world, because India's ancient ideals and truths are meant not for just one country, but for all people everywhere. It is well known that Sister Nivedita was one of the architects of the Indian renaissance, but we know very little about what she did specifically for the revival of Indian art. We know she considered art very important in any scheme of a country's development. In her essay 'The Function of Art in Shaping Nationality' she says, '. . . art offers us the opportunity of a great common speech, and its rebirth is essential to the up-building of the motherland.'

The tenth chapter is about Swami Lokeswarananda's reminiscences about the great men of India. He had the good fortune to meet in his lifetime, including his spiritual guru Swami Sivananda, eminent personalities like Mahatma Gandhi and Netaji Subhas Bose who influenced him in his early life and spiritual leaders such as Swami Visuddhananda and Swami Madhavananda.

Swami Vivekananda said, education is the panacea for all evil. The eleventh chapter is a compendium on the Indian education system—its role in theory and practice, its impact, goals and strategies toward the same. Education means many things but, first and foremost, it is about preparing a child to face the challenges of life. Education is about training in skills, thoughts, ideas, outlook and attitudes. There is no limit to a child's growth and development, and hence he must be taught the right kind of thoughts and attitudes. He is born with infinite potential and the business of education is to help him realise that potential. His growth should be all-embracing and help him evolve into a man of character in the truest sense of the term.

Chapter twelve discusses the Sri Ramakrishna Movement which has become a great power for unity, peace and happiness in India as well as outside. The strength of the Sri Ramakrishna Movement is not in money or men or organisation, but in the ideas it tries to present. In India, which is the home of numerous religious sects and communities, the idea of tolerance and brotherly feelings towards each other has great relevance. Another factor which contributes much to its popularity is the rational approach it brings to bear upon every vital problem of life. The Ramakrishna Movement lays great stress on selfless service as a means of God-realisation. The service it gives is open to all, irrespective of caste or creed or language.

The final chapter sketches the life and times of Swami Lokeswarananda which is sure to inspire the younger generation.

Swami Chidrupananda

Publisher's Note

Born on 19 April 1909, Swami Lokeswarananda was an eminent monk of the Ramakrishna Order and a distinguished thinker, accomplished orator and a gifted writer who wrote and edited several books in English and Bengali, all of which have received much appreciation from spiritual seekers all over the world. This book is a collection of the best of his writings and talks on the wisdom and heritage of India. We would like to express our sincere thanks to Swami Chidrupananda for his efforts in compiling this volume.

This is our humble homage to Swami Lokeswarananda on the occasion of his birth centenary year, and we hope that his deep insight into India's wisdom and heritage will help today's readers understand our country and her message better.

India: Philosophy, Culture and Civilisation

- *The Message of India*
- *Outlines of the Upanishads*
- *The Brahma Sutras: A Brief Sketch*
- *The Bhagavad Gita: An Introduction*
- *The Ganga: The Élan-vital and Soul of India*
- *Some Special Features of Indian Civilisation*
- *The Essence of Indian Culture*
- *India and Democracy*

The Message of India

WE OFTEN USE THE WORD *SPIRITUAL*, AND USE IT VERY LOOSELY. But what exactly is meant by *spiritual*? Suppose I say 'What I am doing is spiritual.' What do I mean? I mean that what I am doing is bringing me closer to God. Whether we are aware of it or not, or whether we admit it or not, whatever we do or say or think has an impact on our spiritual life.

But if we take the word 'spiritual' in the meaning in which it is used in the scriptures, then everything is spiritual and our work itself is worship. You may ask: 'Who is your authority? Who defines this for you?' This is what is said in the *Isa Upanishad*:

Isa vasyam idam sarvam
Yat kimca jagattyam jagat,
tena tyaktena bhunjitha
magridhah kasya sviddhanam.

Isavasyamidam sarvam means everything is covered by God, everything is controlled by God. *Jagatyam jagat kimca* means whatever there is in this ever changing world of names and forms is short-lived. Nothing in this world is permanent. God alone is permanent. Yet, God is underlying everything in this world. This is why nothing we do is secular. Everything is covered and controlled by God.

So, if the criterion is that everything is controlled by God then we can say that everything is spiritual. The scriptures say we should take this as the fundamental principle of our life. This is how we surrender to God. And, this is what our traditions are based on.

An important tradition of India is hospitality or the idea of *Athithi devo bhava*—where the guest is looked upon as God. Once when I was in Germany, I was giving a lecture on Indian culture in a university. Afterwards, one of the professors there came up to me and said: 'I have been in your country. I lived nineteen months in the Himalayas, and I never had to go without a meal. People fed me and looked after me. I didn't know their language and they didn't know my language, but we got on very well.'

Recently, a young American boy was here as our guest, and he said, 'I want to see India'. I gave him a letter of introduction, and with that he went round the country. In one place he hired a bicycle and went from one village to another. He visited many places, and when he came back, he said, 'I never missed a meal. Wherever I went, people looked after me. I was not able to speak their language, but they knew what I wanted—that I was hungry and needed food. So, they invited me to their homes and fed me. This is something I never experienced elsewhere.'

According to the Indian tradition: *Vasudhaiva kutumbakam*—the entire world is your home. The whole world is your home and everybody is your relative. Treat everybody as your friend and your relation, and treat the whole world as your home. It is good we still have this tradition—of worshipping a guest as God. It is a tradition we should try to cherish by all means.

Then, *Ma gridhah kasya svit dhanam*—do not covet anyone's wealth. We say Truth is God and God is Truth. In India, there is one thing you notice—people respect character. They respect people who are honest. A person may be poor. He may not be highly educated. It doesn't matter. Honesty is the hallmark of a good person, a pious person. And here in India, you find this sort of honesty in many people. They are good, simple humble people. Though they are very poor, they are not susceptible to any kind of temptation.

Recently, there was an incident that was reported in the papers. A young girl from a very poor family was walking along a road early one morning. She was alone. Perhaps she was searching for something. As she was walking along, she noticed a bundle of papers lying on the road. She picked it up and discovered that it was all money. How much money she didn't know. Maybe, she did not know how to count. But it was obvious to her that it was money. She looked at it, and then she was puzzled. She didn't know what to do with it. Finally, she decided to take it to the police station nearby. She handed the money to the officers there, saying, 'I found this lying on the road. I do not know who it belongs to.' And then she left.

This attitude is what is important—this ability to overcome temptation. The girl was very young. The newspaper said she was barely ten or twelve. But there was the bag of money, and she could have taken it home. At her age, she would know the value of money. But she did not take it. Instead, she turned it over to the police. You would be surprised to find that there are many people who are like that small girl. I do not know if it was her parents who taught her this kind of honesty, but they can be very proud of her.

That is the kind of tradition we have in India: be honest by all means. People often say, 'Honesty is the best policy,' but Gandhiji used to say, 'Honesty is the *only* policy.' We often try to justify dishonesty by saying that the people are very poor and needy. If they are dishonest it is because they come from poor families. But in India, there are lots of people who are needy—really needy—but they would never think of stealing or taking something that belongs to somebody else. This is our tradition. This is our culture.

Then, another tradition in India is that of renunciation. As the Isa Upanishad says: *Tena tyaktena bhunjitha*, strengthen yourself, strengthen the consciousness that the Lord is everywhere and in everything, through renunciation. *Tyaga eva hi sarvesam moksa sadhanam uttamam.* We are all seeking freedom. How do we attain it? Through the practice of renunciation. Renunciation does not mean poverty. Renunciation means that you are not interested in money, you are not interested in power, you are not interested in social status. You are only interested in Truth. You get the highest liberation, *moksam uttamam,* only by practising renunciation.

There is a story in the Katha Upanishad about a young boy named Nachiketa who asks Yama, the king of death, to teach him about the Self. Yama tries in various ways to avoid answering the question by tempting Nachiketa with other things. He says: 'Well, do you want to go to heaven? I can arrange it for you.' But Nachiketa says: 'No, I am not interested in heaven. I am not interested in money, or in any status or power. I am not interested in any of these things. I am only interested in Truth. I have come to you in all humility to know the Truth. Please, teach me the Truth.'

So, in India Truth is above everything. *Na hi satyat para dharmo*—nothing is higher than truth. Truth is the highest. It is freedom itself. It is immortality itself. And, how do you attain it? *Na karmana, na prajaya, na dhanena*—not by work, not by children, not by wealth. *Tyagena eka amrtatvam manasu*—only by renunciation do you attain immortality.

What do we mean by the word *renunciation*? Renunciation means choosing one thing over another. Suppose you are interested in classical music, and you love to go to music concerts. But sometimes other things may attract you. If you really want to go and hear the music, you must have the ability to reject everything else. So, renunciation is a matter of choosing. It is not that you have to be poor to know the Truth. You do not have to be poor. But you have to decide what you want. If you choose Truth and character and selflessness, then material things are no longer important to you. *Na dhanena*—I do not care for money. *Na prajaya*—I do not care for children. *Tyagena eka amrtatvam manasu*—only by renunciation will I attain immortality.

According to Sankara, *Brahma satyam jaganmithya, jivo brahmaiva naparah*—Brahman is real, the world is unreal, and the individual self is nothing but Brahman. You are Brahman. You are God whether you are aware of it or not. You may not be aware of it, but never mind. At least try to think that everything is God, that God is everywhere. God is up above. God is down below. God is on this side, and God is on that side, with me, without me, here, there, everywhere. God exists, and God is everywhere.

Jagat mithya—this world as we see it is *mithya*, unreal. It is unreal because it is always changing. It is short-lived. This world is always in a state of flux, always changing, never the same. But God is always there, always the same. *Brahma satyam*—Brahman is the reality. If there is any reality, it is Brahman. Brahman is real, the world is unreal, and the individual self is nothing but Brahman—this is a very simple declaration. You may say it is difficult to accept. Perhaps it is difficult to accept. But it is actually the simplest thing possible: God is everywhere. This concept gives us a sense of direction to our lives. We know we are answerable to God for everything we do.

Then comes the great message: *Tat tvam asi*—Thou art that. This is the final statement that a teacher gives—the last instruction. *Tat*—that. *Tvam asi*—thou art. You are God. You are talking of a God within you, within me, within every one of us. Now you have to realise it. That is what the saints and seers have said. *Tat tvam asi*—this great truth has been passed from one generation to another in India. Through years of hard life and discipline you prepare yourself to receive this message from your teacher, or perhaps even from your father. This is the tradition.

We do not learn this from books. Books cannot give us this knowledge. It is the life that speaks—the teacher's life. You see the kind of life your teacher lives, the kind of discipline he imposes on himself and the hardship he goes through. He is prepared to make any type of sacrifice in order to be a good teacher, and he has spent years helping you develop your character. After you have gone through years of disciplines, then at last, when the teacher thinks you are ready to receive the message, the crucial moment comes when he transmits the great truth: *Tattvamasi*—That thou art.

This is the Indian tradition. This is the truth which India has cherished through the centuries: *Tattvamasi*—Thou art that. Long ago, some sages experienced this great Truth, and they taught it to the next generation. From one generation to another generation, it has passed. This is what our ancestors have left for us—not money, not jewellery, not landed property, not political power. They have given us Truth.

As they communicated this great Truth they said: '*Srinvantu visve amrtasya putrah*—Hear me, O children of immortal bliss.' 'My children, children of immortal bliss—*amrtasya putrah*,' he says. *A ye dhamani divyani tasthu*—and those living in illumined regions.' Whoever they may be, whoever is prepared to receive this great message. *Vedahametam purusam mahantam aditya varnam tamasah parastat*—I have known that Great Being, who is beyond ignorance and is self-luminous like the sun. *Tameva Viditva atimrityumeti*—by knowing him one goes beyond death. *Nanyah pantha vidyateyanaya*—there is no other path, no other way, to attain the goal. This is the Truth—the Truth which is immortal, *amrita*. The teacher passes on this great Truth. But what do you do with it? First, you must receive it with great humility and care. Then you must preserve it and pass it on. But most of all, you must try to practise it and live up to it. Vedanta says, *Srotavya, mantavya, nidhidhyasitavya*. First, *srotavya*—hear about it. Then, *mantavya*—think about it again and again. And finally, *nidhidhyasitavya*—meditate on it. Go deeper and deeper and still deeper. Go deeper and deeper into yourself. Concentrate your mind on God, on Truth. God means Truth. Think of Truth, and think that this Truth is within you. Truth is not just a sound, or a word. It is something real. When you concentrate your mind on Truth, slowly you become one with Truth. You become Truth itself.

Then, the final message of the Indian tradition is the idea of oneness. We are all one. God exists. Where does he exist? In you, in me, in all of us. God exists everywhere, in everything. The Indian tradition is: We are all one. If I hurt you I hurt myself, and if you hurt me you hurt yourself. We are all together. This philosophy of oneness is something that has helped India survive. Over the centuries, we have lived together. We may belong to different religions. We may speak different languages, but we are still together, and we help each other. If one is in trouble, others will rush to give aid.

We are all one—that is the enduring message that India's ancient scholars and sages taught their children. This is the tradition we have inherited, and it is our duty to preserve it and cherish it and put it into practice. It is not just something to be talked about. We have to live it. Our lives will show our loyalty and our love for this tradition.

Outlines of The Upanishads

THE WORD *UPANISHAD* STANDS FOR 'KNOWLEDGE' AND THIS KNOWLEDGE is *Vedanta*, the conclusion (*anta*), or the essence, of the Vedas. The Upanishads, the Brahma Sutras, and the Bhagavad Gita—these are the three pillars of Vedanta. They are known as the *prasthana traya* of Vedanta, the 'three paths.' The Upanishads (*Sruti prasthana*) are based on the scriptures, the Brahma Sutras (*Nyaya prasthana*) on logic, and the Bhagavad Gita (*Smriti prasthana*) on the *smriti*, or subsidiary scriptures.

Vedanta is the knowledge of the Supreme Reality. It is not meant for everyone, and that is why it is also called *rahasya vidya* or *guhya vidya*, 'secret knowledge'. You have to be specially trained in order to receive this knowledge, and you have that training by going to a competent teacher, a teacher who himself has that knowledge. If the teacher does not know the subject, how can he teach it? Can a blind man lead another blind man?

The word 'Upanishad' is derived thus: *upa+ ni+ sad+ kvip*. *Upa* means going to a teacher, *ni* means totally, and *shad* means to destroy. So, the whole word means that you go to a competent teacher with great humility and receive from him that knowledge which totally destroys your ignorance. Ignorance of what? Ignorance of the Self, the Reality. This ignorance is the root of all our troubles. Somehow or the other we have to know the Self.

According to tradition, this knowledge is not derived from books. It is not book learning. This knowledge is transmitted from a teacher to his son or disciple. It is an experience, a direct and personal experience. The sense organs have nothing to do with this experience, because it is a transcendental experience, a revelation. What is revealed is Truth—an impersonal, universal, and eternal Truth. No one knows for certain who that lucky person was to whom this Truth was first revealed. Some names are mentioned, but very likely they are fictitious names. The names do not matter, however. It is the Truth that matters. This Truth is verified and verifiable. The Upanishads describe this Truth, but every individual has to verify it for himself. And, no pains are too great for this verification.

The Upanishads lie scattered in the Vedas, but they have been culled together and presented in book form. On the surface it seems as if there is no consistent doctrine or dogma in them. There may even seem to be contradictions. But if we scan them carefully, we will find an underlying idea common to all the Upanishads. This idea is that the Supreme Reality is the Self, and that the goal of life is to realise that Self. The Self is everywhere and in everything, and it is one and the same. It is unique. The oneness of things is the basic truth in the Upanishads. There are hints of dualism here and there, but the overriding idea is monism.

The brightest and most powerful exponent of the monistic philosophy of Vedanta was Sankara, who wrote commentaries on the most important Upanishads. Other commentators also have explained the texts of the Upanishads in their own way, and the philosophies thus set forth can be broadly classified as monism, qualified monism, pure monism, and dualism. The commentators were all good debaters, but Sankara was the best. His expositions hold the place of pride among all the commentaries. Some scholars say that there is really no contradiction between one school of philosophy and another. Each school represents a milestone pointing to a single goal, which is monism.

How many Upanishads are there? One view is that they are innumerable. Another view is that they are a hundred and eight. Whatever the exact number is, the following eleven Upanishads are identified as being the most important: Isa, Kena, Katha, Mundaka, Mandukya, Prasna, Taittiriya, Aitareya, Chandogya, Svetasvatara, and Brhadaranyaka.

THE QUALIFICATIONS OF A DISCIPLE

Upanishads teach you about the Self. But what is meant by the Self? What is it like? Where is it? Each of us says 'I'. This sense of I-ness is common to all—men, women, animals, insects, and even plants, according to Vedanta. This query about the Self is very interesting, but it is also very difficult. Most people think the Self is the body and mind together. They think it is a body—mind complex, and that it is subject to birth and death, pain and pleasure, and it is perishable.

The scriptures, however, say that the Self is neither the body nor the mind. It is something beyond both of them. It is beyond pleasure and pain, beyond birth and death. No wonder people are perplexed about it. Most of us are content if our basic needs are met, but there are some people who are impatient to know what the purpose of life is, what happens when a person dies, what the 'I' is, with which we are all obsessed, and how we can be permanently happy.

The Upanishads answer all these questions, but to understand the answers you have to go through a rigorous routine of self-discipline which purifies your mind. What is meant by 'self-discipline'? What does it include? First and foremost, you have to learn to discriminate between the real and the unreal: *nitya-anitya-vastu vivekah*. Next, you have to practise renunciation of the fruits of all actions in this world and in the world hereafter: *iha-amutra-phala-bhoga-viragah*. The third requirement is the acquisition of the six-fold wealth (samadi-satka) of self-restraint: *sama-dama-uparati-titiksa-samadhana-sraddha*—that is, restraint of the sense organs, forbearance, concentration of the mind, and respect for the scriptures and the teacher. The next requirement is *mumuksutvam*, the desire for liberation. It should be an intense desire—like the desire for water of a person whose head is on fire. You then go to a competent teacher and beg for instructions. By following his instructions and by studying the scriptures you eventually attain Self-knowledge. The essence of the teaching would be: Thou art that—that is, you and Brahman are the same. The oneness of the individual self with the Cosmic Self, the oneness of all things—this is the essence of the instruction, and this is the essence of the Upanishads. This One is known as *Brahman* (literally, 'the biggest') or the *Atman* (the Self). The word Brahman is used from the objective standpoint and Atman from the subjective standpoint.

THE INDIVIDUAL SELF AND THE COSMIC SELF

This 'I' is in reality the Cosmic Self. It is our innermost being. It is like a thread running through the pearls in a necklace. There is only one 'I', one 'Being', but out of ignorance we think there are many. We think we are separate individuals. And, because we think we are separate from each other, we use such words as 'I' and 'you', and we either love each other or hate each other. Each of us has a separate body and a separate mind, and we think these bodies and minds are real. But they are not real. They are superimpositions. It is like the moon with many reflections—one in the ocean, another in a lake, another in a glass of water, and so on. The individual selves are like these reflections. There is only One, but this One appears as many in terms of names and forms.

Another example often given is that of gold fashioned into different ornaments, such as a necklace, bangles, or ear-rings. The gold is always gold. The forms are merely superimpositions and they are not permanent. They can change. Similarly, the names and forms we have, and over which we make so much fuss, are not permanent. What is permanent in us is the Self, and that Self is one and the same. It is the Cosmic Self, which is everywhere, in every being.

You and I are one, but because we have separate names and forms and because we are attached to these names and forms we think we have separate identities and are separate selves. This sense of separateness is ignorance. The sense of oneness is knowledge. To think 'I' am this body and this mind is ignorance. To think 'I' am the Self is knowledge.

Brahman and Atman

According to the *Brhadaranyaka Upanishad*, King Janaka taught Gargi about Brahman thus: 'Those who know Brahman say that Brahman is *aksara*, immortal. It is neither fat nor thin; neither short nor tall ... There is nothing before or after it, nothing inside or outside of it.'

'It controls the sun ... also the heaven and the earth.'

'Try to know this Brahman. Without knowing it, performing rites and rituals serves no purpose. The person who dies without knowing Brahman is indeed unfortunate.'

In the same Upanishad, Yajnavalkya says: '[It] is not seen, but it can see everybody. You do not hear any sound from it, but it can hear every sound. It is unknowable, but it knows everything.'

The *Svetasvatara Upanishad* says: 'Both knowledge and ignorance are in Brahman. Under the influence of ignorance, the individual is born again and again and suffers. Again, the same individual attains immortality and liberation when he knows the Self.'

The *Mundaka Upanishad* says: 'There are two kinds of knowledge, *para* [higher] and *apara* [lower]. By the former you know Aksara Brahman and you are blessed. By the latter you merely attain scholarship.'

Knowledge of Brahman is the highest knowledge. It alone is knowledge; everything else is ignorance. This knowledge removes your bonds and makes you free. You then know your 'self' as the Self of all. Nothing can limit you. You are limitless. You are beyond time and space, beyond everything. You are Brahman. You are one with all.

Brahman, i.e. the Self, is the ground of the entire phenomenal world. The world is not real because it is a superimposition. It is like seeing a snake where there is only a rope in the dark. When the light comes, the snake disappears into the rope. Similarly, when knowledge comes, the world disappears into Brahman.

Vedanta defines the word *real* as that which is real *always*. That is, it must be real in the past, in the present, and in the future. The world is not real in that sense. It may be empirically real, but it is not absolutely real. It may be real at a given moment and in a given situation, but it is not real always and everywhere. Brahman alone answers to that description.

But why does the world appear to be real? Sri Ramakrishna used to say, 'The magician alone is real, and not the magic.' The world is like the magic of the magician. When you see the magic, you think it is real. Similarly, this world is an illusion created by the superimposition (*adhyaropa*) of something unreal (*avastu*) on something real (*vastu*). A discriminating person can easily discern which *vastu* is and which *avastu* is. He rejects the *avastu*. This discrimination is *apavada*.

There are two views about the relationship between Brahman and the world. One view, that of the dualists, is that Brahman has become the world. It is a real change (*parinamavada*). The other view, that of the non-dualists, is that the change is not real. It is only a false appearance (*vivartavada*). You see one thing for another, like seeing a snake where there is only a rope. The non-dualists say that Brahman does not create the world. It only manifests itself as the world. In the *Chandogya Upanishad*, Uddalaka says to his son Svetaketu: 'In the beginning *sat* [Existence, Brahman] alone was, without a second. It said to itself, "May I be many."' It then manifested itself as the manifold world, and it did this with the help of its own power, called *maya*. But this change from one to many is only in terms of names and forms. The one *sat* appears to be many because of the superimposition of many names and forms. *Sat* remains *sat*. The superimposition does not affect it.

Brahman, the Absolute, is *suddha chaitanya*, Pure Consciousness. It is *turiya*, the fourth. It is not manifest. When it wants to manifest itself, it seeks the help of *maya*. By *maya's* grace, Brahman then becomes *Isvara*, the Lord who controls everything. It is the material as well as the efficient cause of everything, the cause of all causes, the source from which everything arises and the end into which everything finally merges.

From *Isvara*, the elements then arise in their subtle state. These elements combine with one another and form fine bodies. The sum total of these fine bodies is known as *Hiranyagarbha*, *Sutratma*, or *Prana*. These bodies then become gross, and together they constitute *Vaisvanara*, or *Virat*. Virat includes the whole phenomenal world.

WHAT IS MAYA?

If the Self is my 'I', why do I not know it? Why do I think the body and the mind are my 'I'? Why do I think that the body and the mind, which are mere superimpositions and ephemeral (like the snake in the rope), are real? And, why do I take the phenomenal world as real and permanent when it also is a superimposition and is ephemeral? It is all because of *maya* (also called *avidya*, or ignorance). Because of ignorance we identify ourselves with the body and the mind. We think whatever happens to the body and the mind happens to us, and thus we are sometimes happy and sometimes unhappy, depending on the conditions of the body and the mind. Our condition is like that of a baby lion brought up by a flock of sheep. It thinks it is a sheep and behaves accordingly. One day, another lion comes there and teaches it its real identity. From then on, it is no longer a sheep. It is a lion.

So, is *maya* a separate entity? No, it is the power of Brahman. Like heat and fire, maya and Brahman are inseparable. Maya has two functions: it can conceal as well as distort. For instance, a patch of cloud can conceal the whole sun. That is how *maya* conceals the almighty Brahman. Then again, a patch of cloud hanging a little above the earth can make the sky, which has no colour of its own, appear to have colour. So also, *maya* can make the one Reality, Brahman, appear to be many.

It is difficult to explain maya. *Maya* is real and yet it is not real. What it is no one can say for sure. And, its ways are inscrutable. It is the power for good and it is also the power for evil. No one is outside its clutches. It casts a spell on us and we are mesmerised. As a result, we do things we should not do and pay heavily for our mistakes. We may be intelligent yet we are still ignorant. Ignorant of the Self. It is a ridiculous situation: we may know everything about this world, but we know nothing about our 'self,' our real identity. The scriptures and wise people say this is why we suffer. Somehow or other we have to know the Self. When we know the Self, *maya* withdraws and disappears into the Self. Just as the magician alone is real and the magic is unreal, similarly, Brahman alone is real and the world is unreal.

SELF-KNOWLEDGE

Self-knowledge means knowing the Self as Brahman. To know Brahman is to be Brahman. You have always been Brahman, but you did not know it. A veil of ignorance hid your identity, just as a patch of cloud hides the sun. This veil is removed when you go through rigorous self-discipline and also practise negating this world of names and forms (*neti, neti* i.e. not this, not this). You should also study the scriptures and receive instructions from a competent teacher. The teacher tells you, '*Tat tvam asi*, That thou art' that is, 'You are Brahman.' Then, suddenly, the Self reveals itself to you.

There is no experience comparable to the experience of Self-realisation. And, there is no way of describing it either. Only the fortunate one knows it. It is like a river plunging into the ocean, leaving behind its name and form. You were nobody compared to the infinite. Now you are the vast, infinite. You are All. So long you have always felt you were missing something. Now you feel you are full. You feel you are free. You are *Sat-Cit-Ananda* (Existence Absolute, Consciousness Absolute, and Bliss Absolute). You are the Absolute.

The Brahma Sutras: A Brief Sketch

BEFORE WE BEGIN OUR STUDY OF THE BRAHMA SUTRAS, WE SHOULD bear in mind that the whole philosophy of Vedanta is derived from three sources: the Upanishads, the Brahma Sutras, and the Bhagavad Gita. These are called the *prasthana traya*, the three pillars—the *sruti prasthana*, the *nyaya prasthana*, and the *smrti prasthana*, respectively.

When we speak of the Upanishads we are not referring to any particular books. We mean knowledge. What kind of knowledge? Knowledge of the Self, knowledge of the 'I'. 'Who am 'I'?' is the most fundamental question for all of us. We all say 'I', but who is this 'I'? Is it the body, the mind, the intellect or something else—or all these put together? Vedanta says that the reality behind this 'I' is Brahman. The word *Brahman* means 'the biggest.' Brahman is 'the biggest' because it is all-pervasive. It is everywhere. It is this 'I' in you, in me, in a tiny insect, in a plant, in everything.

These ideas about Brahman, or the Self, are scattered throughout the Vedas, but they are particularly discussed in the Upanishads. By the word *Upanishad* is meant the knowledge derived from a competent teacher who knows what this 'I' is. If you want to know the Truth, the reality, you have to have great yearning for it. You must want to know it immediately. It is as if your head is on fire and you cannot wait any longer. You then go to a teacher who himself has known the Truth. You must approach the teacher with great humility. It was customary in ancient days to carry some firewood to the teacher as a token of humility. The teachers would make offerings to a fire throughout the day, so they required much fuel. Fire stands for knowledge because it gives light. It removes the darkness of our ignorance and consumes all our weaknesses.

In those days, the students stayed with the teacher, serving him, watching his life, and studying. When the teacher becomes pleased with you, he teaches you. He gives you the knowledge that totally destroys your ignorance. The knowledge that he gives is called *sruti,* 'what is heard,' because it is given by word of mouth. The teacher gives the knowledge from his own realisation. The Upanishads, then, are called the *sruti prasthana.*

In the Upanishads, however, the teachings are not organised or systematised, and this can lead to confusion. Sometime, the same Upanishad will have verses on both non-dualism and dualism, Brahman without qualities and Brahman with qualities. It was at one time felt that the thoughts needed to be systematised and arranged logically, step by step. This was done then in the Brahma Sutras. They are called the *Nyaya prasthana,* which is based on logic. In the Brahma Sutras the thoughts have been arranged so well, it is as if the author has anticipated all our doubts and has cleared them one by one.

Then the *smrti prasthana* is the Bhagavad Gita. It forms part of the *Mahabharata,* the great Indian epic, which is sometimes referred to as the fifth Veda. It is called *smrti* because it is 'what is remembered.' Through the years, some people have been of the opinion that the Bhagavad Gita was originally an independent book which was later incorporated into the *Mahabharata.* Scholars have debated this point for a long time, and now the consensus of opinion is that the Gita was originally part of the *Mahabharata.* The Gita gives the essence of the Upanishads. There is a saying that if you imagine the Upanishads to be a cow, the Gita would be the milk.

The Brahma Sutras are said to have been written by Badarayana. We know very little about him, but the tradition is that Vyasa, who wrote the *Mahabharata* and Badarayana are the same person. Because Vyasa is supposed to have written the Brahma Sutras at Badarinarayana, or, as it is sometimes called, Badrikasrama, he is also called Badarayana. There is a dispute about this, however, some scholars saying that they are two different people. But the general consensus is that they are the same person.

The text we refer to as the Brahma Sutras is also known by other names, such as *Vedanta Sutras, Sariraka Sutras,* or *Bhiksu Sutras.* Why is it called Bhiksu Sutras? *Bhiksus* are monks. As they live by begging for their food *(bhiksa),* they are called *bhiksus.* This suggests that the path which the Brahma Sutras is going to show us is meant only for those who are prepared to renounce their home, to renounce the whole world—to renounce everything for the sake of this knowledge of the Self.

What is a sutra? The word *sutra* literally means a clue, a hint. Many times we find in the scriptures a statement which is very elaborate, with many words and phrases, but what is the essence of that statement? The essence of that statement is something which is clear, precise, and succinct.

A sutra is defined as a statement which has *alpaksaram*—that is, *alpa-aksaram,* very few words, the fewest possible words. It is concise and brief. Next, a sutra is *asandigdham,* without any ambiguity. Though it is concise, there should be no room for any doubt about its meaning. Again, it is *saravat*—full of meaning. There is not a word which is irrelevant. Every word, every syllable, in the sutra is meaningful. Then, it is *visvatamukham*—it deals with all aspects of the subject. Everything relevant is covered, and nothing is left out. *Astavam*—there is no repetition. And finally, *anavadyam*—it is beautiful. The language is flawless. These are the criteria of a sutra.

Altogether, there are five hundred and fifty-five sutras in the Brahma Sutras. They are very terse, and, in spite of what the definition of a sutra says, the Brahma Sutras are extremely difficult to understand and are capable of being interpreted in different ways. For this reason we need the help of a commentary *(bhasya).* There have been many commentaries written on the Brahma Sutras, each written according to the author's own school of thought, but there are five important ones. Sankara's is, of course, the most outstanding. As Sankara is a non-dualist, he interprets all the sutras to support the philosophy of non-dualism. He says that the Ultimate Reality is Brahman, which is *nirguna* (without qualities), *nirakara* (without form), *nirvisesa* (without distinctions)—one without a second.

Sankara's commentary is very popular and highly respected, but he has many opponents. One of them is Ramanuja, who says that Brahman is *saguna* (with qualities). According to him, Brahman is benign and compassionate and this whole universe is his guna, his quality. Ramanuja named his commentary *Bhasya,* after Lakshmi, the consort of Vishnu. His philosophy is called Visisthadvaita, or qualified monism.

Next is the philosophy called Dvaita, dualism, which was propounded by Madhva. Then, there is Nimbarka, whose philosophy is Dvaitadvaita—that is, different yet non-different. At one level Brahman and this world are different and at another level they are non-different. The fifth school is Suddhadvaita, pure non-dualism, which was taught by Vallabha. This philosophy, however, is not non-dualism in the sense of Sankara's non-dualism.

Throughout these commentaries there are many clashes. There is a constant battle of uncompromising wits. These philosophies are so subtle that a commentator alone is not enough to make things clear. We have to have yet further explanations and notes on those commentaries. These are called *karikas* or *vrttis* or *tikas*. For instance, one of the commentaries on Sankara's commentary is called *Bhamati*. It is by Vacaspati Misra. Unless you study *Bhamati*, you will find it difficult to understand Sankara.

Before Sankara begins his commentary, he raises the question: What is the relationship of this 'I' to the phenomenal world? Vedanta says that when we use such words as 'I' and 'you', we only betray our ignorance. 'I', 'you', 'this', 'that'—this is dualism. But Vedanta says there is no dualism; there is only one. Let us admit for the time being that Vedanta is right, that there is only one reality. Now, how do we explain the experience we have of diversity? We all see multiplicity—so many things, so many people, both living and non-living things. We all agree on that. But how do we explain it?

Vedanta says it is nothing but *adhyasa*, superimposition. They give an example: Suppose, you are going along a road at night. It is dark, and there is a rope lying across the road. Seeing something in the darkness, you think it is a snake and you start shouting, 'Snake! Snake!' Then, people from nearby houses come rushing out, bringing lights and sticks. When the light comes, you discover it is only a rope. You had merely superimposed the snake on the rope. All along it was nothing but a rope. This experience is a result of superimposition.

Or, suppose you are walking through a desert and you are very thirsty and are looking for some water. You start walking quickly spotting a distant oasis with a beautiful pond. You walk and walk but you never reach it. It was only a mirage. Similarly, when we see this diversity, this duality, it is nothing but a superimposition.

Again, when you watch a movie, the picture is projected on a screen. You see many things on the screen. You may see people talking to each other or fighting. There may be bloodshed—real blood, you say. But this experience is nothing but the result of superimposition. The screen is the substratum, and on the screen whatever pictures you see are superimposed. This is *adhyasa*.

Then the question arises, is Brahman—that is, Ultimate Reality which Vedanta says is one—transformed into this phenomenal world? Many schools of philosophy will say, Brahman (or God, or the Ultimate Reality) is actually transformed into this diversity. It is a real transformation. This is called *parinama*. It is like milk becoming curds, or like clay taking the form of a pot. Something is transformed into something else. Sankara, however, disagrees. He says it is not a real transformation. It is an apparent transformation—*vivarta*. The one Reality appears to be many due to superimposition, but the one remains one.

Now, there are a couple of objections that arise from the rope/snake illustration: What is superimposed on what? Is Brahman superimposed on the world, or is the world superimposed on Brahman? If Brahman is superimposed on the world, then the phenomenal world is the Reality, which Vedanta says is not so. But if the phenomenal world is superimposed on Brahman, then that would make Brahman an object, just as the rope is an object in the illustration. Yet, Vedanta says that Brahman is never an object, because Brahman is without any name, without any form, without any attributes, without any qualities.

Again, if the world is superimposed on Brahman, a previous experience of the world as real is necessary, just as a previous experience of a real snake is necessary in order to superimpose an illusory snake on a rope. How does Sankara justify his claim of superimposition against these arguments?

Sankara says that it is not necessary that Brahman be an object of perception (such as the rope) on which something is superimposed, because it is well known that we superimpose the idea of blueness on the sky, which we cannot see.

As to the other argument, it is not necessary, that the superimposed be something that we have had a real experience of. The thing that is superimposed could just as well be something that we have an illusory knowledge of. A real snake is not superimposed on the rope; it is an illusory snake. And, this superimposition is due to our own ignorance.

Brahman is the material cause as well as the efficient cause of the world. It alone is the creator, preserver, and destroyer of the world. But the world is not a creation in the sense that something is created out of nothing. The world is a phenomenal appearance of Brahman. Brahman is Pure Consciousness, Supreme, and the world is its projection. This projection comes about by Brahman's own power called *maya*.

Brahman is omnipotent, omniscient, and omnipresent. It is the only reality. There is nothing else but Brahman. If we see diversity, it is because of *avidya*, ignorance. But when we realise the true nature of Brahman—that is, when we know that Brahman is our own Self and that that Self is the Self of all—ignorance disappears. Then there is no more diversity; there is no enjoyer, no enjoyed, no world—nothing, all having merged into Brahman.

In reality there is no diversity. There is just one. This universe was never there; but you thought it was there and that it was an object of perception. But Brahman is always Brahman and is never affected by what we may experience.

The Bhagavad Gita: An Introduction

THE GITA IS A UNIVERSAL SCRIPTURE. IT CONTAINS THE ESSENCE OF all the Hindu scriptures. It presents the verbatim speeches of Lord Krishna. The Gita is said to be the song of God. So, it is given the same status as that of the Upanishads. If we compare the Upanishads to a cow, then the Gita is its milk. The Gita is also regarded as the Vedanta or the science of the Brahman. Of the three major pillars of Vedanta (the Upanishads, the Brahma sutras and the Bhagavad Gita), the Gita is a great favourite of all, because the Gita has very beautifully synthesised the four Yogas, viz., the Jnana Yoga, the Bhakti Yoga, the Karma Yoga and the Raja Yoga. Yoga means unification with God, with Brahman or with Atman. In the Gita, the Lord has discussed the ways to practise all these four Yogas. By following any one of the Yogas or by synthesising all the four Yogas, man can attain self-realisation. If one can understand the Gita well, one will also get a fine conception of the entire gamut of the Vedanta. However, it is not very easy to comprehend the deep spiritual meaning of the Gita, so one needs the help of annotations and commentaries to understand the Gita. Of the commentaries, the one given by Shankaracharya is quite logical and acceptable.

The teaching of the Gita is meant for all nations, for all types of people and for all times. Its aim is to advance men in the path of spirituality, to lead men from lower truth to higher truth. Therefore, the Gita opens in a tumultuous battlefield, where the extreme forms of violence, hatred and selfishness are manifested. It is in such dreary circumstances of life, that the Gita shows us light and gives us hope. It urges us to move ahead, it admonishes us not to stop or lag behind in dire and bleak situations of life, but to go ahead. So, the Gita is meant for all—the monks as well as the householders.

The Gita originated from a turbulent battlefield, which is also called the *Dharmakshetra* or the centre of virtuous activity. On one side there is virtue and on the other there is vice, and in between these two, Lord Krishna delivered the immortal speeches of the Gita. Arjuna is the interrogator; he interrogates the Lord on behalf of the entire humankind. His questions are those of the whole mankind—worldly as well as spiritual.

The Gita begins with the *Arjuna-Vishada-Yoga* or the grief of Arjuna; where Arjuna discerning the opponent camp cries—'I find my enemies consist of my dear ones, my kindred. How can I kill them just for the sake of my throne? This is impossible, this is a great sin! I can never do this. My limbs are failing me, I am sweating, my bow *Gandiva* is slipping from my hand, I can never commit such a heinous crime as slaughtering my kinsmen.' Saying so, Arjuna sank into his chariot, with a heavy heart.

Perceiving Arjuna's plight, Lord Krishna rebukes him. 'The war is about to begin and at this juncture from where did such dejection and ignorance come upon you? You are talking like an impious non-Aryan. This does not befit you. You are an Aryan—honest, intelligent and judicious. If you lose your sense, you will never be able to attain divinity. If you refuse to engage in the righteous warfare, you will earn disrepute. The world will hold you in reprobation and call you a coward. But you are a Kshatriya; a King!'

The Lord says, *klaibyam masma gamah partha naitat tvayyupapadyate, kshudram hridayadaurbalyam tyaktvottistha parantapa.* O Arjuna, do not yield to unmanliness. Do not be timid or a coward. This cowardice does not suit you. Cast off this mean faint-heartedness and get ready for the combat. You are refusing to fight in the war, just out of your cowardice and weakness, and you are talking of non-violence. This is not right. Non-violence is not meant for the timid and poltroon. If you have the strength to fight against your enemies, it is only then you have the right to forgive or pity them. Leave all your chicken-heartedness and get ready for the holy war. In this regard, Swami Vivekananda has said that 'one attains self-realisation sooner by playing football rather than by reading the Gita.' Swamiji meant to say that if you are weak, you will be unable to apprehend the real meaning of the scriptures. You will fail to realise the true significance of the Gita. You will have to acquire courage and strength first, because only a brave or courageous person can vow that, however difficult or inaccessible be the path of Truth, I will realise Him by any means.

In order to conceal his fear and weakness, Arjuna cites several reasons. He says, 'I do not want to enjoy the pleasures of a kingdom or wealth by slaying my kinsmen. I will incur great sin if I do so. It would be much better to eat the bread of beggary. Besides, I cannot decide what would be better. My heart is overwhelmed with grief at the thought of slaying my kindred. I am perplexed about my duty. So, my dear friend, I supplicate you. Say what is good for me. I am your disciple and have taken refuge in you. Please, advise me.'

Krishna smiles and says, 'You are giving reasons and talking just like the wise men, but you are mourning for those who should not be mourned for. The true wise men grieve neither for the living nor for the dead, for they know that the physical body is transitory, so it is useless to lament for it. The body will die one day but the spirit or the Atman will never die. The Atman is eternal and imperishable. One who is wise, i.e. one who has realised the Self never laments for birth or death unnecessarily.'

The Lord, in order to eradicate Arjuna's grief or ignorance, imparts instructions on self-realisation; for man's ignorance is wiped out on hearing it: What is Atman? We speak of birth and death—who is born and who is it that dies? *Na jayate, mriyate va kadachit*—The Atman is never born, nor does it die. The Hindus believe in this theory and do not consider themselves as mere physical bodies. What has birth has death also, that what has a beginning has an end too, but what has no beginning also has no end. The Atman or Self is such a being which is immortal and eternal. The ancient sages discovered this Truth. They said, *Na hanyate hanyamane sarire*—you may kill me, you may slay my body, break it but I shall not die. *Nainam chhindanti sastrani*—you cannot cut this Self with weapons, *Nainam dahati pavakah*—you cannot burn this with fire. *Na chainam kledayanti apah*—neither can you wet this with water. *Na sasayati marutah*—nor dry this with wind. What is the nature of this Self? *Nityah sarvagatah*—it is changeless and all-pervading. The Self is unmoving, immovable and eternal. *Avyaktah*—it cannot be expressed in words. *Achintyah*—it is beyond our speech and mind. The Self is unthinkable. *Avikaryah*—it is unchangeable. If you can realise this Self, then you will never have any reason to mourn.

Consoling Arjuna Krishna says, 'You should engage yourself in this war to establish truth, justice and virtue. This war is indispensable and inevitable. This is called *Prakriti*—our nature. It cannot be resisted. Arjuna, you are saying that you will not fight and this shows your vanity. You are saying all these out of your ego and self-conceit. But you are a *Kshatriya*. Your duty is to take part in war. To get engaged in war to fight is very natural for you. To fight in war is your duty. Do your duty casting away all your attachments. Even if you die by fighting in this war, you will reach heaven.'

'Do not imitate or follow others' dharma or duty. You said that you would beg but begging for your own is a sin. Begging is the duty of the mendicants and the Brahmans. But as *Kshatriya* and a king, begging is a vice for you. The duty of a *Kshatriya* is to fight and even if you fail to achieve any success in your dharma, that does not matter much. Better is one's own dharma, though imperfect, than the dharma of other well-performed. *Svadharme nidhanam sreya*—you may die performing your own duty or dharma, but that is deemed as the most honourable demise. *Tasmat uttistha Kaunteya yuddhaya kritanischaya*—therefore, O Arjuna, gather courage and firmly resolve to fight. Moreover, happiness and misery, profit and loss, victory and defeat all are equal to us. This is our ideal. Never deviate from this ideal.

So, Arjuna, your one and only duty at present is to take part in war and fight. You will not commit any sin if you do that. Moreover, you have the right only to work. *Karmanyevadhikaraste ma phalesu kadachana*—your right is to work only, but never to the fruits thereof. However, every action will produce some fruits but we should not enjoy them. We should work for the wellbeing of the others, for the welfare of the world. Our work and worship are not separate for us. Work is worship. Our life itself is worship, a prayer. As a result, our thoughts, our words and our actions are all devotional and spiritual. Nothing is secular in life, everything is spiritual.

The Gita teaches us to work without any attachment. However, this does not imply negligence of duty or fleeing from work. Action is the means and so we should work with the greatest possible diligence and care. We should not allow any flow or indolence to creep into our work and good consequences will follow automatically. Never work seeking any result for yourself. The Gita teaches us to remove our egoism, to win our narrow senses of 'I' and 'mine'. This is the goal of religion. Our mind gets purified by desireless action and when the mind gets purified, knowledge dawns on it spontaneously. Whether you are an ascetic or a householder, or a student or a businessman, self-realisation is possible through selfless or desireless work.

The common people are slaves of action. None can rest for even an instant, without performing any action. We are working all the time either with our body or with our mind or with out speech.

It is our *Prakriti* which forces us to act and since we must act, we should do it with dexterity. Our actions should not bind us. The Gita shows us the way to work, so that our action may lead to our liberation, without causing any bondage.

The greatest teaching of the Gita is to become *Sthitaprajna*, i.e. a man of steady wisdom. A *Sthitaprajna* is the ideal of our life. Happiness and misery, joy and sorrow—all will occur in our life in turn; but the person, who can treat joy and pain alike, who can accept both with indifference is said to be a man of steady wisdom. He is neither overwhelmed with joy nor moved with grief. Arjuna asks Krishna, 'How does a man of steady wisdom speak, how does he live or move about?'—*Sthitaprajnasya ka bhasa, Sthitadhi kim prabhaseta, kimasit, vrajeta kim.*

Here, Sthitaprajna means one whose wisdom rests in the Supreme Self. *Prajna* means wisdom. In other words, one who is firm or established in the sense that 'I am the Brahman' is a *Sthitaprajna*. His mind is always directed towards God. For him, nothing exists except God. The Supreme Self is his refuge and he is firmly established in the Supreme Self. Krishna speaks about a person of steady wisdom, that a man who has completely cast away all his longings and desires and remains absorbed only in the thoughts of the Supreme Self, in the Absolute Bliss, is said to be a *Sthitaprajna*. His happiness no longer depends on any external object. The aim of our life is to become a *Sthitaprajna*. This is called *Brahmi Sthiti* or having one's being in the Brahman or the Paramatman; to be established in the knowledge of the Supreme Self, with the sense that 'I am the Brahman.' This stage or condition is called *Jivanmukti*, i.e. liberation from all the fetters of life. This is a state of complete detachment—the person has neither fear nor anger. He has neither affection nor hatred and accepts both the pleasant and unpleasant situations equally. His senses remain under control and his mind remains occupied with the thoughts of the Almighty only, with himself established in the Absolute.

The principal teaching of the Vedanta is to attain self-realisation and the means to attain it is by synthesising the four Yogas; the Jnana Yoga or the way of knowledge; the Karma Yoga or the way of action; the Bhakti Yoga or the way of devotion and the Raja Yoga or the way of meditation. In the subsequent chapters of the Gita, all these Yogas have been discussed in detail.

Action implies selfless work. Such action purifies the mind and a pure mind realises the Self. So, Lord Krishna is telling Arjuna over and again that, 'We cannot while away a single moment without performing any action.' But how shall we work? *Tasmat asakta*—we shall have to work without any attachment. Sri Ramakrishna said, 'Oil your hands before breaking the jackfruit.' Here, oil means detachment. We should live in this world but must not allow it to seize us. We should live detached from the world. We should be in the world but not of the world. This should be our ideal, our motto. He who performs all his duties in this way, with detachment, attains the Supreme Soul. Work should be our worship, our devotion to attain God. As desireless action helps us to attain the Absolute Self, it is regarded as the Karma Yoga.

Krishna says to Arjuna, 'Whatsoever the superior and honourable persons do, it is followed by others. Arjuna, you are a king and a learned man. So, if you do not perform your duty or do what is just, then people will also do the same. How will you work? *Mayi sarvani karmani sannyasya adhyatmachetasa*—renounce all your actions and the fruits thereof to me, renounce everything to God, get rid of all hopes and egoism and perform your duties. Remove from your mind all weaknesses and with your mind centred on the Self perform your duties like a machine.'

After this, Krishna tells Arjuna about the Jnana Yoga or the way of knowledge. Simultaneously, he also reveals his real nature. He indicates that he is an incarnation of God. 'You are saying that your relatives will die, but do you know how many times you were born and died? I know how many times I have taken birth because

I am an incarnation of God. I have taken birth out of my own will. *Aja api san*—but I have never been born. *Avyay atma*—I am the unchanging Self. I have no birth or death. *Bhutanam Ishvarah api san*—I am God of all, directing and governing everybody. *Prakritim svamadhisthaya*—with the aid of my *maya*, I take birth or assume mortal frames again and again. Shankaracharya says, 'As if He assumes a body.' The Lord does not come into being as other do.

Yada yada hi dharmasya glanirbhavati bharata—whenever, O Arjuna, there take place the decline of virtue and rise of vice, *tadatmanam srijamyaham*—then I manifest Myself forth. Why do I do so? *Paritranaya sadhunam*—for the protection of the good and virtue. *Vinasaya cha duskritam*—for the destruction of the wicked and vice. *Dharma samsthapanarthaya sambhavami yuge yuge*—for the establishment of dharma or virtue I come into being in every age.

Besides, *ye yatha mam prapadyante*—in whatever way men worship me, according to their taste and will; I accept all their tributes. Everyone is following me. They are treading on my way. They are following me in different ways.

Then, Krishna says, *Yogayukta vishuddhatma vijitatma jitendriya*—always remain attached to God. He is inside you and also beyond. Always feel you are with God, in God, on God, God within, God without, God onward me. In this way, we remain concentrated in God. With the mind purified by devotion to performance of selfless action, and the body conquered and sense subdued; one who realises one's self, as the Self in all beings, is unified with God and though acting, one's action is not tainted.

The wise person always works but knows for certain that he is doing nothing at all. God is the Master and He is making him work. He is so deeply attached to God, that he feels that God is doing everything. He believes that he is only an instrument and the Lord Almighty is the operator. Though it appears to us that the knower of Truth or the wise man is performing all the worldly activities like seeing, hearing, touching, smelling, eating, going, sleeping, breathing, yet he is convinced that he is not the doer of any action. He knows that it is his senses which are working and not he. His work centres around God and He is making his devotee perform all the duties.

If we work with this ideal, what will be the result? *Lipyate na sa papena*—no sin will ever touch you, *Padmapatramivaambhasa*—just like a lotus leaf. The lotus leaf floats on water yet the leaf never gets wet. Likewise, we should execute all our worldly duties but have the knowledge that we are not doing anything.

Now, the question is, will anyone in this world help me to progress in life? In the Gita, the Lord while discussing the way of meditation or the Dhyana Yoga says, the mind can be freed from all desires and made calm by way of meditation. The entire mind should be directed towards God and thus will one attain the state of Samadhi or spiritual ecstasy. But this can be achieved only through assiduous practice by oneself. *Uddharedatmanatmanam*—a man should uplift himself by himself, through sharpening his mind and intellect. He should never cause his own downfall. For this 'self' is the friend of oneself and the 'self' is the enemy of oneself. I am the maker of my own fate. I can make myself wise and also I can make myself a sinner. So, no one should ever consider oneself to be small, weak and powerless. Swami Vivekananda said, 'Only those who are cowardly and stupid speak of fate. But people who are strong and courageous say that they will build their own fate and fortune.'

This Yoga is not possible in a day. *Abhyasayogayuktena*—it is only through arduous practice of meditation that one gets unified with God. The Lord says, *Yunjanneva*—one who is always united with me is called Yogi. *Sadatmanam niyatamanasa*—he always keeps his mind under control. *Shantim nirvana-paramam*—he gets infinite peace. 'Nirvana' is Lord's real nature. '*Nirvana*' or '*Moksha*' means liberation. When one attains this, all his desires get extinguished and he attains eternal peace. A Yogi, who has realised the Supreme Self, always remains absorbed in me, i.e. in God. As a lamp, when kept in a place, sheltered from the wind, does not flicker, so also a Yogi's subdued mind, practising concentration in the Self, remains calm and motionless in the contemplation of God.

When a Yogi realises the Atman or the Brahman, i.e. The Highest Self, he attains Supreme knowledge and infinite bliss. Nothing else is left for him to be known or to be enjoyed. Nothing is superior to self-realisation. The Gita says, to know the Brahman or the Self is to be the Brahman. One who has realised the Supreme Self becomes free from the worldly bondage.

Under such a condition, a man sees the God not only in himself but also outside himself. *Yo mam pasyati sarvatra sarvam cha mayi pasyati*—he sees Me in everything and again sees everything in Me. *Tasyaham na pranasyami*—I am never away from his mind for a single moment, and *sa cha me na pranasyati*—I too never forget him. In this regard Sri Ramakrishna says, 'You can see God when you close your eyes, and cannot you see Him when you open them?' This implies the vision of God in all things and everywhere.

God is one and again He has become many. Every form is actually His form. In fact, this world is His manifestation. The Lord says, 'One who worships Me, sees Me, under all conditions—*Sa yogi mayi vartate*—that worshipper gets absorbed in Me and gets united with Me. Even, one who at the time of death, meditates on Me, gets united with God.' The Lord says, *antakale cha mameva smaran muktva kalevaram yah prayati*—he, who chants My name at the time of death comes to Me and gets absorbed in My Being. But this is possible only through constant practice. If we chant the Master's name all the time in our life, then only at the time of death, His holy name will come to our mind spontaneously. But if we engage our mind always in worldly affairs, then while dying too the same thoughts will occur in our mind. Whatever is remembered, at the end, that alone is realised by one, because of one's constant thought of that object. Hence, the Lord says, *tasmat sarvesu kalesu mamanusmara*—therefore, at all times, constantly think of Me. Surrender your mind and your intellect to Me. Then only you will reach Me. There is no doubt about it.

Actually, our mind should be fully occupied with the thoughts of the Divine Lord. It should not be allowed to stray anywhere other than God. Irrespective of whether You love me or not, O Almighty, O God, I love You alone. God wants nothing from us but only our love. God says, *patram pushpam phalam toyam*—He wants us to worship Him with only a leaf, a flower, a fruit, water and nothing else. He does not desire gold or riches from us. He only wants our whole-hearted devotion and love for Him.

The Lord says *bhakti upahritam*—whatever a devotee offers to the Lord with love and devotion, *tadaham asnami*—He accepts that. Whatever we do is a worship of God. *Yat karosi yadasnasi yajjuhosi dadasi yat*—whatever you do, whatever you eat, whatever you offer or give away, *yat tapasyasi*—whatever austerity you practise, O Arjuna, *tat kurusva madarpanam*—offer all those to Me. Our body, our mind, our life, all whatever we are doing and all whatever we possess, should be offered to God.

The Lord says, *manmana bhava*—give your mind to Me. Constantly think about Me and My activities, *madbhakta*—love Me, *madyaji*—desire Me. Do not desire anything else in this world. *Mam namaskuru*—pray to Me and bow down to Me. *Mameva esyasi*—then you will get Me and at the end of your life you will get united with Me.

Krishna wishes to consolidate Arjuna's faith in Him, by revealing His real nature to His beloved disciple. Usually we do not believe anything at once. Our mind is generally very much suspicious. So, Krishna reveals His all pervading nature to Arjuna. Krishna says 'I am giving you super-sensuous sight, so that you may perceive me—*Divyam dadami te chakshu*. Behold my Supreme Form.

On seeing Krishna's Universal Form, Arjuna was left speechless. He says, *pasyami devamstava deva dehe*—I find all the Gods and Goddesses merging in you. All the animals and everything of the world are entering you. All the hands are yours, all the eyes are yours, all the mouths are yours, everything is you. You assume countless forms. *Na antam na madhyam na punastavadim*—you have no beginning, no middle and no end. Seeing your marvellous and awe-inspiring form the three worlds are trembling with fear.

At length, Arjuna says, 'What a great mistake I have committed considering you as my friend, I addressed you as "*Sakha*", I called you by name, I did not know who you are. Please forgive me. I am ignorant, so I did not realise your real nature. I am very terrified to see you in this form. Please, get back to your earlier form. I cannot tolerate your present form anymore.'

Krishna returns from His Divine Form to His earlier human form. Seeing the Lord in human form Arjuna becomes glad. He said, 'Having seen your gentle human form, my thoughts are now composed and I am restored to my nature.' The Lord says, 'He who works for Me alone without any desire and has Me as his goal, who is devoted to Me and has no attachment towards his relatives, has no enmity towards any creature, nor even in his enemies; such a man alone attains Me.'

Krishna again exhorts Arjuna, to get rid of egoism and self-conceit. Your duty is to fight now. Engage yourself in this holy war. Besides, vain is your resolve, your *Prakriti* will constrain you to combat. Offering all your senses of 'I' and 'mine' to Me, do your duty. Remember that you are my instrument only. *Isvara sarvabhutanam hriddese Arjuna tisthati*—the Lord dwells in the heart of all beings. He is causing all beings to act like tools. He is the operator and all the beings are his machines. He is working on us by the power of His Maya.

The Lord then says to Arjuna 'Now, I shall share with you a profound truth for your own good, because you are my beloved. Do not go for excessive argument or deliberation. *Manmana bhava*—always occupy your mind with me, be devoted to me, worship me, bow down to me. If you can thus engross your mind with me then only you will attain me. *Satyam te pratijane*—this is my promise to you, believe Me.

The Lord speaks of *sharanagati* or refuge in the Supreme Self. *Sarva dharman parityajya mamekam saranam vraja*—relinquishing all dharma, i.e. all kinds of deliberation, all actions, righteous and unrighteous, take refuge in Me alone. I will liberate you from all sins, do not worry or fear.

Receiving such assurance and promise from the Lord, Arjuna says 'My delusion is destroyed.' *Tvatprasadat*—By your grace now my ignorance is removed and I am firm. *Gatasandehah*—all my doubts have evaporated. From now onwards, I shall abide by Your words.

The Gita closes with the speech of Sanjaya, the narrator of the Gita to the blind king Dhritarashtra. He says, *Yatra yogesvarah Krishno yatra Partho dhanudharah*—where Lord Krishna Himself is present and where an archer like Partha (Arjuna) exists, truth, prosperity, victory, success, progress and justice will definitely be there—this is my firm conviction.'

The Ganga: Élan-vital and Soul of India

SRI RAMAKRISHNA USED TO SAY, '*GANGA-VARI* IS *BRAHMA-VARI*'—GANGA water is as good as Brahman itself. Brahman is without any quality and form, but if we need to imagine it in the shape of a river then it is Ganga itself. So, Ganga is equivalent to Brahman. Like Brahman, Ganga is very near, dear and pure. It is the essence and source of everything like Brahman. This was not only Sri Ramakrishna's faith, but the faith of all Hindus. To touch Ganga, to see Ganga, to bathe in Ganga—all these banish sins and help to attain salvation. It is the eternal Hindu belief. Valmiki said in his *Ganga-ashtakam strotram*—'Mother, you are the beauty of the world and the victory banner of heaven. I pray to you that I may live on your bank, drink your water, see your ripples, remember your name and leave my body while seeing you.' Shankaracharya in one of his verses said, 'Mother, you are Goddess Ganga, your abode is in the locks of lord Shiva, you rescue the sinner, you are mother Bhuvaneswari, even the Vedas speak of your divine power, and anybody who has faith in you and worships you can easily attain salvation.' In spite of being a monist, Sankara had made this remark on Ganga.

The word 'Ganga' is derived from—Gam+*Gan*+*Tap*. *Gamyate Brahmapadamanaya*—by whom we attain the Brahman is Ganga. Ganga has numerous names. Some of them are—Vishnupadi;

Bhagirathi, Tirtharaja, Harashekhara, Suradhuni, Alakananda, Jahnavi, etc. As if Ganga is drenched in spirituality, continuously flowing. Our life is also flowing onward, constantly moving forward. One who is not flowing is dead. That is the reason why scriptures say *Charaiveti*. But flowing for what? In search of the infinite, what we call God, the Brahman or the Atman. I am moving towards that Atman. Who am I? Small? Finite? Or, the Supreme Being? The Infinite. Even the possibility of that Supreme Being is inside me, but I am unaware of it. It is sleeping within me. It has to be awakened. Life is the arduous practice of revealing the infinite power that is within us in the form of a seed. To start with it is a small humble stream but after travelling a long distance, after a prolonged period of penance, it ultimately unites with the Infinite. That Infinite is its aim when it reaches the sea. So, expansion is life, contraction is death. Our aim is to expand, to reach that Infinite Self. As Ganga merges with the sea, it becomes one with it and our aim is also to unite with that Supreme Being, that Brahman, that is, to become infinite. *Brahma veda Brahmaiva bhavati.* The arduous endeavour of a being is the arduous practice for infinite. River Ganga is an instance that inspires, telling, 'learn from me, be as great as me.' This is the message of India, the eternal Indian message. As Ganga teaches us this message of courage and self-confidence, Ganga is also known as the 'rescuer of all who sin.' That is one who thinks oneself a sinner and weak, Ganga reminds one of one's infinite strength. And, that one should not lose hope but work hard to utilise that strength. In the true sense man is not a sinner. He is great but he has forgotten it.

Ganga is the soul of India. We cannot think of India without Ganga. From time immemorial Ganga is being worshipped in this land. It is mentioned in *Rig Veda, Katyayan Sautrasutra, Satapath Brahmana* and other ancient Hindu texts. We also find Ganga mentioned in *Puranas, Upa-Puranas* and history. There are numerous stories regarding Ganga. In Valmiki's *Ramayana*, Ganga is the daughter of the Himalayas. As long as Himalaya exists, Ganga exists and hence India exists. India is the offspring of Himalaya and Ganga. As the spirituality of India is nourished by the Himalayas, so is the river Ganga. Himalaya is divine, meditative, Self-absorbed, as though it is the yogi engrossed in meditation. And, river Ganga is carrying the holy message of the Himalaya. She is like the messenger from the abode of Gods, so we also know her by the mythical name of *Mandakini* and *Suradhani*. But what message has she carried on to this mortal earth? The message of renunciation. The message, that only through the path of renunciation one attains salvation. That is the reason, mostly in her course, she is clad in saffron. She is saffron in colour. Shun the transitory and the impermanent and search for what is eternal and infinite—this is the perpetual Indian message. And, Ganga is the embodiment of this eternal message. This is the reason, why Ganga is the purest of all waters, greatest of all pilgrimages and the presence of Ganga is so much desired; a land without Ganga is barren and so a person on his deathbed happily leaves his mortal body taking Ganga water in his mouth. If Ganga dries up the world will become extinct—as mentioned in *Brahma Purana*. We find innumerable pilgrims, temples and dwelling places of sadhus and saints on the banks of river Ganga.

Ganga originates from the heart of the Himalayas, the Gangotri. Travelling 1556 miles she unites with the Bay of Bengal. She is the daughter of Himalaya, but the gods took her to heaven, they also wished her company. The gods prayed for her presence in heaven which Himalaya could not deny. On the other hand, the sons of king Sagara, under the curse of sage Kapila, were burnt down to ashes. They could only be revived if they could receive the holy touch of Ganga. But the Ganga is in heaven. Then the question arose, who would bring her down to earth? So, Bhagirath, a descendant of the Sagara family, did penance to bring Ganga down to this earth as a saviour of his ancestors. Thus, Ganga is the object of endeavour. Just like Truth and God. She can be obtained through austerity.

But who would hold Ganga as she descends to earth from heaven? Only Lord Siva had the potentiality and he did that. He held her on his head. But the worship place of sage Jahnu was drowned in her current. And, out of rage he drank the river Ganga in a gulp. It was possible because he was an austere sage. And, only when the gods started singing hymns praising and glorifying him, that he released Ganga through his ear. It is said, the wrath of a sage is like a stroke of water. From then onwards, Ganga is also known by the name *Jahnavi*. Ganga is like the daughter of Bhagirath. Thus, she is also known by the name *Bhagirathi*. Heaven, Nether-World and Earth—in all three worlds Ganga is flowing. So, she is also called *Tripathaga*. None of the worlds want to be devoid of Ganga.

Ganga is four-armed, fair-complexioned, and is riding on a crocodile. She is worshipped especially on the tenth day of the lunar fortnight of *Jaistha*. If anybody takes bath in the Ganga on this day he or she will be sanctified. This day is called *Dashahara*. Ganga is also known by this name. Impurity can never touch Ganga. Her sanctity is omnipotent and omnipresent. Ganga could be smeared with mud, polluted with impurities and factory wastes, yet her sanctifying power remains unimpaired. Ganga is always pure, that is, she is the way to attain Brahman. The ashes of the dead person become sanctified by the touch of the Ganga and he or she attains heaven.

Ganga is not only our spiritual guide but also helps us in our day-to-day life. From the Himalayas to the Bay of Bengal, Ganga makes this huge part of our motherland fertile. Her banks are green with crops, many cities, towns, ports are built up on its bank. Boats and steamers carrying people and their goods cross Ganga. She is really the strength of India. Her banks are so beautiful; full of greenery and her beauty is changing every now and then. She is ever old as well as ever young. She is our mother, our saviour, our strength of life and the very soul of India. The last will of Jawaharlal Nehru comes to the mind. He held Ganga as the symbol of Indian civilisation and culture. This civilisation and culture are age-old and infinite. Though every day it is changing, it is very old from time immemorial. Ganga is also like that. So, it was his last wish that his ashes should be immersed in the Ganga. And, this might be the reason why all Indians wish to unite with Ganga from time immemorial.

Some Special Features of Indian Civilisation

THE TOPIC IS RATHER DIFFICULT. AND, IF IT IS DIFFICULT, IT IS ALSO controversial. There was a time when many Western people thought India was not a civilised country. But there were among Western people some who again thought that India was highly civilised. To our surprise, these western scholars began to say Indian civilisation is very advanced. I say 'to our surprise' because many of our own people thought we are not civilised. We thought civilisation meant big buildings, clean roads, good food, high standard of material well-being. Of course, a civilised country should not be poor. But, suppose, a civilised country is poor for some reason or other, could you say the country is uncivilised?

India had passed through phases when it was materially poor. If we accept material prosperity is the only hallmark of civilisation, then India was not civilised. But if you think civilisation means mental and spiritual development, India was very much civilised. Compared to United States of America, India was definitely a poor country in terms of material standard.

Some time ago, a few Soviet intellectuals came to India. As they came out of the Dum Dum Airport they felt—so they told us—as if they had arrived on a new planet. The squalor and filth all around gave them such an impression. People like them judge your civilisation by the amount of clothing you use and the quantity of food you consume. But how about your character? How about your moral standard and manners? How do you deal with other people? How honest are you? How far will you go out of your way to help others?

Let us see what the criteria of civilisation are, what kind of civilisation India has, and, what its special features are?

By material standard, India, of course, is not a civilised country. Maybe Pakistan, Singapore, or Bangladesh are civilised. But if civilisation means a certain amount of mental and intellectual development, if that is the criterion, we, of course, are a highly civilised people.

If we go back to Vedic times we will understand this point very clearly. Vedas do not mean some books. It is rather a body of knowledge which always governed the course of life of the people of this land. What kind of knowledge? There was a time when people of this country had a remarkable level of thinking. In the Upanishads, the *Puranas*, Bhagavad Gita and *Bhagavat* the level of thinking, the level of argumentation, the incisive level of questioning in grappling with the question of natural phenomenon, is really baffling. If you bear all these aspects in your mind, how can you tell India is not a civilised country? If you go by the accounts of foreign travellers like Fa-Hien, Hieu-en Tsang and others who had recorded the impressions of their stay in India and who had opined that India was a remarkable country, can you reasonably say that India is not a civilised country?

We do not have connected accounts. It is something related to our process of thinking, related to our mental attitude. We are more concerned with attitude than physical or material achievements. Therefore, Indian history is not the history of persons, events, battles, territorial conquests or violence. It is a history of ideas, evolution of mental attitudes and ethos. This is the peculiarity of the Indian civilisation.

You cannot tell when this civilisation dawned. No one can date it either. It seems it is the source of civilisations of the entire world, for it has raised human thinking to the highest level.

There were Greek, Roman and other civilisations where you had records of their achievements. But those civilisations are now extinct. Maybe they have their vestiges in European Culture. Because European Culture is, after all, nothing but the progeny of the Greek and Roman civilisation. But where is the Greek civilisation? At one time it reached great heights. But now you trace its ruins in a few places. That is all.

But the Indian civilisation is still dynamic and going strong. If somebody who had lived in India 5000 years ago, who was familiar with the conditions of the then India, comes back now, if that is possible, what would he see in India? He would find India has remained the same. He would find India has maintained her cultural and moral life at the same Himalayan level. Is it not surprising?

Nonetheless, there have been changes. But what is remarkable is that she adapted herself to the new situation. She realised if she was to survive she must accept the changes. New races, invaders, marauders came to loot her and they went away with their booty. But India remained India. India's style of thinking remained unchanged.

For example, look at our dress. We are not wearing the kind of dress we used, say, fifty or hundred years ago. But our ways of thinking, outlook of life, approach and our philosophy have never changed. It is the same civilisation. Certain truths were discovered by our sages, which inspired our civilisation. They are at the root of our civilisation. Those truths are eternal. So India, which represents those truths, is also eternal.

Dr S. Radhakrishnan once said 'India is an idea.' It is a way of life, a way of looking at things, what interpretations you put around the natural phenomenon, meaning of life, on your obligation to society and so on. The truths our sages discovered are still valid. It is difficult to say when they were discovered. But they are very much alive. Our government after Independence, therefore, accepted the ageless motto—*Satyameva Jayate.* That is, Truth always triumphs. People collectively tried to live up to this ideal. Because the meaning of life, according to India, is the search for Truth. If I am alive, that is for this purpose only and not for enjoying sensual pleasures. Nothing is more sacred than this quest.

There are certain features of the Indian civilisation which you do not find anywhere. China's civilisation is also very old. No one knows if that is older than India's. But Indian civilisation is unique in respect of its unbroken continuity. The essence of our civilisation is the same.

For instance, we always accept others. We are a people who are ready to welcome new ideas, always prepared to have a close look at anything that came from abroad. If we find they are good and valid, we absorb and assimilate them.

India was attacked by various races from time to time, by the Huns, the Mongols, the Greeks, and the Persians and so on. At first they came to rob. But at last they accepted this country as their own homeland. And, we welcomed them all. Today they have merged with the Indian identity. When you talk of the Indian identity, it is composite.

In India, if you are not cultured by my standard, you may be referred to as non-Aryan and vice versa. It has, however, no ethnic connotation.

It is also surprising that those who came from outside accepted our ethos, our philosophy of life. There is a distinct Indianness, which characterises our people, no matter whether they are Hindu, Muslim, Aryan or non-Aryan. We better stop using these terms. Today, it is very difficult to say who is a Hindu and who is a Muslim. True, there are still some communities which retain their separate identity. But they are a minority.

We always loved to assimilate. But our basic thoughts and philosophy have remained the same. Surprisingly, this basic approach to life, which, India always preserved, proved to be a factor that always sustained India.

If you say Indian civilisation always remained other-worldly by stressing moral values, if you say Indians turned away from the battle of life to attain things of the other world, if you argue that Indians ignored starvation on earth, to be too much occupied with esoteric and spiritual questions, it is not true. A well-known historian said that not only in art, literature, philosophy and religion, India made tremendous progress over the centuries on all fronts including material ones. This prompted Swami Vivekananda to tell a group of people in London that 'You people tell you are civilised. But will you please tell me, how long have you become civilised? The other day you kept robbing other people. Today you have accumulated wealth and you say you are aristocrats, as if aristocracy is synonymous with wealth! But in India, aristocracy is something, which is related to character. If you are a man of character, deeply religious, then you are really an aristocrat. Aristocrat certainly does not mean being rich. A rich man is not necessarily a good man.'

Sister Nivedita said in a similar vein: 'India, when you were completely absorbed in meditation, when you were thinking of God, of higher things, you were taken unawares by a band of robbers. Today, the British and other colonial powers say you are a subject nation'.

Swami Vivekananda referred to the same phenomenon and thundered: 'You people think you are more civilised because you think you use more clothes than we do in a warm country. But it is not the amount of clothes which determines whether you are civilised'.

More thoughtful, more penetrating, more discriminating is our approach. Indian intellect always engaged itself in the task of separating the husk from the grain, he added.

Noted historian and Ideologist A.L. Basham commented that not only in religion, art and social life, but also India has attained a degree of excellence in other fields as well including political organisation.

Swami Vivekananda said we have had religious leaders at certain periods of history and national life. They showed us the way and we tried to follow them. As a result, we attained progress not only on spiritual plane but also on material plane. In fact, India saw no conflict between spiritual and material progress. Both can go hand in hand. And, that has been the character of the Indian civilisation.

Some say our civilisation is 6000 years old. Some say it is ageless, eternal. I think neither is it possible to determine its antiquity nor is it necessary to debate on the question. What is really important is to study the roots of this civilisation, the sources of its strength and the values that gave the civilisation its distinctive shape and flavour. It is also essential to know that Indian civilisation flourished despite repeated political upheavals. So far as the ideals are concerned, India still remains the same. This is the distinctive character of our civilisation. Given this kind of loyalty to the higher values of life, Indian civilisation will continue to thrive.

Look at what has happened to other civilisations. They certainly have high standards of living. Yet, they feel the ground is slipping away from under their feet. They have nothing on which they can sustain themselves. They are about to collapse. They feel they are going to perish, they are doomed. Comparatively, India has had many crises, but somehow it managed to survive. And not only that, India today is a strong, dynamic, vigorous, active power. India remains the same India with the same ideas, outlook, values of life and philosophy. I hope India will live and continue to move ahead, as Swamiji wished, not for her own sake, but for the whole world.

May I ask if it is not possible to combine the secular with the spiritual? India had been a very rich country. It has good natural resources. She was also industrially very much advanced. But India has not stopped there. It has endeavoured and struggled to attain higher truths of life, truths which are far more enduring. And, this is precisely the reason why despite all odds, India seems so vibrant and lively as it had been all through.

II

Every civilisation has some peculiarities of its own. India is no exception. It is commonly argued that Indians lacked a sense of history. But what is meant by the term 'Sense of history'? Our people valued ideas. They did not attach too much importance to recording data and dry information. People, as a whole, were influenced by certain ideas, which slowly spread to all corners and these ideas have carried the seeds of history of the entire population.

We do not possess connected accounts of our past. There were, of course, kings, emperors and outstanding military generals. But they were not considered very important. What was important was the outlook on life, philosophy, approach and thinking. They explain why we do not find a connected account of how Indian civilisation came into being. Nevertheless, some connected links are there which moulded our attitude towards life and the universe. This was something peculiar to India. And, you do not find this peculiarity anywhere.

Continuity of thoughts always influenced our people. That was considered vital. We love those ideas that have made what we are. You may say, 'you are outwardly, you are more concerned with things unrealistic or idealistic, or that you are living in ivory towers'. We will say, 'no, you have misunderstood us. If you scan our history carefully, you will find we paid more attention to ethics and ideals. We build good temples, developed high standard of literature and music. But we also cared about science. It is necessary to point out here that several branches of science were first developed in India. India did not believe in the dichotomy between the secular and the spiritual. We have always asserted that you have to take life as a whole. Life cannot be divided into two water-tight compartments. Everything in life—*Dharma, Artha, Kama,* and *Moksha*—are interlinked.

What is *Artha*, by the way? It is materialism which incorporates, among other things, politics and economics management. They are certainly important. One may ask, if the goal of life is *Moksha* (liberation), why do you attach importance to these things, especially, *Artha* and *Kama* (desire)? The answer is, if you have to have a good healthy life, a good social structure, a sound political system is necessary. That will give you safety, security so that you can try to attain *Moksha*.

India was always dominated by this kind of approach that you need everything including *Artha* and *Kama*, as you have to struggle hard in order to reach the supreme goal of *Moksha*. This approach existed all along. It did not develop at a certain point of time. Nor, that people became suddenly aware of this at a given period of our history. They continuously and steadily pursued this goal of life. That is peculiar about India.

Another feature of the Indian civilisation is that India always tolerated pluralism. We had fighting here. But what kind of fighting? Ideological fighting. We had never used arms as such but employed sharpest possible arguments. This was encouraged by the process of free of thinking, arguments, and debates and eventually India evolved a philosophy that appeared quite unique.

India is a country of ideas and not facts. Maybe, we also produced great statesmen and heroes, but we did not attach too much importance to them. We attached importance to ideology. I want to draw particular attention to this aspect of our civilisation. I also urge you not to pay too much attention to facts when studying Indian history.

Ours is, perhaps, the oldest civilisation. Our people were always curious about nature. The riddles of life ceaselessly haunted them. They kept on asking question: where do we come from? Who sustains us? Or, where do we go after death? Remember the question

Nachiketa asked Yama. Such questions were never asked anywhere in the world. This kind of curiosity about the cosmos, life, and existence always haunted us.

The earliest example of our civilisation is found in Mohenjodaro and Harappa where houses built of bricks, efficient sewerage system and other amenities of a decent modern life were available. From the ruins and remains and other related evidence, we can conclude that we were able to develop our cities to a degree which is unparalled and unprecedented, and people then quite enjoyed their lives. People, nevertheless, misunderstand us. They think we ignored our material needs, which is far from the truth.

It is, however, true that we were more active on the ideological plane. We have always welcomed new ideas. It is on record that an Indian scholar met the Greek philosopher Socrates in Greece. He found Socrates too much preoccupied with matters related to mankind and this world. He asked the wisest Greek why he was wasting so much time being so much concerned with humanity. Socrates replied he has to understand what kind of creature man is! The Indian scholar said in reply, 'You cannot understand man unless you understand God.' What the scholar purported to say is that things so obvious to us are not the actual reality or reality as a whole. That has to be realised at a transcendental level. In other words, truth is something beyond the scope of our sense organs. In India, this experience on the transcendental plane is considered the only way to realise truth. In civilisation elsewhere, including China, this concept of transcendentalism is absent.

In India, knowledge enjoyed highest esteem over money or wealth. Here, we respect scholarship. We even go to the extent of worshipping a wise man, a man who is selfless, a man of character. But this knowledge is not book-learning. It is intuitive knowledge. It is experience acquired from your transcendental understanding. This is something in India.

Among the ideas, the concept of sacrifice is of paramount importance to an Indian. The idea that my life is meant for others is one, which always inspired us.

Then, contrary to the popular belief, Indian attitude towards life is one of affirmation and not negation. Life here is described as '*Karma bhumi*'. Here, you are required to perform your duties, which are referred to as your '*Dharma*'. If you do not perform them, you are committing a sin. Then, you are deviating from the path leading to your '*Moksha*'. Every little bit of work, in Indian view, is important as it takes you closer to God.

Romain Rolland said, 'If there is one place on the face of earth where all the dreams of living men have found a home from the earliest time, where men have begun their dreams of existence, it is India.'

Swami Vivekananda said: 'India, you must live not for your own sake, but for the humanity. The outsiders also added to what we already possessed. This shows our capacity to assimilate'.

The main source of our history is the Vedic literature, which contained the germs of what later on came to be known as Vedanta. It reflects a level of thinking that represents the highest and fullest development of mind ever possible anywhere. The Vedic religion or Brahmanism ended as a number of ceremonialism. Only a group of privileged people was able to take an active part in the ritual-bound religion. Common people started feeling that they were debarred from their legitimate rights. As a result, a sense of revolt was steadily gathering momentum. And this revolt found expression in Buddhism, which neglected ceremonialism.

Buddha was the greatest individual thinker India has ever produced. He was not a Brahmin. But he knew what Brahmanism was about. He went into the roots of Brahmanism. He was one who was deadly against speculative philosophy. Only one question bothered him: How can we overcome sorrow? For the first time someone raised this basic question without quoting the Vedic scriptures.

Buddha had remarkable commonsense. He did not talk in Sanskrit. He used common man's language. As a result, he received almost an instantaneous response from the people. Buddhism began to spread.

However, it is interesting to note, that Buddha was disseminating old wine in new bottle. True, he was simple, straightforward and not pedantic. But he was preaching nothing but the essence of the Upanishads. He was a rebel, no doubt. But he served the old Upanishadic truths in a new garb to be readily accepted by people who got frustrated with the Brahmanical ritualism. Thus, Buddha saved India from stagnation. People were groping in the dark. They seemed confused. They wanted someone to tell what religion was about. And, Buddha came forward to dispel their ignorance and saved them. Later, however, Buddhism merged into Hinduism; every Hindu is therefore a Buddhist, and every Buddhist a Hindu whether you agree or not.

With the advent of Buddhism, India began to flourish again. A new spark of life was visible. A fresh spurt of activities was evident. In art, architecture, music as well as on material and ideological planes India's progress was remarkable. Buddhism had drawn all people into the mainstream of national life. Even the Greeks came and settled here. It was also at this time Indian thoughts for the first time began to cross the national frontiers. Buddha's overwhelming influence on the South-East Asian countries is evident even today.

Thus, Buddha unified for the first time the whole of India. Many would say it was Emperor Asoka and not Buddha who did this. But there is no doubt that Buddha's image was the greatest cementing factor which integrated different linguistic groups and even brought foreign countries closer to India.

One may reasonably ask, did the Brahmins offer any resistance to the burgeoning spell of Buddhism? Perhaps, yes. But there was no bloodshed. No violence. Scholars fought each other on the ideological plane with reason. In later years, there were minor wars, with Hindu kings attacking monasteries. But they were localised. Events like these were few and far between. For, the Hindus consider Buddha to be one of the '*Avatars*' or incarnations of God.

In his teachings, Buddha asked all not to try to conquer other people. He advised his followers to live a life of '*Dhamma*', of righteousness. He laid stress on truth, non-violence, self-control, charity, straightforwardness. He condemned stealing and asked all to be content with what they had.

As Buddha's teachings spread throughout the country, the whole mass of people arose for the first time to become involved in religious activities, ignoring cast barriers. Throughout, Buddha preached the Truth, the essence of Brahmanism, which got enmeshed in too much ceremonialism. Buddha thus saved Brahmanism, saved Dharma and at the same time saved India.

This occurred again and again which saved India's identity and her civilisation. We have not changed much. Changes, which we notice, are only on the surface. In our approach towards life and philosophy, we are almost the same.

III

We have already noted that the history of India is the history of ideas, not a history of facts. It is not a well-documented, continuous account of one group of people dominating another or one distinct political force ruling over another. India is nothing but a sort of vast crucible into which poured nation after nations to merge into one. The present Indian society is the offspring of that harmonising process. Look, what is the character of the present-day India? Is it Hindu India? Muslim India? Or, a Christian India? The answer to this question is, it is the sum total of so many factors that characterises the Indian civilisation today.

It has already been said that Buddha himself was a non-Brahmin. We do not know with certainty if he was a good scholar. Most probably not. In his teachings he made no mention whatsoever of the scriptures. Still more surprising was the fact that he did not ever discuss the question whether God existed or not. He avoided metaphysics as a whole. He was evidently more concerned with the question of human suffering. He in fact, suggested a way out. This was something remarkably new. He addressed the masses in their own language and not in Sanskrit, the accepted language of the day. This was something never attempted before. This was sort of a turning point in the history of the Indian civilisation where Buddha emerged as the leader of a populist movement.

Buddha was a common man except for the fact that he was born a prince. He did not claim special powers. As gold is tested in fire, similarly he would ask all to taste whatever he was saying in the fire of reasoning. He never posed that he was delivering a message on behalf of God. On the contrary, he felt he should talk to people and explain to them the way to get rid of the burden of sufferings oppressing them.

Consequently, he seemed to have a tremendous appeal to the people. Not only the peasants and the rural, but even the educated people flocked to him. This charisma can only be explained by the fact that Buddha was a great soul. And, his message was simple and clear, free from all kinds of pedantry, something which was practical and also acceptable.

Since the advent of Buddha till the decline of Brahmanism (though such a clear-cut division is not appropriate as Brahmanism never faded out completely in the real sense) one notices an upsurge of creative activities in the fields of art, architecture, literature, music and even in sciences. Such a spurt is always visible whenever a new religious movement begins. This shows religion in India is not life-negating, not other-worldly as many people tend to think.

In India nothing is rejected. Nothing is secular. On the contrary, everything, all aspects of our life, all activities of our choice is geared up to spirituality. Swami Vivekananda once said, when a Hindu steals, he steals religiously. Though spoken with a tinge of his inimitable humour, what Swamiji meant is that such an immoral action was bound to interfere with his spiritual growth. Because, in the Hindu view of life, everything you do is an attempt to develop your spiritual character. This is our contention, and India always nourished such a view.

Buddhism gradually spread to the neighbouring countries, now broadly referred to as South-East Asia, and left its indelible imprint on all spheres of lives of the people living there, so much so that historians were tempted to describe these countries as 'greater India'. If the description is acceptable at all, let us see what kind of India it was. It was, of course, a Buddhist India. In China, Japan, Tibet, Malaysia, Sri Lanka, Kampuchea and other countries of the region, Buddhism is still practised as a religion.

This happened not because India went out and imposed the religion on these people. Far from it, India never believed in the policy of closed frontier. If Buddhism spread out from India, then it is also true that India stretched out its arms to welcome outsiders. The Sakas, the Huns, the Mongols—all came and settled here. Even the Jews, who were persecuted and driven out from many places, made India their permanent abode. It will not be out of place to mention that I know some members of this community who went to Israel a couple of years ago for the purpose of living there. But they soon started feeling uncomfortable there. Eventually, they returned to India which they have accepted as their permanent homeland.

The 'Gujjars' who are still to be found in northern India, settled in Kashmir region. The place called 'Gujranwalla' in Punjab bears testimony of its association with the nomadic central-Asian tribes long ago.

Jawaharlal Nehru once said, if you examine the blood of Indians, you will find that some of their ancestors possibly came from Mexico, some from Africa while others from some other country. Each community and each group thus brought along with them a brand of their own culture and finally they went into the making of what is known as the Indian civilisation today. It is like a mosaic where you have all sorts of colours. Perhaps, such an admixture took place in all countries, but not to the extent as it happened in India.

India is very much alive and vibrant and remains the same in spirit as it had been thousands of years ago. Barring some changes which are on the surface only and without which the civilisation would have become stagnant, India has once again become a country strong and dynamic. This capacity to absorb anything that came to the soil, this quality of resilience is remarkable.

The Mohammedans at first came to rob our people of their immense wealth. Later, they tried to impose their own culture and religion on us. They were visibly very much intolerant. According to the Koran, polytheism is a sin. So, they did not like us and wanted us to embrace their religion. Nevertheless, as they started living here, India began to exert its influence on them. Otherwise, how do you explain the phenomenon of Sufism? In essence, it is nothing but Vedanta.

Let me explain. The Sufis too observed some sort of idolatry. If you are a 'Pir', they will put up a mound on your grave and drape it with a satin cloth. The place becomes holy and they will worship the same and offer prayers and sweets. Is it not idolatry?

Thus, the Hindus tried to transform the alien religion into something, which was closer to their faith. The Muslims thus appeared to have changed much over the centuries. The Indians, on the other hand, accepted their language, food and living habits. Many people accepted their religion too for one reason or another. A movement under the leadership of saints like Kabir, Dadu, Nanak and Chaitanya slowly started in the middle ages. The movement intended to bridge the gap between the two poles—Hinduism and Islam. That process of reconciliation is still on.

The Muslim emperors, at least some of them, were great admirers of Hindu sages and saints. They trusted the Hindu officials who were given important positions in the court and general administration. This also helped the process of assimilation.

One interesting feature of the Indian civilisation is that, at first, it seems that India, by being humble and non-resistant, was losing ground. But on closer look, it will be revealed to discerning eyes that slowly and steadily India was asserting itself.

Next to the Muslims came the British, who were very proud people. Initially they appeared to be very humble. But their attitude changed. They professed India was a backward country waiting to be civilised by the British culture and developed the concept of the 'white man's burden'. They thought very poorly of our culture. But surprisingly, among the British administrators, there were again some intellectuals who discovered the genius of India. They declared India was a highly civilised country and the world owed much to India for so many things it possessed. An English Indologist wrote: 'Those Indians have a poor idea of their country's greatness, who do not realise how it had tamed and civilised the nomads of Central Asia so that wild Turcoman have been transformed into some of the royal Rajput races.'

Thus, India never thrust itself upon the will of the neighbouring countries. Its attraction spread on its own. Recognising this aspect of Indian character, Swami Vivekananda addressed India as 'Oh, Truth!' India and truth were two synonymous words to Swamiji.

Slowly, the British felt it would be a good idea to rule over the Indians. The traders calculated they would not be able to carry on trade profitably unless they wielded political power. So, ultimately, they seized political power.

Some Indians thought Indian civilisation was, perhaps, dead. So, they reasoned it was God's will, which had sent the British to save India. Raja Ram Mohun Roy was one of them. But later, he was disillusioned with the British. Slowly, our eyes were opened and a movement started gaining ground that Indians should not accept everything and anything that came from Britain.

There were Englishmen who respected Indian culture and the Indian ways of life. Their attitude, no doubt, emboldened the consciousness about our own cultural heritage. Here again, the spirit of resilience prevailed in the face of great military and political strength of the British. Today, India is a free land once again. Once it seemed impossible.

Modern researchers have been puzzled to find that India has not changed much despite some superficial changes. This is a phenomenon very difficult to explain. But, all the same, it is true. And this truth has enabled India to withstand the foreign onslaughts again and again. And, you can feel proud that here is a country after all, whose outlook, philosophy, approach to life, have remained the same. It does not matter much what food I eat or what dress I wear. But my outlook is more important. Because that makes a country really great. We are fortunate that our basic attitude remained unaltered in spite of the many vicissitudes we have undergone over the years. That we have cherished with love and care what had been handed down to us by our forefathers long ago.

One may argue that India may stand to lose by not responding to the forces of changes visible everywhere. No, that is not our attitude. We must be humble to learn from other people, from our neighbours. But at the same time, we will preserve the great ideas our ancestors had developed which continue to attract respectful attention from all corners of the world. People from all over the world come to India believing that India can show the way. Arnold Toynbee said, 'If you want peace, want to survive, you have to follow the Indian ways.' He mentioned in this context three names—Sri Ramakrishna, Rishi Aurobindo and Mahatma Gandhi.

This civilisation, therefore, must be preserved, for it is very much valid and alive, which can give us a fresh lease of life. No denying, India has problems. Yet, she survives because she is anchored in its old values. It must be borne in mind that science, technology and development—all are important. But they can go hand in hand with our old values. Our future reformers must give due importance to the forces which held us together as Indians. We do believe in diversity. We do not believe in uniformity. But, be sure, there lies a substratum of unity beneath that apparent diversity. Let us maintain that unity.

The Essence of Indian Culture

WHAT IS CULTURE? IT IS DIFFICULT TO DEFINE. BUT YOU KNOW WHAT culture is when you meet a cultured man. I meet a cultured man and think, here is a man I really love and admire. But when I go back to my home I start to think—'What are the qualities I saw in that person that made me feel so drawn to him? How I wish I could be like him! What a wonderful man he is! But what are those qualities I admire?'

Sometimes, you like something and say in admiration—'Isn't it good?' People ask you, 'What is good about it?' You say, 'I just like it.' You say it is good, but can you define what exactly is the quality which makes you think that it is good? Indeed, it is difficult to tell. But somehow you feel it, you know it is good. Similarly, you like a person and you remember him, maybe for a long time. That is just what happens when you meet a cultured man, no matter who he is or where he comes from.

A cultured man is indeed a citizen of the world. When you meet a cultured man, you are so impressed that you do not care to know what his background is, where he is from, what kind of language he speaks, or whether he is a religious man at all. Maybe, he is not religious, or, maybe, he does have some kind of religion, but it is different from the religion you profess and practise. Still you cannot help admiring him.

British administrators used to say—'Beware of Gandhi! Never approach him. But now? Meet him! He has a sort of spell which he casts on anybody who happens to approach him.' Maybe initially, you had nothing but dislike for him. You had been hearing all sorts of stories about him, perhaps that he was a mystic and impractical. Yet, when you met him, though you were warning yourself: 'Look, here I am in the presence of Gandhi, I must be careful so that he does not cast his spell on me; I am going to study, watch him. I want to be sure that I can size him up properly.' But when you leave him, you say he is indeed a remarkable man! Thus, the 'spell' has started working on you.

Culture is something like fragrance of flower. Can you define the fragrance of a flower? What is that fragrance really? You do not know. Yet, it is pleasant. You like it. Similarly, culture is something hard to define. But when you meet a cultured man you know what culture means, though it is difficult for you to identify its particular qualities.

Is it in his clothes? If he is well-dressed, I say, here is a man of good taste! Look at his dress—the colour, the cut, everything is so pleasing! But then, would you call Sri Ramakrishna a cultured man? He was a man who was totally indifferent to his clothes. Unshaven, rustic, lacking in sophistication and of course, very outspoken. Would you call such a person cultured? Still, you will say, 'Yes, verily, he was a man of the highest culture.' Thus, it is very difficult to tell what culture really is. It is like the aura that surrounds a good person, an invisible aura, very delicate, indefinable, yet you feel the impact of such a cultured man.

THE SUM TOTAL

Similarly, the culture of a nation—when you say 'Indian culture', what exactly do you mean? You mean everything. You mean its temples, its slums, its roads; you mean its dirt, filth, poverty; you mean its holy men, its cheats and fools—everything. His base may be very ugly, but the peak is something wonderful. You do not exclude anything—the attitudes, beliefs, the institutions, the prejudices, the art, literature, music, religion, philosophy, rituals and superstitions and so on. The sum total is called 'culture'. We often say, let us have a cultural programme. We know that we are going to have some good music. But is that all that culture means? You cannot really compartmentalise culture. Everything that characterises a particular nation is included in its culture.

INDIAN CULTURE

When you think of Indian culture, what is it that strikes you most? First of all, it is not the same thing in every part of the country, not something which is uniform. You go to South India and meet there one kind of people with their religious practices and art forms, their sense of humour, their idea of what is right and what is wrong, so on. But go to North India, and you find another set of values! But somehow or other, you also feel that this diversity, this difference, is on the surface. Beneath that, there is something which is common. And, it is this common element, whatever it may be, which holds together this vast diversity which is India. There is a unity somewhere which is sustaining India in spite of all the vicissitudes through which it has passed. Sometimes it has received sharp jolts. There have been foreign aggressions. Sometimes there have been internal dissensions. But India still lives. India somehow has come through every form of adversity almost unscathed. This kind of resilience has puzzled many people. Any other country might have fallen apart if it had been exposed to the kind of adverse forces which have now, and then overtaken this country. But India still thrives like a riddle and amazes us.

There are scholars who say India has no history as such, which is true, in a way. In another way, the statement is not true. It is true if by 'history' you mean history of wars and warriors. Other countries have their history and it so happens that their history is a history of wars that they have fought and the great warriors that they have thrown up. But India has no such history.

HISTORY OF IDEAS

India has another kind of history—a history of ideas, not of persons. The impersonal history believes in being interested in ideas, not in persons. Indian history is therefore, a history of ideas. And, what are the characteristics of these ideas? It is the search for something. You find that every few hundred years a new idea grips the minds of the people. There is some individual who symbolises that idea. But they are not so much interested in who the individual is. They are interested in the idea which that individual puts forward. Maybe, they will completely forget the person who first preached that idea.

People say India is idolatrous! Yes, it is idolatrous. But India worships only the ideas. If they worship any deity, it does not matter what name and what form that deity assumes. What matters is the idea which they try to see behind that deity. The deity is important to the extent that he or she represents some particular idea and that idea appeals to the minds of the people. They love that idea and try to live up to it.

The history of India is the history of such ideas which have stirred and still continue to stir the imagination of the people. They may not be able to prove that the person to whom they attribute those ideas really existed in history, maybe he never existed, or maybe he did, it does not matter; but it is the idea that matters to India. When you talk of culture, and ask what the Indian culture is like, you find that it has been inspired by those ideas. And, that culture is still growing. Indian culture is not static but always growing, changing. This is something remarkable.

A GROWING CULTURE

It grows because it is open to new thoughts, new ideas, and new influences. I come across something new, something entirely different from what I always believed in; but because you preach something which strikes me as very original, very convincing, very satisfying, I do not mind throwing overboard everything that I cherished so long. I do this because I am searching for Truth.

The chief characteristic of India is this search for Truth. Truth is above everything. And, India decided long ago somehow or other that Truth has to be realised. We must realise Truth; know what is meant by Truth. And I am ready to stake every dear thing in order that I may realise this Truth. Swami Vivekananda in one place says that you may laugh at the idea that anybody should strip himself completely, go and stand in ice-cold water right up to his neck. But he stands there the whole day defying the cold and the ridicule of sophisticated people. Some of us will say—'isn't he a fool, isn't he mad?' Or, 'isn't he an imposter?' It does not matter what other people think. He is there firm in his conviction that the purpose of life is to realise the Truth, and he must realise it. This is something which people of this country, especially of the present generation, cannot understand. This is what is called India.

Go to a 'Kumbh Mela' and you find huge multitude of people, and what trouble they take just to be there! But they do not care! If you ask them: 'Why are you here?' They smile and say 'Oh, I just love to be here; I enjoy being here.' They cannot explain. When you enjoy something which is very personal, your own, such as an esoteric experience, you cannot share it with other people. You only smile. A simple man from the village is not very articulate, he is not able to communicate his thoughts to others, and he does not try to; but looking at his face you can see how happy he is! And, he means what he says, 'I enjoy being here.' Now, this search for Truth is typical of India.

EVERYTHING IS SPIRITUAL

Another aspect of Indian culture is that India says: 'I make no distinction between the secular and the spiritual. Everything is spiritual to me. Whatever I do is nothing but an act of worship. I am worshipping God who is no other than Truth. If I am eating, or if I go and work in the fields—it is all worship.' There is no difference between the secular and spiritual in the Indian tradition.

I am searching for Truth. I search outside, and I search inside also. Sometimes I may go to the end of the world, trying to find Truth. Similarly, I may sometimes turn my gaze inward. I shut out the whole world that is so attractive, so pleasing to others and it ceases to exist for me. This search for Truth, this relentless, ceaseless quest for Truth, is what has always engaged India. This is the peculiarity of Indian culture.

BEING IS IMPORTANT

Of course, India has big palaces, big factories, industrial complexes, big firms. There are many other things that India can be proud of in terms of her achievement on the material plane. But India says—all this is good; I am not rejecting them; but more important to me is what I am. 'Being' is more important. I may possess the whole world. But if I do not know who I am, if I am not able to control myself, if I do not know what Truth is, what is abiding, what that is which will never perish—then all is vain. If I have an empire, that will perish. My dear body will one day perish. The power which I wield today will go someday. Everything will perish, but Truth. Truth will always prevail. And, I want to know that Truth, nothing but that Truth. Indian culture is the result of that incessant search for Truth.

This search started long ago. It is difficult to say when or how it started and who the people were. But it seems that as long as

India remains India, this search will continue. It is true there are countries which are very powerful and rich. But they are not so much concerned with this question of Truth, which is eternal, universal and impersonal.

NOT LIFE-NEGATING

Lots of people think this kind of attitude is life-negating. A learned man of Albert Schweitzer's standing said so. Isn't it then ridiculous, the critics point out, that Indians should turn their mind to something which is chimerical or absolutely visionary—something which perhaps does not even exist?

Our stand is that the charge is baseless. This is however, not to say that there are no problems. They are certainly there. Yet, this vision, this so-called chimera, has seized the soul of the nation and it is fully absorbed in the quest for this amorphous truth. But does it mean that India has neglected her material needs? Would you say, because of this obsession with the search for truth, India has neglected her material needs and has always been a poor, backward country? Has India really neglected science and technology? Today's historians, Western as well as the Eastern say, no.

The charge is strange. India cannot be otherworldly, as there are really no two worlds. There is only one, and it is not that India neglects her material needs. In fact, historians say, whenever there has been a spiritual upsurge in the country following the advent of a great spiritual leader, a marked progress on all fronts is visible.

Take the coming of Buddha. In the wake of his advent, there was growth in India in all spheres including the material. Art, architecture, literature, music, science—all flourished. This has happened again and again following the advent of great religious teachers. Long after the great spiritual leader has left the stage, there may be a period when everything seems to be in a low state. You may find inertia, laziness; or there may be a feeling of euphoria that we are the greatest, the best. But that is just for a while. Let the new leader come. And, he does come and preach the truth that he has experienced. It is not his scholarship which attracts Indians. India is not interested in the so-called scholarship which is superficial, which is nothing but beating about the bush. India is interested in something which you can grasp in your hand as real. Truth, therefore, has to be experienced.

If you say you are preaching Truth, how do I know that you are preaching the Truth? I know through your very being, your character, and not by what you say. I would judge you by that criterion alone—what you are. If you are really one who has experienced the Truth in your own innermost being, you are then totally transformed, you are a different kind of person altogether, and I would feel inclined to go and sit at your feet and listen to whatever you have to say. The test of the pudding is in the eating. That is how again and again a new teacher has come and taught new ideas. At first there may be resistance. But soon the whole country rallies round him and accepts him. And, at once you experience a new release of power, vigour and energy. You find a new efflorescence in literature, art, music and architecture throughout the country. That is what happens.

Please, do not think that as India is too much preoccupied with things which some people think otherworldly and spiritual, India's secular life has suffered. I would like to read to you what Aurobindo says on this, 'On this firm and noble basis Indian civilisation grew to its maturity and became a thing—rich, splendid and unique. While it took the view from the ... supreme spiritual elevation, it did not neglect the life of the levels.' What he meant is that you are looking at the high peaks of spirituality. But that is not to say that you are neglecting where you are, your surroundings, or your obligations to your family, to your society, the lower levels, the ground. Aurobindo therefore said: 'it did not neglect the life of the levels. It lived between the busy life of the city and village, the freedom and seclusion of the forest and the last overarching illimitable ether.' The feet here on the earth, the head high in the sky. Aurobindo further said: 'Moving firmly between life and death, it saw beyond both, and cut out a hundred high roads to immortality.'

Truth is this Immortality. Therefore, Truth is the goal. In searching for Truth, you do not have to neglect your immediate duties, the duties which you, as a man of the world, have accepted by virtue of being what you are. You fulfil those obligations. But you do not stay stuck there. You look beyond and above. You look to the highest. That is the peculiarity of Indian culture.

India and Democracy

PEOPLE, LIKE EACH INDIVIDUAL, CHOOSE THEIR OWN DESTINY. THE choice may not always be deliberate, for circumstances often make a choice imperative, unavoidable. At least in the case of India, her choice of democracy in 1947 was so. History had shaped her for it, and she could not possibly help it. Her long association with Britain did not suit her for any other form of government. Her intelligentsia, who had long been nourished on democratic ideas, would not have tolerated any other form of government. Willy-nilly, India had to choose it, and the choice now seems to be final and complete. It is final, in the sense that the predominant mood in the country today is democratic. Not only the intelligentsia, but the mass also now would not like any other form of government. Democracy has conferred much power on them, and having tasted power once, they are not likely to barter it away for anything. Judging by the evidences in hand, democracy has come to stay. The choice is complete, because democracy now prevails in all the tiers of the country's administration. Not only at the Centre or at the States, but in the villages also, the administration is now committed to be democratic. A Panchayat Raj is slowly taking shape in India. Power really belongs to her people now.

AN EXPERIMENT

It is a big experiment that India has embarked upon. It is big as well as exciting, for not only does it involve hundreds of millions of people, it is full of hazards also. It is the biggest democracy in the East. Some other countries in the East toyed with democracy for some time, but in the end rejected it. A continuing chaos and confusion forced them to do so. And, when democracy ended in those countries, people heaved a sigh of relief, because they suffered most under it. They were glad to be rid of the cruel farce to which they were being subjected in the name of democracy. It is precisely because of the failure of democracy in other countries in the East that the Indian experiment is being watched with great interest throughout the world. The success or failure of the experiment would decide the fate of democracy in Asia. If the Indian experiment succeeds, there is a possibility that other countries also will some day return to democracy. If it fails, it will seal the fate of democracy in the East for good. There is an impression in many quarters that the oriental mind is not suited for democracy. The results of the Indian experiment will determine the truth or otherwise of this.

CONDITIONS OF A TRUE DEMOCRACY

To put it naively, democracy means a people's government—a government by the people and for the people. It is a government where the whole body of citizens rules through their chosen representatives. Clearly, such a government can function if only the people are intelligent and educated. Statecraft, as is well known, has now become extremely intricate; only the brainiest and most enlightened persons can run a government now. But only brains will not do, there must be also ability and desire to serve. Those who run the administration must be not only capable, but also true representatives of the masses. They must be able to understand the wishes of the people and try sincerely and assiduously to meet them. They must be the true servants of the people. They have no other duty and no other interest than that they will serve the people. They will uphold their rights, secure justice for them, and also safeguard their interests. When the people have their true representatives in the legislature, and when those representatives form a government, there is a true people's government; in other words, there is a true democracy. The people can choose anyone they like, but they must choose right men, for otherwise their own interests will be in jeopardy. Much therefore depends upon whom they choose and how they choose them. They cannot make a good choice unless they know the persons who are wooing their votes. They must know each one of them. They must know the problems of the country. They must know the political and economic forces that are at work in the country, as well as outside. A fair knowledge of these forces has nowadays become essential for the people, for otherwise they will not know in what direction their interests lie, or who are the people they can trust to look after their well-being. Democracy becomes a mockery where this knowledge is lacking. It becomes a mockery also when they are not able to exercise some check on the activities of their representatives. They must keep a constant watch on them and, where necessary, prod them or pull them up. They cannot remain passive when legislations are being put on the statute-book, or when decisions are being taken by the administration which vitally affects them. They have, in fact, to tell their representatives what they want and see to it that their demands are fully met.

CONDITIONS IN INDIA

Only where there is such an electorate, democracy is a success. The question is whether India possesses such an electorate. No one, who has any acquaintance with the conditions in India, will suggest that she has such an electorate. No doubt, her people are shrewd and intelligent, but these are not enough qualifications to ensure that they will be able to choose the right men for the legislature or, after choosing them, will be able to control them when they go wrong. Similarly, that understanding which is essential to decide what is good and necessary for the country, few in India possess today. And yet, every adult has the right to vote today, and that right is being exercised too. Obviously, the danger of this giving rise to an all-powerful bureaucracy or a vicious and corrupt oligarchy has been ignored. But the danger is very real in the present conditions of India. This is why many critics cross their fingers and predict an early and ignominious exit of democracy from the Indian scene. They say, democracy in India will go the same way as it has in other countries of Asia. They point to the growing discontent in the country and say it is a question of time when an explosion will take place, which will completely destroy the present flimsy democracy of India.

THE REMEDY

Whether the explosion will take place or not, the fact cannot be denied that the climate necessary for a strong and healthy democracy does not exist in India yet. What is the remedy? What must be done to assure the safety of democracy in India or, for that matter, in Asia? What are the constructive steps to be taken in this regard? Clearly, the first and most important step is *education*. Through education, the mass should be taught what the needs of the country are and what they are required to do. The people are slowly growing conscious of their power; they realise that in the final analysis, it is their vote alone that decides everything in the country. If they use their vote discreetly, they can have everything their own way. But they do not understand the great responsibility that comes with it. They complain about the government's ineptitude, about taxation, about high prices and about many such things. Some of their complaints are certainly genuine, but some are altogether baseless. They often complain, not because there are valid reasons for complaining, but because they are under the impression that, if they complain, the government will become more solicitous, and they will get all they want. The spirit of complaining stems from some basic misconceptions. People think that it is the duty of the government to give them everything they ask for. If a government cannot give them what they want, it has no right to exist. It will then be open to them to overthrow it. They are only too conscious of their demands. They do not seem to remember that they have some duties, too.

GOVERNMENT—A SPEARHEAD OF THE PEOPLE

In a democracy, there is no essential difference between government and the people. They have identical interests and objects. The government is expected to serve as the spearhead of the people in their efforts towards progress. An enlightened government is the people's leader; it creates enthusiasm in them about its plans and projects and makes them conscious of their duties and responsibilities. It sees to it that they give it their whole-hearted support and cooperation. The test of a democracy is how far it is able to carry the people with it. It is not too sensitive about criticisms, nor is it too vain to ignore suggestions. It welcomes both, but sticks to its own views unless there are some overriding reasons to the contrary. There may be times when the government will find compelled to ask people to practise austerities. Sometimes, it may give directions which are hard to follow. But in their own interest, the people will gladly accept the advice of the government, no matter what sacrifice this may involve. A relation based on trust and understanding exists between the two, which is an essential condition for the success of a democracy.

THE ORDEAL OF THE INDIAN GOVERNMENT

Unfortunately, this relation does not exist between the government and the people in India today. Far from trusting the government, the people are suspicious of its bonafides, and blame it for every little misfortune of theirs. They are not ready to admit that the government is well-meaning, and if it fails, it is because of circumstances beyond its control. Similarly, where credit is due, they are not ready to give it. There is no denying the fact that the present government has done some good work. But the people are not prepared to admit it. It is true at the same time, that the government would have achieved more success if the people had cooperated. Unfortunately, that cooperation has not taken place. Everyone knows how slow and half-hearted the people are when they have to contribute to a public cause. This makes a sad contrast with the alacrity they show when they have to make a demand on the government. They are perfectly justified in making their demands. It is a happy sign that they are conscious of their needs, and they can agitate and demand. But they are not equally conscious that, as citizens of a democracy, they have certain obligations, too. Even when the government policies and plans are directly for their good, they do not cooperate.

Nowadays, the government has made it a rule, that in all developmental programmes, the people will be asked to cooperate. In some cases they are asked to pay money; in some, they are asked to contribute labour. This is certainly a fair and reasonable arrangement. It is vitally necessary that the people should be associated with these programmes, for otherwise they will not take any interest in them. The paradox about these programmes is that, though they are implemented for their own good, the people are suspicious about them. What is wrong is that they are not aware of their social duties and obligations. They are extremely individualistic, and think only in terms of their individual interests. This counters the basic principle of democracy, which requires that every individual under it should place the interests of the community above his own. This social awareness is, unfortunately, absent in India today. This is what constitutes the greatest stumbling-block to her progress.

THE ROLE OF EDUCATION

The need of education in the circumstances cannot be over-emphasised. If the attitude of the Indian population is to be changed, it must be done through education. Through education, love for the community has to be inculcated. That there is no individual well-being, as apart from communal well-being, should be the first lesson taught. Education broadens a man's outlook and makes him conscious of his social duties and obligations. At the moment, the people are apathetic to what goes on around them. They are much too occupied with their own problems, their own struggles. That they cannot live in isolation, they do not seem to know. Their horizons are limited to their families, their villages, or, at the most, their States. They are scarcely able to think in terms of the country. It is the business of education to make them conscious of the country as a whole. Indeed, education's prime object is to strike at the roots of parochialism—religious, linguistic, or racial. Education is nothing if it does not enable a man to love his fellow-men, irrespective of anything.

NEED TO REVIEW ANCIENT IDEALS

India clearly needs this kind of education today. Not only India, in fact, the whole world needs it. But it must be said that India needs it more than any other country. Love for the community or fellow-feeling is now practically non-existent in India. No one cares for the country or the community. This is ominous, not only for the future of democracy, but for the future of the country itself. No country or community can prosper where respect for fellow-men or consideration for the community is lacking. India's future is doomed if there is no improvement in the outlook of her people. That, of all countries, India should be lacking in the spirit of service, in love for others, for the community and so on, is surprising. It is surprising, because she has always been a believer in the ideals of service. Her philosophy has always been a philosophy of selflessness, of humility, of the conquest of the ego, of love towards all. It is a strange irony of fate that these ideals should now be forgotten by her people. Somehow or other, these ideals seem to have been forgotten. Some may still pay them a lip-service, but most people either know nothing about them, or never care to follow them. What is needed is that these ideals should be revitalised. It may be possible to raise the mental levels of the people through education; it may be possible also to teach them the difficult art of government through education; but this will not guarantee that democracy will be a success in India. There are countries where people are intelligent and educated, and who are also mentally equipped to understand the intricacies of statecraft. Even in such countries, democracy has either never been planted or, if planted, has not flourished. This is because they lacked the zeal for those ideals which alone can ensure the success of democracy—ideals of tolerance, respect for others, humility, and a sense of common well-being. These are the ideals which flow from religion; but because religion is very much at stake, those countries and democracies have not been popular and has not succeeded also.

ABUSE OF POWER RAMPANT

As democracy means that power belongs to the people, it is necessary that the people should learn to use that power with moderation and for the common good of all. Abuse of power is already rampant in the world, and the danger is only too real, that democracy will further spread the evil, since it gives power to all and sundry irrespective of their character, irrespective of how they are likely to use it. There is practically no outside agency by which the tendency to abuse power can be curbed. The only existing check is voluntary, that which the people may exercise out of sheer goodwill, out of consideration for others, for the welfare of the community as a whole. This involves much self-restraint, a spirit of sacrifice, which is not possible unless religion provides the incentive for it. This is why it seems that a condition necessary for the success of democracy is that religion or a suitable substitute should be present to influence people towards these ideals. In the West, the ideal to which everyone owes allegiance is good citizenship. This does for them what religion does for others, though, of course, not to the same extent. Where the true spirit of religion prevails, there is every reason to expect that there will be no abuse of power.

RELIGION—AN ADVANTAGE

The fact that India is deeply religious is therefore an advantage. So long as religion continues to hold its sway over the country, it may be argued that a favourable condition for the success of democracy exists. It is true that religion, that is dogmatic religion, also has its pitfalls; it might give rise to intolerance and to factors deterrent to the democratic spirit. But in religion lies the corrective to intolerance and such other evils which dogmatism may produce. The true spirit of religion abhors intolerance as well as all its concomitants. This is why where religion prevails, it is reasonable to expect that the democratic ideals will also prevail. India may be educationally backward; she may be inexperienced in the art of democratic government; but because of her deep religious temperament, she ought to succeed in her democratic experiment. At least, the basic ideas which make for the success of democracy—individual freedom, freedom of opinion, etc.—have always been familiar to India.

The misgivings that one may feel about the success of Indian democracy are therefore groundless. That is, there is nothing basically wrong with India and it may be logically argued that her experiment with democracy is not going to succeed; rather, there are conditions which fully justify the hope that the experiment will succeed. She may lack political education, she may lack also experience in the art of administration; but as against this, she has what constitutes the most important single factor in favour of democracy, namely, love of individual freedom. This she has through her religion. This is a great advantage; this is also a ground for hope that her democracy will succeed. Given that India is truly motivated by the spirit of religion, her democracy may even be better than those hitherto known.

Religion and Spirituality

- *The Necessity of Prayer*
- *The Effect of Meditation*
- *Self-surrender*
- *Philosophy of Peace*
- *Role of Religion in a Modern Secular State*
- *Religion and Social Tension*
- *Religious Harmony: An Impossible Dream?*
- *Religion: Ends and Means*
- *Religion: Man's Quest for Freedom*
- *Science and Religion*

The Necessity of Prayer

Why do we pray? What do we gain or expect to gain by it? Is there any known benefit it confers on man? If so, what is it?

These questions have become pertinent these days, for a great many people have now not only stopped praying but have also stopped believing that prayer can serve any useful purpose. There are some who even regard with pity and contempt, those who are in the habit of praying, for to them they represent an age which is long past. They see in this practice the last traces of medievalism which still persist but which must go as scientific knowledge spreads.

The chief objection to prayer, according to those who accept the standpoint of material sciences, is that, there being no satisfactory proof that God exists. No intelligent man should waste his valuable time in an undertaking of such dubious value as this. Another objection to prayer is that, even assuming that God exists, it is not likely that prayer will yield any worthwhile advantage. The argument on which this contention seems to be based is that the universe is governed by some inflexible laws which even God, probably their maker, cannot alter. He is just as much bound by them as any mortal. So, what purpose would it serve if anyone prayed to Him?

Now, it is not possible to convince anybody by argument that God exists. Only direct experience can do so. But direct experience of God is a rare fortune which few in the world can claim to have had. The price of it is a life-long effort, though there is no guarantee even then that it will come. There is, however, the curious fact that to some lucky souls it comes almost unasked, taking those, as it were, unawares. It came so to St Paul, to St Francis of Assisi, to Guru Nanak. It came so to numerous others, though their names do not appear in history. But the question is: So long as this experience does not come to you, either as a gift or as a reward for your toils, how can you bring yourself to pray?

The answer to this is that you should go on praying as if you have already had that direct experience. In other words, you should accept God on trust. The proposition is not as illogical as it may sound initially. Even in applied science where the scientist claims to go by severely objective evidence he has to accept a great many things on trust, at least to begin with. This is an inescapable necessity. He first makes an assumption and then proceeds to examine if *it* is correct or not. At any rate the assumption is his starting-point. Without an assumption he cannot make a beginning.

In religion also, you start by accepting that God exists and then go on investigating whether He does or not. You investigate the question thoroughly and in all its aspects till you have satisfied yourself that you know as much about it as possible. In religion the only acceptable test of truth is in personal experience. You must have a direct personal experience of God before you are competent to say that God exists. Till then the question is open to doubt and you reserve final judgement, though your investigation must go on.

The name chosen for this sort of investigation in the field of religion is prayer. Not a happy name to be sure, but then there is nothing better at any rate more easily understood. Whatever the word may connote literally, it is used to cover, with a stretch of its meaning, of course, any effort that a religious aspirant may make with regard to God. It may be that he does not specifically seek knowledge of God, being modest or being, as the case may be, not too inquisitive. Nevertheless, God is such a self-revealing force that the aspirant gets to know about Him in the course of his investigation.

In any case there is nothing in the field of religion that is to be taken for granted. The whole field is open to exploration, and everyone has to explore the field himself. The discoveries made by others cannot satisfy your needs. The problem is a personal problem and you have to solve it yourself. If another man eats for you, it does not satisfy your hunger. It is just like that in the matter of religious problems, also.

The point that needs to be emphasised is that in the process of prayer nothing is as important as mental health; mental faculties must be kept intact and used to the full. Even a slight deterioration of these, or slackness in their application, would retard progress. Almost the very qualities that a scientific worker is required to possess in order that he may succeed in his experiments, a religious aspirant also must possess. In fact, more, for here the field of the experiment is inside the experimenter himself. He must possess a sound and strong body, for, in his endeavours, the body plays as vital a part as the mind. Anyone who has the least knowledge of the lives of saints knows what ordeals, physical and mental, they had to pass through before they reached the final goal. Only the strongest body and the keenest mind could have withstood them.

It is well known that, just like any experimental science, religion also has its own rules, its own technique, which those who want to pursue it seriously, must observe. These rules are very exacting and even a slight deviation has a vitiating effect. Further, like science, religion also guarantees a large measure of success, provided the rules are strictly followed. The difference, however, is that even if you do not follow the rules correctly, due to ignorance, or due, say, to laziness, your effort is not altogether wasted. Prayer, no matter how ill-performed, is never in vain. But if the rules are observed, the result is so much greater.

A remarkable thing is that these rules are very much the same in different countries and different ages. Mystics all over the world, irrespective of the denomination or the age to which they belonged have prayed in the same manner, sometimes even in the same words. And as might be expected, they have had the same experience, too. They may have described this experience differently, but it is obvious enough that it is the same. One definition of truth is that it is valid in all countries and at all times. If the experience did not have a core truth, it could not have been the same everywhere.

Advocates of religion do not believe in academic discussions. They say it involves making statements about religion which must inevitably be vague and inadequate. Religion is essentially a matter of experience. Only by experience can any idea be had of what it means and what it stands for. Words, rather than helping to understand it, may even confuse. That is why they stress the need for practice, for only by practice can the truths of religion be experienced.

But what are the advantages of prayer? Again, only experience can provide the answer to this. 'The proof of the pudding is in the eating.' Unless you pray and with sincerity, devotion and longing, that is to say, in the manner prescribed by teachers, you are not likely to understand what advantages prayer has to offer. The fact that to this day, a large number of people are found in the habit of praying is proof that prayer undoubtedly yields a good return. It is well known that religious aspirants have often undergone incredible hardship. If they can still go on, it clearly implies that they find something in prayer which sustains them and gives them hope of ultimate success. Saints of all ages testify that no prayer is altogether wasted. Provided the necessary conditions are fulfilled, every prayer is answered.

But it must be understood that there are different ways in which a prayer can be answered. There are instances showing that even prayers for material gifts may be answered. Miracles of that kind have happened all over the world. But it is a wrong way of judging the benefit of prayer to insist upon a miracle of this kind. The object of prayer is not to merely solve the problems of physical existence, though, indirectly, it does help to solve them. There are far more difficult problems inside one which have to be solved and to solve which prayer is necessary. Until these problems are solved, one is not a complete being, not even a normal being. Everyone is only too well aware of the tangles within himself and how they warp his personality, making him utterly miserable. Prayer, being an exercise in self-understanding, helps to remove these tangles; and the best miracle that can happen is the removal of these tangles.

Prayer has truly a corrective effect on man. Passions, which eat into a man's soul eventually overpowering his reason and judgement, can be conquered only by prayer. And, in being so conquered, they turn into a great benign force. This is why saints are found to possess incredible energy and vitality which they devote to the service of humanity. An illustrious example of this was Mahatma Gandhi.

It is not that prayer brings to a man that which is not already in him. It rather sets free in him forces which ordinarily remain inactive, but which, if properly organised, coordinated and disciplined, can prove of immense value. Moral courage, devotion to duty in the face of utmost difficulties, a keen sense of right and wrong, love of his fellow-beings, cheerfulness—all these, which usually adorn the character of a saint, do not come from without, but from within. Like the fragrance of a flower, they are an integral part of his personality. They come not at the end of a special search, but naturally, almost inevitably, for prayer have so transformed his personality that he cannot help being what he is—kind, good, selfless, strong and bold. He is like that, again not as a matter of policy, nor from a narrow appeal of party or country, but because it is his nature. He is like that unconditionally, also unreservedly.

There is much that is dross in a man and this needs purging. Selfishness, egotism and jealousy are what may be called the dross in a man. They come from ignorance—ignorance of the basic purpose of life. Through prayer this ignorance is dispelled, as is seen in the lives of saints. Truth reveals itself to the man whose ignorance has thus been removed. It is only saints who can possess true knowledge and understanding. It is remarkable how when intricate questions are simple and clear to saints, scholars utterly fail to grasp them. This is because saints apprehend a truth through something higher than intellect—superconsciousness (which develops when the limitations of the ego have been overcome through prayer), while scholars try to understand it through the weak medium of intellect.

The peace, joy and blessedness which saints possess and radiate, are well known. Their love and goodwill towards others transcend all geographical and racial boundaries. When afflicted, humanity turns to saints for comfort and guidance rather than to scholars or political leaders. To this day, men and women owe more to Christ and Buddha than to the tallest among political leaders. It is from them (and others of their kind) that the best that humanity now possesses has been derived. And, in the future also, it is to them that humanity must turn for help and guidance to elevate itself.

In these days when, thanks to industrial civilisation, everybody finds his nerves shattered and temper frayed, the healing effects of prayer should prove most welcome. Today, pride and conceit which man feels because of his achievements in the domain of science have blurred his vision; and he is not able even to see his own follies. Only prayer will give him the humility necessary for him to have a true and correct understanding. Never before was man in greater need for the habit of prayer.

The Effect of Meditation

WHAT IS MEDITATION? HISTORIANS SAY THAT EVEN AS FAR BACK AS Mohenjodaro civilisation, there is evidence that meditation was a common practice among the people of India. In fact, a statue has been found where you see a yogi meditating. So, meditation has been known to us since the very beginning of our civilisation. Our people have practised meditation. Now the question is, do we meditate according to a common code of meditation, or does each individual decide how he or she would meditate? Each individual has his/her own way of meditation. Although we find books where instructions are given as to how you should meditate, you find that the instructions are not very clear to you. In fact, you may even find instructions which you may not understand or do not know what exactly is expected of you.

Now, this is something very subjective. You may have a good textbook on meditation, a book that is written by somebody known to be a good Yogi. He says, your mind is the bee and your mind is fixed on the flower, the ideal figure that you have chosen for yourself. And you keep thinking of that figure all the time. It is true, you find in the scriptures that you have to sit in a particular posture, you choose a good place, a quiet place. As Sri Ramakrishna says, when you meditate, try to meditate in a corner of your house so that there are not too many people around. You alone, with your ideal, God or deity, you sit down and meditate; or you meditate inside the mosquito-curtain, he says. The place is not very important. You would like to have a quiet place. But it may be that you have a kind of environment where it is difficult for you to have a quiet place. But it is expected that you withdraw your mind entirely from things around. There may be people talking but you do not hear. If your mind is occupied with something within, people might be talking but you do not hear what they are saying. It is possible that by practice you withdraw your outgoing organs; all our organs are outgoing, the organs that you have in the body are outgoing. But there are moments when you are not even aware of where you are. When we are absent-minded or when our mind is on a higher plane or some other plane or our mind is totally occupied with something—thought or object—and it may be somebody is calling us and we do not hear, or somebody is before us and talking, trying to draw our attention but we do not hear. We are absolutely indrawn. This is what is called contemplation. You are indrawn, you are inside. Inside there is a world that is much more real than the world that we see with our eyes, the world that we perceive through our sense organs.

A real Yogi lives in a world of his own. He is within himself. He is not conscious of what is going on around him. It is this kind of withdrawal from the world outside, which is called Yoga. That is to say, you are in communion with your own self within and the world outside ceases to exist for you. So, this kind of concentration of the mind we need. When we talk of meditation we think, thinking of some object, something which we are fond of, something which we think is good for us, thinking deeply, constantly like pouring oil from one pot to another in an unbroken stream. It is like you are pouring yourself into something that you love, something that you think is good for you—may be a form of God, if you are a religious person. If you are not a religious person, how do you meditate or what would you meditate on? If you are not a religious person, you certainly are a person who would like to see himself transformed in terms of character. I am good perhaps but I can be better, I would like to be better, I would like to be pure in all respects. Of course, it helps if you are religious. Then you have the direction; you know the direction that you should follow. But if you are not religious, let us say you want to be a morally perfect person. You want to attain perfection in terms of character. Think of yourself as a perfect person you are within. You are perfect, always perfect and if you keep thinking all the time that you are perfect, you are good, you are pure, you are honest, and you are transformed. You become honest. You can never do anything wrong. It hurts you when you find you are thinking of something which is not good, which is not clear, not pure.

Why should we meditate? Because somehow or the other we feel I am not happy, I am not satisfied. All of us have that feeling. Why are we not happy—we do not know? Maybe we have problems. But of course, life has problems. We cannot imagine a life where there are not problems. You may be a really successful person, you may be a rich man, maybe a powerful man but you have problems. And you know, there is a wonderful statement in the scriptures which says: how can I go beyond fear. I have a fear haunting me all the time. I am rich: that does not mean that I have no problems; that does not mean that I have no worry. I am rich, I have money, but I still worry. I worry because my money may be grabbed by somebody else. People around, my own relatives may cheat me, or take my money away. Therefore, the loss of money, health, beauty, youth, and position which now I occupy in society, is perishable. So the idea, the fear of loss—the Hindu scriptures say somehow or other you have to go beyond fear, '*Abhayam*'. We have to attain a state where we are free from fear, we are not afraid of anything.

So, I have problems and I keep worrying. A rich man has his own problems; a scholar has his own problems; a political leader has his own problems—each individual has his own problems. So we worry, and are unhappy. Everyone is disturbed in the mind. We are advancing in many directions. Nevertheless we have problems, we worry all the time. The more you advance, the more complicated life becomes and the more worries trouble your mind.

Now, what can meditation do about this? They say you practise meditation. Turn your mind away from things outside. Direct your mind inside and keep thinking yourself as a perfect man, a good man, an honest man. Each individual has his own concept of what is called perfect. So, keep thinking of perfection, of purity, goodness, beauty, honesty and morality. You are not a religious person. But surely, you admit you have to be a good and a moral person. Think of your moral life, values and try to fix your mind on a certain level where you are satisfied with yourself. Your satisfaction, not what other people think about you. Other people may think you are a perfect man already. But you know yourself. If you are a perfect man you will always go on finding fault with yourself. You will say 'No, I am not perfect. I am not as perfect as I would like to be. I go on finding fault with myself. But meditation, if I keep meditating on myself, I imagine myself at a level when I am perfect i.e., I love everybody, I have no enemy. I do not bear ill-will towards anybody; I cherish goodwill, friendship, a sense of unity and a sense of oneness. If I hurt you, I hurt myself. This sense of oneness, sense of feeling that I have to care for everybody, I cannot afford to be selfish. A selfish man is never happy and I am not going to be a selfish man. I will be unselfish. I will think more of others than of myself. I will love people and serve them. I will be happy if I can provide some service to others.' This sort of life you have to practise if you are not religious.

If you are religious, then of course, things are easier. If you are religious you have some ideal. Let us say, you think of Buddha. You imagine that you are Buddha. All the time you have that figure within yourself. And, thinking of Buddha, according to Hindu scriptures, will transform you into a Buddha, you become a Buddha. You are what you think you are. Again and again this idea is repeated in the *Gospel of Sri Ramakrishna*. Sri Ramakrishna used to say if you think you are a sinner, you become a sinner. But if you think you are pure, you are good, you are honest, you are beautiful, you are what you think you are. So, thinking of Buddha, you will transform your life as Buddha. Look at the face of Buddha—so calm, peaceful. There is an aura of happiness, joy and purity around him.

Therefore, the trouble is within our mind. The mind is always restless, running about all the time. We have to practise what Sri Ramakrishna used to do whenever he dealt with his mind. He used to say, 'Look mind, stay here. Do not run about. I won't let you do that. Stay here. Stay at rest. Stay here at the feet of the Mother.' So, if you are religious, the problem is easier to solve. Otherwise you do not know where you are going to fix your mind on—some abstract thought, some principle, some idea, etc.

Swami Vivekananda said you can fix your mind on some idea. But something abstract keeps eluding you all the time. You would like to have something concrete, something tangible, something real. So, you choose somebody. Let us say, you choose Buddha or Christ or Krishna or Sri Ramakrishna or somebody else as your ideal and you keep thinking of that ideal. Gradually, you are happy and peaceful in mind.

Our saints and the scriptures say, all power is within you. You can realise it only by practice. Keep practising and slowly you find you are able to control your mind. As of now, the mind is restless, always running about from one thing to another, wasting time. But if you keep practising, you look within yourself. Your eyes, your ears, your organs of perception—restrict their areas of operation. Slowly, the world ceases to exist for you and you are within yourself. Inside, there is a much bigger world than the world you see outside. You are within that world and you have your chosen ideal and you are in constant contact with that ideal. You are always thinking of that ideal. And, meditation is the only way by which we can control our mind.

If you keep thinking of Buddha, it means that you are going to be Buddha. You are one with Buddha. To begin with, you and Buddha are separate but as you keep thinking of Buddha you become one with Buddha. You forget yourself. You think of Buddha alone. You think you are Buddha. And slowly, you begin to develop within yourself the qualities that characterise Buddha. And you become Buddha. And, peace and happiness and a sense of fulfilment reigns. But meditation is not easy; it takes time and depends on continuous practice.

Sometimes, you meet people in your neighbourhood, very humble, honest and good, always trying to go out of his way to help others. Why shouldn't I want to be like that? It is a matter of being and becoming. I cannot be satisfied with myself. There is that expression 'divine discontent'. There is in all of us this discontent. And, this discontent is a divine gift. That I am not satisfied with myself, I judge myself and find my weaknesses. But I must get rid of them. I must be perfect—perfect by my own standard. I want peace of mind and happiness. Look around, there are people—they may be poor, they may not be very rich, they may not be learned but cheerful, happy, smiling, good, always trying to help others—all such qualities can give us a sense of fulfilment. If I feel for others, if I love others, if I am ready to sacrifice my own interest for the sake of others, I will be a happy man.

The more I think of myself, the more I think of my own well being, I will be unhappy. The less we think of ourselves, the more will be the possibility of our being happy. You can be happy if you are unselfish. Today, we think that happiness depends upon money, scholarship, position in society, etc. But all this is wrong. Happiness depends upon what sort of a person I am, according to my own judgement. I am not going to attach any importance about what other people think about me. They may think I am bad. But I know I am not bad, not that bad at least, that they think I am. It is like that you begin with a certain piece of stone and you are a sculptor, you have your hammer and chisel and you start working on that stone. And, you are working there alone. People do not know what you are doing. They know you are inside, you are doing something, you are busy, you never allow people to come and interfere with your work. You are working alone. And after a while, there is an exhibition and there, to the amazement of everybody, there is a beautiful statue of Buddha. I am the architect of my own fate.

The concept of meditation arises from the fact that what you are today or what you are going to be tomorrow. It is all up to you. You have to decide what you are going to be. You have to have an idea of your own perfection. You want to be perfect. Perfect, in terms of your character. You are not a selfish person. You are a person who feels for others, who cares for others, ready to share the suffering, the hardship of others—that sort of person is happy. A selfish man can never be happy. A selfish man is very likely to be immoral. He thinks his family exists for his own sake, his neighbours for his own sake; the whole world exists for his own sake. He thinks of himself alone and he is never happy.

So, by constant practice of meditation, you realise that you are improving which encourages you to continue. Suppose my ideal is my Self and concentrate on that ideal. I meditate and slowly I begin to change. Gradually you become a different individual altogether, a perfect person, happy, kind, generous, pleasant, always thinking for others, caring for others. You are a happy person when you are able to feel for others, love others. You do not think of yourself only, you think of others more than you think of yourself. That is what is necessary. Your life has been totally changed. That is the purpose of meditation. Meditation—all your perfect representation, yourself perfect, perfect according to you.

Self-surrender

ALL RELIGIONS STRESS THE NECESSITY OF SELF-SURRENDER. 'THY WILL be done'—this is advocated as the attitude for a religious aspirant. The rule is laid down that under no circumstances should one allow one's judgement or will to prevail. Surrender to God should be complete and unreserved.

Of illustrations given to indicate what self-surrender is, to be like that of a small kitten is typical. A small kitten depends on its mother completely, absolutely. Not only has it no wish or choice about anything, it does not even know what is good and bad for it. All it does know is to meow, i.e. to call on its mother (so that she may always remain with it). The mother may place it, on turns, on a heap of ash or on a bed of down. It is all the same to it. With the mother at hand, it is content to be wherever she may place it. Without her there is no comfort for it; with her there is no discomfort for it. In joy as well as in sorrow, the mother must take complete charge of it. It has no independent will, no independent thought or action. The mother is the pivot of its existence.

Obviously, this sort of self-surrender does not come easily. It comes, if at all, only at an advanced stage of spiritual evolution. It is almost the culmination of a long and sustained struggle. 'The Old Adam' is a tough fighter; few can overcome it. And, it has much guile. You can never be sure that you have shaken yourself free from it. Perhaps, when you are flattering yourself that you have conquered it, it may be it has merely gone into hiding and is preparing a new attack on you. 'Vigilance is the price of freedom'. Indeed, this is very much the case where freedom has to be won and kept from the ego.

Again and again it is pointed out that so long as there is the least trace of the ego in a man, he is not likely to get God's grace. Just as 'even a little fibre can prevent the thread from passing through the needle's eye', similarly even a mere suggestion of the ego can debar a man from God's grace. God is truly a 'jealous' God. He insists that you depend on Him and Him alone. A parable of Sri Ramakrishna brings out how complete dependence on God must be:

'Once Lakshmi and Narayana were seated in Vaikuntha, when Narayana suddenly stood up. Lakshmi had been stroking his feet. She said 'Lord, where are you going?' Narayana answered: 'One of my devotees is in great danger. I must save him.' With these words he went out. But he came back immediately. Lakshmi said, 'Lord, why have you returned so soon?' 'Narayana smiled and said, 'The devotee was going along the road overwhelmed with love for me. Some washermen were drying clothes on the grass and the devotee walked over the clothes. At this the washermen chased him and were going to beat him with their sticks. So, I ran to protect him.' 'But why have you come back?' asked Lakshmi. Narayana laughed and said, 'I saw the devotee picking up a brick to throw at them. So I came back!'

Obviously, the devotee felt he could cope with the situation himself. In the circumstances, the God had nothing to do but to withdraw.

The question then arises: Is there no room for self-help where self-surrender is concerned? Certainly there is, but naturally its scope is limited. If you depend upon God, then depend upon Him only. You cannot depend partially upon Him and partially upon yourself.

Your dependence upon Him must be complete or nothing at all. You must not have any desire, any plan of your own; you leave everything to God and you are content to accept all that may happen to you. You are a tool in His hands and He does with you anything He pleases. You do nothing on your own; whatever you do, you do because you are convinced God wants you to do it.

And, you are not interested in the consequences. You may suffer bitterly, but you do not complain. You believe it is willed by God and, therefore, must be good for you. All that you may ask is that God be with you and give you strength to suffer. In fact, you welcome such suffering, since you know it is a sign of His love for you. A story is related which illustrates this very poignantly. Once there was a devotee who depended upon God completely. One day he was bitten by a snake. As he felt death creeping up his body, he began to shout with ecstatic joy, 'Oh, the Lord be praised. He has sent a messenger to fetch His beloved.'

Job said, 'Let come on me what will. Though He slay me, yet will I trust in Him.'

It is just this attitude which a devotee should adopt. The surrender must be complete and unconditional.

Suffering does not frighten a devotee. Thomas A Kempis said, 'So long as suffering appears grievous to thee and thou seekest to fly from it, so long will it be ill with thee . . .'

The attitude of Christian devotees is typical. Far from running away from suffering, they seek it. They believe God is nearer to them when they suffer. An act of suffering is an act of love—love of God. The Cross is regarded as the highest symbol of love of God and suffering for His sake. While not all are ready for it, they must seek it, strive for it. It is in this spirit that teachers of the Gospel look upon suffering. They are glad, even grateful, that God tries them. Suffering is the best reward they ask of God for their labours.

Self-surrender is not passive. It is active and dynamic. It is a process in which we negate the self, the ego. By reasoning, we realise that the ego is the root of all our troubles. Because of the ego we are selfish and mean, because of the ego we stoop to falsehood and deceit, we cannot see the beauty of reason and truth, we are vain and dull. So, we feel urgently that we must try and conquer it. But how can you conquer it? By love of God. The more you love God, the less you love yourself. The ego automatically goes under if love of God is strong. All attempts to conquer the ego fail where love of God is not present. God is just the antithesis of the ego. Love God more and more; the ego will cease to trouble you. All religious teachers point to this truth.

There is yet another way of conquering the ego, more difficult. That is by meditating on the impermanence of what is called the ego. What is this ego we make much of? We are so very fond of ourselves. But do we ever care to examine what exactly we are fond of? What we call our 'selves' is nothing but a chain of contradictory experiences and organs through which those experiences are acquired. On a close examination, we will see there is nothing in them which we can call permanent. They are more an 'appearance' than a 'reality.' The fact that we run after this phantom and let it dominate our life and character is really a surprise. The best and wisest among us ignore it altogether. They treat it as if it does not exist. They watch it and its pranks with the same concern as you watch a stupid drama.

Man's real 'Ego' is very different from what it is supposed to be. It, i.e. the 'Self' of man, is above all contradictions, all dualities. It is always the same. Nothing can affect it, for there is nothing outside it. It is always full and complete. Man need not desire anything, for he already has what he may desire. He will have no clash with others, for to him 'others' do not exist. Clearly, knowledge of this 'Self' can confer on man the highest peace and joy. And rightly, therefore, this knowledge is regarded as the real aim of life. The ego is no problem to a man who possesses this knowledge, for it has lost its *locus standi*. In him self-surrender is already an accomplished fact, for his self-knowledge is the result of self-surrender—surrender of the (untrue) self to the (true) Self.

Whichever way is preferred, self-surrender must be attained. Though the aim is complete self-surrender, in the beginning it has to be a compromise between the self and God, or between the self and the Self. Progressively less and less of the self, and more and more of the Self—that is how one has to proceed. It is a long process, but it pays dividends all the way. At no stage is it useless. If not for spiritual reasons, at least, for social reasons, the ego has to be checked, and, if possible, conquered. All egotists are social despots. It is from their ranks that political dictators arise. There can be no peace in the world so long as egotists continue to be heads of States. History proves how such people have reduced life to an agony. Love of the self is their strongest motive. Intelligent and efficient, they are ready to send the world to pieces for their petty and parochial interests. By all means leadership must be saved from them. Only such people should be allowed to lead as are able to check the ego. Egotism is not merely a personal problem; it is a social evil also.

Philosophy of Peace

WHEN PEACE BECOMES A MATTER OF EXPEDIENCY, IT CANNOT LAST long. Unfortunately, this is exactly how the problem of peace is dealt with by the world leaders. If they have a dispute, either they use force to settle it, or arrive at some sort of patchwork agreement, in their anxiety to avoid an armed conflict. Neither side is satisfied with the agreement, but as they are not yet quite ready to launch a full scale war, they buy a temporary reprieve this way. They do not go into the basic issues which lie at the root of the dispute; they fight shy of them, for they know they cannot be solved unless there is a complete change in their outlook, a change for which they are not yet ready. Therefore, they have to be content with a make-shift settlement, which means that the root of the dispute remains untouched, with every possibility of a fresh flare-up of the dispute in the near future. Often, this kind of temporary settlement is reached only as a face-saving device or to buy time in which better preparations can be made for the next round of negotiations, if not actual clashes. The relations between the conflicting nations never really become normal. Outwardly, the nations are formal and correct with each other, showing even flamboyant expressions of friendship and goodwill on suitable occasions but all these are only an eyewash. Inwardly, they are hostile, always looking for an opportunity to harm each other. In fact, international relations today are based on mutual suspicion and distrust, each trying to take advantage of the other under one pretext or another. If there is a budding friendship between one nation and another, or between one group of nations and another, it is because they have some common interests which they feel can be best served if they are together. If they have a unity, it is not a unity of hearts; it is only a temporary coming together to resist the aggression of a common enemy or to exploit jointly another country. It is their greed and the savage instinct of robbing the weak and defenceless that brings them together. But between themselves, there is always an undercurrent of suspicion and distrust, and the make-shift unity which they strike up for the time being, cracks at the first hint of a dispute over the spoils of their joint international gangsterism. If they talk of peace it is not from the heart they do so; it is only make-believe. They always follow a cloak and dagger policy. Their own interests are supreme to them. To sub serve their interests they will use any means they find expedient.

Even when they talk, they may have some evil designs in their hearts. Even if they mean what they say, others will not take them at their word, for past experience has taught them to be wary about such talk. It is possible that some leaders do want peace. But they do not know what to do to achieve it. Will they stop buying arms and weapons? Will they disband their armies? Will they stop spending money on defence altogether? Can they follow a policy like this unilaterally? What if the neighbouring countries attack them? Indeed, the crucial question is how far you can go in following the policy of peace. If there is a territorial dispute with a neighbouring country which is not amenable to any peaceful settlement, what will you do to defend your country's territorial integrity? Can you avoid going to war in the face of naked aggression? Will you watch your country's honour and rights being violated without a protest? What if your protest goes unheeded? Can you—should you—remain peaceful when innocent men and women of your country are being butchered?

Indeed, there can be no peace in the world unless all countries simultaneously decide to abjure war as a means of resolving international disputes. There will always be disputes but the nations have to decide once for all to settle their disputes by peaceful means. War is no solution to disputes. It is irrational, an offence against civilisation, an unqualified evil. It is a betrayal of God and man, both. War to uphold justice, to enforce equality and freedom, is always self-defeating. War, once begun never ends, only it changes in the degrees and forms of violence accompanying it. It always leaves behind a trail of bitterness and hatred which go on smoldering till they burst out again in another conflagration. The roots of war are in the mind. If you hate anybody, you have already taken the first step towards war. If there has to be peace it has to begin in the mind. You cannot have peace with hatred in the heart and love on the lips. Love in the heart is the first condition of peace. It is not love for one's own people; it must be love for everybody. You cannot love others for the sake of peace or some other expediency; love, in such a case, is a pretence and not genuine.

Genuine love is spontaneous; it is love which springs from deeper sources, from a conviction. 'A large-hearted man looks upon every being as his own,' goes a Sanskrit saying. Race, religion, language—these are barriers that divide mankind into smaller units. How can these barriers be overcome? How can an individual feel one with the rest of mankind? Here comes in the need of a philosophy, the kind of philosophy that embraces all mankind as one. If mankind is one, there can be no question of one country or community fighting another. Countries, communities or races have to hold on to each other, for they are parts of a whole, they are one. It is on this philosophy of oneness that future attempts at peace have to be based. Is there such a philosophy? Luckily for the world there is such a philosophy, it is the philosophy of Vedanta, an Indian heritage. Let us have a look at this philosophy to see how it can give us the sense of oneness which we miss today and which alone can provide a basis for future peace efforts.

Vedanta briefly says that in essence all that exists, animate or inanimate, comes from one single source. We do not know what this source is like, since it is not susceptible to sense perception. But since we derive our common essence from it, it is our common self. It is the Self, the Cosmic Self that inheres in all of us, that binds us together. In other words, we are all one, though in terms of names and forms we are different from each other. 'Unity in diversity'—this is the basic characteristic of the phenomenal world. That is to say, the diversity that we see is only in details, not in the real nature of things which is one and the same everywhere. It is this concept of oneness on which Vedanta hinges. In fact, it goes to the extent of describing the diversity as *unreal*, unreal in the sense that it is subject to change.

If there has to be peace in the world, it has to flow from this concept of unity. The concept of one world is already known in the West, but this oneness is physical. The time has come when we have to realise our spiritual unity. What is the implication of this spiritual unity? The implication is that we have one self, one consciousness, one mind, we are one. If I hurt you, I hurt myself, since you and I are one in spite of our different names and forms.

What follows from this is that the entire human family is one. There are of course different races, with different pigments of the skin, with different languages, different food habits, different religious beliefs. Underlying these differences there is, however, a basic unity which is constant in spirit. If one race fights another, it is as if the self is fighting the self; it is, in other words, a suicide. This is no ideology, ironically this is reality today. If there is a war today, both winners and losers will suffer, and suffer equally. The nature of war today is such that both sides will be equally affected irrespective of the final upshot of the war. More and more, it is being realised that our destinies are interlinked so that what happens in one part of the world has its repercussions on the rest of it. If there is a war between any two countries it is bound to spread, and soon engulf other countries as well. It is like a stone dropped in a lake: not only the water next to where the stone is dropped is disturbed but the whole mass of water in the lake is disturbed. Gone are the days when war could be contained within a limited geographical area. Now, inevitably, it becomes a global war. This only confirms our physical unity.

But the loss that nations sustain because of war is not to be counted in physical terms only: it completely changes man's psyche, reversing the progress he has made in terms of his feelings and emotions over the centuries. The refinement he has acquired through the evolution process is completely destroyed. He becomes a savage again. If a city is razed to the ground, it can be rebuilt. But the decline which occurs in human nature because of the brutalities accompanying war is hard to mend. One war leads to another war, and each time there is a war, deadlier weapons are used. A chain action follows, leading to more and more cruelty, more and more lowering of the human standards. It is the law of the jungle that prevails. Should this continue? Civilisation will crumble, man will perish if this continues.

What is the way out? How can an international dispute be settled? Some civilised ways have to be devised, certainly not by war. War may be a short-term solution, but it is no solution in the end. It is understandable that there shall always be disputes between nation and nation, but fighting gives no permanent relief to the aggrieved nation. If we are one, we cannot harm others without harming ourselves. We may not yet be ready to accept this idea of oneness, but soon we will be forced to accept it. Perhaps, expediency again will make us accept it. Some more wars and some more battering will teach us the soundness of this philosophy. Only this philosophy of oneness stands as a guard against war. If there has to be peace, it has to be on the basis of this oneness.

The Role of Religion in a Modern Secular State

HAS RELIGION ANY ROLE TO PLAY IN A MODERN SECULAR STATE? THE obvious answer seems to be that it has not. If the State is really secular and modern, how can religion have any place in it? Either the State is altogether opposed to it or at least indifferent to it. China is an example of the former, Russia of the latter. China has banned religion outrightly; Russia has not banned it exactly but makes no bones about the fact that she is not going to encourage it. You may practise religion—there is no law that can prevent you from doing so, but you are left in no doubt that it is not liked.

But China and Russia are not the only offenders in this respect, if, of course, opposing religion or being indifferent to it is an offence. All so-called modern States have more or less the same attitude about religion. They may or may not be secular but they either discourage religion or leave it strictly alone. Somehow or other, there is a widespread belief that a modern State has to be stridently anti-religious, as if opposition to religion is an essential ingredient of modernism. If a concession has to be made, it must at least say that it is secular. India is an instance in point. Her leaders wanted to make India a modern State in the sense the States in the West are. They thought that to do this, they had to eschew religion and declare that they were secular. Later however, they have modified the stand by declaring that as secularists they are not against religion but they do not wish to identify themselves with any particular religion. In the Indian context, this is understandable, for there being many religions in India and there being much rivalry among them, it is a good policy for the State to declare that it is completely neutral in religious matters. It is possible to question if there was no alternative to it, but one derives some comfort from the thought that behind this secularism, there is no hostility to religion as such but simply an anxiety to maintain impartiality towards the various religious groups.

There is yet another argument which can be put forward in support of secularism: Unless a State is strictly secular in its approach to socio-economic problems—that is, if it allows its decisions on such problems to be influenced by religious beliefs and traditions, or the kind of obscurantism which often goes in the name of religion—disastrous consequences will follow. Socio-economic problems are essentially problems of environment, of history, ethnics, traditions, systems, institutions and similar other factors. Religion has no relevance to these problems except in an indirect way. The knowledge needed to solve these problems has to be sought elsewhere. Do we go to an engineer when we have a health problem? If the problem is one of food shortage, epidemic or environmental pollution, religion will not be able to solve the problem, only science can solve it.

The question then arises: What do we need religion for? Do we need it at all? There was a time when we did not know how to explain a solar eclipse, an earthquake or an epidemic. We thought that they happened because we had done something which gave offence to God. We, therefore, tried to appease Him as best we could. We know now why they happen and if we cannot control an earthquake or a solar eclipse, we certainly know how to control an epidemic. There are countries where epidemics are completely unknown. Birth or death is no longer a mystery. We know now how or why it happens and we no longer attribute it to the whims of a supernatural power. Similarly, if a child is born deformed or a woman remains barren it is not due to the malevolence of any deity but to the malfunctioning of some organ or some virus or there is something gone wrong biologically. There is hardly any physiological problem which man does not understand or cannot tackle. There was a time when man worshipped the forces of nature from fear but now he is able to control them and is in fact using them for his own comfort. His power over nature is almost supreme. In the past, man was very much dependent upon his environment but now he can, to a large extent, change the environment as he likes.

The progress that man has made over the past few decades is breathtaking. But what has made this progress possible? It is science and technology, not religion. It is therefore argued, if man has to make further progress, he must depend more and more upon science and technology, and avoid religion altogether. It is a hindrance and cannot stand the test of reason; it is unscientific, encourages daydreaming, and makes man otherworldly. In any case, it is redundant in this age of science and technology. People point to the Western countries and say, 'Look, how they are progressing. They are progressing because they do not make too much fuss over religion as the countries in Asia do.' In fact, critics of religion think India's progress has suffered because her people cannot get away from traditionalism, a weakness directly traceable to religion. There are inhibitions which religion imposes which make man cower before the challenges of life. A man free from religious superstitions is pragmatic, bold and self-confident; a religious man is unsure of himself, suffers from wishful thinking and always hopes for a miracle which never happens. To these critics religion is synonymous with medievalism. It is doomed and is bound to fade out as man progresses in science and technology. A modern State has no use for it.

But can religion be dismissed so easily? Can man do without religion? Protagonists of religion think just as you cannot get out of your skin, similarly you cannot get away from religion. It is something deep within you, something that clings to you despite everything you do to shake it off. It is religion that keeps you dissatisfied with your present situation and drives you on and on till you reach a stage when you feel you have achieved what you wanted to achieve, till you have achieved the best and the highest, and there is nothing further you want to achieve. It is dissatisfaction that is at the root of progress, which gives the motivation to strive for improvement. According to Swami Vivekananda, this dissatisfaction is universal. We are dissatisfied because there is a sense of inadequacy in us, a sense of something we want but which is now missing. We feel we are not what we ought to be or that what is our due has eluded us. There is hunger within us, a hunger for more and more. At first, we begin by thinking that if we have more money or more power or more sense pleasure we will be happy. Some of us have these things to saturation point, yet we are not happy. The richest man is not necessarily the happiest one. Even the most scholarly man is not the happiest man. No man, in fact, is happy.

Because there is this unhappiness, man is never at rest but is always seeking what he thinks will give him a sense of fulfilment, a sense of having achieved what he regards as of supreme value. What he achieves may seem trash to others but so far as he is concerned, he wants nothing better. If you love paintings, you will think nothing of spending a million dollars on a Picasso, if of course, you can afford it. Others may think you are crazy, but you think your money is very well spent. To some, an idea is more real, more important, and more vital than any material object. A noble idea is worth the whole world to them.

But what idea has the greatest appeal to man (or an animal)? Freedom. At first, we are troubled if there is any curb on our physical freedom, that is, if we cannot have as much sense pleasure as we want. But, as Swami Vivekananda says, '... out of this lower consciousness grows and broadens the higher conception of a mental or moral bondage and a longing for spiritual freedom'.[1] The real goal of life is freedom, freedom in its fullest sense. All religions promise this freedom though they describe it differently. It is the embodiment of this freedom which is called God. 'The goal of life is communion with the Supreme. It is a life of realisation, a gnosis, an inner intuitive vision of God, when man achieves absolute freedom and escapes from the blind servitude to ordinary experience.'[2] God may be a mere postulate, an idea, a state of being, but consciously or unconsciously, all of us are striving for this goal called God. The fact of God may be disputed but the fact of man's hunger for freedom and ultimately for God cannot be disputed.

It is wrong to suppose that science and religion are implacable enemies. They are essentially one, one in the sense that both represent man's struggle against nature. Science is the key to man's struggle against external nature whereas religion is the key to his struggle against internal nature. Man has to conquer both external and internal nature: external nature to ensure his physical well-being and internal nature in order that he may be a better man morally, may not suffer from inner conflicts and tensions, and may have peace, joy and happiness. One without the other will leave him incomplete. Man is about to complete his conquest of external nature, but he has done little or nothing so far about conquering internal nature. Despite all his achievements in the field of science and technology, he remains a 'civilised savage'. Thanks to the gadgets we have invented, our physical existence today is easy and pleasant. But what about our minds? Have we been able to conquer our minds? Are we not still prey to our own elemental passions? Buddha used to say that a real hero was he who had conquered not a territory but his

---

1. *The Complete Works* (Advaita Ashram, Mayavati, Himalayas), Vol. I (1962) pp. 336–7.
2. Radhakrishnan: *Occasional Speeches and Writings* (Combined Editions—1952–59), Publication Division, Ministry of Information and Broadcasting, Govt. of India, March, 1960), p. 318.

own mind. All of us are conscious today of the great peril which threatens humanity. The Big Powers have in their armoury such a vast array of atomic weapons that if one of them in a moment of frenzy unleashes war, the whole mankind may be wiped out. The Big Powers themselves know this, but it is doubtful if this knowledge is enough of a deterrent. What is the way out then? Religion is the only way out. Not rituals, theology or faith but what may be regarded as the essence of religion—compassion, truthfulness, justice, fellowship, etc. Science has improved the conditions of life to an extent one never thought possible, but unless this is matched by an improvement in man's moral and spiritual level, man's future is bleak. There is too much hatred, suspicion, and greed among us. We are at constant war with ourselves and our fellow-men. We fight not only big wars; we also fight many small wars, wars which are no less deadly. We fight those wars silently, often imperceptibly, and continually. Though they cause no physical injury they maim the spirit and make us abnormal men and women. It is in the mind that war, small or big, really begins. We must rid the mind of the evil of selfishness, anger and hatred. How do we do it? It is only through religion that we can do it. Religion gives the motivation to fight this evil. All religions teach self-control. We must pledge ourselves to a life of self-control.

By a modern State we understand a State which says that it is going to see that everybody in the State is happy and thriving. In other words, it is a welfare State, a State which holds itself responsible for everything that happens to its citizens whether it is physical or moral. If something goes wrong with the psyche of its citizens, if large sections of them show signs of insanity, the State—that is, if it is a truly modern State—cannot afford to ignore it. The alienation of the younger generation from the older one, essentially a psychological problem, is threatening to disrupt society everywhere. Can a modern State say that the problem does not concern it? There are similar other problems which man faces now which have their origin in his mind. The State must find solutions to those problems; otherwise it is not living up to its promise as a welfare State. Man is not yet man, he is still an animal. His struggle against nature, his evolution, is still going on. Physically he is not likely to change much; perhaps he has already reached the zenith of his development. His progress henceforth will be on the moral plane. There have been great sages and saints born in every age and every society who demonstrated man's great moral and spiritual potential. They are not myths but real. Buddha is a fact of history. If there has been one Buddha, there can be other Buddhas as well. Even if it is an impossible goal, it is well worth trying for. It is the effort we make that is important. Let it be understood that man has limitless possibilities. He is not just body but also spirit, not merely animal but also divine. Every soul is infinite. 'From the lowest worm that crawls under our feet to the noblest and greatest saints, all have this infinite power, infinite purity, and infinite everything. Only the difference is in the degree of manifestation.'[3]

What does religion do? It helps man manifest this infinite power, this infinite purity. It transforms him, makes a sinner a saint, a man a superman. It tells man, 'Look, there is your goal, follow that goal, go on and on till you get there.' It tells him that he must be himself, his true self, here and now. It gives a meaning to his life. Life is not mere existence, but an opportunity, a challenge. When Socrates died he told the citizens of Athens that nothing could deflect him from the pursuit of truth. He did not know what death was like but he did know that a life of ease and comfort, a life without a purpose, a life given to sense-enjoyment, was contemptible. It is religion that makes man spurn wealth, worldly power, social status, and instead seek truth, knowledge and moral excellence. What man has is not important, what he *is* is important. Religion is the science of 'being and becoming', as Swami Vivekananda defined it. It is

---

3. Swami Vivekananda: *op. cit.,* Vol III (1964) p. 407.

growth from within, growth towards better archetypes of manhood. The modern State needs religion, because it wants to improve the quality of its men and women; it wants men and women who are moral, who feel for others, who can sacrifice everything for a truly noble cause, for the cause of truth and justice. Man's flights to the moon are a measure of his supremacy over external nature. He may win more such laurels in the future, but what does it avail if he loses his soul? He must conquer his internal nature also; otherwise the disquiet which haunts him will not go. Civilisation will be at peril if his moral stature is not raised. Industrial development has given man affluence but it has robbed his peace. He is spiritually sick. He needs the care which only religion can offer. The picture of a technologically advanced modern State is an astonishing mixture of success and failure, success where physical welfare is concerned, failure in matters of spiritual care. The State stakes everything to give its citizens physical comfort but where the question is one of their moral and spiritual developments, the State is unconcerned. Is this not a fatal mistake? Has this not cost mankind much already in blood, pain, and misery?

'We help the growth of trees, do we not? Left to nature they would have grown, only they would have taken a longer time; we help them to grow in a shorter time than they would otherwise have taken. We are doing all the time the same thing, hastening the growth of things by artificial means. Why cannot we hasten the growth of man?'[4]

The modern State cannot afford to be indifferent to the religious issue. In its own interest it should promote more and more religion, for otherwise it is going to be overwhelmed by anarchy and violence. The problem of the present age is that passions rule man: his conscience does not. Unless the animal in man is curbed, he may annihilate himself. At this hour of crisis, the State must play its

---

4. Swami Vivekananda: *ibid.* Vol. II (1963), p. 18.

part: it must make man conscious of the God in him by using the influence of religion. There is, therefore, no question of the State discarding religion; it should instead call it more and more to its aid to rehabilitate man in his divinity.

Religion and Social Tension

RELIGION IS SUPPOSED TO TAKE MAN TOWARDS GOD THOUGH HE knows nothing about Him except that he imagines that God is the sum of all that is good, noble and beautiful. If man takes any interest in religion, it is because he values these qualities and he hopes that by practising religion he may some day be good, noble, and beautiful himself. In other words, he is seeking self-improvement and in this, he seeks God's help. The prayers he addresses to God are all for this help. How far God helps him is a matter of personal experience. Some will say He does help and they are so sure about it that it is no use arguing with them about it. The vast majority of people, of course, are not so sure about it. They still keep praying in the hope that some day they will receive help from God as the more fortunate worshippers claim they have. So the purpose of religion is self-improvement and all that man does in the name of religion should be directed to that end.

But if the purpose of religion is to make man good, noble and beautiful, how is it then that, in its name, man commits heinous crimes like murder, or even worse? How much blood has been spilled and is still being spilled in the name of religion! It is, indeed, a paradox that religion has been a cause for violence throughout history. No wonder, many blame religion for this situation. They say that religion creates artificial divisions among mankind and promotes hatred, greed and jealousy between them. They view religion as vicious and suggest that it be banned. Others say that it is obscurantism, obsolete and useless. If it was devised to improve man, it has done just the reverse. Man remains as wicked as ever. If religion has served any purpose, it has served as a cover to hide man's wickedness and cheat others. Religion, in other words, has promoted hypocrisy.

How can man then improve? There are pessimists who will say man can never improve. He will always remain a savage under the thin veneer of civilisation. All his boastful talk of truth, goodness, and beauty is humbug. He is basically selfish, crooked and unscrupulous and he will remain that, religion or no religion.

There are others who say that man can improve only if the social system improves. Several views are current as to what sort of social system is ideal. The ideal social system is that in which there are no vested interests. It is a system which offers equal opportunities for all. It tolerates no exploitation of the weak, and no ever-widening gap between the rich and the poor. It abolishes all class distinctions and gives power to the working people. The idea is good, but has such a system been created anywhere yet? But pertinent is the question: Who will create such a system? Man, of course, but what sort of man? Only men of the highest order, men free from greed and all selfish thoughts, can create such a system, if at all. It has to be a system based entirely upon freedom, equality and justice. One wonders if there shall ever be such a system. Even the attempt to create such a system has to be made by perfect men and women.

But which comes first—the perfect system or the perfect men and women? It must be perfect men and women first. Throughout history, idealists have tried to create a just social order but have failed. They have not been content with good wishes only, but have even used forces. They have been ruthless in their methods, so ruthless that often the remedy has been worse than the malady itself. This has happened because they themselves are imperfect. Whatever an imperfect man does is imperfect. It is imperfect because his means are imperfect. No attempt at social reform can succeed unless the people who make the attempt are good and the means they adopt are good. This is where religion comes in. Religion is important because it insists on perfection, all-round perfection. A good society is a society where everybody is trying to live a good religious life. To be religious means to be committed to the highest principles of religion—truth, goodness, and beauty. To be committed is not enough; one must try hard to practise those principles also. It is only in such a society that peace and justice can prevail, that men and women, irrespective of their varying beliefs and practices, can live with honour and dignity, can feel equal to each other.

But has religion succeeded in achieving this? Buddha and Christ have come, but there is no let-up in wars and conflicts yet. If religion is for perfection, what sort of perfection is it that religious men and women fight each other? How is it that they cause bloodshed? Such people are religious only in name; a truly religious man cannot go against his principles of love and goodwill. Buddha suffered from his adversaries but never uttered a word against them. Christ was crucified but prayed for the forgiveness of those who crucified him.

It is not the fault of religion if people misuse it. If electricity is misused, it is not the fault of electricity. A truly religious man can never hurt others. If he does so by mistake, he takes the earliest opportunity to make amends for it. True religion lies in love, goodwill and friendship. It is truth, justice and equality. A man may say he is religious, but he is not religious if he does not possess these qualities. The test of a truly religious man is in how far he has been able to conquer his ego. He is humble, not only before God but also before man. He may think he is right, but he does not want to impose his view upon others. He does not want to force people to come to his way of thinking. He may think his sect is the best but he respects other sects as much as he respects his own. He never interferes with the freedom of others. Even when he feels his own freedom is being curbed, he will not use violence to protest. He will protest peacefully.

It is not that religion does not permit strong and heroic action for a just cause. It does, in extreme cases. Even this heroic action should be used with caution. In no case should there be the spirit of vindictiveness. A strong action may be taken only as a last resort and only to the extent necessary for self-defence. Only that heroic action is permissible which is used to prevent further violence. It may be used only to uphold justice, truth and peace. Krishna advised Arjuna to fight out the big war at Kurukshetra, in order to reestablish justice in a society where untruth and injustice reigned.

A truly religious man uses even a strong action with moderation, and not for selfish reasons, not even for a particular section of people, but for the entire community irrespective of creed, religion or nationality. Today, there is hardly a society which is not rocked by conflicts of one kind or another. Often, these conflicts are marked by senseless cruelty. Anger, hatred, vengeance and other animal passions seem to have got the upper hand. Man has lost his reason. His sanity is in doubt.

What is the remedy? The remedy is simple: man has to go back to religion. Only light can dispel darkness, only love can conquer hatred. What the world needs today is true religion. Poverty and unemployment no longer pose a challenge to man; they can be tackled and are being tackled. His greatest enemy now is he himself. His very survival is at stake. He can save himself only if he improves his own being, if he becomes, or at least tries to become what religion requires of him: love and goodwill towards all. In other words, he must practise his religion.

Religious Harmony: An Impossible Dream?

THE RIG VEDA DECLARES: 'TRUTH IS ONE, BUT SCHOLARS DEFINE IT in various ways.' What does this mean? It means that the substance which constitutes the phantasmagoria, called the world, is one and the same; but it can be given different names—a profound statement which can form the basis for human unity at all levels of life. But the moot question is: 'Is the substance we daily encounter, amidst the diversity of things and beings, really one?'

The Rig Veda calls the substance 'Truth', but what is that 'Truth'? No two persons will agree about the nature of this 'Truth'. Is the truth relative, or absolute? If it is a relative truth, it cannot be the same for all and for all times. For instance, the temperature 20°C is quite pleasant to some people, but it is unbearable to other people. Eye-witness accounts of the same event may be entirely different from each other, in detail, even in substance. The history of World War II, narrated by scholars of different nationalities, is invariably contradictory. Even scholars of the same nationality will depict the incidents of the war differently if they belong to different generations. The viewpoints change with the passage of time. Each scholar claims he is presenting the truth, but it is only his version of the truth and surely it cannot be acceptable to all. This is the problem if the Rig Veda is referring to a relative truth.

If the Rig Veda is referring to an absolute Truth, the question will then arise: 'What is that absolute Truth?' No one can answer that question. The absolute Truth, if there is such a thing at all, remains unknown, is perhaps also unknowable. Those who believe in it argue that whether we know anything about it or not, its existence is beyond question. If a relative truth has any credibility, it is because there is the absolute Truth behind it. There is one universal Truth which is infallible and therefore eternal; it is also impersonal. It is from this that every relative truth is derived. Without the absolute Truth, there is no relative truth. Religion, according to Hinduism, is a search for this absolute Truth. The search, in the end, changes man's character: he rejects everything relative; he remains stuck with the Absolute only. This Absolute is one and the same. To reach this Absolute is the goal of life. Anything that helps man reach this goal is religion. The Absolute is desirable because it is the Absolute in perfection, in peace and happiness—in everything. It is not an impossible goal, for there are instances of people having reached this goal.

But is this statement about religion and its purpose acceptable to all? Where is God in this scheme of things? How can there be a religion without God? Who is our Master? To whom are we answerable for what we do? To whom shall we pray when we are in trouble? Without God who will run this universe? Can a motor car go without a driver?

Most religions view God as the Supreme Being who presides over everything that goes on in this world. He creates, sustains and destroys. He is supreme. He tells you what you should do and what you should not do. You may expect rewards if you obey Him; if you do not obey Him, you are sure to be punished. He is your Master or your Father. If you are in trouble, you can seek His help and get it too. You can never question His judgement. He is infallible. Without God, man sees no *raison d'etre* for honesty, for caring for others, for self-control. He remains a savage.

Most religions belong to this category. How can there be any agreement between these religions and the religion or religions which deny God, or reduce Him to a principle only? Indeed, no two religions seem to agree about their essentials, not to speak of details. Even common terms have different meanings. It is futile to try to bridge the gulf between them. Any talk of their ends and means being the same is naive.

Against this backdrop, those who believe in the harmony of religions contend that the difference between one religion and another is more apparent than real. In fact, it is only semantic. All religions have one common objective—turning out better men and women. But what is meant by 'better men and women'? Surely, they are honest. Honesty is a *sine qua non* for every truly religious person. All religions, irrespective of God or not, put the highest premium on it. Love of fellow-men is another ingredient common to all religions. More such qualities can be named which all religions want their followers to cultivate. It is these qualities which constitute the essence of what is called religion. Whatever their creeds or dogmas, whatever their practices, all religions try to equip men and women with these qualities. It is in this that they may be said to unite. True, they have differences, but those differences do not militate against their common objectives. Those differences arise from ethnic backgrounds and they are natural. Within the same religious group, there may be differences in terms of expressions of religious feelings and emotions. These differences too are natural and have to be preserved. Each individual worships God in his own way. It is a matter between himself and his God. There should be no interference in this so long as he does not offend others. This may be extended to sects and communities also. They will differ from each other and this difference has to be respected. So long as there is no infringement of the rights of others, each sect and community, even each individual, should have full religious freedom. There can be no regimentation in this.

Attempts are now on in many quarters to explore and see what common ground there is, if any, among the religions. Behind these attempts there is the belief that if that common ground is highlighted, the tensions and conflicts which now prevail between different religious communities may be eliminated. Such attempts are welcome, but it is doubtful if they will ever succeed unless those who initiate such attempts are themselves first convinced that there is indeed much that is common between one religion and another. As part of such attempts sometimes inter-religious dialogues are held, but to what end? They begin with much fanfare, but when the show ends they are back to where they were before. This happens because they never come to grip with the real problems at issue. They talk and talk, but they never ask themselves if they are talking about the same thing. Do the terms they use have the same meaning to all of them? Once, representatives of different religions met in what purported to be inter-religious dialogue. All of them were scholarly people. The discussions started on a very friendly note. Everybody seemed to be eager to come to some sort of agreement. They knew there were issues likely to prove controversial; but they either completely avoided controversial issues, or dealt with them very superficially. Obviously, they did not want to strike a jarring note; they wanted everything smooth and pleasant. What was the result? There was no in-depth discussion, no free and frank exchange of views. The very purpose of the dialogue was defeated.

The dialogue may also flounder over meanings of terms. Each religion has a specific term for what it thinks is the goal of life. Often, it is argued that no matter what that term is, all religions have a common goal. This is a mere conjecture yet to be proved. For instance, many people think the common goal of all religions is perfection. The word may be *Nirvana*, or *Mukti* or 'the Kingdom of Heaven', but the substance is the same: Perfection. To say this is only to beg the question. If you ask what perfection is, the answer will be *Nirvana*, *Mukti*, or the Kingdom of Heaven. The issue remains unsolved. You do not know what you are talking about. Once, in the course of an inter-religious dialogue, the participants came to the point of agreeing that there must be something common in all religions, otherwise it would be difficult to explain the phenomenon of each one of them producing its share of great saints and sages. But when it came to identifying those common elements among the religions, the participants could not agree. Some said that they followed what they taught. Their ends and means both fell within the category of what the holy books and the teachers taught. They never looked beyond. Others defined the means and ends of their religions, but they used terms which others knew nothing about, for they were esoteric.

It transpired that the very word 'God' meant one thing to a Hindu, and another to a Muslim. A Hindu would say, not only is this natural, but 'God' may mean different things to different people even within the same community. This happens because religion is basically an individualistic affair. What an individual thinks of God is his own; he cannot share it with others. When he prays he uses terms of his own coinage, or if he uses the same terms as others, he uses them in an entirely different sense. This exclusiveness increases as his relationship with God deepens. Finally, religion becomes private and personal. At this point, there is no question of sharing your religious feelings and emotions with others. Even if you try to explain what you think and feel about God, people do not understand you. You are on a level to which few others have access. If they are on your level, you enjoy talking to them, for you find your experience is the same as theirs. They give you a sense of certitude and you feel happy. As you advance, the number of people who can share your thoughts and feelings becomes less. When you reach the peak of your religious experience, you are alone. People may admire you from a distance, but they know nothing about the richness of all that you have within yourself. People like you are rare, but, surprisingly, every religion has a number of them to boast of, no matter how different the religions appear to be.

All this is a typical Hindu way of thinking. Other religions would see nothing but blasphemy in this. How can there be any understanding between one religion and another when they are poles apart? What do two gentlemen do when they argue about a political issue and find they cannot agree? They agree to disagree. That is what religious communities have to do—agree to disagree.

The question is: 'Where is the harmony then?' If 'harmony' means complete 'unanimity', there is none and there never will be. Does that mean that there should be conflicts? Not necessarily. Difference is natural; let the difference continue. This is no reason why there should be conflicts. Love of God is the one common ground where all can meet. Given a genuine love of God, the difference will not cause dissension, but will rather bring people closer to each other, may even foster friendship and goodwill. The enthusiasm that one displays may spread and inspire others, but too much display may offend others and lead to conflicts. Religion is not a matter of display, it is a matter of feeling, of 'being and becoming'. If the love of God is genuine, it expresses itself in love and respect for others, no matter how different they may be.

When this happens, there is harmony. Harmony is in the attitude of mind—in mutual understanding, love and goodwill. What all religions can and should strive for is this.

Religion: Ends and Means

IN DISCUSSING WHAT I PERSONALLY FEEL TO BE THE RELIGIOUS GOAL which we should keep in view and the means we should employ in order to achieve that goal, I shall speak more from the collective standpoint than the individual. In my opinion, we are individually still quite religious, but collectively we are becoming less and less religious. This is a dangerous trend. There are individuals who are very good, people who can compare with the saints of old; but when we think of nations or of mankind as a whole, the picture is depressing. Religion has influenced and is still influencing individuals, but if it does not influence nations also then the future of mankind is bleak. It is this problem that I want to discuss here. This is not a new problem; it has been debated again and again in the past, but never before did it become as acute as it is now. Mankind as a whole is now on trial. The question many are asking is, will man survive? There are misgivings on this score because there are frightening trends discernible. It is ironical that such misgivings should arise when man's conquest of his environment is almost complete.

What, then, is the trouble with us? The trouble is that we are behaving like a huge corpus without a head. We are, in brief, suffering from 'mindlessness'. We do not think; we do not wish to think; perhaps we have lost the capacity to think. How else can one explain our lack of concern in the face of the catastrophe which threatens to overtake us? Perhaps, we do not want to think because we want to enjoy for as long as we can the euphoria of our success on the physical plane. We certainly have done well as biological animals, for have we not conquered nature to use it as we like for our pleasure? When we look into our hearts, however, we are forced to admit that our progress in this sphere has been singularly dismal. It is true that we have now a civilisation which, in its power and richness, has far outstripped anything we built in the past; but one wonders if it serves any purpose. It is impressive in its concern for our physical well-being but, surprisingly, it shows no concern whatsoever for our moral well-being. We are inventing new machines every day to increase our physical comfort, but what about our peace and joy, our feelings and emotions, our imagination, our perceptiveness? Is not mind the most important component of the human personality? We have a passion for progress, but progress toward what? Acquisition of more cars, more money, property, more political and economic power? Let us be clear in our minds about our goals. If we are asking for only physical powers and comforts, then we are certainly moving in the right direction and we have every reason to feel proud of what we have so far achieved. Yet, individually and collectively, do we not also want peace and happiness? Do we not also want to increase our moral powers—our powers of honesty, forgiveness, compassion, wisdom, self-control, and so on? All over the world today sociologists are perplexed by the strange phenomenon that in spite of all the wealth we possess now, we are haunted by a sense of insecurity, by a sense of having been cheated out of the things we wanted most. Why is it that the richest man is not also the happiest?

That there is something wrong with our civilisation is now too patent a fact to need much elaboration. There is a kind of sickness from which man is suffering. The sickness is not physical, it is mental. The fact is that we have neglected the mind too long already, and are still neglecting it. The result is that despite our much-vaunted civilisation, mentally we are still in the early stages of our evolution.

We are at best civilised savages. We continue to be ruled by anger, hatred, greed, and the like—the elemental passions of man.

It is in this context that thinking people ask if the present civilisation can last long. Science has put infinite power in man's hands, and if he does not use that power judiciously he will destroy himself. But where is the mechanism to compel man to use his power judiciously? That mechanism should be inside man himself; it should be in his own mind. He should be so trained, so conditioned, that even in the face of great provocation, he would not use his power wrongly. Unfortunately, there is nothing in his present civilisation which gives man the motivation for self-restraint.

A further complication is that men and women are now more organised than ever before. More often than not they are organised to exploit others, even to exploit each other also. No strife today is localised. Since the world has become small as the result of easier communications, and since nations have come close to each other physically but not mentally, being without true friendship and goodwill, a small clash in one area may soon assume the character of a world crisis. Individually and collectively, our only concern today is self-advancement. Some of us, paradoxically, are good individuals if taken separately; but when organised for reasons of self-interest, the same individuals are ruthless and will throw to the winds whatever principles they otherwise swear by. What they hesitate to do individually they have no compunction in doing collectively. When they get together for a common cause, their personal moral code remains suspended. A diplomat may himself be a most moral and humane person where his own personal affairs are concerned, but when he has to act on behalf of his country, he at once switches over to a new code of conduct dictated entirely by his country's interests. On national and international levels, there is a complete disavowal of moral values in spite of the fact that the world has become one, and man has become a single unit.

That great organisation, the United Nations, was founded to settle all international disputes amicably, to ensure world peace, and to protect the interests of the smaller nations; unfortunately, however, it has fallen far short of that ideal. In practice, the United Nations has not been able to look after the interests of the smaller nations to the extent it intended to, neither has it been able to dispel suspicion and hatred or even reduce tension. It is wrong to suppose that differences can be ironed out merely by signing agreements. The seat of differences is in the heart and unless they are tackled at that point no paper agreement will solve the problem. If I think you are going to stab me in the back, every move you make is suspect in my eyes. Somehow or the other you have to convince me that your intentions are good, otherwise your protestations of friendship will merely sound hollow and meaningless to me. Today, most international conferences exude fine sentiments, but no one takes them seriously. There are fine clichés galore at these conferences, but people know they are only a cloak to conceal sinister motives.

We talk of peace but can there be any real peace so long as there is hatred in our hearts? Our trouble lies in the fact that we are trying to fool one another by sweet talk. We do not want to recognise that if we are to have a stable peace, peace must be based on justice, freedom, and equality for all. Mere talk will not do. There is at present a sort of caste system among the nations, in the sense that some nations are 'more equal' than others. There is still exploitation, although it exists in a more subtle form. Many wars to end war have been fought, but peace eludes us because we do not respect the freedom of others and because we do not give them what is their due. In the name of helping others, we impose our wills and our ways of life on them, and this naturally creates resentment among them and causes them to hate us.

All Men are Brothers

The problem before us is not poverty or disease, the problem is how we are to live in peace with each other. It is true that there are still some countries where poverty and disease are basic problems, but with the help of science and technology these problems can be solved within a foreseeable future. In the physical sense, a better world is no longer a dream but without peace such a world will be a mockery. How, then, can we have peace? How can we give each nation, each individual, a sense of security? Tagore, in his *Gitanjali*[5] envisioned a world

> Where the mind is without fear and the head is held high;
> Where knowledge is free;
> Where the world has not been broken up into fragments by narrow domestic walls;
> Where words come out from the depth of truth;
> Where tireless striving stretches its arms towards perfection;

When is such a world going to be a reality? What is it we lack that we have not yet been able to bring about such a world? William Blake in his poem 'The Divine Image' says:

> And all must love the human form, in heathen, Turk or Jew.
> Where Mercy, Love, and Pity dwell, there God is dwelling too.

A poet much older than Blake and Tagore, none other than Vyasa himself says:

> May all beings be happy;
> May all attain bliss,

---

5. London, 1953, p. 27.

> May all see happy days,
> May no one be subject to suffering.

Not to speak of poets and philosophers, even realists like Churchill and Stalin dreamed that there would be a world where there would be justice and equality for everybody. In founding the United Nations they used words usually heard only from religious people. Whether we call these words political or religious, the substance is the same. The task before us, whether we approach it politically or religiously, is to accept all men as brothers, treat them with respect and affection, give them their due and help them if we can. If we cannot, at least let us not hinder them. This we have to do at the individual level as well as at the collective level. There can be no peace so long as we do not recognise that man is essentially one. If I hurt you, I hurt myself. Swami Vivekananda used to emphasise this idea of oneness. He said: 'One atom in this universe cannot move without dragging the whole world along with it.' (*Complete Works of Swami Vivekananda* (Mayavati, 1964) Vol. III, p. 269) Through the centuries religious men have demonstrated that human relationships can be based on this idea of oneness or the brotherhood of man. Even when provoked, they have not hurt others. There have been men and women all over the world and in all ages who, when hit, have refused to hit back. To them no one is an enemy. In the worst days of communal fighting in India, Muslims died for Hindus and Hindus died for Muslims. With truly religious people, friendship and goodwill are part of their daily living, not mere idle sentiments.

LET MAN'S DIVINITY SHINE FORTH

Religion, however, is anathema to many people today. There are those who would not, under any circumstance, invoke the help of religion. It does not matter what they are going to use instead of religion; so long as they give us a better world and a better man we shall be satisfied. Other than religion, however, what can they use?

Will they use some political, economic, or social device? Whatever name they give it, in substance it will be religion, and nothing but religion. If those who are working for a better world mean what they say, then they will have to resort to more and more religion—truth, justice, fraternity, and so on.

The greatest misfortune of history is that we have so far failed to apply religion in practical life. We have come to the conclusion that religion can have no relevance in political or social affairs. This is a mistake. It is a mistake to think that some aspects of life are secular and others spiritual. All our activities, the whole gamut have one common objective, and that is perfection, or God. Whatever we do, takes us either nearer to God or away from him. In this sense, the entire life process is a spiritual exercise. It is impossible to divorce life from religion. Instead of trying to separate our so-called secular activities from religion, we should allow religion to inform and inspire them.

The problem before us is to devise some means by which human nature can improve. If it is said that man cannot improve and that he will *remain* as bad as ever, then there is not much point in all the fuss we make over our achievements in science and technology, art and literature, for they cannot defer for a day the doom to which we have committed ourselves. The prospect is not as bleak as it appears, however. It has been demonstrated again and again that individually we can rise to great heights of selflessness and moral excellence. Even in countries where religion is actively opposed, people have been known to make supreme sacrifices for others. There is an element in man which makes him feel for others. Perhaps, this is what the Upanishads mean when they say that there is one single Self in all men, or what Teilhard de Chardin means by 'one in All and All in one'. Religion makes this element stronger, more active. What we have to do now is to demonstrate that collectively we can rise to the same heights as we can individually, that as nations we can be more moral, more just, treat one another with more goodwill. Julian

Huxley, the great biologist, was never known as a religious man, but he too felt that efforts should be made to help man improve as a species. In an essay on 'Emergence of Darwinism'[6] he wrote:

> Man's most comprehensive aim is seen not as mere survival, not as numerical increase, not as increased complexity of organisation or increased control over his environment, but as greater fulfilment—the fuller realisation of more possibilities by the human species collectively and more of its component members individually.

Julian Huxley also points out that 'man's evolution is not biological but psychosocial... ideological instead of physiological.'[7] One Buddha, one Christ will not solve the problem. The entire human race has to be transformed into a race of Buddha and Christ. This may be a tall order but this is the ideal we should keep in view. Let us by all means control external nature, but in the process let us not forget to control our internal nature also. It is because we have neglected to do this that there is trouble all around us, and there is even talk of our extinction as a race. In *The Phenomenon of Man* Teilhard de Chardin talks of 'rebarbarisation'. That is to say, progress cannot be continuous; there are also periods of regress. Perhaps, we are now passing through a period of regress—at least, that is the impression we gain when we look at the current happenings in the world. Or perhaps, the word 'progress' is a misnomer. What we call progress is perhaps no progress at all. If it is progress, then it is self-defeating; it is progress towards death. In the context of what we call progress how can we explain, for example, the Vietnam War? We know that the majority of people do not want this war. By all tokens its futility and its unspeakable inhumanity are overwhelming. Yet, at the same time, those who are engaged in it will not give

---

6. *Evolution after Darwin*, Chicago University, 1959, Vol. I, p. 20.
7. Op. cit., Vol. III, p. 251.

it up. Neither North Vietnam, nor Nixon, nor Thieu will give it up. They all press on with it, and the pitiable people of Vietnam cannot extricate themselves from it—except, of course, those whom a most horrible death has already extricated. Tragic death is part of all war, of course, but the Vietnam War has been so long-drawn-out. Yet, Vietnam seems such a small and insignificant place; its people must wonder what they have done to deserve such a fate. This applies to all wars. No one wants them, and no one knows why they are being fought. The irony of it is that still such wars continue to be fought.

The long and the short of it all is that this is the penalty we are paying for neglecting the affairs of the Spirit. Matter has so long dominated the world, now let Spirit take over. Let the divinity of man shine forth through everything he does—individually, of course, but also collectively. Whatever we do, let us do it in a spirit of reverence and with conviction in our hearts that we are essentially one. Let religion be the breath of our life—not the religion of creeds and dogmas, but the religion of service, of love for fellow-men, of the worship of God through man. May the agony that we are now going through be the prelude to a new world order so that we may say with Jalalud-Din Rumi:

> For tonight this world is heavy and in travail,
> Striving to give birth to an eternal World,

Religion: Man's Quest for Freedom

EVERYWHERE TODAY, RELIGION IS AT A DISCOUNT BECAUSE, IN COMMON parlance, the word 'religion' means collective religion, organised round a creed or a dogma to which masses of people give blind and often fanatical support, even though there is no scientific proof of its validity. Religion, as it appears to many people, is only a body of beliefs which have to be accepted on trust just because there is the authority of some holy man or some holy book behind them. In this age of reason, this is a proposition which people find it hard to accept. Then they also ask, why should we accept religion? What purpose does it serve? There was a time when people turned to religion for an explanation of the mystery of nature, but today science explains the phenomena of nature and they are no longer mysteries. Thanks to science, what was previously regarded as an act of God is now within human competence. Man is now supreme and he sees no reason why he should recognise any authority outside himself. God has, therefore, become irrelevant, and religion, which provides the channel through which man can communicate with God, superfluous.

People then point to the mischief which religion often does. It is supposed to unite, but instead it creates artificial barriers between man and man. Today, you are either a Hindu or a Christian or a Muslim, and so on, as if this religious label is all there is to you, and you must display this label prominently so that others make no mistake about the special species of humanity that you represent. Then, there is also the long and most disgraceful history of cruelty which the followers of one religion have perpetrated against the followers of other religions in the name of religion. What is particularly shocking is that their religion seems to acquiesce in this cruelty. At least, there is no evidence that its leaders protest against such cruelty or do anything to prevent it.

This is not the only charge against religion in India today. What about the disparities? There are all manner of disparities in society today, and religion, far from condemning them, tends to lend its support to them. At least it cannot say that it tries to combat them.

There is thus today an atmosphere of hostility to religion all over the world, including India. More than hostility, there is also the problem of indifference. Educated people, by and large, are indifferent to religion. They behave as if religion is not for them; it is for the uneducated masses, and especially for women and children. A business executive, a university teacher, a highly placed government official, or an industrial magnate—all such people have no time for the silly things of religion. They may be nice people in themselves—honest, good, and efficient, but if you ask them what they think about God or what is their attitude towards religion, they will smile and say, 'Well, we have never given any thought to it'. This is another way of saying that they have never thought religion important and have therefore not bothered about it. They are 'of the earth, earthy', and what matters to them most is their success in the fields in which they are operating, and they do not care in the least whether God exists or not. They may say with Pippa:

God's in His heaven—
All's right with the world!

It is understandable if a man examines religion and then rejects it; but not to give it a look, not to allow it to trouble one's mind even for a moment, is unpardonable. Religion, after all, is so vital a matter that no educated person can afford to say that he is not interested in it. Whether there is any substance in religion or not, its influence cannot be questioned. It should be studied because of the historic role it has played and is still playing in the lives of large sections of humanity. No responsible person can, therefore, ignore the fact of religion. He may not agree with its claims, but he should certainly study it.

As a corollary to this problem of indifference, another problem now confronts religion. It has fallen into the hands of ignorant people who know nothing about religion. These people are unscrupulous and use it for their selfish ends. It is because of this religion creates problems today. The merits of religion, remain hidden behind this facade of hatred and jealousy.

THE COMPULSION OF INNER FORCES

But what is religion? It is generally agreed that religion is a quest that man undertakes under the compulsion of forces within himself, a quest which leads him to discover himself and to discover thereby a basis on which he can establish relations with himself and the world around him. Religion is also described as being an expression of man's longing. He thinks it will give him supreme peace and joy, for freedom and glory, for a state which gives him the feeling of having achieved the highest and noblest in life. To others, this achievement may mean nothing, but to the individual concerned it is of the highest importance, something for which he is ready to stake his all. This religious goal may seem intangible to others, and it is certainly not possible to define it in terms of objects of common experience, but that does not make it less vivid, less real, or less desirable to those who have set their hearts on it. Because it cannot be defined in terms with which we are familiar, there is a tendency to dismiss the religious goal as an 'airy fairy', a mere fantasy, or something subjective, something we imagine exists but really does not exist, an idea or a state of being which owes its existence entirely to a heated brain. If it is an experience, as indeed religious people claim it to be, it is what one feels in the depths of one's heart; and there is no way of duplicating it or inducing it in others so that there is always room to question its validity.

But what is the goal of religion? Almost all religions agree that the goal of religion is perfection, that is, a state of being in which man feels that he is free from the limitations which now pin him down to a state of helplessness against his environment, his own nature and other factors, all of which take away from the freedom to function in the manner in which he wishes to function. It is said that religion promises man absolute freedom, freedom which is at present denied to him, freedom of the body, mind, and spirit. The Christian idea of this freedom is the 'Kingdom of Heaven'; the Muslim idea is the same as the Christian idea; the Hindus describe it as liberation, *moksha* or *mukti*; and to the Buddhist, this freedom is *nirvana*. Whatever the nomenclature may be, the meaning is the same—release from the state of slavery, which seems to be present in the lot of man. Whether it is slavery due to forces within or without, it is unmitigated slavery to which man feels condemned, but it is a trait of man that he can never accept this slavery as something over which he has no control. Here is the beginning of religion, this revolt against what man thinks is bondage. Thus begins the first step towards that goal, which all of us desire and which religion promises—absolute freedom.

Religion is, therefore, that science which teaches man the secret of how to throw off the shackles which he feels are now crippling him. It is the science of growth towards freedom, towards perfection. All men and women are struggling for this growth, though not all of them are conscious that they do so. Because they are not conscious and because they are, therefore, not able to plan and direct their growth in the manner best suited to their interests, their growth is often slow and halting. Not only men and women, even animals and plants make this struggle, but of course, they make their struggle in their own way and in their case, the growth is feeble and even retarded. Even people who say they are opposed to religion or are indifferent to it are making this struggle, and inasmuch as they are doing so they too are religious whether they care to admit it or not.

It is in fact a characteristic of life to struggle for growth and development, and this struggle never ceases till it reaches a point where there is a feeling of fulfilment, a feeling of having reached the top. So long as there is a sense of inadequacy, sense that one is only finite with many limitations, there is a sense of discontent—'the divine discontent' as it is called—and the struggle to overcome this inadequacy is bound to continue. It is like the river which hastens on its way to the sea, as if the sea is calling it and the call is irresistible so that, whatever the obstacles may be, it will not stop till it reaches the sea. When it joins the sea, it loses its identity and becomes one with the sea. It then sheds the limitations which finiteness imposed on it and becomes infinite. It was to achieve this new infinite status, this freedom, that it made the long, hazardous journey from the hills to the sea, covering hundreds of miles. Religion has aptly been described as a 'call of the infinite, a call of freedom'. It is, indeed, a call to revolt against all forms of slavery, against limitations and a call to achieve freedom which is absolute.

ORGANISED RELIGION

Let us now see what the characteristics of collective or organised religion are, that it falls short of the sophisticated needs of the present generation. Take the case of Islam. As is well known, Islam is a highly organised religion with a single teacher, a single holy book, and a message which is simply and clearly stated. Although

Islam does not recognise any intermediary between God and man, a hierarchy exists of teachers and divines who help the faithful to understand the true import of Mohammed's teachings. The prayer a Muslim has to say is simple, and the code of conduct he has to observe is also simple. In fact, simplicity is Islam's forte. If the Muslims are a compact group, it is because of this simplicity. They can easily understand and practise their Islam, an advantage other religions do not enjoy. The fact that Islam puts in much collective activity makes for further cohesion among its followers. Islam is essentially a collective religion. There is a sense of 'togetherness' in it which other religions scarcely display.

The weakness of Islam, however, is that it is based entirely on faith. If we do not accept Mohammed and the *Quran,* the whole structure of Islam collapses. Mohammed never intended that his personality should be given any importance, but because he was the medium through which the message of God was received, he is naturally the key figure in the whole system of Islam. No formal worship is offered to him, but there is no doubt that without him, Islam could not sustain itself. Similarly, the *Quran*—if we accept it as the word of God there is no problem, but if we do not there is no Islam.

The same applies to Christianity. If we accept Christ as the son of God and the Bible as the word of God, then the whole issue becomes simple, but if we cannot accept them, then Christianity too goes the same way as Islam. Not only Islam and Christianity, in fact, all religion (including Hinduism) go the same way if faith is their only basis.

Hinduism has an advantage, for, it is not as organised and as clearly defined as other religions are. Some argue that this is a weakness, but in reality it is an advantage, for it leaves room for adjustment according to individual tastes and requirements. Hinduism gives due place to faith, but it also encourages reasoning. To Hinduism, however, the decisive factor is experience. The proof of the pudding is in the eating. While faith and reason are important, experience is the only satisfying and acceptable proof of religion. Hinduism insists that the truth of religion must be experienced; otherwise it is only a postulate. Luckily, Hinduism has no organised Church. This gives each individual freedom to think and act as he thinks best. It is individualistic, just as Islam or Christianity is collectivistic. Some say this has led to anarchy in Hinduism. No one knows what Hinduism is or what it stands for. It means different things to different people. Without going into any controversy over this, it may be said that within the broad spectrum of Hinduism, almost every religious belief and action may find a place. Even the basic principles of Christianity and Islam can be fitted into it. Hinduism is all-embracing, from animism to that brand of monism which proclaims the unity of man and God.

MEETING THE CHALLENGE OF THE DAY

Can Hinduism meet the challenge of the day? Not only Hinduism but all religions can meet the challenge, if the underlying spirit is stressed and not the personalities or the letter, of what is projected as the word of God. The questioning spirit of the age must be satisfied. Religion has nothing to fear from reason or from science. Some of this century's greatest scientists have been deeply religious persons. Religion too, is a science, a science of 'being and becoming', as Swami Vivekananda used to say. It is a search, a search for Truth, for understanding and knowledge. We want to know not only the physical world, but also ourselves.

Religion comes in when we want to know ourselves and our relation with the world outside. Has life a purpose or is it just an accident? What happens to us when we die? Is it the end or is there something beyond? Why is it that there is so much inequality between man and man? Is man the maker of his destiny or is there some other power who determines it? There are many such questions which trouble us from time to time. Religion tries to answer some of these questions, though it may be that the answers religion gives are not all satisfactory. It may be that we will never know the real truth, but in the process of trying to know the truth we discipline ourselves, and it is this discipline that is the most important justification of religion. Even if religion was nothing other than discipline, discipline of the body, mind, and heart, it would be well worth all the trouble we might take for its sake. If religion transforms a person, it is the discipline which religion insists upon. 'The tree is known by its fruit', and if religion can produce a character like Buddha, Christ, or Sri Ramakrishna, there can be no doubt about its necessity or validity. Swami Vivekananda used to say that if by worshipping stones and trees a man could become like Sri Ramakrishna, then there must be ample justification for such practice. People often show their aversion to religion, saying they do not see what purpose it serves. Religion must show in concrete terms what good it can do. If nothing else, religion gives man a sense of purpose. He is asked to struggle for the Infinite, for by nature he is 'infinite' and it is only in the Infinite that he can be happy. Swami Vivekananda used to say, 'The infinite human soul can never be happy but by the Infinite itself.'

At first, the struggle is on the physical plane, but from the physical we move on to the intellectual plane, and then the spiritual. Thus, we are always moving from the lower to the higher, from the grosser to the finer. We give up what is small in order that we may get what is big; we give up what is temporary in order to get what is lasting. This is practical religion, in the words of Swami Vivekananda. The Swami says: 'Utilise the things of this world and the next just for one goal—the attainment of freedom.' We attain freedom when we feel that we have had all we want and there is nothing else we want. We have this feeling when we are one with God. We are God himself.

We are all seeking God, only we are not seeking Him where we should. This is why Swami Vivekananda used to say that 'the concept of God is a fundamental element in the constitution of man.'

The fact of God as creator, sustainer, and destroyer of the universe may be disputed, but God as a state of being to which individually and collectively we should look forward cannot be questioned. All religions point to God as being the source of everything. When we want something, say, freedom, or truth, or beauty, or knowledge, we turn to God, not necessarily because we think He will give it, but because God is another name for the state we are trying to reach. God is not far away living, somewhere in the skies, He is everywhere, He is in us. He is our innermost being. He is the 'life of my life', as Tagore says. At first, man searches for God outside himself—in the forests, hills, rivers, skies, in temples, mosques, and churches. After a long search, he discovers that God is within himself.

Swami Vivekananda once wrote a letter to Professor John Henry Wright, and with his letter he sent a poem he had written which beautifully sums up this idea of looking for God outside oneself, and then discovering Him within. Here are a few lines from the poem[8]:

> O'er hill and dale and mountain range,
> In temple, church, and mosque,
> In Vedas, Bible, Al Koran
> I had searched for Thee in vain.
> Years then passed in bitter cry,
> Each moment seemed an age
> Till one day midst my cries and groans
> Someone seemed calling me.
> . . .
> A flash illumined all my soul;
> The heart of my heart opened wide.
> O joy, O bliss, what do I find!
> My love, my love, you are here,
> And you are here, my love, my all!

---

8. *Complete Works of Swami Vivekananda*, Mayavati, 1969, Vol. VII. pp. 448–9.

In the Bible also we have the same idea when Christ says, 'The Kingdom of Heaven is within you'. According to Swami Vivekananda, 'Each soul is potentially divine', and the purpose of life is to manifest that divinity. Consciously or unconsciously, we are all trying to manifest that divinity, in the sense that we are all engaged in the struggle to acquire those qualities which we attribute to God. Freedom is one such quality, and there are others. There are truth, goodness, and beauty. We can compound these qualities into one and call it perfection. God is God—it is no use trying to describe Him or to list the qualities He embodies, he is the repository of everything, He is everything. So long as man tries to be perfect, he is religious. Religion is the technique by which he tries to be perfect. There is no one who says, 'I do not want to improve, I do not want to do better, and I do not care for perfection.' Like the desire for freedom, the desire to improve is inherent in man. We are all trying to improve, though it is not always that we improve, nor do we improve at the same rate. And, in the sense that we are all trying to improve we are being religious, whether we care to admit it or not. We may not profess any recognised religion or observe any religious practice, yet we are religious by this token. Swami Vivekananda used to say: '*Uttisthata jagrata prapya varan nibodhata,* Arise, awake, and stop not till the goal is reached.'[9] We are marching forward, all of us, though our rate of progress is not the same.

A RELIGION FOR EACH INDIVIDUAL

In India, individual religion is still quite strong, but collective religion, that is, religion as a social force is on the wane. There is, of course, community worship still in practice, but this worship has hardly any religious character. At best it is a social get-together. Islam and, in a lesser degree, Christianity too, still have much community worship,

---

9. ibid. Mayavati, 1970 Vol. Ill, p. 193.

but there is unmistakable evidence that even they are not able to evoke the same religious spirit that they used to. As in the case of Hinduism, the upper-income groups, the intelligentsia, and the young people invariably stay away from all forms of community worship, unless they join it for purely social reasons. Young Hindus, of course, are of late taking much interest in community worship, but as is well known, this is only euphemism for social, and also very often, for political activities. They are not interested in religion as such, but if religion provides an opportunity to promote their social and political interests, they do not see why they should spurn it. In any case, the signs are clear that community worship as a form of religious activity is slowly dying out; if it continues at all, it will continue purely as a social activity. For example, in Soviet Russia, Christmas is slowly being revived, but it is no longer a religious ceremony but a social event which the communists tolerate.

Perhaps, it is understandable why community worship has become only a social event. In community worship, people miss the thrill they experience when they worship individually. Religion is essentially a matter of communion with God. One cannot have that communion when praying together with other people. We pray best when we pray alone, for we then pray in our own way and our contact with God is direct and personal. With others, prayer becomes impersonal, even mechanical. It may be a mere pantomime. Each of us is unique and our relations with God are determined by the uniqueness of our individual temperament and character. Can you share Sri Ramakrishna's intensity of longing for God, his renunciation, or his perceptiveness? Is it possible to duplicate the religious experience of the Buddha or of Christ on a mass scale? Can we produce mystics on a conveyer belt? If religion is an experience, it has to be on the individual level. Its quality and content will depend on the kind of individual one is, one's capacity and readiness to receive the shock of contact with God. There is no limit to man's experience of God. It is as infinite as God himself.

Collective religion suffers from uniformity. No two individuals feel or think alike; no two persons have the same needs and interests. To some, religion is pleasure; to others, it is intense pain. Some seek physical comforts through religion; others shun such comforts, welcoming pain and suffering because they feel that they may thus reach their religious goals quicker. What hardships the sages and saints of old suffered for the sake of religion! To them no price was too high for God. Collective religion rules out individual vagaries and insists on a common pattern. But what common pattern of conduct can we expect between a God-intoxicated Sri Ramakrishna and a drink-addict like Girish Ghosh? Do they want the same thing when they pray together? Are their thought levels the same? Have they the same norms, the same criteria of right and wrong?

Is it not an impractical proposition to try to collectivise human thoughts and emotions? It is my contention that, as the years pass by, religion is going to become more and more individualised. As Swami Vivekananda used to say, each individual will have a religion of his own. Some day collective religion, religion based on creeds and dogmas, will go; the frontiers between different religions will disappear and they will become one, giving each individual the option to decide what will be his goal, and he will then try to reach the goal in the best way he can. Already inter-religious sympathy is the order of the day. If this trend continues, its logical culmination will be that the labels we now use in dividing men and women in the name of religion, will become superfluous. We shall all feel one in God. We hope this may happen sooner rather than later. Let us remember that collective religion may bring man closer to man, but it is only individual religion that can bring man closer to God.

COMMITMENT TO TRUTH

Let us now turn to another aspect of religion—the question of conformity. Conformity is insisted upon regarding religious belief and action, and yet there can be no real conformity in these matters even within a single religious group. No two Hindus, no two Muslims, no two Christians think or act alike in religious matters. If there is any similarity between them, that similarity is deceptive. Behind the apparent similarity there may be a deep chasm which keeps them apart. They may say the same prayers but the words they use have different meanings to each of them. Invariably, they evoke different feelings and emotions in their hearts, and they also conjure up different mental images. The difference may be even more fundamental—not only concepts, methods, and approach may differ, but even religious goals may differ too. In these circumstances, to insist on conformity is not only wrong, it may even prove a hindrance to religious growth.

Now, what does a religious man believe in? First and foremost, he believes in an ultimate Reality which he may call God, Spirit, or Ground, depending upon what sort of religious tradition he has been brought up in. The name he uses does not matter; what matters is what he thinks about it. Invariably, man makes God in his own image. He thinks of God in terms of his own personality, his hopes and aspirations. God is 'He' at his best. To a primitive man God is also a primitive man, only very much better off, with more power and pleasures at His command. To a buffalo, God is also a buffalo, only He has more green grass to eat, and more mud to wallow in, as Swami Vivekananda used to say. As man improves, his idea about God also improves. The *Agni Purana* says:

> The child's toy-Gods are made of clay and wood,
> For the average man, Gods live in holy streams;
> For the intelligent, in heavenly orbs;
> The wise man's God is his inner Self.

Man begins by thinking of God as a powerful potentate who rules the world arbitrarily. If a man falls sick or has some mishap, he thinks he must have offended God. He then tries to please God by offering him sacrifices or performing acts which people who claim to know the mind of God recommend. He himself has no idea of what is right or wrong. To decide what is right or wrong he depends upon what is passed round as being God's word on the subject, communicated through a chosen agency—a holy book or a holy man. He tries to follow this supposed word of God, but he often fails; then, from fear of punishment, he throws himself upon the mercy of God. This leads to the theory of God as a kind father. But, still later, man discovers that God is not only transcendental but also immanent, and not only a person but also a spirit. He then comes to feel his presence within himself and even to feel one with him. He feels he is God not only potentially; he is God already and nothing but God. When he reaches this stage, he is then his own master. There is no person or power to challenge him. He is no longer answerable to anybody for his conduct. What he does is the law.

This is the whole range of man's thinking about God. If a man is given the option to think of God as suits him best, then there is no problem; but in the case of organised religion, this freedom is not given. Its followers are told what should be their thinking of God. There is a readymade theology served out to them which they must accept, for good or for ill. They cannot question any aspect of it. They must accept it as it is and without any reservation. This happens when there is a central authority claiming to know what God really intends. It is not ready to make allowances for individual choice. It makes a choice for the entire community and imposes that choice on all and sundry, without considering their individual needs. What follows as a result is that people do what they are told to do, though they do not see why they should do it; in other words, they go through the motions of doing it, though their hearts are not in it. This is insincerity.

Suppose, we are told to worship God in a particular manner and we cannot. What is the choice before us then? Either we revolt or we become insincere. In a rigid society, it is almost impossible to revolt, for that may mean social death. Not many people have the courage of Martin Luther; they can only be silent martyrs. The only course open to us then is to be insincere, that is, to pretend to accept the prescribed form of worship. Nothing could be more harmful to religious life than this insincerity. Religion, it must be remembered, cannot be mere make-believe. If it has to change our character, we must practise what we believe, practise it intensely and with the utmost sincerity. Let me give an example. Sri Ramakrishna once promised to visit a garden-house next door to the Dakshineswar temple where he lived. It happened that he forgot all about his promise and remembered it only at night when everybody had gone to sleep. He ran to the garden-house, but found the gate closed. He called out to the people inside, but nobody came. He then thrust his leg through the bars of the gate and touched the ground with his foot on the other side of the gate, saying thrice, 'I have come.' This may sound absurd, but when we practise truth we must practise it in letter and in spirit, under all circumstances; occupation with truth should be complete and there should be no compromise on this. In fact, one's entire being should be conditioned by it so that one becomes truth itself.

Swami Vivekananda used to describe this state as 'nervous association', for even one's nerves must show one's commitment to truth. Another example from Sri Ramakrishna's life will make this point clear. Sri Ramakrishna had taken a vow to renounce gold, and would not even touch it. His rejection of gold was not only intellectual, it was also physical. That is to say, even his body rejected it. If by accident his body came in contact with gold, he felt intense pain. Renunciation in his case was not only a principle; it was a fact, a physical fact. This becomes possible only by intense practice. But we cannot practise renunciation unless we believe in this.

In religion, we all have to go it alone. We are different from one another, and therefore what is your problem may not be mine.

Even if two people have the same problem, each has to solve it for himself, in his own way. If somebody solves your problem for you, it is like someone else eating for you; it does not serve your purpose. Each of us has to fight our own battle. We are like pilgrims with a common goal before us, but each has to make the journey separately and cross the hurdles as best he can. Sri Ramakrishna always taught according to the needs of the individual to whom he was addressing himself. If he was talking to a group of Brahmo leaders, he would talk of the Godhead as a formless Being. If he was talking to a Vaishnava devotee, he talked like an orthodox Vaishnava, as if Vishnu were the only Deity he worshipped. He took great care not to hurt anybody, and it was farthest from him to try to push anything down anyone's throat. He taught only that which was easily acceptable to the person concerned. To each according to his taste and temperament—this was his motto. He made no attempt to impose his choice upon others.

We grow best when we are free. One reason why religion is unpopular these days is that this freedom is denied, and there is regimentation. We want to study, think, argue, and decide for ourselves; if, instead, a readymade decision is thrust upon us, our natural reaction is to revolt. A little guidance may be welcome, but in the name of guidance, there should be no attempt to curb freedom. To reach God we may choose any one of the many paths open to us. One path is just as good as another, and if we have chosen a path because we think it suits us best, other people should have nothing to say about this.

UNFOLDING THE DIVINITY WITHIN

It must be understood that religion is not merely an intellectual exercise. Whatever may be our idea of the Godhead, we must make a great effort to change ourselves in the light of that particular Godhead. If, for example, we think of God as love, it is not enough to think that God is love; we must show that we really believe that God is love. That is to say, in our dealings with others we must reflect a little, at least, of our thinking. If we declare that we worship God as love, then we should not lack love in our hearts, we should not be cruel, selfish, and should feel for others, otherwise we are not true to our ideal. When we really think of God as love, we become kind and soft-hearted and begin to love everyone. Love then becomes the dominant feature of our personality.

Religion in fact, is three-fourths action and one-fourth belief. Even if our thinking about the Godhead is sound, that is not enough to prove that we are religious. A religious man need not be a scholar; in fact, the world's greatest religious teachers were not scholars; what they learnt about God was gained through intuitive experience and not from books. Intellect or scholarship may be a means, but it is not an end in itself. The 'goods' of the intellect, the emotions, and the imagination are real 'goods', Aldous Huxley pointed out, but they are not the final good, and when we treat them as ends in themselves we fall into idolatry. We may have good brains, but we must use them to judge right from wrong, good from evil. Brains by themselves are not so important; they are important only when we use them in the right manner, as a means to our real progress and development.

Our thinking about God is naturally crude and clumsy. Even the cleverest and most scholarly among us can have only an imperfect idea of God. When we start on our religious journey we may have only a very vague idea about the direction we should follow; but the idea improves as we go on. Even if we make a few mistakes in the beginning, we correct ourselves as we progress. Sri Ramakrishna used to say, 'Suppose you want to go to Puri and you do not know the way. Maybe, you start in a wrong direction, but as you go on you ask people, and soon you know the way. If you are sincere and follow the path people point out to you, you get to Puri all right in spite of the few mistakes you made initially.'

What all religious teachers emphasise is that we should be sincere, patient, and hard-working. Sri Ramakrishna used to say, 'If you take one step towards God, God will take a hundred steps towards you.' The emphasis is on self-help. Help yourself in order that God may help you. It was Eckhart's belief that God expected but one thing of us—'come out of yourself in so far as you are a created being and let God be God in you'. God is anxious to help you, only you must let him help you. 'God is bound to act,' says Eckhart, 'to pour Himself into thee as soon as He shall find Thee ready.' Only we have to be ready, that is, to take the first step. It is the first step that is the most difficult, but once it is taken, the Gordian knot is cut and progress is then comparatively easy. By practice, religion becomes realisation; it is no longer only an idea, it now becomes a fact.

Many people demand proof that religion is no more a fantasy or a figment of heated brains. Only by doing what religion postulates can one verify the truth or otherwise of what it claims. No amount of talk or intellectual argumentation can prove or disprove religion. Sri Ramakrishna used to say, 'As you proceed to the north, you know that you are getting closer to the Himalayas, for it becomes cooler and cooler.' The truth of religion is best known through first-hand experience. This experience is open to all—to you, me, and all of us. Only we must try hard. It is not enough to profess an ideal. We must live up to it. Swami Vivekananda used to say, 'Religion is realisation.' Realisation of what? Realisation of God who is otherwise known as Perfection. We are all trying to attain this perfection, but some of us are doing so consciously and some are doing so unconsciously. The goal of life is to attain this perfection which is also known as Divinity. Said Swami Vivekananda: 'Each soul is potentially divine. The goal is to manifest this divinity within by controlling nature, external and internal. Do this either by work, or worship, or psychic control, or philosophy—by one, or more, or all of these—and be free. This is the whole of religion. Doctrines, or dogmas, or rituals, or books, or temples, or forms, are but secondary details.'[10] It is not only Indian mystics who teach this; Christian mystics voice the same idea. Eckhart says: 'The seed of God is in us. Given an intelligent and hard-working farmer, it will thrive and grow up to God whose seed it is; and accordingly its fruits will be God-nature. Pear seeds grow into pear trees, nut trees into nut trees, and God seed into God.'

Once we know that the goal of life is the attainment of divinity, to be one with God, we should direct all our efforts to that end. This does not mean that we should run away from life. The one charge which one hears most against religion is that it encourages escapism. This charge is altogether unwarranted. No religion says that we can shirk our duties and yet be religious. Religion, in fact, insists that we do our duties well, and that we should do them as if we were doing them only to please God. Whatever we do is an act of worship. Lord Krishna says in the Bhagavad Gita, 'Offer unto me whatever you do, eat, sacrifice, or give.'[11] In short, the entire life-process should be a long stretch of prayer. To a true devotee nothing is secular.

What we are seeking through religion is a change of character. We want to be honest, good, and selfless; we also want to help our fellow-beings. Can anyone object to this? Can anyone say that these good qualities are not necessary? One may, of course, question if religion really produces these qualities. One may say that they do not. But the fact is that all religions emphasise these qualities, among others, as being the essence of true religion. The Mahabharata says, 'Do not do to others what you do not wish done to yourself; and wish for others too what you desire for yourself. This is the whole of Dharma. Heed it well.' Jesus Christ said exactly the same thing, and in almost identical words. 'Whatsoever ye would that men

---

10. ibid. Mayavati, 1963, Vol. I, p.124.
11. Bhagavad Gita IX, 27.

should do to you, do ye even so to them.'[12] This, Jesus described as 'the whole of the law and the prophets'. Echoing the same idea, Mohammed says:

> Noblest religion this—that thou shouldst like
> For others what thou likest for thyself;
> And what thou feelst painful for thyself,
> Hold thou as painful for all others too.

This, in fact, is the crux of religion—love for our fellow-men. It is doubtful if any political or social science can produce this kind of love. At least, it cannot give any *raison d'etre* for loving one's fellow men. Religion alone can give it. According to Hinduism, there is the same Self everywhere, and when we love our fellow-men, we in fact love our own 'self'. Christ says, 'Love thy neighbour as thyself.' John says, 'He that loveth not knoweth not God, for God is love.' It is possible to quote many such passages from different religious sources. If you are a dualist, then a fellow-man is your brother; if you are a non-dualist, then the fellow-man and you are one.

What is important is that these sentiments have not only been expressed, they have also been practised. History is replete with such examples. Let us say that the number of people, who have loved their neighbours as their own selves, or even as brothers, is not great. But is it not wonderful if only one single individual has done so? It is proof that others also may do so. Here is the justification of religion. It points to the great possibilities of man and asks him to achieve them. Men like Einstein cannot be produced on a mass scale; nor can men like Buddha, Christ, or Sri Ramakrishna. Such men are inevitably few and far between. The wonder is that such men have at all walked the earth. If they occurred once, they can occur again; and perhaps, with care and effort, their number might

---

12. Luke 6, 31.

increase. Man's achievements in science and technology have been breath-taking. Obviously, much care and effort have gone into those achievements. Similar breath-taking achievements may be possible in religion also—with care and effort. If man is the centre of civilisation, then more and more care should be directed to the development of man himself. Man's conquest of external nature is almost complete; he has, however, to go a long way before he can say he has conquered his internal nature. More courage, more fortitude, and more strength are called for in this matter. Buddha used to say, 'He is a true hero who has conquered his own nature.' Here is a challenge before us: science and technology have put immense powers into our hands. Unless these powers are matched by those powers which lie hidden within ourselves—powers represented by compassion, wisdom, and selflessness—civilisation is doomed. This is where religion comes in. Religion alone can unfold the divinity which is already within us; let religion do this—and soon.

Science and Religion

No doubt, religion and science are entirely two different disciplines. There are scientists who think that they are not only different, they are opposed to each other. Now, my contention is that, really speaking, there is not much difference between science and religion, if you examine their fundamentals. Let us agree at the outset that science has an objective approach whereas the approach religion has is subjective. Both are trying to understand the mystery behind man and his environment. But in their practical application, both are concerned with the welfare of man. Science, as you all know, is concerned with man's physical well-being. If you have problems about food, clothing, housing, health, better standards of living, then you turn to sciences, but you turn to religion when you are trying to raise your moral standards; for instance, if you want to know how you can improve your relations with your neighbours, how you can have peace and happiness, how you can grow not outwardly but inwardly, how you can become a perfect man! Science is, as you all know, based on well-tested data. There is nothing speculative about it. It is based on hard facts which have been verified and which are always verifiable. The test that leads to the body of knowledge called science can be repeated, that is to say, scientific knowledge is not an exclusive property of some privileged persons, and all are entitled to it, given that they are able to fulfil the requisite conditions. There is nothing secretive about science. The truths, it reveals, are as clear as broad daylight. There is no place for faith in science. It does not recognise that there is any extraneous power or person that controls the destiny of man or the environment in which he lives, that is, the universe. It believes only in reason and observed facts.

But what is religion? It is also a science with the same characteristic of exactitude in its principles, methods and attainable results. In fact, as a discipline, it is more rigorous, perhaps more exacting. Like science, it is as clear as daylight, at least up to a point, but beyond that point it is possible that there is need for secretiveness because one does not want one's privacy encroached upon. Religion is essentially a personal affair; it is something one does with one's own mind and naturally feels shy to share one's thoughts and feelings with others. Nevertheless, the principles of religion are simple and clear and where they are concerned, there is no room for any secretiveness. You can discuss them freely with everybody. Most religions have the same aims and objects, the same methods and the same results. They hold good everywhere and in every age. So, there is no room for secrecy. But if there is secrecy, one may suspect there is something wrong.

Higher religion, however, is a different proposition; it is beyond reason. What a mystic sees and feels, cannot be explained but he himself is proof of its validity. Religion basically is a science of the self. It tries to enquire into the nature of the self—the questions it asks are: 'Who am I? What are my relations with my environment or my fellow-beings, who control my destiny? Why do I commit mistakes for which I suffer much later and so on?' These are questions which trouble all of us at one time or another. Religion tries to answer these and other allied questions. Also, it tries to give a meaning, a purpose to life. What is the purpose of life? According to religion, the purpose of life is to develop, to grow, 'ABHYUDAYA' in Sanskrit. Is it physical development, physical growth it is seeking? Yes, to begin with, physical development, physical and material development, but man soon discovers that physical development or material development alone is not enough. Man is a body-mind complex. So, he soon discovers that along with physical development, mental development is also necessary. He also discovers that progress depends more upon his mind than upon his body. This is why we find religion lays more stress upon man's mental development than upon the physical. According to Hinduism and perhaps other religions also, infinite powers lie coiled up within man. Man has to be made conscious of these powers and also taught how to use them for his own growth and development. This is what religion tries to do. If one man is superior to another, it is because one has used one's powers better than the other. Religion says man can grow to the point of infinity, not physically of course, but morally and spiritually. Physically also he can grow much, he can grow much more than he thinks possible now, but this kind of growth does not satisfy man unless it is matched by moral growth. Theoretically, we have in us the same possibilities as Shakespeare and Einstein had, or as Buddha and Jesus Christ had. The difference between us and those great men is in degree and not in kind.

Religion, however, is concerned with man's internal growth, growth in ethical and spiritual terms. To be perfect is the goal of life, according to religion. As man studies his self, he discovers that he is not only body and mind but also spirit, something which cannot be properly defined, something which is the real core of his being, which, in fact, is his real self—the body and mind being only its tools which it uses for its purpose. How do we know there is such a thing as the self which is separate from the body and the mind? The evidence Vedanta cites is like this: when you are awake, the self functions through your body and mind, which is proof that you have both a body and a mind. But is the mind separate from the body? Yes, for when you sleep you dream you are going places, eating, running, talking to friends and so on. But you are doing none of these things, for you are lying on your bed all the time—physically you are completely at rest. The dreams you have are all mental constructs, which is proof that our mind can operate independent of the body. Just as we have waking and dreaming states, we have also a state in which we sleep soundly, that is, without any dreams. When we wake up from this state, we are not able to recognise at once where we are and what time of day it is. As if we were dead for some time and we are now coming back to life. During this state, both our body and mind were extinct; at least they did not function. If our body and mind were extinct temporarily, what survived that we were able to come back to life again? Vedanta answers 'The self.' The self is the connecting link in all these three states—waking, dreaming and sleeping dreamlessly. It is clear that the self is beyond both body and mind; it is the real coordinating and controlling authority in the whole complex that is man. The self is the man, the body and the mind being only organs it uses for its purposes.

This self is no doubt intangible, but its existence can be felt. Let us try to understand the nature of this self. There is in all of us the feeling of 'I'. We say: 'I eat, I drink, I see, I work and so on.' This I-ness, this sense of identity, is present in all of us. Even an insect has this I-ness. This is why if you hurt it, it will retaliate. But who is this I? Is it the body or the mind? If it is the body, why then can I not reply if you call out to me when I am dead? You may poke at me when I am dead. Yet, why can I not protest? Do I feel any pain when I am dead? Do I feel any resentment within, when I am insulted? Why not? What is missing in me when I am dead? You say life, but what is life? Consciousness? It is difficult to define life. But consciousness is certainly one of its characteristics, at least in the case of man. It is that which makes it possible for us to feel pain and pleasure through our body and mind. We need a body and mind to feel pleasure and pain, but, independent of this consciousness, the body and the mind cannot feel anything. A man may die in perfect health with all his organs intact, yet he feels nothing. But there is one common experience to which I want to draw your attention: When I am absent-minded, you may call out to me, but I will not hear you, or you may pass before me, yet I will not see you. Both my body and mind are in normal condition, yet why do I not then hear you or see you? Obviously, there is something beyond the mind which has withdrawn itself from my organs so that they are not able to perceive the sounds and sights in my immediate vicinity.

Vedanta says it is the self which has withdrawn itself from my sense organs so that they have become useless. This self is what science calls consciousness ('*CHAITANYA*' in Sanskrit) and this is what is meant by I. This is also known as spirit, the soul. This self is the essence of our being. Thus, this self exists, but it is not separate from existence, for existence and that which exists cannot be two separate entities. Similarly, it is also consciousness, for the organs can perceive because of this self. It is also '*ANANDA*' because we can feel joy again because of this self. The essence of our being, that is, the self is thus '*SATT*', which corresponds to existence, '*CHITT*' which corresponds to consciousness and '*ANANDA*' which corresponds to joy. Existence, consciousness and bliss are not qualities of the self. Existence and that which exists, consciousness and the person who is conscious, bliss and the person who feels bliss are not separate entities, they are one. This existence, consciousness and bliss are the nature of the self. They together constitute the self. But what about pain? Sometimes we suffer pain too. What about pain? Is it a separate entity? No, it is only absence of joy like darkness is nothing but absence of light. Still one might doubt the existence of the self. One might argue that the self is nothing but the mind or an extension of the mind. Consciousness itself, one might say, is the same thing as the mind. But the Hindu view is, as I have already said, that the self is something independent of the body and the mind. It operates through them, it makes use of them, but it can also operate independently. This in fact, is the view of other religions also.

There have been mystics in all religions, in all countries and in all ages. These are people who live on a plane where sense organs have no access. In the absence of a better term, we usually call that plane transcendental. It is remarkable that all mystics have experiences which are identical. They say, 'We have seen visions, we have been filled with floods of joy; or we are overwhelmed by oceans of light and so on'. The experiences they have are supersensuous, that is, independent of the sense organs. They apprehend truths directly, not through senses like we do when our visions are invariably coloured by the influence of our sense organs. Is there such a thing as a supersensuous plane? Yes, according to the Hindus, on this plane the self is in direct contact with the reality behind the phenomenal world which we see around us. It apprehends truth directly. According to Hinduism, knowledge is within. It is my own self. Just as light shines through doors and windows, this knowledge within reveals itself through our sense organs, through our body and mind. On the supersensuous plane, this seer and the seen merge into each other, the subject and the object become one. This is not absurd. For am I not part of my own environment, or are we not made of the same stuff as the environment in which we live? As we look around, we see only the facade, the surface of things; we do not see the reality that is behind it. Only when we are able to transcend our sense limitations, we can see the reality which is the self, the essence of everything. At this point the self sees itself as the self of everything and every being, sees it as the only reality. It discovers that the diversity which it had so long seen is not real. Behind that diversity, there is unity which, in fact, is the essence of all things, all beings.

It is this essence, this self which is the common factor that binds us all together. It is like the thread that runs through the pearls to make a necklace. It holds together the universe. It is the support of the universe. Aldous Huxley describes it as the H.C.F.—the Highest Common Factor—among all beings and all things. Without this essence, without this self, nothing can exist. Sri Ramakrishna used to say, 'First, write one and then add a zero, that would make the figure ten, add another zero the figure would be a hundred, go on adding zeros—the figure would correspondingly increase. But if you wipe out the number one, all the zeros will become useless.' This self which is the essence of all beings and all things cannot be proved by laboratory tests, but can easily be presumed from personal experience. I have already pointed out how the self is always present whether I am awake or dreaming or sleeping dreamlessly. This self is the connecting agent through my three states—waking, dreaming and sleeping without dreams. Every one of us has this self, the I-consciousness, whether we are small or big, man or animal. This I-consciousness being common, Hinduism argues that it is one and the same 'i' in all of us, that is to say, there is one common self which in different beings appears as different selves, different because of different names and forms. Underlying this difference in names and forms there is a common self which has these characteristics, namely, it exists, it knows and it can feel. This common self is not material, not at least in the sense we understand the word. You cannot say what life is. Yet, it is the substance of everything that exists. All we can say about it is, as I have already stated, it has in it the seeds of existence, knowledge and bliss—'*SATT*', '*CHITT*', '*ANANDA*'. It fills the universe. It is in every little bit of it. There is no place where it does not exist. There is nothing big or small which is not dependent on it. In fact, all that exists has come out of it, has its being in it and ultimately merges in it. It is like the ocean and its waves. Worlds rise and fall on this infinite ocean of existence. Some worlds are small, some are big. We all are waves on this ocean of existence. All are, in fact, made of the same stuff, the things we see, look different but they can be traced back to the same source. The difference is only on the surface, only in regard to detail; in a sense all is one. The many we see is a delusion, delusion in the sense that it is transitory. Shelly, not a Vedantic by any means, says 'the one remains, the many change and pass.'

Unity in diversity—this is the keynote of India's religious thought. A well-known physicist, J. Kaplan says, 'The atomic theory is the product of the western mind. In his naive way the western scientist generalises the experience that one can subdivide matter until one meets an ultimate particle. The Hindu philosopher goes further and reduces everything to one element.' This one element is what the Hindus call 'BRAHMAN', 'BRAHMAN' because it is everywhere, because it is the biggest. It is also called 'ATMAN'—the self, because it is the self of everything, every being. It is this which we have earlier described as 'SATI' 'CHITI' 'ANANDA'—the I-consciousness, the self. It is the same in all of us—you and I are really one. If I hurt you, I hurt myself. It is from this sense of unity that the ideas of love, compassion and non-violence have come. All religions agree about this unity. Shelly is right when he says, 'The spirit of the worm beneath the sod/In love and worship blends itself with God.' That is, in spirit the worm is one with God. The difference is only in the degree of development. God is perfect, we are not as of now, but if we try hard we can also be perfect like God, since we are one in spirit. As a corollary to this idea of unity, the self in the individual is also the self in the cosmos. The individual self and the cosmic self are one. What is in the microcosm is also in the macrocosm. The English poet, Robert Blake says 'To see a world in a grain of sand/And a Heaven in a wild flower,/Hold Infinity in the palm of your hand/And Eternity in an hour.'

I have earlier referred to the fact that all that exists has come out of one common source. Not only that, it has its being in it and also ultimately merges in it. No one can say what this source is like. It is variously described, but no description quite fits it. Finally, Hindu scholars decide to refer to it only as THAT in Sanskrit 'TAD'. Mark the affinity between the two words 'THAT' and 'TAD', The Rig. Veda[13] for instance says: 'The source from which this universe hath sprung/That source/None else: That That alone.' But where was this universe? In what condition was it? Earlier, the verse I

---

13. X 129 1–7.

have just quoted from the Rig Veda says: '... from out of a seed it came/Asleep within the heart of THAT—the seed/Of vanished worlds that in order wheeled/ Their silent course from eternity/The manifest in the unmanifest they found'. Please mark that the Rig Veda says that there have been many worlds over the centuries that have come and gone like bubbles of water. I draw your special attention to the word 'SEED' and also to the words 'unmanifest' and 'manifest'. At first, the universe was in the state of a seed. It was unmanifested. Then it became manifested. According to Hindu philosophy, there is no creation; there is only manifestation, from the seed to the tree, from the tree back to the seed. This is how the process of creation and destruction is going on all the time. There is really no creation as such. Similarly, there is no destruction as such. There is only change of form. You can never create something out of nothing. For instance, you cannot create life. No one ever created life. Life must have been there always. Only it was not manifest. When the conditions became propitious, it manifested itself. If we try to trace the evolutionary process back to its root, where shall we arrive? We shall arrive at that which is neither organic nor inorganic, neither matter nor spirit. It is only 'THAT', 'TAD', because there is no other way of describing it. All that exists has a common origin, the difference between living and non-living, between organic and inorganic, is in degree, not in kind.

This is what ancient Indian seers claim. And this, as far as I know, this unity of existence was also the thesis of the great seer-cum-scientist in whose honour this lectureship has been founded. The GITA compares this universe to a banyan tree. Where from does a banyan tree come? It comes from a tiny seed, as tiny as a mustard seed. The whole of the tree with its trunk, branches, leaves and shoots lay coiled up within the seed. Conditions being favourable, it burst forth into the huge tree that we see. Everything we see in the tree was in the seed. It is not that anything was added to it later. As far as I know, modern science says everything I have or I am is because of genes. All my physical or mental peculiarities are from my genes. Incidentally, I had a very interesting talk on this subject with Dr Kannel Usef Vosa, Professor of Genetics, Oxford University. He seems to agree with the Hindu view that the universe originated from one single source. Similarly, the self is the gene out of which this universe has come. Well, you may use the word gene, if that suits you. Use any other word if you like, but we have a common source which Hindus call the self. This self is both the material and efficient cause of the universe. It runs through it as its warp and woof. It is both the soul and the body of this universe. The self is never created nor destroyed. It is only sometimes manifest, sometimes unmanifest, sometimes evolved, sometimes involved. According to Hindu cosmogony, first appears life, then sense organs and finally matter. They are, however, one, not different from each other.

At first, they are very subtle, fine and close to each other. As they become gross, their distinctions become marked. According to science, growth is from gross to fine. But Hindus contend that the process is just the reverse—from fine to gross. As in the case of cause and effect, cause is always fine while effect is gross. From one cause, the first cause, the uncaused cause, that is the self, the universe has emerged. The self has become the universe. But the self undergoes no change, it remains the same. The change is only on the surface, only apparent, not real. The universe is the product of the principle of cause and effect. The universe is a vast chain with cause and effect as its links. Hindus say that cause is always present in effect. This is why the first cause, i.e. the self or 'BRAHMAN' is present in everything.

But religion is not so much concerned with cosmogony as with the development of man. The primary concern of religion is to help man become perfect. The GITA says all mankind is born for perfection and each man shall attain it, that being his destiny. All religions point to this goal—perfection, the kind of perfection that Buddha had or Christ had. There have been many men and women throughout history and in every country, who would not deviate from truth and who would not also hurt others for their own sake. They have goodwill for all, even those who hurt them. They were people who were utterly selfless. It is such people, who are the pride of any country, pride of humanity as a whole, the salt of the earth as the BIBLE says. How can people get such perfection? Religion says, 'Kill your own small self, the small self in us, the self which thinks of itself as a separate entity, separate from others, for this is the root of all trouble.' It makes you selfish. It makes you hate others; it makes you think of yourself only. Perfection comes when you identify yourself with others, when you are able to share the fortunes and misfortunes of others. Religion says: 'See yourself in others and see others in yourself.' This is the essence of religion. All religions have this in common. Other things are non-essential or at best, of peripheral interest. Religion is no magic. There is no shortcut in it. You can reach the goal of perfection only through hard work, through strict discipline. Often, people confuse rituals with religion. Rituals may help, help up to a point, but they become a hindrance beyond that point. Through religion, man can develop to a point when he becomes perfect, so perfect, indeed, that the dividing line between man and what is called 'GOD' disappears. For 'GOD' is the name given to that state of perfection which religion is seeking. Science certainly cannot dispute the need for this perfection. Man is indebted to science for physical comforts, but unless these comforts are coupled with man's moral uplift, there is no stability in society, no peace on earth, no real progress.

We seem to have wrong notions about progress. By progress we mean a higher G.N.P., a better standard of living, more affluence. We certainly need material prosperity, but we also need better men and women. Men and women who are more moral, more compassionate, more selfless, men and women who think more of others than of themselves, more of collective welfare than of their own personal welfare. Einstein says that science can change the nature of an element, but it is only religion which can change human nature. It is only religion that can remove hatred from our hearts. It can give us a new outlook, a new attitude towards others that can transform us into saints. It is this change that gives religion its authenticity that proves that religion is also a science. Mystics all over the world tread the same path, apply the same methods and finally reap the same fruits. The changes that come over them are also the same. They achieve perfection at its highest. The experiences may be subjective, but the results they achieve are objective. It is for the whole world to see the changes that religion brings about in their personalities. A tree is known by the fruit it bears. On this token, religion is as much a science as any other experimental science. Physical science is concerned with man's external nature, but religion is concerned with man's internal nature; that's all the difference that exists between the two.

Man may be physically comfortable, but he must also be morally sound, generous and selfless. Not mere intellectual brilliance, but good human qualities are also needed. A scientist must also be religious. A religious man also must be scientific in outlook. Science and religion must combine to make the perfect man, sound in body and morals. A true scientist is also a seer, he is concerned with truth as a whole, not only the truth that is apparent, but the truth that is real, the truth which is beyond the senses, beyond even our understanding. Above all, he has to have an open mind. If religion can demonstrate its results, scientists then have no right to dismiss it as nonsense. Religion does prove that it can transform a sinner into a saint. Religion is also based on experience. Religion is realisation of the highest moral standard. It is in this sense that religion is also a science.

Hinduism
The Eternal Religion

- *What is Hinduism?*
- *Mantra: Its Meaning and Significance*
- *Mother Kali**
- *Mother Durga**
- *Durga Puja: Past and Present**
- *Kumari Puja*
- *Krishna*

What is Hinduism?

HINDUISM DOES NOT DERIVE FROM ANY SINGLE TEACHER AS Christianity, Islam or Buddhism does, but from many teachers most of whom are nameless. Nothing, in fact, is known about those teachers except that they must have been very extraordinary persons, judging from the nature of their thoughts and experiences. Why they chose to remain unknown is difficult to say unless it is that they had a special disinclination towards fame or recognition of any kind. It seems that they were glad to be able to place on record their thoughts and experiences for such use as others might wish to make them, but they never cared for any recognition of any kind in return. They perhaps argued that what mattered was the truth and not who had discovered it.

The most important characteristic of those great souls was that they taught only that which they themselves had experienced, not in their day-to-day care-worn existence, but in a state of superconsciousness they had attained through many years of struggle. They did not guess at the Truth, or speak about it from second-hand information or from what they had learnt through study and reasoning; they spoke about it only when they had known and verified it from personal and direct experience.

This was what lent authority to whatever they said. They need not have spoken about it at all, but because by knowing that truth they had achieved great happiness and peace of mind and had also improved their character to a level of excellence not otherwise possible, they wanted others, too, to share the knowledge of the Truth so that they, too, might be happy like themselves. They assured us that the Truth they had known could be known by others as well, provided of course, they tried hard enough to know it. They added that life's goal was to know that Truth. It is this fact that the knowledge gained by the ancient teachers can be gained by others also and has in fact been so gained at different periods of history that lends validity to that knowledge. According to Hinduism, the only acceptable test of Truth is direct, personal experience. You can talk with authority and you will be heard with respect, provided what you preach you have personally verified to be true and you are a man far superior in intellect and character to the men around you. Why should anyone be interested in the Truth you say you have known unless it is seen that as a result of your having known the Truth, you have indeed become a great man? It is your daily life and character that would prove the truth or otherwise of whether you have truly attained the knowledge that everybody else is trying to get but has not yet got and whether or not the knowledge that you have got is truly worth having. Merely intellectual brilliance or fine talk is not going to impress anyone as any proof of your being a man of knowledge; it is your life and character that may be accepted as a criterion of your being what you say you are—a man who has known the Truth.

It is the direct, personal experiences of many teachers over many hundreds of years which form the corpus of what is known as 'Veda'. The knowledge which the Veda (or Vedas, if the reference is to its various sections) represents is accepted as valid because it is verified and verifiable through personal experience. It is in fact urged that no pains should be spared to attain the knowledge which the Vedas speak of, for it is only by attaining that knowledge that the transformation of character which we all so much desire can take place. The Vedas describe in detail the steps that have to be taken to prepare oneself for the experience of that supreme Truth which the seers of different epochs claim they have known. Though the Vedas thus constitute the storehouse of the knowledge and experience of many seers, it is pointed out that merely reading the Vedas or apprehending intellectually the truth they speak of is not enough, but that the Truth must be known for oneself, for just as one's hunger is not satisfied unless one eats the food oneself, so also unless one has a direct and personal experience of the Truth, one's doubts are never set at rest and one does not reap in full the benefit of the knowledge of the Truth.

Now, what is this Truth that the teachers, that is, the Vedas speak of? In other words, what is the Truth that Hinduism is supposed to stand for? Hinduism believes that there is one Supreme Soul called Brahman which is the common ground for all that exists: man, animal, matter. He is both immanent and transcendent; He is also the instrumental and material cause of this universe. It is from Brahman that we have originated, it is in Him that we have our being, and it is in Him, too, that we will finally merge. We have separate names and forms, but we are in reality all one, one in this Brahman. It is due to ignorance that we behave as if we were separate from each other, sometimes loving and sometimes hating each other; it is also due to ignorance that we behave as if we were puny, little things hemmed in on all sides by barriers, physical as well as moral, a plaything to both internal and external forces that surround us. The goal of life is to penetrate this veil of ignorance and realise that we all are one and the same, differing only in name and form, but not in substance; the goal of life is also to realise that however weak we may appear now, we are essentially one with Brahman and in that sense, divine and infinitely powerful. The body is subject to decay and death, but not the soul which is outside the pale of birth and death, joy and sorrow, it being one with that Supreme Soul called Brahman.

But how do we overcome our ignorance and know our true nature—know that we are all one and that we are one with Brahman? By both physical and mental disciplines, in other words, by practising Yogas. Yoga literally means that which unites, here it means that discipline which leads to the unity of the individual soul with the Cosmic Soul, Brahman. Hinduism preaches four Yogas which are—*Karma* (work, selfless work), *Bhakti* (devotion), *Jnana* (knowledge, discrimination, etc.) and *Raja* Yoga (control of breath and such other methods of physical discipline by which perfect control of the mind is obtained). Because it helps us attain control of the mind, which is the *sine qua non* of all spiritual progress, it is called the Raja Yoga, the best of all Yogas.

Apart from the activities which come within the purview of these Yogas, a Hindu is required to view all his daily chores as acts of worship, acts performed so as to hasten his union with God, Brahman. Nothing he does is entirely mundane inasmuch as it takes him either nearer to God or away from Him, depending upon whether or not he does it with deliberation and with an eye to the goal he has before him, or merely to satisfy his passing whims or passions. He should so organise his life, from birth to death, that not a moment of it is wasted, not a whiff of energy is spent except on acts essential for the purpose of unfolding the divinity which is lying hidden within him. It is urged that it is only by doing sincerely and to the best of his ability, the duties allotted to him, that he can make any progress in spiritual life.

It is wrong to suppose, as many indeed suppose due to ignorance, that the Hindus worship many Gods and Goddesses. They do not. They worship only Brahman, the Supreme Reality, who being Infinite, is naturally beyond thought and speech, without form, without, in fact, any attribute. But it is not possible for man to conceive of something limitless, something without a form and without an attribute. This is why the Hindus, for reasons of convenience and as a purely temporary measure, attribute names, forms and qualities to

Brahman, choosing them according to individual tastes, requirements and levels of thinking, but knowing all the time that they are worshipping the same Brahman, under these varied trappings. Having decided upon the form in which he is going to worship God, a Hindu enters into a close relationship with Him, so close as to behave as if he was His son, servant, brother or even friend. By constant practice, the relationship becomes so real that in course of time, he becomes a different person altogether, that is, a person bearing a character which the relationship would warrant.

Hinduism believes that man is the architect of his own fate. What he is today is largely the result of what he was in the past; similarly, his future will be the result of what he is today. This means that he should so conduct himself in the present that his future may be as good as he wishes it to be. Hinduism believes that man is born again and again, until through his own efforts, he reaches a point at which he is free from desires, a state he can reach only when he realises his true identity, when he knows that he is in his true nature one with God.

Because the Hindus believe that everything is a manifestation of Divinity though in a crude form, they do not wish to hurt anyone or anything, if they can help it. While this explains their general attitude towards all animals, they show a special consideration towards the cow, because she of all animals is the most useful to them.

Hinduism in its vastness includes almost every belief, attitude and concept known in the world of religion. Within a certain framework, it encourages independent thinking and practice to the maximum. This has led to a proliferation of sects and a degree of diversity in the theories and practices of Hinduism which is puzzling to outsiders, but this freedom to think and act according to one's tastes and requirements has also made possible attainment of the highest levels of religious enlightenment in more cases than would have been possible if this freedom had been denied. Long ago the Vedas declared that 'Truth is one, though the sages call it by various names.' Happily, the spirit underlying this saying still animates Hinduism. That is why Hinduism does not claim that it is the only true religion which man must follow or otherwise be damned, but gladly accepts that other religions also are equally capable of taking man to God. What it regards as vitally important is sincerity on the part of the seeker. It believes that even if a seeker does not know what the correct path to reach God is but is sincere and earnest in his search for God, he will surely find his way to God in the end.

The books which may be said to represent Hinduism correctly are first the Upanishads and then the Gita which is nothing but the quintessence of the message of the Upanishads. Next come the epics, the *Ramayana* and the *Mahabharata*, which present a medley of characters illustrating how the principles of religion can be and ought to be practised. There are also other books, written to suit varieties of tastes and levels of understanding, which serve to give further light on Hinduism. There is also a long succession of saints and seers born at different periods of history and in different regions who exemplify how one has to strive for God. Generations of Hindus have derived inspiration from them and they still follow in their steps as best they can to reach God. Some regard union with God as the goal of life while others think the goal of life is to know one's true identity, to know that one is part and parcel of God, one is even God Himself. In substance, both of course mean the same thing.

Coming to the practical side of Hinduism, the principal values that motivate a Hindu to make his struggles are: *Dharma* (righteousness), *Artha* (material possessions), *Kama* (sense-enjoyment) and *Moksha* (liberation). The highest is *Moksha*, i.e. liberation from the cycle of birth and death which happens when one is united with God or when one realises one's true identity. Getting rich and enjoying sense-pleasures are not by themselves bad but they must not involve any deviation from Dharma, i.e. the path of righteousness.

Every Hindu is asked to practise self-control as much as he can, for it is the very essence of religion. He is asked to practise, for instance,

Ahimsa (non-violence), *Satya* (Truthfulness in thought, speech and action), *Asteya* (non-stealing), *Brahmacharyya* (Chastity in thought, speech and action) and *Aparigraha* (non-acceptance of gifts). Other practices which are considered important are: *Soucha* (Cleanliness), *Santosha* (contentment), *Tapas* (austerity), *Swadhyaya* (study of sacred literature) and *Iswara-Pranidhana* (surrender to God).

Hinduism teaches that God is everywhere and in every form of life. A man may be wicked, God is in him too. God may be temporarily hiding behind his evil nature, but if he tries hard, he can make Him show Himself. A Hindu's social virtues come from this belief that God is in every human being. This makes it obligatory for him to love and serve his fellow-men, for by doing so he is in fact serving God Himself.

Superficially, Hinduism may seem to be a dying religion, if not dead already. But if one looks closely, one will find that its forms are changing and have in fact changed much, but in substance it remains the same dynamic religion that it has always been. It is this ability to adapt itself to the altered circumstances of life without in the slightest degree surrendering what it regards as vital, that has saved it from extinction in the past and promises to do so in the future also. Another factor that contributes to its continuity, and also proves that it stands on a sure foundation, is, that again and again, sages have appeared at different periods of history. They have testified from their experience to the truth of its conclusions. It is due to this fact, that the principles of Hinduism are mostly empirical which guarantees its continuity. Science may pose a serious challenge to other religious systems but not to Hinduism, for it is based entirely on experience. What it preaches can be tested by anybody, provided he has the requisite preparation.

Mantra: Its Meaning and Significance

SAINTS AND SEERS ARE PEOPLE WHO HAVE REALISED GOD. THEY are immensely happy. But they are not selfish people. They want others to be happy also. If people approach them for instructions about how to realise God, they gladly teach them. The way to God is not easy. You have to work hard and strictly follow the teacher's instructions. One of the things the teacher asks you to do is to repeat some words. These words are called a *Mantra*. '*Mantra*' means the word or words by repeating which you get liberated. The mantra is secret. You are not supposed to disclose it to others. It is meant only for you. The teacher chooses it for you, taking everything into account—your whole life and character.

A mantra is terse and succinct. It may consist of only one word, or it may consist of several words put together. But it has the power to completely change you as an individual. Once the mantra starts working, you begin to feel you are changing and you are no longer the same person. Gradually you become completely transformed. It is as if you are a lump of clay, and a potter is shaping you as he likes.

The question is: Where does the mantra derive its power from? It derives its power from God. The teacher realises God, and he becomes like God himself. And, when he speaks to you, you feel as if God is speaking to you. Then he whispers a mantra to you. The mantra is the medium through which God is transmitting his power to you.

There is immense power within you, but this power is sleeping. It is like a sleeping snake. If the snake is awakened, it raises its hood and you then see what power it has. Similarly, you have infinite power within you, and all you need to do is to awaken that power. The mantra helps do this, for it comes from a person who has realised God.

The teacher gives you the mantra and tells you how you should repeat it. When you repeat the mantra, no one should hear it. Some people count how many times they repeat it. The minimum number of times is one hundred and eight. But the number is not important. What is important is where the mind is when you are repeating the mantra. Is the mind on God? Repeating the mantra is not a physical exercise; it means communion with God. You should then feel His presence, as if you are one with Him.

As you repeat the mantra, you should meditate on the *ista*, the form of God that is dearest to you. In fact, your teacher tells you who your *ista* is. Your teacher seems to know this better than you do. God is one and the same, but devotees love to think of him with different names and in different forms. God changes His name and form according to the wishes of His devotees. Just as his devotees seek him, He also seeks the devotees. Religion means, in fact, the search by the devotee for God and the search by God for the devotee.

There is a saying in Bengali that the 'name' and the 'named' are not different. This is why you are advised to meditate on God while repeating the mantra. God and the mantra are the same. If you keep practising this, you may see in a vision that the letters of the mantra and the divine figure you have been so long meditating on, have become bright and luminous,. Not only that, you may also see the whole of yourself shining with light. You, the mantra and the deity the mantra represents—all three become one. You have then reached your goal.

The mantra leads you to your goal, but it also sustains you through your troubles and sufferings, which is more important. Some people never stop repeating the mantra. They find great joy in it. There are times when you are haunted by some thoughts. You are confused and you do not know what to do. The mantra then comes to your rescue. If you keep repeating the mantra and thinking of the Lord, you will soon find that your mind is filled with joy and happiness.

If people seek God, it is because they seek happiness. The mantra always keeps you in touch with God and you are happy. Gradually, as you go on repeating the mantra, it becomes a habit and you find you are always repeating it—even in sleep. Some people never stop repeating the mantra. That is, they are always in the presence of God. For a seeker of God, nothing is more satisfying than this.

Mother Kali

THE CONCEPT OF KALI OF THE HINDUS MAY BE QUITE PECULIAR TO many people. In fact, not only the non-Hindus, but many Hindus also have several queries concerning the image of Kali. Kali is our Mother, the Mother of the universe, the Primal Energy. But how can such an awe-inspiring repulsive figure, a blood sucking demoness garlanded with human skulls, be our Mother? The Mother of the world? And, why is Her tongue protruding out? Is it out of shame? What is most distasteful about Her is that She stands on Lord Siva, Her husband. Is She then insane? And, we have to worship Her as our Divine Mother? How mean must be those men who pay their homage to such a heinous deity? This is the attitude of many.

Those who are sympathetic towards the Hindu religion also get dumb-founded while attempting to interpret the image; not to speak of those, who are always on their toes to defame this religion. As a result, while on one hand, the Goddess has several followers, on the other, there are many who cannot tolerate even Her very name. Rabindranath Tagore despised the idol of Kali immensely. When Romain Rolland asked Rabindranath Tagore to discuss Kali with him, he started to tremble in anger. Romain Rolland was probably an admirer of Kali, so was Nivedita. Once, Nivedita delivered a lecture in Kolkata defending the Divine Mother. It was more than a lecture, it was an explosion. The listeners were all Hindus—but soon they disintegrated into two. One group supported Nivedita vehemently while the other differed. The crowd broke into a scuffle in the end and many were injured. After this, Nivedita was invited to deliver another speech on Mother Kali, in the compound of the Kalighat Temple. This time a huge crowd assembled to listen to her. The audience consisted of both the Indians and the Europeans. Fortunately, no fight ensued this time.

In the Gospel, Sri Ramakrishna says; Kali and Brahman are identical. Kali is Brahman and Brahman is Kali. Brahman is the Absolute Truth and Kali is the Relative Truth. Thus one cannot think of Brahman without Shakti, i.e. Kali or of Shakti without Brahman. One cannot think of the Absolute without the Relative, or of the Relative without the Absolute. The relation between the two is like that of the fire and its power to burn. We cannot separate the fire from its burning power. We cannot feel fire without its power to burn. Similarly, we cannot conceive of Brahman if we exclude Kali.

The same Primordial Power when inactive and without attribute is called Brahman and when it is ever at play—creating, preserving and destroying is called Kali, the active and energetic. Kali is verily Brahman, and Brahman is verily Kali. The Reality is one and the same; the difference is in name and form.

This material world is a manifestation, Divine play of Mother Kali is a mixture of the good and the evil, of love and hatred, of joy and sorrow; it is a blend of different contradictory forces. The Hindus often wish to captivate the Impersonal Absolute Being with the help of their imagination, although it can never be apprehended either by the mind or the intellect, and the result is Kali. Brahman is beyond mind and speech. Kali is the ultimate image that man can conceive of Brahman with his limited capacities of mind and brain. The entire contradictory attributes lie dissolved in Brahman and in Kali, all these contradictory forces exist separately. Brahman is like a calm ocean and Kali is its waves.

But then, why Kali bears such a terrifying look? How can it be assumed that she is the manifestation of the Brahman? Beyond the extreme boundaries of word, thought and intellect, Brahman is Brahman. Nothing prevails in that domain but only the Brahman. There is no scope for either imagination or comprehension in this region. But within the periphery of mind and intellect, within the realm of name and form, i.e. in this relative world, Kali is the most effective symbol of the Brahman. Kali stands on Lord Siva because She is another aspect of Siva and a part of Him. Siva is the inactive form and Kali is His active and energetic counterpart. Kali is black because nothing can be said definitely about Her. She is terrifying, yet at the same time kind and merciful. She is slaying and blessing at the same time. Sternness and gentleness—these dual qualities have amalgamated in the image of Kali. The sword in Her hand stands for knowledge and the human skull for action. The Divine Mother is severing all our bondages with her sword of knowledge. Her lolling tongue is devouring all the desires of man, which are the root cause of all our attachments. Kali is the real bestower of salvation to man. In Her horrifying form, the Goddess is eradicating all the weaknesses present in man and as an affectionate mother she is helping to develop all the virtues latent in us. Kali is a symbol—a symbol of power, courage and struggle. She seems to deliver a message and the message is, 'There is no place for the weak and the coward, neither in this world nor in the world hereafter. Face all adversities and overcome them like a hero.'

Mother Durga

According to the Hindu scriptures, God is one and unique. He is the root cause of this universe; He is omnipresent, infinite and unchanging. He is beyond mind and speech. He is attributeless, i.e. above all attributes. There is nothing that can limit Him, mark Him or endow Him with any quality.

However, we live in a world, characterised by name and form. We are finite; we are distinguished by our names and forms only. Hence, we love to assume that the Almighty too bears a name and form like us. We love to imagine Him as a person, though however, as a person he is omnipotent, the most venerable and the most beautiful. We also tend to impose upon this personal God certain human qualities, which we are normally acquainted with. In fact, so long as we identify ourselves with our physical body and we are conscious of the gross material world surrounding us, we can never think of God as a formless, impersonal, being. From form to formless, from personal to impersonal—we shall proceed towards the Infinite Soul through our meditation. But until we can apprehend God as an impersonal being or have the realisation of the Supreme Self, we worship the Almighty as a personal God, possessing a name and a form. From the practical point of view, such an approach to attain God is undoubtedly very rational and useful.

The Hindus are well aware that the name, form and qualities which they associate with God are all the products of their imagination. These are only temporary means to attain the Supreme. Gradually, a time comes when the aspirant has no longer any need to worship God in a human form. The Hindu scholars have gone even one step further to state that: A time comes when the devotee feels that he is one with the God, he and the Supreme Being are the same entity. This realisation is the goal of every ascetic and such a divine realisation is the last word of spiritual discipline. Again, this state is not desired by certain aspirants. For instance, Sri Ramakrishna used to say, 'I do not want to be sugar, I love to taste sugar.'

Now, one may ask that by which name shall we call God or in which form shall we worship Him? The Hindus believe that it is subject to the choice of the devotee. A devotee can worship God or think of Him in any form or name he wishes, according to his taste or liking.

Taste varies from person to person, from community to community. Therefore, different people worship the Divine Soul in different names and different imaginary forms. However, this does not imply that they are worshipping different Gods. They all are worshipping the same Supreme Spirit—but in different names and forms according to their liking. This form of practice make many people presume that Hindus believe in many Gods and Goddesses and that they are polytheist. However, such a notion is entirely baseless. The Hindus never advocate the existence of many Gods—they believe only in one God.

Now, the question arises that, where and when did the image worship of Goddess Durga originate? Most probably it commenced in this very Bengal in the remote past. But from time immemorial, Devi Durga is being worshipped throughout India, in various imaginary forms. The ancient scriptures, like the *Mahabharata*, the *Harivansham*, the *Markandeya Purana* (which includes the legend of Chandi), etc., bear testimony to this fact. Even long before that, as the archaeological surveys of Mohenjodaro and Harappa reveal, the worship of Shakti or the Divine Mother was in vogue in India, though not specifically called the worship of Durga.

The worship of the Supreme Soul in the incarnation of Mother is an age-old tradition of the Bengalis. Durga, Kali, Jagatdhatri, Saraswati, Lakshmi, Shitala, Manasa—we worship the Divine Mother in all these various forms. However, amongst them, Mother Durga is the most adorable to the Bengalis. In our family, just as our mother is our very own, likewise, in this world God is our Mother. She is omnipotent, she is the Mother of this whole world, yet we have made her our very own by addressing her as 'Mother'. The worship of the Mother is a worship of love—it is like a festival of joy and delight. Hence, Durga Puja is often regarded as a festival. It is entirely a ceremony of the Bengalis, very dear to them and their very own. Mother Durga is worshipped in autumn—when the sky remains cloudless, the gentle breeze carries the pleasant fragrance of the harsingar (*shiuli*), the water bodies brim with fullness, and nature seems to spread out her soft verdant remnant over the Mother earth. It is amidst such a radiant atmosphere that the Divine Mother comes infusing hope in us and accepts our tributes. We wait the whole year round for this festive occasion. During the days of the festival, we see the beautiful charming face of the Mother in the pandals, charioted on lion and slaying demons. She is the Primal energy, the remover of all our afflictions and sorrows. She is Devi Durga, (clay image) earthen yet the Supreme conscious soul, Power and Beauty incarnate, a symbol of love and compassion, of wealth and prosperity.

Durga Puja: Past and Present

IN A FEW DAYS THE BENGALIS WILL START CELEBRATING DURGA PUJA. The subtle excitement of celebration can be felt at every nook and corner. The Durga idol is on the verge of completion and the work of pandal decorations is progressing with a rapid pace. People are too busy with their shopping which continues till the last moment, as in spite of much alertness either something is missed out or a lot amount is left to be purchased. Durga Puja is not just a commonplace for worship, it is worship where sacrifices were earlier performed by the kings to establish their supremacy over other kings, so only kings or zamindars had the potential to perform the Puja. Wealth alone was not just enough to make this Puja possible, but sufficient manpower was also necessary. Lest, there is any kind of hindrance while performing the worship, the zamindars distributed some amount of land to some families and kept them as mortgages permanently. Thus, during the Puja, those families could provide their labours or supply the necessary things required for the Puja, and they could also thoroughly execute all the required duties for the Durga Puja.

The zamindar-subject relationship was passed on from generation to generation. This was beneficial to both sides. Starting from the Brahmin priest, washerman and barber, blacksmith and potter, carpenter, confectioner, garland maker, drummer—all communities in a Hindu society, were equally needed by the zamindar while performing the Puja. Each one would have his or her due role to perform. Either they would supply ingredients for the Puja, or during the Puja they would stay with the zamindar and give their service as and when required. In advance, they started to visit the zamindar's house quite frequently. Not only men, but women, young and old everyone would visit—with the hope to do some kind of work. What an anxiety, what an immense happiness! 'Mother is coming', 'Mother to all', Mother to the zamindar and also mother to the peasants, She is the Mother to the rich and the poor, Brahmin and the Sudras, the learned and the ignorant alike; all are allowed to worship the holy Mother according to their capacity. During the puja each one has his duty to perform, and responsibility to carry out so that the puja could be carried out unimpeded. Not only Hindus, even the Muslim community actively involved themselves in this grand festival. They came to adore the idol and even asked for Prasad. Many zamindar houses sacrificed goat on this occasion. And, on many occasions this goat for sacrifice would be offered from the house of a Muslim peasant. The offering would be free of charge because the zamindar had already distributed land to their ancestors a long time back. Maybe, at the time of that deal, the peasant was a Hindu, and later had been converted to Islam religion. In spite of being a Muslim, he personally did not have any objection to offer the goat for sacrifice, but later, due to the social prejudices he would hesitate. At certain times, the zamindars wished to pay back against the offered goat. The fact that the zamindar wished to pay back against the offering, also, at times created a mutual ill-feeling amongst them.

On the occasion of Durga puja, everybody was invited in the village, regardless of caste or race. The maximum priority always used to be given to the Brahmins. They would happily accept the invitation in case the zamindar himself was a Brahmin. The zamindar invited each member of the Brahmin families. The invitation letter would also be quite enjoyable and interesting which would be written in Bengali and Sanskrit language. The invitation was not only meant for the invitees, but the guests of the invitees were also heartily welcomed. The invited Brahmins would be in a dilemma in case there was more than one Brahmin zamindar in the village and all were organising pujas. The house that was visited would be greatly pleased, whereas the house that was unvisited would be quite disappointed. At times, family members would be divided into two to three groups and each was sent to attend a different house. Still, there was no end to the difficulties, because the zamindars kept a watch on which place the head member would visit. This was also the cause to give rise to partiality amongst them. There would be no cooking done in the village if there was a puja in the Brahmin zamindar's house. In case the zamindar was not a Brahmin, the Brahmins would prefer to have their own food. The Brahmins would instead once visit the zamindar's house and accept their due fees and gifts and have some sweets and fruits that the zamindar would offer them.

It was a tradition to have theatrical performances during the puja. The play was selected and kept ready much ahead of the puja. Even the characters were chosen and selected. And there would be frequent rehearsals to make the play a success. Lastly, the play would be enacted on a particular day. And, with what eagerness everybody would wait for the day! Everyone would yearn to watch the enactment of the latest and most popular play in Kolkata. And, the maximum thrill would be derived if they did better than the neighbourhood village with their excellent performance. Everyone would be active and working hard so that the pride and prejudice of the village remained untarnished. Even the zamindar would support with open heart, with decoration and dress material, to make it a success.

A Durga puja in the village includes everybody. This is a national festival. Everybody celebrates—the young and the old, the rich and the poor, the Brahmins and the Sudras. The little ones would impatiently look forward for the puja to arrive, as they could buy the dresses they were eagerly waiting for. And, they would try out the dresses and would not stop asking repeatedly for appreciation. Just being new and elaborate would not suffice; it had to be according to the current trend also. Each year different trends are out in the market, some having a Western look, whereas some with a touch of South India. Whatever it might be, it had to be having a new and extraordinary look, something different from the others.

But in recent times the scenario has changed a lot. Just for name sake the zamindars continue to be zamindars. Neither have they the money power, nor many hands for labour. Thus, the puja is still offered just to maintain their ancestral pride. So, inviting all for feast like earlier times would be out of question. Nowadays, villages have started conducting social puja gathering. There could be more than one puja in the society. Now, it is the *Sarvajanin*, or the public puja for a locality, inclusive of all races, classes, castes and creed and is not limited to a particular family or a section of the society.

The youth participation in the puja is the maximum. They prefer to highlight the social aspects more than the religious aspect, which remains rather subdued. In the social, or the *Barowari puja* only the Brahmins could make the offerings of *Naivedya* or *Bhog* to the Divine Mother but now it is done by the Brahmins and the Sudras or any other caste. Each puja consists of a puja conducting committee. Each one in the locality is a member of this committee and the senior-most is selected as the president. The other capable members are selected and respectively given their suitable posts. Many a time, surprisingly quite a few non-Bengalis or non-Hindus would be selected as members and sometimes also given responsible posts in the committee. This committee is appointed not just for conducting the puja programme, but also aims at various other social works. For example, a part of the puja collection is spent for the needy class, distributing clothes and quilts to them. Many innovative ideas are thought of to serve, more or less, each class of the society. Nowadays, a remarkable aspect of puja is serving and worshipping the human God.

As we know change is the natural process of life, the notion of Durga puja has also undergone a sea change, having both hostile as well as advantageous aspect. We would like to build an organised society where the Brahmin and the Sudras, the rich and the poor or the learned and the ignorant shall have equal rights and importance. The *Sarvajanin* Durga puja is truly a significant step overcoming the so-called social barriers. This puja wonderfully creates a ground for gathering and unites the society. At least for a few days, we tend to forget all the differences and barriers among us and represent the Bengali class, rather the whole nation. This attraction for uniting is such that many a time we find that the non-Bengalis take greater initiative, donate huge money and actively take part in the festival. There are many facets to it that give immense pleasure to the society, the most valuable being the bond of unity that is strengthened by this auspicious festival. The warmth of the hearty embrace of the *Vijaya* significantly enhances the bonding. No where else in India we find such kind of festival that unites people with a single thought, as different flowers woven onto a single thread, to make a garland.

Truly, Durga puja is a festival of joy and unity that helps to organise our life and society harmoniously.

Kumari Puja

GOD IS ALL-PERVASIVE. HE IS BOTH WITHOUT ATTRIBUTES AND WITH attributes. You cannot qualify Him by saying He is like this or like that. He is beyond the reach of both speech and thought.

Since God is everywhere, He must be in all beings—both in animals and plants. Sri Ramakrishna used to say that He manifests Himself in all living beings, in the entire universe, and the twenty-four cosmic principles. In fact, He is everything, He is all that exists. He is without name and form. Yet, all names and forms come from Him. Nothing exists independent of Him. He is within this universe as much as He is without it. He is both immanent and transcendent. He is the female aspect of the Reality as He is the male aspect. He is the boy and He is also the girl. He moves about in diverse names and forms. He alone exists. All forms are His and at the same time, He is formless. He is beyond the reach of the senses. When He divests Himself of names and forms, He is then beyond cognition.

But because we have forms, we want that God should also manifest Himself in some form or the other, preferably in the forms we adore. If He does condescend, we can then share our joys and sorrows with Him and enter into a relationship with Him. The Mother-child relationship is, of course, ideally the best. That explains why the worship of God as Mother is so popular. We worship Her, with great pomp and grandeur in an image made of clay, wood or any metal. But before doing so, we infuse life into the image. How do we do that? We say, 'Mother, you are everywhere, you are in my heart. But I cannot see you or feel your presence. For my sake, will you please come into this image? Please do. I want to see you, feel you, love and caress you. You are infinite and I am finite. Please, be finite for my sake, at least for the time being.' After this prayer, the devotee begins to feel the image is no longer an image; it is mother Herself—living, loving and conscious. Mother is the source of all power. She creates, sustains and destroys. But what is this power? Sri Ramakrishna used to say, 'My Mother Kali is no other than what you call Brahman, the pure and undifferentiated consciousness.' To illustrate the point, he would say—'The snake is the snake, whether it is lying on the ground, or is standing on its tail with its hood raised.' Brahman and Kali are the same reality: the difference is that Brahman is not manifest, Kali is manifest. They are inseparably related like fire and its power to burn. We cannot think of a creator without his creation. Acharya Sankara emphasises this fact in *'Soundarya Lahari'*.

Siva Saktya yukto yadi Bhavati Sak Pravhabitam
Na ChedeamDevam Na Khalu Kusalah Spanditamapi.

Siva can create only if Sakti helps. Without Sakti, Siva is inert.

Swami Vivekananda asserted that a physically weak person shall achieve nothing in this world or in the world beyond. He would quote the Upanishad to reinforce his contention—*Nayamatma Balahinena Labhyah*.

Spiritual discipline is not for a weak person. The Sakti worship traces its origin to the hoary past. It was practised even in the Mohenjodaro period. In Devi Sukta (Rig Veda) the Goddess Mother thus speaks of herself and proclaims—

Aham Rastri—I Lord it over the created world.

Yajnaiyanam prathama—I enjoy precedence over other Gods. I am absolute. I rule over everything—spiritual or secular. Nothing is beyond me.' We worship this incarnate of the Supreme Reality in diverse names and forms. But, obviously, names and forms are all superimpositions and therefore not part of the Reality. Mother is the essence of everything.

Swami Vivekananda used to say, 'Images made of clay or metal are inert, immobile, and inarticulate. As an image, man is living. He can feel and speak. God is everywhere, but He is more manifest in man. Why not worship God in man?' And, among men the divine presence is more pronounced and discernible in these who are honest and God, like you see the moon's reflection, more clear if the water is clear. It follows then that the Divine Mother is more manifest in virgin girls. In **Yogini Tantra** we find

Kumari Pujana Falam Vaktum Na Ahrami Sundari

Siva says to Parvati that there is no end to the merits derived from 'Kumari Puja'. Even the heavenly abode of the Gods can be conquered by such worship.

Kumari Pujanam Kritva Trailokyam Vasam Anayet

It is interesting to note that a girl of any caste whatsoever can be chosen for such worship.

Jati Bhedo na Kartabyah Kumari Pujane Sive

That is why Swami Vivekananda had no hesitation in worshipping a Muslim girl as Kumari in Kashmir. In choosing a girl for worship, choose one who has good features and who is below sixteen years. She should be unwed. Swami Vivekananda himself introduced the worship of Durga Puja and Kumari Puja at the Belur Math. This worship continues in strict conformity to the scriptures. The ardent solicitations of the devotees breathe divine life into the image, living (that is man) or non-living. The surrounding atmosphere is surcharged with religious fervour and solemnity. What fascinate us all the more are the visible reactions and movements of the girl during the whole process of worship. Thousands of devotees feel that the girl is transformed. She no more belongs to the human plane. She has been divinised—she is the Mother Goddess, radiating divinity and adored by the Gods. After the ritualistic worship is gone through, everybody irrespective of age, even the monks pay their homage to the Goddess in the form of the Kumari. It is prescribed that girls of different ages are worshipped as incarnations of different Goddesses.

For instance—a one year-old-virgin is worshipped as *Sandhya*, as *Saraswati* a two-year old, a three-year old as *Tridha* and again a four-year-old girl is worshipped as *Kalika*.

What does the worship lead to?

When we worship a person or a deity, we worship him or her for the good qualities he or she possesses we all wish to acquire. By so worshipping, we hope we should someday be able to acquire those qualities ourselves. I am a weak person in physical or spiritual terms. When I worship Mother, I seek her grace so that I may acquire all the virtues that she represents.

Procedures of worship are detailed: first and foremost, we must keep in mind that the girl as the worshipped is considered to be no other than the Divine Mother. The girl has to be adorned with various ornaments and then placed on a comfortable seat. Her feet are first washed with love and devotion, and then they are tinged with red colour (*aalta*). A dainty spot of vermilion on her forehead is a must. Then, the worship proceeds with a sip of drinking water followed by early breakfast for the girl. The worshipper, while meditating should pray—

> *Balarupanca Trailokya Sundarim Varavarninim*
> *Nana ASri Lankaranamrangim*
> *Bhadra Vidya Prakasinim*
> *Caruhasyam Mahanandahridayam*
> *Subhadam Subham*

Mother, my Mother! You are the object of adoration of *Trailakya*, but Mother, as a matter of grace, you are here now before me in the form of a girl. You present knowledge, joy and benediction.

Thereafter, the rituals of worship should have to be gone through with different items of worship. The rituals may either be very elaborate or relatively brief. It is desirable that there shall be abundant supply of flowers for the Mother, and sweets for distribution among the devotees. After the formal worship, it is prescribed that the worshipper should engage himself in *Pranayam* (control of vital breath) and *Japam* (repetitions of holy names). The worship is rounded off with this hymn:

Om Namami Kulakaminim
Parama Bhagya Sandayinim
Kumararati Caturim Sakala Siddhi Dana Nandinim
Prabala Gutika Srajam
Rajata Raga Vastranvitam
Hiranyatula Bhusanam
Bhuvana Vak Kumarim Bhaje

Oh, Mother, you may, if you so desire, surround me with earthly fortunes. I bow down to you. May I achieve my fulfilment in all respects! You are bedecked with various ornaments made of gold and silver and coral. You are none other than Saraswati (Goddess of Learning). I bow to you.

Kumari Puja is performed at the Belur Math on the Maha Astami Day (Eighth day after autumnal new moon). According to some scriptures, the worship may be performed on the ninth day also. Actually, any day and any place whatsoever is appropriate provided the worship is performed with due devotion.

Krishna

KRISHNA IS THE COMPLETE MAN. HE IS A STATESMAN, A PHILOSOPHER and a warrior, all rolled into one.

As a statesman, he worked for the unity of India. He tried his best to bring about an understanding between the Kauravas and the Pandavas, but he failed. He knew war would cause loss of life and hardship to the survivors, but when he saw war was inevitable, he had no hesitation in siding with the Pandavas. He wanted the Pandavas to win, for they were fighting for their legitimate rights and not out of greed like the Kauravas. He was a well-wisher of the Pandavas, yet he never actually fought for them. He did, of course, urge Arjuna to fight, for without Arjuna the Pandavas could not win and it was necessary that the Pandavas should win, for otherwise there would be chaos in the country, and the Kauravas would dominate and the weak and the honest people would suffer. The Kurukshetra war was a war of peace and justice. Krishna led this war, but he was never in the forefront. Apparently, he played an insignificant role in the war as the chariot-driver of Arjuna but his shrewd judgement of men and things, his commonsense and his knowledge of the art of war were a formidable force. This force, working silently and invisibly, turned the side of the war in favour of the Pandavas and they won. The forces of evil were totally crushed and the ground was prepared for the creation of a new and united India where truth and justice would prevail.

As a warrior, there was no one who could match his skill and courage. He defeated one after another all those small tyrants who were oppressing the innocent people and restored peace and harmony in the whole country. At first, people did not understand him. They thought he was not genuine and some ridiculed him or challenged him to a trial of strength. In every instance, Krishna proved his superiority and in due course, came to be recognised as an extraordinary person. In every assembly of men of prominence, he was given the highest seat of honour. But it was not his physical strength or skill of war alone that brought him this honour; it was his wisdom and personal life and character that made people respect him as a true leader of men. Though born of Kshatriya parents, Krishna spent his childhood among people who tended cows and lived around Brindavan. He was a restless boy and he played many pranks. Yet, he was loved and adored by everybody irrespective of age and sex. The women who loved him had been great sages in their previous lives. They had no body-consciousness. They loved Krishna and their love was pure. According to Swami Vivekananda, this love was totally selfless and only the devotees of the highest order could have such love. Swamiji says, 'A great landmark in the history of religion is here, the ideal of love for love's sake, work for work's sake, duty for duty's sake, and it for the first time fell from the lips of the greatest of incarnations, Krishna, and for the first time in the history of humanity, upon the soil of India.'

We see Krishna as a philosopher when Arjuna said he did not want to fight at the battlefield of Kurukshetra. He taught Arjuna the essence of Vedanta, which is now known as *Srimat Bhagavat Gita*. The Gita is one of the three Prasthanas. If the Upanishads are the cow, the Gita is the milk of the cow. The whole humanity will always remain indebted to Krishna for the Gita. It is in the Gita that for the first time we come across the concept of God assuming a human body whenever there is a moral chaos in the world. *'Krishnastu Bhagavan Svayam'*, that is, Krishna was God Himself. He was '*Yogesvara*', the lord of the Yogas. He declared in the Gita that 'no matter what path you choose, you will surely come to me if you are sincere.' He also said that work is indeed worship if it is done for the sake of God, for the good of others and without expecting anything in return. He also asked man 'to be in the world but not of it', that is to say, to remain always unattached. Krishna stressed much on this art of non-attachment. He taught a new concept of duty. What is duty for a scholar cannot be the duty for a soldier. A scholar may abhor killing but a soldier has to kill, it is his duty. One cannot imitate another. Each has to grow in his own way, according to his genius. Each has to do his duty well, there is no division whatsoever in this. A sweeper who does his duty well is just as good as a priest who does his duty well.

These are some of the loftiest teachings of Krishna. Krishna is the ideal man, judged by any standard. He is the sum total of all that man can wish to have—strength, courage, wisdom, physical beauty, above all, moral grandeur. He saved India from the tyranny of the wicked. He is still the path-finder for all of us.

Buddhism Fulfilment of Hinduism

- *Are you a Buddhist?*
- *Re-reading Buddha in the Light of Swami Vivekananda*
- *Buddhism and Vedanta*
- *Buddham Sharanam Gachhami*

Are you a Buddhist?

SWAMI VIVEKANANDA LOVED TO SPEAK OF BUDDHA AND HE OFTEN spoke of him with such feeling that people would think he was a Buddhist. Even Nivedita, who was so close to him, was confused. She once asked him pointedly if he was a Buddhist. In reply, Swami Vivekananda said, 'I am a servant of the servants of the servants of Buddha.'[14] He had this love for Buddha right from his boyhood. Buddha's renunciation and concern for mankind were always a source of inspiration to him. When under Sri Ramakrishna's influence, his renunciation intensified, he, with two brother disciples, rushed to Bodh Gaya. They chose this place because of its association with Buddha. This is where Buddha had attained nirvana and they too wanted to attain it. They thought the place would help them. They were seized with the same zeal and anguish as Buddha had been before his enlightenment. They spent a few days there absorbed in meditation, and then returned to Cossipore where Sri Ramakrishna, their Master, was dying.

During the days Swami Vivekananda travelled through India as a wandering monk, he often stopped at places where there were big libraries. With the help of friends, he borrowed books from these libraries and spent much of his time studying scriptures of different

---

14. *Life of Swami Vivekananda By His Eastern and Western Disciples*, Vol. II, Advaita Ashrama, Calcutta, 1981, p. 340.

religions and books on different systems of philosophy. Studying Buddhism he became convinced that it was not a new religion, it was only 'a rebel child'[15] of Hinduism. In other words, it rejected ceremonies and sacrifices which then characterised Hinduism. He also opposed philosophical dialectics, in which scholars loved to indulge in those days. Hinduism had become cumbersome with accretions of all sorts. Common people did not know what they were expected to do. It was a critical time for Hinduism. Buddha appeared at this juncture and saved the religion. He offered a version of Hinduism which was simple, clear and practical.

Soon after Swami Vivekananda had read his famous paper on 'Hinduism' at the Parliament of Religions in Chicago, he spoke on 'Buddhism' on 26 September 1893. The title of his speech was significant: 'Buddhism, the fulfilment of Hinduism.' He started by saying, 'I am not a Buddhist, as you have heard, and yet I am. If China, or Japan, or Ceylon follows the teachings of the Great Master, India worships him as God incarnate on earth.'[16] Swami Vivekananda was of the view that 'Shakya Muni' came to preach nothing new. He also, like Jesus, came to fulfil and not to destroy. Only, in the case of Jesus, it was the old people, the Jews, who did not understand him, while in the case of Buddha, it was his own followers who did not understand the import of his teachings. What Christ taught was nothing but the fulfilment of Judaism. The Jews, however, did not understand this and they crucified Jesus. Similarly, Swamiji says, 'Shakya Muni came not to destroy, but he was the fulfilment, the logical conclusion, the logical development of the religion of the Hindus.'[17]

Hinduism may be divided into two parts: the ceremonial and the spiritual. The ceremonial is for householders, the spiritual is

---

15. *The Complete Works of Swami Vivekananda*, Vol.II, Advaita Ashrama, Calcutta, 1964, p. 275.
16. Ibid., Vol. I, 1962, p. 21.
17. Ibid.

for monks. Where spirituality is concerned, there is no place for caste. Caste is essentially a social institution, according to Swami Vivekananda. Religion has nothing to do with it. But, for one reason or another, orthodox Hinduism had held back from sections of people it branded as low castes, the higher Vedic truths. It was given to Lord Buddha to break down this barrier. To quote Swami Vivekananda, 'Shakya Muni himself was a monk, and it was his glory that he had the large-heartedness to bring out the truths from the hidden Vedas and through them broadcast all over the world.'[18] Buddha was also the first missionary in the history of religion. He converted people on a mass scale.

In the same speech, Swami Vivekananda also referred to Buddha's heart. Buddha, he said, felt for everybody, especially the poor and the ignorant. He preached in the language of the masses. Sometimes, his Brahmin disciples would suggest that he preach in Sanskrit, the language of the elite. Buddha always refused saying, 'I am for the poor, for the people; let me speak in the tongue of the people.'[19] And so, to this day the great bulk of his teachings are in the vernacular of that day in India.

Buddha avoided metaphysics altogether. He had seen how scholars got bogged down in the dialectics of metaphysics, losing sight altogether of the purpose of life. He talked of universal suffering and how that suffering could be ended. His approach to the problem was pragmatic. If man suffered, he had to look for the cause within himself and not outside. He was responsible for everything that happened to him. He was the architect of his own fate. Buddha did not refer to the eternal issues like God or the Self. This led many to think that he was an atheist and did not believe in the existence of God or the Self. The fact that he preached *Anatmavad* of the objects of the world, i.e. nothing in the world had an identity of its own,

---

18. Ibid., p.22.
19. Ibid.

it being only an aggregate of things, fuelled this belief further. It is very likely that Buddha, like the Vedantins, wanted to point out the perishable nature of the empirical world. He was not, however, explicit about the Vedantic idea that there was something imperishable which sustained this perishable world, yet Swami Vivekananda, said, 'The Vedanta philosophy is the foundation of Buddhism . . .' He was convinced that what was known as Buddhism of the Northern School was nothing but Vedanta. Referring to Buddhism of the Southern School, he said that it did not accept the Vedantic viewpoint that there was something imperishable in the world. He, however, said in reply to this objection that Vedanta did not think that there were two distinct categories 'Perishable' (phenomenal) and 'Imperishable' (noumenal), there was only one category which appeared so divided. To make himself clear, he said that Reality was one and the same. Seen through the senses that Reality would appear as the phenomenal world, always divided and changing. The Vedantic position was such, that it would make no difference so far as Reality was concerned. It would always remain the same, unchanging and unchangeable.

In answer to a question, Swami Vivekananda said, 'Buddha was one of the Sannyasins of the Vedanta. He started a new sect, just as others are starting even today. The ideas which now are called Buddhism were not his. They were much more ancient. He was a great man who gave the ideas power. The unique element in Buddhism was its social element.'[20]

Talking about the decay of Buddhism in India, Swami Vivekananda said, 'Every movement triumphs by dint of some unusual characteristic, and when it falls, that point of pride becomes its chief element of weakness. The Lord Buddha—greatest of men— was a marvellous organiser and carried the world by this means. But his religion was the religion of a monastic order. It had, therefore, the evil effect of making the very robe of the monk honoured. He

---

20. Ibid., p. 309.

also introduced for the first time the community life of religious houses and thereby necessarily made women inferior to men, since the great abbesses could take no important step without the advice of certain abbots. It ensured its immediate object, the solidarity of the faith, you see, only its far-reaching effects are to be deplored.'[21]

Buddhism saved Hinduism, but itself 'died' in the process. It died in the sense that it lost its separate identity. Perhaps, Buddha never intended that it should remain a separate religion. All he wanted was to remove the embarrassing features Hinduism had acquired over the ages. He was basically a reformer. Hinduism, so reformed, is what is now known as Buddhism.

Re-reading Buddha in the Light of Swami Vivekananda

THERE IS HARDLY ANY DEBATE ABOUT BUDDHA, THE MAN, BECAUSE everything about him is well attested. The same, however, cannot be said about his religion. To avoid debate, Buddha, as far as possible, left alone metaphysics, and reduced his religion to a few working principles of ethics. Yet, the irony is that there was and still is much debate about what he taught. Over the centuries, a series of elders' councils have been held under royal patronage to arrive at some sort of consensus, but the result has been splits and more splits among the followers. Buddha avoided metaphysics in order that people might not be confused, but it is precisely metaphysics which dominates the continuing debate about what exactly Buddha taught.

Buddha and Buddhism cannot be separated. To understand Buddhism one has to refer to Buddha again and again. He was the best Buddhist if there was ever one. Apart from being the first historical prophet, Buddha was one of the finest characters in history. Sir Edwin Arnold acclaimed him as 'The Light of Asia'. More truly, he is 'The Light of the World'. Swami Vivekananda might have had reservations about other prophets, but he was 'a servant of the servants of the servants of Buddha.'[22] He says, 'All my life I have been very

---

22. *His Eastern and Western Disciple, Life of Swami Vivekananda* (Calcutta: Advaita Ashrama), p. 340.

fond of Buddha . . . I have more veneration for that character than for any other . . .'[23]

In the same lecture, he further says, 'If he was great in life, he was also great in death.'[24] He had a meal given him by a poor man, which killed him. The man was naturally upset. Some people also cursed him. But before he died Buddha sent the man word, thanking him, for 'he has done me one of the greatest services of my life—he has released me from the body.'[25]

Buddha taught man to love man. Referring to this Swami Vivekananda said, 'This was the first time they (men) turned to the other God—man. It is man that is to be loved. It was the first wave of intense love for all men—the first wave of true unadulterated wisdom—that, starting from India, gradually inundated country after country, north, south, east and west.'[26]

Brahmanical India reserved her wisdom only for the elite. The masses had no access to it because they were not considered fit for it, intellectually or otherwise. The greatest barrier was Sanskrit, which the masses did not know and the scriptures were all in Sanskrit. Caste also stood in the way. This led to the rise of a special hierarchy of brahmins who taught merely rites and rituals in the name of religion. Even princes did not know what religion was about. If they wanted a favour from God, they tried to please Him by pouring huge quantities of butter into the sacrificial fire and slaughtering animals. Of course, the priests were always with them. Few people realised why they were doing this. The masses did not know where they stood in relation to God. They mechanically did what the priests told them to do—that is all.

According to Swamiji, the time was ripe when someone should come to explain the riddles of religion. So long, brahmins had

---

23. *The Complete Works of Swami Vivekananda* (Calcutta: Advaita Ashrama), viii, 103. (Hereafter, C.W.)
24. C.W., viii, 104.
25. C.W., viii, 104–5.
26. C.W., viii, 100.

monopolised the role of religious teachers. Now, it was the turn of a Kshatriya. Buddha, a prince of the Sakya line, whose kingdom was at the foothills of the Himalayas, was a Kshatriya. In ancient India, a teacher was not competent to teach unless he proved his competence by renunciation. Buddha, heir to his father's throne, left home, wife, the new-born child, everything, and overnight became a beggar. He all but killed himself through the rigours he imposed on himself in his pursuit of knowledge (*bodhi*). He finally got his bodhi, became a 'Buddha', and set his 'wheel of dharma' in motion by preaching his first sermon at Sarnath. Contrary to the practice of the day, he taught in the language of the people, quoted no scriptures, and totally omitted the word 'God' or 'Self' from his sermons. What he taught was a challenge to man to determine his fate. He asked man to control his thought, speech, and action. In other words, always follow the right path, and be a better individual, be a 'Buddha'.

Buddha saw that the root of man's suffering was in his own mind. A person had endless desires and these desires made him act in a manner ultimately injurious to himself. Man was the architect of his own fate. If he did something wrong, he was bound to suffer for it. He had himself to blame for this, not God or any other agency. Buddha's last words to his disciples were 'Be ye lamps unto yourselves. Be ye a refuge to yourselves.'

Buddha never claimed that he was the saviour. He did not even want that anybody to look upon him as his master. Swamiji says, 'None of his adulators could draw from him one remark that he was anything different from any other man.'[27] He merely pointed out the obvious things, the things which were there for everybody to see, though, for one reason or another, people tended to overlook them. He also did not want anybody to accept anything he said on trust; he wanted people to test it and then accept it if they so wished.

---

27. C.W., iii, 527.

As he was dying he said: 'Work out diligently your own salvation. Each one of you is just what I am. I am nothing but one of you. What I am today is what I made myself. Do you struggle and make yourselves what I am.' He also said: 'Believe not because an old book is produced as an authority. Believe not because your fathers said [you should] believe the same. Believe not because other people like you believe it. Test everything, try everything, and then believe it, and if you find it for the good of many, give it to all.'[28]

Swamiji adored Buddha because he thought he was 'the sanest philosopher the world ever saw, its best and its sanest teacher. And never that man bent, even before the power of the tyrannical brahmins. Never that man bent. Direct and everywhere the same; weeping with the miserable, helping the miserable, singing with the singing, strong with the strong, and everywhere the same sane and able man.'[29]

In his speech on 'Buddhism, the Fulfilment of Hinduism' dated 26 September 1893, at the Parliament of Religions, Swamiji said: 'You have just now heard that I am going to criticise Buddhism, but by that I wish you to understand only this. Far be it from me to criticise him whom I worship as God incarnate on earth. But our views about Buddha are that he was not understood properly by his disciples. The relation between Hinduism (by Hinduism, I mean the religion of the Vedas) and what is called Buddhism at the present day is nearly the same as between Judaism and Christianity. Jesus Christ was a Jew, and Sakya Muni was a Hindu. The Jews rejected Jesus Christ, nay, crucified him, and the Hindus have accepted Sakya Muni as God and worship him. But the real difference that we Hindus want to show between modern Buddhism and what we should understand as the teachings of Lord Buddha lies principally in this: Sakya Muni came to preach nothing new. He also, like Jesus,

---

28. C.W., iii, 528.
29. C.W., iii, 528.

came to fulfil and not to destroy. Only, in the case of Jesus, it was the old people, the Jews, who did not understand him, while in the case of Buddha, it was his own followers who did not realise the import of his teachings. As the Jew did not understand the fulfilment of the Old Testament, so the Buddhist did not understand the fulfilment of the truths of the Hindu religion. Again, I repeat, Sakya Muni came not to destroy, but he was the fulfilment, the logical conclusion, the logical development of the religion of the Hindus.[30]

In what sense was Buddhism 'The logical fulfilment' of Hinduism? Hinduism, in those days, meant only ceremonialism. If you wanted something, you performed one ceremony after another. It was a time when people confused religion with ceremonialism and scholarship. Buddha pointed out that religion was nothing but the practice of being good and doing good. This is exactly what the Upanishads demanded of man. In this sense, Buddhism is nothing but Vedanta. To be more precise, it is practical Vedanta.

Vedanta begins where ceremonialism ends. In fact, ceremonialism prepares the ground for Vedanta. It helps man realise the hollowness of the things of the world. He gets rid of his desires and begins to enquire about the nature of the ultimate reality. To get rid of the desires is the means; to get an answer to the enquiry is the end. Buddhism talks about the means, but is silent about the end. This silence has been misunderstood. It is not that there is no end, but it is difficult to explain the end. Scholars have tried, but have miserably failed. Buddha describes the end as nirvana, but what the word means is still debated. Buddha disliked metaphysical speculations. All scholastic discussions were a waste of time to him. If there was a wound, first and foremost that wound had to be healed. Who caused the wound, why he did it, what caste he belonged to—all these were useless questions. Given the means, the end would be clear soon. Buddha was pragmatic: He pointed out the steps leading

---

30. C.W., i, 21.

to the roof. He asked man to go and discover for himself what was there on the roof. He might have tried to give an idea about what was there, but that would not have served any purpose. Hearing the word water would not satisfy a man's thirst; he has to drink the water himself. Buddha had good reason to be silent on questions about God or the Self. The answer to those questions could best be found when Buddhism was practised.

Swami Vivekananda had once described Buddhism as 'a rebel child' of Hinduism. What did he mean by this? Buddhism was a rebel child of the kind of Hinduism that prevailed in his time, not of Hinduism as such. He refused to believe that ceremonialism, which comprised pouring butter into fire, distributing wealth in charity, or slaughtering animals, could remove the evils which were in the mind of a man. Only good could remove evil, just as light could dispel darkness. In rejecting ceremonialism, Buddha was only rejecting the non-essentials for essentials. The essentials are implicit in the word 'Buddha'. In this is 'the fulfilment', 'the logical development' of Hinduism, as Swami Vivekananda said.

Edmond Holmes in his scholarly work, *The Creed of Buddha* says: '. . . Buddha's ethical scheme was a practical interpretation, an exposition in terms of human conduct and human life, of the paramount idea of the Upanishads . . .'[31] Explaining Buddha's silence on questions of God or the Self, the scholar says: '. . . the reason is that Buddha, though he worked out the idea, as a principle of action, with consistent thoroughness and consummate skill, not only made no attempt to expound it, but even turned back, on the threshold of their inquiry, all who sought to go behind the scheme to the philosophy that it embodied. But this difficulty will vanish when we remind ourselves that if Buddha, who made it his life's work to preach the gospel of deliverance to all men, had accepted the

---

31. Edmond Holmes *The Creed of Buddha*, (London: The Bodley Head), Reprint 1949, p. 156.

paramount idea of the Upanishads and made it his own, he would have been bound by the very strength and depth of his faith in it to wall it round with inviolable silence.'[32]

The silence was well intended, but it has done much damage to the cause too. Swami Vivekananda rightly said that Buddha's disciples 'misunderstood' him. If they misunderstood him, it was because of his silence on issues like 'Self' and 'God'. The disciples naturally concluded that Buddha denied the existence of an ultimate reality.

This, among other things, also led the disciples to conclude that Buddha had totally broken with the Hindu tradition. Swami Vivekananda, on the other hand, thought that he saved Hinduism. Dr Rhys Davids, the most authoritative specialist in Buddhism, says '. . . that Buddha's whole training was Brahmanism and that he probably deemed himself to be the most correct exponent of the spirit as distinct from the letter of the ancient faith.'[33] Buddha's insistence on the unreality of the self has always been a bone of contention among the scholars. Edmond Holmes thinks Buddha was merely clearing the way for the exposition '. . . of the profound conception which is the very quintessence of the 'ancient faith,'—the conception 'that Brahma and the Self—the true Self—are One.'[34] Buddha cleared the way to the supreme truth of Vedanta, but deliberately left the truth a mystery. People were already confused. He did not want to confuse them further.

Caste, according to Swami Vivekananda, was a social institution, not religious. Yet the Vedic truths had been reserved only for the higher castes. This made society weak. He admired Buddha because 'he had the large-heartedness to bring out the truths from the hidden Vedas and broadcast it all over the world.'[35] Incidently, this was also

---

32. Ibid. p. 157.
33. Ibid. p. 175.
34. Ibid. p. 176.
35. C.W., i, 22.

the Swami's own plan when he said that he would bring Vedanta from the depths of the forests to the cottage door of every poor man.

Like caste, language had also been a barrier to transmission of spiritual truths in ancient India. Buddha's brahmin disciples wanted to translate his teachings into Sanskrit, the language of the elite. Buddha rejected the idea. He said, 'I am for the poor, for the people; let me speak in the tongue of the people.'[36] This is why the bulk of his teachings are in the people's language of that day.

Man needs a God to stand by him in his difficulty. But Buddhism, has no God to offer to man. This, according to Swami Vivekananda, cost Buddhism its independent survival. Wherever it went, it absorbed local deities to make up for the absence of God. It had its 'natural death in India' and lost its original identity in the process, first because it did not have a God for the common people, and, secondly, because it had no strong philosophical base. The death of Buddhism was a great loss to Brahminism: the loss was in terms of 'that reforming zeal, that wonderful sympathy and charity for everybody, that wonderful leaven which Buddhism had brought to the masses . . . ,' as Swami Vivekananda said in his speech.[37] Buddhism had given society a high moral tone. Quoting a Greek historian Swamiji says, '. . . no Hindu was known to tell an untruth and no Hindu woman was known to be unchaste.'[38] This was when Buddhism still had its hold on society.

Buddhism has now lost its separate entity in India. It has merged into the broad spectrum of what is now called Hinduism. Every Hindu is now a Buddhist, as every Buddhist is a Hindu. Buddha continues to receive the worship given to a Hindu Avatara. But Swami

---

36. C.W., i, 22.
37. C.W., i, 23.
38. C.W., i, 23.

Vivekananda thinks, 'Hinduism cannot live without Buddhism . . .'[39]. He describes Buddhism as the heart of India, and Hinduism her brain. India's downfall, according to him, is due to the separation of the two. India along with every country needs the humanising power of the Great Master. It was Buddha's heart which attracted Swami Vivekananda more than his head. But a religion which is all heart with no brain cannot survive. Buddhism died because it rejected the support of its parental brain. But if Hinduism tries to live by its brain only, it is doomed. This is why Swami Vivekananda says, 'Hinduism cannot live without Buddhism.'

---

39. C.W., i, 23.

Buddhism and Vedanta

I

RELIGIOUS SITUATION IN INDIA BEFORE BUDDHA'S TIME

WHEN ONE COMPARES THE TWO SYSTEMS, BUDDHISM AND VEDANTA, one is so struck by their similarity that one is tempted to ask if they are not one and the same thing. Buddha, it will be recalled, did not claim that he was preaching anything new. He said he was preaching the ancient way, the Aryan Path, the eternal Dharma. Somehow or other, people had lost sight of this path. They had got caught in the meshes of sacerdotalism. They did all kinds of crazy things thinking they would get whatever they wanted through them. We get a true picture of the situation in *Lalita-vistara*[40] which says:

'Stupid men seek to purify their persons by diverse modes of austerity and penance, and inculcate the same. Some of them cannot make out their mantras; some lick their hands; some are uncleanly; some have no mantras; some wander after different sources; some adore cows, deer, horses, hogs, monkeys or elephants. Some attempt to accomplish their penance by gazing at the sun . . . resting on one foot or with an arm perpetually uplifted or moving about the knees . . .'

---

40. *Radhakrishnan's Indian Philosophy*, Vol. 1, George Allen and Unwin Ltd. 1941 reprint p. 356.

Vedanta, with its literature mostly in Sanskrit, was a closed book to the common people. What Buddha taught was essentially this Vedanta, only he taught it in more practical terms, in terms that people would understand, in terms, independent of dogmas, priesthood and sacrament. He presented it in a new garb, stripped of vague phrases, laying the greatest stress on reason and experience. He did not quote any scriptures, for they confused people and people did not understand them. Also, it is doubtful if he recognised their authority at all. 'The test of the pudding is in the eating'—this was the criterion he asked people to apply. The doctrine is not based on hearsay, it means 'Come and see.'[41] He once said to Kalamas: 'This I have said to you, O Kalamas, but you may accept it not because it is a report or because it is a tradition. Not because it is so said in the past, not because it is given from (our) basket (or scripture, *pitaka*), not for the sake of discussion, nor for the sake of a particular method, nor for the sake of careful consideration, nor for the sake of the forbearance with wrong views nor because it appears to be suitable, nor because your preceptor is a recluse, but if you yourselves understand that this is so meritorious and blameless, and when accepted, is for benefit and happiness, then you may accept it.'[42]

The onus is entirely on you, you yourself have to work out your destiny, not that somebody else will be responsible for what you do or what you are. There is no magic, no mystical force controlling man's destiny; it is just as he wills and works, entirely a question of his choice and effort. If he succeeds, it is because he has made the right choice and he has also worked hard; but if he fails, he himself is responsible for it, because he did not make the correct decision and he did not perhaps work hard enough, either. It was

---

41. Ibid.
42. *The Basic Conception of Buddhism* by Vidhusekhar Bhattacharya. University of Calcutta', 1934 p. 10.

for people to try and see whether what he taught worked or not. If it did not work, they were free to reject it. 'Try it as gold is tried in fire', he said. Not that Buddha held out liberation as a gift to be offered to those who supplicated him; it was something to be had only by those who were prepared to work hard. There was no such thing as grace or miraculous intervention in Buddha's scheme of things. He disowned that he was a saviour. People had to save themselves—*Uddhared Atmanatmanam*[43]. 'Therefore, O Ananda, be ye lamps unto yourselves. Be a refuge to yourselves. Betake yourselves to no external refuge... Look not for refuge to anyone except yourselves.'[44]

Manu says, *na lingam dharmakaranam* (External symbols are no criterion of a religious man). Buddha also attached no importance to external symbols. What to him was important was a man's way of life and character. Was he honest? Was he able to control his passions? Was he a man of renunciation? If so, he was a spiritually advanced person. The essence of spiritual life is self-control, *Yogah Chittavrittinirodhah*[45], both Buddhism and Hinduism hold. He also underlined the importance of reason. He said one should follow one's own reason (*yukti-sarana*) and not any other individual (*pudgala-sarana*), whenever he might be. This is not to say that one must always ignore what others say. If what others say is sound and good, one might accept it but not otherwise. It is not the age or the status of the person who gives the advice that counts but whether or not one's own judgement says that the advice is good.

What Buddha taught was something based on his own experience. It was also clear, straightforward and readily efficacious. Because it produced results immediately, as if inviting people to try and see

---

43. Gita VI, 5.
44. The Creed of Buddha, Holmes, The Bodley Head, London, 1949 reprint.
45. Patanjali, Yogasutra.

whether it works or not, it was often referred to as *ehipassika* (to be seen immediately) or *samakristika* (to be experienced in this very life). In giving it these appellations, people wanted to point out its contrast with the Brahminical rites and rituals, which bore fruit, if at all, not in this life but in the life hereafter.

No Hindu accepts the whole of the spectrum of Hindu faiths and beliefs. There are aspects of it he finds repulsive and he, therefore, rejects them. This does not make him less Hindu than any other Hindu. Buddha, in that sense, was a Hindu to the last day. Dr Rhys Davids has said, 'Gautama was born and brought up and lived and died a Hindu... There was not much in the metaphysics and principles of Gautama which cannot be found in one or other of the orthodox systems, and a great deal of his morality could be matched from earlier or later Hindu books. Such originality as Gautama possessed lay in the way in which he adopted, enlarged, ennobled and systematised that which had already been well said by others; in the way in which he carried out to their logical conclusion principles of equity and justice already acknowledged by some of the most prominent Hindu thinkers.'[46] Buddha has been described by Swami Vivekananda as 'a rebel child of Hinduism', but this is not to say that he rejected everything Hindu and taught something new, something not known to Hinduism. Buddhism is no freak, not an accident of history but a bye-product of the process of thinking which had long been going on in the Hindu mind. According to Rhys Davids 'Buddihism grew and flourished within the fold of orthodox belief.'[47]

Yet, it must be admitted that Buddha broke away from what then passed as Hinduism. The religious scene in India was then dominated by two extreme groups: the Charvakas on the one hand, and the votaries of *Karma Kanda* (the ceremonialists) on the other.

---

46. Radhakrishnan's Indilan Philosophy Vol. 1, p. 361.
47. Ibid.

The Charvakas were after physical pleasure; they were sensualists, pure and simple. They must have been very strong in Buddha's time, which is why perhaps Buddha never tired of harping on *Anatmavada* (no substance to the phenomena world), *Anityata* (the impermanence of things) and universal suffering (*Sabbadukha*). He felt sorry for people who ran after sense-pleasure, for they did not know they could never be happy that way. This was why the recurrent note underlying his teachings was the concept of universal suffering. He talked of this suffering so often that many thought and still think that he was a pessimist. What he was really doing was only making a statement of fact, not palatable to many, though. Then, there were people who believed in *Karma Kanda*, people who performed rituals hoping they would get whatever they wanted through them. Some wanted money, some long life, some children; some wanted to get into heaven after death. There was nothing wrong in asking for these things, but people forgot they were all short-lived. Even if they got into heaven and became Gods and Goddesses, they could enjoy this privileged status only for a while. They would have to return to earth as men and women and begin life all over again. If they satisfy one desire, another soon takes its place. It is like trying to put out fire by butter. It only makes the blaze stronger. (*Najatu kamanam upabhogena shamyati/Havisha Krisnavartmeva bhuyah eva abhivardhate.*)

This state of eternal thirst in man is described by Buddha as:

What he sees he does not wish for,
But something he does not see;
Methinks he will wander long.
And what he wishes, not obtain.
He is not pleased with what he gets;
No sooner gained it meets his scorn.
Insatiate are wishes all!
The wish-free, therefore, we adore![48]

---

48. Warren's *Buddhism* in translations, Radhakrishnan's *Indian Philosophy*, p. 154.

Hindu scriptures also praise people who are 'wish-free' *Apta-kamah*, i.e. people who are able to overcome their craving for perishable things. The *Padma Purana* says:

Indriyani vase Kritva yatra tatra vasennarah
Tatra tasya Kurukshetram Prayagam Pushkaram tatha.

'If you are able to control your mind, then you need not visit holy places. Wherever you are, the place is holy.' The Gita also extols the man who is able to control himself. Such a man, according to it attains peace and nirvana (VI. 15). Such a man, i.e. the man, who is free from all desires, is considered by both Hinduism and Buddhism as the ideal man. The object of life is to try and become such a man. The business of religion is to help man reach a state in which he is able to say that there is nothing he wants outside of himself, he is full and he has nothing to ask for. Such a man is 'free', free in the sense that he is his own master, and because he is his own master, he never succumbs to any temptation of any kind.

Buddha felt distressed when he found people did not know the real meaning of religion. They performed rituals but why they performed them they did not know. On the one hand, there was ignorance, on the other, there was the tyranny of the selfish priests. What pained him more was that there were scholars who did nothing to help the masses. They kept debating among themselves about high metaphysical matters. Not that they were deeply religious or interested in religious contents, but they found pleasure in discussing philosophy, they just wanted to show themselves off—that's all. This was why perhaps Buddha always discouraged idle discussions. If people asked him metaphysical questions, he either parried them or remained silent. *Viveka Chudamani*, a work on Vedanta, says *Sastrajalam Maharanyam Chittabhramanakaranam* (The scriptures are like a vast forest where one easily gets lost). If there was a real seeker, Buddha would gladly answer his questions. But most people asked questions just for the fun of asking, without any intention of applying the knowledge that Buddha might impart to them. It was a fashion with people in those days to engage in scholarly debates about metaphysical matters but it was not that they were dying to know the truth. They were superficial people who blabbered and got nowhere near the truth, and perhaps never wanted to get near the truth, either. They were confused people and if Buddha said anything to them they would have got more confused. The best knowledge is personal knowledge. People must discover the truth themselves and not by proxy. This was why he showed them the way to the truth, but never tried to explain to them what exactly the truth was like or what happened when one realised, the truth, for that would have been an impossible task. Between these materialists and pseudo-intellectuals, there were many splinter groups of people (*Niganthas. Ajivakas* and *Shramanas*) whose philosophies varied in degrees of aimlessness of life and sensualism.

BUDDHA'S ADVENT

It was at this juncture that Buddha appeared, as if to save humanity. He taught Vedanta, the essence, in Aldous Huxley's language the H.C.F., (Highest Common Factor) of all religions. Vedanta had so long been treated as the close preserve of a few. Only those who were highly educated had access to it. In fact, not only Vedanta, but all other systems were a sealed book to the common people, for books on those systems were all in Sanskrit. Buddha taught Vedanta but taught it in the language of the people. He was perhaps the first religious teacher in Indian history to do so. He avoided dialectical Vedanta, he taught only those aspects of it which everybody could understand. His Vedanta was simple, clear and practical. He wanted people to fix their minds on the problem which was immediate and which bothered them the most. What is that problem? The problem of suffering. There is suffering everywhere; high and low, rich and poor, no one is exempted from it. There is physical, as well as mental suffering. Whether desired or not, it is a fact of life which one must face.

BUDDHA'S TEACHINGS

He reduced the whole question of religion to four basic truths, truths he called 'four Aryan truths' (*Catvari Arya-Satyani*). They are:

1. Life is full of suffering.
2. The cause of this suffering is desire.
3. Suffering can be overcome only by overcoming desire.
4. Self-discipline is the only key to the control of desire.

But how can this self-discipline be attained? There is no magic about it, only by practice. Practising what? Buddha recommends an eightfold path. Practise, he says, (1) Right Faith (2) Right Resolve (3) Right Speech (4) Right Action (5) Right Living (6) Right Effort (7) Right Thought (8) Right Self-concentration.

SELF-CONTROL—KEYNOTE OF VEDANTA AND BUDDHISM

The emphasis here is on the word 'Right' that is to say, you have to tread your path very carefully and stick to it. The onus is entirely on you. If you make a wrong choice you have yourself to blame for it. The advice may be difficult to follow, but there is no haziness about it. Surprisingly, Vedanta also gives the same advice. It asks you to examine what is enduring and what is not and then choose only that which is enduring (*Nity-anitya-vastu-viveka-ihamutraphala-bhoga-viraga*). It asks you to eschew even life in heaven, for that too is ephemeral. The choice must be your own and it must be a correct choice. Vedanta also asks you to practise self-restraint. By self-restraint, it understands *Shama* (control of the mind) *Dama* (control of the sense organs), *Uparati* (withdrawal from sense pleasure) and *Titiksha* (austerity). As part of this practice, one should also concentrate on things conducive to spiritual growth and have faith in oneself. Thus, both Vedanta and Buddha attach the greatest importance to the sense of discrimination and self-restraint. There is no place here for miracle. The only miracle they recognise is the miracle of self-discipline. Self-discipline, according to them, is the whole of religion. Both reject rituals out of hand, for it can, at best, produce some temporary benefit, but not change the mind of man where the seat of all trouble lies. Vedanta emphatically declares that the ultimate truth can never be known through ritualism. *Na Karmana na Prajaya dhanena amrtatvamanashuh* (Not by rituals nor by children nor by wealth, only by renunciation, can you get immortality), says Kaivalya Upanishad 2. One of the Upanishads (Br. Up. I, IV, 10) even think that the Gods do not feel happy at the prospect that man should know the ultimate truth, for then they will miss the sacrificial offerings which man gives them and which they covet. This is why they hold back the ultimate truth from man so that they can continue to receive man's sacrificial offerings. But man will for ever remain in bondage unless he gains mastery over himself. The importance that Buddhism attaches to self-control can be gauged from the following remarks of Buddha.

'If a man were to conquer in battle a thousand times a thousand men, and another conquers one, himself, he indeed is the greatest of conquerors', says Dhammapada 103.

Dhammapada (105) also says: 'Not even a God can change into defeat, the victory of a man who has vanquished himself.'

Chittadhino Dharmo Dharmadhino Bodhih (on the mind depends Dharma, on the practice of Dharma depends enlightenment).[49]

AVIDYA

But why is it that people run after ephemeral things? Due to ignorance (*Avidya*), both Buddhism and Vedanta aver. Ignorance is, according

---

49. Radhakrishnan's *Indian Philosophy*, p. 423.

to Buddhism, one of the links in the chain of existence that binds man. Vedanta also regards it as the root of all trouble. But when did ignorance start? How did it start? Both Buddhism and Vedanta dismiss these questions as irrelevant. What is relevant is to know how it can be ended and then try to end it. Because of this ignorance, man has endless desires and he keeps running after perishable objects. He sees the world crumbling around him, he sees how brittle it is, yet he finds himself running after it.

Shelley says:

Worlds on worlds are rolling over
From creation to decay.
Like the bubbles on a river,
Sparkling, bursting, borne away[50]

Indeed, the world which we love and to which we are so much attached is only a bubble on the ocean of infinity. It is said that it is this impermanence of things that spurred Buddha to take to the life of a recluse. He had, while out on a drive through his town, seen signs of decay in the shape of old age, disease and death. Against this, he had also seen signs of peace and joy on the face of a hermit. This set him thinking.

He understood that only through renunciation, renunciation of perishable objects, that one could be happy—*tena tyaktena bhunjitha* (Therefore, save yourself through renunciation) *Isa Upanisad* I. Those who run after this sense-world, plunge deeper and deeper into darkness—*Andham tamah pravisanti ye asambhutim upasante. Isa Upanisad* 1, 12. If you run after sense-pleasure, sometimes you may enjoy yourself for a while, but your enjoyment cannot last for long. Soon, you will find the pleasure has slipped through your fingers. But if you can say, 'I do not care for external pleasure, I have everything I need within me, I am content, I am full, and that is to say, if

---

50. Radhakrishnan's *Indian Philosophy* p. 368.

you can overcome your craving, then you are indeed happy. This is the ideal that is held out by both these systems. They follow the maxim, 'That which is in the hands of other people is a cause for sorrow, that which is within your grasp is a cause for happiness.' *Sarvam Paravasham duhkham Sarvam atmavasham Sukham*. In other words, you have to be your own master.

The contrast between the one who runs after sense-pleasure and one who does not is very well brought out in the following verse of the *Mundakopanisad*:

Dva Suparna Sayuja Sakhaya
Samanam Vriksham Parishashvajate
Tayoranyah pippalam Svadu-atti
Anashnan-anyoh abhichakashiti

Two birds are on the same tree; they look exactly alike; one runs from one fruit to another; sometimes the fruit turns out to be sweet, sometimes bitter. The other bird, however, is calm, quiet, only watching.

DETACHMENT

It is this complete withdrawal from the world that both Vedanta and Buddhism advocate. The withdrawal need not be physical but it must be mental. That is to say, you may work like anybody else does but while others work with an eye to the fruits of their labour, you will have to work with a spirit of detachment. Ordinarily, we work because we have something in view, something we want to get; we have some desire in our mind and it is this desire that drives us to do, what we do. We are, in other words, at the mercy of our desires. If we succeed in our endeavour, we are overjoyed, but if we fail, we break down. We are like that bird, sometimes eating sweet fruits, sometimes bitter, sometimes happy, sometimes unhappy. Our goal is to be like the other bird, the bird which does not allow its happiness to depend upon external factors, which has complete mastery over itself. Buddha had this mastery over himself, so he had 'changeless bliss'[51]. It is not that Buddhism or Vedanta is advocating inertia. Buddha himself was an active man. To the last day he worked, worked ceaselessly trying to save mankind. He never allowed himself to rest. He, however, enjoyed infinite rest in the midst of infinite activity. This was possible because he worked not for himself but for others, he worked with complete detachment, he worked not under the compulsion of desire but out of compassion. In the Gita also we find Krishna urging Arjuna to work, but he cautioned that he must work with detachment (*Karmanyeva adhikaraste ma phaleshu kadachana*). Gita II. 47.

In explaining why there is suffering, Buddha propounds the well-known theory of *Pratityasamutpada*, conditioned origination. The theory means that nothing comes into being just out of nothing; something must have been its cause which existed earlier. Buddha describes this as Dharma, the law that governs the whole world-process. There is suffering in the form of old age, disease, death or despair, grief, etc., (in other words, *Jara-marana*) because of birth (*Jati*). Where there is birth there is death. But between birth and death, there are many experiences which one must go through, they being a logical corollary to the fact of birth (*Jati*). So the goal, according to both Vedanta and Buddhism, is to go beyond birth and death, to break through this cycle, the wheel of becoming (*Bhava chakra*). It is Avidya (ignorance) which keeps this wheel moving. The chain of causation, put in the reverse order, is like this:

From Avidya spring the *samskaras* (impressions), from impressions the initial consciousness of the embryo (*Vijnana*), from consciousness name and form (*Nama* and *Rupa*), from name and from six organs of knowledge (*Sadayatana*), from the organs contact (*sparsa*), from contact sense-experience (*Vedana*), from sense-experience thirst, i.e. desire (*trisna*), from desire attachment (*upadana*), from attachment

---

51. Light of Asia, pp. 51–52.

the tendency to be born (*bhava*), from this tendency birth (*Jati*), from birth old age, death, etc. (*Jara-marana*).

Both Vedanta and Buddhism hold that this ignorance is cosmic. How and when this ignorance started they do not discuss, but the interesting point is that both think that this ignorance is 'real' as well as 'unreal', 'real' if you think it is real and act accordingly, 'unreal' if you refuse to recognise that it exists and behave as if it does not.

Both Buddhism and Vedanta accept the law of Karma and its corollary, reincarnation. How long does this law of Karma operate? So long as you think you have a 'self' and so thinking, run after sense-enjoyment, says Buddhism. Vedanta thinks this law of Karma operates so long as you do not know your true self. You think your body is your self. So, you try to keep the body in comfort. If the body is in pain, you think you are in pain, if the body enjoys something, you think you are enjoying it. In the case of Vedanta, your ignorance of your true Self is the root of your trouble. The dictum of Vedanta is—'Know thy Self' *Atmanam Viddhi*.

Buddhism does not speak of there being any permanent Self, rather discourages the idea that there is such a thing as 'Self'. It keeps harping that there is no 'Self', perhaps because it is observsd that it is from this idea of 'Self' that attachment grows. When Buddhism says there is no such thing as 'self' it obviously refers to the phenomenal world which is without substance. Ananda once asked Buddha why he preferred to remain silent when people asked him whether there was a self or not. Buddha replied that this was because he did not want to confuse people. If he said that there was no self, people might then become completely nihilistic in outlook, thinking annihilation was the end of everything. If he said that there was a self, then people would mistake the body for the self and run after sense-enjoyment. In essence, however, both the standpoints mean the same thing. The problem is the problem of overcoming attachment to the phenomenal world. Buddhism says you can overcome this by knowing that it is false. Vedanta says that you should know that it is false but should try to shift your attachment to your true 'self' which is free and independent under all circumstances, without birth and without death, which is Existence, Knowledge and Bliss Absolute, and which needs no help of the phenomenal world for its happiness. If the surface of the mirror is clean, you have a good reflection of yourself on it. The layer of dust that has accumulated on it is the hindrance. This hindrance has to be removed. Similarly, there is the hindrance of the false ego and consequential attachment to the world to your knowledge of the Self. If you remove this hindrance, you automatically know your Self. Buddha stressed the need to remove this hindrance, the false ego and the attachment to the world. He perhaps argued that if he talked about the Self, people would get confused, so he wanted that they should concentrate on the removal of the hindrance rather than try to understand a subject which is really beyond understanding. The self is something 'words cannot express'—'the mind comes away from it baffled, unable to reach it' (Taittiriya Upanishad, II. 4).

Renunciation is thus the keynote of both Vedanta and Buddhism. Renunciation of what? Renunciation of that which is *Anitya*, ephemeral. Both also point out that you are the architect of your own fate. If you are what you are today, it is entirely because of what you were yesterday. What you are going to be tomorrow will be determined by what you are today. Everything, therefore, depends upon you. Here again, *Pratitya-samutpada* operates your own action leading to the reaction to which you are subject now.

Buddhism and Vedanta are more a science than a religion. They are based on observed facts. They prescribe methods which lead to predictable results. Both are dominated by commonsense, reason and experience. Both deny a personal God and therefore the necessity of prayers. Both hold life is full of suffering, man is caught in the 'wheel of becoming' (Bhava chakra), the goal is to get out of the cycle of birth and death, to attain Nirvana, *Mukti* or *Moksha*, so that there is no more birth, no more 'becoming'. But how to get this Nirvana? By practising self-restraint, by practising *asta-marga* (the eightfold path). It is the same thing as *Shama, Dama, Uparati*. etc. of Vedanta. In either case, the aim is to prevent the mind from running after this world which both recognise as *Anitya* (transitory), the cause of all suffering.

II

BUDDHA, A PRAGMATIST

Both Buddhism and Vedanta lay stress on the need to practise self-restraint. Perhaps, all religions feel self-restraint is the first step towards religious progress. It is the first step, but it is also a step from which there is no withdrawal. At no point of time can a truly religious man say that he needs no self-restraint unless he is a person to whom self-restraint is not a matter of effort but has become his second nature. Where this is the case, there is no mystery in religion which he cannot unravel. Why did Buddha have so much aversion to metaphysical discussions? It was because he found people talked and talked, they seldom got down to solving the problem before them, the problem of how to end the suffering which was the common misfortune of mankind as a whole. He wanted that people should concentrate on this rather than waste time discussing academic questions. Perhaps, he had also found that those who asked him questions about God or soul did so out of idle curiosity, rather than with any serious intent to know the truth, to unravel the mystery of life. Sometimes, he scolded the questioner saying that he had better turn his attention to more urgent matters in hand rather than trouble himself about matters not of immediate concern. In this connection, the story of Malukya's encounter with Buddha as narrated by Dr Oldenberg may be of interest.

'The venerable Malukya comes to the Master and expresses his astonishment that the Master's discourse leaves a series of the very most important and deepest questions unanswered. Is the world eternal or is it limited by bounds of time? Does the Perfect Buddha live on beyond death? Does the Perfect one not live on beyond death? It pleases me not, says the monk, that all this shall remain unanswered and I do not think it right; therefore I am come to the Master to interrogate him about these doubts. May it please Buddha to answer them if he can. But when one does not understand a matter and does not know it, then a straightforward man says I do not understand that, I do not know that.'[52].

Buddha was far from pleased with this question. Malukya seemed to suggest that Buddha was not being fair to his disciples. There were questions to which Buddha perhaps did not know the right answers. If he did not know, he should frankly admit it, but it was not right that he should refuse to answer the questions, for that only kept the people guessing. Buddha asked Malukya with a touch of irony if he had ever invited Malukya to be his disciple. Malukya replied he had not. Buddha then pointed out to him how irrelevant the questions he had raised were. The questions related to the nature of the soul and the world. Buddha said: 'If a man were struck by a poisoned arrow, and his friends and relations called in a skilful physician, what if the man said: 'I shall not allow my wound to be treated until I know who the man is by whom I have been wounded, whether he is a noble, a Brahman, a Vaishya, a Sudra'—or if he said: 'I shall not allow my wound to be treated until I know what they call the man who has wounded me, and of what family he is, whether he is tall or small or of middle stature, and how his weapon was made with which he has struck me.' What would the end of the case be? The man would die of his wound.'

BUDDHA'S IMPATIENCE WITH METAPHYSICS

But why did Buddha show this impatience? One reason may be that he knew it was not essential that man should know answers to these

---

52. *The Creed of Buddha* by Holmes, p. 143.

questions. It is also possible that he thought that if he said 'yes' or 'no' in reply to these questions, it would only increase the confusion that already prevailed. It would perhaps raise more questions and however he might try to explain and clear their doubts, people would get caught in the maze of metaphysical subtleties. The knowledge Malukya was seeking was not essential. Buddha had already said enough on the subject of whether the world was permanent or not, and whether there was such a thing as a soul and if that soul survived after a man's death. This is why Buddha, with a degree of finality, said to Malukya, 'Therefore, Malukyaputta, whatsoever has not been revealed by me, let that remain unrevealed, what has been revealed, let it be revealed.'[53]

It must be understood that there are certain truths which the human mind can never fully comprehend. Even if a man can comprehend them, he cannot communicate his knowledge or understanding to others. The truths are so vast, so profound that when asked about them one can do no better than remain silent. To drive this point home, nun Khema asked King Pasendai of Kosala, 'O great king, hast thou an accountant or a mint-master, or a treasurer who could measure the water in the great ocean, who could say: there are therein so many measures of water or so many hundreds or thousands or hundreds of thousands of measures of water?' The king replied, 'No'. 'And why not? The great ocean is deep, immeasurable and unfathomable. So also, O great king, if the existence of the Perfect one be measured by the predicates of corporeal form; these predicates of the corporeal form are abolished in the Perfect one, their root is severed, they are hewn away like a palm tree and laid aside, so that they cannot germinate again in the future.' There is no frame of reference, no *Nama* and *Rupa* (name and form), by which what happens when the Perfect one passes away can be described. It is like a river falling into the ocean when it loses its separate identity—*Yatha nadyah syandamanah*

---

53. *The Creed of Buddha*, p. 144.

samudre astam gachhanti name-rupe vihaya. (Mundaka Upanishad 3.2.8). The phenomenon can be guessed, but certainly not described. Buddha wanted that his disciples should first practise *Asta-marga* and somehow or other overcome their attachment to sense enjoyment. If they did, they would then be able to enter the world of transcendental experience where Truth would automatically reveal itself to them. It was this kind of direct experience that could dispel all doubts and not merely scholarship. Scholarship is also a kind of enjoyment which like Buddha Vedanta discourages. Vivekachudamani says that scholars debate endlessly and display great skill while they argue, but, all this may be good grist to the mill of those who are seeking enjoyment but if they are seeking liberation, it can never take them nearer to their goal. Scholarship is no knowledge, no way of removing *avidya* (ignorance). Only direct and personal experience can remove ignorance. This is why 'seeing is believing'.

So long as there is ignorance, trouble will continue. Practice of Asta-marga (self-restraint) induces the state of mind in which the transcendental experience becomes possible. Both Vedanta and Buddhism hold that there is no escape from suffering so long as ignorance lasts. So all efforts should be put in to remove ignorance. To underscore this, Buddha once said that if you wanted to build a *Kutagara* (peaked house), all rafters should then point upwards and meet at a common point. He said all troubles originate from ignorance—*avijjamulaka*. Because of this ignorance, man is deluded into thinking what is unreal as real. Thinking the unreal as real, he feels drawn towards it and soon gets attached to it. The state of bondage to which both Buddhism and Vedanta again and again refer, and from which man is urged to extricate himself is this state of attachment to sense-pleasure which is perishable and therefore unreal.

BUDDHA MISUNDERSTOOD

But Buddha's silence on questions of God, soul, etc., has been misunderstood, misinterpreted. Perhaps even when he was alive, people had never completely stopped debating about them. However much he might have wished to avoid philosophical wranglings, these always continued and perhaps intensified when he passed away. As doubts persisted about the real import of what Buddha had taught, elders of the Buddhist Order called a council at Rajagriha in 483 BC immediately after Buddha's passing away. 500 monks attended it. Mahakasyapa presided and Ananda recited the Dhamma. There must have been much acrimonious debate at this council but one has no record of it. Whatever might have happened, the doubts were never completely set at rest.

That people should misunderstand and have doubts about what exactly Buddha taught is natural, seeing that no written records were available. As more and more doubts arose, a second Buddhist council was held at Vesali in 383 BC, i.e. one hundred years after the first. 700 monks attended the council. The council lasted for eighteen months which must be an indication that the debates were hot and exciting. It is said that a section of monks called Mahasanghikas were condemned as corrupt. On the other hand, Mahasanghikas who numbered 10,000 held a parallel council and condemned the orthodox Theravadis. They claimed that they represented the true Buddha spirit. A split among the followers of Buddha seemed inevitable and it took place. The issues, over which the split took place, are difficult to decipher. One group constituted what is known as Mahayana (the great vessel) and the other group Hinayana (the small vessel). The lines of distinction between the two groups are not very clear except that Mahayana is more broad-based and admits all and sundry to its ranks, its literature is in Sanskrit and it looks upon Bodhisatva as its ideal, that is to say, a Mahayani is not satisfied with his own salvation but works for the salvation of others also. Hinayana, on the other hand, is more orthodox and insists that one should work for one's own salvation only. Its literature is all in Pali. Mahayanis are also known as Northern Buddhists and Hinayanis as Southern Buddhists.

As the years went by, more splits took place. It is said that there were altogether thirty schools of Buddhism in later days. These divisions, it should be noted, were all over philosophical questions. The fundamentals of what Buddha had taught were never in dispute. They formed the common ground among them all. Soon, a whole system of Buddhist philosophy developed. It will be recalled that Buddha had refused to be drawn into any discussion about God, soul or the ultimate reality, all synonyms of the same thing. Paradoxically, in spite of or just because of his reluctance to discuss metaphysics, his followers spent much time debating metaphysics. This was perhaps inevitable, for man cannot help wanting to know the truth behind this riddle of the phenomenal world. A typical example of how this matter troubles man is Nachiketa of the Katha Upanisad. He went to the abode of Death seeking an answer to the question of what was there beyond death. Did something linger after death or was death the end of everything? What, in other worlds, was the ultimate reality? Was there such a thing as the soul or the self? The world, as we see it, is constantly changing, always in a state of flux, 'a stream of becoming'; is there something behind it which never changes, which is permanent, eternal?

This is a question that has been troubling man through the ages. Much depends upon the answer to the question. The question is so vital that even Ananda did not like the idea that Buddha should refuse to throw any light over this question. So, he once asked Buddha why he refused to answer this question. Buddha said that if he said that there was such a thing as a soul or self, people would then think that ths body was the soul. They were already too attached to it. They would become *Deha-atmavadins* (identifying the self with the body). It is such people who think sense-pleasure is the only pleasure. It is among such people that hedonists, materialists and sensualists are to be found. No civilisation can survive when people ignore the higher aims of life, whose only concern is the pursuit of the pleasure of the senses. Buddha appeared at a time when there were too many people in India who took the phenomenal world for granted. They seemed to forget that the phenomenal world, however attractive it might be, was only ephemeral. It is only to caution such people that Buddha harped on the theory of *dukha* (suffering) and *Anityata* (impermanence). What Buddha wanted was the kind of attitude that Nachiketa displayed during his encounter with Death. Death tried to dissuade Nachiketa from pressing him for an answer to the question whether anything survived after death, if there was a soul or not, and if there was, what it was like. Death tempted Nachiketa in many ways: he offered him gold, women, even the office of a God. Nachiketa would have none of these; the only thing he wanted was the transcendental knowledge of the self. It is only with people like Nachiketa, i.e. people who have their minds fixed on the supreme goal of life and who, under no circumstances, would deviate from it that you can discuss the intricate question of whether there is a self or not. If you discussed this with other people, they would not understand, this being too subtle for them. This is why he also said to Ananda that if he said that there was no *Atma* (self), people would then think that he was preaching nihilism (*uchchedavada*). The Hindu tradition is to teach a disciple according to his capacity. You cannot offer the great philosophy of the self to all and sundry; you can give it to only those who, like Nachiketa, are able to overcome the temptation of the phenomenal world and concentrate on the self which is 'subtler than the subtlest'.

What passes as Buddhist philosophy in mainly over this question of the ultimate reality. Three replies are possible to this question: There is no reality; there is reality but that reality is only mental; there is reality and it is both mental and external.

There is a school of philosophers who hold that there is no Reality but only void. They are known as Sunyavadins or Nihilists. Another school of philosophers believe that there is a Reality but it exists only in the mind. They are known as Yoga-charas or Vijnanavadins or subjective idealists. Yet another school, known as

Sarvastitvavadins believe that Reality is both subjective and objective, internal and external. These Sarvastitvavadins known also as Realists, are divided into two groups, Vaibhasikas and Sautantrikas. According to Vaibhasikas, Reality can be directly perceived (this is why their theory is called *Vahya-pratyaksavada*) while, according to Sautantrikas, Reality can only be inferred (this is why their theory is known as *Vahya-anumeyavada*).

Sunyavadins and Vijnanavadins belong to the Mahayana school whereas Sarvaastitvavadins (i.e. those who are of the Sautantrika and the Vaibhasika group) belong to the Hinayana school. Thus, except Sunyavadins, all the schools of Buddhist philosophers acknowledge that there is such a thing as Reality. Even Sunyavadins did not completely deny Reality. They neither denied it nor admitted it. Their position was in between, Madhyama, so they came to be known as Madhyamikas (those of the Middle Path). Some scholars even say that Sunya is not just 'void' or 'nothing', it is something positive but something that cannot be described, beyond thought and speech, almost corresponding to the Brahman of Vedanta.

Buddha did not say anything about Reality, but, somehow or the other, Reality has now carved out a place in Buddhist philosophy. One wonders if Buddha ever wanted it.

But what is the position of Vedanta regarding Reality? Does Vedanta admit that there is such a thing as Reality? How does this Reality square with its theory of *Anityata* (Impermanence) which it shares with Buddhism? If, like Buddhism, it believes that the empirical world with which we deal is an appearance, an illusion[54]. What is real then? Vedanta agrees that the phenomenal world is unreal, but it says that behind this phenomenal world, the world of appearance, there is the world of reality, the ultimate Reality, which according to Vedanta terminology, is called Brahman or Paramatman.

---

54. *Mayaya Kalpitam Jagat*, Mahanirvana, 14. 113, the world is only an illusion.

It is on this Brahman that the phenomenal world is projected. It is like cinema pictures being projected on a screen. When we see a film, we see so many things happening before us—people laughing, loving each other, quarelling, fighting, in varying moods, in varying situations, a Kaleidoscopic view of the fun called life; we see them and feel excited: our reactions vary, depending upon what we see; when we watch the film, we forget that what we are seeing are not real but only pictures. We feel so involved with them that we feel happy when they are happy and unhappy when they are unhappy. We forget, for the time being, that they are all imaginary, old pictures and that appearances are not real. The only real thing in this case is the screen without which the pictures would not have been possible. Another apt example which Sri Ramakrishna used to give is that, when you have first the figure 1, then zeros have a meaning, a value; otherwise zeros are only zeros. Similarly, there must be something, something solid and something real, on which this world of experience rests. This in Vedanta, is called *Brahman* which literally means the biggest. It is also called *Paramatman*, the soul of souls, the over-soul. This Brahman is the support (*Adhisthana*), the ground on which the empirical world rests.

Without this Brahman, there would have been no world of experience. *Tasya bhasa sarvam idam vibhati* (Katha Upanishad 2.2.15). This is why Vedanta again and again says, *Brahma satyam jagat mithya* (Mahanirvana 14.113). Brahma alone is real, the world is unreal. It is like the magician and his magic, the dreamer and his dreams. Brahman is the source as well as the end of everything, (*Sarvajiva* and *Sarva-samstha*, Svetasvatara Upanishad 1.6), it is both the materal and efficient cause of this universe. When Vedanta says Brahma Satyam, Brahma is real, it means that Brahman is eternal (*Nitya*). Other things change, but not Brahman who is always the same, *Sanatana*, not subject to modifications. He is unconditioned, unique, one without a second, without any attributes, uncreated, without birth, without death,—Supreme, *Nirguna, nirvishesha, Advaya, Svayambhu, Swarat,*

Ajara, Amara and so on. You can never say, 'He is this, he is like this', for whatever predicate you may use with reference to him will fall short of him. According to Udana, vii 3, 'There is an unborn, an unoriginated, an unmade, an uncompounded; were there not, O mendicants, there would be no escape from the world of the born, the originated, the made and the compounded.'

BUDDHA'S VIEW ABOUT THE ULTIMATE REALITY

The question is: Did Buddha subscribe to this view? Did he believe that there was any reality, a phenomenon, behind this phenomenal world? Most scholars think he did. If he did, if he truly thought that there was something real behind this appearance, why did he not say so? Vedanta, one finds, again and again repeats the falsity of things, the *mithyatva*, the *anityatva*, the impermanence of things but, at the same time, draws attention to the reality of Brahman. Why does not Buddha do the same thing? Why is he silent about the ultimate Reality? Not merely silent, he even shows impatience if anybody persists in asking him about it. It is difficult to say why he does not like to talk about the ultimate Reality unless it be that after having indicated how that ultimate Reality can be reached, he thinks it unnecessary to launch into a discussion of the nature of that ultimate Reality. He tells us what happens if you follow the path he has indicated, how you can attain Nirvana the happy state of no more 'becoming', the state of dissolution of the individual self. This exactly is the state which Vedanta looks forward to, which it holds up as being the goal of life. Buddha is rather cryptic about what this state is like, but is there not ample reason for his not saying much about it? Is it possible for anybody to describe the transition from finitude to infinitude? It is like a drop of rain falling into the sea. All your fetters of individuality are gone, you are infinite, you are free, *Bhidyate hridaya-granthih, chidyante sarva samsayah Kshiyante chasya karmani tasmin driste paravare* (Mundaka Upanishad. 2.2.9).

This is *mukti* or *moksha*, liberation, according to Vedanta; in this the individual ceases to exist as individual, the microcosm becomes the macrocosm.

This, in brief, is the anatomy of *moksha* or *nirvana*. Buddha did not go into details, but he gave enough hints to suggest that nirvana is not annihilation as some people tend to think. He once said that it was a 'heresy' to describe nirvana as annihilation. It is a positive state, a state in which man has full mastery over himself, he is no more troubled by desires, his mind is at complete rest. There is, therefore, no more question of birth and death for him. Buddha urges us to direct all our efforts to reach this state. Once we can get into this state, there will no more be *dukha* (suffering for us. This state is not just an idea, a theory or a dream; it is a reality, he himself being the best testimony to it. He calls our attention to this reality and also chalks out the path as to how to reach it. He points out the steps we have to climb to get on to the roof, but does not say much as to what we may expect to see when we get on the roof. He shows us how we may escape from the fire in which we are being consumed but can we blame him if he has not said what we may experience when the fire has been extinguished? Is it necessary to tell us about the relief, the joy, the happiness that we shall feel when we escape from the fire, when our suffering has come to an end? Vedanta says, all activities, good or bad, cease in this state, your mind is calm and quiet, you rest within yourself: you enjoy infinite peace, *Chittasya hi prasadena hanti karma subha-subham. Prasanna-atmani, sthitva sukham avyayam asnute.* (Maityyani Upanishad. 6. 34). Buddha, on the other hand, does not spell out the contents of your exprience but does it make any difference?

SELF

But there is the question of self over which it seems that the viewpoints of Vedanta and Buddhism are like two poles. Buddha preached

Anityatva (the impermanence of things), but, with equal emphasis, he preached also *Anatma vada* (the doctrine of no-self). Vedanta believes there are two kinds of self, *Jivatma* (the individual self) and *Paramatma* (the cosmic self). They are not separate, they are one and the same *Jiva Brahmaiva naparoh* (Mahanirvana 14.113), though they appear separate. Why do they appear separate? Because of Maya, cosmic ignorance. Because of this ignorance, the individual selves think they are separate from each other and separate from the cosmic Self also. Each individual self has a name (*nama*) and form (*rupa*) and on the basis of this name and form, they behave as if they are separate entities. They love or hate each other, they form communities or nations, they go to war or agree to live in peace with each other.

Not only men and women, but all living beings suffer from this delusion that they are separate, separate from each other and separate from the cosmic Self. Because they feel they are separate from the cosmic Self, because they do not know their identity, because they think they are the body and the mind that they have, because they have many desires which keep them running after *anitya* (perishable) objects, they suffer continuously. Life, with all of them, is nothing but suffering. They have to practise self-restraint (something corresponding to Buddha's eightfold path) and when they have acquired self-mastery, the Self reveals itself to them, *Tasya esa atma Vivrnuete tanum Svam.* (Katha Upanishad, 1.2.29). This Self is the Self of all, the common denominator, the common indwelling spirit *eka eva hi bhutatma bhute bhute vyavasthita.* It is like the one moon appearing as many because of its reflections on water; *ekadha vahudha chaiva drisyate Jalachandravat* (Panchadashi 15.8). This Self, this Brahman, this Paramatma, is the common substratum of all that exists in the world, *Isa vasyam idam sarvam yatkinch jagatyam jagat* (Isa Upanisad, 1.1). To know that the same self is everywhere, know that the individual self and the cosmic Self are one and the same, to know that the phenomenal world that we see is an illusion (*mithya*), only a superimposition, is true knowledge, and is that knowledge that liberates, *Para-Vidya*. True knowledge is to know that unity of existence, to know that only one exists and not many, *Neha nana asti kinchana*.

But, as we have seen, Buddha has talked about *Anatmavada*, emphasising again and again the unreality of the self; the self, according to him, is nothing but a conglomeration of several constituents like *Rupa* (matter), *Vedana* (feeling) *Samjna* (perception), *Samskara* (impression) and *Vijnana* (consciousness). It is like a chariot which, as such, is no entity, being only a combination of so many things—the wheels, the axle, the frame, etc. Buddha enunciated the theory of 'conditioned origination', *Pratitya-samutpada*, 'that being, this is, if that ceases, this ceases also', according to which nothing that has no independent origin (*Swabhava*) is real. The self, in this sense, does not exist. Here, obviously Buddha is talking about the empirical self. Vedanta will readily agree that independent of the real Self, there is no empirical self, just as there can be no reflection of the moon without a moon. The reflection is unreal but the moon is real. Talking of the chariot, one may ask: who puts its parts together? who holds them together? According to Vedanta, the chariot could not have come into being without there being someone behind it. Giving the example of the chariot, Vedanta says that there is a charioteer who controls it. This charioteer is the Self—*Atmanam RathinamViddhi*. Comparing the body-mind complex to a chariot, the *Katha Upanisad* says, 'Know the Self to be the charioteer, the body the chariot, the intellect the driver, the mind the reins, the senses the horses and the objects the roads.'

THE EMPIRICAL SELF

According to Buddhism, everything is in a state of flux; life is motion, change; we see this motion, this movement and we think we are seeing an object. Human life is only a moment in the cosmic wheel of time which is always moving. It is like the wheel of a moving chariot resting on the ground only for a fraction of a second. According to this idea of flux (*Kshanika vada*, momentariness), no individual, no object is the same for two seconds together. Referring to an individual if you say, 'Mr X,' by the time you say it he has ceased to exist. According to this logic, you can never punish the man who commits a crime. The man who committed the crime is gone; there is a new man in his place. By punishing him you are punishing an innocent man. If you push this *Anatmavad* to its logical end, it would then look as if—

Misery only both exist, none miserable,
No doer is there; naught save the deed is found
Nirvana is, but not the man who seeks it
The path exists, but not the traveller on it.

On this basis, the law of Karma would mean that there is no receptacle on which the fruits of action are carried along; there are only deed-forms and thought-forms which gather at a particular point, depending upon a certain concentration of circumstances. That is to say, there is no rebirth; no transmigration of a soul, there is only a rebirth of deed-forms and thought-forms. It is like one lamp being lighted by another, a leech travelling from one leaf to another. According to Buddhism, there are two kinds of *nairatmya* (the theory of non-self): *Pudgala-nairatmya* and *dharma-nairatmya*. Pudgala is another name for Jiva. The theory of *Pudgala-nairatmya* is preached only to emphasise *Jiva* as such has no independent existence; it is no *vastusat*, something with a substance of its own. It is only a name used to serve empirical needs.

Similarly, we see things around us which exist only because certain other things exist, *Pratityasamutpada*, they have no existence of their own. So, these things also are false, *Dharma-nairatmya*. Thus, both subject and object are false. If both subject and object are false, there is no room for desire, the cause for attachment. It is to help man overcome his desires that Buddha propounded this theory of *Pudgala-nairatmya* and *Dharma-nairatmya*. If there is no self, how can there be any desire? It is for the sake of the self that things become dear to an individual—wife, gold, long life, etc. This is the contention of both Vedanta and Buddhism. For instance, in the Brhadaranyaka upanisad, Yajnavalkya says to his wife Maitreyi: *Atmanastu kamaya sarvam priyam bhavati.*

HISTORICAL REASONS

There were perhaps good historical reasons why Buddha asserted *Anatmavada, Anityatva* or *Pratitya-samutpada* (which he called the Dharma, the Law, governing the world) in the manner, he did. All these theories, pointing to the perishable nature of the world, warn us against being entangled in it. This is not pessimism but facing facts as they are. It must be borne in mind that he was rejecting only the phenomenal world. Here, Vedanta is completely at one with him. Vedanta also negates the phenomenal world including God. Buddha's advent was at a time when people had forgotten the purpose of life, when the craze for pleasure had driven them mad and when they turned to religion only to enjoy more pleasure. They seemed to think, as Buddha said. 'This is the world and this is the self, and I shall continue to be in the future, permanent, immutable eternal, of a nature that knows no change...'[55] Buddha, out of the fullness of his heart, told them the truth. He took much trouble to impress on them the transitoriness of things. The Self is described by Vedanta as being Existence Absolute, Consciousness Absolute and Bliss Absolute. Buddha would take this as the criterion to show that nothing in the phenomenal world answers to this description. The entire phenomenal world is only an appearance (*Prajnaptisat*) and no reality (*Dravyasat*). Everything in this world is made up of five *skandhas* (aggregates), viz., *rupa* (form), *vedana* (feeling), *samjna* (perception), samskara (impressions) and *vijnana* (consciousness). Referring to this Buddha

---

55. Radhakrishnan's *Indian Philosophy*, p. 385.

once said that a discriminating person has an aversion (*nirveda*) for composite things, things made up of *skandhas*. Such a person is free from attachment (*viraga*). Being free from attachment, he has no more rebirth, he therefore attains nirvana.

Somehow or other, the sense of ego (*ahankara*) has to be got rid of. Because Buddha pointed this out he is praised in a hymn as being the only teacher who knew where real trouble lay and his message was the only message that can liberate. Chandrakirth in his Madhyamakavatara (vi. 123) says: 'A wise yogin denies the existence of the ego (Satkayadrsti), for he observes that all his troubles arise from the ego and centre round it.'

Buddha also says that the worlds are only *Citta* or *Vijnana*, i.e. consciousness. Does he mean by this that the worlds are only a projection of the mind and have no objective existence? In any case, this probably has led to the rise of the school known as *Yogacharas* or *Vijnana-vadins*, philosophers who hold that external things are made of the same stuff as our dreams. Buddha also said on many occasions that all things were void (*Sunya eva dharmah*). Here is another pronouncement which probably led to the rise of the school of philosophers known as *Madhyamikas*. Many such schools arose whose chief concern was metaphysics, the subject which Buddha so studiously avoided.

DIFFERENT SCHOOLS OF BUDDHIST PHILOSOPHY

Although Buddha was silent about the ultimate Reality, Buddhism, in the course of its evolution has done much speculation about it. The question whether there is an ultimate Reality and if there is, if it can be known, has exercised the Buddhist mind much. One school of philosophers, the *Madhyamikas*, hold that there is no reality, mental or non-mental, there is only a void. These philosophers are known as nihilists or *Sunya-vadins*. Another school of philosophers say that there is a reality, but that reality is mental; there is nothing outside the mind. These philosophers are known as *Yogacharas*, or *Vijnanavadins* or subjective idealists. There is yet another school of philosophers who say that reality is both subjective or objective, internal and external, mental and non-mental. These philosophers are called realists, sometimes also *Sarvastitvavadins*.

Now, there is an epistemological question: if there is an external reality, how can it be known. One group of *Sarvastitvavadins*, called Sautantrikas say that the external reality can be known only through inference. Others, called Vaibhasikas hold that the external reality can be perceived directly.

MADHYAMIKAVADA

Madhyamikavada is often referred to as Sunyavada, but the former seems to be a more appropriate term. Buddha had used the word *Sunya*, but it is doubtful if he had used it in the sense that we understood the word void. By 'Sunya', Buddha wanted to mean that the phenomenal world was without substance. Nagarjuna who expounded the *Madhyamika* philosophy, says that the real nature of things is indescribable (*Anirvachaniya*) because it is dependent upon other things (*Pratitya-samutpada*). Because it is indescribable, it is called *Sunya*, that which is indeterminate, which cannot be predicted, which cannot be categorised. In fact, one can say nothing about it, the only thing one can say about it is that it has a conditioned origination. Because one cannot say it has an absolute Reality or an absolute unreality, it may be regarded as somewhere in between *Madhyama*[56]. It is from this peculiar position of this school of philosophy that it has come to be known as *Madhyamikavada*.[57]

---

56. Ibid., Vol. V, 1964, p. 279.
57. 'It exists not for even the Buddha has not seen it; Nor, is it non-existent as it is the essence or basis of this *Samsara* and beyond'—translation of a short prayer composed by Karmapa Rangjung Dorji in Tibetan (Translated by Sri. T.D. Densapa).

As no appellation can be used in the case of the ultimate Reality, Asva Ghosha (AD 80) used the word That (*Tatha*), his theory being known as the theory of Thatness (*Tathata*). This 'That' is eternal, immutable, without any attributes, just like Brahman. In Vedanta, Brahman is also referred to as 'That', That thou art, O Svetaketu (*tat tvam asi O Svetaketu*). Since this 'That' cannot be particularised, it may be called '*Sunya*', i.e., without any attributes. According to this theory, *Avidya* 'perfumes' *Sunya* as a result of which the world appearence bursts out. This exactly is the stand of Vedanta which says that Brahman by itself is *Nirguna* (unconditioned, without attributes), but when its power, *Maya* or *Avidya* operates, the world-delusion takes place. The goal of life, according to Vedanta is to realise one's identity with this Brahman, the ultimate reality. The goal of life, often called *Mukti* or *Moksha*, is also called *Nirvana*. *Nirvana* is not a negative state, a state of annihilation, but a positive state in which one has a transcendental experience of the ultimate Reality. According to Nagarjuna, there are two truths on which Buddha's Dharma is based, one is *Samvriti-satya* (empirical truth) and another is *Paramarthasatya* (transcendental truths). Those who are not able to distinguish the two cannot understand Buddha.

Thus, Vedanta and Buddhism agree so far as the goal of life and the means of reaching that goal are concerned. The agreement between them is so much that Gaurapada, the first well-known exponent of Vedanta and teacher of Sankara's teacher, is described by some scholars as a Buddhist. Even Sankara, notwithstanding his reputation as being the man responsible for the elimination of the Buddhist influence from India, is charged by his critics as being nothing but a Buddhist in disguise (*Prachhana Bauddha*). Buddhist or no Buddhist, that Sankara held Buddha in the highest esteem is beyond doubt for he said, *Ya aste kalau Yoginam cakravarti, Sa Buddhah prabuddho astu machchittavarii* (I adore Buddha who is the leading Yogi in this Kali Yuga). Buddha himself is looked upon by the Hindus as an incarnation of God. The poet-saint Jaydeva said about him, *Keshava Dhrita-Buddha-sharira jaya Jagadisha Hare* (You are Lord Vishnu himself, you have assumed the form of Buddha, glory unto you, O Lord of the universe, O Hari).

But why is it then that Buddhism is extinct from India? It is wrong to say that it is extinct, it is very much present, but present in the form of Vedanta. Or perhaps, one may put it this way; They are complementary to each other in the sense that Vedanta is theory, Buddhism practice; Vedanta is philosophy, Buddhism is religion.

Buddham Saranam Gachhami

THE MAHABODHI SOCIETY AND THE RAMAKRISHNA MISSION, BORN about the same time and inspired by two great men who knew each other and had much in common between themselves, symbolise awakening of what is now called South Asia. At one time, the whole of the East was known as backward, waiting to be raised by the West. People of this region were considered as 'the White Man's burden'. Surprisingly, there were even people in this part of the world who gladly accepted this inferior position. Not only that, they even welcomed foreign rule, saying it was God's blessing. A real slave mentality!

But Rev Anagarika Dharmapala and Swami Vivekananda had other ideas. They were conscious of the fact that militarily their countries were surely inferior to the Western countries, but that was no reason for shame. Both India and Sri Lanka, in fact most Asiatic countries, are not ashamed to admit their military weakness. They are not countries which take pride in being able to dominate over others; they rather take pride in the fact that they never dominated over others. Buddha said, 'A real conqueror is he who conquers himself.' It is that dictum that had inspired both India and Sri Lanka over the centuries. These countries could have seized neighbouring countries by force, but they never did. They are proud that they did not. Their policy has always been 'Live and let live.' Again, it is Buddha's influence that is responsible for this. The history of

South Asia is not the history of wars, it is the history of peace and harmony, of 'live and let live.' In the West, the big countries have swallowed the small countries again and again, and then the big countries have fought among themselves over those small countries. This has been going on over the centuries. Many people have been rendered homeless and there are homeless people even today. Maps have been drawn and redrawn. It is difficult to keep track of the cartographic changes that have occurred. As against this, the picture in Asia is one of continuity, peace and harmony.

Both Swami Vivekananda and Dharmapala were conscious of this contrast between East and West. Goodness is not weakness. The best way to conquer is to, conquer by love. This is the way of Buddha, this is the way of South East Asia.

Dharmapala and Swami Vivekananda, both were delegates to the Parliament of Religions held in Chicago in 1893. That is where they came to know each other. They became friends and their friendship lasted to the last day of their lives. Both made a great impact on the USA. Western people heard for the first time about eastern thoughts from Eastern people. Earlier they had heard about them from Western people. There had been Western scholars who had written about both Hinduism and Buddhism. Rarely did they do justice to either. Bishop Heber, for instance, says the people of Sri Lanka worship wood and stone. Can there be anything more preposterous? There have been exceptions no doubt, and we remember them with gratitude, but they are few and far between. Most of them did not understand Eastern mysticism, because they did not want to. Eastern people were all heathens in their eyes, just because they differed from them in the pigment of their skin, in their habits and ways of life, that was enough reason to set them down as backward, even as savages. When they heard Dharmapala and Vivekananda expound their religious tenets, it was an eye-opener to them. Could they be so profound that they become liberal and yet rational? They began to feel ashamed that they had so long held a poor opinion about them. Dharmapala and Vivekananda might not have agreed on every religious issue but there is not at least any evidence about their disagreement. As regards Swami Vivekananda, his adoration for Buddha is well-known. He had a vision of Buddha as a young man. Once when he was admiring Buddha, an American asked, 'Are you a Buddhist?' He replied, 'I am a servant of a servant of Buddha.' Between themselves, Vivekananda and Dharmapala totally reversed the thinking of the people of Sri Lanka and India. They no longer thought that everything Western was good and everything Eastern was bad. When the Western people themselves began to praise Eastern religion and philosophy, they at first felt intrigued, then it dawned on them that there must be something to their own heritage that Western critics, normally suspicious about everything Eastern, had started praising their religion and philosophy. It was this that roused in them a sense of pride about their own region, philosophy, art and culture. This marked the beginning of a national awakening in this religion which finally culminated in foreign rule being wiped out from the whole of South Asia.

But Dharmapala will be remembered for launching the Mahabodhi Movement. He felt there should be a worldwide organisation which will treasure as well as spread the Gospel of Buddha. The motto should be, as Lord Buddha himself had said, 'Go ye, O Bhikkhus and wander for the benefit of the many, for the welfare of many, out of compassion for worldly beings, for the benefit, good, and happiness of men and Gods.' Inspired by this motto, he founded The Bodh-Gaya Mahabodhi Society at Colombo on 31 May 1891. Dharmapala was its General Secretary.

There are now Mahabodi Societies in many places. They are like windows through which you can get the Light of Truth, 'the Light of Asia.' We are grateful to Dharmapala for this.

Medieval Saints of India

- *Jnanesvar*
- *Namadeva*
- *Ekanatha*
- *Dadu*
- *Mirabai**
- *Chaitanya**

Jnaneswar

MAHARASHTRA HAS PRODUCED NOT ONLY GREAT WARRIORS BUT ALSO great saints, some of them well-known even beyond the borders of Maharashtra. Everybody in India knows, for instance, the name of Tukaram whose life and *Abhangas* (short lyrical poems full of religious fervour) are still a source of inspiration to all religious aspirants in the country. Less well-known outside Maharashtra, but in Maharashtra equally respected (if not more) is Jnaneswar, another saint who flourished about 300 years before Tukaram. True to his name (lit. 'Lord of Knowledge'), Jnaneswar was a great scholar and his work—Jnaneswari—is still regarded in Maharashtra as almost the last word on mystical literature. It is a work of rare beauty and grandeur and may rank among the world's best classics. Following Jnaneswar, a long succession of saints have enriched Maharashtra's religious life, but everyone of them has drawn inspiration from him and some have had, it is said, even direct help from him through mystical visions.

Jnaneswar was born in a free and prosperous Maharashtra—a Maharashtra still unmolested by foreign invasion. The exact date of his birth is not known, but it is fairly certain that he was born somewhere in the 70s of the thirteenth century. As for the date of his death various surmises are made, but the probability is that he died in the closing years of that century. This means that he had a very brief span of life, not even thirty years. Naturally, this makes his achievements as a scholar or saint all the more remarkable.

Vithalpant, Jnaneswar's father, was 'Kulkarni' of his village, Apegaon,—an office he had inherited from his ancestors. Apegaon, a small village on the bank of the Godavari, belonged to the territory over which the kings of Devagiri ruled, and the king who ruled then was Jaitrapala, the best in the whole dynasty and a disciple of Maharashtra's first great poet and saint, Mukundaraja. Jnaneswar was second among his brothers and sisters, four in number and, curiously enough, each a saint. Vithalpant was a monk who had turned a householder under instructions from his Guru, and this was an offence in the eyes of the society for which he and his family had to pay heavy penalties. It is said that, as a consequence of his father's premature death, he had felt disgusted with the world. With his wife's consent, he had gone to Benaras where he took orders from the famous Ramananda (or some one of his school) as his Guru. Shortly after this, his Guru happened to visit his village where he met his young wife who was pining for him. The Guru who was very human was so shocked to see this that, on his own, he ordered Vithalpant to return home and rejoin his wife, which the disciple did. This was clearly a breach of monastic vows and naturally society looked upon this with great disfavour.

Vithalpant was immediately ostracised and till the last day, was a victim of all manner of social persecution. Life became impossible for him in his village and he was compelled to move to Nasik with his wife and children. Nothing further is known about Vithalpant and he may be presumed to have met with death not long after this. Social persecution, did not, however, cease with Vithalpant's death and his family remained ostracised as before. At last the children, all still pretty young, went to the Brahmins of Paithana, leaders of the orthodox section and chiefly responsible for the persecution, to plead that the ban on them might be lifted and their re-entry into society allowed. They fought their case so vigorously and intelligently that the Brahmins relaxed and acceded to their request, rather gladly.

It appears Nivrittinath, Jnaneswar's elder brother, was Jnaneswar's Guru. A story is related as to how Nivrittinath himself attained spiritual illumination. During a visit to the Brahmagiri, a sacred hillock near Tryambakeswar at Nasik, the family encountered a tiger. All escaped unhurt but Nivrittinath was found missing. For several days no trace was found of him and he was taken to be lost. At last, he reappeared one day to the great relief of the family. What had happened was that, frightened at the sight of the tiger, Nivrittinath had taken shelter in a cave. There he was received by a saint of the Nath sect, Gaihininath. The saint at once saw his rich spiritual possibilities and was so impressed that he not only gave him shelter, but also set about effecting his spiritual unfoldment, presumably unasked as teachers sometimes do. Nivrittinath's response was extraordinarily quick and in a few days' time, he emerged from the cave, a full-fledged saint.

A word ought to be said here about the Naths, for next to the Mahanubhavs, they were a great influence in those days. No one knows where the Naths originally lived. Bengal, U.P., and Maharashtra—these three places claim their origin. Most probably, they were an itinerant people owing allegiance to no particular place. The first of all Naths was Matsyendranath—perhaps a legendary figure. His probable disciple, Gorakshanath—a more well-known figure—is, however, historical.

Tryambakanath, great-grandfather of Jnaneswar, was a disciple of Gorakshanath. Another disciple was Gaihininath, Guru of Nivrittinath. Jnaneswar, himself a Nath, made the Naths widely known. In the opinion of many, he was the best product of the Nath movement. Broadly speaking, the Naths were Yogis, i.e. followers of the Yoga system. They did not, however, adhere to the letter and spirit of the Yogic scriptures. They followed them only when it suited them. They were a class of people who did not want to be bound down by anything. Wherever the movement might have originated, it must have, at one time, been very popular in Bengal and evidence of its influence is to be found, among other things, in the title 'Nath' which many in the province still bear.

Mention has been made of the Mahanubhavs. They were another class of people whose influence was very great in those days. They had a rich literature which provided an appropriate background for Jnaneswar's great work *Jnaneswari*. The Mahanubhavs did not recognise the authority of the Vedas, and to them Krishna was the only God. They wore dark blue garments resembling Krishna's colour. They did not believe in the caste system and they differed from the Hindus in many other respects. In the beginning, they behaved as if they were distinct from the Hindus. Later, they gave up this attitude and tried to narrow down their differences with them. In due course, they were completely absorbed in the parent body.

About 1293, Jnaneswar visited Pandharpur accompanied by his brothers and sister. There he made acquaintance with the famous saint of the Pandhari Sampradaya, Namadev. Instinctively he felt drawn towards him and became his admirer. It is said Namadev was responsible for Jnaneswar's joining the Pandhari sect. Whether this was the case or not, we find Namadev always at the side of Jnaneswar after this. Together they undertook an extensive tour of upper India visiting Delhi and Benaras among other places and spending about three years over it. They returned to Pandharpur probably in 1296.

Soon after this, Jnaneswar told Namadev that as he would like to give up his body, he wanted to go to Alandi. Namadev went with him and also his brothers and sister. Jnaneswar named the day when he would pass away. For some days before his death, religious songs were sung day and night, Jnaneswar himself joining in them. On the appointed day, he passed away singing songs with others. Nivrittinath (his Guru) placed a slab on the spot where his last remains were deposited. The place is in front of the temple of Siddheswari, which still stands. Before Jnaneswar, Alandi was a place of pilgrimage. Now, Jnaneswar's tomb is an added attraction.

Unfortunately, not much is known of Jnaneswar's spiritual career—the particular methods he followed in order to attain spiritual illumination, in which that most coveted experience is of the manner the Yogis finally came to him and the struggles that preceded it. All these are only matters of conjecture. The only thing that can be presumed with any precision is that, like all Yogis, he must have had many difficulties on the way, for there is no such thing as cheap success in spiritual life. Another thing of which his works furnish ample evidence is that his success as a Yogi must have been most complete. His works are not only proof of his scholarship but also of his enlightenment. Only personal experience can enable a man to speak of mystical truths with any clarity and precision. That Jnaneswar does so must be taken as proof of the fact that he had experienced those truths. Indeed, there are many remarkable passages in his work showing rich mystical sentiments possible only for those whose minds dwell on them constantly.

Several books are attributed to Jnaneswar—*Jnaneswari*, the *Abhangas*, *Amritanubhava* and *Chengadeva Prasasti*. Of these the best known are *Jnaneswari* and *Amritanubhava* (or *Anubhavamrita* as Jnaneswar preferred to call it). Some think these two are by the same author, and the other two books are by another author. Those who hold this view argue that the former are altogether different from the latter in language and thought. Side by side with this view there is also the view held by some that there were two Jnaneswars. They further allege that the two Jnaneswars belonged to two different religious sects—one a Mahanubhavic (partially, at least) and yet a worshipper of Pandhar, and the other a Shaiva and having nothing to do with the Pandhari Sampradaya. They base this contention chiefly on the fact that there are two tombs dedicated to Jnaneswar—one at Alandi and the other at Apegaon.

Both the views are, however, wrong. The books do contain evidences suggesting different authorship, but a closer examination will reveal that they are nothing but evidences of different landmarks in the evolution of Jnaneswar's career as an author. In essentials his literary genius shows a marked consistency in all the books, though that consistency is attended with different degrees in the qualities of thought and style. As for the fact that there are two tombs at two different places, there is the quite plausible explanation that the Hindu practice does not rule out such a thing.

Between the two books—*Jnaneswari* and *Amritanubhava*—the former appears to be more mature. This has led some to suppose that it was a later work. This may or may not be the case. There is, however, no convincing proof either way. At any rate *Jnaneswari* is almost without parallel as a philosophical work. It is wonderful in knowledge, wisdom, and experience. In style also it is superb. Few works can excel it in flights of imagination or in the use of analogy which Jnaneswar often employs in order to explain subtle points of philosophy.

It is said that Jnaneswar dictated the text of the book and one Satchidananda took it down. Satchidananda did this service to him, it is said, as a mark of gratitude, for Jnaneswar had once saved him from sure death. A pillar at Nevase on the southern bank of the Godavari marks the place where the composition of the book took place. The text dictated to Satchidananda is not available. Only the text as edited by Eknath in 1594 is available. Eknath undertook editing the book because he was directed to do so by Jnaneswar in a vision, as it is said. He did not, however, change the text materially, for that would have been, he feared, 'putting nectar in a disc of coconut shell'. In his edition, the book contains exactly nine thousand verses.

Jnaneswar pays profound respect to his Guru in this book. He attributes all his wisdom to his Guru's grace. He says he was originally most unworthy and it was the grace of the Guru that transformed him into what he was. He compares himself to a Chataka bird, which, though thirsty, can carry in its beak only a few drops of rain, though it may be pouring at the time. Similarly, his Guru was so vast and he so small that he either could not represent him at all or represent him only very inadequately. All the wisdom that is in the book is his Guru's but that is only an infinitesimal part of the real wisdom of his Guru. He says it is like the infinite sky mirrored in a small pond.

It is said, Nivrittinath did not think much of the book. He said it was a mere commentary on the Gita. He wanted Jnaneswar to write a more original book. It was this which prompted Jnaneswar to write *Anubhvamrita*. It is not on record whether the book pleased the Guru, but there is evidence that it pleased Jnaneswar. He claimed the book would show the way to final emancipation. He 'served this dish of spiritual experience in order that the whole world might enjoy a general feast.' He could not keep it to himself, for that would have meant acting against the strict injunction of his Guru. The Guru had bestowed on him the supreme knowledge of the Truth on the express condition that he would pass it on to mankind. 'God endowed the sun,' he used to say, 'with light not for his own sake, but that he may illumine the whole world with it.' It is to be noted that the book throughout shows preponderance of the Vedantic trend of thought.

Here and there glimpses of Jnaneswar's spiritual experiences may be had in his books. In one place in *Amritanubhava* he declares most ecstatically that he has been made 'the sole sovereign of the kingdom of supreme bliss'. Elsewhere he says in a similar strain, 'I have become merged in God . . . God indeed fills the inside and the outside, and as one goes to embrace Him, one becomes identified with Him.' Again, 'I have seen the God of Gods. My doubt is at an end. Duality has disappeared.' Expressing his gratitude to his Guru Nivrittinath, he says, 'I was a blind man and a lame man and illusion had encircled me. My hands and feet were unable to work. Then I saw Nivritti, who initiated me into spiritual knowledge by seating me under a tree and dispelling all my ignorance. Blessed be the spiritual knowledge of Nivritti, blessed be the name of God.

The fruit of my action is at an end; my doubt is dispelled; all my desires have been fulfilled... My mind is engrossed for ever in divine joy... In all directions there is spiritual bliss. Everything now appears to me to be Brahman.' Speaking of God he says, 'The cool south wind cannot be made to drop like water from a piece of cloth. The fragrance of flowers cannot be tied by a string... the sky cannot be enveloped. So, who can understand God?'

It ought to be pointed out that, though in these quotations Vedantic monism is most prominent, he always sought to reconcile both dualism and monism in his philosophy. He was essentially a synthesist, and if we bear this in mind, it will not be difficult for us to understand the puzzling fact that he was in sympathy with several sects at the same time, one apparently antagonistic to another.

Namadeva

CENTERING ROUND THE DEITY VITTHALA OF PANDHARPUR, A LONG succession of saints, headed by Jnaneswara, flourished in Maharashtra for nearly four centuries beginning from the thirteenth. Of the many strikingly common features which marked their characters was the catholicity of their views as well as the simplicity of their faith. Never allowing themselves to be identified with any particular creed, they would concentrate on what they considered the essence of religion, strictly leaving alone all forms which they held in great contempt. Indifferent to all theological disputes, they concerned themselves only with the ultimate goal of God realisation, to which they bent all their energy. Love of God was their chief trait which in some of them took on the form of a passion totally eclipsing all other aspects of life. Many of them were gifted poets who wrote short lyrical poems ('Abhangas') which in flights of imagination, in the beauty and grandeur of diction, or in the profundity of wisdom remain unexcelled.

One such saint of Maharashtra was Namadeva who claimed all the distinctions mentioned above, besides a few others not attained by any other who either preceded or followed after him. Hailed by Jnaneswara as 'the light of the world', he was a contemporary of that great soul and also his peer in many respects. Together they toured many places of India, and though having contrasting temperaments they found much in common between themselves so that a friendship sprang up between them which continued till the last day. Jnaneswara, whose approach to questions of religion was essentially intellectual and analytical, was nevertheless so drawn towards Namadeva (despite the latter's well-known bias towards emotionalism) that he often sought his advice and followed it, sometimes even against his own reasoning. The relation between the two was so close that their difference in outlooks was scarcely known outside the narrow circle of intimate associates, and a still more interesting fact is that after the premature passing away of Jnaneswara, his admirers and disciples accepted him (Namadeva) as the natural successor of their leader.

From the evidence furnished by his own writings, Namadeva's date of birth may be placed somewhere around 1270. Unlike Jnaneswara who died very young, he lived to a great age, eighty or more. Son of a tailor, Namadeva's early life gave no indication of the saint that he was to become in later years. Uncontrolled and uncontrollable, he found much delight in mischief-making which ranged from playing relatively innocent pranks on the unwary to committing violence. As he grew in years, the ferocity of the trait so increased that such crimes as murder, loot, and arson began to figure prominently among his daily doings. The climax, which proved also the turning-point in his life, occurred when one day he with his accomplices attacked and killed eighty-four horsemen. Visiting the temple of Amvadhva shortly after this, he found there a boy crying from hunger while his mother scolded him for being so unreasonable, for had she not already told him that she had no food to give him? On enquiry, he learnt that the father of the boy was one of those unfortunate horsemen who had fallen victim to his cupidity. Stung by conscience he entered the temple and striking his neck with a sharp weapon made an offering of his blood to the deity as a mark of his atonement. He was turned out from the temple and from there he went directly to Pandharpur, determined that he would spend there the remaining years of his life in repentance and prayer. With the same ferocity which marked his earlier misdeeds he now began his new life—a life of utmost poverty, a life of ceaseless prayer and bitter repentance. He continued like this for several years till at the end he had a vision of God. By now he had won recognition as a religious man and many began to visit him to receive instructions from him in matters relating to spiritual life. About this time, a congregation of religious men took place at Pandharpur—it had to be Pandharpur, for, thanks to the influence of Jnaneswara, it had become the centre of attraction to all seekers of truth,—and with such eminent men as Jnaneswara, Namadeva also joined it. It so happened that among the leaders of the congregation there was one called Gora, who declared that a test should be held to decide about the fitness of those present to join a congregation meant for monks of the highest order. The idea was accepted and he undertook the test. Passing before each monk he pronounced judgement saying whether he was 'baked' or 'unbaked', that is, whether as a spiritual aspirant he had reached his goal or not. Coming to Namadeva he declared that he was entirely 'unbaked' and it would be many years before his 'baking' could be said to be complete.

Utterly dejected, Namadeva left the place and also Pandharpur resolving that he would not return till he could feel sure about his position among the monks of Pandharpur. He felt what he needed was the instruction of a competent teacher who would guide his steps to the goal. So, he began to look for such a teacher and found him in one called Visoba Khechara. When he first met Visoba, it is said that Visoba was lying and his legs were on a Shivalinga. Shocked, Namadeva began to scold him for such sacrilegious conduct. In reply Visoba suggested that he (i.e. Namadeva) might take the trouble to put his legs elsewhere, if he so objected to his legs being where they were. Indignant Namadeva removed his legs and as he put them elsewhere, another Shivalinga sprang up on the spot immediately. He was struck by the extraordinary power of Visoba and decided that he was the teacher he was looking for. He besought him for his guidance which the latter agreed to confer on him, and from then onward, he remained with his teacher till he had satisfied himself that he had received spiritual illumination in full measure.

Soon after this, he returned to Pandharpur where the brotherhood of monks accorded him a warm welcome, Jnaneswara himself at their head. Although Jnaneswara was the first to draw the attention of the country to the deity Vitthala, and the brotherhood of monks which his personality brought into being, none made both more popular than Namadeva.

Namadeva in one place describes what he experienced when he had his first vision of God. He says he saw a flood of light suddenly coming out from the skies—light as brilliant as that of a thousand suns shining at once. Voices, probably of saints, told him that God was coming. And when God came, He came, just as 'a cow rejoins her calf' after a long time. In another place he says, in the vein of a Vedantin, 'What lamp can we light in order to see our Self? He who gives light to the sun and the moon needs no light to be seen.'

Namadeva, as the name implies, was an apostle who preached that the Lord and the name of the Lord were one and the same. He used to say: 'The name of God is the form of God and the form of God is the name of God'; 'In the eighteen Puranas, the only remedy suggested for the cure of man's evil nature is the repetition of the name of God'; 'God may conceal Himself but He cannot conceal His name'; 'Cling fast to the Lord's name, O young and old!' Namadeva was, in his time, the greatest singer of devotional songs. With the *vina* in his hand, he would sing and dance with an ecstasy that was most touching. In his house, which still stands, there is the deity Kesiraja before whom his daily devotions in the form of singing and daucing used to be a great attraction to the people around. He would say that, if allowed, he would continue in this way throughout day and night, and he would not stop even for food and drink. Such was his habit that at no time of the day would he stop repeating the name of God, no matter how he was occupied;

and he would say if ever the tongue failed to keep on uttering the name of God, he would prefer that it were destroyed.

Namadeva has many Abhangas to his credit, all of them remarkable for their simplicity and clarity. And, they had such a universal appeal that many of them have transcended barriers of narrow sects, having found acceptance among varying communities of people including the Sikhs. What is most characteristic of these Abhangas is Namadeva's yearning for God, which is the common note which all of them strike. In utter desolation he says; 'Although you are called the Lord, strangely enough I remain helpless, a destitute, an orphan'; 'While people praise you as one who grants redemption to those fallen, I remain a fallen man all the same'; 'You are the Lord of the universe who controls everything; yet it looks as if the world has overcome you, for why else should your presence not be known.'; 'I care for nobody except you. Is it not, therefore, a shame that you should remain indifferent to me?'; 'I hate this world, yet you have made me cling to it. Is this not an act of betrayal? 'With tears in his eyes and hands stretched out to you, Namadeva cries out to you, O Lord!.'

Many stories are related bearing on the saintly character of Namadeva. Typical of them is one in which it is said that once a dog snatched away from him a piece of bread he was eating. With a pot of curd he ran after it, begging that it might kindly accept the curd also. Namadeva was lucky in being of a generation in which many saints nourished. Most of them were simple men and women, unlettered and of lowly birth. Those who deserve special mention among them are: Samvata, the gardener; Narahari, the goldsmith; Chokha, the untouchable; Kanhopatra, the dancing girl; Jana, the maidservant. The last named was Namadeva's maidservant, who was with him till his last day. Like her master and teacher, she also sang and danced ecstatically before the Lord, and among women saints she was only second to Muktabai, sister of Jnaneswara. Kanhopatra, whose famed beauty brought her many suitors, declared that she would marry only him whose beauty equalled hers. And, as according to her the only person who fulfilled that condition was Vitthala, she would regard herself as his betrothed. Soon after this, the chief of a neighbouring State sent word asking for her hand. As it was impossible to refuse him, she stood before Vitthala and put an end to her life. There is an unidentified tree marking the spot where she was buried and the tree stands to this day and is worshipped.

Describing the characteristics of a saint, Namadeva says that he is a spiritual washerman. He applies the soap of illumination, beats his linens on the rock of tranquillity and washes it in the river of knowledge. It is thus that he removes the spots of sins. His further signs are that he sees God in every being and to him gold is as is a clod or earth. His heart is free from anger and passion, and peace and forgiveness rule there. To him, honour and dishonour are of the same value as they are to a tree. He recognises no one as his enemy and his tongue is ever busy praising the Lord.

As to what we should ask of God, Namadeva says that all we need to ask of Him is that we may always think of Him alone in our hearts, utter His name alone with our lips, see nothing but Him alone with our eyes, use our hands in His service and worship only, hear only of His kindness, and that He should always be with us in this life and hereafter. Of such all-absorbing love for God, there could not have been a better example than Namadeva himself, with whom it was like a fire which consumed him day and night. Till the day he passed away in 1350, his life was one long prayer, in which all his thoughts, feelings, and actions found themselves working in unison.

Ekanatha

OF THE SAINTS WHO FOLLOWED AFTER JNANESWARA AND NAMADEVA to uphold the traditions, which, they together with other Natha saints had built up, the most important was Ekanatha, born, probably, in 1533 at Paithana. Both his father, Suryanarayana, and his mother, Rukminibai, having passed away when he was a mere infant, he was brought up by his grandparents, who naturally bestowed on him the care and affection which the child would have enjoyed had his parents been living. But, as if conscious of the loss he had sustained, Ekanatha became increasingly grave and aloof with the growing years, taking no interest whatsoever in games and other childlike occupations. Instead, he found more joy in reading stories about saints and contemplating the beauty and the astonishing purity of their characters. A favourite place where he would often retire to occupy himself with the thoughts of the saints was a Shiva temple situated outside Paithana.

It is said that when he was barely twelve he heard a voice telling him to proceed to a village called Devagaon where he would meet a saint, Janardanapant, who would initiate him into the spiritual life. Accordingly, he went to Devagaon and met the saint, who, after satisfying himself that he fulfilled the conditions of a disciple, agreed to accept him as one. Soon after this, and under instructions from his teacher, Ekanatha retired to a lonely place nearby where he spent six years in intense and uninterrupted meditation, realising in the end his spiritual aims. It was at this time that his teacher introduced him to Jnaneswara's two books, *Jnaneswari* and *Amritanubhava*, the two books which exercised a profound influence on his character in the years to come.

Shortly after this, Ekanatha's teacher asked him to undertake a tour of the holy places, adding that when he had completed this, he was to return home and settle down to the normal life of a householder after marriage. It was probably the teacher's intention that Ekanatha should be an ideal householder rather than an ideal monk, for it was in the former role that he was likely to serve the community better than in the latter. However that may be, in strict obedience to his teacher's instructions, Ekanatha returned home after the tour, and marrying a girl called Girijabai began the life of a householder.

As a householder, he lived a life which soon began to attract widespread notice and rouse conflicting comments in the neighbourhood. While some thought very highly of him, paying him the respect due only to the best and noblest among saints, others thought he was a fool or a cheat. Some came to him expecting to see him perform miracles; others came with the hope that they would find in him a scholar of the first grade. As he did not answer to their expectations, they went away disappointed, abusing him roundly for befooling them. But among his visitors were some, who were discerning enough to recognise that under the surface of what appeared commonplace and ordinary in his character, there were traits which unmistakably pointed to his greatness. What was most striking about him was that he would treat everybody with utmost courtesy and consideration, irrespective of any treatment that he himself might receive from others. Numerous stories are current illustrating this side of his character. His own son might defy him and insult him, because he thought he was more learned than his father, but Ekanatha would overlook it good-humouredly, never failing to give him the father's love and goodwill. A Mussulman might spit at him just to show how much contempt he felt for him, but unruffled, Ekanatha would acknowledge it as if he had just been offered a kiss of honour. Similarly, thieves might break into his house at dead of night, but he would receive them and treat them as if they were guests of honour.

What Ekanatha's life specially demonstrates is that it is possible to live the highest truths of religion even within the framework of a poor householder's life. Toiling and struggling for bare subsistence like everybody else of the common folk among whom he lived and moved, he yet practised those noble principles which many may talk of but are far from realising. It was in Ekanatha's daily routine that one might find proof of the feasibility of combining happily what is regarded as the mundane and the spiritual. While he went about his daily duties just like everybody else, yet he found time to perform his usual devotions, though it was, of course, his attitude towards life which underlined his greatness rather than anything he did or did not do during the day. He would leave his bed long before dawn when he would sit down to meditate. Afterwards he would go to the river to take a bath and coming back home would spend some time reading the Gita and the *Bhagavata*. From then till meal-time, he would occupy himself with family duties. At meal-time it was his practice to have some guests to share with him whatever modest fare he was able to provide for them. To give an example of what lengths he might go to in order to entertain his guests, reference might be made to the well-known story which records how he used for fuel the only bed he had because all the fuel in the house had been exhausted during a specially long spell of rainy weather, in order to serve cooked food to guests who had demanded it. However, in the afternoon, he would give discourses on the *Jnaneswari* or the *Bhagavata* and in the evening, he would meditate again. Afterwards he would sing devotional songs till it was time to go to bed. Thus, between work and worship he divided all his time. Though apparently a devotee and a dualist, Ekanatha was, as far as can be judged from his writings, a strict non-dualist, a Vedantin of Shankara's school. It is remarkable how, without knowing any Sanskrit, and without having many vernacular books to help him in its study, he had mastered the difficult philosophy of Vedanta. The fact deserves special mention that it was through his writings that Vedanta became accessible to the masses. It is probable that he owed his interest in and understanding of Vedanta to his study of the *Jnaneswari* and the *Amritanubhava*, especially the latter, which was predominantly a treatise on Vedanta, as is well known.

It is said that once Ekanatha was suffering from a throat disease when Jnaneswara, appearing in a dream, told him that he would get well if he removed a root of the *ajana* tree, which, having got into his tomb at Alandi, was choking him. As Ekanatha removed the root, he heard a voice purporting to be that of Jnaneswara, dictating to him the text of *Jnaneswari*, which had at that time got out of sight. It is, therefore, to Ekanatha that the world owes the only version of the book it knows and has grown to love so much.

Ekanatha himself was a writer of no mean order, having written some Abhangas which mark him out as a poet of the highest merit. But he took no credit for this, for he said it was Jnaneswara who was the real author, while he was only his agent. It was, however, surprising to him that Jnaneswara should have chosen such a 'fool' as he to be his agent.

His respect for his teacher was comparable only to that Jnaneswara had for his. To give an idea how much he loved and adored his teacher he would describe how he would like to worship him. First, he would purify his mind completely and then instal him on a seat there. By way of incense he would burn his own egoism at his feet, his best emotions would serve as the light to be waved and all his sense-impressions would be the food that he would invite him to partake of. He would say that his teacher had done a miracle in that he had kindled in him a light which never knew any diminishing. As a mark of respect for his teacher, he coupled his teacher's name with his in each Abhanga that he wrote. Referring to the role that the teacher played in unfolding the latent spiritual qualities in a disciple, he would say that the teacher was indispensable and more important than even God.

Ekanatha thought that he was the most fortunate who could meet a true saint. According to him, it was easy enough to meet persons possessing miraculous powers, such as changing the courses of the planets or walking over water, but to meet a real saint was most difficult. In describing the signs of a saint, he said that a saint was a person who was never influenced by the objective conditions of life. He might be struck by an enemy, but he would not like to retaliate. He might lose his only son, or his very dear wife, or whatever earthly possessions he might have, but he would remain cheerful. Equally indifferent to adversity and prosperity, he would never lose control over his mind, never give way to joy or to sorrow.

He did not believe in leaving home and going to the forest in search of God. Ridiculing the idea that God might be found in the forest, he would ask if the forest was not also the home of pigs. He stressed the need of overcoming the attraction for women and gold, which was the greatest impediment in the path of realising God. He made no special distinction between Sanskrit and the popular vernacular languages, for, he expressed the view that if God had created Sanskrit, was it Satan who had created the vernaculars? If one prayed to God sincerely, God would be pleased, and it did not matter in what language one prayed.

He would say that devotion made the devotee bigger than even God. In one place he described the devotee as the father of God. To indicate the relations between God and the devotee, he would say that while God was impersonal, the devotee was personal; while God was the ocean, the devotee was the waves; while God was gold, the devotee was the ornament made of it; while God was the flower, the devotee was the scent of the flower.

Like Namadeva he laid much stress on the name of God. He would say that while everything else in the world was perishable, the name of God was not. Similarly, he would advise everybody to practise meditation. He would say that by intense meditation one could become united with the object of his meditation. To give an example, he would refer to the insect which, when under the power of the bee, became itself transformed into a bee as a result of its dread for the bee. If this was possible for an insect, it might be possible for a man also. He would say that the aim of life was God realisation and if a man did not bend all his energy to the fulfilment of this aim, he had only lived in vain.

Ekanatha lived a fairly long life, passing away in 1599, at the age of sixty-six. All his life, he followed his routine which has already been described, and preached God in the clearest and most convincing way. He lived a life which in itself was the best argu-ment that could be advanced for religion, and it is, therefore, no wonder that, despite all the limitations to which he was subject either by choice or by necessity, he became one of the most potent forces in popularising the fundamental principles of religion in medieval India.

Dadu

MEDIEVAL INDIA WITNESSED AN INTERESTING PHENOMENON: SHE saw for the first time an attempt—and a fairly successful attempt at that—at reconciliation between Hinduism and Islam. And oddly enough, this attempt was initiated not by intellectual India but by what may roughly be called India of the ignorant masses.

Before this, Hinduism and Islam were regarded as irreconcilable. They were like two poles asunder. To the Mussalmans, Hinduism was mere idolatry, a mass of blind superstitions. Its ideals and practices—everything was repugnant to them. It was the very contradiction of all they held dear and sacred in Islam. The Hindu reaction to Islam was, of course, a bit different. The Hindus have all along been tolerant. They have been used to all kinds of vagaries in the religious world. Within their own fold they have seen all manner of ideals and practices. They have not treated any with contempt. Far less have they tried to smother any. To them everything is welcome, provided it originates from a sincere and earnest quest for the Truth. And, they know they must allow for differences in tastes and temperaments. They do not treat religion like a strait jacket to pin down man to fixed beliefs and dogmas. This explains why there is this amazing diversity in the Hindu religious thought. Moreover, through all this apparent diversity they try to seek a real unity. So, they were not essentially hostile to Islam. Rather, they were curious and interested. Here was a new pattern of religious thought and they wanted to examine it and see if there was anything in it they could accept with profit. In course of time, perhaps, they would have absorbed and assimilated Islam as they have done myriads of such ideas and ideologies through countless ages. In that case, the Mussalmans would have been today only another sect in the Hindu fold.

But this was not to be. Unfortunately—yes, unfortunately, Islam strode into India with the sword of a political conqueror. It did not come purely as a religious movement. It came as an attack, an assault. It was an attack on the political integrity and the religious freedom of the Hindus. This fact made the whole of Islam suspect to the Hindus. And, being politically conquered, they could not but feel a sting of humiliation in accepting Islam. It hurt their pride. Hence, though so unlike themselves, they assumed an attitude of sullen indifference; they would have no truck with it. And, to prevent defections, they hardened the caste rules and made social ostracism the price of accepting Islam. Almost an unprecedented step in Hindu history, and how deplorable!

Thus, a barrier came to be established between the Hindus and the Mussalmans. It did not, of course, extend so far as to make social intercourse impossible between the two communities. Also, it did not deter their representative theologians from engaging now and then in healthy debates under the auspices of Moghul courts. And true to the Indian traditions, these debates were always characterised by an atmosphere of friendship and good humour. Nevertheless, the barrier remained and the idea persisted that Hinduism and Islam were fundamentally different, nay, even antagonistic to each other and reconciliation between them was thought impossible.

Against this background of religious conflicts and confusions appeared a great mystic who addressed himself to the task of bridging the gulf between Hinduism and Islam and also partially succeeded. This was Dadu. Born a Mussulman, he accepted a Hindu as his guru. By this very fact he brought Islam and Hinduism nearer to each other. He practised a religion which did not answer to any rigid type. It was neither Islam nor Hinduism. It was something constituting both. It was the essence of religion.

It was his chief endeavour to synthesise, to harmonise all religious views. This he did by emphasising that the contents of all religious ideals were the same though their forms differed. To him 'Hindu' and 'Mussalman' were arbitrary and artificial labels and they surely had no sanction from God. When accused of breaking down the barriers between the Hindus and the Mussalmans his emphatic reply was that such barriers had no right to exist, for man was the same everywhere and God the same God in every religion and there was no sense in creating barriers among men which, far from helping, hindered their progress towards God. To him, religion was intensely personal and it must vary according to individual tastes and requirements.

It was more by conduct, by his own personal example, than by his teachings, that he brought about a reconciliation between Hinduism and Islam. Religious disputes arise when the fundamentals of religion are forgotten. Dadu stressed as well as embodied these fundamentals. And, what are they? They are: God alone matters and nothing else. And, to attain Him what is necessary is love and sincere longing of the heart. Quarrels about creeds and dogmas are foolish; they are the idle sport of intellectual fools. Dadu himself is the best example of all these. He is the example of a man attaining to the highest spiritual grandeur aided solely by the devotions of a longing heart. For, his was an approach to God not through the devious ways of scholarship, not through dry contentious intellectualism, but through a burning faith, through an all-devouring love.

Details about Dadu's origin are a matter of dispute. Many stories are current and it is difficult to tell which are true and which are not. Nevertheless, it is fairly established that he was born of a poor Mohammedan family somewhere in the 40s of the sixteenth century and by caste he was a cobbler. As a boy he showed nothing remarkable, nothing that bore any promise of what he was to be in future; he was like any other boy of his station. At the age of eleven, he met in his village Budhan (Briddhananda), a Hindu monk of Kabir's school, and this marked the turning-point of his life. Evidently, Buddhan was able to see the tremendous possibilities of the boy and was impressed; so he singled him out from among a host of other boys and taking him aside instructed him about God. What exactly he told him we do not know, nor how Dadu reacted to it. We do not know also how Dadu passed the next seven years before Buddhan visited him again. Outwardly, it is possible, he simply drudged at his family trade as he had been doing before; but, inwardly, it may be presumed, the seed planted by Budhan in his heart must have been growing, drawing nourishment from those hidden sources of which only Budhan was aware. So that by the time Budhan came again, he was ready in his own conscious mind to take a real plunge into spiritual life. Budhan, too, must have been waiting for this happy development and when he came again, he lost no time to give Dadu fuller instructions about God and to introduce him to the secrets of the esoteric life according to his school. And, we know what Dadu's reaction this time was: as soon as Budhan left, Dadu discovered he could not live the life he was so long living—the life of a petty workman earning a few coppers honestly and being content with it. He felt a call—an irresistible call, the same to which many have succumbed, beginning with Buddha. This made him throw down his tools, snap all ties with the family and rush out into the big wide world in quest of truth. Roaming about ceaselessly he visited innumerable places and wherever he was he took care to contact sages of different cults and to study their ways. He was like an ever thirsty traveller drinking at whatever fountains he met on the way.

    He was equally at home with the Hindus as well as the Mohammedans, with the Shaktas as well as the Vaishnavas, with the Buddhists as well as the Jains. He was like a sturdy plant thriving alike in all climates. He, however, did not commit himself to any particular creed or dogma. For he had no use for any man-made institution. Nor was he to get bound by any fixed belief or custom. He was a true universalist who accepted everything and rejected nothing. Nevertheless, he believed in one Godhead and in the ultimate identity of the individual soul with that Godhead. In this he was on a par with the Vedantist.

How Dadu acquired such broadness of outlook, it is difficult to say. Of course, Kabir to whose school his guru belonged and who influenced him more than any other single individual, held similar views. Still, they were not so pronounced in their comprehensiveness and width of vision. It must have been Dadu's own intuitive experience of Truth coupled with wide travels and close observation that lent such catholicity to his character. He brought about a synthesis not only between Hinduism and Islam but also among other warring creeds of the time. And, this he did not by a process of mere juxtaposition or that more grandiosely called eclecticism but by realising as well as uploading that common truth underlying all the varying creeds and by emphasising the organic harmony that naturally exists between them. It is a great thing to do at any time and it is wonderful Dadu did it as early as the sixteenth century.

At the end of his long itinerary, we find Dadu settled somewhere in Rajputana. He had married some time or other and here he lived a quiet life with his wife and children. His quiet life could not remain quiet, for Dadu's fame soon spread far. People began to flock to him in numbers. He received all with equal courtesy and tried to solve their doubts. Some came to test and some to tease only, but Dadu was unruffled and they went away tremendously impressed. Some, again, came to tempt or to threaten, but Dadu went on, unswayed, with his teaching of the Truth and guiding the genuine seekers. Hindus as well as Mohammedans came and sat at his feet and many became his ardent followers. Among his visitors were common men as well as royalty, and among the latter, there was Akbar the Great himself. And, how interesting reads the story of his interview with

Akbar! It reveals the characteristic qualities of both the great souls and it is a matter fit to be recorded in some detail.

Dadu, emperor of the spiritual world, was in his ramshackle house surrounded by his admirers. A messenger from Akbar, the biggest emperor of the temporal world of the time, arrived to say that Dadu was wanted. 'The Emperor wants me? What have I to do with him—I, a poor fakir! Excuse me, I cannot go.' This was Dadu's reply with no sign of elation or indecent hurry to oblige the emperor!

Soon, the messenger came again. This time he knew better what to say. He said the emperor wanted to meet him because he wanted to profit by having a religious talk with him. So, would he please accept the invitation? Dadu replied he would, but he could not go and meet the emperor in Delhi. His significant excuse was that he lived in a world altogether different from the emperor's and if he went to the emperor's world, he would not be himself any longer. To this Akbar sent a clever reply, full of understanding, full of that nobility of spirit of which only he was capable. He said it was not his intention that Dadu should go to Delhi. He had sense enough to understand how foolish it would be to take him out of his environment. It would be like taking a piece of rock from the Himalayas and trying to judge their beauty and grandeur from it. But it was, at the same time, Akbar's misfortune that he was an emperor. If he went to Dadu's place, a whole host of ministers and courtiers would then rush to the place and defile its simple native beauty. So, would he mind coming over to Fatehpur Sikri, that city which Akbar meant to be a seat of deep spirituality? Fatehpur Sikri suited Dadu quite well for he would often go to places around it, and he readily agreed. Accordingly, the time and place were fixed for the meeting.

They met in the quiet deserts outside the city and they met for forty days! It was like two masterminds locked in grips with each other. They discussed almost everything bearing on spiritual life and they differed and argued and fought. Together they journeyed far into the spiritual realm, Dadu guiding and Akbar always doubting, questioning and challenging. It is well known that Akbar, though illiterate, was a profound student of philosophy and was himself a mystic of a sort. His thirst for knowledge was great and he was no bigot to refuse to add to his knowledge from new or even from alien sources. It is this fact that explains why he felt impelled to seek an interview with Dadu, and to secure it he would let no false prestige stand in the way.

In the discussions that took place Dadu must have been impressed by his keen intellect, his deep understanding as well as his wide range of vision, and he must have felt glad at heart to be able to share his spiritual knowledge with him. Akbar, too, with his shrewd understanding of what was genuine and what was spurious, must have been struck by the rich contents of Dadu's spiritual experience—his great wisdom, his catholicity and, above all, his wonderful synthesis of all seemingly antagonistic and contradictory creeds and dogmas. And, he drank in his words instinct with the living experience of reality. When, in course of discussions, Dadu incidentally pointed out to him that no creed, however perfect and comprehensive, can embody the full truth, 'just as no bird can contain in its beak the whole of sea-water', it must have given Akbar the shock of a new discovery and in this perhaps lies a partial explanation of that large-hearted toleration which characterised Akbar's treatment towards religions supposed to be hostile to Islam.

At last, they parted and they parted the best of friends. Each conceived great admiration for the other and their exchange of ideas continued from a distance. It is difficult to say what influence Dadu had on Akbar. Who knows if his deep indrawn moods, his religious ecstasies and his increased abhorrence of bigotry which were all so prominent a characteristic of Akbar's last days were not the outcome of his contact with Dadu!

Dadu founded a sect named after Brahma and its chief articles of faith were: conquest of ego, prayer, indifference to conditions of body and mind, and love for all. It was a truly non-sectarian sect, for it was open to all and it preached and practised nothing with the least hint of narrowness of outlook. It had on its rolls Hindus as well as Mohammedans, and all enjoyed equal rights, and there was no question of change of religion on the part of those who sought its membership. It was not intended to replace any existing religious ideology but to supplement it, to broaden it, and to free it from all tendencies to collectivise everything stultifying the individual taste and requirement. It did not enjoin any complex rituals and ceremonies or anything tending to interfere with normal pursuits of life. It left every individual free to choose his own mode of approach to God, laying down the only condition that he should not infringe the articles of faith quoted above.

By necessity, but one would like to believe more by choice, Dadu did all his teaching through the popular dialect of Hindi. Among his disciples were men who were deep scholars of Sanskrit; still Hindi continued to receive special preference and thanks to this, Dadu's spiritual wisdom did not become a close preserve of the learned and its wide diffusion among the masses became possible. In addition, his disciples translated many Sanskrit books into Hindi in order that common folks might derive their benefit. It was, in short, the interest of the common folks that was always put in the forefront and in every sense, the movement became a real people's movement.

Another feature of the movement was that, besides Dadu, it drew inspiration from various saints, ancient or contemporary, and it became a sort of common pool to which all sects of all religions contributed their share. The idea was to help man advance in his spiritual struggles and not to create a hard crystallised sect centering round a particular personality or principle, so that, rather than cooperate, it would compete with the innumerable sects already existing. That is why sayings of saints belonging to different sects were carefully collected, preserved, and read with the same respect as Dadu's own sayings in the monasteries dedicated to him.

Names of Dadu's prominent disciples are on record and they include both Hindus and Mohammedans. His own son, Garibdas, was a disciple and, after Dadu's passing away at an approximate age of sixty, it was he who was chosen leader of the movement. Some of his disciples were brilliant men, and their gifted writings greatly influenced the religious thoughts of the time. It must be said to the credit of Dadu's disciples that, unlike what has happened in the case of most saints, they did not tamper with his utterances trying to improve upon them or to suit them more to the popular taste. Not only that, they also remained loyal to their spirit and tried to live up to them.

As time passed, the movement gathered in volume and more and more men came under its influence. As Dadu's catholic ideas seeped into popular minds, the old atmosphere of religious rivalry disappeared and a general sense of understanding and sympathy towards religions other than one's own became widespread and habitual with the people. Partly because of its catholicity and partly because it had fulfilled its purpose, the movement lost its distinctive role and eventually disappeared. The services rendered by it and its originator, Dadu, can never be overrated for if, until recent times, relations between Hindus and Mohammedans or between one sect and another, Hindu or Mohammedan, have been friendly and sympathetic, it can be safely concluded that it has been largely due to Dadu and his movement.[58]

Mirabai

THE LEGEND OF MIRABAI DATES BACK TO ABOUT FIVE HUNDRED years. Mirabai's father Ratan Singh was the grandson of Rana Rao Yoodhaji, the founder of the Jodhpur kingdom. Ratan Singh was a devout Vaishnava and a very pious man. Helping others was his life's motto. Visitors, guests, particularly, Vaishnava monks and mendicants, were received very warmly in his household. Ratan Singh's father Dudaji was also an ardent votary of Lord Krishna and the shrine of Giridharilal in his house, always reverberated with the songs of the devotees.

It was in such a holy environment that Mirabai was born in 1504, in the village of Kudki in Medhta. From her very childhood, everyone was drawn to Mira's melodious voice, sharp intellect and exquisite beauty. When sitting in her mother's lap, she would listen to the devotional songs and later on, she would recite them sweetly and perfectly; everybody would be spellbound. Collecting flowers for her grandfather's worship was Mira's daily duty. Sometimes, while collecting flowers or while playing with her friends, she used to make a clay model of Lord Krishna and start dancing and singing around it. People would then gather to watch her elegant performance.

One day having observed a marriage ceremony, she said to her mother, 'Who is my husband?' Her mother answered jokingly, 'Your husband is none but our household God, Giridharilal.' Hearing this,

Mira sang, overwhelmed with joy—*mere to Giridhargopala dusro na koi...*—I have no one in this world but only Giridhargopala.

Once, a monk came to Kudki, Mirabai's village, with a stone image of Lord Krishna in his hand. Mira found a striking resemblance between this idol and that of her Giridharilal. Mira pleaded for the idol but the monk was not ready to give the same to a child making a capricious demand, for he used to worship this idol everyday. That night, the monk received a divine command in his dream and he gave the idol to Mira very gladly. From that time onwards, Mira used to worship the idol regularly. Gradually, it became her constant companion and playmate.

Apart from being a good singer, Mira was also a fine poetess. From a very tender age, she could compose devotional songs, and charmed her audience with her marvellous compositions.

In due time, Mira's fame spread all over Rajasthan. The ruler of Chitor, Sangram Singh sent a marriage proposal to Mirabai's father for his son, Prince Bhojraj. Ratan Singh, Mira's father, accepted it very gladly, on behalf of Mira. Mira's wedding was arranged and on the day of her marriage, when Mira's companions adorned her with jewellery and fine clothing, Mira sang *Main Girdhar ki ghar jaun...*—I am going to Giridhar's house.

While leaving for her husband's house, Mira did not forget to take her constant companion, the stone idol of Lord Krishna, with her. Her conversations with the idol were at first mistaken for a mere expression of childishness in her in-law's house. But within a few days, the king Rana noticed her true devotion and set up a temple of Giridharilal for Mira, though the king himself was a devotee of Mother Bhawani. Mira composed many beautiful songs in this temple and sang them to her beloved deity. Her husband, mother-in-law and sister-in-law all watched her in amazement. Slowly, many devotees too started coming to Mira's temple, attracted by her wonderful songs.

Gradually time passed on. Mira lost her husband after a lapse of ten years. Yet, Mira did not lead the life of a Hindu widow, for she strongly believed that Giridharilal had been her one and only husband. After a few days, Mira was initiated by saint Ruidas in Varanasi. Mira now devoted herself more deeply than ever in her spiritual practice. Sometimes, she used to go out in the streets with monks and saints, chanting the name of God and singing His praise. The holy name of the Almighty showered upon her divine joy and she sang—*Payo ji main to naam rattan dhan payo* . . .—I have got the priceless gem of Lord's name.

However, Mira's brother-in-law, Vikramjit detested these practices of Mira. One day he sent his sister, Udabai, to ask Mira to stop mingling with monks and saints. In reply, Mira sang *Bala main bairagan hungi* . . .—I will be an anchorite. After this, Vikramjit engaged two maids, named Champa and Chameli to teach Mira a good lesson. They brought with them by the King's order, a basket containing a venomous snake, a bowl of poison and a bed of thorns for Mira; but could do no harm to her. Mira saw a *Salagrama* (a black stone worshipped as Vishnu) instead of a snake and placed it with great care on the altar of her Giridharilal. Then, she drank the poison as *charanamrita* (water washed off the Lord's feet) with deep respect. Champa and Chameli were shocked. They fell at Mira's feet, begging pardon for their heinous deed. Mira sang in ecstasy—*Mira magan bhai Hari ke gun gaye* . . .—Mira sang the song in praise of the Lord Hari, absorbed in pure joy.

From then on, Champa and Chameli devoted themselves wholeheartedly to the service of Mira, to atone for their past misdeed.

Mira spent her night in spiritual practice. While meditating, she would often feel the close proximity of her divine Lord and she would sing—*Chhor mat jajoji maharaj* . . .—Do not leave me, O my Lord.

Hearing Mira singing at night, some wicked men of the royal household reported to King Vikramjit, that Mira would sing, dance and talk with an unknown man at night in her room. Furious, the king went straight to Mira's room and when he heard Mira singing inside, he rushed into her room with his sword and asked Mira to show the stranger in her room or he would kill her. Mira, in her reverie, just pointed to the idol of Krishna in her room. But Vikramjit did not believe her and gave orders to banish Mira from their kingdom. When Mira was about to leave the palace, thousands of devotees blocked her way. They would not allow their beloved queen to leave the kingdom. The king realised his fault and begged Mira for forgiveness. Mira condoned her brother-in-law but she had already made up her mind to leave Chitor for good. She was free today and wanted to set out in search of her beloved Lord Krishna. Bidding farewell to all, she sang *Tero koi nehi rokan har* . . . No one can stop you.

Accustomed to a comfortable and luxurious lifestyle, Mira could not sustain the exertion from her journey for long and getting tired one day, she almost fainted nearby a wood. A cowboy noticing this nursed her and when she came round, the boy asked Mira, 'Where are you going?' Mira replied that she was going to Vrindavan but did not know the way. The cowboy smiled and assured her, 'Do not worry. I will show you the way.' Mira reached Vrindavan but on reaching there, she could not find the cowboy anymore. He seemed to have vanished all of a sudden. Mira now realised that this cowboy was none other than her Lord Krishna. Then she sang in deep fervour—*Tumre karan sab kuch chhora* . . . I gave up all my pleasures just because of you. . . . The people of Vrindavan were delighted to have Mira amongst them. Everyone flocked around her to listen to her melodious bhajans.

Roop Goswami was a famous saint of Vrindavan at that time and Mira expressed her desire to meet him. But his disciples informed her that Roop Goswami would never meet any women. Having learnt this fact, Mira wrote to Goswamiji—Lord Krishna is the only man in this Vrajadham and all others are women. If Goswamiji is unaware of this fact, he should leave the place. Reading Mirabai's letter, Goswami became aware of his folly and he himself went to meet Mira. Seeing him, Mira sang—*Sadhan karna chahiye manua, bhajan karna chahiye . . . bina premse nahi mile Nandalala . . .* O mind, you will have to pray and worship, you will have to undergo austere ascetic practice . . . without Love, Nandalala (Krishna) cannot be achieved.

Days passed and so did many festivals; but Mira's yearning for her deity piled up year after year. The pain of estrangement from her Lord now seemed to be almost unbearable.

Mira travelled to many holy places in her life and started for Dwaraka. She had become old and feeble but did not stop. Mira went on and on. The nature with her exquisite beauty seemed to be too busy to make her forget all her tiredness. Finally, Mira had reached Dwaraka.

In the mean time, Chitor had been invaded several times by enemies. The royal priests and preceptor advised the king to bring back Mira for the welfare and peace of the kingdom. The king soon sent his men in search of Mirabai and finally they spotted her in Dwaraka. They narrated to her the miserable plight of their state. The news grieved Mira and she waited for her Lord's permission to leave for the kingdom of Chitor. Sitting in the temple compound of Ranchhorji, she sang *Prabhuji main araj karu chhu, Mero bero lagajyo paar* . . . O Lord, I earnestly request you, to kindly ferry me across this worldly ocean. Mirabai perceived in her ecstasy that her beloved Lord was beckoning her and she sang with deep passion—*Jyogi mat jaa, mat jaa, mat jaa* . . . Please, do not go, O my Lord. When the song was over, the deity and the devotee became one with each other and the other devotees, who had assembled there, were overwhelmed with joy. They, too, could see the smiling countenance of Balkrishna and shouted in joy—*Bolo bhakta aur bhagawan ki jai* Hail to the devotee and the Deity!

Chaitanya

IN EVERY *AVATARA-LILA* (DIVINE PLAY) IT IS FOUND THAT THE DEITIES come to see the *avataras* when they take birth on earth. When Jesus Christ was born—'Wise men of the East' came to see him. In the case of Chaitanya also, it is seen that the saints came to see him. All and sundry cannot apprehend the birth of an Avatara, only a blessed few can realise the Avatara. The saints went to Navadwipa in disguise to see Chaitanyadeva when he was born on 18 February 1484. Nemai or Gouranga (other name of Chaitanyadeva) was born to mother Sachi Devi and father Jagannath Mishra.

Krishna is the incarnation of love, as he manifested himself in his *Vrindavanalila*. Chaitanyadeva is said to be the incarnation of Krishna. People, therefore, worship Chaitanyadeva as the incarnation of love. Thus, we could see that throughout his life he had been in search of Krishna at Vrindavana, for in the form of Krishna Avatara, he indulged in a divine play at the Vrindavana and in this life he was searching for those items, related to his divine play—at the sacred river Yamuna, Vrindavana, the Gopis, Radha, the tree Bansibat and the small cowherds. Today, what we know as Vrindavana is after all the discovery of Chaitanyadeva. It is said that he synthesised Radha and Krishna in one mortal frame. Outwardly he is Radha, but inwardly he is Krishna. He has through his life proved that the divine sport of Radha–Krishna is not false or mere imagination. It is, in fact, Vrindavanlila where the devotee and the Divine meet in a divine play.

In his childhood, Gouranga of Navadwipa resembles Krishna of Vrindvana much. As a child Gouranga was very naughty and playful, still he was loved by many at Navadwipa. When devotees were busy performing puja on the bathing ghat of the Ganga, Nimai used to snatch their offerings in a playful manner. That was his benign game. God is snatching or taking the offering from the devotee out of love. The devotees are unable to understand this *lila* and consequently get annoyed. Yet, devotees are so fortunate that God accepts readily their offerings in a playful manner. Women, on the other hand, loved Nemai. Nemai's sudden departure pains them and they try to satisfy him out of benign affection by offering food.

One day, a Brahmin called at Nemai's house as a guest. He cooked food with his own hands for his Lord Bal Gopala. As soon as he closed his eyes to offer it to Gopala, Nemai came and ate the same. Noticing this, Brahmin shouted with vexation. He was unable to make the offerings to God as the boy had spoiled everything. Nemai's parents pleaded before the Brahmin, and also made arrangement for the offerings. But, consecutively, three times Nemai had eaten before it was offered to God. Nemai said to Brahmin, 'What can I do? You are calling me.' Then, the Brahmin realised that Nemai had been Gopala himself.

Though Nemai was naughty, yet he used to love his mother very much. He was very much obedient to his mother. Sometimes, he would go into a trance that was wrongly interpreted by people as a disease. But one who knew Sastras and Sadhanas believed that the same had been due to the practice of Yoga.

Nemai was very much keen on studies. He learned grammar very well. When he grew up he opened a traditional school, where many boys came to study. Everyone was very happy with his teaching and gradually he became popular as Nemai Pandit. Soon, it was found that not only in grammar but in Nyaya, Sankhya and in various other branches of Indian philosophy, he was a scholar. He contested with many Pandits and no one could defeat him.

In his early days Chaitanya married Lakshmi Devi, but her life was cut short by death due to snake-bite. Later, he married Vishnupriya Devi. During this period, Nemai went to Gaya to perform the last rites of his father. In Gaya, when he saw the footprint of Lord Vishnu, he got spiritually transformed. After he had taken initiation from Ishwarpuri, he could hardly concentrate on his teaching. He became absorbed in the thought of God and at last abstained from teaching. He used to take the name of Krishna day and night. Frequently, due to deeply spiritual emotion, he used to fall on the ground. During this time, there were a few Vaishnavas who used to live in Navadwip—Srivasa, Mukunda, Gadhadhara, Murari etc. Nemai used to go with them taking the name of Krishna or participating in *kirtan*. Advaitacharya also joined them. On the other hand, Nityananda, a wandering Brahmachari, after searching for Nemai, found him at Navadwip and joined his group. Both were in search of one another. They could also recognise one another. Their union was necessary for the divine play. In the Bible, we find a similar instance about Jesus Christ and Saint Paul. In this age, we also witness the union of Sri Ramakrishna and Vivekananda. On seeing Nityananda, Nemai said that he had already seen him in his dream.

In Navadwip, Srivasa's house was a centre for their *Kirtana* or song in praise of Lord Krishna and they used to get immersed day and night in the thought of Krishna. They used to roam about and sang Kirtana in a procession. Jagai and Madhai were notorious persons and one day they disturbed the Kirtana procession. Being drunk, they threw a pitcher towards Nityananda's head. There was profuse bleeding. Yet, Nityananda was calm and quiet. He embraced Jagai and Madhai out of love. This is God's mercy. There is no limitation in the love of God. He loves unconditionally and a sinner also gets his love. Nityananda's love made the two brothers overwhelmed. They fell at his feet and asked for mercy. Nityananda forgave them but Nemai was unable to forgive them. He became very angry as his loved one was hurt. Then, Nityananda on behalf of Jagai and Madhai prayed to him for mercy. However through this their life got finally transformed. After that incident, they had recourse to the feet of Chaitanya and followed the path of devotion.

Chaitanya appeared on the soil of India to immerse the people of India in the love of God. Nemai's mother Sachidevi on seeing Srivasa, began to cry and said 'Nemai pays no attention to the household duties.' His movements were suspicious and she felt that like her elder son, Vishwarupa, he would also become a sannyasin. Nemai embraced Srivasa, 'My only desire is to be with my beloved Krishna'. Srivasa saw that all the time Nemai's eyes were filled with tears of love. Intense love for God made the body tremble, sweat, and the eyes filled with tears.

Nemai became more like a hermit, he could no longer remain there in the *samsara* (familial life). At the age of twenty-four, he left his home so as to spread the message of Krishna, i.e. selfless and benign love. He took *sannyasa* 'initiation' from Keshav Bharati of Katwa. His sannyasa name was Krishnachaitanya. In order to satisfy mother Sachidevi, he decided to stay in Nilachala or Puri in Orissa, the place of Lord Jagannatha. From that place, he spread the message of love of Krishna to all.

Had Chaitanyadeva not have been there, we would have ignored Radha–Krishna *lila* to be imagination or at best an imagination conducive to the spiritual practice of love. Essentially, he is an *Advaitin* or a monist but his outward appearance was that of a devotee accepting Dualism. For the sake of others' betterment, he had such a loving nature. What a sacrifice he made and what austerity! If there is no sacrifice then there cannot develop a spiritual love, and the best example for this is Chaitanyadeva himself. It is said about him that one of his favourite disciples once took alms from a female devotee, and so Chaitanyadeva left him. This was done to establish the strict principle of spirituality. All was meant for the betterment of the masses. On the other hand, we see his love, his mercy! From door-to-door he moved about to spread the name of Krishna and even offered refuge to the sinners. Later on, this sacrifice gave way to love. One, who can make an unconditional sacrifice, can alone unconditionally love others.

It is said about Chaitanyadeva that he is both Radha and Krishna synthesised in one frame, inwardly Krishna and outwardly Radha. Had Chaitanya not been there, we would not have realised Radha's glory, Radha's love—we would never have understood, the great spirituality of love. He has made us aware of the significance of *Vrindavana-lila*. He showed us the proper path of appreciation of spiritual emotion, or *bhava* of Gopi and the devotees of the Vrindavana. Sri Chaitanya in his life taught what *Radha bhava* is. He is the symbol of Radha's love for Sri Krishna. He is the epitome of the union of *Jivatman* with *Paramatman*.

Chaitanya in his own words narrated how he felt being far away from Krishna—'Days are all fruitless miserably. Every moment seems to be like a decade. Through the eyes, rain of tears is coming down! I didn't get Govinda and thus the world seems to me dark. This pain of separation haunts me. Death would have been better. The fire of separation burns me constantly.'

Narahari Sarkar, one of his biographers, offers also a description of this painful separation—'Chaitanyadeva's golden complexion has become grey. Sometimes, he shivers as if he is feeling cold. Sometimes, he is speechless like a picture. But a sigh of grief is coming from within him. Sometimes, tears are rolling down his cheeks—like that of Mandakini, sometimes, he sweats profusely, sometimes he sings, sometimes he cries, sometimes uttering words in an unusual manner.'

This is Radha–Krishna's *Vrindavana-lila* which Chaitanyadeva rejuvenated. In the history of religion, the discovery of Vrindavana is of great significance. Vrindavana was covered with trees then. People forgot where this Vrindavana had been. Chaitanyadeva discovered Vrindavana. One of his biographers once wrote that while roaming he came to Vrindavana; till then he did not know that the place had actually been Vrindavana. The trees, animals, birds of Vrindavana recognised him—'Here is the man who had done several *lilas* and we were the witness. Today, he has come again in a different form.' They were discussing among themselves what unique divine play had been played by God. 'Krishna who is clever enough to deceive others—He is doing the same with us again. This is a new way of deceiving, so He has taken such a guise. Look at Him! He has hidden his black complexion. Our beloved Krishna had a black complexion, but where has He hidden his black complexion? He has taken the guise of Radha.' But we have understood, in your body there is Krishna's name—in reality you are that Krishna—outwardly you are Radha. In your sayings you utter that name of 'Krishna'. Other than that there is no sign of Krishna. Radha Krishna, is for the betterment of the people; for the reason of *lila*, Chaitanyadeva has emerged in a single body.'

The biographer writes—all plants and trees could recognise their beloved Krishna. They, with their branches, leaves, flowers and fruits are all bestowing their love at the feet of Chaitanyadeva as if a friend is giving gift of love to another friend. Chaitanyadeva also embraced them. He heard the sweet voice of birds Suk and Sari. They were talking between themselves. Chaitanyadeva understood their language as Suk was telling—'Krishna is playing the flute. The sweet sound of flute had mesmerised the womenfolk.' Here 'women' does not mean the ladies but his beloved devotees. In this world, the only male is Krishna and the others are all female. Krishna with the sweet sound of his flute had mesmerised His beloved devotees. So, sing the glory of His victory.' Then other bird Sari replied—'You eulogise the victory of Krishna and in doing so you have forgotten our beloved Radha. If Radha stands near Krishna then only Krishna is Madanamohana. If Radha is not present then he is not Madanamohana as Radha is his *Shakti*. Though he has spellbound the whole world, yet he himself is immersed in ecstatic pleasure by Radha. How strange!

Brahman and Maya, *Purusha* and *Praktriti*, Siva and *Shakti*—are not different in essence.'

Chaitanya was surprised to listen to the conversation between the two birds. The wise conversation made him aware that the place had been no other place than Vrindavana. Vrindavana was discovered in this way. If it is just imagination, then what an excellent deep and noble imagination! This imagination makes our life happy. This is not the imagination of a devotee, but a reality. Chaitanyadeva discovered Vrindavana, Radha's love for Krishna and at the same time that passion between devotee and God; he accepted that in his own life. That thirst or passion for God took the form in his life. On seeing this, people can realise the truth that love for God is not impossible and not even impracticable. Sri Ramakrishna says, *prema*, ecstatic love, is an extremely rare thing. Chaitanya had that love. When one has *prema* one forgets all outer things. One forgets the world. One even forgets one's own body, which is so dear to a being. If one drop of such love occurs in someone's life one becomes frantic for God. What a love or what a passion for God! Chaitanyadeva experienced it.

Sri Ramakrishna
The Soul of India

- *Sri Ramakrishna*
- *Sri Ramakrishna's Earliest Appraiser: Srinivas*
- *Sri Ramakrishna as Portrayed in Brahmo Journals*
- *Sri Ramakrishna: Householder or Sannyasin?*
- *Sri Ramakrishna, the Complete Teacher*
- *Sri Ramakrishna—Lived in and with God*
- *The Religion of Sri Ramakrishna*

Sri Ramakrishna

SRI RAMAKRISHNA WAS BORN GADADHAR CHATTOPADHYAYA IN THE village of Kamarpukur, approximately 60 miles from Calcutta, in the year 1836. His father, Khudiram, was poor but commanded respect from all classes of people in the village because of his character. Chandra Devi, Sri Ramakrishna's mother, was a simple woman who loved to feed people; no visitor could leave without eating whatever food she had to give. This sometimes meant she had nothing left for herself. The family was poor but happy.

Even as a boy Sri Ramakrishna was independent-minded. He did not like school, for, he said, at school you learned how to earn money, but nothing about God. He preferred to roam open fields outside the village—alone, or with other boys, singing with them, or staging popular dramas. He was a versatile artist with a degree of mastery in every form of art—singing, dancing, painting and so on. He loved nature. Once, the sight of a line of white cranes against dark monsoon clouds sent him into ecstasy. Thinking of God also sometimes sent him into ecstasy. Once, Sri Ramakrishna accompanied some elderly women to a temple dedicated to a Goddess, in a nearby village. The ladies asked Sri Ramakrishna to sing songs about Mother as they walked along. Listening to his songs, the ladies were enchanted. But at one point, Sri Ramakrishna stopped singing and stood still with tears streaming down his cheeks. He was in ecstasy!

On another occasion, Sri Ramakrishna, still a boy, was to play the role of Shiva in a drama in his village. When he appeared as Shiva on the stage, people greeted him with shouts of joy, for he looked like the real Shiva. Sri Ramakrishna too must have felt like Shiva, for he was lost in ecstasy. Not knowing what exactly was happening, people took alarm at his condition and the play did not even begin. They, however, felt relieved when they found that Sri Ramakrishna showed no signs of abnormality afterwards, and was, as ever, lively, intelligent and witty. They did not know why he behaved like this from time to time. At first, they thought it was hysteria, but they dismissed the idea when they noticed that the ecstasy was invariably the outcome of a deep spiritual experience. They always regarded Sri Ramakrishna as extraordinary. He was a mere boy, yet his comments on any topic were wise and far-sighted. He played his share of boyish pranks, but he never erred when he had to make a choice between right and wrong. Everybody recognised him as a rare combination of man and God. He was the pet of the whole village, but also an object of awe. An old man well-versed in the scriptures privately worshipped Sri Ramakrishna as an Avatara.

Sri Ramakrishna was seventeen when he first came to Calcutta. Meanwhile, his father had died and the whole family looked up to him to start earning to mitigate the financial hardship. His eldest brother, Ramkumar, who was in Calcutta, sent for him. Ramkumar ran a Sanskrit school and also worshipped deities at different places. He wanted Sri Ramakrishna to take Sanskrit lessons from him and assist him in worshipping deities. The object of both was to earn money—an object repugnant to Sri Ramakrishna. He flatly refused to do either. He said the only thing he was interested in was God-realisation. Ramkumar did not argue with him, for he knew arguing would be futile. Sri Ramakrishna was one who would not budge an inch from his position. For the next three years, Sri Ramakrishna did nothing but visit nearby temples where he sang devotional songs, and some families where he was much sought after because of his songs and funny stories.

In 1855, Rani Rashmani, a rich widow of Calcutta, founded a temple complex with Mother Kali as the chief deity, at Dakshineswar in the suburbs of Calcutta. She appointed Ramkumar as priest at the temple of Mother Kali. After much persuasion, Sri Ramakrishna agreed to help with dressing the deity. Hriday, his nephew, was his assistant in this work. On Ramkumar's retirement in 1856, Sri Ramakrishna took over as priest at the Kali Temple. As he worshipped Mother Kali, he began to question what Kali was—a piece of stone or Divinity in that form. If She was divine, could She not give some hint that She was pleased with his worship? He begged Mother Kali to let him know who or what She was. He would say, 'Mother, I am your child just as the seers of the past were. You revealed your true nature to them, Why should you not do the same to me? Are you neglecting me because I am ignorant? Can a mother love one child more than another?' As the days passed, his yearning for God increased. He would not sleep at night, and sometimes he even refused food. As the sun set, he would cry out, 'Mother, yet another day has passed and I have not seen you.' He would roll on the ground crying 'Mother'. He would rub his face on rough ground till it bled. Bystanders thought he had lost his mother and he was mourning the loss. Some thought he had gone mad. Luckily, Hriday looked after him, or else he would have died. It was becoming increasingly difficult for him to perform the formal worship, for he would burst into crying when he worshipped, and he gave every sign that he was not in his right mind. His condition was reported to the authorities. Rani Rashmani, accompanied by her son-in-law Mathur Babu, paid a surprise visit to see what the truth was. They were moved to see so much love of God in any human being at this age. They were convinced that he was no ordinary man, and left, giving instructions to the temple employees that Sri Ramakrishna was to be treated with the greatest respect.

But as the days passed, Sri Ramakrishna's impatience for a vision of Kali increased. Instead of performing the puja, he would go on crying, 'Mother, how long will you make me suffer? Are you heartless?' One day, as he was crying like this, his eyes fell on the sword, meant for animal sacrifice, hanging on the wall. Seizing the sword he said, 'Mother, look, I'm going to kill myself, for life no longer has any meaning to me!' As he was about to kill himself with the sword, he, in Sri Ramakrishna's own words (as quoted by Isherwood), 'had a marvellous vision of the Mother, and fell down unconscious... It was as if houses, doors, temples and everything else vanished altogether; as if there was nothing anywhere! And, what I saw was an infinite shore-less sea of light; a sea that was consciousness. However far and in whatever direction I looked, I saw shining waves, one after another, coming towards me. They were raging and storming upon me with great speed. Very soon they were upon me; they made me sink down into unknown depths. I panted and struggled and lost consciousness.' After that, Mother Kali was always alive, a real mother, and the relationship between them was like that between an indulgent mother and a petulant child. Ramakrishna, like a small child, could not bear to let Mother out of his sight even for a moment. Mother also seemed to demand his presence all the time. Mother and son talked, teased each other, laughed, and played together, though to others all this seemed nonsense. It was, however, clear that, physically, Sri Ramakrishna was no longer able to perform any formal puja. He was, therefore, relieved of his duties as priest.

But Mother seemed to possess him: he forgot his surroundings; he forgot even his physical needs. He would not eat or sleep. Hriday forced him to eat; otherwise he would have died of starvation. He was a mere skeleton now. Yet, most of the time he was in ecstasy. Soon, word spread that he had gone mad. When his mother came to know of this, she sent word that he should be sent back home immediately. Under his mother's care, Sri Ramakrishna slowly improved. At least, there was no sign of insanity in him. On the advice of her neighbours, Sri Ramakrishna's mother arranged his marriage, which surprisingly, Sri Ramakrishna welcomed. Still more surprising, he suggested the girl who was to be his bride and where she was to be found. Sri Ramakrishna was then twenty-four while the bride turned out to be the five-year-old Sarada of Jayrambati, a neighbouring village.

Soon after his marriage, Sri Ramakrishna returned to Dakshineswar. With Mother Kali's consent, he now started practising different branches of Hinduism, one after another. For each branch, a guru arrived just as he was about to start the practice. One peculiarity about him was that he reached the goal that the branch concerned had in view in the shortest possible time. Hinduism's most difficult path is known to be non-dualism. Few ever attempt it, or having attempted, succeed in realising its goal. Sri Ramakrishna, however, mastered it in one day while his teacher Totapuri, on his own admission, had taken forty years to do so.

When you reach the goal of non-dualism, you attain *nirvikalpa samadhi*. Samadhi is ecstasy, something with which Sri Ramakrishna had been familiar from his boyhood. Samadhi is of two kinds, *savikalpa* and *nirvikalpa*. In *savikalpa samadhi*, the devotee is in communion with his Lord, but does not get lost in Him. He is like a bee sitting on a flower and sucking its honey. In *nirvikalpa samadhi*, he is like salt melting into water. The knower and the known become one. The individual merges into the collective, like a drop of water falling into the sea. The sense of separateness disappears. There is only the sense of Oneness, there is only one Self. Unity of existence—this is what one experiences through *nirvikalpa samadhi*. Sri Ramakrishna attained this Oneness, and, as such, saw himself in everything and in every being. When two boatmen hit each other, Sri Ramakrishna felt he had been hit and he cried out in pain. Surprisingly, his back bore marks of the assault too. Seeing someone pluck a flower, Sri Ramakrishna felt his heart was being plucked out. When a man beat his bullock, Sri Ramakrishna rolled on the ground in pain. This is what it means to be a non-dualist.

But what exactly happens when one is in *samadhi*? It is like too much light blinding you for the time being; you cannot feel anything else. When all your consciousness is concentrated on one object, you become temporarily unconscious of other objects. If you are experiencing *savikalpa samadhi*, you have a vague perception of yourself and the object of your love, the Lord. You are not aware of anything else. If the samadhi is *nirvikalpa*, the knower, the known, and the knowledge—all three become one. When carried to completion, your consciousness becomes Pure Consciousness, free from its association with the sense-organs.

Pure Consciousness, like the midday sun, is too bright for the eyes to see. It is difficult for us to comprehend. But it can be seen as a beatific smile on the face of the person in *nirvikalpa samadhi*. The man is otherwise apparently dead.

Sri Ramakrishna's *samadhi* perplexed many. Village people said, 'Here is one who dies seven times a day, yet revives each time. Isn't it wonderful?' Dr Mahendra Lal Sarkar, a pioneer in Indian scientific research, was puzzled but not impressed. Sri Ramakrishna told him that he was not simulating. Yet, Sarkar rightly decided to test him. Amidst protests from those present he thrust his fingers into the fixed eyeball of Sri Ramakrishna. Sri Ramakrishna did not even blink. He was not breathing, his heart was not beating. To all appearances he was a dead man, yet he wore a bewitching smile on his face! Sarkar never understood this phenomenon and nobody else did, either. When the *samadhi* passed, Sri Ramakrishna was again his usual self, pouring out words of wisdom spiced with humour and interspersed with soul-stirring songs, stories and anecdotes. There is never a dull moment when you are with Sri Ramakrishna!

Sri Ramakrishna also experienced a whole range of *bhavas* and *mahabhavas* which all mystics who are dualists experience. His world of mystic experience was infinite, just as his love of God assumed myriads of forms. The ways to God are not limited; there are as many ways as there are men and women. No one has kept track of all the ways Sri Ramakrishna followed to reach God, nor of the visions and ecstasies he was rewarded with. He walked the well-trod paths, but he was also driven by his love of God to discover many paths long forgotten and no longer heard of. To give an example, he once decided to practise the *dasya bhava* in which God is your Master and you are His servant. Sri Ramakrishna chose as his model the monkey Hanuman who knew nothing but his Master, not even what day or time it was. Sri Ramakrishna wanted to be another Hanuman. He was not content with loving God as intensely as Hanuman did; he felt he must also look like him. He dressed like Hanuman, complete with a long tail, walked on all fours, dropped his human speech, spent most of the time on trees, and so on. If people thought he was crazy, they could not be blamed.

The next thing he did was to practise Islam, something unprecedented for a Hindu. As always, a guru arrived to help him with the practice. He said his *Namaz*, read the Koran, dressed like a Muslim, even toyed with the idea of eating beef. But Mathur told him Islam did not require Muslims to eat beef, as beef-eating was no part of Islam. This went on for three days. Finally, Sri Ramakrishna had a vision of Mohammed, a figure surrounded by light. Sri Ramakrishna had the same experience with Jesus and Chaitanya, both merging into him. The mystic experiences Sri Ramakrishna had through the practice of those religions convinced him that all religions were like different paths leading to the same goal. Religions differed in details, but in essence they were one and the same. You might like your own religion better than another, but you have no right to think that your religion is the best or the only true religion. Holiness is not the monopoly of any particular religion; every religion has produced great saints and sages. People tend to argue about God and other religious matters. According to Sri Ramakrishna, this is a waste of time; this also shows that such people are ignorant. When bees settle on a flower, they no longer buzz; they are quiet and happy. Because those people have had no experience, they love to talk, though they do not know what they are talking about. Religion is love of God. 'Love God sincerely and intensely. Weep for Him; He will then reveal Himself to you',—this was the burden of his message. He favoured no particular creed or dogma; no particular ritual or practice; he rejected none either. Even things seemingly bizarre were acceptable to him, provided they were prompted by a genuine love of God.

Sri Ramakrishna used to say, 'When flowers are in blossom, bees start coming on their own.' This is exactly what happened in the case of Sri Ramakrishna. Soon, word spread that there was a remarkable man at Dakshineswar who always seemed to live with God. The ecstasies he had were also a much-talked-about subject. Curiously, a Christian missionary serving as principal in a big college in Calcutta was the first, on record, to have talked about these ecstasies to his students. Next to be struck by Sri Ramakrishna's unusual spiritual character was Keshab Chandra Sen, a highly Westernised person and himself the head of a powerful religious community. He wrote about Sri Ramakrishna in his journals, quoting his wonderful teachings. One by one, leading figures among Calcutta's intelligentsia saw him and were impressed. Finally, a few young men came, all of good families and with a fair amount of education. Sri Ramakrishna received them as if he were waiting for them. He was, in fact, anxious to have some followers who not only understood but lived his message. First and foremost, he taught his wife, Sarada Devi, who joined him when she was in her late teens. Sri Ramakrishna was awed by her spiritual potential and trained her so that she could take his place when he was gone. Among the young men he trained was Naren, who, as Swami Vivekananda, later became a world teacher, as Sri Ramakrishna had predicted. He initiated some of these young men into monastic vows and later, with the blessings of Sarada Devi, these young men, led by Vivekananda, were to form the nucleus of the future Ramakrishna Order.

After Sri Ramakrishna's death in 1886, they formed themselves into the Ramakrishna Order and a little later founded the Sri Ramakrishna Math and Ramakrishna Mission. This twin organisation, with branches now spread all over the world, emphasises God-realisation and service to God in man. It regards both of these objectives as equally important for the welfare of all. The Math and Mission do not believe in conversion. That is why among its rank and file can be found men and women from many different countries, communities and religions. It is the epitome of Sri Ramakrishna's ideal of Oneness.

Mahendra Nath Gupta (M), a popular school teacher, had started coming to Sri Ramakrishna a short while before these earnest young men arrived. He had been greatly disturbed in mind by some family problems and had been contemplating suicide. But Sri Ramakrishna's personality and his words so fascinated him that he found a meaning and purpose in life and became a new man altogether. He was in the habit of maintaining a diary, and his acquaintance with Sri Ramakrishna had been such a momentous event in his life that he naturally entered in his diary everything that happened during his many visits to him. These entries were for his own use. He never intended to make them public. But under pressure from many people, he tentatively sent some expanded diary entries to different journals. They at once became popular and there was a demand for more such material. One by one, M published five volumes in Bengali, entitled *Sri Ramakrishna Kathamrita*. This book was later translated into English by Swami Nikhilananda and published under the title '*The Gospel of Sri Ramakrishna*'.

The book has been translated into many other languages and is now a source of inspiration for people all over the world.

Sri Ramakrishna's Earliest Appraiser: Srinivas

ALL AVAILABLE RECORDS TESTIFY TO SRI RAMAKRISHNA'S GREAT popularity in his village. This popularity began even when he was a mere baby. Womenfolk of his village would daily come and shower their caresses on him. They had their own children; still this visit was a 'must' with them. They felt miserable if they missed seeing him for a single day. Everyone treated him as if he was exclusively hers. They would vie with one another in this, and sometimes there would be so many of them eagerly waiting their turns to caress him that for a long time his own mother, Chandramani, would have no opportunity to do so herself.

As he grew into a boy, this popularity increased, and he became the idol of the whole village. There was no one in the village who did not regard him with special affection and kindliness. There was no home in which he was not welcome. Wherever he went, he radiated peace and joy. Everyone sought his company—young and old, high and low. Boys of his age followed him to the mango-grove outside the village to receive lessons in drama and music. Women gathered round him to listen to his readings from the *Ramayana* and the *Mahabharata* or to hear him sing. Older men loved his company for his lively conversation, which was also full of wisdom and humour. Except when he performed appointed duties connected with the worship of the family deity, he was rarely at home. His laughter rang through the village; his songs filled its air. He lived as if he did not belong to a particular family, but to the whole village.

But however popular he was, Sri Ramakrishna was not above playing boyish pranks. There is the story of how he once duped a neighbour who boasted that no male visitor could ever enter the inner apartments of his house. Disguised as a lady-weaver, Sri Ramakrishna one evening appeared before this gentleman and sought a night's shelter. He said 'she' had come to the marketplace with other lady-weavers to sell thread, but as evening fell, they had left 'her' behind, and 'she' had now nowhere to go. So complete was the verisimilitude and so convincing was the case presented, that the gentleman had not even a moment's hesitation in inviting Sri Ramakrishna to go into the inner apartments of the house and stay with the womenfolk there. The deception was not detected until Sri Ramakrishna's elder brother arrived there. As Sri Ramakrishna had not returned home, anxiety was felt on his account, and his elder brother came out to look for him. He went from house to house and called out for Sri Ramakrishna. When he arrived at the house in question, Sri Ramakrishna answered his brother's call. One imagines that he did this rather loudly, for he must have been anxious for everybody to know where he was!

The stir that the discovery created in the household can very well be imagined. What a blow it must have been to the boastful head of the family! The whole village must have had a good laugh over his discomfiture. As for Sri Ramakrishna, he became dearer still to the village as a result of this incident.

But Sri Ramakrishna's popularity did not rest on such pranks only. Neither did it rest on his sweet innocence, his songs, his power of mimicry, or his sense of humour only. There was another side to his nature, which, too, contributed much to his popularity. This was his great wisdom.

Though still a boy, he often spoke like one with a mature mind. People in the village had learnt to respect him because of his judgement and understanding. He showed an uncanny power of solving problems that baffled scholars. If there was a discussion in the village on a subject of social and religious import, there would often appear a deep and unbridgeable gulf between opposing views. In the course of discussions, tempers would rise, arguments would become involved, and the issue more and more complicated. Just then Sri Ramakrishna might make a casual remark as if in spite of himself. At once, all arguments would stop, for as everybody saw, the remark indicated a possible meeting-ground between the differing viewpoints. He had a knack of ignoring superficialities and getting down to the root of a problem. He would make a brief analysis of the problem, and the solution would then become obvious to everybody. The fact that so obvious a solution had not occurred to others would then seem very strange.

Once, a great debate took place at the house of the Lahas—his next door neighbours. The occasion was a ceremony connected with a death in the family. As was customary in those days, scholars from several places were invited. Many eminent men came, and soon discussions started. The issues chosen were of perennial interest—issues concerning God, man's relation with God, life's purpose, etc. The discussions were long and acrimonious, for the scholars represented different schools of philosophy, and their differences in outlook were sharp. The whole village had turned out to listen to the debate. As might be expected, Sri Ramakrishna with his friends was also present. They had come merely out of curiosity, for they did not want to miss this opportunity to see the great scholars that had come and hear them argue. As the debate proceeded, the main issues were soon lost sight of, and the scholars got bogged down in arguments which hardly had any bearing on the subjects they were discussing. Sri Ramakrishna was listening with rapt attention, as was everybody else; but while others were not able to follow the arguments, he was. And, it must have been a shock to him to see that the scholars were more concerned with the shell of an argument rather than its substance.

While this was going on, something happened that no one including Sri Ramakrishna ever expected. Sri Ramakrishna, a mere boy, found himself making some remarks that took the whole assembly by surprise. A particular point in the scriptures was being discussed by the scholars, and no conclusion was in sight. Sri Ramakrishna, who was intently following the discussion, said to a pundit known to him, 'Can't the point at issue be decided this way?' The pundit heard what Sri Ramakrishna had to say and felt convinced that it was the right conclusion. He then told about it to some other scholars, who realised the correctness of the solution offered by Sri Ramakrishna. They felt that it was the only possible solution regarding the disputed point and explained it to all others. All the scholars present unanimously admitted that it was the only rational solution and expressed surprise and satisfaction at the performance of the boy. They made enquiries about the family background of the boy, predicted a great future for him, and offered him their blessings. The whole village was excited and proud; the talk of what Sri Ramakrishna had done was on everybody's lips. But Sri Ramakrishna himself was least concerned; he was hardly conscious that he had done something unusual.

Sri Ramakrishna was now a real hero to the people of his village. Everybody knew about his great commonsense, his wisdom, his ability to disentangle a problem from unnecessary details. Still, no one in his wildest thoughts imagined that he was capable of performing this astonishing feat. They did not know how to explain this. They were happy and proud, though perplexed, at this wonderful and inexplicable capacity of Sri Ramakrishna.

Did anyone of them ever suspect that this might have been possible because of some divine power working through him? Did it ever occur to them that all that Sri Ramakrishna did could be explained, if only it was accepted that he had something of the divine in him? There is no evidence that anyone in the village, nor even his closest associates, thought that Sri Ramakrishna was anything beyond a young boy of some extraordinary intelligence. Some perhaps thought that he was a little crazy, and some of the unusual things that he did or said, according to them, stemmed from his craziness. That he had a streak of divinity in him, that all his lovable qualities flowed from some divine source within him, that he was a man with a divine mission, who was destined to influence large masses of people, no one in the village ever believed or dreamt of.

There was, however, one exception. This was Srinivas, or Chinoo, the conch-shell dealer. He was the only man in the whole village who knew who Sri Ramakrishna was. Of all of Sri Ramakrishna's acquaintances, he was the first to recognise Sri Ramakrishna's divinity. So far as this goes, he occupies a unique position. Although by caste Srinivas was a conch-shell dealer, in reality, he ran a small grocer's shop. He had a modest income, and was able to make both ends meet with some difficulty. He had no pretensions to scholarship, but he was well-read in the *Bhagavata* and similar sacred books of the dualistic school. He was older than Sri Ramakrishna by many years— the records say that he might as well have been Sri Ramakrishna's grandfather. In spite of this difference in age, and in spite of the fact that he belonged to an inferior caste, there was the deepest friendship between the two. Sri Ramakrishna had many friends in the village—in fact, everyone in the village was his friend, irrespective of age and caste, but his friendship with Chinoo was of a special kind. There was not a single day when he did not call at Chinoo's house. Chinoo, too, would eagerly wait for his visit. As soon as Sri Ramakrishna came, he would rush forward to greet him and make him sit. He might have had important work in hand, but that would not deter him from being engrossed with Sri Ramakrishna. Even if a customer came, he would refuse to attend to him. For hours together, they would talk; while talking, they would be completely oblivious of their surroundings. Sri Ramakrishna would sometimes climb on to Chinoo's shoulders, and this Chinoo would consider a great favour. He was a fat big man, dark complexioned, with all his hair grey. Sri Ramakrishna, on the other hand, was a small lean boy, fair, and good-looking. The contrast between them was most striking. People would wonder about what was the common ground between them, that they found joy in each other's company. Sri Ramakrishna called Chinoo 'Dada' (elder brother), and to Chinoo, Sri Ramakrishna was a 'Bhai' (brother). When Sri Ramakrishna was with him, Chinoo forgot his age and his family cares; he then behaved as if he was a boy himself.

He would feed Sri Ramakrishna with his own hands, and feed him with the best sweets that he could afford. To him, this gave the greatest satisfaction. He would keep his eyes fixed on Sri Ramakrishna as if he was hypnotised. Often, tears would come to his eyes from the joy that he felt.

While talking, they would often get excited, and sometimes they would have sharp and bitter disagreements, too. For long they would argue, each maintaining his position with tenacity and vehemence. Chinoo would argue from the orthodox point of view, drawing on scriptures and his lifelong experience. Sri Ramakrishna, on the other hand, would argue from intuition and commonsense, without leaning towards any particular point of view. No wonder that there was disagreement between them.

Chinoo loved Sri Ramakrishna, loved him more than his life. He also sensed that, beneath his little body, Sri Ramakrishna hid a great soul. He was filled with awe for this soul; still, where vital issues were concerned, he held his own view, and he did not see why he should forsake them. Sri Ramakrishna, though full of love and respect for Chinoo, thought that Chinoo was being unnecessarily an obscurant. He could not see how so good a soul could be so obstinate. One imagines that, besides arguments, he also used his characteristic humour to demolish Chinoo's case. As is well known, his humour could be more deadly than his arguments. However that may be, the clashes between them often left them in a fury. Tempers would be so frayed that they would refuse to talk to each other. They would rush away from each other, giving the impression that a complete rupture had taken place between them. That they were the best of friends would then seem a thing of the past.

But the next day, the picture would change completely. Chinoo would begin to miss Sri Ramakrishna very much soon. He would be sorry that he had quarrelled the previous day. He would hope and pray that Sri Ramakrishna would not mind it, and come to his house as usual. Again and again, he would look out and see if he was not already in sight. Sri Ramakrishna, too, would feel the same. It was impossible for him to stay away from Chinoo. Soon, he would wend his way to Chinoo's. Scenes of tumultuous joy would mark their meeting. They would rush forward to meet each other. Chinoo would snatch up Sri Ramakrishna in his arms, with tears rolling down his cheeks. He would feel an overwhelming sense of joy and relief that Sri Ramakrishna had forgiven him. Soon, he would buy him the choicest sweets and feed him. Discussions also would begin and then arguments. Almost the same scene would enact itself again. Thus, day after day, they would meet, argue, and quarrel.

Although a humble man, Chinoo commanded respect because of his character. A God-fearing man, he cared more about God than about anything else. God was his sole passion, and he had spent his whole life searching for Him. When he first met Sri Ramakrishna, he was drawn towards him by his appearance, his music, his cheerful nature, etc. But when he came to know him closely, he was struck by his other qualities. He saw, for instance, that Sri Ramakrishna knew more than what the scriptures that he had read contained. Profoundest truths fell from his lips easily and naturally. He spoke as if a great wise man was speaking. His words had an irresistible charm and power. They brought light as well as peace unto his soul.

Sri Ramakrishna lifted his soul on to a new plane altogether. What he had vaguely yearned for seemed to be within his grasp now.

It is true that he had difficulties in accepting Sri Ramakrishna in the beginning. As has been seen, he was not in the habit of accepting a statement from Sri Ramakrishna without challenging it or examining it in all its implications. This involved entering into long and heated arguments, but he risked it. In fairness to Sri Ramakrishna, it may be added that he was the last man to demand unquestioning acquiescence. As was seen in later years, he preferred a disciple who questioned and argued, rather than one who never questioned and, therefore, never understood.

Through daily contact, Chinoo had understood the power that Sri Ramakrishna represented. He understood that he was a born teacher, who was destined to mould the spiritual life of others. He had seen in his own case how he had transformed him. The more he studied Sri Ramakrishna, the more he wondered at the magnitude of his powers. He at once recognised that a great teacher was at work in the form of Sri Ramakrishna. He felt sure that he was going to do great things in later years. It was his regret that he would not live to see him do them, for he was old and would soon die. But he wished to welcome him and accord him due honour on his own behalf and on behalf of the future generations. He wished to be the first in this—a privilege he very much wished for himself.

A wealth of details is given in the books as to how he did it. One day, with the best flowers and sweets that he could procure, he took Sri Ramakrishna into the fields. He chose a spot where he thought he was not likely to be seen by others. What he was going to do was so intimate, so personal, that he was anxious that others should not know about it. This was going to be his final surrender to Sri Ramakrishna. It was a privilege, also an achievement. He wanted to have it all to himself. First, he fed Sri Ramakrishna with the sweets that he had brought; then, he knelt before him and worshipped him with flowers. Next, with folded hands and tears trickling down his cheeks, he began to pray to him. What he said was more or less to this effect: 'Oh Lord, it is not for me to judge you. I do not know who you are, but I am convinced that you are born to lead mankind to light. You already have performed some miracles, but you are going to perform many more in the future. Alas, I will not live to see them. I am old, and will soon depart this life. But before I die, I wish you to know what I feel about you. I wish to offer myself at your feet. Please, accept me, please, bless me.'

It is a pity that what Sri Ramakrishna said in reply is not recorded. But did he say anything at all? Most probably he did—he perhaps scolded Chinoo for the foolish things he was saying. As was his wont in later years, he ridiculed the suggestion that he was divine. But there are also instances in which he allowed it, even enjoyed it. His reaction depended upon many things, especially upon the character of the person from whom it came.

Thus, it happens that it was Chinoo who first recognised Sri Ramakrishna's divinity. This appraisal was unique, because it came from a humble tradesman. Later, many scholars and religious leaders loudly proclaimed Sri Ramakrishna as an incarnation of God. But Chinoo, the small village grocer, had the distinction of being the first to do so.

Sri Ramakrishna as Portrayed in Brahmo Journals

WHO FIRST INTRODUCED SRI RAMAKRISHNA TO THE PUBLIC? Curiously enough, not an orthodox Hindu, but one who was scarcely a Hindu—Keshab Chandra Sen. The great Brahmo leader first met Sri Ramakrishna on 15 March 1875. He was at once so fascinated by Sri Ramakrishna that he often sought his company in later years. Either he himself visited Sri Ramakrishna at Dakshineswar or had him come to his meetings and conferences. He loved to hear him talk, and whatever Sri Ramakrishna said impressed him deeply. Many feel that Keshab's religious thoughts underwent a distinct change after he came in touch with Sri Ramakrishna. There is some proof of this in the fact that like Sri Ramakrishna, Keshab too began to refer to God as Mother in his later speeches and writings. He also had interesting accounts of Sri Ramakrishna's visits to the Brahmo Samaj, with his talks, published in his journals.

One such journal was *Dharma Tatwa* in Bengali. Readers might be interested to read a report which appeared in its issue of 1 November 1879, about Sri Ramakrishna's visit to a Brahmo gathering. The report is taken from the Bengali book entitled *Sama samaika Dristitey Sri Ramakrishna Paramahamsa* by Brajendra Bandopadhyaya and Sajanikanta Das, General Printers and Publishers Ltd.

'On *Bhadra* 31 last, Saka 1801 (1879 A.A.) 25 to 30 Brahmos met at the holy garden-retreat of Belgharia. The much-respected Sri

Ramakrishna Paramahamsa happened to grace the occasion. Everyone present on this occasion saw with bewilderment what fathomless love he has for God and how it often takes him into flights of super-consciousness. There is not a second person among us today in whom one can see such evidence of divine bliss. *Srimat Bhagavata* thus recounts the signs of God-intoxicated devotees: 'While meditating on God, devotees sometimes weep, sometimes laugh; sometimes go into raptures, or talk of miraculous things; sometimes they dance, or chant His name, or shed tears of joy as they sing about Him.' In the Paramahamsa are all these signs present in their fullness.

'On this day he discussed profound subjects like God-realisation, yoga and love of God, besides singing songs. He was often overwhelmed with emotions, and completely lost his self-control. Sometimes, he went into ecstasy and sat inert like a statue. Sometimes, he laughed, wept or danced; sometimes he behaved as if he was drunk or was no more than a mere child. While he was in his emotionally intoxicated state, he said words of deep spiritual meaning, leaving everyone stunned. When you see him in this divine mood you feel yourself a chastened man—all your wicked tendencies gone, your atheism crushed.

'The Paramahamsa also visited the Master (i.e. Keshab Chandra Sen) in his house on the afternoon of Sunday, the 6th. On that occasion too, there was no lack of his characteristic devotional fervour. The only thing one missed was his exquisite dances. He sang soul-stirring songs in his melodious voice which moved even the stoniest heart present. Subsequently, a picture was taken catching him in his ecstatic mood. He fell into a trance at the mere mention of the words "Satchidananda Ghana" (i.e. God, the embodiment of Existence, Knowledge and Bliss).'

It was given to the great Brahmo leader, Keshab Chandra Sen, to draw public attention to the luminous personality of Sri Ramakrishna. He did so through the journals of the Brahmo Samaj in which he had articles appear dealing with Sri Ramakrishna's life and teachings. He liked Sri Ramakrishna so much that whenever he had an opportunity, he visited him accompanied by friends and followers. Often, he had Sri Ramakrishna come to special Brahmo services, for Sri Ramakrishna's very presence made such services alive with God-consciousness.

In the same issue, we also gave an English version of a report which had appeared in a Bengali journal of the time conducted by the Brahmo Samaj, *Dharma Tatwa*. The report was about Sri Ramakrishna's visit to a special Brahmo service. Here, we reproduce another report from the same journal concerning a visit which the Brahmo leader himself made to Sri Ramakrishna at Dakshineswar on a special occasion. The report, translated into English, runs as follows:

> Last Wednesday (Kartick 13) was the full-moon night of autumn. The day was marked by the celebration of the autumn festival. First, there was a service at the temple in the forenoon. The notes struck during the service indicated scholarship as well as love of God. The idea was stressed that God's presence might be felt in food. Food was cited as proof of God's existence and His concern for His children.
>
> This was followed by a boat trip made to Dakshineswar at 1 p.m. About eighty pilgrims including ten to twelve ladies made this trip. They occupied a houseboat, six *Bhowalias* (boats made in Bhowal, Dacca) and two small crafts. The houseboat was decorated with flowers and festoons. The journey began in the midst of singing accompanied by trumpets, drums, cymbals, etc. As the pilgrims reached the landing place at Dakshineswar, the Paramahamsa's nephew Hriday boarded the houseboat singing. He sang, "Who is this man singing about Hari on the bank of the Ganges? It must be Nitai, the bestower of divine love, else how is it that scorched hearts are being cooled and the wicked are

being subdued by the name of Hari?' He sang and danced in a state of frenzy. Several devotees joined in this. It was a most touching sight.

Later, the whole party proceeded towards the Paramahamnsa's room. They first went round the places hallowed by the religious disciplines he had gone through there, and then came to his room. As they moved around, they sang the song. 'One who is the very embodiment of divine bliss . . .' The Paramahamsa went into a trance when he saw the assemblage of devotees and heard them sing this song. On regaining normal consciousness, he dwelt on the subject of Supreme God and the struggle one has to make to overcome one's ego. In this connection, he made some profound observations.

Next, a brief service was held at the landing-place. Keshab stood up and spoke with special reference to the moon and the Ganges. His speech showed, among other things, how great his love for God was. Even the most unfeeling among the audience were touched, and felt a rush of deep emotions. The Paramahamsa was delighted to hear the sermon and applauded Keshab again and again.

After the sermon, a newly composed song about God as Mother was beautifully sung. Moved by this, the Paramahamsa began to dance, overwhelmed with joy. Later, he sang some songs which induced in the people a God-intoxicated state. One of the songs he sang was—'Man, if you want to enjoy life with God's name on your lips, then come here . . .' As he sang this song, he cast a spell over the entire audience. It was a sight too holy for words. At this point the Paramahamsa stood up and fell into a trance again.

The party started back for Calcutta at eight in the night. This year's autumn festival was much more enjoyable and inspiring than last year's.

Like the *Dharmatatwa* there was another Brahmo journal called the *Sulabha Samachar* which often published reports about Sri Ramakrishna's activities. It was a more powerful and popular journal than the *Dharmatatwa*, and was regularly read by both the Hindus and Brahmos. This was because it had some very capable Editors, who used their talents to preach the particular religious viewpoint represented by the Brahmo Samaj and also to preach the broad spectrum of Hindu thoughts common to all sects. It was perhaps this fact which made the journal take a very favourable notice of Sri Ramakrishna and his teachings although he was by no means a Brahmo and his pronouncements were not always sympathetic to the Brahmo Movement. It is significant that there was hardly any Brahmo journal of the time which did not at one time or another publish accounts of Sri Ramakrishna's life and teachings. While most of these accounts were certainly inspired by the great Brahmo leader, Keshab Chandra Sen, some, one suspects, might have been written by the leader himself. Below is one such report which appeared in the *Sulabha Samachar* in its issue dated 30 July 1881 under the heading 'Sri Ramakrishna Paramahamsa of Dakshineswar':

> Readers have many times heard the name of the above saint. He is living at the Kali temple of Rani Rashmoni in the village of Dakshineswar about three miles to the north of Calcutta. Every time we see him we are struck by his elevated life and character. In our estimate, he is truly a man of God-realisation. We doubt if there is a second man like him in this country. Through Yoga he has reached a stage in which his mind is constantly absorbed in God. To him God is, as material possessions are to us. Just as we constantly think and talk of our family, money, prestige, etc., he thinks and talks of God and God alone all the time. He is as simple as a child. Often, so intense is his love of God that he is simply overwhelmed by it. With Hari's name

on his lips, he now dances with ecstasy as Chaitanya did; next moment, he calls on God as Mother with touching affection. When he does so, one can see in him the example of an ideal Shakta. Sometimes, he also worships God as Brahman, i.e. in His formless aspect. Then, he is completely immersed in God-consciousness like the old Yogis. He has thus, different attitudes at different times towards God. But the interesting point is that whatever may be his attitude at a given moment, it is so complete, so overpowering, that it makes him lose all outer consciousness. His body then becomes inert as if it were a block of wood. Despite the change that comes over his body, his mind remains steeped in God-consciousness. He believes both in God with form and God without form. But he emphatically declares that if he is mad about anything, it is certainly not the clay-limbed Kali or Krishna. The Kali or Krishna that he worships and is so excited about is without form; it is made of spirit and can be felt only in mind. He says that the formless God is like the infinite ocean. Sometimes, waves appear on this ocean corresponding to a devotee's particular spiritual moods. The forms that God takes on are the products of those waves. Recently, he came to the house of a respectable gentleman in Calcutta. During this visit he created an atmosphere in which almost all present felt compelled to join in a mass dance in praise of God. On another occasion he accompanied us on a steamer-journey. On this occasion he confided to us some of his mystic experiments which left us completely speechless with wonder. He said that at one time in the past he saw himself as a black baby-cat snuggling up to his mother and mewing. The Mother, in her turn, was pleased at this and licked his body and talked to him affectionately. Those were days when night was for him a very happy time. Sometimes, he considered himself a woman. As a woman, he looked upon God as husband and spent a happy time talking to Him with love. There were again times when he felt as if he was being overwhelmed by the ocean of Brahman. He then felt he was submerged in the water of Satchidananda (Existence–Knowledge–Bliss). When he was in this state, it became impossible for him to take care of his body. Even such simple things as eating were not possible for him. If ever the intensity of this state abated a bit, he would tell his attendant, 'Hurry and give me some food now; I am slightly better now, give it rightaway.' But hardly had he finished when he would again be overwhelmed by the ocean of Brahman. When this happened he was helpless, as helpless as a man caught in a flood. As if a high tide had again come over the ocean of Brahman and he was being carried away by it! He was trying to catch at something, but there was nothing he could catch at. He again fell down unconscious as before. God played tricks with him. The other day he was with us on board a steamer when somebody came along with a telescope and asked him to look through it. He was annoyed. He said angrily, 'My mind is now absorbed in Brahman, I am very happy in this state; why should I withdraw my mind from Brahman in order to look through the telescope? Is it such a novel thing that I should forgo the joy that I am now having?'

How sublime and new are his thoughts! How wonderful and varied are the moods one can see in him! If one were to describe them, one would then use all the columns of the *Sulabha*. Today, we are presenting to the readers only a brief account of those moods and thoughts. We hope readers will enjoy reading it.

Sri Ramakrishna: Householder or Sannyasin?

'Was Sri Ramakrishna a householder, or a sannyasin?' This is a ridiculous question. He was the King of Sannyasins, the Emperor of Renunciation. He could not even touch a coin. The wealthy Marwari devotee, Lachminarayan, wanted to give him ten thousand rupees. Living on alms, penniless, depending only on God, Sri Ramakrishna would not accept it. The rule for sannyasins is *aparigraha*, non-acceptance of gifts. But in order to test Sarada Devi, he asked her if she would like to accept the money. She also refused. She was the Empress of Renunciation. Though she never came to the forefront, preferred to remain always veiled, hidden, she too had renounced the world—silently, secretly.

Sri Ramakrishna, by the performance of the *viraja homa* ceremony, had taken the vows of sannyas, renouncing all worldly desires. Sarada Devi used to say that renunciation was Sri Ramakrishna's most prominent characteristic. He had renounced everything through the ceremony of the *homa* fire, had made an offering to Kali, the Divine Mother, of his good and evil, sin and virtue and even his very self. Truth, for him was dharma, religion and righteousness. Swami Vivekananda used to say, 'For Truth everything can be given up, but one must not give up Truth for anything.'

Still, one may ask, if renunciation is Ramakrishna's most prominent characteristic, why did he not renounce family life as sannyasins do? There are several marks of a traditional sannyasin. Ordinarily, a sannyasin either shaves his head or wears his hair in matted locks; he wears a *guerrua (saffron coloured)* cloth, carries a *kamandalu* (certain type of water pitcher) and a staff; he lives in a monastery and begs for his food. Surprisingly, Sri Ramakrishna did not do any of these things. He was married and did not renounce his wife. He chewed pan and smoked tobacco, dressed in an ordinary manner, and slept on a bed. He was unable to go anywhere without a carriage. He mixed with the influential and wealthy. How could he live this way and still be a sannyasin?

This question naturally arises. But before we can know the answer to this, we must understand what renunciation is. Renunciation is not giving up betel leaf and tobacco; it is not going about barefooted; it is not refraining from eating meat. Mirabai used to sing a song which said in essence that outer renunciation is not real renunciation. Inner, mental renunciation is the real renunciation. 'Turn your thought to God, love Him—that is real renunciation,' accords Mirabai.

Many have a wrong conception of the word 'renunciation'. They look for its outward marks. If outward renunciation were real renunciation, the beggar on the street would be the greatest renouncer of all. His poverty would be a mark of renunciation. But we find that the poor beggar is holding on to his tattered rags and cracked begging-bowl for dear life. If anyone touches them he will create a big scene.

Poverty and renunciation are not the same thing. Renunciation means giving up the lesser for the greater good. It means that poverty is freely chosen for the sake of an ideal. Those who are dedicated to science think nothing of their physical comfort. In the same way, those who are dedicated to the search for God consider worldly enjoyment contemptible. Both of these—the man dedicated to science and the man dedicated to God are renouncers. They are expert in their own disciplines. Their minds are so engrossed in their work that they are indifferent to bodily comforts. Renunciation has come natural to them.

The royal sage, Janaka, said 'I am the ruler of Mithila. If Mithila were destroyed today, nothing that is mine would be lost.' He had no attachment whatsoever to his kingdom. Non-attachment is a sign of renunciation. What I have or what I do not have is of no importance to me if I am a person of renunciation. He who lives a life of luxury but has no desire for sense objects is a renouncer. But a person, living in poverty may still hanker after enjoyment; such a person is a 'bhogi', a sensual person and not a renouncer.

Sri Ramakrishna's mind was immersed in the bliss of Brahman; worldly joys held no attraction for him. There was no place in his mind for anything but God. He had no body-consciousness at all. Our scriptures say that a knower of Brahman is like a mad person. Sri Ramakrishna was this kind of madman. It didn't matter to him if he wore the white cloth of a householder or the *gerrua* cloth of a sannyasin. Many times, he would wear nothing at all. He had no need to wear the garb of an ascetic. A true sannyasin is not to be known by his appearance—his dress, his name. His life and character are the only proof of his renunciation.

Renunciation means not only the renunciation of sense objects, but also the renunciation of desire for sense objects. This is the negative aspect of renunciation. There is a positive aspect also. If an intense love for God arises in a person, then the desire for worldly sense pleasures disappears. If you once taste nectar, can you bear to eat molasses? Intense love for God is like nectar. Sri Ramakrishna was absorbed in this love, so he could not feel the attraction of sense objects. God was his all.

Sri Ramakrishna was a *paramahamsa*, belonging to the highest order of sannyasin but he had no reason to behave as a *paramahamsa*. He was established in God-consciousness; the world was unreal to him. He was indifferent to all worldly affairs. We cannot define him. He was unique. He was a sannyasin yet to teach the world, he served his old mother and gave honour to his divine companion, Sarada Devi. He gave to each his due; still he was a *jivanmukta*—a free soul. He easily cut all worldly bondages; but in order to teach people, he lived among ordinary men and women. Although he tried to behave like an ordinary man, everyone could see that he was not ordinary. Whether he was called a householder or a sannyasin, everyone honoured him as a sannyasin. He was a world-teacher. What he taught was real religion. His life demonstrated what he taught and showed everyone what true religion is. He proved that truth is not the monopoly of any one religion. Truth is for all people, for all times. No sectarian religion can limit it. What is true for a householder is also true for a sannyasin. Sri Ramakrishna was an embodiment of Truth—the eternal, everlasting Truth. Truth is Truth, as much to a sannyasin as to a householder.

Sri Ramakrishna the Complete Teacher

SRI RAMAKRISHNA WAS AN UNPOLISHED RUSTIC, POOR, AND WITHOUT any formal education. Yet, his admirers were mostly sophisticated Westernised people whom he often designated as 'Englishmen'. How he attracted such people is a paradox.

One of his admirers, Pratap Chandra Majumdar, says: 'What is there common between him and me? I, a Europeanised, civilised, self-centred, semi-sceptical, so-called educated reasoner, and he, a poor, illiterate, shrunken, unpolished, diseased, half-dressed, half-idolatrous, friendless Hindu devotee? Why should I sit long hours to attend to him, I who have listened to Disareli and Fawcett, Stanley and Max Muller, and a whole host of European scholars and divines? Why should I be spell-bound to hear him? And, it is not I only, but dozens like me who do the same.' Going on, Mazumdar adds, 'He most vehemently repudiates the title of being called a teacher or guru . . .'

True, Sri Ramakrishna did not like being called a teacher, but he was a teacher par excellence all the same. The peculiarity about him was that he never thrust anything on you; he only took you forward from where you were. His advice to everybody was: 'Go forward'. That is to say, never think what you know or what you are, is enough. You certainly can know more and grow more, too.

Keep growing all the time. If you do not grow, if you stay stuck at some point, you stagnate.'

A man may be very primitive in his religious outlook. How would Sri Ramakrishna receive him? He would not condemn him. He was incapable of condemning anybody, however stupid and crude his religious ideas might be. He would probably say, 'Yes, what you say is fine, but do not say that is final. What is final you do not know, you have only to explore it. It is like exploring the ocean. Go deeper and deeper; at each level you have surprises waiting for you.' Religion, according to Sri Ramakrishna, is a process of exploration. You do not know where it begins and where it ends. You simply go on and on; each forward step you take has its own reward. It is possible to describe what you experience as you go on, but the final experience is so overwhelming that it is impossible to put it into words. It is for each individual to experience that state to know what it is like. But he would urge you not to stop before you reach the goal. Always aspire to the highest, he would say.

By 'religion', Sri Ramakrishna meant 'realisation'. You cannot guess what sugar tastes like unless you put some grains of it into your mouth. 'The test of the pudding is in the eating.' A mere intellectual grasp of a religious truth is not enough, it has to be practised and made part of your being. To know is to be. A parrot is not religious because it has learnt to speak some religious words. Mere speaking is not enough, religion has to be 'lived'. A scholar is not necessarily a religious man unless what he has learnt from holy books, he is able to reflect in his daily life. 'Even Satan can quote the scriptures.' Scholarship, by itself, has no value unless it is used as a means to attain spiritual illumination.

The records show Sri Ramakrishna had among his visitors people who were highly intellectual as well as people who had no pretensions to being intellectual. He warmly received both kinds, provided they were true seekers. Just as there were men like Pratap Chandra Mazumdar at one extreme, there were also men like Latu at the other. He would teach each of them according to what he liked, or believed in. Mazumdar, a member of the Brahmo Samaj, believed in God without form. Perhaps, he was a bit fanatical about it, and had nothing but contempt for those who believed in God with form. To him, Sri Ramakrishna would say, 'Good, you worship God without form, but please do not say that God cannot have any form and those who worship Him with form are to be pitied. We just do not know what God is like. If you say you know everything about God, you're mistaken. It's all right that you prefer to worship Him as being formless. But it will be a mistake if you say that's all there is to God. God can be both with form and without. He can even be many things more than that. Everything is possible for Him.' Mazumdar found this logical. He did not contradict Sri Ramakrishna. Perhaps, he also learnt to be humble where God was concerned.

But what did Sri Ramakrishna teach the illiterate Latu? Again, he applied the same principle—taking him forward from where he was. Latu, judging from what he later turned out to be, must have had great spiritual potential. Sri Ramakrishna recognised this almost at first sight. He drew him closer and closer and finally made him stay with him. Perhaps, he thought this would be a better way to teach him than give him merely some oral lessons. Living with a teacher is always a more effective way of learning than merely receiving oral instructions. Fresh from the village, young Latu was simple, and innocent of the ways of the world. In Sri Ramakrishna he had a living example of everything he needed to learn about religion. And, he took full advantage of this opportunity presented to him.

Perhaps, the most striking example of how Sri Ramakrishna taught different types of his disciples is furnished by Girish. Girish was a profligate. There was hardly a vice he did not have and he was proud of this fact. Yet, paradoxically enough, he came under Sri Ramakrishna's spell. He wanted to make a complete turn round and asked the Master if he should give up drinking. Sri Ramakrishna knew it would be impossible for him to give up drinking right away. He therefore advised him first to offer the liquor to Mother and then, drink it, as *prasad*. Sri Ramakrishna must have been a wonderful psychologist. True discipline is discipline which is self-imposed. If Sri Ramakrishna told Girish not to drink, Girish would have revolted. He would have said, 'Why should I not drink? Who are you to tell me what I should do or what I should not do? Am I not my own master?' Seeing the kind of man that Girish was, this would have been his reaction. But offering the drink to Mother first did not interfere with his freedom to drink. And, what Sri Ramakrishna said was only by way of advice, there was no injunction. This suited Girish fine. He was free to drink as and when he liked, but could he drink happily after offering the liquor first to Mother? The thought troubled him that he was offering liquor to Mother, while her other children offered her higher and better things—love and devotion, for instance. This naturally acted as a constraint on his drinking. This also made him think more of God.

As part of his attempt to reform, Girish thought he should completely withdraw from the theatre movement—in which his role had been that of a pioneer. When he sought Sri Ramakrishna's opinion about this, Sri Ramakrishna objected. He said he had been doing very good work through the theatre, for he was educating the masses; he would not like that work stopped in any circumstance. Sri Ramakrishna's far-sight saved the Bengali theatre. More than that, it saved Girish, for his life, at that point, centred round the theatre. If he had left this theatre, he would have been dead for all practical purposes, his talents, his inclinations all choked.

Swami Vivekananda is another typical example of how Sri Ramakrishna taught. Swamiji was a born rebel. He was not used to being told by anybody what he should do or should not do. He was a member of the Brahmo Samaj when he first met Sri Ramakrishna. He believed in a personal God who was good and kind. The monistic idea that man and God, apparently separate, were ultimately one, was shocking to him. Sri Ramakrishna did not want him to be dogmatic. He wanted him to study monism and then decide whether he could accept it or not. So, whenever Swami Vivekananda came alone and was able to spend some time with Sri Ramakrishna, the Master would ask him to read out to him a monistic book. At first, Swamiji would revolt, saying, 'What's all this nonsense the book is saying—God being one with man, and so on? I do not like it.' The Master never argued with him, trying to defend monistic thoughts. He merely said, 'Never mind what the book says; you do not have to agree with what it says. Only do me the favour of reading out the book to me. It's for my sake that you're reading it. Somehow or the other, I enjoy listening to its arguments.' As it turned out later, Swamiji became a strong votary of monism. Sri Ramakrishna, however, taught more by his own example than by what he said. That is exactly what a complete teacher does. He represented in himself the best of every religious point of view. Looking at him one could see religion at its best, in essence as well as in details.

Sri Ramakrishna taught not only individuals, he taught also different religious groups and communities. He taught them just what they lacked in their thinking.

Sri Ramakrishna—Lived in and with God

SRI RAMAKRISHNA DID NOT PERFORM ANY MIRACLES: HE HIMSELF was one. Alien to common experience, his life was a wonder, to many a puzzle.

If it inspired reverence and awe, it also aroused doubt, even some disparagement. People asked if Sri Ramakrishna was the latest incarnation of God. On the other hand, even his chief disciple, Swami Vivekananda, wondered during their first meetings whether he was normal.

Ten years after Sri Ramakrishna's death, Max Müller introduced him to the Western World as 'not only a high-souled man, a real Mahatman, but a man of original thought'. Later, Romain Rolland presented him to the West as 'the consummation of two thousand years of the spiritual life of three hundred million people'. And, a great representative of these people, Mahatma Gandhi, described the story of Sri Ramakrishna's life as 'a story of religion in practice', observing further that 'his life enables us to see God face-to-face'.

Yet, it is not a life easy to understand. The Goddess Kali, Sri Ramakrishna's Chosen Ideal, who is no other than Time herself, alone knew who he was (The word 'Kali' comes from the word Kala, 'time.' Both Kali and time are all-consuming and all-devouring. Kali is frequently called the 'Mistress of Time'). Though many years have passed, Sri Ramakrishna remains an enigma, provoking diverse reactions and interpretations.

The debate continues. Perhaps, it will continue forever. A characteristic of men such as Sri Ramakrishna is that they always remain controversial. Many of Buddha's and Christ's teachings are still debated, and divisions among their followers continue to multiply. The difficulty is that people try to understand them through their little intellects. That is just not possible. These persons belong to another world, the world of spirituality. If you are not familiar with that world, you will never understand them. Sri Ramakrishna would ask: 'How can an egg-plant seller determine the value of a diamond?'

Another difficulty in the case of Sri Ramakrishna's predecessors is a lack of reliable records. In this respect, Sri Ramakrishna is fortunate: He is not known by hearsay; everything about him is authenticated. Sri Ramakrishna's disciple M. kept a diary which is known today as *The Gospel of Sri Ramakrishna*. In this diary M. meticulously recorded Sri Ramakrishna's everyday life, including his message to mankind. He is also the first incarnation of God to have been photographed.

Sri Ramakrishna's *samadhi* is a phenomenon which may baffle some. What was it? Was it hysteria? Fortunately for future generations, the *samadhi* was critically examined by Dr Mahendra Sarkar, founder of the Indian Association for the Cultivation of Science and a scientist of eminence. Dr Sarkar, an M.D. and a leading medical practitioner, pronounced no judgement on Sri Ramakrishna's *samadhi*: he was simply perplexed. He found Sri Ramakrishna a normal person, lovable, intelligent, and extremely yet he enjoyed his talks. In fact, he had decreed that so long as he was with him, Sri Ramakrishna was to talk to him only. And, Dr Sarkar spent hours on end listening to Sri Ramakrishna. His practice suffered, but he did not mind. Sri Ramakrishna held him captive by what he said. What Sri Ramakrishna did not say but meant is best seen in his *samadhi*, caught in a photograph all can now see. It is a call to the ultimate in religious experience. The smile on his face is proof of the bliss a mystic experiences in *samadhi*. Sri Ramakrishna's message is in this smile.

Sri Ramakrishna was the antithesis of most of his contemporaries, who desperately tried to copy their British masters. At a time when a little bit of English education was a password to employment, Sri Ramakrishna refused to have anything to do with it. The only English words he knew and sometimes used were 'Very good, thank you.' He had perhaps picked them up from the conversations he had heard between English-educated Indians who loved to spice their native dialect with English words. On the same grounds, he also had no interest in Sanskrit education, for he noticed that the motive behind such education was the same as the motive behind English education—earning money. If he wanted any education at all, it was that education which would give him knowledge of the highest Truth which he termed God.

When Sri Ramakrishna was young, he often skipped his village school to attend popular plays, where under the cover of mythology; the highest spiritual truths were presented. The characters in those plays were such as one often meets in real life: representatives of good and evil, their inevitable clashes and the ultimate victory of good. Sri Ramakrishna had a remarkable memory. He knew most of these plays by heart, particularly the songs that were included in them.

Nineteenth-century rural Bengal might have been ravaged by malaria, famine, and a host of other problems, but by and large, people were simple and friendly to one other. The cinema was unknown, but there were varieties of entertainment provided by religious festivals, which came in close succession throughout the year. Sri Ramakrishna always looked forward to them. He enjoyed them, but also found much to learn from them.

Sri Ramakrishna was a keen observer of everything, including human character. Nothing passed in the village from which he did not draw a lesson. Because he was discerning, he saw through things easily, and he had a strong commonsense. Mankind and nature were the source of his education.

Sri Ramakrishna was a versatile artist. He sang, danced, and told stories with superb artistry and could act the roles of various characters in the same play. He also made images of deities like a professional. Even professionals sometimes sought his help to put the final touches to the eyes of the images they had made. That was the most difficult part of the art of image-making.

As a boy Sri Ramakrishna was totally guileless, and was much sought after by the young and the old alike. Interestingly, he also commanded respect from his elders, inside the family as well as outside. If there was ever a disagreement about what was right and what was wrong, invariably Sri Ramakrishna's view prevailed. Some felt he was divine. One old man, well-versed in the scriptures, formally worshipped him, saying, 'Lord, a time will come when many will recognise you as Avatar. I will not live to see that. So, please remember that I have been the first to do you the honour due to you.' This, however, did not turn his head. He continued to be the simple playful child that he was.

When the time came for Sri Ramakrishna's sacred thread ceremony, a great dispute arose in the family over who should be the first person to give alms to the boy. This ceremony is central in the life of a brahmin boy. The person who gives the first food that the boy begs to, is an important figure in the ritual. The custom was that only a brahmin could give the first alms, for it marks the formal recognition of the boy as a brahmin by the entire brahmin community.

But Sri Ramakrishna would have none of this. As a nine-year-old boy, he had promised a woman from the blacksmith caste, the midwife at his birth, that he would take his first food from her. He must do this, he said, because he had given her his word. The whole family was aghast. Everyone in the family and even neighbours pointed out that this was never done. But the boy was adamant. His argument was that a brahmin must keep his word; if he did not, the sacred thread would be a mockery. And, this argument clinched the issue.

Even as a boy Sri Ramakrishna was highly sensitive to any reference to God or any natural phenomenon of great beauty. His first spiritual experience came when he saw a flight of white cranes silhouetted against a bank of dark monsoon clouds. The sight so thrilled him that he lost consciousness. On another occasion, he was called upon to act as the God Shiva in a play. He was so overwhelmed with the feeling that he became Shiva and lost external consciousness, when he appeared before the audience. He stood still looking like Shiva and people cheered him. At another time he was going to a temple of the Divine Mother manifest in one of Her special aspects, with some elderly women. The women asked him to sing some devotional songs. Soon after he began to sing, he was choked with emotion and was lost in ecstasy, as if he was possessed by the Divine Mother!

At the age of sixteen, Sri Ramakrishna came to Calcutta and stayed with his eldest brother, Ramkumar. Ramkumar ran a Sanskrit school and wanted his brother to have a Sanskrit education, but Sri Ramakrishna's mind was elsewhere. He made it clear that he was not interested in the kind of education which was meant for earning money; he was only interested in learning about God. Ramkumar did not insist, for he knew it was of no use. He was, however, happy to notice that Sri Ramakrishna loved to worship deities in different houses of the neighbourhood, and that everybody who came to know him loved him.

Soon after this, Ramkumar moved to Dakshineswar to serve as the chief priest at the Kali temple there. Sri Ramakrishna followed him, rather reluctantly, and became his assistant. His job was to decorate the image; this work was closest to his heart since he was an artist par excellence. He not only made Kali look exquisite, she looked alive under the touch of his artistic fingers.

Ramkumar was getting old and was not keeping well. So, after some time, Sri Ramakrishna took over as the chief priest at the Kali temple. He began worshipping Kali with great enthusiasm and meticulous care. But soon, he began to ask himself if Kali were a mere piece of stone. Why didn't she respond to his prayers? There was no sign that she was a living being and was pleased with his worship. He then began to wonder if there was anything lacking in himself. Perhaps, he was not earnest enough to make Mother Kali talk to him. She had talked to the saint–poet Ramprasad and to other devotees; perhaps, he thought, they loved her more and their yearning was deeper. Sometimes in the midst of his worship, Sri Ramakrishna would cry aloud, 'Mother, why are you so partial? I know I'm ignorant, a fool. Is that why you neglect me?' As evening approached, he would rub his face on the hard ground till it bled. He would say, 'Mother, another day is gone and yet you did not reveal yourself to me. What is this life for?' Seeing him, bystanders thought he had gone mad or he had just lost his mother. One day as he was doing his worship, he began to cry, saying, 'I cannot bear to live without seeing you. I must end my life.' His eyes fell on the sword hanging on the wall. Seizing the sword he was about to strike himself when he saw a light emanating from Kali and advancing towards him. As it came closer, it grew in volume. He was soon enveloped by it. He fell down and lost consciousness.

After that, the relationship between Sri Ramakrishna and Kali was as intimate as between a petulant child and an indulgent mother. Sri Ramakrishna would demand from Mother Kali that she reveal herself to him in all her aspects. If she did not seem to immediately oblige, he would cry until she yielded. People thought he was mad. He was—mad for God. In his madness he often forgot to eat or bathe; he rarely slept. His nephew Hriday attended to his needs, otherwise he would have very likely died.

The relationship between Kali and Sri Ramakrishna has almost no parallel in religious history. Kali was Sri Ramakrishna's mother, guardian, friend, and playmate. He would not do anything without first asking her. To Sri Ramakrishna, Kali was the only reality. She filled his world.

Where most mystics are satisfied with experiencing one aspect of God, Sri Ramakrishna wanted to practise the spiritual disciplines of other religions also. In the years that followed, Sri Ramakrishna practised almost every faith and spiritual discipline known to religion. But, invariably, before embarking on a new experiment, he first obtained Kali's consent. He would ask, 'Mother, show me how other people worship you.' Kali seemed to like the idea and encouraged him. It was like a mother feeling happy that her child was keen to progress in education.

One interesting feature of Sri Ramakrishna's spiritual practices was that whenever he wanted to follow a new spiritual path, a teacher would appear—as if out of nowhere—in order to help him. Tota Puri, for example, came this way. In fact, Sri Ramakrishna had not even thought of practising non-dualism, but Tota Puri came and offered to teach him Advaita Vedanta. Sri Ramakrishna said he would have to ask his 'Mother'. Kali told him that she had arranged for Tota Puri to come, so that Sri Ramakrishna could learn non-dualism from him. If non-dualism is a difficult concept to grasp, it is more difficult to practise. Sri Ramakrishna, however, mastered it within a few days, much to Tota Puri's amazement.

After following the different paths of Hinduism, Sri Ramakrishna practised the spiritual disciplines of Islam. For a Hindu to practise Islam is unprecedented, if not unthinkable. Nevertheless, Sri Ramakrishna took initiation from a Muslim spiritual teacher, and during this period, did not even enter the courtyard of the Kali temple. He wore his cloth like a Muslim, repeated the name of Allah, and said the daily prayers of Islam. No doubt, Kali approved all this. Perhaps, it will be more correct to say that Sri Ramakrishna did whatever he did at his Mother's bidding. Sri Ramakrishna followed the Islamic path until he attained its highest realisation. How did

Kali feel during this time? She must have missed him, but she must have felt proud of her son.

After following the path of Islam, Sri Ramakrishna practised Christianity. One day, while visiting a devotee's house, Sri Ramakrishna's eyes fell upon a picture of the child Jesus seated on the Virgin Mary's lap. He must have been looking at Jesus for quite some time. As he gazed at the picture, a ray of light emanated from it and entered his body. Immediately all of Sri Ramakrishna's Hindu ideas and tendencies were pushed to the back of his mind, and he was filled with Jesus. He also had visions in which he saw Christian priests burning incense, and Christian devotees praying in churches. For three days he did not enter the Kali temple; he was completely absorbed in his devotion to Christ. On the third day, he saw a tall God-like man walking towards him. The tall stranger was wearing foreign garments; a voice from within told Sri Ramakrishna that this man was none other than Jesus. Approaching Sri Ramakrishna, Jesus embraced him and entered into his body. Sri Ramakrishna went into deep Samadhi. They became one.

Sri Ramakrishna's spiritual experiences convinced him that all religions essentially taught one common truth: perfection—perfection in the spiritual sense. As Jesus said, 'Be ye perfect, even as the Father which is in heaven is perfect.' This is the essence of religion: everything else is peripheral. If there is a dispute between one religion and another, it is over non-essentials. Non-essentials vary and have to vary because of different tastes and temperaments, social and cultural contexts. Ignore them and go to the essentials. There, all religions are one.

Sri Ramakrishna respected every religious belief and practice. He never argued with anybody. He respected every point of view, no matter how crude it might be. He tried to point out how rich and varied religious perceptions were. It was wrong to think that there was only one path leading to God. According to Sri Ramakrishna, there were many paths. Each path was good and valid—he knew because he had traversed each of those paths just for the joy of it. He encouraged everyone to follow the path that he or she had chosen, but he also advised people not to stop midway in their path. They must continue until they have reached the end of the path. He also advised everybody not to think that his path was the only path.

As long as the goal is the same, the path one chooses does not matter. It is like choosing food according to one's taste. Christians, Hindus, Buddhists, and Muslims will all eventually reach the same goal. There should be no quarrels about the way; Sri Ramakrishna wanted to see everyone follow his or her own path, suited to his or her own temperament, to reach the goal. Each religion has produced great saints and sages, and this is the proof of its validity. He upheld not one particular religion, but each and every religion. He was as much a Hindu as a Christian, a Muslim or Buddhist. He was the sum-total of all religions. He was the representative of the beginning as well as the end of religion. What he taught was Hinduism to a Hindu, Islam to a Muslim, Christianity to a Christian. He taught the essence of religion.

Sri Ramakrishna lived in and with God. God alone was real to him. But Sri Ramakrishna's experience was that God was everywhere, in everything, and in every being. Sri Ramakrishna felt that the Supreme Being was his being. Sri Ramakrishna's realisations showed him that there was in fact one single Being. But that single Being appeared to be many, because of the diverse names and forms superimposed on it. The saint and the sinner were one and the same. The same divinity was present in them, but it did not show itself equally. In the saint, the divinity was shining; in the sinner, it was concealed. Given love and encouragement, however, the sinner's divinity would begin to reveal itself. Gold is always gold, even if it is covered with dirt.

Sri Ramakrishna did not preach any creed or dogma. Nor did he reject any. His sole concern was that men and women achieve their full potential in terms of moral and spiritual growth. As far as spiritual growth is concerned, man is limitless as God. Not only that, man's love and compassion are also limitless. We have the potential of feeling ourselves to be one with everyone and everything. If there is pain anywhere, we can feel that pain as our own. If others are happy, we too can be happy. Religion is a process of growth. God is the ultimate in this process of growth. The goal of life is to reach this ultimate. This is why Sri Ramakrishna says the goal of life is God-realisation. To know God is to be God. You see Him inside yourself and you see Him also outside. You see Him everywhere and in everything. You see nothing but God.

The world is divine, so is humanity. Sri Ramakrishna realised this. This was also his message. In short, Sri Ramakrishna was his own message.

The Religion of Sri Ramakrishna

MOST OF US KNOW WHAT SRI RAMAKRISHNA TAUGHT. WHY DO WE then discuss it? What prompted me to choose this topic among others? The reason is that there is a lot of debate now going on about Sri Ramakrishna's religion. What exactly was it? The matter has in fact gone to court; it is, indeed, surprising that the question of what Sri Ramakrishna's religion was is going to be decided by a court of law. But that is what is apparently going to happen.

The problem is that though Sri Ramakrishna was born a Hindu, he practised other religions also. Is there another instance of any Hindu practising non-Hindu religions? Of course, there are instances of Hindus changing their religion—a Hindu becoming a Muslim, or a Christian, or a Brahmo. But Sri Ramakrishna switched from one religion to another and back. First, what made him do that? And secondly, what did he finally become, did he remain a Hindu?

Let us take a brief survey of his religious life. He was born a Hindu, an orthodox Hindu; but right from the beginning, he showed some unorthodox tendencies. As one born into an orthodox Brahmin family, he would be expected to be an orthodox Brahmin. But how can we explain the fact that after his sacred thread ceremony, *upanayana*, he accepted his first alms from a Sudra woman? It is the custom for a Brahmin boy, after receiving his sacred thread, to accept alms from a Brahmin woman. But Sri Ramakrishna said, 'No, I have promised to accept alms from so-and-so, a Sudra woman.' (She had attended his mother at the time of his birth.) This was something unheard of—a Brahmin boy accepting alms from a Sudra. But Sri Ramakrishna stood firm, though everyone protested. He told them that as a Brahmin he must be true to his word, and he took his alms from the hands of the Sudra woman. He would be truthful at all costs—even in opposition to orthodox customs.

Sri Ramakrishna came to Calcutta and settled there as a priest in a Kali temple, where he worshipped Mother Kali. He started worshipping ritualistically conforming to the standards laid down by the scriptures. But soon, he began to worship in his own way. Thus, a tendency to unorthodox behaviour was once again noticed in him. After having worshipped Kali for some years, he turned to Tantricism. That is understandable. But why did he have to cover all the sixty-four disciplines found in Tantra books? And, why did he become the disciple of a woman? Normally, a man goes to another man to learn religion. But the remarkable fact is that the guru came to him and the guru happened to be a woman, Bhairavi Brahmani. She taught him all the Tantras. He might have said, 'Well I am a Sakta and I worship Mother Kali as a sattvic Tantric.' But he went through all the disciplines of the Tantras—even to the extent of eating dead human flesh.

One may have an encounter with God, a vision, or experience of God, but Sri Ramakrishna did not stop there. After having gone through the sixty-four ways of the Tantras, he switched to Vaishnavism. At this time a monk with matted hair (Jatadhari) appeared. He was a great Vaishnava devotee. He had with him a Ramlala, an image of the child Rama. Sri Ramakrishna also started worshipping Ramlala. And Ramlala, who had received love and worship from Jatadhari, left him and came to Sri Ramakrishna, preferring his company. Sri Ramakrishna looked on him as his son and would take him into the Ganga, bathe him, feed him, caress him; sometimes, a strict father, he would even slap him. (All these things we find in Vaishnava literature, in the Bhakti marga—God as father, and you his son, or God as son, and you his father, etc.)

He had all the experiences that this path leads to, but he could not stop there. In the Bhakti literature, in the Dasya discipline you play the role of a servant, with God as your master. Sri Ramakrishna started to practise the Dasya sadhana and became a monkey, a Hanuman. Hanuman is the epitome, the best embodiment of Bhakti—a devotee who is also a servant. As a Hanuman he would walk on all fours, live in a tree and never speak. He had started by being a devotee of Kali. But when he became a Vaishnava, he did not visit the Kali temple. He was no longer a Sakta, he was a Vaishnava practising the Dasya discipline. Alright, there is no harm, if you want to practise the attitude of a servant of God. He might have stopped there; but he did not.

Next he went on to practise the *Madhura*, the most difficult path according to Vaishnava authorities. God is your beloved and you are His beloved. This *bhava* is known as the Gopi *bhava*. Sri Ramakrishna dressed himself as a woman in order to practise this discipline. He had all the experiences, which this kind of devotee is supposed to have. He had all those wonderful experiences but did he stop there? No he did not stop there.

Suddenly a Punjabi Naga monk, Totapuri, appeared. Note one thing: Generally an aspirant searches for a guru, but in the case of Sri Ramakrishna, the gurus looked for him. At the right moment, gurus of different sects came to him. When Sri Ramakrishna had completed the dualistic disciplines, Totapuri, a non-dualist teacher, appeared. He came to Sri Ramakrishna and asked 'Will you practise non-dualism?' Sri Ramakrishna replied, 'I have to ask my Mother.' So, he went to the temple and asked Mother Kali; with her permission he started the non-dualist *sadhana* and became a non-dualist. As a non-dualist he had nothing to do with Mother Kali; he would not go to any temple and would not practise any sort of dualism. In three days, he attained *nirvikalpa samadhi*, the highest goal a non-dualist can attain.

Hinduism has a very broad spectrum. In this spectrum, there are many ways of worship which are not widely known. Sri Ramakrishna seems to have practised all of them. These are mostly offshoots of Hinduism and Buddhism in a decadent form. For example, there is one community known as 'Sahajiya'; but there are also others. Sri Ramakrishna was familiar with all the kinds of worship known in India.

But now he went to Mother Kali and asked Her to help him worship God in other ways—other than those found in Hinduism. Mother Kali knew the nature of Sri Ramakrishna and obliged him. All of a sudden, a Sufi, Govinda Roy, appeared. This man was a Muslim but belonged to the Sufi sect. Sufis are people who are very close to Hindus. In fact, Muslims do not recognise them as Muslims. At one time Sufism had spread across northern India; even now you might come across Sufis there. What I want to point out is that, being a non-dualist, Sri Ramakrishna found that Islam was very close to what he personally believed in and practised.

Dakshineswar was a place which was open to everybody. Even Muslims came and stayed there. Sri Ramakrishna would go around meeting them and talking with them. This way he discovered Govinda Roy. He was very impressed by his life and character, and when he discovered that he was a Muslim, he asked him to help him understand Islam. Govinda Roy agreed and explained to him the basic principles of Islam, taught him how to say the *Namaz*, and how to say *Ajana*. Surprisingly enough, for a time Sri Ramakrishna was one hundred percent Muslim. He would not go into a Hindu temple and preferred to eat the kind of food Muslims eat. He dressed like a Muslim and visited mosques. At last, he had a vision of Mohammed, whom he later described as having bright, burning eyes, a long black shining beard, and a brilliant personality.

One peculiarity of Sri Ramakrishna was that whatever might be the path he had chosen to practise at a particular period of time, he was totally devoted to it and totally identified himself with it.

If he was a Muslim, he was a one hundred percent Muslim; if he was a Vaishnava, he was a one hundred percent Vaishnava,

Next was Christianity. Once, someone read to him from the Bible, and taught him about Christ, his life and message. Later, when he was one day visiting Jadu Mallick's nearby garden-house, he saw in the large drawing-room, a beautiful picture of the Madonna, Mother Mary, with the baby Jesus. (That picture is now in the hands of the Ramakrishna Mission, not in India, but in San Francisco, America.) Sri Ramakrishna began to meditate on this picture, and soon he found light coming from it and entering his body. For several days he was completely immersed in the consciousness of Christ as an Incarnation of God, who had come to help the poor, the oppressed and degraded. He also had another vision at Dakshineswar. He saw a procession coming towards him, with Christ at its head. Christ came and merged into Sri Ramakrishna, who became overwhelmed with the consciousness of Jesus Christ. Incidentally, he noticed that Jesus Christ was very handsome and that his nose was blunt. Normally, we find in pictures that Christ had a sharp, aquiline nose. Now, it has been discovered that there are pictures where Christ is shown, with a snub nose, the way Sri Ramakrishna saw him.

Sri Ramakrishna thus, experienced full Christ-consciousness. He seemed to have a thirst for religious experiences, which was never to be quenched. If we get some religious experiences, we are happy. Normally, we hear of saints and sages having some kind of mystic experience, such as a vision. They are very satisfied with that, and stop there. But here is a man who seems to be always impatient for more experiences. He never tired of looking for new areas of religion.

The Brahmo Samaj in his time was a powerful movement. He discovered that most of the educated persons, the elite of Calcutta society, were members of this organisation. He met many of these people, attended the Brahmo services, and invited the members to Dakshineswar. He had the greatest intimacy with Keshab Sen, whose home he used to visit but he was also intimate with Pratap

Mazumdar and others. Then, there was Swami Dayananda Saraswati, the founder of the Arya Samaj whom he met and exchanged ideas with. He also met Vaishnava Bhagwan Das Baba. We find that Sri Ramakrishna was always a seeker; he would never stop. He would never say, 'Now I know everything.' He used to say that God is a subject that you can never know everything about.

Sri Ramakrishna covered from A to Z the entire field of religious experience. Fetishism is the crudest form of religion. Tribal people have this kind of religion in which they worship a fetish, yet Sri Ramakrishna would accept even that. He would not reject anything that is called religion—any practice, any ritual that to us may seem a waste of time. Sri Ramakrishna accepted any religion if its devotees were sincere. The most important thing is, you must be sincere. What you are practising does not matter; it may appear to others as silly and primitive. Never mind, start from anywhere with sincerity; then proceed onward and discover the Truth.

The two things which Sri Ramakrishna would insist upon are: First, you must be sincere; and secondly, you must not think that the path you have chosen for yourself is the best or only path. It may be the best for you, but not for all; there are other paths also. The Upanishads say the same thing: *Ekam sat vipra bahudha vadanti*—Truth is one; wise men speak of it in various ways. Our ancient rishis said this, but has anybody in the history of religion in India or elsewhere tried to find out through experience whether or not it is true?

But Sri Ramakrishna verified this great principle. He practised all the major religions of the world and also the minor, less known religions some of which are not even recognised as good religions. Sri Ramakrishna practised everything, as we have noted, from fetishism to non-dualism. He covered the entire gamut of religious thinking and religious practices. He would say, 'I must know from personal experience. People say that God is one, but I have to know that. I must testify to the truth which the rishis proclaimed thousands of years ago.'

He sometimes had arguments with his own disciples who would object to a particular religion; Swami Vivekananda would sometimes make such an objection. But according to Sri Ramakrishna, though a form of religion may not suit you, you have no right to condemn it. What is important is the end result. He would say, 'Judge the tree by the fruit it bears. Do not condemn anything.' That was Sri Ramakrishna's attitude towards different religious paths.

Please note that Sri Ramakrishna's attitude towards other religions was not one of 'tolerance'. Swami Vivekananda elaborated on this by saying, 'Not tolerance'; when you say 'I tolerate, I am a tolerant man. I do not mind what you practise and am ready to allow you the privilege of worshipping the way you want to worship. I have nothing to do with it; I will not interfere,' you are being arrogant in that you are assuming the attitude of being superior. You are not going to interfere with another man's way of worship, but you are thinking, 'Well he doesn't know that he is a fool. Never mind, let him stew in his own juice; I do not care.' This attitude is nothing but arrogance. So, Sri Ramakrishna would say, 'No, not tolerance, but acceptance; you have to accept. This is also a path leading to the goal; it may not be your path. Never mind, allow that man to follow his own path and respect him.'

This is something unprecedented, something never preached—even in our own country which has always been known as very tolerant, a country where there is a great deal of diversity in terms of language, religion, food habits, etc, and yet where there is a wonderful unity in the midst of the diversity.

But Sri Ramakrishna is a living example of the spirit of acceptance—the spirit of deep respect for others' viewpoints, others' religions. He would bow down and say, 'I respect those who worship God with form, those who worship God without form, those who believe in the Impersonal God, and those who worship the Personal God.' He seemed to say to us, 'Never mind what you think about God. It is up to you, you choose. You are free to choose anything you like and other people have no right to interfere with you'. The only thing he did not like is for you to say, 'Mine is the best path; mine is the only path.'

But what exactly was the religion of Sri Ramakrishna? Was he a Hindu? This question is agitating the minds of many people, even people who are initiated disciples of the Ramakrishna Mission. They are asking, 'Do you mean to say that we are not Hindus because we worship Sri Ramakrishna and had our initiation from Belur Math?' That is a big question. I will try to discuss what, in my opinion, is the religion that Sri Ramakrishna taught. Some people have called it 'Sri Ramakrishnaism', a new religion. Perhaps, Sri Ramakrishna himself would be shocked to hear that there is a religion being taught to people in his name.

I have made a brief survey of Sri Ramakrishna's religious career. He started by worshipping Mother Kali, then having practised all the branches of the Hindu faith, he switched over to non-Hindu faiths. He practised Islam, Christianity, and a number of other faiths which might be partly Buddhist. Some of those faiths seem to have totally disappeared from the face of India; if they are still there we cannot identity them. Lots of religious faiths are still underground not on the surface. But Sri Ramakrishna, having practised all the known and little-known religious faiths came to the conclusion that all religions lead to the same goal. Religions are so many paths which lead to the same place apparently they differ in detail but the essence of all religions is the same. Thus, through his own experience he reaffirmed the truth which the sages of the Rig Veda had declared long ago *'Ekam sat vipra bahudha vadanti'*—Truth is one, wise men speak of it in various ways.

He is the only man known to history who has experimented with different religions and has from his own experience come to the conclusion that 'Truth is one, the paths to it are various.' The methods, of course, are different; different because of our different temperaments, different racial, geographical and historical backgrounds; but basically, all of us are trying to reach the same goal, which we define as 'God'. As he often said, '*Yata mat, tata path*'—As many faiths, so many paths.

Now, the question still remains, 'What was Sri Ramakrishna's own religion?' We want to know: 'What did he end up being finally? Did he remain a Hindu or was he something else? If he remained a Hindu, then what sort of Hindu was he?' It is clear to everybody that he was not a sectarian Hindu. He was a Hindu, perhaps, or perhaps we cannot pigeonhole him. When we say that he was a Hindu, it means that he was not a Muslim, nor a Christian, Buddhist or anything else. If you say that he is a Hindu, you at once categorise him. But you cannot pigeonhole him like that; you cannot limit him. You cannot identify him with any particular religion. He is everything—everything that passes in the name of religion.

As I said, he accepted everything from gross fetishism to the highest nondualism—the whole gamut of religious beliefs and practices. He was everything. He would welcome all religions because to him religion was nothing but an expression of love for God. If you love God, you are a religious man; it doesn't matter how you express your love. What is important is love, whether you go to a mosque, or a temple, or nowhere at all. But you must love God, no matter what deity you worship, or if you worship your Self. If a man worships himself thinking that he is God, that is fine. That was Sri Ramakrishna's attitude.

Now, when we say 'God', we usually mean a personal God. But, of course, we do not mean that God is a person high up in the heavens, watching over us, keeping an eye out whatever we are doing here below and then some day punishing us, or rewarding us, depending upon whether we do bad things or good things. By 'personal God', we mean somebody who is perfect. We are not perfect, but God is. But God can be impersonal as well as personal. By 'impersonal God', we mean a state of being, a degree of excellence and a degree of moral and spiritual development—the highest level of development.

We do not know what God is really like. Sri Ramakrishna said again and again, 'You can talk about everything else under the sun, but you cannot talk about God, because you have no idea about Him.' He also said, very aptly, 'Can you look at the sun at midday? No, the glare of the midday sun will burn your eyes. But you can look at the sun when it is just rising—the morning sun. It is very pleasant, beautiful.'

God is like the noonday sun—beyond thought and speech. But the same God, like the morning sun which we can see and enjoy, can be seen manifested in human beings. He is in fact manifest everywhere—in you, in me, in the whole world, in the cosmos. But he is most manifest in human beings, and even more in good, holy, and honest people.

In reality, Truth was Sri Ramakrishna's God. Truth, God, Self—he used these words interchangeably. It doesn't matter which word you use, he would say. It depends on the angle from which you are looking at the Ultimate Reality. 'Ultimate Reality'—another expression for God. Still other expressions: 'Pure Being', or 'The Supreme Being.' There are so many qualifying words, but no word can fully explain the nature of God; no holy book, no holy man, nothing on earth can truly represent Him. How can you define the Infinite, the Limitless, the Unique? That was Sri Ramakrishna's attitude.

What Sri Ramakrishna really believed in, was the religion he practised. It is the religion which is Islam to the Muslim, Christianity to the Christian, and Hinduism to the Hindu. There is an English saying, 'Religion is one; religions are many.' True religion is one—it is an approach to the Ultimate Truth. It is eternal, universal; I cannot explain what Truth is but I feel there is such a thing as Truth, and I want to reach that Absolute Truth.

I begin in a clumsy way. When I begin I know nothing about Truth; but slowly as I grow morally and spiritually, my vision changes and I begin to understand the Ultimate Truth. It is the Truth of all religions, the Ultimate Reality which is the substratum of all that exists, which upholds all that we see around us. It is the Truth, which is called 'God' or 'Self'.

What I am hinting at is that Sri Ramakrishna was a non-dualist, and because he was a non-dualist, he could very well be a Muslim, a Christian, a Buddhist, or a Hindu. If you are a non-dualist, you feel that God is the only Reality, and that that Reality is in you, in me, in everything and in every being. That Reality lends whatever reality there is to you, to me, to everyone and everything. Without that Self, you are nothing—you are a mere shadow, non-existent. It is that Reality which runs through all of us, sustains us, is the essence of our being. Sri Ramakrishna believed in that non-dual Self.

I have already discussed Sri Ramakrishna's initiation from Totapuri, and how he attained to the highest goal envisaged by non-dualism. But if he was a non-dualist, why did he go to a temple? Why did he continue to worship Kali and other deities? He had realised that Self which is the common Self of all. There is only one Self; so why did he go to worship in the temple? The wonderful thing about Sri Ramakrishna was that he did not reject anything. He was a non-dualist, true, but he did not reject dualism. You may remember that Sankaracharya did the same thing—Sankaracharya, who was the doyen of all non-dualists. What made him compose hymns to the Ganga and to Bhavani and others? Isn't that dualism? And, Sankaracharya was a non-dualist, a one hundred percent non-dualist.

We are mistaken when we think that if you are a non-dualist you cannot respect any form of God. There are so many forms but there is one Self common to all. That common Self, the cosmic Self can have many forms and many names. You are one form, I am another form; you have a name, I have another name; we are different from each other but in reality, in our essence we are one—we are the same. This is what Sri Ramakrishna believed in. He was a true non-dualist.

But though Sri Ramakrishna was a non-dualist, I would like to point out again, that he was not exclusive. He regarded dualism as a stepping stone to non-dualism. As you proceed, you use one stepping stone after another, but you do not reject them. When you start your education, you go to primary school then you go on to secondary school, higher secondary, and perhaps then to the University. In the same way, Sri Ramakrishna would say, Always go forward—on and on in your pursuit of Truth; there is no end. He would say, 'Suppose you have reached the highest level, does that mean that you reject all that you have left behind, all that you covered at one stage or another? All the steps you have taken in the course of your journey to the Ultimate Goal are valid, as valid as the final step.'

Sri Ramakrishna in fact covers everything—from the crassest dualism to the highest, finest, subtlest non-dualism—everything. If you worship a tree as God, what would be Sri Ramakrishna's reaction? Would he condemn you? No. 'Worship it,' he would say. 'Go ahead and worship it, but do not stop there. Do not say that this is all; this tree is everything to me. Worship the tree as God, not just the tree.' Here in India, you will find people worshipping trees, mountains, rivers—so many other things—as God. Sri Ramakrishna accepted all this; but he said, 'Look, your goal is non-dualism; so do not stop where you are. Worshipping the tree is just the beginning; go on and on till you have reached the highest, which is non-dualism.'

It is in non-dualism that you feel that you are one with God, one with the universe. There is only one Existence, one Self, and you are that Self. If somebody is in pain, you are in pain; if somebody is happy, you are happy. You are not separate from the rest of the universe—this is the feeling of oneness. That is what Sri Ramakrishna felt. When somebody was walking over the green grass, he felt pain. He said, 'Someone is plucking out my heart.' He had identified himself with the grass. A bullock was being beaten. Sri Ramakrishna rolled on the ground in agony. He cried, 'I am being beaten; I cannot bear it any longer.' Two boatmen were fighting, and he felt that he was receiving their blows. He had this sense of oneness with every being, everything. Krishna also had this experience. One day, Naren (later Swami Vivekananda) came to Sri Ramakrishna and said, 'Sir, please grant that I may have what is called *nirvikalpa samadhi*. I would like to have that ecstasy and stay immersed in it, forgetful of my body and surroundings. Once in a while I would become conscious of my body, take a morsel of food, and then go back into *samadhi*. Please, grant me this.' Sri Ramakrishna replied, 'I am surprised. I thought you were meant for something bigger, something higher and nobler. I could not believe that you would be so selfish as to think of your own ecstasy and liberation.' He wanted Swamiji to serve others—the ignorant, the poor, the downtrodden, the weak, seeing the Lord in them. That would be worshipping God in the best way, the way of non-dualism.

Sri Ramakrishna himself practised this. Once, when he was on his way to Varanasi, he noticed the famine-stricken people at Deoghar. He left the group he was travelling with, went to the place where the poor people were squatting and sat with them. He said to Mathur Babu, his guardian as well as his disciple, 'Feed these people. Give them cloth and whatever else they need.' Mathur Babu pleaded, 'Sir, that will take a lot of money and I cannot afford it. Already we have spent so much arranging for this pilgrimage. It is also a question of time; we will be held up here if we have to send for provisions for the people.' What was Sri Ramakrishna's reply? 'I do not care to go to any holy places. These are my Gods; let me stay here among them. I want to share their sufferings; I and these people are not separate.'

This sense of oneness is the logical sequel to non-dualism. If you are a non-dualist, you do not feel that you are separate from other people. You feel that you are one with everybody—good or bad—even the wicked, even the simple. As Swami Vivekananda said, 'From an amoeba to the highest God—everything is Brahman.' Only, the manifestation of divinity differs. That divinity is present in all its grandeur, in all its fullness, in all creatures. When you see a wicked man, or a very simple man, remember that they are Brahman, but in their case, their divinity is less manifest. That was what Sri Ramakrishna taught.

But please note that, though he taught non-dualism to Swami Vivekananda and some of his other disciples, he taught dualism to people whom he knew were not yet ready to receive the highest teaching—the difficult, abstruse concepts of non-dualism. He taught each person according to his capacity, temperament, and taste. You cannot preach the same thing to everybody. What Swami Vivekananda could understand and practise, others could not; he knew that.

Swamiji became a staunch supporter of non-dualism, as is well known. You may remember the incident in which he found a picture of Sri Ramakrishna being worshipped at the Advaita Ashrama at Mayavati. He scolded those responsible for setting up a shrine there. He said, 'What is this? There should be at least one place where there is no worship of God with form. I thought this would be the place, but I find that Sri Ramakrishna is receiving worship here, as he is in other places.' The monks who had set up the shrine were perplexed. Why did Swami Vivekananda object so much to the worship of his own Master? So, they referred the matter to Mother Sarada Devi. What was her reply? 'Naren is right. The Master was a non-dualist.'

Sri Ramakrishna was obviously a non-dualist. 'Non-dualism is what we can call 'Sri Ramakrishna's religion.' But when I say that he was a non-dualist, I mean that he was all-inclusive, all-embracing; he was Religion itself, the whole of Religion. You cannot say that he was this or that; you cannot put a label on him, such as Hindu, Buddhist, Christian. Study his life and what do you see? On the wall of his room were many pictures of Gods and Goddesses. When he rises in the morning, he goes to each one, and bows his head in worship. Is this not dualism? But the next moment he comes back to his bed, sits down, meditates and goes into samadhi where he is in communion with his own Self. Everything else has been blotted out; the world does not exist for him. All that exists is the Self, Brahman. So, he is a non-dualist. He would say, 'I climb up to the roof of the building, but I come down, too.' When he is in ecstasy, in *samadhi*, he is on the roof—then he is a non-dualist. But when he comes down, he meets people, talks to them. Most of them are not interested in non-dualism, so he talks to them as a dualist. He helps them as much as he does the non-dualists.

He would say, 'You talk of Brahman—good. Brahman is the only reality. It is also true that *jagat mithya*—the world is illusory. But the next step is *jiva brahamaiva na parah*—the *jiva* (living creature) is nothing but Brahman. Sri Ramakrishna says that when we talk of Brahman, we do not include the cosmos; but how can we explain its existence? He gave the example of the *bel*-fruit. When we speak of the bel-fruit, do we mean only the pulp? Don't we mean also the shell and the seeds? In the same way, when we say Brahman, we include also this cosmos, this universe. Where did it come from? From Brahman it comes, and then it goes back into Brahman—back and forth, all the time. This cosmos is nothing but the manifestation of Brahman. If we view the cosmos as something separate from Brahman, it is unreal and we have every right to reject it. But eventually, you will see Brahman everywhere; nothing but Brahman exists. This *jagat*, this empirical world, is Brahman. That is why we find in Sri Ramakrishna so much concern for all creatures.

He also said that though God is present in all creatures, he is most manifest in human beings. Swami Vivekananda learned this from him. He used to say, 'Among all the creations of God, man is the Taj Mahal—the most remarkable creation of God.' Then he would say, 'My God, the poor, my God, the ignorant, my God, the superstitious, my God, the wicked.' The only God I believe in is He whom the ignorant call man.'

Sri Ramakrishna by his non-dualism, and by his acceptance of dualism as a necessary step towards non-dualism, has mixed together all the different religions, which always seemed to have been at odds with each other. Each religion was claiming, 'I am superior to other religions.' But Sri Ramakrishna points to the Truth underlying every religion. Though apparently one religion differs from another, if you go down to the essence of each, you find one common truth underlying them all. Sri Ramakrishna would point to that truth. He would say that, of course, there are non-essentials in every religion, but there are essentials, too. Ignore the non-essentials. Even in Hinduism itself there are many sects and sub-sects—so many differences. But the differences are not in the essentials, which are the same for all Hindus.

Notice, as days pass, Hinduism is changing; slowly people are turning more and more to the essence of Hinduism. And, the essence of Hinduism is also the essence of Islam and the essence of Christianity—the essence of religion itself. By stressing this oneness of religion, mankind, existence, Sri Ramakrishna has tried to remove all conflicts. He has tried to give us peace, harmony, unity. He has taught us to respect other religions, other viewpoints. He says that if you respect your own religion, you should also respect other religions, because the same truth that is in your religion is also in other religions.

What, in fact, is religion? It is a commitment to certain moral principles; it is the science of growth, of becoming better. Religion always tells you to try to be better and better and better—there is no limit to your growth. This is what religion is. Sri Ramakrishna would say that religion is not creeds or dogmas; what is important is not just worship or knowledge, but practice. Practice is important; being and becoming is the core of religions. I judge you by what you are, not by what rituals you practise, if you fast or how many baths you take in the Ganga. These are all unnecessary details. As Swami Vivekananda said, 'God is within you; God is in all of us. Manifest that God. Show that you are God Himself. You do not have to become God; you are already God.'

Sri Ramakrishna used to say that God-realisation is the goal of life. God is hidden within you, but you are not aware of it. You have to become aware of your inner divinity and manifest it in your daily life, in your conduct. That is what Sri Ramakrishna taught; that was his religion. And, he himself was the best example of Religion.

Then, was Sri Ramakrishna a Hindu? I will give my own opinion. You may not agree with me. The Vedas teach Hinduism. Sri Ramakrishna was that kind of Hindu. He was not the kind of Hindu we find in the *Puranas*, the *Smritis*, etc. He embraces everything; he was the whole. According to Sri Ramakrishna, no holy book can exhaust God; no holy man can exhaust Him; no holy word can exhaust Him. Swami Vivekananda once criticised the Tantras saying that they were all nonsense, and wicked. Sri Ramakrishna responded that all religions have their shortcomings inasmuch as they try to define God who is limitless but we should not criticise any one of them. Each one is helpful to certain people.

So, Rarmakrishna was a Hindu, but also a Muslim, also a Christian, and everything else in the sense that he represented in his life and character the whole of what is called Truth, or God, or *Paramatman*, or the Absolute, or Ultimate Reality. He was That, the only one of his kind known to history. Without any narrowness or exclusiveness, he was the whole. He was Religion itself.

Sarada Devi
Motherhood Embodied

- *Sarada Devi*
- *Sarada Devi—A Unique Personality*
- *Ma Sarada Devi—the Highest Ideal of Womanhood*
- *Sarada Devi—The Universal Mother*
- *Is Sarada Devi—The Last of an Old Order or the Beginning of a New?*

Sarada Devi

RUMOURS SPREAD TO KAMARPUKUR THAT SRI RAMAKRISHNA HAD turned mad as a result of the over-taxing spiritual exercises he had been going through at Dakshineswar. Alarmed, Chandra Devi brought him home and arranged that he might have the best medical care available in a village. The doctors who examined him declared that there was nothing abnormal about him. Chandra Devi who studied him closely also found he was absolutely normal. As he had always done, Sri Ramakrishna sang songs, told stories, cut jokes and made people laugh—that is all. He was interested in everything except in the financial affairs of the family.

Chandra Devi's neighbours advised that if Sri Ramakrishna could be persuaded to marry, he might then be more conscious of his responsibilities to the family and accordingly, pay more attention to its financial needs. Chandra Devi started looking for a suitable bride. She did not want Sri Ramakrishna to know anything about her plan, for she feared that he might see marriage as a hindrance to his spiritual progress. Sri Ramakrishna, however, came to know, and so far from objecting to the marriage, began to take an active interest in the selection of the bride. He, in fact, mentioned Jayrambati, three miles to the north-west of Kamarpukur, as being the village where the bride could be found at the house of one Ramchandra Mukherjee. The bride, six-year-old and bearing the name, Sarada, was found. The marriage was duly solemnised; the bride went back to her father's house and Sri Ramakrishna to Dakshineswar to resume his spiritual practices.

Years passed and the bride and the bridegroom seldom met. Sarada continued to live at her father's house, helping her poor peasant parents with the usual chores of feeding the cattle, carrying food to the paddyfields for labourers working for her parents, cooking, cleaning, looking after the younger brothers, and so on. Once, famine gripped Jayrambati and its surrounding areas. Starving people went about searching for food, but there was no food anywhere. Sarada's parents had saved some foodgrains that year. They decided to cook some food everyday and distribute it to the starving people, fresh and hot. Sometimes, the hungry people would burn their fingers in eating hot food. Sarada, still a tiny girl, would fan the food to help it cool. She did it on her own.

As Sarada grew older, neighbours began to gossip about her misfortune. They would say that her husband had gone mad. Sarada overheard such remarks and was naturally very disturbed. She decided to go to Dakshineswar and see for herself the condition of her husband. So, she started for Calcutta with her father. In those days, one came to Calcutta from Jayrambati walking most of the way. She reached Dakshineswar and found her husband Sri Ramakrishna quite normal. She stayed with him for some time and then returned to Jayrambati. After some years, she permanently stayed with him.

In a way, Sarada Devi was Sri Ramakrishna's first disciple. He taught her as much religion as philosophy. He taught her everything he had learnt from his various Gurus. Sri Ramakrishna must have been pleased to see that she mastered every religious secret as quickly as he himself had done, perhaps even more quickly. Impressed by her great religious potential, he began to treat her as the Universal Mother Herself. Once, she asked him what he thought of her. He said, 'I look upon you as my own mother and as the Mother who is in the temple.'

Sri Ramakrishna fell sick with cancer of the throat. He was removed from Dakshineswar to Cossipore for treatment. By now he had come to be known as a great religious teacher. Many of the Calcutta elite came under his influence, but Sri Ramakrishna was not satisfied until he had a band of young men who were prepared to mould themselves strictly according to his instructions. Such young men came, fifteen or sixteen in number, all with a good family background and modern education. All of them are now well known for their achievements as religious teachers. It is Swami Vivekananda who led them from the front. It is this band of young men who later formed the Ramakrishna Mission.

Before passing away, in 1886, Sri Ramakrishna made Sarada Devi feel as if she was the mother of those young men, nay, of the entire humanity. At first, Sarada Devi was shy about playing this role, but slowly, she filled that role, and even became a religious teacher in her own right.

For the thirty-four years or so that she lived after Sri Ramakrishna's passing away, she inspired people, both monastic and lay, with the ideals that Sri Ramakrishna himself had preached and practised. She did the same way as Sri Ramakrishna—she lived those ideals.

Sarada Devi—a Unique Personality

IN A SENSE, SARADA DEVI'S LIFE WAS MORE COLOURFUL THAN SRI Ramakrishna's. And certainly, more testing and more complicated, Sri Ramakrishna never knew the rigours of a householder's life, its challenges, and its bitternesses. He, the ideal monk, always kept away from the cross-currents of family life. He was a child of nature, free, happy, and gay; he loved to watch the fun called life, but was careful enough never to be drawn into its maelstroms. Sarada Devi, on the contrary, was at the very heart of it. She was the head of a large family comprising men and women, most of them not even distantly related to her. And, what an assortment of characters they were! Some of them were great souls by any standard, but there were also some who were mean, jealous, and positively mischievous. How she managed to keep them all together without losing her balance of mind in the process is a mystery. And, each of them was convinced that she loved him or her best. They were all of them dependent on her, not only spiritually but also materially. She was not only their 'mother' but also their guru. She gave them full satisfaction on both scores.

Sarada Devi had a hard life from beginning to end. As daughter, wife, and finally, as the beloved mother of a large community of people cutting across race and language, there were demands on her much more than a woman in her circumstances has to meet. She fulfilled them in a manner possible only for her. But what is remarkable is that, in the midst of all her cares, she maintained a degree of aloofness which Hinduism attributes to the highest and best among men and women. Through the skein of all the varying situations which she faced, she remained absolutely calm as if these were no concern of hers. Her fortitude, courage, and wisdom, tested again and again, amazed everybody.

But the most amazing thing about her was her renunciation, a quality she shared with her husband in a measure equal to, if not more than, his. She often found herself in a situation in which starvation seemed certain, but under no circumstances would she seek aid from any quarter. Even when her disciples had grown to a considerable number and there were people among them with means to keep her in comfort and also anxious to be of service to her, she would never so far as even drop a hint that she had any difficulty.

She taught not by precepts but by example. There were irritants galore in the way people around her behaved. But she was an indulgent mother, who knew, the best way to educate an erring child was to set an example before him. She had seen the worst side of man, but she never lost faith in him, knowing that, given affection, sympathy, and guidance, be could overcome all his limitations.

She was human, yet divine. Her divinity shone through everything she did, even if it was something entirely mundane. She was a simple woman, but in thought, speech, and action she was attuned to God. She demonstrated how one could be in the world and yet not of it. Because her mind rested constantly on God, her whole life was a continuous prayer. She was a true saint, but she never claimed she was. She passed as an ordinary woman, but everything about her was extraordinary.

When her husband died, the mantle of leadership of the small group of ardent seekers of God that Sri Ramakrishna had created fell on her. Not that she sought it; it did not fall on her immediately either. The question could not arise, for she was a stranger to most of Sri Ramakrishna's devotees. If they knew anything about her, it was that she was a simple village woman, shy, without any education, without any knowledge of the world, but utterly devoted to her husband. Many had not even seen her face. With Sri Ramakrishna's passing away, she first returned to Kamarpukur and later settled at Jayrambati. Few among the disciples remembered her.

In fact, it never occurred to anybody that Sarada Devi was an extraordinary person. Most people thought that she was a lucky woman in that Sri Ramakrishna had married her. That she was great in her own right, nobody understood. It was Swami Vivekananda who first made the discovery. At least, it was he who first said what he thought she was. In a letter to Swami Sivananda written from the United States he described her as 'living Durga'. He also said that if he lived long enough, he would prove to the world what stuff she was, made of. In this connection, one remembers that the great Swami, not being able to decide whether he should go to the West, wrote to Sarada Devi of all persons and sought her advice. What made him do so is indeed a wonder, for what did she know of the implications of this journey? Surprisingly, Sarada Devi approved the idea. She wrote back to him saying that he should embark on this tour, for this, she said, would pave the way for the fulfilment of Sri Ramakrishna's mission. Vivekananda had no more hesitation when he received this letter. In the letter to Swami Sivananda referred to above, he said that his success in the West was entirely due to her grace. He repeated this statement later on many occasions. He was very keen that a suitable piece of land be found on the Ganges for Sarada Devi's use. He used to write to his brother-disciples urging that they make every possible effort in this direction. The land was found—the present site of Belur Math, and he begged Sarada Devi to come and see it. He was not happy until she saw it and liked it. On her behalf, the land was duly dedicated to Sri Ramakrishna.

A very interesting incident took place shortly after this: Vivekananda wanted to sell this land because he needed money to give relief to those suffering from the plague in Calcutta. She opposed the idea. She said, 'You cannot sell the land because you bought it to be dedicated by me to Sri Ramakrishna.' Her further argument was that Belur Math was not meant to give relief just once; it must continue to give relief to distressed people for generations to come. Vivekananda had no answer to this argument.

Sri Ramakrishna had begged that Sarada Devi do her share of work in giving spiritual light to people groping in the dark. She declined saying that being a woman she was not fit for that kind of work, Sri Ramakrishna remarked that she would, nevertheless, do much more than he himself had done. That is exactly what happened. But how did it happen? It is difficult to explain, but one notices that she was the first to recognise the need for the monks to have a home of their own. They were young people who, inspired by Sri Ramakrishna, had left home in search of God. If they were to make a permanent impact on society by spreading Sri Ramakrishna's message, they must stay together; attract more young people and work together to uplift the mankind. Instead, it distressed her to see that the young monks were wandering about like traditional monks, homeless, dependent upon food they got by begging. What a hard life they lived! Once, on a visit to Gaya, she had noticed how monks of the Sankar Math lived together happily in a permanent home of their own. She prayed to Sri Ramakrishna that her children also might have such a home. As if in answer to that prayer, the Ramakrishna Mission eventually had a home of its own at Belur Math. No wonder Vivekananda later gave her the name 'Sangha Janani', Mother of the Mission. She looked upon every member of the Mission as her own child, holding herself responsible for his spiritual and physical well-being. She encouraged everybody to intensify his spiritual efforts, but if anyone taxed himself too much in doing so, she strictly forbade it. Again, if she found anybody taking things easy, not trying as hard as he might, she would mildly scold him, or drop hints which left the individual in no doubt about her displeasure. Also, if anybody came to her with a spiritual problem, she would solve it, often by quoting Sri Ramakrishna or through a parable or some song.

When the centre at Mayavati was started, it was given the name *Advaita Ashrama*, for it was Swamiji's wish that amongst all the centres of the Mission, there should be at least one where non-dualism would be practised. That is to say, it would be a place where there would be no ritualistic worship and God would be meditated upon in His formless aspect. When Swamiji visited Mayavati, he however, discovered that a portrait of Sri Ramakrishna had been installed somewhere and some sort of worship was being offered to him. He did not like it though he did not specifically say that the worship was to be stopped. The worship was however, stopped. Those who had started the worship felt quite a jolt that Swamiji objected to Sri Ramakrishna being worshipped. They found it hard to reconcile themselves to this situation. So, though not immediately but after quite some time they referred the matter to Sarada Devi for her opinion. She wrote back in unambiguous terms that Swamiji was right. She said that since Sri Ramakrishna himself was a non-dualist, they, his followers, also fell into that category. That put a seal of finality to the controversy and it has never been raised again.

Sarada Devi never asserted herself where organisational matters were concerned. She, in fact, never even expressed an opinion about any policy or action of those who ran the organisation unless her opinion was sought, or she felt a grave error of judegment had taken place. In the early years of the Ramakrishna Mission, there were doubts in some quarters about the propriety of the monks doing the kind of work they were doing—running schools, hospitals, etc. The objection against it was that Sri Ramakrishna had never referred to it as a way of spiritual development. Some even suspected that Vivekananda introduced this work among the monks in imitation of the Christian missionaries. All doubts were, however, set at rest when Sarada Devi, after a visit to the Sevashrama (hospital) at Varanasi, remarked that she saw Sri Ramakrishna himself present there. She also donated a ten-rupee note as a token of her appreciation of the selfless service the monks were rendering to the sick. The note is still preserved with much care. Those who objected to this kind of work had misunderstood Sri Ramakrishna. They obviously forgot that Sri Ramakrishna himself had urged Mathur Babu to distribute food and clothing to distressed people at Deoghar and also at a place called Kalaighata, near Ranaghat in Nadia. He refused to budge an inch from those places till this was carried out to his satisfaction. He had also taught Vivekananda to serve men *(Jiva)* as God *(Siva)* Himself, describing this as the highest spiritual ideal for man.

Sarada Devi, who had known much suffering herself, was easily moved when she saw suffering in others. A Muslim youth, despised and feared by others for his record of crime, was a son to her. Every time he visited her, she welcomed him and fed him. An old destitute *Majhi* (one of the lowest castes in Hindu society) widow lost her only son, Sarada Devi cried with her loudly as if she had lost her own son. A junior monk had been told to leave the Math premises because of some offence he had committed. He went to Sarada Devi seeking refuge. She sent him back to the president of the Mission pleading that he be forgiven. He was. She would often tell her disciples to remember in their difficulties that they had a 'mother' in her who was looking after them. She used to say, 'Look upon me as your real mother; it's not a relation based on mutual choice, or by virtue of the fact that I'm your guru's wife.' She would also add, 'I'm mother to all, irrespective of what they are—good or bad.'

All of Sri Ramakrishna's disciples regarded her with awe. Slowly, they came to recognise that spiritually she was Sri Ramakrishna's equal, if not better. Sri Ramakrishna's power was there for all to see—in his ecstasies, wisdom, intellectual acumen, witty sayings and so on. Sarada Devi was like a live wire, her power seen only in flashes. Sri Ramakrishna himself treated her with great respect and consideration. 'She has come to bestow knowledge on mankind,' he used to say. Swami Vivekananda would sprinkle the water of the Ganges on himself again and again before he felt he was pure enough to appear before her. Swami Brahmananda, whom both Sri Ramakrishna and Sarada Devi regarded as their own son, trembled in her presence. Swami Saradananda, secretary of the Sri Ramakrishna Math and Ramakrishna Mission, and, in a way, also secretary to her, regarded her as the Mother of the Universe. The same was the attitude of the other disciples of Sri Ramakrishna also. Any wish she expressed, even if in an indirect manner, was a command that must be carried out. She, however, seldom if ever at all expressed her wish about anything.

Sri Ramakrishna left behind a small band of inspired young men, devoted to their Master and to each other. Swami Vivekananda preached his Master's message, laid the foundations of an organisation and died, leaving the care of the organisation in the hands of his brother-disciples. Sarada Devi lent a hand in nurturing this organisation, first by the example of her own life, then, also by encouragement and by offering wise counsels whenever sought. She however, always remained in the background, the over-watchful loving mother whose influence was more felt than seen. But, more than that, she drew hundreds of people to herself, people of all classes and communities, whom she initiated in the principles of spiritual life as taught by Sri Ramakrishna. Her husband restricted his choice to a dozen or so disciples, but she accepted anyone who came, regardless of how qualified he or she was—a testimony to her great power as a religious teacher.

Those were days of intense terrorist activity against the British government. Many monks had been terrorists (revolutionists) at one time, but after becoming monks, they had given up politics altogether. The police, however, did not trust them. They thought their monastic robe was only a camouflage. Carmichael was Governor of Bengal then. He declared that Belur Math was a den of the terrorists, referring to the presence of the erstwhile terrorists. People stopped visiting Belur Math or keeping contact with the monks to avoid police suspicion. Some well-wishers even suggested that those monks who had adverse police reports against them should be expelled from the Mission to prove to the government that the Mission was a loyal organisation. When the matter was referred to Sarada Devi, she firmly ruled it out. She said those who had come in the name of God were honest and they must be protected. She advised Swami Saradananda to see the Governor and explain to him the aims and objects of the Mission and to impress upon him the fact that ex-terrorists had completely eschewed politics and were now dedicated to religion and selfless service to mankind. The Governor later withdrew his allegation. Terrorists, however, kept coming to Sarada Devi for spiritual instructions. The police were watching and she knew it, still she never turned them away. Once, a pregnant woman was forced to walk several miles to answer a police summons. When this was reported to Sarada Devi, she indignantly remarked, 'Was there no man there to give the police a beating and then rescue the woman?'

As the years passed, more and more people began to come to her. She sometimes visited other states of India. Wherever she went, people came to see her in droves. Language was no barrier. The mere sight of her was a comfort, a blessing. It was as if she was launching a movement, not by design, but unconsciously, perhaps by divine dispensation. Many Western people also came to her and they were warmly welcomed. The movement began to grow and now it has spread across the world, known as the Sri Ramakrishna Movement.

Sarada Devi preferred her rural home but, partly for reasons of health and partly because of importunities from her devotees, she was sometimes forced to come to Calcutta. Whether she was at

Jayrambati or Calcutta, the last few years saw her at the height of her spiritual powers. A glance, a word or a touch was enough grace to uplift a man. But her health was fast declining. The last words she uttered on her deathbed were characteristic: 'My blessings to all those who are already here, those who are on the way and those who will come in future.'

Sarada Devi: The Highest Ideal of Womanhood

MANY BOOKS ARE BEING PUBLISHED AND MANY DISCUSSIONS ARE ALSO being held on the Holy Mother Sarada Devi nowadays. It seems that with the passage of time, the Mother is getting exposed and exalted. Sometimes, I wonder if the Mother might even excel Sri Ramakrishna. However, very few people knew about the Holy Mother before her birth centenary. Let me recount an incident: A person, who had been initiated by the Mother, longed to have one photograph of hers, so that he could keep it in his room. He tried hard but failed to manage a single photograph of the Holy Mother from anybody. Finally, he came to Swami Saradananda with his plea: 'Could you please give me a photograph of the Mother?' On hearing this, Saradananda replied, 'Mother's photo—why? Do you think she is Queen Victoria?' Indeed, the Mother kept herself hidden throughout her life. She was ever veiled. But today we find that the Divine Mother is slowly unveiling herself. We can discern the various novel facets of her personality. So many new incidents, which were once kept hidden like a treasure, are coming to light.

I feel very scared to say or write anything about the Mother, lest I belittle her or write anything wrong about her. Nivedita had once written a letter to the Mother. It was no ordinary letter—it was literature. It is only possible for people like Nivedita to write such a letter. Nivedita wrote the letter from abroad. She had gone to the church for prayer and was musing on Mother Mary, when all of a sudden she had a vision of the Holy Mother Sarada Devi sitting in Mary's place– clad in sari and wearing her bangle. Returning home, Nivedita wrote a letter to the Mother. She wrote: 'Dearest Mother—I wish we could send you a wonderful hymn, or a prayer. But somehow even that would seem too *loud*, too full of noise!' Nivedita could say no more, her speech seemed to have been exhausted. Unable to express herself any further, she wrote: 'Surely you are the most wonderful thing of God—Sri Ramakrishna's own chalice of His Love for the world—a token left with His children, in these lonely days, and we should be very still and quiet before you—except indeed for a little fun!' Then in her attempt to explain, she says, 'Surely the 'wonderful things of God' are all quiet—stealing unnoticed into our lives—for instance, the light of the sun, the breeze that flows over the Ganges, the sweet fragrance of the garden, etc. These are the silent things that are like you. They help me to understand you a little.'

Sarada Devi was very silent by nature. Neither did she write any book nor did she deliver any lecture. But her life itself was a great encyclopaedia. She taught everyone the basic truths of life by practising them in her own life.

We can recall those days in Cossipore, when Sri Ramakrishna was on his deathbed. His mortal life was slowly coming to an end. One day, he asked the Holy Mother, 'Shall I go on working alone? Won't you do anything?' Sri Ramakrishna was as if making an appeal to her. He very well knew that their advent on this earth had significance, but the Holy Mother seemed to be unaware of her role till then. So, Sri Ramakrishna was making her alert of her duty, before his departure form this mortal world. He said, 'What have I done? You will have to do a lot more.' The advent of Sri Ramakrishna and Sarada Devi in this world had one and only one great significance. They had come to show an ideal to us– this ideal was the eternal ideal of India. India has always advocated that if you want to acquire wealth then acquire it, if you desire to attain social status then attain it, if you wish to have education then gain it, but you should remember that all these are not the ultimate or highest goal in life. There is something even greater or bigger than these goals, which cannot be expressed in words and this is called the Supreme Being, the Omnipresent—nothing is greater or better than Him. Try to achieve this highest being. Ultimately, however, it will be found that this Supreme Being is not external, rather it is internal. It is not that we have to gain it, but we have to become it. To get is to be. To become means to build own self. A man is not great by wealth, or by education. He is great by his life, by character and by the development of his humane qualities. This is the chief tenet of religion and it is this religion, which Sri Ramakrishna and Sarada Devi wanted to hold up before us. They did not come to propagate any new religious doctrine; rather they came to show everyone the basic principle of religion by their own life and behaviour. In this respect, Sri Ramakrishna and Sarada Devi were same, as their ideals were the same.

We perceive in Sri Ramakrishna the glorious ideal of renunciation. If he was given more than one cloth, he would keep only one and return the other. Once, the Holy Mother gave him some aniseeds after his meal as a digestive, he was unable to save even those little grains. Mathurbabu had once attempted to give a small part of his property to Sri Ramakrishna and the latter became angry and was about to hit him. His renunciation was cent percent. However, Sri Ramakrishna was an ascetic and renunciation is the trait of any true ascetic. But Sarada Devi was apparently a simple housewife, yet we notice the same quality of renunciation in her, too.

Marwari Lakshminarayan had come to offer a sum of ten thousand rupees to Sri Ramakrishna which he declined. He then offered it to the Holy Mother. But Mother refused to accept it instantly. After the demise of Sri Ramakrishna, Sarada Devi started living at Kamarpukur. Her clothes were ragged and patched. She could not even buy the salt to season her food. She could have easily reported her plight to the disciples of Sri Ramakrishna through a post card and they certainly would have made some arrangements for her livelihood. But she never informed them about her miseries. She never begged anything from anybody. I usually say that, if Sri Ramakrishna was an emperor in the realm of renunciation, Sarada Devi was its empress. We observe that Sri Ramakrishna's ideal, his renunciation, his forgiveness, his love, purity, generosity and his dependence on God are also entirely present in Sarada Devi. Moreover, she held on to this lofty ideal, while remaining within the ambits of family life, performing its different duties and responsibilities. We perceive in her an extraordinary sense of responsibility and non-attachment. She remained ever calm, poised, unmoved, unflinching and a stoic seer in all conditions—her mind always contemplating the lotus feet of the Lord.

We see what a profound reverence the disciples of Sri Ramakrishna had for their Holy Mother! Swami Vivekananda wrote to one of his brother-disciples, 'You have not yet understood the wonderful significance of Mother's life—none of you. But gradually you will know. Without Shakti (Power) there is no regeneration for the world. Why is it that our country is the weakest and the most backward of all countries?—Because Shakti is held in dishonour there. Mother has been born to revive that wonderful Shakti in India; and making her the nucleus, once more will Gargis and Maitreyis be born into the world.' 'To me, Mother's grace is a hundred thousand times more valuable than the Father's. Mother's grace, Mother's blessings are all paramount to me. Please, pardon me, I am a little bigoted here as regards Mother. If but Mother orders, her demons can work anything... Brother, I shall show how to worship the living Durga and then only shall I be worthy of my name. I shall be relieved when you will have purchased a plot of land and established there the living Durga, the Mother... of Sri Ramakrishna, you may aver, my brother, that he was an Incarnation or whatever else you may like but fie on him who has no devotion for the Mother.'

Durga Puja was settled to be held at the Belur Math. The question of animal sacrifice arose. Swamiji wanted to have animal sacrifice, but the Mother said, 'There will be no sacrifice' and Swamiji readily accepted her verdict, without any argument. Had Sri Ramakrishna proposed the same, Swamiji would have definitely argued, quoting from the scriptures. But when Sarada Devi expressed her views, Swamiji said nothing to refute her.

Before going to meet the Mother, Swamiji used to drink holy water from the Ganges and sprinkle it over his head and body, ignoring his ill-health. He said, 'We have such impure minds, so before going to the Mother, I am purifying myself.' It is to be noted that the speaker here is not a layman, but a pure soul like Swamiji.

Likewise, Swami Brahmananda also remained very alert while going to pay his respect to the Holy Mother; he used to tremble even. A senior monk once narrated an incident to me, which he himself had witnessed before becoming a monk. At that time, he had only heard the name of Swami Brahmananda, but did not have the opportunity to see him. He had a great desire to have a glimpse of this great disciple of the Master. A friend informed him that Swami Brahmananda was going to Bhubaneswar by a train from the Howrah station, on such and such date and at such time. So, he went to the Howrah station on the specified date and time and waited for the much-coveted moment. At last, Swami Brahmananda arrived in a white Rolls Royce Car—it was the car of the king of Coochbehar, and Maharaj came down from the magnificent car just like a king. Then, instead of moving towards his train, he proceeded towards another platform, where a Bankura-bound train was standing. The narrator and his companion followed Maharaj and soon found him standing near a reserved third class compartment. Inside sat a lady with a huge veil over her face and Raja Maharaj lay flat on the ground to pay his homage to this lady, paying no heed to the dirty and dusty platform. Then, he stood with folded hands and the Holy Mother was heard saying from under her veil, 'Take care of yourself, son. Malaria has broken out in Bhubaneswar. Do not forget to boil the water before drinking', and Swami Brahmananda answering, 'Yes, Mother, yes, Mother' walked backwards with his face towards the Mother. It must be remembered that this deep regard was not meant for any common person, nor also because Sarada Devi was the better-half of their divine master, Sri Ramakrishna, but it was purely for a person, whose noble life and divine character had left them astounded. Nivedita was a foreigner. Why was she so charmed with the Mother? It is true that the Holy Mother showered her affection on her and lovingly called her 'My little girl', 'Naren's daughter', etc. But this cannot be the reason behind Nivedita's devotion or her emotional outburst. Actually, they all honoured an ideal—the ideal which these people perceived in Sri Ramakrishna, the ideal which they observed among his disciples, the same ideal was also found to be sparkling in Sarada Devi. It is this lofty ideal to which they had paid their deep respect and reverence.

We say that Sarada Devi is the Mother of the Sri Ramakrishna Mission. This is because she wanted all the disciples of Sri Ramakrishna to stay together under one roof and in this way an order be built up. After the demise of Sri Ramakrishna, the Mother had prayed earnestly: 'You came and went away and will everything finish with you? Then, why did you come to this world taking so much pain? I cannot bear to see your sons begging.' Whether it was because of her prayer or not, we find that gradually the Math developed and it owned its land. Then, Swamiji brought the Holy Mother to the Math and said, 'Mother, now you can move about freely in your own place.'

All these are correct, but Sarada Devi is not regarded as the Mother of the Mission just for this reason only. Sarada Devi is called the Mother of Ramakrishna Mission for keeping up the ideal of Sri Ramakrishna—his ideal of renunciation, of devotion to God, the ideal which is the foundation of the Mission, the ideal for whose propagation stands the Mission. She always tried to keep up this ennobling lofty ideal not only in herself but also in her disciples and in those she loved. She could never tolerate any deviation from the ideal. She reminded everyone about this high ideal over and over again. It is for this cause, that Sarada Devi is the Mother of the Mission.

Sri Ramakrishna left his mortal frame in 1886 and Sarada Devi lived for thirty-four years more after that. Thakur had said, 'You will have to do a lot more' and she did that 'lot more' during these thirty-four years. She assured all men—good or bad, sinner or virtuous, monastic or lay—and said to them, 'Always remember that you have a mother, who is sheltering you all.' Now, what does this 'sheltering' imply? Is it only affection, tolerance and love? No, it is not. Undoubtedly, the Mother has profound love for us but this love is not the love of the feeble or the weaker mind. The Mother's love admonishes us not to deviate from the path of our noble ideal and virtue. She encourages us to move towards our goal and assures us, 'I am there with you, I shall help you and show the way and if necessary, I may even chastise you.' This is called true love. When someone gives a present, that is also a kind of love; but when one helps us, encourages us and shows us the way, so that we may develop into an ideal human being, then that love is the true love. This kind of love emancipates a man forever. The love of the Holy Mother is like that.

Another thing to be noted in her personality is that she revealed no occult power or spiritual glamour. Her spirituality had no external manifestation. Even in Sri Ramakrishna, some mystical powers were revealed. He went into deep trance from time to time, he could sing very well, he could dance, his speech had a wonderful intoxicating quality and all these attracted the common men. But Sarada Devi had no such grandeur. If she possessed any, it was the grandeur of love. Silently, she drew the teeming villagers towards herself, with the purity of her love, taking the responsibility for their present life and their life beyond. Sri Ramakrishna used to say about the Mother: 'She is like a cat hidden under the ashes, a cat smeared with ashes, is as if sitting on a heap of ashes. No one can see it.' Similarly, the Holy Mother also remained in the domesticity concealing her true self. Everyone took her to be just another mother or aunt or grandmother next-door, but the speciality of the Mother is that despite living in the trash, in the drab and dingy environment of the domestic life, she stuck firmly to her principles and ideal. Swami Premananda said about the Mother: 'The queen of queens is mopping the house, washing utensils, winnowing rice, even cleaning up the leftovers from the plates of her children, like a beggar-woman, at her own will—yet she is the queen of queens, an empress!'

However, the Mother's divinity was sometimes revealed and people were astounded. The following is an incident of those days, when the Mother was living at the Udbodhan House. One morning, Swami Shuddhananda, Chandra Mohan Dutta and another monk were going to the Ganges for a bath. Chandrababu was a disciple of the Mother and had free access to her. The Mother also loved him very much and he used to carry out various small errands for the Mother. Swami Suddhananda said to Chandrababu: 'You always ask the Mother for this and that. Why do not you ask for your salvation? Go to the Mother and ask for it today.' Chandrababu replied, 'I will definitely ask for it from the Holy Mother. It is no big deal.' After his bath, Chandrababu went straight to the Mother's room. She was engaged in her daily worship then. Chandrababu stood near her but could not utter a single word. A strange awe fell on him and he was trembling. The Mother looked up at him and enquired in a solemn voice, 'What do you want?' But Chandrababu could not ask for his salvation. Instead, he said, 'I want *prasad*.' The Mother beckoned and said 'It is kept over there. Take it.' Chandrababu came back with the prasad, he was still shaking. His trembling persisted for a couple of hours or more.

Sindhubala Dasi was a pregnant woman. She had been arrested by the police, who made her walk a long distance. Hearing this, the Mother said, 'Was there no man there to give the police a beating and then rescue the woman?' When Mother spoke like this, everyone seemed to be thunderstruck. The Mother's personality, her divinity was thus manifested from time to time.

Actually, it is not possible for us to understand or apprehend the Holy Mother. How shall we define her? Shall we call her a householder or was she an ascetic? Or, shall we describe her as a bridge between these two? She represented all these and again, she was over and above all these, too. She cannot be specified by any adjective. She is a Goddess, yet she lived like a common woman. She was human and yet her divinity was revealed from time to time. Nothing can be ascertained about her. If we look for supernatural or miraculous incidents in her life, we shall hardly find any. The Mother herself was a miracle. Nivedita wrote in her letter, mentioned earlier—'The most wonderful thing of God—Sri Ramakrishna's own chalice of His Love for the world—a token left with His children . . . ' Bringing that chalice, Sri Ramakrishna seems to be saying to the people: 'See how wonderful and noble can a person be. Apparently, so ordinary yet so extraordinary, when judged by human standards.' We understand no other miracle. The greatest miracle is a man's life and his character. From that viewpoint, Sarada Devi is a great miracle. She is not present among us any more physically but her love for us still exists. The Mother had said, 'My blessing will be with everybody—those who have come, those who are coming and those who will come in the future.' The Mother's blessing and love will persist forever and always, for all those, who want to follow the path of virtue, renunciation, salvation and divine joy.

Sarada Devi—The Universal Mother

PERHAPS, MANY OF US HAVE NOTICED THAT EVERY YEAR THE VOLUME of Sri Ramakrishna Vivekananda literature is increasing in size and the Holy Mother Sarada Devi is at the heart of this literature. The readers seem to have a deep curiosity and eagerness regarding the Holy Mother. Even if we have read about the Mother, and know of many incidents of her life, still we wish to know or read about them all over again. We feel as if we are reading them anew, every incident seems so novel to us.

Mother Sarada Devi has been designated as the Universal Mother, although no one claims that a certain specific title suits the Mother best or can describe her personality fully. But the Holy Mother is the real Universal Mother; this title is only applicable to her and to no one else.

We cannot assert that even Sri Ramakrishna regarded everybody impartially or equally as the Holy Mother did. Sarada Devi is the mother of all; she is the mother of both the virtuous and the wicked. Sri Ramakrishna was not so liberal like her. He used to select his disciples very carefully and then transformed them gradually. Others only visited his place and the Master had good wishes for all. But the Holy Mother seemed to take the entire responsibility of her children. She did not merely cherish good wishes or motherly love for them,' she assured her children, saying: 'Do not worry. Your mother is with you.' In our childhood, we all have heard such words of solace, strength and assurance from our mothers; Sarada Devi also said just like that: 'I am there with you. Why do you worry? Do not worry.' Whenever anyone committed some mistake or wrong, she used to say, 'If the son gets dirty, it is the mother's duty to clean him up. The mother knows that her child is wrong but after all it belongs to her. The son's responsibility rests upon the mother.' This is called responsibility. Sri Ramakrishna might have taken the responsibility of some of his disciples but he never admitted it like this in public. He had understood what would be the role of the Mother after his absence.

The Sri Ramakrishna Movement is spreading very fast to every corner of the world. Recently, I had gone to Germany. There in the German University, a lady read an article on the Holy Mother. This lady, who had written the article, was the Departmental Head of Philosophy of that University. Our topic was Sri Ramakrishna Movement, the centenary of Ramakrishna Mission; but how could the Mother have a place in it? Sarada Devi did not belong to the Ramakrishna Mission. She was neither its member nor its President. She was neither the Secretary nor the Trustee of the Mission, yet whenever we discuss anything about the Ramakrishna Mission, we cannot exclude or ignore the Holy Mother from our discourse, otherwise it remains incomplete. I found that the German lady had studied the life of the Divine Mother very well.

Whenever we try to talk about the Mother, we often use words like 'extraordinary woman', 'Goddess', 'universal mother' etc. in our zeal and excitement. I remember once having regarded the Mother as the 'universal mother' in one of my lectures, a monk of the Belur Math had rebuked me for this—'Oh, so you think you have understood the mother quite well. You have realised that she is the universal mother.' In fact, no word can sufficiently describe the Mother. How can we describe the Mother? It is better to keep mum. No one is greater than the Mother, we hardly need any adjective to qualify her. Mother does not need such attributes as affectionate, kind-hearted or merciful. In the Gospel, we find Sri Ramakrishna telling one of his favourite disciples, 'Listen my child, try to understand only your relation with me'. Sri Ramakrishna indirectly meant to say, 'I am yours and you are mine. I am very close to you. You have every right on me. Love me.' Actually, this love is the essence of every religion—to love God and to think Him as one's own. Why should I praise Him so much? He is my very own. I have every right on Him, why should I glorify Him? Therefore, that monk had reproached me for using such title as universal mother. Again, whether I say it or not, the truth remains the same; whether I know or not, Mother remains Mother. 'Universal mother' means the mother of all. The Mother had herself admitted, 'I am the mother of all. I am the mother of both Sarat (Swami Saradananda) and Amzad.' So, she is herself disclosing her identity.

The Mother always remained veiled. She sat with a long veil over her face. But when she remained at Jayrambati, she did not use any veil, as it was her father's place. There, she was someone's aunt, or sister and the like. She made no discrimination of caste and creed. She belonged to all. It was like a big family. When Mother used to return to Calcutta, a bullock cart would come to take her and as she boarded the cart, half the village assembled there shedding tears for her. She belonged to them all. Whether we address her as mother or as sister or as anything else, she is our very own.

Sarada Devi used to say, 'The Master had left me to propagate this ideal of motherhood throughout the world.' In other words, 'I am the Mother, the Mother of all, regard me as your mother and love me as your mother. This is your worship, your meditation and your study of scriptures. Only know this much that I am your mother. You need not feel shy before me.'

Sri Ramakrishna passed away in 1886 and the Holy Mother in 1920. In other words, the Mother lived for thirty-four years after the demise of the Master and in this period, Mother did many things which the Master did not. Sri Ramakrishna had rightly said, 'What have I done? You will have to do a lot more.' In short, the mother gave shape to the Sri Ramakrishna Mission. She was the creator of this Mission. Swamiji gave her the name 'Sangha-janani' or the Mother of the Mission. He declared, 'Do not think Mother is merely the wife of our Master, she is the creator of our Mission, its preserver and protector. She is the "Mother of the Mission" and this is a fact.'

And, what about her intelligence? We often speak of commonsense. The Mother's commonsense was matchless. Every man, in his life, faces moments of crisis, at one time or the other, which he finds very difficult to cope with. A great presence of mind is needed to deal with such situations. Similar dire situations are also not rare in the history of Ramakrishna Mission. During such times, the Holy Mother, who had no connection with the Mission as such, i.e. she was not a member of the trustee, yet very adroitly handled the situation and led the Mission out of the crisis. However, we cannot assert that she led from the forefront, as she actually gave the leadership from behind her veil. She gave all the suggestions and advice from there. Her advice was not shallow or superficial; rather they were very much realistic and practical.

For instance, when Swamiji was busy building up the Mission, purchasing land, collecting money from abroad, the Mission was in its initial stage, it had just started to grow. During that time, plague spread in Calcutta as an epidemic. Swamiji hurried down to Calcutta from Darjeeling, urging everyone to serve the victims and work hand-in-hand against the epidemic. He chalked out several big plans in this regard. A few asked him from where he would get the money to materialise his plans. Swamiji retorted that if there were men, then money would definitely pour in. And if necessary, he would even sell Belur Math. 'We are monks and ascetics' he said, 'we are supposed to wander about and live under the trees and we shall revert to such a life, if necessary.' When Mother heard this, she said to Swamiji, 'How is that possible? You cannot sell the land because you bought it to be dedicated by me to Sri Ramakrishna.' Swamiji realised that Mother was right—the property of Belur Math actually belonged to Her. Then, the Holy Mother adduced a reason, which was very significant. The Mother suggested, 'Belur Math was not meant to give relief just once. Many such calamities may come in the future, what would you do then?' The Mother meant to say: 'Will there be no crisis or danger or natural calamity in our country in the days ahead? When people will be in distress and seek help from you, then what will be left for them?' Just a few words and Swamiji accepted Mother's advice readily.

When any crisis comes, sometimes, we cannot decide what to do or how to tackle the situation. But the Holy Mother's presence of mind was incomparable. She had protected the Mission from all odds with her unparalleled presence of mind, several times. Even Sri Ramakrishna used to do what the Mother proposed. Another crisis befell the Mission, when the Governor of Bengal, in the convocation address of the University, remarked—'Belur Math, it is a den of all the terrorists.' After this, many monks of the Math suggested to make a list of those monastic members, who were involved in politics or who were members of revolutionary organisations, prior to their joining the Mission and to expel them from the Math immediately. A list was made which included the names of Bharat Maharaj, Surya Maharaj, whom many of us know. There were many others like Ram Maharaj, who had gone to jail innumerable times. They heard that they would be expelled. They went to the Mother and fell at her feet, crying: 'Mother, what kind of decision is this? Shall we be driven out?' No one spoke a word on their behalf, so they themselves went to seek protection from the Holy Mother. They seemed to say 'Mother, we are being driven out, how can such injustice be done to us in your presence?' The Mother then called Swami Saradananda and told him: 'These boys are all worshippers of Truth. Our Master was an embodiment of Truth and these boys are worshippers of that Truth. What they are saying is true. They are saying that previously they were involved in politics but now they have left all that in order to join Sri Ramakrishna's Mission. There is no falsehood in what they are saying. You go and meet the Governor and explain to him the aims and objects of the Mission and to impress upon him the fact that ex-terrorists had completely eschewed politics and were now dedicated to religion and selfless service to mankind. He will surely understand.' When does such confidence come? When truth is in your favour, when you are clinging to truth and standing on the path of truth; then you can raise your voice to say who you are. Swami Saradananda, with the assistance of Miss MacLeod went to meet the Governor of Bengal and explained everything to him. Then, the Governor came to visit Belur Math. Later, in Dhaka, when the next convocation was held, he admitted that what he had said about Belur Math in the last convocation was not true, the monks of the Math were doing a noble job. In this way, the Mother saved the Sri Ramakrishna Mission.

The Mother gave her own introduction—'I am the mother of all. Thakur (Sri Ramakrishna) left me behind to manifest the Motherhood of God to the world.' A cat was mewing. Hearing it, the Holy Mother said, 'Look, Gyan, this cat is depending upon us. Take care of the cats. Give them some milk to drink everyday.' Again she added, 'Do not beat the cat. I am present in it. If you beat the cat, it will be same as beating me.' A parrot was twittering, the Mother said fondly 'I am coming, my child.' She herself admitted—'I am the mother of all.'

At Dakshineswar, while massaging the feet of the Master, the Holy Mother all of a sudden asked Sri Ramakrishna, 'What do you think of me?' It was as if she wanted to hear and also make others hear, what the Master thought about her, how he estimated her; she would not say anything about herself. Sri Ramakrishna uttered without any hesitation: 'The Mother who resides in the Temple is the one who has given birth to this body and is presently living at the Nahabat and it is she, who is now massaging my feet.' In other words, 'You are that Universal Mother.'

Sri Ramakrishna introduced the Mother to us all consciously. Sri Ramakrishna said, 'Is she any ordinary woman? She is my Shakti (the creative power of Brahman).' Sri Ramakrishna had once addressed the Mother as 'Tui' (a disrespectful pronominal address), by mistake. The Master was lying in his bed, with his eyes closed. Someone had entered the room and Sri Ramakrishna thought it was Lakshmi Didi. Then when she was going out, she kept the door open, the Master said, 'Close the door when you leave.' Holy Mother answered, 'Okay.' Sri Ramakrishna was startled to hear the voice of the Holy mother and said 'Oh! It was you. I thought it was Lakshmi, please do not mind.' Then, he could not sleep and fidgeted the whole night. Next day, at daybreak, he rushed to the Mother apologising 'Look, I could not sleep the whole night thinking as to why I uttered such harsh words.' He said this in such a way as if he had committed a crime. The Mother consoled him by saying: 'So what? You did not say it willingly and even if you did so, it is not an offence.' What a high esteem the Master had for her! What profound respect they had for each other! The Mother herself admitted, 'We are inseparable.' *Yathagnerdahikashakti*—The fire and its power to burn are inseparable. Water and its liquidity, milk and its white colour, can these be separated? Likewise, power and the powerful. Sri Ramakrishna said, 'She is like a cat smeared with ashes. A cat sometimes lies in a heap of ashes and no one can detect that it is there.' Our Holy Mother is also like that.

This universal motherhood is very strange. The Mother was ill, she was suffering from arthritis in her feet, yet she worked the whole day trudging on her feet. Even on her birthday, she insisted on cooking all by herself, serve food to her children and then would she have her own meal. Once, all the monks protested together against this practice, 'We won't allow this anymore. You will have to dine first and then we shall have your Prasad.' But the Mother was unable to accept their proposal. She said, 'How can I have my meal before feeding my children? I cannot do that. First, you eat and then I will.'

There are many more wonderful incidents—all centering round the Mother. One day, while everyone was taking rest, a gentle rapping sound could be heard from the courtyard. Someone came out to find that a brick was protruding from the ground and the Mother unable to pick the heavy brick up, was trying to crush it with another brick, lest her sons stumble over it and get injured;—and hence this rapping sound. There were so many devotees and people around, no body cared for such things but the Mother did.

Once, Swamiji faced a grave problem. Foreigners were pouring into his Mission from abroad. American devotees, British devotees were all coming. From our viewpoint, they were all *Mlechchhas*, the untouchable non-Hindus. No one would touch them. Swamiji wrote to Nivedita: 'Since you wish to come to this country, you should also have some knowledge about this land beforehand. The people for whom you are coming, whom you will serve, they will not even touch you. You are an untouchable in their eyes.' Nivedita and Miss MacLeod had come. Swamiji knew how good they were. But our society would not accept them. So, what to do? Swamiji just told the Mother: 'They have all come. They want to see you and pay their respect to you.' The Mother replied 'Very well. Let them come.' Then, she greeted them very warmly and dined with them. She not only touched them but also had her meal with them. This is the contribution of the Holy Mother.

Nivedita often lamented, 'If I am reborn as an Indian in my next life, then I will be able to work a lot more than now.' All these foreign ladies appealed to the Mother that they wanted to take a photograph of hers. With folded hands, they prayed to the Mother—'Mother, it is our misfortune that we were not born in this nation, we were born elsewhere. We are untouchables. But still, we are your children. We need at least a photograph of yours.' Moved by their grief, the Holy Mother consented. The photograph of the Mother that we find today was taken by them.

Mother had a unique attitude. Use of foreign articles was being boycotted in those days. Everyone refused to buy foreign articles and clothes. Now, the Mother's nieces, they preferred the fine foreign clothes to the coarse indigenous ones or *khaddar*. So, the Mother returned the coarse clothes to buy some finer foreign ones for them. The person who had bought the clothes was very displeased; he grumbled, 'How can I buy those foreign clothes?' The Mother replied, 'My son, they too are my children. I have to deal with all; how can I be so partial? If my son soils himself in the dust or mud, it is me who has to wipe all the dirt off his body and take him in my lap.'

Nivedita had made an excellent remark about Sarada Devi. She said, 'To me it has always appeared that Sarada Devi is Sri Ramakrishna's final word as to the ideal of Indian womanhood. But is she the last of an old order, or the beginning of a new? In her, one sees realised that wisdom and sweetness to which the simplest of women may attain. And yet, to myself the stateliness of her courtesy and her great open mind are almost as wonderful as her sainthood. I have never known her hesitate, in giving utterance to large and generous judgement, however new or complex might be the question put before her. Her life is one long stillness of prayer. Her whole experience is of theocratic civilisation. Yet, she rises to the height of every situation.'

Sarada Devi: The Last of an Old Order or the Beginning of a New?

THE *MASTER AS I SAW HIM*, THE BOOK ON SWAMIJI BY SISTER NIVEDITA raised a question: 'Holy Mother, Sarada Devi—is she the last of an old order, or the beginning of a new?' Not only do we love and respect the Holy Mother but we also believe in her philosophy. The aim was to educate the common mass. Sri Ramakrishna came at a juncture of two ages when everybody was copying the occident at random. As if offering a passive resistance, he came to say—'Look at me. Here I am, the very soul of India.' A very simple man, very innocent, poor and knowing nothing of literacy but we see the contemporary elites of Calcutta visiting him. From the *Gospel of Sri Ramakrishna* (*Kathamrita*) we learn that most of the visitors and guests visiting Sri Ramakrishna were educated and well-versed in English, whereas Sri Ramakrishna was just an ordinary priest of the Dakshineswar Kali Temple. In spite of this, it is worth mentioning that people meeting him looked upon him as the incarnation of God and they were finally inspired. There was a benign pleasure in his company. From where does this sweetness come? He did not use a very refined language but what brilliant and enlightened thoughts did he convey. Similarly, we can compare his message with that of Jesus Christ in the *Sermon on the Mount*. They came to show us a way and unfolded philosophical ideals through their life. There is a saying of Swamiji, 'Let work be your voice, Let it speak for itself.'

We are not differentiating Sri Ramakrishna and Sarada Devi as two distinct identities. They are one and undifferentiated like the body and its shadow or the fire and its heat. Sri Ramakrishna confessed Sarada Devi to be his power Goddess Saraswati, who had come to bestow knowledge upon the ignorant people. And, Sarada Devi said, 'Who am I? He is everything.' They came to enlighten the mass with the knowledge of aim of life. This is what we call religion; what else is being religious? Swamiji said religion is a science. It is a science of 'being and becoming.' It is a science of how one unfolds one's life and extends one's help to unfold that of others'—'Being and becoming.' We accept science when we find out that the truth science is providing holds good for everybody. And, it is equal and same to all, irrespective of difference in time, place and individuality. So what they said was Truth only. Truth is God, Truth is religion, Truth is everything. Truth is truth, so not to deviate from truth is the eternal Indian ideal. We would like to respect only those who are committed to truth; not the politician, not a man of power not an established man, but to a man committed to honesty, we pay our maximum respect. Truth is a truth at any point of time and is not differentiated as new or old.

Once, Swamiji said that Sri Ramakrishna is like a mould. We should follow the path he showed and shape our lives accordingly. Sri Ramakrishna has shown the path for all, even for householders. How should they lead their life? The Holy Mother was a housewife. They wanted to show us that religion is a proved science. Swamiji says, 'Religion is realisation.' Therefore, everything should be put into action, only words are not sufficient. Sri Ramakrishna suggests, just to follow their life. Their life was committed to Truth and love for all.

Who is a great man? A person who has got money or who has power? No, people often forget them. But we shall never forget Gautam Buddha, or Chaitanya. Similarly, we can never forget Sri Ramakrishna and Sarada Devi. It is strange to know how rapidly their voice has spread widely. Are we doing it? What ability do we have to spread their voice? Rather, it is the greatness of truth that is comparable to the sun. Does anyone question the sun, 'Oh sun, you are giving light; but who gave you the right?' Sri Ramakrishna, a stammering villager who could not even speak proper Bengali, now has his sayings imprinted on texts. Moreover, he attracted and inspired contemporary people. Romain Rolland said while describing him, that he is 'God intoxicated' and 'the symphony of India.' Max Muller regarded Sri Ramakrishnas 'not only a high-souled man, a real Mahatma, but a man of original thought.'

It was rightly quoted by Karl Marx, 'Religion is still opium of the masses.' Again, it was stated by Karl Marx, 'Religion is the only heart in a heartless world.' And, Sri Ramakrishna is that 'Only Heart'. Men search after God at different places but Sri Ramakrishna shows the way of God and says, 'I belong here, it's my place, now there is no need to wander.'

Religion, according to Swamiji, is comparable to sunlight. There is nothing to hide because where there is something to hide, which is sure to be untrue. They have come to show true love. To be precise they showed us what truth is and what love is. Sri Ramakrishna is not referring to any God or Goddesses. Nor, does he assure that by Kali worship you will get all. He is not even emphasising reciting *mantra* or *japa* or conviction of oneself to any Math or sector. He is rather asking for something simpler than that. The greatest truth is—realising God which is the aim of life. But how should we start?

Sri Ramakrishna wants us to go towards that sea of knowledge, that infinite sky of knowledge. He insisted on moving towards that Infinite and he always insisted on making a continuous movement, never to be just satisfied and stop. Truth is vast and infinite like the sky and deep like the sea—the omnipresent. As one develops, Truth unveils its vastness gradually. Then only the person understands what Truth is. They had come to spread the knowledge of this Truth.

They told us to realise that Truth. Truth, which is nothing but God. Never to deviate from Truth, because that is everything. But where is God? He is within each one of us, so love all, serve all and feel satisfied with this opportunity—these are also Sri Ramakrishna's and Sarada Devi's teachings.

Now, can we judge them as old or new? Does their teaching ever become old? Was that true in the past and can it be false at the present? That can never happen. Truth is Truth. Sarada Devi showed us a simple mould. Sri Ramakrishna is quite far away. It is very difficult for us to understand him. Many a times, we do not understand him, he remains mystically unknown to us, whereas Sarada Devi is a woman resembling our mother, aunt or like our elder sister, very simple, really near and dear. Taking care, feeding all, asking for one's needs. Skipping her own food, feeding others and with her service and sincerity, taking care of them. She is not giving lectures, nor asking to study the Gita or the Upanishad, the *Ramayana* or the *Mahabharata*. Instead, she shows us the perfect way of living as we cannot find anywhere else. From her very childhood she showed us what love is, what truth is and what courage or perseverance is.

If Sarada Devi said something, Vivekananda dared not oppose it. Her words were final. There was an incident—Durga Puja would be celebrated in Belur Math and Swamiji insisted on sacrificing a goat. No one could go against Swamiji's decision. As this decision was conveyed to the Mother, she said, 'You are all monks, you all assure that no harm shall come to any being, therefore, you cannot sacrifice goat.' And, that was enough. If the same would have been said by Sri Ramakrishna, Swami Vivekananda would have certainly opposed him quoting extracts from the scriptures and by logical reasoning. But when it was said by Sarada Devi that it was wrong to sacrifice the goat, Swamiji accepted it as truth. Why does he abstain from reasoning? Why does he feel that monks should give assurance of no harm, and give love to all, not only limited to human beings but also to all beings—animal, plants, etc.? This is religion, love to all.

Again, we can see with the outburst of plague in the city of Calcutta, Swamiji hurriedly returned from Darjeeling and asked for immediately relief. Sister Nivedita and Swami Sadananda were there. They at once started the relief work. Then came up the need for money. In order to meet the urgent need, Swamiji decided to sell off Belur Math. When the news reached the Holy Mother, she said, 'First, you do not have the right to sell Belur Math, as it was willed after my name. So, as long as you do not get my permission you cannot sell it.' Then she said, 'Is everything done with this one relief by selling Belur Math? Will there be no more sadness, no more starvation or no more plague? So, you cannot sell Belur Math. You arrange for money in some other way.' What a steady and intelligent approach! Swamiji could not say a word after that. Even Sri Ramakrishna had acknowledged Sarada Devi and said that she had come to bestow wisdom and knowledge.

Sarada Devi never read the Vedanta. But her life and sayings were practical Vedanta. Once, Swami Vivekananda had longed for an Ashram in Mayavati (Himalaya), where there would be no idol worship but only meditation on Truth of Advaita philosophy. When Swamiji reached Mayavati, he could not appreciate the portrait of Sri Ramakrishna being worshipped with flowers. Swamiji remarked, 'Oh! The old man has made his presence even here! I wanted a place where there would be no idol worship.' Those who worshipped the portrait were confused and consequently approached the Holy Mother for help.

What do you think was the answer of the illiterate village lady? She had studied neither the scriptures nor the Vedanta. She wrote, 'Naren (Vivekananda) is right, your Master, Sri Ramakrishna was Advaitin, the follower of Advaita philosophy. You are all his followers—so you are all Advaitins. I can strongly confirm that you are all Advaitins.'

Sarada Devi's wisdom and knowledge are really incomparable, but above all, there is her unconditional love for all. The Advaita philosophy states the omnipresence of the Brahman. It is everywhere and in every being. Though we state this easily, can we act accordingly? It was truly practised by Sarada Devi. She said, 'Like Sarat (Swami Saradananda), Amjad (a Muslim poor man) is also my son.' Amjad who is not only Muslim but also a thief and is often imprisoned. In spite of that when he had come to see mother with some vegetables, she would enquire about his well-being, and with motherly love and care, feed him.

Again, we have also seen how a village lady—an old destitute widow came to mother crying on the death of her only son. And, both of them started crying loudly. Everybody came running when they heard mother crying so loudly, as if the Holy Mother herself had lost her son. We can find this kind of unaltered and unconditional love for all in her, regardless of whether they were adult and children. She said that if someone practises meditation and prayer religiously, one can see that Atman,—the same Almighty God residing in all of us. How naturally she says, 'I am mother to the honest and dishonest alike. If any of my sons is covered with dirt and dust, I shall clean him and embrace him.' She embraced all with the same love, as if all were near and dear.

At the tender age of five or six, we see how she served the famine-hit people. Nobody told her to do so, but we find her fanning the hot meal so that the hungry men and women would not have to wait.

Among devotees, some women were unwelcome in the eyes of the respected, elite families. But Mother was determined that she would not say no to anybody who came to her. Usually, Mother carried the meals to Sri Ramakrishna. One day, a woman of bad repute came to mother and asked, 'Mother, give it to me, I shall take it to Thakur.' On the other hand, Sri Ramakrishna's sense of sanctity was so high that he could not tolerate the least of impurity. He would suffer from immense pain in contact with the slightest impurity. So, he decided not to accept it. When Sri Ramakrishna refused to take the meal,

Mother prayed, 'Accept it for today at least.' Sri Ramakrishna said, 'Then promise me that you will not send food with just anybody and everybody.' Then Mother became conscious, 'I cannot do that.' She confessed, 'If someone calls me "Mother" and confides in me I cannot turn them away.' Thus, we find the vastness of love in Sarada Devi. Love for all regardless of any age.

Once, it so happened that in search of a political freedom fighter named Sindhu Bala, the British police arrested an innocent woman, a would-be mother having the same name, Sindhu Bala. Mother was shocked on hearing this, and in total surprise, exclaimed, 'How could the police arrest that innocent lady? Was there no man there to give the police a beating and then rescue the woman?' And, she was not afraid to foresee the imminent fall of the unjust British government.

Apparently, we do not find much in the life of Sarada Devi but if we can probe deeper and deeper, slowly it unwinds itself. If truth is religion and love means religion, then these two are uniquely personified in Sarada Devi. Sri Ramakrishna is not so easy to understand, most of the time being self-absorbed in God consciousness and trance. We can hardly come across such a personality who neither by her meditation nor by her words fascinated people. Just by virtue of her way of life she attracts people. How interesting it is to know about Mother!

Swamiji brought Nivedita, 'the lioness' as he used to call her, to this country for enlightening the women and also for their uplift. Sister Nivedita decided to establish a school. So, on the first day a meeting was held at the Balaram Basu's house for the selection of students. Swamiji appeared unexpectedly to deal with the matter. Many devotees were present and Nivedita said to them, 'Who would be interested in giving their daughter, since no fees would be required for it?' Our society was so rigid and conservative that nobody dared to be interested. With Swamiji's push, one person raised his hand a little. Swamiji pointed to him and said, 'Sister, here is a man who wants to send his daughter to your school.'

In a letter to Nivedita Swamiji wrote, 'You want to serve this country. This society can only give hatred in return. They will treat you as an untouchable...' Swamiji sent this Nivedita along with other foreigners to Sarada Devi. Mother treated them as her daughters. She received them, spoke to them and also fed them. And, when they requested her to eat along with them, she also had food together with them. Everybody protested saying how could Mother eat along with those untouchable girls? In a letter Nivedita had written that the Holy Mother was always conservative in customs and practices. She kept it all aside, when for the first time the two British ladies visited her. 'As soon as we had gone, we were treated with food. With this we could overcome the caste barrier and could also strengthen our commitment towards our decided goal, which would not have been possible in any other condition.' Again, another day, Nivedita had cooked some porridge and handed over to Mother for Thakur. In spite of opposition Mother said, 'She is my daughter, so if you all will abandon me, I do not care. I am determined.' In a letter Nivedita writes, 'Mata Devi is our mother forever—her unaltered and ineffable divine grace along with unlimited glory is so smoothing.' The other day Mata Devi had come to visit Nivedita. Nivedita had become seriously ill. 'Mother had come to me to release me from any troubles. How happy I had become. Never did I come across such a face, filled with love. She looks so young, always working but so cheerful in spite of being more than sixty-five years of age. And, I am not even forty-five but I look older! Her voice is like that of a girl of eleven. It is filled with young smile, filled with happiness. Her each and every word captivates the mind...'

Nivedita said about Mother, 'Can you all differentiate whether she is the follower of the ancient or the modern age? With what should we differentiate, by her colour or by her thoughts?' According to Sarada Devi, the principle to deal with others is '*jakhan jeman takhan teman*'—through commonsense adopt yourself according to time and place. It is not like changing of fashion that changes every moment. This is an eternal perception; to take decision in accordance with time, place and subject. For example, when in your office, you have to wear a proper uniform.

Life is ever changing. India would not have survived if she could not have accepted the series of changes. One without change is stagnant, is dead and lifeless. So, one should go on. Change is definite. But of what? Does food, fashion and skin colour make you modern? Or, is it your power of thought and expression? The kind of person you are—are you a rational human being, free of superstitions, open-minded and do you accept the truth as it is? Thus, one should be open to accept all. This is the speciality of India. India has always accepted, with an open mind all kind of thoughts. She never liked monotony. Sri Ramakrishna spoke about synthesis and harmony. We have to accept change though we will judge it rationally. Your character, behaviour towards others, love for others, ability to accept all as dear ones. To be sad in others' sadness, to be happy in others' good times is the eternal truth. Change of fashion is indeed needed but the most important is the open-mindedness and the logical sense and the power of reasoning. Again, Swamiji mentioned giving our good to the West—give and take, the best of East and West. There is no narrow-mindedness, no mean-mindedness in this Indian outlook. This we call modern. In Sarada Devi we see this when Sri Ramakrishna asks, 'Do you come to bind me to this worldly life?' 'I have come to help you in your spiritual life' was her bold answer.

In Indian philosophy, husband and wife complement each other and do not compete with each other. The sacrifice made by each is not to be measured always but there should be happiness in sacrificing. We see in Sarada Devi—what a devoted service! Again, we find how much Sri Ramakrishna cared for her. Sri Ramakrishna said to his nephew Hriday, that he should not harm Sarada Devi's sentiments, otherwise everything would be at stake. And again, he could achieve everything if she was contented. He worshipped Sarada Devi in a traditional way to show his respect.

Here, they form an ideal and an ideal never perishes. The truth neither changes nor dies. The concept of modernisation lies in the open-mindedness and the rational power, the logical and scientific outlook. Only then the person is modern. Sarada Devi wanted us to imbibe this modern outlook and let education infiltrate our country. Women need to be intellectually at par with men, as it is the need of modern times. The question is not 'what is modern.' Rather, it is 'what is an ideal?' And, to stick to this toughest of ideals is the philosophy. They have created a synthesis—an amalgamation between ancient and modern. And, Sarada Devi has bridged the gap between the two poles of womanhood. 'I have never seen such presence of mind with such clear thought,' confessed Nivedita, 'everything seems to be empty in Her absence.'

We have noticed that intellectual persons like Swami Brahmananda, Swami Saradananda and even Swami Vivekananda would accept Mother's wise advice. In one lecture Swamiji said, 'there had been an inner conflict as to how to establish my Master's philosophy in this world for the betterment of human race and on the other side, how to feed my hungry brothers and mother. There were no kith and kin after our Master, Sri Ramakrishna, had left this mortal world. Thus, the conflict within grew stronger with the passage of days and months. What an intense pain—an unbearable pain! There was no one to give solace except one. Solace from the only person that brought blessings and hope along with it. A woman—the follower of the Master's principles and ideals, Sarada Devi. Whereas she was all alone, poorer than we were.'

In a letter to a brother-disciple, Swamiji wrote, 'You have not yet understood the wonderful significance of Mother's life—none of you. But gradually you will know. Without Shakti (Power) there is no regeneration for the world. Why is it that our country is the weakest and the most backward of all countries?—Because 'Shakti' is held in dishonour there. Mother has been born to revive that wonderful 'Shakti' in India; and making here the nucleus, once again Gargis and Maitreyis will be born in the world.' 'To me, Mother's grace is a hundred thousand times more valuable than Father's. Mother's grace, Mother's blessings are all paramount to me. Please, pardon me, I am a little bigoted as regards the Mother. If but Mother orders, her demons can work anything . . .' 'Brother, I shall show how to worship the living Durga and then only shall I be worthy of my name. I shall be relieved when you will have purchased a piece of land and established there the living Durga, the Mother . . .'

One woman who never comes into the focus but is the constant source of inspiration—in every step of life, in every struggle of life, she is love and truth personified. Thus, Sister Nivedita says, 'Sarada Devi, our Holy Mother as we call her—who is only a simple Hindu woman, and yet, as I think, the greatest woman in the world today . . . the most wonderful thing of God—Sri Ramakrishna's own chalice of His Love for the world . . .' So, with Sri Ramakrishna's ultimate statement about the modernity of Sarada Devi, Nivedita forwards this invaluable question—'To me it has always appeared that she is Sri Ramakrishna's final word as to the ideal of Indian womanhood. But is she the last of an old order, or the beginning of a new? In her, one sees realised that wisdom and sweetness to which the simplest of women may attain.'

Swami Vivekananda As Condensed India

- *Swami Vivekananda and Indian Renaissance*
- *Swami Vivekananda and India's Spiritual Heritage*
- *Swami Vivekananda's Philosophy and Religion*
- *Swami Vivekananda's Approach to Social Work*
- *Swami Vivekananda's Vision of a New Social Order*

Swami Vivekananda and Indian Renaissance

SWAMI VIVEKANANDA'S (1863–1902), PRE-MONASTIC NAME WAS Narendranath Dutta; he was the only son of a well-known lawyer of Calcutta, Biswanath Dutta, and a very intelligent and pious lady, Bhuvaneswari Devi. Once he described himself as 'condensed India'. If by this he meant he represented every individual, every sect and community of India, he was not exaggerating; by this token, he might as well have said that he was the condensed world. He was a man who truly identified himself with mankind as a whole; creed, caste or language was of no consequence to him. He was a true citizen of the world.

India, of course, occupied a special place in his heart, but that was because India was a land of great idealism. He thought no other country had such idealism, or had suffered so much for that idealism. He wanted India to retain that idealism, but, at the same time, acquire western skill and efficiency to improve her material life. He believed East and West had much to give to each other, and in so giving both could grow and prosper. Artificial divisions between one country and another, between man and man repelled him. To him mankind was one, so also the world.

He taught three truths: first, Oneness of the world. He felt at home wherever he went and said: this is my home—*Vasudhaiva kutumbakam*—all people are my people. This oneness of the world, one world, that was one of the truths that he preached. Secondly, another truth he preached—divinity of man. Again and again, he would say man is divine. 'He is the image of God, he is next to God.' The greatest attraction among things that man has created is the Taj Mahal. And man is a Taj Mahal among the creations of God, according to Swami Vivekananda. Thirdly, he preached the harmony of religions. He did not like the idea of tolerance. He said, when you say you tolerate others you are being arrogant. You feel you are superior to others. You could have rejected them outright, but you are very magnanimous—you tolerate them—this is arrogance. No, accept, accept them as they are. Each religion is a way to God and you ought to pay equal respect to each religion. If one religion is true, all religions are true. Not that any religion can claim the monopoly of holiness. Holiness is something we find in every community, everywhere, in every country, in every age. Swamiji says, we only travel from a lower truth to a higher truth. Religion is nothing but an interpretation of truth. That interpretation may not suit everybody, it may suit some people. Well, choose whatever interpretation appeals to you, but do not condemn another interpretation. Because you do not accept it, you have no right to condemn it.

In a sense, India's renaissance can be said to have begun from 11 September 1893, i.e. on the day on which Swami Vivekananda made his first speech on India at the Parliament of Religions in the United States. He spoke many times in the Parliament and later at many places in the country, since then and later also in England but wherever he spoke, he spoke of his country and its heritage in glorious terms. He introduced himself as the condensed India. He spoke so convincingly that many began to feel ashamed that they had once thought poorly of this great land. It was the habit of the missionaries in those days to raise funds for their work in India by presenting to the American public distorted pictures of the social conditions of India. Unfortunately for the country, there were even Indians—and some of them quite distinguished, too—who joined hands with them in misrepresenting the country's conditions, either because they honestly believed that India's salvation lay in totally rejecting her ancient traditions and in re-orienting herself on the western model, or they were just ignorant of the greatness of the country's heritage. These were the people who saw nothing good in India; to them everything Western was good, and they went so far as to welcome the British presence in India as if it was a gift of God.

It is against this background that Swamiji's work in the West has to be seen. Since the British conquest of India, the country was groping for an identity and it was this identity that Swami Vivekananda gave it. He had much success in the West, but that success was not his, but his country's. For the first time, the Western countries saw a true Indian, one who could speak of India with authority. If people applauded him, they applauded the India that he represented, the India that they had so long ridiculed. They now came to love and respect India, which they did because they understood her better now, after having known him.

Swami Vivekananda introduced true India to the Western world, which was no doubt a great achievement, but a greater achievement on his part was that he introduced India to the Indians who knew nothing about the country except that it was a country of which they had every reason to feel ashamed, a mental depravity which was largely the consequence of Western education. Not that Swami Vivekananda was blind to India's shortcomings; he knew them just as much as anybody else, but he knew also that whereas no society in the world was completely blameless, in India's case the merits far outweighed the demerits. He pointed to the thought, which India was the first and perhaps the only country in the world had conceived, namely, the divinity of man, but where India had failed was that it was only individuals who practised it, not society as a whole. Indian philosophy is full of such gems of idealism. India has no need to borrow idealism from the West, what she needs to learn from the West is its practical sense.

It was never his contention that everything was perfect in India and there was nothing she could learn from the West. In fact, while dealing with India's lapses, no one was more scathing than Swamiji, but, at the same time, no one was more rapturous while praising her philosophy. His forerunners, starting from Raja Rammohun Roy, wanted that India should reorient herself on the Western model, as if this was where India's salvation lay, but it was Swamiji's hope that India would rise again by her own strength and not by imitating others. He, in fact, was opposed to the idea that India should imitate any other country, for no country could prosper by imitating other countries. He, however, was a believer in 'give and take'—he wanted that India should learn science and technology from the West and, in return, teach it philosophy. If India needed anything, it was material prosperity which could be got only by the application of sciences and technology. He used to deplore the neglect of the masses which, according to him, was a national sin that India had committed and to which could be traced most of the ills from which India suffered. A handful of scholars or one or two spiritual giants did not make a nation, though their presence did indicate the vitality of the national genius, but the real strength of the nation lay in the masses. The masses of India possessed great human qualities, but due to centuries of neglect by the upper classes, crushing poverty and lack of opportunities for education, have been reduced to a state of 'next to brutes.' Swamiji condemned this policy of neglect of the masses, but did not suggest that they have to be uplifted at the cost of others. His advice to those who claimed to be patriots was to pay more attention to the masses, and do something tangible for them, rather than merely talk of social problems or widow remarriage.

When Swami Vivekananda appeared on the Western scene, not only the West, even his own country knew nothing about him.

But after the accolade he had won by explaining to the Western audiences the secret sources of India's strength and beauty, he had overnight become a national hero and his name a household word in India. When he returned to the country, a grateful India gave him a reception unprecedented in scale and grandeur. This was no wonder, for the young monk had instilled into them a sense of pride and self-respect by opening their eyes to the greatness of their country's civilisation and culture, religion, philosophy, language and literature, art and architecture. Through him, they discovered India, the aged mother who had so long hid from them her great treasures. They also discovered themselves, their great past and the possibility of a still greater future. This was the beginning of the renaissance which culminated in Indian independence and which has paved the way to the progress India has the choice to make.

Swami Vivekananda and India's Spiritual Heritage

RELIGION IS OFTEN SEEN AS A MATTER OF FAITH. GOD, CHURCH, worship—all these odd components of religion—hang on faith. Nineteenth-century man, aided by science, started dismantling this faith. The process still continues, though twentieth-century man, again aided by science, is less sure of the grounds on which he has so long taken his iconoclastic stand. This has been a global trend, and, paradoxically, India has been no exception to it though she has always held religion as truth. As truth, it can be experienced and therefore verifiable. India defines religion as *dharma*, that which sustains. It sustains because it is wisdom resulting from experience, because it is the truth. Generations of people have experienced it. Accordingly, religion, truth, and experience are synonymous in India. If faith has any place in religion, it is because it is an off-shoot of experience. The experience that sustains has to be direct and personal, otherwise it is meaningless. Sugar has to be tasted in order to know that it is sweet.

Indian history is a history of spiritual giants, the way they shaped the Indian mind and how they left their stamp on the country's polity, social structure, art, architecture and literature. They taught us how to conquer ourselves, but they saw no conflict between spirit and matter, between the spiritual and the secular. A person of the highest spiritual attainment can also be very efficient and successful in his secular activities. A sage can be a prince and a prince a sage. 'Be in the world but not of it'—that was the motto of our spiritual giants, and they not only preached it but practised it. Other things they taught:

   a) The key to happiness is non-attachment.
   b) Be your own master; do not let anything overwhelm you—success or failure.
   c) Have faith in yourself.

Right from Vedic times, Indian saints and sages have stressed the truth that the essence of religion is 'being'... not 'doing' or 'knowing'. Much of the paraphernalia that religion has can be dispensed with. Rituals are simply expressions, which become redundant after a time. When the being grow in intensity and depth, exhibitionism seems vulgar. The being is the end; everything we do in the name of religion should be directed to the unfolding of that being. The man who has perfected his being, that is himself, is the ideal man. He is a hero to whom the whole world pays homage. India has produced many such heroes and it is remarkable that whenever the country has been threatened by disintegrating forces, a spiritual leader has appeared with the right kind of message to put the house in order. It is always the same message—the message that India has always believed in—the message that Truth is the highest end in life, it alone prevails, and everything can be and should be sacrificed for it. It is this one message that India has preached again and again, though in different idioms dictated by changed circumstances. The content has always been the same—Truth.

India's history is the history of her search for that Truth, as if destiny had assigned her this role from the very beginning. The quest for Truth has sometimes preoccupied her to the exclusion of everything else. Truth is the highest thing to achieve in life. 'Everything can be sacrificed for Truth, but Truth cannot be sacrificed for anything.' Indians would go to the end of the world, searching for Truth. They would leave home, retire into the forests and brave every conceivable hardship, trying to understand Truth. Often, this has been misinterpreted as being other-worldly, but in their scheme of things, there is no this-world or that-world; there is only one world.[59]

That is to say, she views the secular and the spiritual as one; everything is spiritual. This idea is emphasised in the Gita.[60] Work is truly worship if it is done for others. The highest religion is living for others. At first, people look for God in temples and mosques outside of themselves; soon they discover that God is also within themselves. Finally, they discover that all that exists is God. The difference is only in the degree of manifestation. The goal of life is to realise the unity of existence, to understand that the same Being is in you and me; the difference is artificial and false. When this sense of unity dawns, love overflows all barriers, uniting all. This is the culmination of *Yoga* (union). It is the consummation that man aspires to. He is no longer a fragment, he is the whole, he is All—Bhuma, the ultimate in man's growth. This is his destiny.

India has always regarded this development as the highest goal of life. Political power, high social standing, money, scholarship—all these are nothing compared to this kind of development. It in the highest, the best, and the most prized state of being. Real peace, happiness, the sense of fulfilment is to be found in this state. Nothing short of this can satisfy man. The Kingdom of Heaven, *Nirvana*, Immortality—these are various inadequate names applied to this state. One has to experience it to know what it is like.

It is not that these are mere words without substance. Again and again, there have been people, in every country and every age, who

---

59. *The Complete Works of Swami Vivekananda*, Advaita Ashrama, Calcutta, 1989, Vol. V, p. 410, (hereafter, CW).
60. *Bhagavad Gita* 9/27; *Commentary of Shankara*, 3/19, 20.

have demonstrated the reality of this state. They may be the poorest and humblest in society, yet they are the happiest. How do you explain this? It is what they are inside, their being, which makes the difference. Happiness is not in what a man possesses, it is in what he is. In Indian society, such people enjoy the highest honour. History remembers such people, easily forgetting its empire-builders, if there have been any. They sustain India by their self-imposed poverty, by their total rejection of sense-pleasures, by their preoccupation with spiritual conquests, and above all, by their selflessness. Their only concern in life is the welfare of others. They live only because they want to serve others.

Such people have come and gone without even caring to leave behind any trace of who they were. The details that are available show what sort of people they were, but often they remain anonymous, or they use a pseudonym. Janaka, Yajnavalkya, Sanaka are names that occur again and again. Their wisdom and their greatness as men are beyond doubt, but they disclose practically nothing about their lineage. They obviously argue that it is the ideal that is important and not the person in whom the ideal is embodied. It is these ideals that have nourished India and sustained her in all her travails. Much of India remains a riddle if we do not recognise this.

Many races have come from outside and settled in India, each of them distinct. Some of them dominated India militarily and politically, yet as time went by, they adopted the Indian ethos and became thoroughly Indian. If they showed their separateness, it was only in details. The story of Indian art, architecture, music, language, in short, Indian culture, is a story that depicts the fusion of diverse ethnic traditions into a unique mosaic. India is one country where each race has been respected for what it is. There is no evidence of interference with what any race has, or imposition of something it does not want. It is difficult to find another country where diversity has been welcomed and unity has been maintained in spite of the diversity.

Of all the intruders, the British were the only people whose conquest of India was not only military, but also largely cultural. Many among the Indian intelligentsia felt the British presence was a blessing and they imitated the British in every possible way. When the debate on whether the indigenous system of education should continue with its emphasis on Sanskrit, most Indian leaders said 'No'. They preferred the English system. Lord Macaulay in his famous *Minute on Education* declared that he would introduce a system of education that would make the Indians British in every respect except in the colour of their skin. This did happen in many cases, especially in the case of those who came under the influence of Derozio, a highly talented Anglo-Indian teacher of English at Hindu College in the mid-twenties of the nineteenth century. These young men had nothing but contempt for everything Indian. Some of them embraced Christianity, others, if not Christians, were thoroughly Western in outlook.

There were several reactions to this from the Indian community: The orthodox became more orthodox, more rigid—some of them wanted to go back to the Vedic way of life. Another group wanted to avoid contact with Western thought as far as possible and continued to follow their own system of education, Hindus in Sanskrit, Muslims in Arabic and Persian. There was yet another group who modernised Hinduism in such a way that it remained Hinduism only in name.

Ordinary people were confused. They always followed the upper castes, but the upper castes themselves were in disarray under the British impact. Besides their traditional beliefs about the Avataras, caste practices were all that remained of religion with them. Proselytising missions took advantage of the situation, bringing as many of them as they could into their fold, by temptation, even by coercion.

SRI RAMAKRISHNA

Against this backdrop, Sri Ramakrishna appeared on the Calcutta scene—illiterate, poor, a mere temple priest. People hardly took any notice of him. Paradoxically, among the first to take notice of this humble man, was a Christian missionary, Professor Hastie, Principal of Scottish Church College in Calcutta. One day, while teaching his students Wordsworth's poem, *Excursion*, Principal Hastie told them about Sri Ramakrishna and his ecstasies.[61]

Soon, word spread from other quarters about Sri Ramakrishna's eccentricities, about his love of God, his constant flow of words of the highest mystical order, above all, his ecstasies. Both believers and non-believers, mostly Westernised, began to come to him in an endless stream. The most significant event was the coming of Keshab Chandra Sen, the doyen among the religious leaders and social reformers of the time. Sri Ramakrishna and Keshab fell in love with each other. Keshab invited him to his religious meetings where Sri Ramakrishna, with his wit and wisdom, was invariably the centre of attraction. Keshab also wrote about him in the Brahmo papers. Thus, Sri Ramakrishna came to be known among the elite of Calcutta and had access to many distinguished homes in Calcutta.

This did not satisfy Sri Ramakrishna. He was looking for people, preferably young, who would gladly renounce everything to realise God and then serve mankind in a spirit of worship. Surprisingly, such young men, all below thirty, and around twenty in number, did arrive in the closing years of his life. The Master trained them in monastic life, giving them the ochre robe, sometimes even sending them into the neighbourhood to beg. The brightest among them was Narendranath Dutta, later known as Swami Vivekananda. Sri Ramakrishna chose him as their leader and took pains to fit him for that role.

---

61. *The Life of Swami Vivekananda* by his Eastern and Western Disciples, Advaita Ashrama, Calcutta, 1979, Vol. I, p. 48 (hereafter, Life).

Thus, Swami Vivekananda's appearance at the Parliament of Religions was the climax of a drama which began the day he first met Sri Ramakrishna in 1881. The meeting took place at the house of a neighbour, Suresh Mitra. At that time, Sri Ramakrishna asked Swamiji to visit him at Dakshineswar, which he did after some time. When he finally went, Sri Ramakrishna received him warmly, and treated him as if he were a divine being. Swamiji felt embarrassed and began to wonder if Sri Ramakrishna was completely normal. He soon discovered, however, that Sri Ramakrishna's behaviour was eccentric only in regard to him; he was perfectly normal with others. In the days that followed, Swamiji tested Sri Ramakrishna in many ways, and at last came to the conclusion that he was truly an extraordinary man. He began to feel that his future lay in Sri Ramakrishna's hands.

Sometimes, the two were involved in prolonged arguments. At one time, Sri Ramakrishna decided to test Swamiji by refusing to talk to him when he came. This did not deter his coming. When the period of testing was over and Sri Ramakrishna asked him why he had continued to come, Swamiji gave a reply that was typical of him, 'I come to you because I love you, not for what you say'. Thus, he passed the test and also gave expression to his love for his Master. In addition, he showed his independent thinking when he said he didn't come to Sri Ramakrishna for what he said. He would not accept everything he said without proving it for himself. Sri Ramakrishna greatly valued this trait in his extraordinary disciple.

Sri Ramakrishna taught no creed or dogma; he taught only Truth, the Truth that is common to all religions. He had practised all the major religions and had found from experience that they all lead to the same goal. Each religion is true, though it may not represent the Truth in its entirety. Sri Ramakrishna would say that just as food tastes vary from one individual to another, religious tastes also vary. Each person should feel free to choose his own religion.

He said that the goal of life is spiritual illumination, and that this can best be attained by worshipping God in man. 'Treat every *jiva* as Shiva', he said. He scolded Swami Vivekananda for seeking only his own liberation. Selfishness is repugnant to true religion. Renunciation and service should be practised by everybody. Swamiji later said that these two were India's national ideals.

THE SRI RAMAKRISHNA MISSION

Sri Ramakrishna not only taught high spiritual ideals, he practised them himself and made his disciples practise them. He was a hard taskmaster, imposing on his disciples the strictest spiritual disciplines, and controlling everything they did and said. He wanted them to be perfect in every respect.

They did not disappoint him. Under his relentless training, each of them became a spiritual model for future generations to follow. The best, of course, was his beloved Naren, Swami Vivekananda, who was to be the leader of this band of dedicated young men.

Sri Ramakrishna passed away in August 1886 at Cossipore near Calcutta. Most of his disciples returned home to resume their studies; but some of them refused to go back to there families, taking shelter wherever they could. The future seemed uncertain for all of them. Their leader, Swamiji, however knew what his Master and he himself wanted: They must be monks and serve humanity. He would visit the young disciples without the knowledge of their guardians and keep urging them to be ready to renounce as soon as the time was propitious. People who had at one time thought of Swamiji as a promising young man, began to say that he had ruined his own future and now was busy ruining the future of other young men. He was, in their eyes, a misguided youth.

At this juncture, a householder disciple of Sri Ramakrishna, Surendranath Mitra, offered Swamiji the money needed to hire a house where the young disciples could live together. The house, at

Baranagar, became the first monastery of the future Sri Ramakrishna Mission. There, they got their food by begging, as monks do, and as their Master would have liked them to do. This meant privation, but they were dauntless. The more hardship, the more they felt they were nearing the standard their Master had set for them. Reminiscing about their life at this time, Swamiji once said, 'There were days at the Math when we had nothing to eat. If there was rice, salt was lacking. Some days that was all we had, but nobody cared... Come what may we were indifferent... The more circumstances are against you, the more manifest becomes your inner power.'[62]

The monastery later shifted to another house at Alambazar. (Before finally shifting to its own premises at its present site in Belur in 1897, it occupied for a while Nilambar Mukherjee's adjacent house.)

For a decade or more after Sri Ramakrishna's passing away, his young disciples either lived in these make-shift monasteries, or roamed the hills and plains of India, braving every possible discomfort. Each was on his own and the idea of having a monastic order never occurred to them. But they were devoted to each other, and Swami Vivekananda, as their informal leader, kept track of each of them, always inspiring and guiding them and making sure that they took no undue risks. He himself wanted to wander about like his brother-monks, penniless and dependent entirely upon God.

But he was not free. His father had suddenly died, and his mother and his brothers and sisters were starving. Taking advantage of their helplessness, some of his relatives had started a lawsuit claiming title to their house. If they had won the suit, Swamiji's family would have been thrown out of their home. So, Swamiji had to contest the claim, and he himself sometimes argued before the court. It is said that the English judges before whom he argued were highly impressed by his skill in advocacy. Finally, he won his case.

---

62. Ibid., p. 203.

SWAMIJI AS A WANDERING MONK

Now Swamiji was free to savour the life as a wandering monk. First, he visited a few, not far from Calcutta, but when he left the monastery in July 1890, he did not return till after his great success in the West. Just before leaving, he met Holy Mother Sarada Devi to seek her blessings. He told her that he would not return until he was able to prove that he was a 'man'. And, she replied, 'of course, you will return, and return as a man.' How true that prediction proved!

His first halt was at Bhagalpur in Bihar. He then stopped at Badrinarayan and other holy places in the Himalayas. Coming down to the plains, he spent some days in Meerut and Delhi. It is difficult to see any plan in his itinerary. He moved from one place to another, sometimes on foot, sometimes by rail, sometimes staying in a dharmasala, sometimes enjoying the luxurious hospitality of a prince. Whoever met him, high or low, was drawn to him. His picture as a wandering monk shows him shaven-headed, staff and water-pot in hand, in a majestic stance. He was conspicuous wherever he went. When he walked along the street, passers-by found it difficult to take their eyes off him.

If he stayed with anybody, the host would invite all his acquaintances to come and share with him the pleasure of the guest's lively company. Swamiji would discuss religion, philosophy, literature, art, architecture—almost everything under the sun. He would also draw the attention of his audience to the problems of the country; poverty, ignorance, caste, selfishness, discrimination against women, and so on. Everyone was charmed by his enlightened views. Another thing that impressed them was his music. Swamiji had been trained in classical music as a boy. Later, he learned devotional songs. And his voice was superb. He also played percussion instruments with great skill.

All over the country Swamiji left admirers from different walks of life and different communities. Nevertheless, there were times when he had nothing to eat day after day. Once, after he fainted from hunger, a Muslim fakir gave him a cucumber to eat and saved his life.

Swamiji travelled from one end of the country to the other for three years, totally penniless. He was always on the move, a restless spirit. But why was he restless? Why was he always travelling? If he was seeking God, why did he not settle down somewhere and start meditating? It is difficult to find an answer to this question. But there must have been some divine purpose behind his restless journey, for he never did anything unless his Master wanted him to do it. His Master had taught him that higher than finding God within oneself was finding God in others. This was a truth only Indian seers had discovered. This is the highest spiritual achievement possible for man.

Yet, why was man so maltreated in this very India? Why were India's people exploited by the rich and the upper castes? Why did India have so many problems?

How could those problems be solved? He had to find the answer to these vital questions. Perhaps, the divine purpose of his restless travels was for that very reasons. He was to discover for himself what India's problems were, and set about finding their solution.

In the process of discovering India and her problems, Swamiji discovered himself. He began to feel the growth of a new power within him, and a great expansion of heart. As he was to say to his brother-monk, Swami Turiyananda, a little later, 'I cannot understand your so-called religion, but my heart has grown much, much larger, and I have learnt to feel the sufferings of others.'

THE WORLD'S COLUMBIAN EXPOSITION

Meanwhile, preparations had been going on in the city of Chicago in the United States to hold a World Fair. It was to be called The World's Columbian Exposition in honour of Christopher Columbus who had discovered America in 1493, four hundred years previously. During these years, immigrants had poured in not only from Columbus's country, Spain, but also from England and other European countries. At first, these Europeans clashed with the local people and sometimes with one another. In addition, there was a devastating Civil War.

Despite everything, the country had made amazing progress and it was proud of itself. It felt that this would be a good time to exhibit America's wonderful inventions. According to the well-known research scholar on Swami Vivekananda, Marie Louise Burke, the purpose of the Exposition was to show 'not only the achievements of Western civilisation but, the better to show these off, to exhibit life-size models of the more backward cultures of the world.'[63] To put it more bluntly, the purpose was to show the contrast between the West and the East. They further decided to have 'congresses' where the superiority of Western thought would be proved beyond a doubt. One such congress was to be a 'World's Parliament of Religions.'

THE CHRISTIAN REACTION

When the idea of a Parliament of Religions was first mooted, many Christian leaders were aghast. They were firmly of the opinion that there was only one true religion and that religion was Christianity. To ask other religions to join the Parliament would be an insult to Christianity. It was like asking truth to share the same platform with untruth, here truth standing for Christianity and untruth for other religions. Another group, however, argued that the Parliament would offer an opportunity to convince the followers of other religions of the superiority of Christianity. They might then be converted to Christianity. This was the opinion that prevailed, and many Christian leaders took part in the Parliament.

---

63. Ibid., p. 388.

SWAMIJI'S JOURNEY TO THE WEST[64]

Representatives of different religions were invited to participate in the Parliament, but no one had been invited to represent Hinduism. Some young South-Indian admirers of Swami Vivekananda began to press him to attend the Parliament as Hinduism's representative. They even started raising funds for this purpose. But he declined; he was not sure he should go to the West. Soon after, he visited Cape Comorin and swam across to a rock in the sea. After meditating there for several days, he had a mystic vision which made him feel that it was the wish of his Master that he should attend the Parliament of Religions. So sure he was of this that he told Swami Turiyananda whom he accidentally met at Mount Abu that the Parliament was being arranged just for him.[65]

Now bursting with self-confidence, he gave his permission to those who wanted to raise money for his journey to the West. They raised the money and booked his passage on the Empress of India, which was to leave Bombay on 31 May 1893. They bought him a second-class ticket which the Dewan of Khetri changed to a first-class one. He also bought him, among other things, the red silk robe which later became an embarrassment to Swamiji by its conspicuousness.

No one realised that what he needed most was warm clothing, the lack of which was to cause him much suffering in the freezing cold of North America.

The ship left as scheduled and berthed at Vancouver, Canada on 25 July. Swamiji took a train for Chicago the next day, arriving there on 30 July. Two shattering discoveries were awaiting him: First, there was no way of his being admitted as a delegate to the Parliament as he carried no letter of accreditation from any recognised authority saying that he represented Hinduism; secondly, the hotel

---

64. *Swami Vivekananda in the West.* New Discoveries. Marie Louise Burke. Advaita Ashrama, 1983. Vol. I, p. 66, (hereafter, New Disc.)
65. Life, p. 385.

bill at Chicago was prohibitive and unless a miracle happened, he would starve.

He decided to go to Boston where prices were not so high, and there he stayed at the country home of Miss Kate Sanborn, an elderly woman he had met on the train. Miss Sanborn treated Swamiji as a 'curio'. Most Americans had never seen an Indian before. Apart from his colour and features, it was his dress that attracted the most notice. In Chicago people would follow him, at times pulling on his turban and pushing him. Once, someone even threw stones at him.

Staying with Miss Sanborn, Swamiji was protected from that kind of harassment; still it must not have been pleasant to be treated as a 'curio'. A press report says:

> Miss Kate Sanborn, who has recently returned from the West, last week entertained the Indian Rajah, Swami Vivekananda. Behind a pair of horses furnished by liveryman F.W. Phipps, Miss Sanborn and the Rajah drove through town on Friday (August 18) enroute for Hunnewall's.[66]

The drive was to show off her acquisition to the local people. Swamiji took all this in his stride. As he wrote to a friend, 'All this must be borne.'

In spite of how Miss Sanborn made use of Swamiji, she did him a service for which she will be remembered with gratitude. She introduced him to Professor John Henry Wright of Harvard University. Professor Wright discussed many subjects with Swamiji and was tremendously impressed by Swamiji's range of knowledge. He asked Swamiji why he was not speaking at the Parliament of Religions. When Swamiji replied that he had no credentials, Professor Wright compared him to the sun and said that like the sun, he did not need any credentials.

---

66. *New Disc*, Vol I, p. 22.

Nevertheless, Professor Wright wrote a letter to the proper authorities describing Swamiji as one 'who is more learned than all our learned professors put together.'[67] He did not stop there. He also bought him a ticket to Chicago, gave him some money and handed him several letters of introduction.

RETURN TO CHICAGO

When Swamiji reached Chicago it was night and too late to look for a place to stay, so he spent the night in a boxcar in the rail yard. The next day, he woke up to discover that he had lost the addresses Professor Wright had given him. He was tired, hungry and badly in need of a bath. The neighbourhood was mostly non-English speaking. If he asked anybody about hotels, either the person did not reply or muttered something in an unfamiliar language.

He then decided to knock on doors and beg. As a monk he was entitled to do so. He did knock on some doors, but either nobody opened the door, or opened it and slammed it on his face. One person even pointed a gun at him thinking he might be a robber. Utterly frustrated, he sat down under a roadside tree and said to himself: 'He who brought me here has to look after me. I'm not going to go begging any longer; if it is His wish that I should starve, I will starve.'

Soon, a middle-aged lady appeared from across the street. She asked him if he were a delegate to the Parliament of Religions. When he answered in the affirmative, she invited him into her house. Her name was Mrs George Hale; she became his mother and her house his home. He had the sweetest relations with the family till the last day. Mrs Hale, like a true mother, took care of all his needs. She even arranged for his admission to the Parliament.

---

67. Ibid., p. 27.

The first Press roport following Swamiji's acceptance as a delegate said that 'his face is bright and intelligent... His English is very good.'

It quotes Swamiji as saying that the Parliament may have an important bearing on the religious history of the world.[68] How prophetic Swamiji was! The Chicago Evening Post said about the upcoming Parliament:

> 'We look for great results from this great gathering and not at once, not perhaps in the near future. But in the wisdom of that Providence which men of all creeds prefer to worship, and whose movements are slow but sure, the energy here concentrated will be felt upon all over the world and its effect will be for the unification and uplift of mankind.'[69]

It is gratifying to see that the thoughts Swamiji had in his mind had already begun to find expression elsewhere.

THE PARLIAMENT OF RELIGIONS

The Parliament opened exactly at 10 o'clock on Monday, 11 September 1893 befittingly with a prayer. An eye-witness has written:

> The sight was most remarkable. There were strange robes, turbans and tunics, crosses and crescents, flowing hair and tonsured heads... The supreme moment of the nineteenth century was reached.[70]

And, where was Swami Vivekananda? He sat amidst this impressive gathering, conspicuous in his 'gorgeous red apparel, his bronze face surmounted with a turban of yellow'[71] as noted by the Revered Mr Wente.

---

68. Ibid., p. 60.
69. Ibid., pp. 73, 74.
70. Ibid., p. 77.
71. Ibid., p. 78.

The solemnity and grandeur of the occasion must have overawed Swamiji. He felt nervous and when asked to speak in the forenoon, he declined several times. As he was later to say, 'I was so nervous, and could not venture to speak in the morning.'[72] At last he spoke, late in the afternoon, greeting the audience as 'Sisters and brothers of America'. At these few words people rose to their feet, shouted with joy and threw hats and handkerchiefs into the air. The President had difficulty in controlling them. When quiet prevailed, Swami Vivekananda made a breathtaking speech. He did not praise Hinduism, he only praised the spirit of tolerance, but even 'tolerance' was not enough for him; he preferred 'acceptance'. Each religion must be accepted and honoured. He quoted a Sanskrit verse which says:

> As the different streams having their sources in different places all mingle their water in the sea, so, O Lord, the different paths which men take through different tendencies, various though they appear, crooked or straight, all lead to Thee.[73]

No religion has a monopoly on holiness. All religions have had their share of great saints. This is proof of their equal validity.

This set the tone for the proceedings at the Parliament of Religions. If any delegate secretly hoped to prove the supremacy of his religion, he refrained from saying so; the atmosphere changed. Peace and harmony were in the very air. This was aptly expressed by Swamiji in his concluding remarks when he said, 'The Christian is not to become a Hindu or a Buddhist, nor a Hindu or a Buddhist to become a Christian . . . Upon the banner of every religion will soon be written, in spite of resistance: 'Help and not fight', 'Assimilation and not Destruction'.'[74]

---

72. *Letters of Swami Vivekananda*, Advaita Ashrama, Calcutta, 1970, p. 53 (hereafter, Letters).
73. CW, Vol. I, p. 4.
74. Ibid., p. 24.

REACTIONS TO SWAMIJI

The impact of Swamiji's speeches was electrifying. From obscurity he leaped into worldwide fame. Hundreds followed him wherever he went. People merely wanted to be near him or at best, shake hands with him. In his official report, Dr Barrows, President of the Parliament of Religion characterised Swamiji's address as 'noble and sublime'.[75] The *Boston Evening Transcript* said, 'Vivekananda's address before the Parliament was broad as the heaven above us, embracing the best in all religions, as the ultimate universal religion'.[76] The Press hailed him as a Prophet and a Seer. The *New York Herald* said, 'He is undoubtedly the greatest figure in the Parliament of Religions. After hearing him we feel how foolish it is to send missionaries to this learned nation.'[77]

Dr Annie Besant was present at the Parliament of Religions, probably as a delegate from the Theosophical Society. Giving her impression of Swamiji she uses such expressions as, 'A striking figure, clad in yellow and orange, shining like the sun of India . . . a lion head, piercing eyes, mobile lips, movements swift and abrupt.'[78] He was a monk, no doubt; to her, however, Swamiji was a warrior-monk, for if anybody said anything derogatory about India, he would at once react sharply, 'The queen of his adoration was his Motherland,'[79] as Nivedita would later say.

The Honourable Merwin-Marie Snell, President of the Scientific Section of the Exposition, wrote:

'Swami Vivekananda . . . in fact, was beyond question the most popular and influential man in the Parliament. . . . The people thronged about him wherever he went and hung with eagerness

---

75. *Life*, p. 435.
76. Ibid., p. 432.
77. Ibid., p. 428.
78. Ibid., p. 429.
79. *The Master As I Saw Him*. Sister Nivedita, Udbodhan office, Calcutta, 1977, p. 41.

on his every word... The most rigid of orthodox Christians say of him, "He is indeed a prince among men." [80]

It was not only his oratory that impressed people; his life and character impressed them more. Some regarded him as another Christ or Buddha. They were ready to follow him to the ends of the earth.

But Swamiji received not only 'bouquets'; he also got many 'brickbats'. Christian missionaries took alarm at his popularity. They were in the habit of raising funds by preaching that India was a land of heathens waiting to be saved by Christianity. The American press now began to say that it was a mistake to try to teach India religion; rather the world should sit at her feet to learn religion. And, Swamiji said India needed bread, not religion. The missionaries found that the donations they had so long been receiving from the people were steadily declining, and they blamed this on Swamiji. They started denigrating him in many ways, even slandering his personal character. Some of his own countrymen joined them in this. But 'Truth alone prevails,' as Swamiji always insisted, and he did not try to defend himself. Others stood up for him and vehemently protested against the slanders. Finally, all such mean attempts failed and Swamiji's reputation rose higher than ever.

Christians were not the only ones to challenge Swamiji. Once a group of so-called free-thinkers challenged him to a debate. The group included all kinds of people—atheists, materialists, agnostics, rationalists, and so on. They were confident they would be able to easily crush him with the help of their Western science and philosophy, in which they claimed to be expert. Swamiji gladly accepted the challenge and the debate began. An eye-witness has given an account of this encounter:

> I shall never forget that evening when the Swami appeared single-handed to face the forces of materialism, arrayed in the

---

80. *Life*, pp 428–29.

heaviest armour of law, and reason, and logic, and commonsense, of matter and force, and heredity, and all the stock phrases calculated to awe and terrify the ignorant. Imagine their surprise when they found that, far from being intimidated by these big words, he proved himself a master in wielding their own weapons, and as familiar with the arguments of materialism as with those of Advaita philosophy... With an irresistable logic he demonstrated that their knowledge proved itself incorrect, not by comparison with that which was true, but by the very laws upon which it depended for its basis.[81]

Swamiji was not elated by such victories; he had not gone to the West with personal ambitions. His concern was for mankind as a whole, and especially for the poor in India. Sometimes, rich people invited him to stay with them, but he could never enjoy the comforts they provided. How could he? The miseries of the people back in India haunted him. He had at one time considered raising funds in America for his people, though he never tried it. He sensed that this was not the way to work. He did not even ask his new American disciples for money for himself. As a monk, he should never have anything to do with money.

THE WORLD TEACHER

Sri Ramakrishna had once scribbled on the floor of his room at Cossipore that Naren would be a world-teacher. Naren knew his Master's habit of praising him, and did not like it, so he protested, saying that he was not going to be a world-teacher or anything of the kind. But the Master told him that he had no choice in the matter; he was bound to play that role in the future. Later events proved that

---

81. Ibid., p. 342.

Sri Ramakrishna was right. Swami Vivekananda, whether he liked it or not, did become a world-teacher. Sri Ramakrishna gave him the mandate to teach. And, in order that he could carry out that mandate, he transmitted to him his own power. When Swami Vivekananda was carrying out his work, he always felt that Sri Ramakrishna was working through him. Sometimes, that power within him so overwhelmed him that he felt he could not contain it.

That is no doubt why he earned the sobriquet 'the cyclonic Hindu.'[82] The power he had received from his great Master propelled him like a cyclone through America, teaching everyone, as Sri Ramakrishna had predicted he would. His lecture engagements carried him far and wide. One day he might be lecturing on the borders of Canada, the next week, somewhere in the South. Sometimes, he gave three or four lectures a day. He lectured in churches, public halls, universities and private homes, and once in an open field. It was killing, but he never balked. He was an inspired soul and he felt he had no right to withhold the message he carried. 'I have a truth to teach, I, the child of God,' he once wrote to Alasinga, a disciple in India.[83]

But what was that Truth? It was the Truth common to all religions—the Truth that:

> Each soul is potentially divine. The goal is to manifest this Divinity within by controlling nature, external and internal. Do this either by work, or worship, or psychic control, or philosophy—by one, or more, or all of these—and be free. This is the whole of religion. Doctrines, or dogmas, or rituals, or books, or temples or forms, are but secondary details.[84]

---

82. Ibid., p. 461.
83. CW, Vol. V, p. 93.
84. Ibid., Vol. 1, p. 124.

This was the burden of what he taught the universal element in religion—How can man be perfect? Every religion is universal, if the focus is on this universal element.

If man is divine, he is one and the same everywhere, different languages, pigments of the skin and other features notwithstanding. A sequel to this is that love is the obvious basis on which all relationships should rest. This is the central theme of what Swamiji preached. He may have talked about history, philosophy, religion, literature, and science, but the gist of whatever he taught was Love.

This is not to say that he lived in an ivory tower. Man was his supreme love and concern, especially the oppressed, the poor, the backward. And, he had a high conception of man. He described him in many ways: 'Man is God, he is Narayana', 'Man is divine', 'Man is the greatest of all beings', 'Man is the epitome of all things', 'Man is the best mirror, and the purer the man, the more clearly he can reflect God', 'the Real man, therefore, is one and infinite', 'Man is individual and at the same time universal', 'The highest concept we can have of God is man', 'Our God is man and man is God.'

Such utterances, scattered throughout his writings and speeches, reflect Swami Vivekananda's attitude towards man. But when he uses the word 'man', does he mean a man of a particular country, caste, or community? No. He means mankind itself, every human being, everybody of every race, every country every community. He saw God in everybody and everybody was an object of worship to him, be he good or bad, white or black, brahmin or sudra, rich or poor. Everyone was God to him, but, as we have seen, he was especially concerned for God the poor, God the sick, God the ignorant.

Once, in America, some Negroes came and congratulated him, saying that they were proud that one of their own race had become so great. Swamiji thanked them and never told them he was not a Negro. Similarly, a barber once mistook him for a Negro and refused to cut his hair. Swamiji took the humiliation without protesting. When someone asked him why he hadn't disclosed his identity and told the barber he was not a Negro, Swamiji promptly replied that he was not born to prosper at the expense of others. He gladly let people think that he was a Negro, for his heart always went out to those who suffered oppression. Even women of dubious morals received his sympathy. To him, they were also divine.

In his letter of 9 July 1897, to Mary Hale, he wrote:

> May I be born again and again, and suffer thousands of miseries so that I may worship the only God that exists, the only God I believe in, the sum total of all souls; and above all, my God the wicked, my God the miserable, my God the poor of all races, of all species, is the special object of my worship.[85]

This, and the declaration he made in a letter to Alasinga Perumal dated August 1895, 'Truth is my God, the universe my country'[86] sums up his philosophy of life. These words, which had their source in the Indian spiritual tradition, also represent the essence of what he taught.

INDIA AND THE WEST

One of Swamiji's Western admirers said of him and his message, 'He was young with an ageless youth and yet old with the wisdom of ancient times. For the first time we heard the age-old message of India, teaching of the Atman, the true Self.'[87] This age-old message appealed to many, and as Swamiji and his message became popular, his country also began to command respect from the people in the West. Earlier, India was viewed as a barbarous country waiting to

---

85. Letters, p. 350.
86. CW. Vol. V, p. 92.
87. *Reminiscences of Swami Vivekananda*, Advaita Ashrama, Calcutta, 1961, p. 149 (Here after, ReminiscenCses).

be civilised by the West. After hearing him, many became convinced that India was a highly cultured country.

Swamiji spoke not for Hindus alone, but for the entire population of India. Never before had a representative gone abroad who was truly 'Indian', and who always spoke about India with pride and authority. Those who had gone before were full of apologies for their country. Not so Swamiji. He knew India very well and was proud of her. If anybody attacked his country, he knew how to counter-attack. Not that he was trying to hide his country's weaknesses. He only wanted to have India judged objectively and in its true perspective.

It took some time before Swamiji's countrymen came to know of his struggle and triumph in the West. When the news of his success first trickled into the Indian Press, the whole country was thrilled. That such a thing could happen was unbelievable! It was like bearding the lion in his own den. But when more reports came and the picture became clearer, ecstasy followed. 'So, we are not as worthless as we so long thought ourselves to be'—this was the dominant reaction; and, this was a turning-point, in the Indian attitude towards themselves.

RETURN TO INDIA

Swami Vivekananda returned to India in 1897, and was received by the people as a conquering hero. He was driven through the streets in decorated coaches drawn by admiring crowds. In one instance, the ruling prince of a state with his court officials joined the people in drawing the coach. The story was the same wherever he went. On his journey from Colombo to Almora, he inspired everyone.

The nation had long been asleep, now it awoke at his call, 'Arise, awake, and stop not till the goal is reached.' What is the goal he set for India? She has to be herself, not just a copy of the West as she was then trying to be. India should assimilate whatever good there is in the West, but surely not at the cost of what she now possesses and which has served her well through the centuries. 'Give and take'—that is the law of Nature. India has much to take from the West—science and technology, for instance, but she can also give much to the West in return—religion and spirituality. Through science and technology India can prosper materially, but she has to hold on to her spiritual traditions so that her growth may be well-balanced.[88]

It is interesting to note the contrast between what he said to the people of the West and what he said to his own people. He was impressed by Western progress, but he did not mince words in pointing out how the craze for money and the comforts it bought could some day boomerang. In talking to his own people he was equally blunt: He saw no special merit in a starving people indulging in moral and spiritual dialectics. His teacher, Sri Ramakrishna, used to say that there could be no religion on an empty stomach.[89] Swami Vivekananda also thought that what India needed first and foremost was bread. In his travels through India before leaving for the West, he had had first-hand experience of India's debilitating poverty.

Next to poverty, the heinous caste system of India troubled him. No one else attacked it so strongly as he did. He said India's downfall began from the day she coined the word 'untouchable'. In theory, man is divine in India, but in practice, he can be treated as a brute; this is the irony, how it happened is difficult to understand. The original idea of caste was good. Based on the principle of division of labour, it was an ideal institution. It was intended to give each individual a chance to grow as best he could according to his genius, but when it became stratified and hereditary, it was stultifying and therefore self-defeating.

And, what is the remedy for this? Swamiji would say, 'Education.' The common people who had long been neglected and had had no

---

88. CW, Vol. VII, p. 151.
89. *Letters*, pp. 81–82.

access to education should now receive special attention so that they can quickly overcome their initial drawbacks. He wanted education to reach out to them rather than their coming to education. He had rightly seen that making education free was not enough. A further incentive was necessary: education should be available to them at their doorstep. And, not only should it be free, a working man's child should have five teachers to one for a child coming from an enlightened family. This is what he said to the ruler of Mysore when the latter was planning to introduce free education within his state.

But what kind of education? Education to him was not information; it was something more meaningful. He saw that the prevailing system of education turned out only clerks. He did not care for this. He wanted 'man-making' and 'character-building' education.[90] He said, 'Education is not the amount of information that is put into your brains... We must have life-building, man-making, character-making assimilation of ideas.'[91]

In addition, Swamiji insisted that education should include acquisition of skills so that it could be productive. He thought it a pity that the existing system of education did not enable a man to stand on his own feet, nor did it teach him self-respect and self-confidence. He wanted an education which would combine Indian idealism with Western efficiency.

To accomplish this, Swamiji wanted India in her education schemes to take full advantage of modern science and technology. He advised the young Jamshed Tata (later to become one of India's most successful industrialists), to create a strong industrial base in India, and as a first step, to set up an Institute of Science and Technology. Acting on this advice, Tata started such an Institute that is now famous all over India. Interestingly, Tata invited Swamiji to be its first Director, an offer, he obviously could not accept as a monk.

---

90. CW, Vol. II p. 15; Vol. III, pp. 224, 302; Vol.V, p. 342.
91. CW, Vol. III, p. 302.

SWAMIJI'S PREDICTIONS

Swamiji felt that India had greatly harmed herself by neglecting the people. He described this as a national sin. She has had some stray great men, but the common people, by and large, have remained poor and backward.

He was no politician, but he had no doubt in his mind that the British had no right to impose their colonial rule over India. He predicted that India would be independent in a most extraordinary manner within the next fifty years.[92] He said this some time in 1897. Exactly fifty years after this India became independent. The Second World War had completely exhausted England. She had her hands full rebuilding herself and had not the power or inclination to keep under check a disgruntled giant of a country like India.

Swamiji also predicted the emergence of the *sudra* power,[93] that is, the power of the working people. His understanding of history had convinced him, that revolution was bound to come sooner or later. He mentioned two countries where it would come first—Russia and China. This was some time in the 90s of the last century. How he had this hunch no one knows. Neither does one know if he would have approved of the way revolution took place in these two countries.

As for India, it is clear that he preferred evolution to revolution. He wanted the working people to have the opportunity to catch up with the intelligentsia of the country. It is not that the intelligentsia has to go down to make room for the working people. It was Swamiji's hope that the upper classes would welcome any move for the progress of the backward classes, and they would make any sacrifice necessary to help quicken the process.

---

92. *Reminiscences*, p. 367; *Yuganayak Vivekananda*. Vol. III, Udhodhan Karyalaya. Calcutta. 3rd edition, p. 420.
93. CW, Vol. VI, 380, 381.

Another of Swamiji's predictions is waiting to be fulfilled. It was his prediction that India would some day rise to great heights of prosperity and power, far more than she had done in the past. Swamiji wanted that risen India to be a classless, casteless society. He visualised the future India as being 'a junction of the two great systems, Hinduism and Islam—Vedanta brain and Islam body.'[94] All will have an equal social status, but they will also aspire to the highest spiritual development, as found in Vedanta.

There is hardly any problem he did not touch upon. He was distressed by the neglect to which Indian women were subjected. They were not even allowed to go to school. They were given away in marriage before eight and by fourteen they had become mothers. Swamiji was prepared to 'murder' people responsible for child marriages. Women should have the same status as men in society. If they cannot contribute their share towards social growth, society is the loser. He said, 'It is not possible for a bird to fly on only one wing.'[95] Swamiji was struck by Western women's capabilities. He invited some of them to come and work in India. The most notable among them was Nivedita who served India till her death, working in every field of the country's life. India still remembers her with gratitude.

THE AWAKENING OF INDIA

Swami Vivekananda was still in his thirties when he began to have a premonition that death was close at hand. He was in fact only thirty-nine when on July 1902, he serenely gave up his body in meditation. He was satisfied that he had been able to launch a movement for the regeneration of India, and that the movement was flourishing. He had written to a friend on 9 July 1897: Only one idea was burning in my brain—to start the machine for elevating the Indian masses—and that I have succeeded in doing to a certain extent . . .

---

94. Letters, p. 380.
95. Ibid., p. 201.

I feel my task is done—at most three or four years more of life are left. I have lost all wish for my salvation. I never wanted earthly enjoyments. I must see my machine in strong working order, and then knowing for sure that I have put in a lever for the good of humanity, in India at least, which no power can drive back. I will sleep, without caring what will be next; and may I be born again and again, and suffer thousands of miseries so that I may worship the only God that exists, the only God I believe in, the sum total of all souls—and above all, my God the wicked, my God the miserable, my God the poor of all races, of all species, is the special object of my worship.[96]

History has proved that Swamiji had indeed succeeded in starting 'the machine for elevating the Indian masses'. 'Arise, awake, and stop not till the goal is reached'—this was his call and the nation heeded it. The awakening that we witness in India in the present century can be traced to Swami Vivekananda's influence. Gone is the inertia that once paralysed the country. Gone also is the mentality that insisted that India could prosper only by imitating the West. Everyone has come to realise that India must stay India, whatever her problems are.

Swamiji was no politician, but he inspired every political leader who has shaped India's destiny. Tilak, Aurobindo, Gandhiji, Netaji—in fact every national leader has acknowledged his indebtedness to him. As C. Rajagopalachari has written, 'Swami Vivekananda saved Hinduism and saved India. But for him we would have lost our religion and would not have gained our freedom.

We, therefore, owe everything to Swami Vivekananda.'[97]

---

96. CW, Vol.V, pp. 136–37.
97. *Swami Vivekahanda Centenary Memorial Volume*, Calcutta, p. xiii.

PRACTICAL VEDANTA

Can we identify anything as being Swami Vivekananda's distinct contribution? His distinct contribution is Vedanta. It is not that he created Vedanta; he recreated it. Vedanta had always been known in India, but not known in the form in which he presented it. It had been known only among a certain class of scholars who enjoyed studying and debating its propositions.

That it had or could have any bearing on life never seemed to have occurred to those scholars. They pursued their daily life as if Vedanta meant nothing to them. They were generally caste-ridden, and an individual was important or not important depending upon the caste he belonged to. Religion was rituals which they performed with great care, never questioning what purpose they served. These men were intelligent, also scholarly, but they were more concerned with the crust than with the essence of religion. They turned away from the freedom Vedanta offered; they preferred to stay in their sects.

Swamiji loved India for her idealism, but her failure at the practical level disgusted him. India says that man is divine but in practice she simply treats him as a brute. The West is more practical: it does not give man a divine status, but treats him exactly as he is—human. Swamiji was also much impressed with western efficiency. It was his hope that India would show how religion and science could be combined to promote material prosperity and moral excellence. The purpose of life is to improve, both materially and morally.

India owes much to Swami Vivekananda, but so does the world. He was a true citizen of the world. Of all countries India was the dearest to him, but that was because India was the land where the highest thoughts had been conceived. India was Truth itself to him. 'Shall India die? Then, from the world all spirituality will be extinct, all moral perfection will be extinct,'[98] he said. India should live for

---

98. CW, Vol IV, p. 348.

the sake of the world because man everywhere was his concern; man was God Himself to Swamiji.

This is not humanism, it is much more than that. This is Vedanta which sees God everywhere and in everything. Man is the very image of God, for God is most manifest in him. Since God is the same everywhere, man is the same everywhere. Colour, country or religion makes no difference. There is only one human family and there is also only one world. To a Vedantin, there is no East or West. It is all one. Swami Vivekananda was at home everywhere—in the West as well as in the East.

Although Swamiji had love for all, he saw how material prosperity had blunted the moral perceptions of people in the West. They had a craze for sense-pleasure which he did not like. He said in one of his letters:

> The Americans are drunk with new wine. A hundred waves of prosperity have come and gone over my country. We have learned the lesson which no child can yet understand. It is vanity. This hideous world is Maya. Renounce and be happy. Give up the idea of sex and possessions. There is no other bond... As these fall off, the eyes open to spiritual vision. The soul regains its own infinite power.[99]

CONCLUSION

Swamiji had preached this Practical Vedanta in the West—he must have been the first to do so. He had watched with joy the response it evoked. The people in the West had grown sick of their own sensual outlook and of the narrow creeds their church leaders preached. The people in India were equally sick of the stereotyped beliefs and practices handed down to them as religion. Swamiji brought them fresh air for which they were gasping. He rejuvenated them, giving them a new life.

---

99. Ibid., Vol.V, p.137.

According to his teaching of Vedanta, weakness is the root of all problems, both for individuals and nations, for the East and the West. He wanted strong men and women everywhere. 'Atman is not accessible to the weak,'[100] he used to say, quoting from the *Mundakopanishad*.[101] He had no sympathy for any religion that robbed people of their faith in themselves. Nothing can be more degrading than losing faith in oneself. A man may have faith in all the Gods and Goddesses, but if he has no faith in himself, he is doomed, according to Swamiji.[102]

Vedanta, which says man is divine, everything is divine, is a message that needs to be preached, and not the debilitating creeds and dogmas which make people depend upon an arbitrary God. Vedanta had long remained the monopoly of a handful of scholars. Swamiji wanted to carry it to everybody—scholar or no scholar. The West, as much as India, remains grateful to him for unravelling this closely-guarded secret, fully, freely. More important, he lived what he preached.

Swami Vivekananda brought the East and the West closer to each other. In fact, he pulled down the artificial barriers that divided them, and demonstrated that man was the same everywhere; distinctions of race and religion are only superficial.

'Live and let live' has been India's way. She has always been a believer in the philosophy of Unity in Diversity. This diversity is natural—each must be allowed to grow in his or her own way, otherwise there will be no growth at all. Where then is unity? Unity is in the divinity that is the essential characteristic of all. In our divine essence we are one. It is because of this feeling of oneness that we are careful not to injure anyone; we see ourselves in others. Thus, each group, while sticking firmly to its own essential beliefs,

---

100. *Letters*, p. 142.
101. *Mundakopanishad*, 3/2/4.
102. CW, Vol. III, p.190.

accepts and respects the religion and social customs of other groups. Not only that, people are urged to serve those of other religions and nationalities in time of natural or man-made catastrophes, thus creating a bond of love and friendship. This is the way integration is possible in the midst of a diverse, multiracial, multi-religious society.

Swamiji passed away just as the present century was beginning. Two World Wars have taken place since then, and there has been astounding progress in science and technology. As a result, the world as a whole has changed; man's outlook and style of living have also changed. We face problems unknown in Swamiji's time. So is Swami Vivekananda relevant today?

The answer to that is an unequivocal 'yes', because Vedanta, which contains India's eternal truths, and which Swamiji based his teaching on, is never dependent on the nature of the problems we face, but on the spirit with which those problems are tackled. The stress of India's spiritual teaching is on man himself, for, given the right kind of man, no problem need be daunting. 'Man-making is my mission,' Swamiji used to say.

Swami Vivekananda was always positive, never negative. It is easy to condemn, difficult to uplift. Swamiji was for the uplift of everybody, everywhere. A friend of all, he wanted people to grow in the way best suited for themselves, and at last realise the divinity within themselves and in everyone else.

Swami Vivekananda's Philosophy and Religion

SWAMI VIVEKANANDA'S PHILOSOPHY WAS VEDANTA, WHICH LITERALLY means the essence of the Vedas, or the conclusions the Vedas arrived at. Vedanta is a general term used for monism, qualified monism or dualism. Swami Vivekananda, however, believed in monism though he did not reject qualified monism or dualism, for he regarded them as steps which ultimately led to monism.

But what is monism? According to monism, the Ultimate Reality is One, though it has many names and forms. These names and forms are attributes and therefore without any substance of their own. They, of course, have some empirical value, but that is all. This Ultimate Reality is the source to which all that exists can be traced. On this Reality all that exists rests, and to this Reality all that exists returns on its dissolution. It is an Infinite Ocean of Existence. On this ocean things are mere waves, some small and some big. The universe itself is such a wave. It has the appearance of reality because it has its basis in the Ultimate reality, but it does not exist independent of that Reality, the Ocean of Existence. And, that which is Existence (*Sat*) is also Consciousness (*Chit*) and Bliss (*Ananda*). The three are in fact identical.

This Ultimate Reality is therefore called *Sat-Chit-Ananda. Sachchidananda, Existence–Consciousness–Bliss Absolute.* It is also called

Brahman because It is the biggest, being in every thing, in every being, everywhere. It is the essence, the self, of everything. Since It is the same Self in all, It must be One. It is this one common Self that holds together all that exists, like a thread running through everything. It is the Ground on which everything rests, from which everything comes, and into which everything goes back.

Since the Self is one, we are all one in the essence of our being, though we have different names and forms. This unity of existence is beautifully illustrated in one verse of the *Svetasvatara Upanishad* in which this Self is described as being the same in a woman, in a man, in a boy, in a girl, in a baby that has just been born, in an old man who walks with the support of a stick—in everyone. The names and forms differ but the Self remains the same. Oneness in spite of diverse names and forms, the same Self under the surface, Unity in diversity—this is the central theme of monism that Swami Vivekananda believed in and preached.

This *Sachchidananda* or *Brahman* is also called God, Isvara, because He is the Overlord, being the Soul of all souls. He is impersonal, but he can also be personal when perfectly manifest in an individual, as in the case of an Incarnation of God. What is the difference between an Incarnation of God and an ordinary individual? Both are divine in essence, but in an Incarnation, the divinity is more manifest. The goal of life, according to Swamiji, is to make our inner divinity more and more manifest, so that we become more and more God-like.

VEDANTA IN PRACTICE

Swami Vivekananda, as is well-known, exercised tremendous influence on a long succession of national leaders and also on the youth of India. His influence on the young has not waned even today. It is, in fact, on the increase. This is because Swamiji, like the great Buddha, was not so much interested in speculative philosophy as in its application for human welfare. If man was divine in essence, why should he live as if he were 'next-door to brutes' in Swamiji's words? It distressed him to see such human misery. It distressed him even more when he saw man's callousness to the suffering of others. Man to him was a living God, and the best way to worship this living God was to serve him. In his poem 'To a Friend', he wrote,

> From highest Brahman to yonder worm,
> And to the minutest atom,
> Everywhere is the same God, the All love;
> Friend, offer mind, soul, body, at their feet.
> These are His manifold forms before thee,
> Rejecting them, where seekest thou for God?
> Who loves all beings without distinction.
> He indeed is worshipping best his God.[103]

To serve man as God was, in his view, the real meaning of Vedanta. This, he said, was practical Vedanta, the religion of this age. If you sincerely believe that God is everywhere and that in man is His best manifestation, how can you turn away a hungry man when he comes to you for food? You will serve him with reverence and humility and with a feeling that you are privileged to be able to help him. If you serve him with an attitude of condescension, you are insulting him—you are insulting God Himself. You should not expect any thanks. Swamiji said that we should expect nothing in return for whatever we do for the good of others. We should be completely selfless.

In founding the Ramakrishna Mission, Swamiji declared that its ideals were self-liberation and service to humanity. Many demurred. They could understand self-liberation, but not service to humanity. How could service to humanity be compatible with self-liberation? If you reject this world, how could you then concern yourself

---

103. *In Search of God and Other Poems*, Swami Vivekananda, Advaita Ashrama, 1981, p. 45.

with its welfare? You cannot renounce the world and then try to improve it.

But if Swamiji had to make a choice, he would prefer happiness for others rather than his own salvation. He had seen God everywhere, in every being. This explains the concern he felt for man. This is in perfect conformity with the sprit of Vedantic scriptures. The Bhagavad Gita, for instance, extols selflless service as a way of realising the Ultimate Reality. Selfless service means service to God in man without expecting any return. In advocating this, Swamiji was in fact preaching religion in its highest form; and he was also taking his stand on the soundest philosophy.

SWAMIJI'S RELIGION

In practising religion, Swamiji placed little emphasis on rituals. He had noticed how they tend to cloud the vision of the worshipper. They are useful up to a point, but if overdone, they defeat their very purpose. In his view, they should be reduced to a minimum. In regard to this, he once wrote the following to his brother-disciple, Swami Brahmananda, concerning relief work started at Berhampore by Swami Akhandananda, another brother-disciple:

> The kind of work that is going on at Berhampore is exceedingly nice. It is those works that will triumph—can doctrines and dogmas touch the heart? Work, work—live the life—what do doctrines and dogmas count? Philosophy and yoga and penance—the worship room—our sunned rice or vegetable offerings—all these constitute the religion of one man or one country; doing good to others is the one great, universal religion. Men and women, young and old, down to the Pariah, nay, the very animal—all can grasp this religion.
>
> Can a merely negative religion be of any avail? The stone is never unchaste, the cow never tells a lie, nor do

trees commit theft or robbery, but what matters it after all? That work, little as it is, that you have done has brought Berhampore to your feet for ever—now people will do whatever you wish them to . . . kindness and love can buy you the whole world; lectures and books and philosophy—all stand lower than these. . . . Curtail the expenses of worship. . . . The children of the Lord are dying of starvation. Let the allowance for His Bhoga (food offerings) be spent in offering food to the Living God who dwells in persons of the poor . . . then will His grace descend on everything.[104]

In this connection, we recall Swamiji's plan to sell the Belur Math property and use the money for the relief of the plague-stricken people of Calcutta. Holy Mother Sarada Devi dissuaded him from this by superior arguments. However, he continued to decry placing too much emphasis on rituals.

THE DIVINITY OF MAN

To Swami Vivekananda, religion is a science of growth, a science of Being and Becoming. You have to grow through your own effort—there is no other way. Religion is no magic; it is hard work, constant struggle, always pushing ahead till you meet God—your own Self. It is unfoldment of the power that lies within. What others have achieved, you can also achieve—perhaps even more.

All of us are potential Buddhas, potential Christs. Buddha, Christ and other great men and we common mortals are all one in the Self.

The idea that man is a sinner was repugnant to Swamiji. How can man be a sinner if his essential nature is divine? He said, 'Ye divinities on earth—sinners! It is a sin to call a man so; it is a standing

---

104. *The Complete Works of Swami Vivekananda*, Advaita Ashrama, Calcutta, 1989) Vol.VI, p. 403 (hereafter, CW).

libel on human nature.[105] It may be that your divinity is temporarily hidden, like the sun hidden behind clouds, but sooner or later that divinity will become manifest. The task before you is to strive hard to manifest that divinity. There is nothing you cannot achieve. You must have faith in yourself. Swamiji calls that person an atheist who has no faith in himself. He says:

> If you have faith in the three hundred and thirty millions of your mythological Gods, and in all the Gods which, foreigners have introduced into your midst, and still have no faith in yourselves, there is no salvation for you. Have faith in yourselves and stand up on that faith.[106]

That faith will come when you remind yourself that you are the Atman, the storehouse of infinite power and knowledge. Potentially you are God Himself, whether you know it or not. 'Come up, lions, and shake off the delusion that you are sheep; you are souls immortal, spirits free, blest and eternal; ye are not matter, ye are not bodies; matter is your servant, not you the servant of matter,'[107] Swamiji cried out at the Parliament of Religions.

It is the man of faith who fashions the history of the world. To lose faith is to court death. Swamiji's gospel is the gospel of strength, courage, and manliness. You may commit a few blunders, but if you are strong, you can rectify them.

Swamiji made no distinction between the secular and the spiritual. In his philosophy and religion, everything is spiritual. The daily chores that you perform are spiritual, viewed in Swamiji's perspective. A shoemaker is no less important than a scholar. The vocation does not make the man; it is your character that makes you what you are. Work is worship, provided you do it as a means to manifest the God within. Echoing Swamiji, Nivedita quotes a Christian saying, 'To labour is

---

105. CW Vol. I, p. 11.
106. CW Vol. III, p. 190.
107. CW Vol. I, p. 11.

to pray.' Keeping this in mind, Swamiji asked the monks of the Sri Ramakrishna Mission to run school, hospitals, orphanages and other institutions of service. It is not social work these monks do; they are worshipping God. This work is part of their spiritual discipline.

Swamiji's philosophy of monism implies unity of existence, therefore a monist does not recognise distinctions based on caste, race, or religion. To the follower of this philosophy, mankind is one and the world is one. The only difference between man and man is in the degree of manifestation of the Self. The same Self is in all of us, so we can only love, and never hurt one another.

SWAMI VIVEKANANDA AND RELIGIOUS HARMONY

Swami Vivekananda, like his Master, was more concerned with the essence of a religion than with its practices, which they knew were peripheral. They saw the same essence in all religions, and that essence was Truth. Here, they were in agreement with the Indian seers who declared, 'Truth is one; the wise speak of it in various ways.' This Truth is called Brahman, God, Allah, and many other names. Truth is Impersonal, but it can be personal when manifest in a person, Buddha, Christ and others like them represent that Truth within a human framework. The goal of life is to reach the level that those great souls represent.

Perhaps, we will never reach that level, but let us try. If we cannot reach that level by our own efforts, perhaps they will come down and carry us up to where they are. Is there not such a thing as divine grace? What path we choose is not very important. Any path is good, provided we are sincere. That is what counts. Swami Vivekananda said, 'We travel from lower truth to higher truth.' Truth remains Truth, only at first our understanding of it is not clear; it improves as we continue along the way. Because Truth is one and each religion is a way to reach that Truth, Sri Ramakrishna was able to practise different religions.

The harmony of religions may be too distant a goal to realise, but if we learn to 'live and let live', that will be something. Today, even this minimum seems difficult to achieve. What is it that stands in the way? Could it be our 'holier than thou' attitude? Do we believe that we are superior to others? Do we think that everyone should behave as we do, practise religion as we do? That is where we err. Religious practices vary from country to country, from one ethnic group to another. Even within the same religious group there is no uniformity, so far as practices are concerned. But why should there be uniformity? There is no uniformity even between any two members of the same family. One cannot be a carbon copy of someone else.

You have to be yourself in outlook, tastes and understanding of the purpose of life. If this freedom is denied, there is no growth. In religious matters, freedom of thought is essential. Religion is something personal—a matter between you and your God. You should be free to express your love of God in your own way. And, you should give others freedom to express their love of God in their own way. If more and more people arrive at this broadminded outlook, we will have true religious harmony. Swami Vivekananda gave expression to his own universal views on religious harmony when he declared at the Parliament of Religions:

> I accept all religions that were in the past, and worship with them all; I worship God with every one of them, in whatever form they worship Him. I shall go to the mosque of the Mohammedan; I shall enter the Christian's church and kneel before the crucifix; I shall enter the Buddhistic temple, where I shall take refuge in Buddha and in his Law. I shall go into the forest and sit down in meditation with the Hindu, who is trying to see the Light which enlightens the heart of every one.[108]

---

108. CW, Vol II, p. 374.

Swami Vivekananda's Approach to Social Work

WHAT SWAMIJI STRESSED MOST IN HIS IDEAS ON SOCIAL WORK WAS the kind of attitude that one brought to bear on it—in other words, one's approach to it. In any programme of social work that we may adopt, it is essential that there be a correct approach; otherwise it is possible that the work will defeat its own purpose. But if the approach is the right one, then even if there is a lack of resources or technical skill, we may be able to do some good.

A man may be very efficient, highly trained and a specialist in some particular field of activity; he may have vast resources and a large organisation at his command; but if he doesn't have the right attitude, he is not likely to be of much service to the people he is trying to serve. For example, a doctor may be highly qualified and have the latest instruments and technical skill to give relief to a patient. But if he does not have the right kind of attitude, if he is only interested in earning money and nothing else, he may not be able to give much relief to his patients. This is because there is no understanding between him and his patient—that kind of fellowship, that spirit of mutual respect and confidence that should form the basis for a joint attack on the patient's disease. The patient must feel that the doctor really cares for him and feels his misfortune as his own—a friend and well-wisher who will ungrudgingly place all his knowledge and skill at his service. When a doctor is like this, kind and sympathetic and anxious to understand and care for his patients, he is bound to be a great blessing to his patients, as well as a successful professional man.

THE SPIRIT BEHIND SOCIAL WORK

Just as a doctor needs this feeling for others, those in other occupations also need this feeling. This is especially true for a social worker, who should develop a spirit of understanding and fellowship towards those he is serving. With this attitude, half of his work is accomplished.

We do not suggest that you do not need other qualifications to be successful in your mission of service. It will be helpful to have some specialised training, some equipment, and the backing of an organisation for supplying manpower and resources, and other things as well. These however, are secondary. The main requisite is that you have sympathy, fellow-feeling, a sense of selflessness, a spirit of service. With these, you will be a good social worker.

But Swamiji did not use the expression social work or social service; he simply used service. In Bengali and in Sanskrit it is *seva*. He said, 'Serve others.' You should consider yourself fortunate to be able to do this, because you have the opportunity to express your love. When you serve someone with this attitude, both of you are happy—he in receiving love through this service, and you in giving love through it. You should have this kind of kinship with those you serve.

ONE COMMON DIVINITY

It is necessary to understand that when Swamiji preached this service, he based his teaching on the awareness of the one divine spirit in everyone. You and I are not essentially different. You have a body that is different from mine; we have different minds also, but we belong to one common, divine source from which everyone and everything is derived. We are one spirit, having different forms. We have to realise this unity.

Our ancient sages taught that the goal of life is to realise this oneness at the centre of all creation. Not only are human beings one in essence, animals and all things are one. Everything is but a manifestation of the same divinity.

We recall an interesting incident in which Swamiji taught a Mathematics professor the concept of oneness. When he was staying at Lahore, he was invited to lunch by a professor of Mathematics. After they had eaten, the Professor took his watch from his pocket and offered it to Swamiji, saying, 'Swamiji, you have been so kind to visit me. Please accept this watch and keep it with you. It will remind you of me and of your visit to my home.' Swamiji accepted the watch but at once put it back into the professor's pocket and said, 'I shall use the watch in this pocket. You and I are not different.' At this the professor said, 'Swamiji, will you give me a message that I may try to practise in my life?' Swamiji took out the watch from the professor's pocket and said, 'Look, it is one o'clock. Try to realise this oneness.'

The professor later took sannyasa at the suggestion of Swamiji and came to be known as Swami Ramatirtha. Swamiji advised him to go to the West and preach Vedanta, which he did with considerable success. He tried to practise the message Swamiji had given him, and whenever he addressed any meeting he would begin his lecture by saying. 'Myself in the form of you, ladies and gentlemen present!'

It is this recognition of one common divinity pervading everything that is the basis of Swamiji's gospel of service. Whatever you see around you is nothing but a manifestation of the same divinity. There is no essential difference between a good man and a bad man; they are both divine in essence. That is why we find Swamiji using expressions such as 'My God the wicked', 'my God the sinner.' We should serve those who are bad—perhaps even more than the good. They need our service more; they need more sympathy, more understanding.

SRI RAMAKRISHNA'S EXPERIENCE OF ONENESS

One incident in Sri Ramakrishna's life clearly shows how deeply Sri Ramakrishna had absorbed this spirit of oneness, and how this had become a fact of daily experience with him. When he was suffering from cancer of the throat and was unable to eat or drink anything, some of his disciples, including Swamiji, begged him to ask his Divine Mother Kali to allow him to eat and drink something. He replied, 'How can I do that? I have no will of my own. Mother knows best what I should do about eating and drinking.' But the disciples would not give up. They continued to urge him to ask Mother Kali to let him eat and drink something. Finding it difficult to refuse the disciples, Sri Ramakrishna prayed to Kali that, for the sake of his disciples, he might eat a little. At once he had a wonderful vision, in which the Divine Mother revealed to him that he was already eating through millions of mouths. 'What does it matter if you do not eat through that one mouth of yours?' She said.

Sri Ramakrishna was greatly annoyed with himself because he had yielded to the pressure of his disciples. He turned to the boys and said, 'It is because of you that I have been put to such shame! I should have known better. As long as other people eat, why should I care whether I myself eat or not. There is no one but me. Bodies differ, but within them all there is one single soul—one Supreme Soul in all bodies.'

Another incident in Sri Ramakrishna's life illustrates how real his sense of oneness was. Once, when he was sitting on the Western verandah of his room, he suddenly cried out in pain saying, 'Look, they have beaten me, they have beaten me!' People came running. They could not imagine who could be so wicked as to beat a holy person like him. 'Who has beaten you?' they asked. He pointed to a boat on which one brother was beating the other. The people noticed that there were red marks on Sri Ramakrishna's back, as if he himself had been beaten.

Romain Rolland has tried to explain this phenomenon in his book on Sri Ramakrishna. He says that when you feel intensely for others, when you share their suffering, you have this kind of manifestation in your body. You have such a sense of oneness with others that you suffer the same way that others suffer. When others are happy you are also happy.

The Christian experience called *stigmata* is an example of this kind of sensitivity. When Christ was crucified, he was placed on a cross and nails were driven through his palms and feet. He suffered great agony, and there was profuse bleeding. Some Christians meditate on the sufferings of Christ, and visualise the wounds on his body. As they continue their meditation, wounds like those on Christ's body appear on their bodies also. Cases such as this have been well-documented.

Swamiji stressed this same spirit in his *gospel of service*, only he wants us not only to feel for those who suffer, but serve them in such a way as to relieve their suffering. Because of the Oneness at the centre of all creatures, when we serve others we are in fact serving ourselves. We are not doing others a favour when we serve them, or pitying them—that is not the true attitude of Service. When we serve with a feeling of humility and with a sense that it is a privilege to serve, we are true social workers.

THE TASK AHEAD

As we look into the future, an important question arises. Suppose, there comes a time in India when there is no poverty, no lack of hospitals or any material want or hardship. If India develops into a good welfare state, it is possible that poverty, illiteracy, and many other problems that we face today will be eradicated. At that time, India will have trained social workers such as are now found in most Western countries. They are specialists who work among those who are physically or mentally handicapped, and are employees of the government.

What will be the place then for a worker who wants to serve others out of love, voluntarily? How will the Sri Ramakrishna monks, for example, be able to serve the people as they do now. Will our religious social workers then remain idle? Will there be no scope for real, loving social service then? This is the basic question: What role will voluntary, dedicated social workers play in a welfare state?

The answer to this question is that there will always be a need for people who feel for others. There are some forms of suffering that are more painful than physical suffering. For these we need something more—we need sympathy, a sense of security, a feeling that there are others who care for us.

The welfare state may take care of my body, but it is not its purpose to build up a system of relationships among the people on the basis of friendship and sympathy. There is a need for voluntary organisations and individuals to promote peace and brotherhood among diverse races and classes. In other words, it is not enough to have an efficient system for looking after the physical needs of people. There should also be organisations and individuals who will develop warm human relationships so that a sense of unity, a sense of love and respect for one another, will develop among the people.

The real criterion of what sort of man you are, is whether you feel for others or not. Whatever you may be, you are not human unless you have this feeling and concern, unless you feel that when others suffer you have no right to live in luxury. You must share what you have with others. When you have learned to feel as one with others, when you feel their misery and happiness as your own, then you are a true human being, and can become an ideal social worker.

Swami Vivekananda's Vision of a New Social Order

MAN HIMSELF MAY BE IMPERFECT, YET HE CANNOT HELP DREAMING OF a social order that will be perfect. What exactly a perfect social order is he doesn't know, still this has been one of his major preoccupations through the centuries. Is it only a question of a just distribution of wealth? Or, that of equality in respect to status, opportunities, rights and privileges? Or, is there something more to it?

In regard to material resources, we are in a position today in which no one need feel deprived or discriminated against. Nevertheless, there are large sections of people everywhere who have the feeling that they are not getting their due. Although they are the people who produce wealth, they receive only a fraction of it, the major portion going to people who do not work at all. Thus, there are two broad divisions in society: people who produce the wealth but remain poor, and people who do little, yet manage to grab most of the wealth. The poor remain poor and may get even poorer, while the rich become richer. Although the rich are few in number, they are able to keep the vast masses of the poor in a state of perpetual poverty. This kind of exploitation has been going on throughout history. Cannot this be changed? Cannot we have a social order that guarantees justice and equality to all?

In India, society is divided more on the basis of caste than on wealth. A Brahmin is a privileged person even if he is poor. He is authoritative, imposes his will on others, and enjoys more power than he can wisely use. A *sudra* may be rich, yet he is the social underdog. Economic or social, such divisions in society are cruel and arbitrary, because they put too much power into the hands of a few and deny the majority their basic rights.

SWAMI VIVEKANANDA'S OUTLOOK

As a monk, Swami Vivekananda need not have bothered about these social problems, but he did bother about them very much because he was concerned about everything that concerned man. To him, man was God Himself, 'the only God that I believe in'. How could he be unconcerned when he saw that God suffer? He had travelled extensively through the world; wherever he went he saw human suffering. The suffering, he observed, was in most cases man-made—the rich taking advantage of the poor, the strong of the weak, the brahmin of the *sudra*, the educated of the illiterate. Could this worldwide phenomenon of social disparity be stopped? Could there be a social order with no loopholes for the strong to exploit the weak?

Religion was Swamiji's first concern, but religion as he understood it could not be indifferent to human suffering. In an outburst of anger against the callousness to suffering he noticed in those who called themselves religious, he said, 'I do not care for a God who cannot wipe the widow's tears and provide food to the hungry orphans.' Religion, according to him, implied work to relieve human suffering. If this action was slow in producing results, he was prepared to accept a compromise: socialism. He knew socialism was not perfect, yet he saw in it an attempt to end exploitation of the poor—perhaps not a successful attempt, yet an attempt. As he said, 'Half a loaf is better than no bread.'

Man's history is a history of rosy dreams; dreams often shattered against stark reality. Again and again, man has set ambitious goals for himself, but he has never got far from where he was. Justice, freedom, equality—all these are great ideals, but stern reality only mocks at them. New systems and institutions come into being amidst much fanfare, but they do not live up to their promise. Man's best efforts seem to produce little of lasting value. Can this dismal story be ended?

THE IMPORTANCE OF MAN

To Swami Vivekananda, what was important was man himself, and not so much the system. However good a system might appear on paper, in practice it might turn out to be a travesty of what it was intended to be unless it was manned by good, honest people. This is why he said again and again that man-making was his mission. Given good and capable men, any system would work; without such men, any system, however perfect on paper, would fail. This came to him as a revelation when he saw the parliamentary system in operation. He must have admired it at one time, but when he saw it operating at close quarters, he found it was a mockery—a fraud on the people. Not that the system was inherently bad, but the way those in power ran it did little to fulfil the purpose for which it was created. Despite all the talk about equality and fair play that the parliamentary system was to bring about, people continued to suffer under oppression of one kind or another.

So, Swamiji directed most of his efforts in the field of social reconstruction to the work of man-making. In carrying out this work, he did not overlook the differences between one individual and another—differences in outlook, in aptitudes in skills, and attitudes. Such differences are natural and necessary. Any attempt to suppress these differences is likely to thwart the individual's growth. Each person has to grow in his own way, according to his genius. Nobody can grow according to a prescribed model; everyone grows best in an atmosphere of freedom. It is the duty of society to provide such an atmosphere.

But even in such an atmosphere there is no guarantee that an individual's growth will be assured. Freedom and equality of opportunity are not enough to ensure a person's growth to the desired level. He may need some special assistance, because he may have drawbacks which he cannot overcome left to himself, and also because, having made a late start, he may need special help in order to catch up. In Swamiji's view, the more educated, cultured people should maintain their own standards, but they should try to raise the less fortunate to an equal level. He was for 'levelling up', not 'levelling down'. 'Be and make' should be the motto for all. He charged every educated man to help educate those who have not had the benefit of education.

'Expansion is life, contraction is death,' he used to say. To be occupied only with oneself to the exclusion of others is death; to be truly human, one must be concerned with others, and think and feel in terms of the whole community. One cannot have education or anything else exclusively for oneself. A happy and progressive society is one in which there are no class barriers to prevent an individual's moving from one class to another—totally and permanently. But what do we mean by 'class' in an ideal society?

Since no two persons are alike, it is perhaps inevitable that society will divide itself into groups and classes based upon common interests. For instance, lovers of music or sports may form groups or classes for themselves; similarly, there may be groups formed on the basis of occupation. However, these divisions should not be rigid nor should they carry with them any idea of high or low. 'Each is great in its own place,' Swami Vivekananda said. The question of one being superior to another by virtue of one's occupation should not rise at all. The real test of greatness is in the character of the person and not in his profession. A butcher may be a saint while a scholar may be a moral wreck. Any work done in the right spirit can be worship.

ISLAM BODY AND VEDANTA BRAIN

In a letter written to a Muslim friend, Swami Vivekananda wrote that the ideal society was one which had 'an Islam body and a Vedanta brain'. By an 'Islam body' he obviously meant an egalitarian, casteless society. In spite of the proclamation by religion of the ideal of equality, society everywhere is divided into high and low classes. Of all religions, Islam alone has been able to achieve equality to a large extent. This equality is not the kind that an all-powerful state may impose; it is founded on the sincere conviction among followers of Islam that, before God all are equal. This has given Muslims a sense of unity scarcely seen among the followers of other religions. This has also given them a sense of dignity and self-respect.

But Swamiji wanted the casteless society to have a 'Vedanta brain'. An egalitarian society is welcome, but it should be a society where everybody is committed to the ideal of trying to be perfect. As a Vedantin, he believed the 'each soul is potentially divine', and that 'the goal of life is to manifest that divinity.' An ideal society is not merely a society where all are equal, with equal rights and privileges, but where conditions are conducive to maximum moral and spiritual growth. Society should certainly attend to everyone's material needs, but it should also try to foster in him an urge for moral and spiritual excellence. Swamiji had observed that in the West disproportionate importance was attached to material prosperity, as if this alone was enough to guarantee happiness. There had, no doubt, been great saints among the people in the West, especially in Europe, but the average man there had a materialistic outlook that Swamiji deplored. Lest this same outlook should become prevalent in India, he wanted her to preserve her spiritual heritage by all means.

It was his belief that if a country remained spiritually strong then no matter how weak she was otherwise, she would survive. To emphasise this he would refer to the examples of great powers like Greece and Rome. Despite their prosperity and military strength, they had crumbled only because of their neglect of spiritual values. India, on the other hand, notwithstanding her many ups and downs had retained her distinct identity because she had pursued her spiritual goals even at the expense of her other interests.

Not that he was prepared to acquiesce in the kind of dehumanising poverty from which India suffered. He hated it most because like his guru Sri Ramakrishna, he was aware that there could be no religion on an empty stomach. But physical well-being is not enough; this has to be backed by moral well-being. No society can thrive where men and women are selfish and dishonest. Swamiji would say again and again that man-making was his mission. By this, he meant that whatever he taught was intended to improve human beings. His gospel was a gospel of strength, courage, and hard work. His call to man everywhere was, 'Arise, awake and stop not till the goal is reached.' What does he mean by 'the goal'? What is the goal he wants man to achieve? That goal according to Swamiji is the manifestation of his essential divinity.

RELIGION AND SCIENCE

Man is by nature divine, but somehow or other that divinity has become obscured. The task before us is to manifest that divinity. In Swamiji's view, we can manifest this divinity by controlling nature, external and internal. To control external nature man uses science, and to control internal nature he has to use religion. We must combine the two—religion and science: science to take care of our physical well-being and religion to foster our moral and spiritual growth. For this reason, Swamiji wanted India to learn science and technology from the West and in return teach it spirituality, which has been India's speciality through the ages.

He especially admired Western efficiency and wanted India to learn that, but he also wanted to 'introduce Vedantic thoughts, conceived long ago in the forest, to the poorest of the poor living in cottages.' The poor in India were 'next door to brutes', and the rich and those in a position to help them were callous about it. He warned these people that their days were numbered; they already belonged to the past—they had become 'mummies'. Swamiji hated the idea of privilege—especially in the field of religion, where those who were expected to help the poor and the ignorant actually exploited them. This was completely contrary to the teachings of Vedanta which emphasise the oneness of all, and urge man to serve others, seeing his own self in them.

But the question is: How can the kind of social order that Swamiji envisages be brought about? Does he advocate revolution? No. Though he was convinced of the inevitability of social change, he wanted that change to come peacefully and not through violence. As a student of history, he had seen how every revolution tends to defeat itself. He was for the slow process of evolution in order to ensure a lasting change. But, as we have seen, no change can sustain itself unless there are good and capable men behind it. That is why Swami Vivekananda laid so much stress on man-making.

Whether or not Swamiji's vision of an ideal social order will ever become a reality is difficult to tell, but it is a goal worth striving for. It was his hope that India would show the way in this matter. Will she succeed in doing this? Will she be able to combine material prosperity with spiritual greatness—not just for a few individuals as she has done in the past, but for the whole community? Will she be able to create a society based on equality and justice with a strong spiritual mooring?

For the good of the whole world, which needs India and its great spiritual treasures if it is to survive, and for India herself, it is imperative that these questions be answered with a clear affirmative Yes.

Sister Nivedita and Indian Art

- *Sister Nivedita*
- *Nivedita and the Revival of Indian Art*
- *Nivedita's Contribution to the Development of Indian Art*

Sister Nivedita

LET ME INTRODUCE A DAUGHTER OF IRELAND, MISS MARGARET Elizabeth Nobel, later known as Sister Nivedita. Elizabeth Nobel was born on 28 October 1867. She was the daughter of a priest. After having received her education, she had been running a Kindergarten school but in spite of that she had a deep quest for spiritual illumination. This quest brought her in contact with Swami Vivekananda in 1895 when he visited London. There she accepted Swami Vivekananda as her guru. She came to India in 1898 with the invitation of her guru and having adopted India as her own country, breathed her last on its sacred soil in 1911. Swami Vivekananda felt keenly that there was no chance for the welfare of the country unless the condition of women was improved; he used to say, 'It is not possible for a bird to fly on only one wing.' So, he paid great attention to the uplift of women in India, in his scheme for the regeneration of the nation. He used to say, 'My duty would not be complete, if I die without starting two places, one for the sannyasins, the other for the women.' 'Education, education, education alone! . . . Education was the answer I got . . . It will be necessary to start centres for women exactly like those for men.' At the time, he could not find any woman in this country who could undertake this tremendous task. Swamiji appealed, 'Will there be no woman in the land of Maitreyi, Khana, Lilavati, Savitri and Ubhayabharati, who will venture to do this?' This fervent appeal of Swamiji did not touch the heart of any educated woman in India.

But in a far-off land the light of its inspiration broke upon the soul of Margaret Nobel.

Swamiji knew that Margaret was serious and sincere, and that she desired to dedicate her life to the service of the Indian women. Swamiji invited Margaret to India for his work. He wrote to her, 'Let me tell you frankly that I am now convinced that you have a great future in the work for India. What was wanted was not a man but a woman, a real lioness, to work for the Indians, women especially.' Sister Nivedita responded to this call of her Guru and came to India to fulfil his dream of women's education. Nivedita used to say, 'I love India as the birthplace of the highest and best of all religions, as the country that has the grandest mountains, the Himalayas. The country where the homes are simple, where domestic happiness is most to be found, and where the women unselfishly, unobtrusively, ungrudgingly serve the dear ones from early morn to dewy eve.'

Swamiji spoke to Nivedita about the kind of work she would have to do and the conditions in which she would have to work. Nivedita said, 'It was only on the ship, during the voyage to England, that he fully expressed the ideal that was in him. 'You must give up all visiting, and live in strict seclusion,' he said one day, as he discussed the future of women's work. 'You have to set yourself to Hinduise your thoughts, your needs, your conceptions, and your habits. Your life, internal and external, has to become all that an orthodox Hindu Brahman Brahmacharini's ought to be. But you have to forget your own past, and to cause it to be forgotten. You have to lose even its memory.'[109]

In advising Nivedita about the work in education she was to take up, he emphasised the fact that the ancient Indian culture was so rich in so many ways, with all its myths, spiritual practices and family customs, etc., that these should be adapted to the modern age in the work of educating women and children. The teachers should

---

109. *The Master As I Saw Him*. Nivedita, Udbodhan Office, Calcutta, 1977. pp. 255.

borrow from the West only those concepts that were absolutely essential, and in harmony with Indian ideals.

Slowly and painfully, Nivedita shed her deep-rooted British character and became what she and Swamiji wanted her to be, Nivedita, a totally selfless worker for her guru and for the regeneration of the country she now identified herself with—India. She had not just changed her allegiance from one country to another. She had completely given up her narrow patriotism. In adopting India as her own country, she was in fact adopting the whole world, because India's ancient ideals and truths are meant not for just one country, but for all people everywhere. Just as the law of gravity, though discovered in England by the Englishman Newton, is true for the whole world, the truths which the ancient Rishis in India discovered are also true for the whole world, for every religion. They are truly universal principles.

Though Nivedita was so thoroughly trained by her great guru, her transformation into a perfect receptacle of these Indian truths and ideals was brought to completion by her utter devotion to him. We tend to become like those we deeply love and revere. Nivedita was no exception to this rule. She became permeated with Swamiji's thoughts and ideas through her devotion to him.

Nivedita was finally able to give herself whole-heartedly to India because she saw in India the personification of Truth—the Truth that is universal—that is valid for all countries, all religions, all times. It is the Truth that avers that we are at heart all one. The supreme goal of life is to manifest that oneness in all our thoughts, words, and deeds.

This Truth is beautifully expressed in Swamiji's poem, 'To A Friend', which ends:

Everywhere is the same God, the All-Love;
Friend, offer mind, soul, body, at their feet.
These are His manifold forms before thee,
Rejecting them, where seekest thou for God?
Who loves all beings, without distinction,
He indeed is worshipping best his God.

Nivedita and the Revival of Indian Art

I CHOSE TO DISCUSS NIVEDITA'S ROLE IN THE REVIVAL OF INDIAN art because I felt that not much has been said on the subject by those who have dealt with Nivedita and that I might perhaps make a beginning so that others more competent might throw light on it. It is well known that Nivedita was one of the architects of the Indian renaissance, but we know very little about what she did specifically for the revival of Indian art. We know she considered art very important in any scheme that the country might have for its development. In her essay 'The Function of Art in Shaping Nationality' she says, '... art offers us the opportunity of a great common speech, and its rebirth is essential to the up-building of the motherland'.[110]

Now the question arises, How did Nivedita come to be interested in Indian art? More pertinently, How did she come to have so much esoteric knowledge of it? Nandalal Bose has said, 'I do not know whether Havell has mentioned the name of the Sister anywhere in his books; but she made him understand the viewpoints of Indian aesthetics and philosophy of art.'[111] How did it happen that even the great Havell sought light from her on Indian art? Most Westerners

---

110. *The Complete Works of Sister Nivedita*, Vol. III, Calcutta. 1967, p. 3.
111. Pravrajika Atmaprana, *Sister Nivedita*, Calcutta, 1961, p. 269.

found Indian art baffling. Some even thought it puerile, bizarre, or at best, a vulgar imitation of Greek art. Yet, how did Nivedita understand art so well? Who introduced her to its mystique? I will try to answer these questions. Indirectly, Nivedita herself provides the answer in her book *Notes of Some Wanderings with the Swami Vivekananda*. She says, 'Beautiful have been the days of this year. In them the Ideal has become the Real. First, in our river-side cottage at Belur; then in the Himalayas, at Naini Tal and Almora; afterwards wandering here and there through Kashmir;—everywhere have come hours never to be forgotten, words that will echo through our lives for ever . . .'[112] Whose words is Nivedita referring to here? She is referring to the words of her Master, to the talks Swami Vivekananda gave to her and his other Western disciples when they stayed at Belur and when they accompanied him on his North Indian tours. Those talks covered wide-ranging subjects but history, religion, art, and literature were given special attention. Through those talks, the Swami was trying to introduce them to India, 'the crown of his adoration'. Nivedita's own account of the talks runs as follows:

> For the most part, it was the Indian religions that he portrayed for us, today dealing with one, and tomorrow with another, his choice guided, seemingly, by the whim of the moment. But it was not religion only that he poured out upon us. Sometimes, it would be history. Again, it would be folk-lore. On still another occasion, it would be the manifold anomalies and inconsistencies of race, caste, and custom. In fact India herself became, as heard in him, as the last and noblest of the *Puranas*, uttering itself through his lips.'[113]
>
> And, carried by his burning enthusiasm it was possible to enter into these things, and dimly, even then, to

---

112. *The Complete Works of Sister Nivedita*, Vol. I, Calcutta, 1967, p. 277.
113. *Notes of Some Wanderings with the Swami Vivekananda*, Calcutta, 1957, p. 5.

apprehend their meaning. Whatever might be the subject of the conversation, it ended always on the note of the Infinite.'[114]

One imagines those talks were meant primarily for Nivedita's edification, for Swamiji expected that she of all his Western disciples was going to serve India most. Once, he wrote to her: 'Let me tell you frankly that I am now convinced that you have a great future in the work for India.'[115] How prophetic this proved to be! But while it was his hope that Nivedita would do great things for India, he knew her services would not amount to much if she did not understand India. Superficially, India was a country teeming with poor and ignorant people. Most Westerners judged her by what they saw around them—abysmally low standard of living, unhygienic conditions, and a caste-ridden society. Again and again, Vivekananda warned Nivedita about what she was likely to see in India, that is, if she looked only superficially. He welcomed the idea that she should come and work in India but, at the same time, gave her a true picture of what it was like in India lest she should come with false notions and then be disappointed. No Westerner could have given a grimmer picture of the country. While welcoming her he said:

> Yet, the difficulties are many. You cannot form any idea of the misers', the superstition, and the slavery that are here. You will be in the midst of a mass of half-naked men and women with quaint ideas of caste and isolation, shunning the white skin through fear or hatred and hated by them intensely. On the other hand, you will be looked upon by the white people as a crank, and every one of your movements will be watched with suspicion.

---

114. ibid. p. 6.
115. *Complete Works of Swami Vivekananda*, Vol. VII (Calcutta, 1963) p. 507.

The climate is fearfully hot; our winter in most places being like your summer, and in the south it is always blazing.

Not one European comfort is to be had in places out of the cities... You must think well before you plunge in...'[116]

THE BEGINNING OF NIVEDITA'S EDUCATION IN THINGS INDIAN

Vivekananda warned Nivedita in such clear terms because he did not want her to come to India with false notions and then to start condemning the country because conditions were different from what she thought they would be. Vivekananda, as is well known, was most sensitive where India was concerned. He used to say to his Western disciples, 'Remember, not a word of condemnation.' He must have observed that there were many Europeans who sincerely loved India, but the way they loved her showed that they did not understand her. Often, they suffered from a sense of superiority and there was a patronising attitude behind their love. Vivekananda made it clear to his Western disciples that he would tolerate no such nonsense from them. They would be doing harm to the country if they did not have a proper attitude towards their work. After all, what was important was that the country's self-respect should not suffer while she was being helped to stand on her own feet. India should grow out of her own strength and not out of strength injected into her from outside. She had her own traditions to which she must remain true, for they had sustained her through the centuries and could sustain her in the future also. In other words, India must remain India and not try to be some other country. It was, therefore, necessary that his workers should understand those traditions, and accept them without reservation.

---

116. ibid, pp. 507–8.

Vivekananda once said that if the country was first deluged with spirituality, then the task of reconstruction would be comparatively easy. He laid so much stress on spirituality because he believed that was where India's strength lay.

He expected much from Nivedita but he knew if she did not accept the traditions of India, all her efforts would be futile. She would be like any other missionary woman from the West who worked for India but did not understand or respect her culture and civilisation. He wanted Nivedita to be different; she should not only understand India, but also accept her and completely identify herself with India. He once handed a brief poem to Nivedita which was at once a testament and a mandate. He said in his poem[117]:

The mother's heart, the hero's will.
The sweetness of the southern breeze,
The sacred charm and strength that dwell
On Aryan altars, flaming, free;
All these be yours, and many more
No sincere soul could dream before—
Be thou to India's future son
The mistress, servant, friend in one.

It was a big role that Vivekananda was assigning to Nivedita, but he had faith in her and knew she would be able to fulfil his expectations provided she had the requisite training.

First and foremost, she must understand that religion was the main source of inspiration for India and all India's endeavours in art, literature, history, sociology, science, and philosophy were only the means by which she was trying to reach her religious goals. Those who thought these activities were merely secular would be making a grave mistake. Nothing in India was in fact secular. The Swami wanted Nivedita to grasp this, for otherwise her approach

---

117. ibid. Vol. VI, p. 178.

to her work would be entirely wrong. Nivedita had seen India's famished body covered with disease and filth, but he now wanted her to see India's soul, which was as fresh and as healthy as ever. This was why he took pains to explain to Nivedita at great length India's history, philosophy, art, and literature. Nivedita herself was a keen student of these subjects, but she now studied them from a new angle and was able to see in each familiar fact a meaning she had never suspected before. Thanks to the training and education she received from the Swamiji, she realised that it was important that India should never deviate from the course she had followed through the centuries. She realised that while change was necessary it should not be a purposeless change or a change basically against the genius of the country; that kind of change was bound to prove ruinous. Later, Nivedita herself was to warn India against thoughtless change or change in the wrong direction. In an article she said, 'Re-adjustments are necessary in all directions, and in making those very re-adjustments, it may be, we shall become, we are actually becoming, a nation. For it is not change that is destructive, but *aimless or wrongly-purposed change.* And, precisely from such it is that the ideal of nationality, with its overwhelming impulse of moral direction and ethical stability, is to deliver us.'[118]

When Nivedita arrived in India, she wanted to start work right away. She expected the Swami to tell her what he wanted her to do. Vivekananda, however, did nothing of the kind. Once or twice she raised the question but he brushed it aside. Evidently, he had decided that Nivedita was not yet ready to work in the manner that he thought she should work. In the first place, she was too much of a Britisher. By her own admission, the dearest thing to her was the British flag. Her patriotism was such that the Swami once remarked, 'Patriotism such as you have is a sin.' Secondly, she did not understand the peculiar phenomenon that India was. To her

---

118. *The Complete Works of Sister Nivedita,* Vol. III, p. 1.

India was just another unfortunate country waiting to be saved by people like her. Vivekananda knew that Nivedita would be useless as a worker so long as she had her strong British predilections and did not learn to respect and appreciate India's rich spiritual heritage. In a letter to her he wrote: 'Only I do believe the Western people have the peculiarity of trying to force upon others whatever seems good to them, forgetting that what is good for you may not be good for others.'[119] He did not want Nivedita to commit this kind of blunder while serving India. This was why he took pains to train her. He was not content even after he had thoroughly explained to her India's history, art, literature, and religion; he did not stop then but felt it would be good for Nivedita to see the country a bit so that she could judge for herself the correctness or otherwise of the interpretations that he had given regarding India's heritage.

Accordingly, he asked Nivedita to accompany him when he started on his North India tour in May 1898, with his other Western disciples. The process of educating Nivedita continued throughout the period of the tour. It was a painful process for Nivedita, for it involved abandoning views she had so long held dear. Referring to this she once remarked, '... it seemed as if a going-to-school had commenced.' An idea of the impact which Vivekananda's discourses made on Nivedita can be had from the book Nivedita wrote following this tour, *Notes of Some Wanderings with the Swami Vivekananda*. The tour, lasting for five months, covered the whole of North India. What an education it was! And, what a revelation also! It was almost a spiritual experience, for it was during this tour that she came face-to-face with the soul of India; she discovered that in spite of the poverty and squalor which one saw on the surface of things in India, her religious life still ran strong. It was during this tour that Nivedita had her first demonstration of the ideas behind Indian art and architecture. When the party visited the Pandrenthan temple in Kashmir, the Swami explained to them every aspect of the architecture

---

119. *Complete Works of Swami Vivekananda*, Vol. VI, p. 435.

of the temple in order that they might grasp how the religious ideas of the Hindus and Buddhists had found expression through it. About this visit Nivedita's comment was—'... this was our first peep at Indian archaeology.' The change that came over Nivedita after this tour was to surprise many. She now understood India better than even many Indians. Referring to her attitude towards India and things Indian, Lady Minto was to observe later, 'She is an idealist and sees wonderful meanings in the Hindu religion.'

NIVEDITA LEARNS THE PHILOSOPHY BEHIND INDIAN ART

Nivedita had studied art in England under Mr Ebenezer Cook, an art teacher of repute. She had eventually become an art critic also, but Indian art was entirely a new world and she could never hope to know anything about it unless Vivekananda taught her its fundamentals. How he himself came to know so much about art is not known, but we find him giving lectures on the subject in America and elsewhere. Some of his recorded comments suggest that he was thoroughly acquainted with the basic philosophy behind Indian art and architecture. Perhaps, he had read source-books in Sanskrit—at least that is the impression one has when one reads his comments. He must have been familiar with the characteristics of Greek art also. Comparing Greek art with Indian art, he once said:

> The secret of Greek art is its imitation of nature even to the minutest details; whereas the secret of Indian art is to represent the ideal. The energy of the Greek painter is spent in perhaps painting a piece of flesh, and he is so successful that a dog is deluded into taking it to be a real bit of meat and so goes to bite it. Now, what glory is there in merely imitating nature? Why not place an actual bit of flesh before the dog?'[120]

---

120. *Complete Works of Swami Vivekananda*, Vol. V, Calcutta, 1963, p. 258.

He made a very important point when he compared Greek art with Indian art. He said that while Greek art tried to idealise the real, Indian art tried to realise the ideal. Dr S.N. Das Gupta, the well-known philosopher, also says the same thing in his book *Fundamentals of Indian Art* (London, 1960). He says:

> If we look at the plastic creation of Greece, we find that the conception of Greek Gods was the idealisation of forms of human beauty. The Greek Gods represented in themselves the ideal perfection of human beauty. They did not involve any superior ideal or connote any superior meaning. The case, however, is different in India. Here, though the Gods are mostly human figures, they are not conceived on the pattern or types of human beauty. Their forms do not always resemble human forms.' (p. 12)

Within proper limits this was perfectly alright, but if it was carried too far, as it often was, the results were by no means happy. Referring to Indian art as it was then, Vivekananda said, 'The Indian tendency, on the other hand, to represent the ideal, the super-sensual, has become degraded in painting grotesque images.'[121] He condemned this and said that art must be in touch with nature, and wherever that touch was gone, it degenerated. Art, he said, must represent the beautiful. Incidentally, he regarded Sri Ramakrishna as highly artistic and quoted him as saying that a person devoid of the artistic faculty could not be truly spiritual.

Talking of architecture, Vivekananda once said that the difference between architecture and building was that the former expressed an idea, while the latter was merely a structure built on economic principles.

He must have visited countless art galleries and museums during his tours in the West. It is on record that he stood enthralled before

---

121. *Complete Works of Swami Vivekananda*, p. 258.

Da Vinci's 'Last Supper' at Milan. When he visited the pyramids in Egypt, he showed a keen interest in everything he saw there. Whether in the East or in the West, no work of beauty escaped his attention. About the Taj Mahal he remarked with feeling: 'a dimness, and again a dimness, and there—a grave!' What a keen student of architecture he was may be gauged from the following account given by Nivedita of their visit to the temple of Marttand in Kashmir:

> The Swami was hard at work, in an instant, on observations and theories, pointing out the cornice that ran along the nave from the entrance to the sanctuary, to the west, surmounted by the high trefoils of the two arches and also by a frieze; or showing us the panels containing cherubs; and before we had done, had picked up a couple of coins.'[122]

Vivekananda was the first in modern times to point out wherein lay the distinctiveness of Indian art. Like everything else an Indian does, art was, according to him, an attempt to realise God, an attempt to bring about a union between the worshipper and the worshipped, between the object and the subject. Art represented what one felt in the depths of one's heart about the Infinite. The exciting cause of this feeling might be some object in nature or some experience or some idea. When this feeling became compelling, the artist then looked for some medium through which he could express himself. The medium might be a song, a picture, a statue, or a building, depending upon the nature of the artist's talents.

It is interesting to see that those who have tried to interpret Indian art after Vivekananda have virtually echoed his views. I have earlier quoted the views of the well-known philosopher Dr S. N. Das Gupta, which, as you might have observed, were identical with the views of Vivekananda. Another person who, as an exponent of Indian art, had

---

122. The *Complete Works of Sister Nivedita*, Vol. I, Calcutta, 1967, p. 345.

quite a name was the Swami's own brother Mahendranath Dutta. In his book *Dissertation on Painting,* he tried to develop the idea given by Vivekananda. This book, published in 1922, was dedicated to Swami Brahmananda and carried a preface written by Abanindranath Tagore. Referring to this book Romain Rolland says, 'Vivekananda's own brother... has filled in the lines indicated by the Master. I cannot urge European aesthetes too strongly to read his *Dissertation on Painting* (dedicated to the memory of Brahmananda, the first Abbot of the Ramakrishna Mission, with a preface by Abanindranath Tagore, 1922...). The great Indian religious artist places himself face-to-face with the object he wishes to represent in the attitude of a Yogi in search of Truth: to him the object becomes the subject...'[123] I might add here also the comments of Dr Stella Kramrisch, that outstanding exponent of Indian art. She also confirms Vivekananda's views about Indian art. She says:

> In India, the ultimate aim of life is Release (*moksha*), and art is one means of attaining this aim...
>
> 'The temples and statues are so many stages in the approach to *moksha*. They are halting places, providing rest and support for the one unanimous Tradition, that flows through the word of the *Veda* and is borne along by the ritual in inviolable and multifold patterns.[124]

After Vivekananda many scholars have tried to explain the philosophy behind Indian art, but the point I wish to make is that in modern times he was the first to do so and that if Nivedita later became a champion of Indian art and also its most successful exponent, it was entirely because of him. It was Vivekananda who first refuted the theory that Greek art had influenced Indian art. Later, many others followed suit and now no one seriously suggests

---

123. *The Life of Vivekananda,* Calcutta, 1960, p. 227.
124. *The Art of India,* London, 1954, pp. 9–10.

that there is any evidence that Greek art exerted any influence on Indian art.

We are all aware of Havell's interest in Indian art and his contribution to its renaissance; we are also aware of the love Okakura and Ananda Coomaraswamy had for Indian art and their masterly works on it. If Indian art today commands respect, it is entirely due to the efforts of these four—Nivedita, Okakura, Havell, and Coomaraswamy. Among these four, Nivedita occupies a special place, for it was she alone who knew the philosophical background of Indian art. Whenever the true import of a picture had to be unravelled, Havell and others turned to Nivedita. Nandalal Bose says, 'Havell, Abanindranath, Okakura (a Japanese artist and art-critic), Jagadish Bose, etc., all used to discuss about art with Sister Nivedita. All of them were inspired by the Ideal of the Sister.'[125] I have shown that Nivedita owed her knowledge of, and passion for, Indian art to her Master. Since it was his hope that Nivedita would dedicate herself to the service of the country he spared no pains to transmit to her some of his own knowledge about India. This was how Nivedita became an authority on India. It is not that she merely understood India, but she also accepted her. She so much identified herself with India that she became as sensitive about her as the Swami himself was. If Nivedita was able to do what she did for Indian art, it was because she had thus been trained by her Master.

We will see in the following chapter how she helped to bring about the revival of Indian art. We have dealt at such length about her training because unless we understand the manner and extent of her training, we shall not be able to understand what gave her such an insight into Indian art and also so much love for it.

---

125. Bhupendranath Dutta, *Swami Vivekananda: Patriot and Prophet*, Calcutta, 1954, p. 311.

Nivedita's Contribution to the Development of Indian Art

WE HAVE SEEN HOW NIVEDITA CAME TO LOVE AND UNDERSTAND Indian art, it was she who instructed Havell and others in the metaphysics of Indian art, and that it was largely through her efforts that Indian art was rehabilitated and commands the respect it has today.

Let us now turn to her work in this field more specifically and also in greater detail. However, to appreciate the value of her work we ought to understand first the great tragedy that had struck Indian art. Like every thing else in India, art went into complete eclipse with the onset of British rule. It languished because both the rulers and the ruled neglected it. We have already seen how Indian art baffled Western critics and how some of them thought it was puerile or, at best, a vulgar imitation of Greek art. Educated Indians, however, were no better; they neither understood Indian art nor did they have any sympathy for it. Havell sums up the Indian attitude by saying, 'We have succeeded in persuading educated Indians that they have no Art of their own . . .'

Somehow Indians had come to believe that everything Indian was bad and everything British was good. This attitude was, in fact, symptomatic of a general sense of defeatism from which most Indians then suffered. The fact of the matter is that British rule had ruined the country, physically as well as morally. Nivedita saw what was going on and cried in agony:

> The process by which the peoples of a vast continent may become mere hewers of wood and drawers of water have already begun is already well afoot. Their indigenous institutions are all in decay. . . . Their arts and industries are dead or dying. They have lapsed into customers for other men's cheap wares. Even their thought would seem to be imitative . . . [126]

Nivedita pointed out that even in thinking, India had become imitative. As a matter of fact, India became imitative in every field of activity, including art and architecture. The rich invariably, built their houses in imitation of Western architecture. In some cases the result was hideous; yet, they felt proud because it had the Western touch. Nivedita always hated imitation wherever she saw it; she prefered originality even if it was modest. A sidelight on her reactions to imitative architecture may be had from a portion of Aurobindo's memoirs. Referring to Nivedita's visit to Baroda, Aurobindo says:

> I do not remember whether she was invited but I think she was there as a State guest. Khasirao and myself went to receive her at the station . . . On the way from the station to the town she cried out against the ugliness of the College building and its top-heavy dome and praised the Dharmashala near it. Khasirao stared at her and opined that she must be at least slightly cracked to have such ideas![127]

The rich spent huge sums not only in building ugly houses but also in decorating them. They often paid high prices for furniture, paintings, and other art objects from the West, most of which were

---

126. Pravrajika Atmaprana, *Sister Nivedita*, Calcutta, 1961, p. 196.
127. Ibid, p. 145.

tawdry. If they wanted a picture, they would rather commission a visiting minor artist from the West than engage an Indian genius.

THE INSULARITY OF THE ANGLO-SAXON MIND

Nivedita deplored the fact that Indian tastes had degenerated so. She said, 'All lovers of the East stand dismayed at this moment before the disintegration of taste and ideals which is coming about in consequence of competition with the West.'[128]

Havell also felt unhappy that Indian art was being neglected and he blamed his own countrymen for this. He said:

> Twenty-four years ago, I was sent out to India to instruct Indians in art, and having instructed them, and myself to the best of my ability, I returned filled with amazement at the insularity of the Anglo-Saxon mind, which has taken more than a century to discover that we have far more to learn from India in Art than India has to learn from Europe.'[129]

I may cite here an example of the insularity of the Anglo-Saxon to which Havell refers by quoting what Sir George Birdwood once said about a certain well-known Buddha image:

> This senseless similitude in its immemorial fixed pose is nothing more than an uninspired brazen imago, vacuously squinting down its nose to its thumbs and knees and toes. A boiled suet pudding would serve equally well as a symbol of passionless purity and serenity of soul.[130]

Pity the man who thus speaks of the Buddha image! But the plain fact is that Birdwood, otherwise sympathetic to India, just did

---

128. K. Okakura, *The Ideals of the East*, London, 1905, p. xx.
129. O.C. Ganguly, *Indian Art and My Reminiscences*, 1969.
130. E.B. Havell, *The Art Heritage of India*, Bombay, 1964, p. vi.

not understand the philosophical background of Indian art. No one can understand Indian art unless he also understands Indian religion and philosophy. Most Westerners knew nothing about the religion and philosophy of India; this was why they did not understand Indian art. Havell, for one, knew how difficult it was for Western critics. He writes:

> I do not anticipate that all my fellow-artists in Europe will at once accept the views which have forced themselves upon me gradually, and after long years of study. Having entered upon my study of Indian art, with a full equipment of European academic prejudices, I know that they are not easily shaken off. No European can appreciate Indian art until he divests himself of his western prepossessions, endeavour to understand Indian thought, and place himself at the Indian point of view. I am convinced that those who do so will find my artistic conclusions inevitable; but there will always be many who believe it more interesting to use the wrong end of the telescope.[131]

Havell was unhappy that his government's policy regarding Indian art was most unsympathetic. Referring to this he says:

> We no longer desecrate and destroy the masterpieces of the Moguls and the great monuments of ancient India: we patch them up and try to admire them. But there is still that insidious form of vandalism in our departmental system—much more cruel and deadly than active iconoclasm, because it acts through mind instead of matter—which continues blindly to crush out the means by which India might yet surpass the greatness of her ancient art.[132]

---

131. ibid. p. 2.
132. ibid. p. 2.

How the departmental system did grave injustice to Indian art is best illustrated by the educational policy which was being followed then. Lord Macaulay, who was the author of the educational policy in India at that time, thought Indian art worthless. That was why no provision had been made by him for the teaching of Indian art in the educational institutions of the country. Universities, museums, art galleries, and schools of art had been established but there was no Indian art there. To most Britishers, Indian art and architecture were examples of fine craftsmanship accompanied by much pomp, but that was all. The basic difficulty for the Western critics was that they could not understand that art could be a vehicle for expressing the feeling that one had about the Infinite. According to them, all this talk about the Infinite, the Ideal or the Absolute, was nonsense.

THE REVIVAL OF INDIAN ART

As we have seen, the educated Indians saw no virtue in their own art; their infatuation with everything British was so great that nothing Indian appealed to them. According to O.C. Ganguly, contributing factor of the decline of Indian art, was the absence of any outstanding artist who could continue the old traditions. Molaram of Garhwal was the last of the great masters. When he died in 1832, the last link with the old traditions had snapped. There was no one left who was as familiar with the old traditions and whose work was in any way representative of the old style. There were minor artists here and there, but they were by no means effective in keeping the old traditions going or in resisting the influence of the West. Art had flourished in India because it received patronage from the ruling princes as well as from the aristocracy. That patronage was no longer forthcoming; on the contrary, the State was definitely hostile and the public apathetic. The State was also partial to Western art; that is to say, it gave every possible encouragement to Western art and not only did it fail to encourage Indian art but in the beginning was even hostile towards it. According to Havell, the government even practised ruthless vandalism. As regards patronage, young students were given scholarships to study British art, but none were given to those who wanted to study Indian art. The building of New Delhi was just the kind of opportunity needed to boost Indian art and architecture, but they were completely ignored by those in power. Surveying the situation, Pramod Chandra, Curator of the Art Section of the Prince of Wales Museum of western India, Bombay, says in the Preface to the new edition of *The Art Heritage of India*:

> With the end of the Pahari schools of painting in the nineteenth century the last vestiges of traditional art can be said to have disappeared from this country, and strange to say even its memory was all but lost within the passing of a few generations.' (p.v)

He goes on to say that people not only lost touch with their traditions but even forgot that their country possessed artistic objects of the highest standards. It was the British scholars who first discovered them, but, as Pramod Chandra says, '. . . by temperament and training they were unable to assess their true significance. Their reaction was a mixture of astonishment and revulsion, couched often in extreme language, which sought to deny the very existence of anything like Indian art . . .' (ibid. p. v)

Like O.C. Ganguly, Pramod Chandra also mentions how Indians themselves began to lose interest in Indian art. The first casualty to 'alien pressures', according to him, was Indian art. Speaking of patronage, Pramod Chandra says, 'Patronage shifted from traditional objects of art to tawdry works of European manufacture or its feeble native imitations.' (ibid. p. v)

It was at this juncture that Ravi Varma appeared on the scene. He was the first important product of Western influence. According to Pramod Chandra, 'he possessed academic realism of the most debased kind.' O.C. Ganguly also thought poorly of him as an artist; but it was Swami Vivekananda who was the first to decry Ravi Varma's abilities as an artist. When the Swami criticised him, Ravi Varma was at the height of his fame and it took much courage to say anything against him. But why was Ravi Varma still popular? He was popular because, as Pramod Chandra explains, he had a 'false religiosity' about him. He knew he must satisfy the religious sentiments of the people or else his pictures would not sell. Therefore, he used religious themes in his drawings, but in reality they were least inspired by religion.

This was the state of Indian art when Havell took over as Principal of the Government Art College in Calcutta in 1896. Before this he had served as Principal of the Government Art College in Madras for several years. He had come to India to teach Western art, but as the years went by, he began to take an interest in Indian art and became conscious of its richness. When his first book, *Venares, the Sacred City* appeared in 1906, people were struck by his respect for India and Indian culture. How did it happen that he became such an Indophile? Could Nivedita have influenced him in any way? Nivedita, as we have seen, became a changed person after her tour of North India with Swami Vivekananda. At first, she did not understand India but thanks to the Swami's instruction, she now not only understood India but had become an authority on her.

According to Nandalal Bose, it was she who explained to Havell the aesthetics and philosophy of Indian art. This testimony of Nandalal Bose cannot be lightly dismissed, for he was close to both and had met them on many occasions. It may be that Havell had already felt the greatness of Indian art but, not being familiar with its philosophy, his appreciation was rather amateurish. It was only when, in 1902, he came to know Nivedita that he began to understand the esoteric character of Indian art. That he was greatly influenced by Nivedita cannot be doubted. Rabindranath Tagore has called Havell 'the guiding spirit that led to the revival of true Indian art'. Undoubtedly, Havell deserves this tribute, for by virtue of his official position, he was able to initiate as well as guide the process which ultimately culminated in the rebirth of Indian art. But if it is true that Nivedita influenced Havell, as seems to be the case, no tribute is too high for her. It is not my wish to suggest that Havell's love for Indian art was entirely due to Nivedita. What I am trying to say is that without Nivedita his understanding of Indian art would have been incomplete and, not having understood its full significance, he would not have worked for its revival in the way he did.

In this connexion, it is well to remember that Nivedita herself was anxious to see the rebirth of Indian art. She once said, 'Art must be reborn. Not the miserable travesty of would-be Europeanism that we at present know. There is no voice like that of art to reach the people... And, art *will* be reborn, for she has found a new subject—India herself. Ah, to be a thinker in bronze and give to the world the beauty of the Southern *Pariah*, as he swings, scarce-clad, along the Beach Road at Madras! All, to be a Millet, and paint the women worshipping at dawn beside the sea! Oh, for a pencil that would interpret the beauty of the Indian sari; the gentle life of village and temple; the coming and going at the Ganges side; the play of the children; the faces, and the labours, of the cows!'[133] Could Nivedita have imparted some of this enthusiasm to Havell, while explaining to him the philosophy and science of Indian art?

THE BEGINNING OF A NEW AGE

It is known that Havell asked Abanindranath Tagore to join the Art College as Vice-Principal, which he did in 1905, three years after

---

133. *The Complete Works of Sister Nivdita,* Calcutta, 1967, Vol. III, pp. 518–19.

Havell had met Nivedita. Why did Havell invite Abanindranath Tagore to join his College? How did he come to know about him? Is it possible that Nivedita had told Havell about Abanindranath? Nivedita, it should be noted, had been visiting the Tagores for a long time now and she must have been familiar with the work of Abanindranath. There is, however, nothing on record to suggest that Nivedita had any hand in the appointment of Abanindranath. Maybe, Havell had come to know of him independently, for Abanindranath had exhibited his work earlier. On joining the College, Abanindranath spent two hours daily taking lessons from Havell in the history and philosophy of Oriental art. This is what Abanindranath himself says in his book *Jorasankor Dharey*. Would it have been possible for Havell to instruct Abanindranath in this way if he himself had not been taught in turn by Nivedita? Abanindranath had studied Western art under Ghilardi and Palmer who were then conducting classes in Calcutta. All his work so far had been in the Western tradition. Havell now asked him to draw according to the Indian tradition. Abanindranath was at first diffident, but finally he produced what turned out to be a masterpiece, his famous picture *Bharat-Mata*. It was not entirely Indian perhaps, still it was the first picture after many years in which the artist had consciously followed the Indian tradition. The picture marked a real breakthrough in Indian art. Ecstatically Nivedita wrote:

> We have here a picture which bids fair to prove the beginning of a new age in Indian art. Using all the added means of expression which the modern period has bestowed upon him, the artist has here given expression, nevertheless, to a purely Indian idea, in Indian form . . . We see in this drawing something for which Indian art has long been waiting, the birth of the idea of those new combinations which are to mark the modern age in India.[134]

---

134. *The Complete Works of Sister Nivedita*, Calcutta, 1967, Vol.III, pp. 58–9.

'From beginning to end the picture is an appeal, in the Indian language, to the Indian heart. It is the first great masterpiece in a new style. I would reprint it, if I could, by tens of thousands, and scatter it broadcast over the land, till there was not a peasant's cottage, or a craftman's hut, between Kedar Nath and Cape Comorin, that had not this presentment of Bharat-Mata somewhere on its walls... Up to this time, Mr Tagore has been mastering his language, creating his style. Now, he has begun to write poems. May he never cease!'[135]

I do not know if the picture deserved all this praise. It may not have been Abanindranath's best picture; yet why did Nivedita feel so excited about it? She behaved as a mother behaves when she sees her child receive his first school-prize. Nivedita used to say again and again, 'Art must be reborn'. It was her hope and her wish that art should be reborn. Here was proof that her hope and her wish, cherished ever since she came to learn from the Swami the significance of Indian art, were about to be fulfilled. She herself had worked hard to make this possible and she felt happy and proud that her efforts had not gone in vain.

Soon after this, a new department was added to the Art College, with Abanindranath Tagore in charge, which was devoted entirely to Indian art. Soon, several young men joined this department, the foremost among them being Nandalal Bose, Surendranath Ganguly, Asit Haldar, and Venkatappa. Each one of them became famous later. When Nandalal Bose's picture *Dasaratha's Death* appeared, Nivedita welcomed it by saying:

Mr Abanindra Nath Tagore can no longer be said to represent his own School of Painting by himself. He has succeeded in creating a following... It may be noted that Modern Indian

---

135. ibid. p. 61.

Art—at once genuinely Indian and genuinely Modern—is born at last.[136]

She always encouraged the younger artists, but if they merely imitated the West or if their works lacked an Indian feeling, she strongly criticised them. Once, Nandalal drew a picture of Kali which Nivedita generally liked but there were some details in it which she did not like. For instance, she did not like the idea that there should be so many garments on Kali. She said, 'Kali is sky-clad.' She asked Nandalal to read Vivekananda's poem on Kali to understand her character.

There was another picture by Nandalal in which he showed Dasaratha in grief because Ramachandra had gone into exile in the forest. In the picture, he showed Kausalya fanning Dasaratha with an ordinary palm-leaf fan. Nivedita pointed out that this did not look right, for a queen could not use an ordinary palm-leaf fan, she must use an ivory fan. She then advised Nandalal to visit the museum to study what an ivory fan was like. She also said, 'But the picture has a lovely peaceful atmosphere. It reminds me of the room of the Holy Mother, hence it pleases me much.'

Later, when Nandalal showed his new painting *Jagai and Maddhai* to Nivedita, she was very pleased. She particularly liked the way Nandalal pictured the two ruffians. When she asked how he had captured the expressions on the faces of the ruffians, Nandalal replied that Girish Babu's face had given him the idea. Nivedita laughed at this and told him to always draw after meditation as this was the principle of Indian drawing. Nandalal said that he could never say enough about the encouragement he had received from Nivedita. He said, 'When she died it was like being deprived of the presence of a guiding angel.'

Asit Haldar said once:

---

136. *Modern Review*, October 1907, p. 391.

'Nandalal and I often went to meet her at Baghbazar... Nivedita told us that on us depended the revival of ancient Indian art which was rapidly approaching extinction and that the revival of national art would be our great contribution in the movement of national awakening and freedom. She urged us to try our best. As long as she lived, she visited our exhibitions at the Oriental Art Society and encouraged the artists.[137]

It was at this time that Lady Harrington came to India to get copies done of the frescoes of Ajanta by local artists. Nivedita got in touch with her and suggested that she commission the artists of Bengal. At first Lady Harrington agreed, but later she backed out saying that the artists of Bengal were too young and inexperienced, and she had already engaged the artists of Bombay. Nivedita insisted that she utilise the services of the Bengal artists and without giving her an opportunity to refuse, she promptly sent a group of young artists like Nandalal Bose to Ajanta to do the copying. As food was a big problem at Ajanta, she sent Brahmachari Ganen to attend to it. Not being content with this, she herself arrived there soon after to see how the work of the young artists was progressing. The reason why she was so keen that the artists do this work was that she felt that it would help them improve their skill and technique.

Nivedita's reviews of the pictures of Abanindranath and his students appeared in the leading journals of India including *The Statesman* and the *Modern Review*. These attracted the notice of the Viceroy at that time, Lord Minto, who became a great patron of Indian art. He once said in a speech that Indian art was important not only to India but to the whole world. Among those who became patrons of Indian art under the influence of Nivedita were Lord Kitchener, Lord Ronaldshay, and Mr S.K. Ratcliffe. I have already mentioned how, according to Nandalal, Nivedita influenced Havell. When Havell's book

---

137. Mani Bagchi, *Nivedita*, 1957, p. 143.

Indian Sculpture and Painting appeared, she reviewed it in the *Modern Review*. She also wrote a few articles in the same journal explaining what Havell was trying to do for Indian art. Even before this, she had written an introduction to Okakura's *Ideals of the East*. Okakura's thoughts are so close to Nivedita's that one wonders if she did not influence him also. Coomaraswami later became a great exponent of Indian art in the Western world. His book *Myths of the Hindus and Buddhists*, written in collaboration with Nivedita, is well known. It is more than likely that he too was influenced by Nivedita. Thus, starting with Havell, everybody who came within her orbit became a patron of Indian art, and, according to Abanindranath, no one was her equal in her love for Indian art and culture.

Nivedita made significant contributions in many fields, but what she did for Indian art stands out as the most constructive and fruitful. When she started her work, Indian art was obscure, even despised; within a decade she was able to see it fully rehabilitated, and commanding respect from the highest quarters.

Men I Have Seen

- *Swami Sivananda: A Direct Disciple of Sri Ramakrishna*
- *Swami Visuddhananda: An Apostle of God-awareness*
- *A Real Gentleman: Swami Madhavananda*
- *Gandhi, the Great Experimenter*
- *Netaji Subhas Chandra Bose, in the Light of Swami Vivekananda**

Swami Sivananda: A Direct Disciple of Sri Ramakrishna

WHEN THEY TOOK THEIR MONASTIC VOWS, THE DISCIPLES OF SRI Ramakrishna were each given a new name. Tarak was given the name Sivananda, but his more popular name was Mahapurush Maharaj, which Swami Vivekananda gave him. Why did Swamiji give him that name? It was in recognition of his austere life and character. Tarak—that is, Mahapurush Maharaj—lived throughout his life an austere life. When he left home to live as a monk, he had nowhere to stay. For a while he stayed in a garden belonging to Ramchandra Dutta, a brother-disciple. There were times when he spent his nights there in the open.

After the passing away of Sri Ramakrishna, he lived as a wandering monk, visiting holy places. He was in Benaras for some time, living on the bank of the river. He was there when he received a message from Swamiji asking him to return to Calcutta immediately. A householder-disciple of Sri Ramakrishna had had a vision in which Sri Ramakrishna directed him to give some money to Swami Vivekananda so that he could start a monastery forthwith. Swami Vivekananda had hired an old house in a suburb of Calcutta. He felt the best person to start the monastery was Swami Sivananda, so Swamiji sent a message to him urging him to return to Calcutta.

Swami Sivananda came and with Swami Vivekananda proceeded to the house destined to be the first home of the future Ramakrishna Mission. The holy relics of Sri Ramakrishna, which had so long been lying in the house of Balaram Bose, were now placed in a suitable room in the monastery. Soon, word spread that a monastery was started and other young monks started coming. The story of their monastic life and zeal is more interesting than any work of fiction. Most of the physical work of the monastery Swami Sivananda reserved for himself, for he was the oldest.

After spending a few years at the monastery, Swami Sivananda left for the Himalayas. For several years he travelled around India, visiting different places of pilgrimage. Meanwhile, Swami Vivekananda had gone to the West and had been very successful in preaching Vedanta. Swami Sivananda went to South India. Few people there knew anything about the Master and Swamiji, so he talked to them about Sri Ramakrishna's message of religious harmony.

When Swami Vivekananda returned from the West, Swami Sivananda was among those who received him. Soon after, at Swamiji's request, Swami Sivananda toured Sri Lanka and preached Vedanta. He next founded the Advaita Ashrama at Benaras. Almora was a place he loved very much. He and Swami Turiyananda often spent months together there. It was the Himalayas that attracted them. They never tired of looking at them.

Meanwhile, Belur Math had grown. Scores of young men had come to join the Mission. Swami Premananda was in charge of training the young men, but he fell sick and finally died. Swami Sivananda was now called upon to look after everything, from the worship in the shrine to the training of the junior monks. Swami Premananda was love personified, but Mahapurush Maharaj was a grave and serious-looking person. People avoided him as much as they could. But as days passed he began to change, and people discovered the soft side of his nature. One day, Mahapurush Maharaj declared that there would be scripture classes and that attendance at the classes was compulsory. To ensure that everybody came, he himself attended them. There was no rule laid down that he himself did not obey. If anybody was ill, he was the first to arrive and enquire if there was anything he could do for him.

The Swami became softer when he began to initiate disciples. Whenever anybody approached him for initiation, he would say: 'I am nobody's guru. There is only one guru and that is Sri Ramakrishna. I can only help you get to him. For this age, he is the way to freedom. Surrender to him.'

Swami Sivananda had lost his mother at an early age. But from the day he saw Sri Ramakrishna, the Master became his mother. If anybody brought him a gift, he would say, 'Go and give it to Mother.' He meant that the person should take it to the shrine and hand it over to the monks there to be offered to the Master. From his childhood, Swami Sivananda loved dogs. They even shared his bed with him. Towards the end of his life he had a black dog named Kelo. Referring to Kelo, he would say, 'Just as Kelo is my dog, I am [pointing to the shrine] his dog.'

In later days, when he had become feeble, he was not steady on his feet. It was difficult for him to walk out of his room. Once, he came out and stood before a photo hanging on the wall. It was a photo of Swamiji and some of his brother-disciples, including Mahapurush Maharaj himself. He bowed to Swamiji, saying: 'Swamiji, you were indeed unique. How much you loved humanity! We do not know of anyone else with such a large heart.' He next bowed to Maharaj (Swami Brahmananda) and said: 'Maharaj, you were truly a Raja. How much we miss you!' He went on talking in this way to each one in the picture. Finally, he came to himself. He looked shocked. He asked: 'Who is this man? How dare he occupy a seat among these men of God! He has no right to be here.'

Many such intriguing incidents happened. There is a very interesting story about the fun he once made over his meal. He was a strict vegetarian, and his meal consisted of rice and a vegetable soup. The food was simple, if not tasteless. People would often describe his food as being a medical decoction. No one even cared to taste it. One day, however, Mahapurush Maharaj declared, to the surprise of all, that he wanted to taste each of the items of food that had been offered to the Master. Everybody was alarmed. First and foremost, the food would not agree with him at all. It would be too rich for him. And then, there were too many items. He always had only the blandest curry possible. And, any deviation from such a diet might totally upset his internal delicacy.

Mahapurush Maharaj's attendants begged him not to insist on deviating from his normal food. But he was adamant. He was the head servant of the Lord, and it was his duty to see that the Lord had the right kind of food. He trusted the workers, but what if they erred? Once in a while, he thought, he must check and be sure that the Master was being well looked after. He told his attendants: 'Bring the food after it is offered to the Master. Do not miss anything.'

When the food was brought and placed before him, Swami Gangeshananda, the chief attendant, appeared on the scene. He said, with folded hands: 'Sir, you can do whatever you please to do with me. You can curse me to hell, I would never mind. I will accept any punishment you inflict. But I won't let you eat that food.'

Swami Sivananda flared up. He said: 'How dare you talk like that! Do not you know I am "Mahapurush"? Swamiji gave me that name. Here, I shall eat whatever I like.' With these words, he dipped the forefinger of his right hand into each of the items of food one after another, and then licked the finger. 'Do you think it was for nothing,' he said, 'that Swamiji gave me that name? Am I a greedy man? Has anybody ever seen in me a sign of greed?' With these words, he pushed away the plates. Then, he said once again: 'I am the chief of all the servants here. My duty is not only to serve the Lord but also to supervise everything so that all of us here serve the Lord as best we can.' All the attendants were struck by the depth of his love for the Master. They apologised to him with folded hands for misunderstanding him.

His concern for the poor was beyond measure. Often, a poor man would appear wearing torn clothes. Mahapurush Maharaj could not bear the sight. He would at once give him a new cloth. More people would then come to get such gifts from him. Most likely, they were cheating him, but he did not mind. They were poor, and that was reason enough for them to receive whatever they wanted. One day, a thief was caught red-handed. The monks were in a fix. What should they do with him? Should they hand him over to the police or let him go free? The monks reported the matter to Mahapurush Maharaj. He called for the thief and asked him, 'Did you not know that this was a monastery?' 'Yes, I did,' answered the thief. 'Do not you know that we ourselves are poor and live by begging? Why did you come to the home of beggars to steal?' With tears in his eyes and folded hands, the thief replied: 'Sir, I am very poor. I have not eaten anything the whole day.' Mahapurush Maharaj became very upset hearing this. He said: 'Look, the man is very poor. He has not eaten anything all day. First and foremost, give him some food. Then, give him a new cloth and also ten rupees.' He was in tears when he said this.

There was a fisherman who caught fish in the river near Belur Math. Mahapurush Maharaj would stand on the verandah of the building and watch him. If the fisherman did not have a good catch on a certain day, Mahapurush Maharaj would give him some money. Once, Mahapurush Maharaj noticed that the man had not come for a few days. He had much affection for the fisherman, so he was unhappy that he had stopped coming. He wondered what the reason was and began making enquiries. Finally, he learned that the fisherman had died. Mahapurush Maharaj was very upset. He wanted to help the poor man's family, but he did not know where they lived. One day, the fisherman's wife came to the Math and narrated her sad story. After that Mahapurush Maharaj used to give her some money every month for herself and her children.

Every morning the monks would go to Mahapurush Maharaj to pay their respects. Some of the senior monks would ask, 'Sir, how was your night?' Mahapurush Maharaj would smile and say: 'If you are asking about my health, well, I must remind you that my body is about to fall apart. But as far as my self is concerned, I know, by the grace of the Lord, I will never die.'

One evening after dinner, the monks had gathered in the room underneath Mahapurush Maharaj's room. They were teasing each other, and there was much laughing and shouting. This was nothing unusual, but on that evening the shouting went beyond all limits. Mahapurush Maharaj was heard to say: 'Mother, these children have left home and taken shelter in you. They seem to be very happy. May they always be happy.'

AT THE FEET OF MAHAPURUSH MAHARAJ

It was 1925, I was still a school student. I was at home on vacation. One of my uncles came at that time and one day asked me, 'You have a holiday now, would you like to go somewhere with me?' Naturally, I jumped at the idea; I always liked to move about. So, we went to his place at Lalmanirhat, a very small town in Bangladesh. There was a high school. The headmaster of that school was a great devotee of Belur Math. He was a nephew of Swami Atmabodhananda (Satyen Maharaj). He asked me, 'Would you like to study here for your last year of school?' I agreed. When I was visiting there, I used to go to visit the headmaster every day after school in his home; he was very affectionate to me and I would spend much time listening to his talk. At his home, his mother and wife were disciples of the Holy Mother. I used to read Gospel of Sri Ramakrishna (Bengali) to his mother.

I did not know what I was to be. Everybody used to say I must get a scholarship and become a judge or a magistrate. But the headmaster said, 'No, do not listen to these people. You must be a very good sadhu, that is what I want.' One day, his wife overheard it and became irritated, 'What are you telling him? You are asking somebody else's son to become a sadhu, and not your own son. What about your own son?' Then, the headmaster replied, 'If one of my sons becomes a sadhu, I shall deem it a great good fortune.'

He used to tell us about Maharaj, Baburam Maharaj, Mahapurush Maharaj and others. And, he would tell me, 'Mahapurush Maharaj is still in Math at this time, go to him, ask for his blessings and try to get initiation from him.' So, from that time onward in my mind I accepted Mahapurush Maharaj as my guru. When my school finals were over, I took leave of my teachers and went to Calcutta. The headmaster gave me a letter of introduction to his uncle, Swami Atmabodhananda. He did not know that the swami was at that time in Mayavati, but I had no difficulty. As far as I remember I bought a newspaper on my way to Calcutta in the train. On the first page itself I found Mahapurush Maharaj's picture. He was blessing the devotees. I went to my elder brother's house in Calcutta, and one day set out on a cycle to find Belur Math. I had no idea how far it was. After inquiring of many people along the way, I ultimately reached Belur Math. I started at ten o'clock and reached there at four o'clock.

As soon as I came in front of the old temple of Sri Ramakrishna near a mango tree, I found one swami. I bowed down to him and went to see the shrine. At that time, suddenly one window opened and I found a beautiful figure of a swami and I was very much impressed. He looked very happy and asked, 'Wherefrom do you come? Come, come to me.' I was a little taken aback. I did not know what to do. Then he asked, 'Go and salute *Thakur* and come.' I did that. In the meantime, two swamis came to take me to Mahapurush Maharaj's room. So he enquired of me. He was astonished to hear that I had finished my school finals and that I had come all the way from Khidirpur by cycle. He began to say,

'How could this small boy have finished his school finals? How could he come through these crowded streets of Calcutta by cycle? It is unthinkable.' He began to call everybody and say, 'See, this little boy has finished all this.'

Of course, I had doubt whether I was so small or not. I was sixteen years at that time and I probably looked a little small. He asked me many questions. I was always shy before such a big personality. I was not very free in talking. After questioning and making me talk, he asked his attendant, 'Introduce him to Jnan Maharaj and give him some prasad.' Then, he asked me to go cautiously back home. Jnan Maharaj was very popular among the young students.

I felt such an attraction to Mahapurush Maharaj that next day I came again to the Math. Seeing me, he said, 'You have come again.' I said, 'Yes, Maharaj, my examination is over, I have nothing to study now.' He said, 'That may be, but if you come so often, then the people of your home will blame us and will say that we are taking you away from them.' My people at home were more generous, but I could not tell him that point.

After a day or two, again I went there. I was a little afraid. That day he did not talk much so I became more nervous, but I had to go because I was going back home, that is to our country home, and I wanted to take leave, but even that I could not tell him.

After the results of the examination were out, I came to Calcutta for studying. From that time I used to go every Sunday to Belur Math. I would go in the morning and come back in the evening. Sometimes, during celebrations I used to spend nights also. I would bow down to Mahapurush Maharaj and he would sometimes make inquiries. As I was going on visiting the Math for three or four months, a few of the swamis became my guardians. They used to take an interest in me. One of them asked me one day whether I had thought about initiation. I had been meditating every day according to my own ideas, but I was afraid to tell Maharaj anything. So, I told the swami when he asked, 'If you would please arrange it, it would be nice.' So, he must have told Satyen Maharaj, because one day he called me and said, 'Come with me.' One or two other swamis also encouraged me. So, with trepidation of heart I one day went with him. Satyen Maharaj said to Mahapurush, 'Maharaj, he is a nice boy, he wants to tell you something.' I did not think that he would push me forward like this and I was not prepared for it and I did not know what to say in such a situation. Somehow or the other I got out the words, 'Maharaj, please bless me' and I burst into tears. He smiled a little and said, 'Oh, you want initiation. All right, my child, but we are not professional gurus. You will take Thakur's name, that's a very good thing. All right, repeat with me.' So saying, he began to tell the mantra. His eyes were closed. Sitting cross-legged on the bed, he began to recite the mantra. In the meantime, all the swamis went out closing the door behind. I also repeated the mantra. I do not know how much time we spent that way. Suddenly his voice came to my ears, 'Now, go to the shrine.' When I came down, a swami said, 'Take your bath and sit in the verandah of the shrine. Mahapurush will again give initiation in the shrine.' I did so, but Mahapurush did not call me further.

One day I told him, 'Maharaj, where I live, the other boys cut jokes if I meditate. That's why I often take the name of the Lord while walking on the street.' On hearing this, Mahapurush Maharaj was very happy. He said, 'Wherever possible, take the name of the Lord. As much as you can, repeat his name and be blessed by reciting his name.' Then, after keeping quiet a little, he said, 'But, my child, see that you do not get run over by a car.' And, he smiled a little. I also smiled. Mahapurushji still thought that I was a boy even though I was at that time a college student.

Then, after some time, suddenly he touched my chest and told me something. I could not understand the meaning of all he said. Even now I do not understand the meaning. He told me at the end what my relationship was with Thakur. Even now when I think of it, I become astonished.

In later days, when I went, I would rarely get Mahapurush Maharaj alone, and very rarely would I ask him questions, but I would notice that somebody or the other would ask the question I would like to ask, and I would get the answer. But he would look at me sometimes, especially when I felt that way and it was as if he would be speaking to me, saying, 'Go on, go on, you will have everything.' Probably that was my imagination, but I would get much courage through that.

In the meantime, I joined the Mission and was sent to Deoghar Vidyapith, a residential school. Then, I told him, 'Maharaj, I am now going to Vidyapith.' He with firmness said, 'Yes, my child, go there. Baba Vaidyanath (Lord Shiva) is there, he will look after you. Do not worry.' Later, he began to call me the Kanai of Deoghar, or Tall Kanai, because by that time I had become quite tall.

Once, there was an interesting incident. A friend of mine came with me to Belur Math. I took him and I do not know wherefrom I got the courage to say to Mahapurush Maharaj, 'Please bless him'. 'He smiled and said, 'All right, sit down.' Then he looked at me and said, 'What mantra did I give you?' I was taken aback, how could I tell the mantra before others? As he found me hesitating, he said, 'You fellow! You have objection even to tell me.' Then I told him the mantra, and strangely, Mahapurushji gave my companion the same mantra in the same way, i.e. without going to the shrine. But he was an intelligent boy and brought some fruits and flowers and offered them to him.

There was a big celebration on his birthday. At that time, I went several times to bow down to him. I was feeling so much attracted to him and his wonderful beauty. Whenever I went and bowed down to him, he smiled and gave me a gracious look. One attendant noticed me going several times and said, 'How many times are you going to do *pranams*?' That day I boldly said, 'Today is a holy day. I shall do as many times as I want.' Mahapurush only smiled.

In this way many small incidents come to my mind, they are very valuable to me, but I do not expect that they would be equally valuable to others. Through these small incidents, I have got his grace and that sustains me at this age now. I was not fit, I was quite ordinary, but he blessed me and whatever grace I got, was not because of my fitness but because of his motiveless grace. I feel blessed.

Swami Visuddhananda: An Apostle of God-awareness

I DO NOT REMEMBER WHEN I FIRST SAW SWAMI VISUDDHANANDA—IT was, I think, sometime in the late 1920s. Long before I saw him I had been hearing people refer to him as a great contemplative. Being young, I liked men of action and thought rather poorly of a contemplative. Why should a man spend all his time thinking of God? I would argue, why should he not do something for the good of society also? Did not Swamiji preach service to man as a kind of worship? Yet, I found people refer to Swami Visuddhananda with great respect and admiration. This rather puzzled me. How could people be so much enamoured of a man who was a mere contemplative?

I did not have to wait long for my answer, for I soon came to know Swami Visuddhananda personally and having once known him, had no difficulty in discovering the secret of his charm. I remember the first time I saw him. He was then head of the centre at Ranchi and had just come down to the Math to attend a meeting. Without knowing who he was, I felt drawn towards him at first sight. It was his fine chiselled face, auburn complexion and poise that attracted me. He was not imposing, not even striking by any standard, but there was an aura of sweetness around him which one could not but notice. When I was introduced to him, I was a bit nervous, but he soon put me at ease by treating me with utmost affection and by speaking to me as if he had known me a long time. He was a soft-spoken man who knew also the real art of conversation, for he never spoke much himself, but made others speak as much as they wanted to speak, himself putting in a word or two when he must. Having known him once I began to watch him closely, for I wanted to know what exactly was the distinctive quality that made him the object of universal love and respect. The first and most distinctive among all the qualities he possessed, as I observed, was that he led an organised and well-regulated life. Nothing could happen that would make him deviate from his well-thought-out routine which included, among other things, three-hours' meditation in the morning and evening. I also noticed how tip-top everything in his room was. Not only was there not a speck of dust, but the few articles he had in his room—his clothes, books, bottles of medicines, one or two pieces of furniture, etc., all were well arranged. I also liked the way he dressed. There was a distinctive taste which was unmistakable.

Another striking thing was his disinclination to talk about mundane affairs. He would gladly discuss a religious topic, but if the topic was non-religious, he would probably refrain from making any comments. It was also interesting to note that whenever he talked about religion, he would talk about it from the practical point of view and not so much about its theories. He would make religious experience seem not only the most desirable thing in life, but also a thing easy of attainment, as if even you and I could have it if only we tried. In his religious talks, there would always be a fair sprinkling of quotations from popular religious books, especially the *Gospel of Sri Ramakrishna* and anecdotes from the lives of saints of all religions, so that it was always interesting to listen to him. He would disclaim any pretension to being a good speaker, but, in reality, he was a very interesting speaker, always to the point, brief and inspiring. He never made any attempt at oratory; he in fact spoke as if he was talking to a group of friends across the table. He spoke from the heart and his simple words, backed by conviction, appealed to monks and laymen alike.

II

Swami Visuddhananda was born at a village in Hooghly District about 50 miles from Calcutta in the year 1883. Having lost both his parents at an early age he was brought up by the relatives of his mother. As a boy he was quiet, introspective and deeply religious. The question that often troubled him was: 'What is the purpose of life?' The question became more and more pressing as he grew up in years. When he finished his school education in 1900, he became quite restless looking for an answer to this question. He often spent the whole day at what was then known as the Imperial Library (now known as the National Library) rummaging among books for what he thought might provide the answer he was looking for. The British Librarian, John McFarlance, struck by the young man's seriousness of purpose, often helped him choose the sort of books that would help in his quest. It is not known if he directed him to it, but once Swami Visudhhananda came upon Max Muller's *Sri Ramakrishna—His Life and Sayings* and this proved a turning point in his life. He went through the book with bated breath. He was elated to discover that Dakshineswar, the place where Sri Ramakrishna lived, was only four miles to the north of Calcutta. He lost no time in visiting Dakshineswar and kept visiting it again and again. The place, hallowed by its associations with Sri Ramakrishna filled him with inspiration. Every time he went there, he spent the whole day thinking of God. He soon came to know Ramlal, Sri Ramakrishna's nephew, who was then the Chief Priest at Dakshineswar. Ramlal's company gave him much impetus in his religious endeavours. Not long after this he came to know also M, the compiler of the *Gospel of Sri Ramakrishna*, when the latter came on a visit to Dakshineswar. M, in his inimitable way, talked to him about Sri Ramakrishna, adding further to the intensity of his longing for God. Previously, he used to have his meals at the temple of Dakshineswar, but M pointed out that it was wrong that he should thus tax the hospitality of the temple authorities. From then on, the only food he would have, was one-anna worth of meal consisting of some flattened rice mixed with sugar and lemon juice.

While Swami Visuddhananda was once on a visit to Dakshineswar, Sarat Chakravarty, the disciple of Swami Vivekananda who compiled the book *Swami-Shishya Samvad,* i.e. conversations between Swami and Disciple, came there. Ramlal Chatterjee introduced Swami Visuddhananda to Sarat Chakravarty and the latter held him spellbound by telling him stories about Swamiji. Once, while he was thus talking to him, Sarat Chakravaty turned to Ramlal and asked him, 'How is Mother?' This led Swami Visuddhananda to enquire who this Mother was and when he discovered that this was Sarada Devi, he at once resolved to take the earliest opportunity to visit her at Jayrambati to pay his respects to her. So one day, not long after this, he started for Jayrambati following the route via Burdwan, walking most of the way. When, travel-weary and dust-laden, he finally arrived at Jayrambati, Mother received him as if he was her dear child whom she was long expecting. She asked, 'How are you, my child? Has the journey been very difficult?' The warmth with which Mother said these words was a balm to his body and mind. He had never known Mother's affection, but now he felt as if he had found the Mother he had lost as a child. He spent a happy week with Mother and then returned to Calcutta. Before he left Jayrambati, Mother graciously initiated him.

The initiation increased his longing for God-realisation tenfold. It now became an all-consuming passion with him. He decided to leave home in search of God, but felt he must have Mother's blessings before he did so. He, therefore, returned to Jayrambati for Mother's consent within a few months. This time he walked the whole distance and had two friends with him who later came to be known as Swamis Girijananda and Shantananda. Mother was as warm as before, but when they declared that it was their firm resolve to live the lives of wandering monks depending upon what chance brought them, she firmly ruled it out. At their request, she, however, gave them Gerua cloth, but directed them to go to Varanasi to have their monastic names from Swami Sivananda who was then there. She handed them a letter introducing them to him and asking him to look after them. This was in 1907.

Armed with her blessings, they started for Varanasi walking the whole distance. It took them three months to reach Varanasi. Swami Sivananda welcomed them and they stayed there almost a year. It may be mentioned here that Swami Visuddhananda had his formal monastic vows from Swami Brahmananda at Varanasi in 1921.

Sometime in 1908, he proceeded to Madras to assist Swami Sri Ramakrishnananda in his work. Later, he worked at Bangalore also for some years. In 1916, he was transferred to Mayavati where he served for nearly four years. While at Mayavati he was in charge of accounts for some time. Referring to his work as accountant Swami Madhavananda once remarked, 'He had a wonderful power of concentration. He totalled up figures without ever making a mistake; he would get the correct total at the very first attempt. He was so sure of himself that he would not care to check a second time.' After a brief interlude in Calcutta when he lived in close touch with Swami Brahmananda and when he was appointed a member of the Governing Body of the Mission and a trustee, he was again sent to South India for some years. After a year's stay at Bhuvaneswar as the head of the monastery there, he was posted to Ranchi where he served continuously for a quarter century from 1927 to 1952.

His life at Ranchi was the life of a recluse. He seldom, if ever at all, left the monastery or received visitors. Only one or two select devotees could come once in a while to read with him the *Gospel of Sri Ramakrishna*. Most of the time he would keep himself immersed in meditation and study. There are people living who bear witness to the austerity of his life and the state of God-consciousness in which he lived there. Some of them feel blessed that they knew him then and refer to those days with joy and gratitude as if they themselves were privy to the religious experience of this great soul. A road bears his name as a tribute of the people of Ranchi to his memory.

From 1952 onwards, a marked change was discernible in Swami Visuddhananda. He was appointed Vice-President of the Sri Ramakrishna Math and Mission that year and in that capacity, he had many responsibilities, chief of them being to meet people and attend to their spiritual needs. Gone were the happy days of seclusion for him! From now on he spent at least a couple of hours daily meeting people and replying to their religious questions. Hundreds of people came to him, people of all ages and all communities. He was patient with all and his answers were simple, straightforward and convincing. Once a person came to see him, he would come back again and again, very often with friends and relations. Soon, his reputation as a religious teacher spread. He was in demand all over the country and he in his turn, travelled far and wide ministering to the religious needs of the people. It was at this time that an Indian barrister-at-law who also happens to be an all-India political leader once declared in a public speech, 'I deem Swami Visuddhananda to be the greatest saint in India today.' When this was reported to Swami Visuddhananda, he was embarrassed and visibly annoyed. He said, 'What does he know of saints?'

Swami Visuddhananda visited Assam more times than any President or Vice-President of the Sri Ramakrishna Math and Mission before him did. Mentioning this with pride, many people in Assam claim that their State occupied a special place in the heart of Swami Visuddhananda. Whether this is true or not, the fact remains that his visits created a religious ferment, in both Bengali and Assamese populations, large sections of whom flocked to him as if drawn by a magnet. People who saw him then still remember him as if he was a symbol of a great experience. If there are today a large number of Sri Ramakrishna Ashramas throughout Assam, it may be attributed largely to the influence of Swami Visuddhananda. He set in motion the powerful Sri Ramakrishna Movement which is now sweeping through Assam and its neighbouring states in the Eastern Region.

In the year 1962, Swami Visuddhananda succeeded as President of the Sri Ramakrishna Math and Mission following the death of Swami Sankarananda. He was already eighty and his health was indifferent, yet when the call came to him to shoulder the responsibilities of the office of President, he did not demur. As President he stayed mostly at Varanasi where he had begun his monastic career sixty years earlier. He was now at the zenith of his monastic virtues. As usual he had many visitors every day. However taxing it might be for him to talk to them in his feeble health, he never turned away anybody. He continued to exhort people to try to realise God. So inspiring were his talks and so kind and affectionate he himself was that many people visited Varanasi from Calcutta and other far-off places merely to see him and listen to his talks.

For some years, he had been having trouble with his urinary system and doctors had advised an operation. At first, he was unwilling to have the operation, but when the trouble persisted he decided in favour of it. He came down to Belur Math and soon entered a nursing home. Before leaving for the nursing home, he approached almost everybody at Belur Math with folded hands and begged for forgiveness for any offence he might have given him. The behaviour was unusual, but no one thought that this was his final leave-taking. On 13 June 1962, he had his operation done by the best surgeons of Calcutta. Contrary to everybody's expectations, his condition began to deteriorate from the midnight of the 15th and on the 16th morning he passed away. His lips were seen moving and his hands were joined together across his chest. Even his last moments were marked by his God-awareness.

III

Two incidents may be mentioned here which serve as a pointer to what made Swami Visuddhananda the man he was. Once, a vain young man who had atheistic leanings asked him, 'Sir, have you seen God?' Swami Visuddhananda, instead of giving him a direct answer, told him that since religious men of all countries and all ages had claimed that God existed and He could also be seen, it was wrong to have any doubt about His existence. The young man was not satisfied with this, but asked, 'I want to know, Sir, if you yourself have seen Him.' Again, Swami Visuddhananda spoke at some length about how God answered one's prayers if one was earnest enough and how if one sincerely wanted to see Him, one could surely have His vision. Swami Visuddhananda thus parried the question a few times, but the young man was insistent and kept asking if he himself had seen God. At this impertinence of the young man, the atmosphere became tense and people present held their breath, worried about how Swami Visuddhananda was going to react. As people looked, they were amazed to see a great change slowly come over Swami Visuddhananda; he looked as if a halo surrounded his body. In words ringing with conviction he said, 'I have seen God as I see my own limbs.' A hush fell over the awed audience. The cheeky young man sat speechless. Without a further word, Swami Visuddhananda retired to his room and was not seen for the rest of that evening. People returned home with a sense of having experienced something breathtaking.

The next incident happened when Swami Visuddhananda was staying at Varanasi towards the close of his life. A leading surgeon of the town happened to lose his son, and this so upset the surgeon that he was no longer able to attend to his patients. He, in fact, was so distraught with grief that he was not even his normal self. Everybody in the town felt distressed at this because the surgeon was extremely popular. Also, there was nobody in the town who could match his skill as a surgeon which meant that the entire population in the town felt helpless without his services. Swami Visuddhananda who knew the surgeon felt sorry that the surgeon should thus suffer and with him also the citizens of Varanasi. He was so moved that he declared that he would gladly forgo the fruits of his lifelong prayers if that would make the surgeon normal and enable him to serve the community as before. Strangely enough, the surgeon began to show signs of recovery soon after this and within a week he was able to resume his work. One day, he appeared before Swami Visuddhananda and said, 'Sir, I have just completed a very difficult operation and I think it is going to be successful.' He came to give him this news as if he knew that his recovery was due to Swami Visuddhananda. The happiest man on hearing this news was Swami Visuddhananda.

A Real Gentleman: Swami Madhavananda

When the President of the Ramakrishna Math and Mission, Swami Madhavananda, passed away on 6 October 1965, someone sighed: 'A true gentleman is gone.' This brief comment expressed what almost everybody who knew the Swami well felt at that time.

There are not many who knew Swami Madhavananda intimately, but those who did, will always remember him with affection and gratitude. This was because he made you feel that you were not the stupid, worthless fellow that you imagined you were. It is not that he lectured you in order to make you feel this, but that he treated you in such a way that you could not help feeling that you were important—to him as well as to the world. He increased your self-esteem, made you conscious of your good qualities and also created in you a sense of urgency so that you might work hard to improve yourself. When you left him after spending a few minutes with him, you were thoroughly convinced that you were capable of achieving whatever you wanted to achieve, no matter how difficult it was, and all that you needed to do in this connection was only to try hard.

And yet, Swami Madhavananda was not a man easy to deal with. If you were a junior monk who wanted to have some discussion with him, you had better be sure that you had all your thoughts carefully arranged and then, while speaking, you used the right word in the right place, for if you said something which was not quite clear or to the point, woe to you! He would at once pounce on and scold you that you were wasting his time as well as yours. He wanted you to say whatever you wanted to say in a minimum number of words, and then also, clearly and pointedly, without beating about the bush as most of us do, for he was a believer in mental discipline, that kind of mental discipline which ensures clear thinking and clear expression. He would watch every word that you said and if you ever said a word that was not quite appropriate or he thought irrelevant and unnecessary, he would not hesitate to point it out. Or, if you happened to mispronounce a word, he would not hesitate to pull you up and correct you, though of course, he would be careful while doing so, not to hurt you. Once, a young monk had said in the course of a discussion he was having with the Swami, 'Give a dog a bad name and hang it.' The young monk was referring to the treatment he had earlier received in connection with an incident in which his seniors had, according to him, misjudged his motives and had wrongly blamed him. Swami Madhavananda interrupted him by quietly saying, 'hang him', and though he made no further comment on the mistake the young monk had committed, the latter, aghast that he had committed such a silly mistake, did not wish to continue further with his protests.

Swami Madhavananda was a great stickler for accuracy and if he ever had any doubt about the precise meaning of a word, its usage or spelling, he would go to any length to make sure that he had got the right answer to his question. Once, he was seen worrying about the use of the article 'a' in a particular place, for he thought it had not been correctly used. He asked many people if they knew how to justify it, but they did not know. He asked even a college student, perhaps arguing that because he had just finished school, he might remember his grammar better.

As a student he was very good, having always been near the top among the successful students who appeared for the public examinations with him. He stood second in the Entrance Examination, but in the F.A. Examination, he did not get a high place because he had fallen ill. His result in the B.A. Examination too was not good either,—he got a second class in English, but this was because he had already transferred his love to religion, and studying for a university degree had by then become an intolerable chore. He joined the post-graduate course but was not able to finish it. He soon joined the Sri Ramakrishna Monastery. Commenting on his brilliance, a fellow-student once remarked, 'It will be wrong to judge Swami Madhavananda by his examination results. Those who knew him well would unhesitatingly say he was the most brilliant among us. If we ever had any problem about the subjects we were studying, we always turned to him, for we knew he alone among us knew the answer. Others might know, too, but they were not as thorough and dependable as he was.' It was Swami Madhavananda's habit, which he maintained to the last day, never to give an answer about whose correctness he was not sure. If he had any doubt in his mind as to what the correct answer was, he would then take endless trouble till he knew what the correct answer was. He did not believe in guessing. Similarly, he would not give an answer which he thought was not clear or did not help remove the doubts of the questioner. He would humorously mention how the explanation given by scholars was sometimes more difficult and more perplexing than the problem itself. By way of example, he mentioned about a book he had once come across in which an attempt was made to give the meaning of the word 'father'. He said, according to the book, the word meant 'male parent'!

Those who know anything about the difficulty of rendering abstruse philosophical concepts from Sanskrit into English, say that his English translation of Sankara's commentary on the *Brihadaranyaka Upanishad* is a masterpiece. It is an example not only of his scholarship and grasp of the subject, but also of the amount of hard work he would put in and the care he would take to achieve precision. There have not been many translations of this great Upanishad before or after which can have any pretensions to parity with his, and to the extent that he has given to the scholastic world a correct and precise translation of this book he has laid it under a deep debt of gratitude.

Swami Madhavananda translated a few more such books and it is scarcely a mere coincidence that each one of those books bore the same stamp of scholarship and precision. The fact that he always insisted on exactitude to the extent that he would not mind sacrificing everything for its sake, perhaps explains the relative smallness of his literary output. He had great command over English, Bengali and Hindi, and if he so wished he could have written much in any one of these three languages, but being naturally shy and having from an early age acquired the painful habit of worrying too much as to the words he should use to say what he wanted to say, he restricted himself to translating a few books and writing a number of articles, only. Another factor which made it difficult for him to write as much as he would have liked to, was, that he was for the entire period that he was in the Ramakrishna Mission saddled with such exacting administrative duties that he had very little time left to devote to intellectual exercises. This makes all the more remarkable the fact that he had written as much as he had written and that, too, of such a high quality. He wrote many articles, some under his own name and some under a *nom-de-plume,* all of them characteristic of his personality—sharp, clear and cut to size. There was nothing in them that need not have been said just as there was nothing that needed to be said but was not there. They were brief but complete, informative but not flabby or burdened with too many details; they were interesting and always pleasant to read, though, at the same time, scholarly.

Apart from what he wrote, he edited many books and articles by others. There is hardly any book published by the Ramakrishna

Mission over the last thirty years which he did not go through in manuscript, examine its matter and language critically and helped to improve. Even Christopher Isherwood's book on Shri Sri Ramakrishna which appeared in 1965 shortly before Swami Madhavananda's death, is no exception, for, as Isherwood mentions in the preface, he had had every chapter of the book examined by him before sending it to the press. Isherwood did it especially to ensure accuracy of facts, for he knew there could be no better person to whom he could refer to be sure of his facts than Swami Madhavananda. One wonders if it may not be that Swami Madhavananda enjoyed doing this kind of work, for otherwise it is difficult to explain why he did it even when he had not been asked to do it. Or it may perhaps be more plausible to say that it was irksome to him to see any sign of carelessness anywhere, and when he saw someone had been clumsy and careless in anything he had written, he hastened to correct it, if of course, he could do so without causing hurt to him.

Once, a young man had written an article in a daily paper, to which he later drew Swami Madhavananda's attention, perhaps with the object of eliciting the latter's opinion about it. Swami Madhavananda read it and then made some appreciative remarks about it, but presumably having noticed many blemishes in it, unasked, he started editing it and when finished doing so, the article had infinitely improved! It was a great surprise to the young man that the improvement had been accomplished by merely changing a word here and a phrase there. What Swami Madhavananda had really done was to replace certain words and phrases which the young writer had used, probably without giving due thought to their meaning and usage, by others which, in his opinion, more precisely conveyed the meaning of the writer. Having done this, Swami Madhavananda perhaps later felt that he had unwittingly censured the young man, so that, to make amends, he remarked apologetically that he had merely tried to 'impart lustre to what was already good', which of course, was an understatement.

A point to be specially emphasised in this connection is that Swami Madhavananda was a man who sincerely believed that work is worship if done in the right spirit. There was no work too insignificant for him if it was work done in the service of God. He was often found correcting proofs—an occupation few people ever care for. The way he did it gave one the impression that he thoroughly enjoyed it. The truth of the matter is that he knew that others did not like this kind of work and if it was entrusted to them, they were likely to do it perfunctorily. This was why he often took this tedious work upon himself rather than ask somebody else to do it, in spite of the fact that he was already overworked, being the Chief Executive of the Mission. And, with what devotion he would do this universally disliked work! He had so completely mastered the art of proof-reading that once he had gone through a proof, it was impossible to find a single mistake left in it, which was yet to be corrected. It is interesting to note that he often did proof-reading and similar such tedious work immediately after his meals. If somebody pointed out to him that this was the time when, for the sake of better digestion, he should take some rest and not engage in such dull, specially taxing work, his reply would be, 'I *am* taking rest. Taking rest does not mean doing nothing; it means change of occupation.'

Indeed, there was hardly a moment when he was not active, when he was not doing something or other. He was a frail man, but he conserved his energy in such a way that even though he carried on his shoulders the burdens of an exacting office which imposed on him much physical and mental strain, he never tired. This was because he was careful not to waste his time and energy over activities not particularly relevant to the office he occupied, or not useful to himself or others. This was why he was not only always up-to-date with his work, but also had time to receive visitors, answer letters and do a vast amount of reading. He daily had a large number of people coming to see him, but while most of them came on business, there were some who came not because they had anything in particular to discuss with him but only because he happened to be the executive head of a big organisation! And, it was such people who often stayed with him much longer than there was any seeming justification for, with the result that Swami Madhavananda had to sacrifice a big chunk of the little time that he usually set apart for his personal needs—bath, meals, etc. Even in a situation like this, he was too polite to protest. The utmost he would do was to hint gently to such people that they might perhaps find it interesting to visit the temples of the Math! On the days when there were festivals at Belur Math which attracted big crowds, it was often impossible for him to find time for his meal, for he would have people visiting him throughout the day. It caused him tremendous strain, but he never showed it nor did he turn away a visitor. The only time when he would be alone and free to attend to his personal needs was when the bell rang to announce that meals were ready, for his visitors would then hastily leave, apologising that they were hungry and did not wish to miss their meals!

One of his most distinctive traits was consideration for others, which marked him out as a gentleman of rare charm. He would not allow himself the luxury of a moving fan if it was not particularly warm, but if somebody called on him and if it was a warm day, he would at once turn the fan on. If he had to be late for his meal for some reason or other, he would send word that his meal be put away somewhere so that he might easily find it when he was free to go and eat it, but he would not like that anyone should wait for him. Nor would he like that because he was going to be late, someone should bring his meal to his room and leave it there. He would, in short, object to any special consideration being shown to him on account of his age and status, and if anyone acted against his wishes in this regard, he would be annoyed. On one occasion, he refused to take his meal because someone had, in disregard of his express instructions on the subject, brought his meal to his room and left it there, knowing he had gone out and would not be back till long after the mealtime, so that there was every chance that he might miss his meal unless it was left in his room waiting for his return. On another occasion, he and his younger brother, also a monk of the Ramakrishna Mission, went to see their aged parents who were then ailing. They had planned to arrive in the evening, but the train was late. So, when they arrived at their destination, it was night and everybody in the house, including the parents, had gone to bed. Lest they cause them any inconvenience by waking them, they decided to spend the night outside the house without sleep and without food.

In his last illness, Swami Madhavananda needed an electric fan and when a friend came to know about it, he purchased one and sent it to him. It was the friend's intention to give this as a present to him, but Swami Madhavananda insisted that he accept payment, for, as he pointed out, the gentleman, a man of moderate means, had already made much sacrifice for the Mission so that he thought it would be wrong to accept any present from him, even though he might be anxious to make one. The gentleman tried every possible excuse he could think of to dissuade Swami Madhavananda from paying for the fan and for some time he even stopped visiting him, but it was of no avail, for he kept sending for him and did not stop till he had accepted the money.

Swami Madhavananda was also loth to accept any service from anybody. Once, a junior monk offered to wash his shaving instruments after he had shaved, at which he reprimanded him saying, 'Why do not you go and pray in the temple, instead?' On another occasion, the same monk had taken care of his shoes when he had entered a hall where shoes were not allowed and when he came out, the monk placed the shoes near his feet. This was hardly a service, but Swami Madhavananda did not like that even this little service to be rendered to him and he scolded the monk because he had bothered about his shoes. Even when he became old and found it difficult to walk, he would not allow anybody to support him. It used to be a torment to see him climb down steps, but he always insisted that he do this without anybody's help. When he became too ill to take care of himself, he naturally had to depend upon others even for his smallest needs. Some junior monks were appointed to attend on him, which often led him to speak as if he felt guilty that those monks had to interrupt their regular work in order to look after him. There were instances in which those who were looking after him had committed mistakes due either to ignorance or negligence, but Swami Madhavananda would smile indulgently and make light of the mistakes when shame-facedly they tried to explain how those mistakes had occurred.

He was at first assistant secretary to the Sri Ramakrishna Math and Mission, and then became its General Secretary, a position in which he continued for more than two decades. He was known to be a strict administrator, but his strictness was of a kind which seldom hurt. It is not that he turned a blind eye to the shortcomings of those for whose welfare he, as executive head, was mainly responsible. He could be severe and if necessary, take drastic action, but the way he behaved on such occasions gave one the impression that he was in torment that he had to take the step that he was taking. It often happened that the man he punished became a greater admirer of his after the punishment than he had been before, and he also never questioned the justness of Swami Madhavananda or that in taking the action that he had taken, he had been prompted by the highest and purest of motives. Swami Madhavananda was a man to whom principles were more important than persons, and when necessary, he never hesitated to scold or take such other action as the circumstances of the case might demand against a dear friend for the sake of principles. But at the same time, he was fully aware that if a man committed a mistake, it did not mean that he was lost forever, but that with affection and encouragement, he could improve and it was his duty as leader to see that the erring member of the Mission had every opportunity to correct himself. There were sometimes complaints that he showed undue softness towards men who had erred not once but again and again, but his softness stemmed from the fact that he was convinced that, notwithstanding the weaknesses such men temporarily showed, they had great potentialities and all that was needed to help them shed their weaknesses and fulfill the promise which they possessed was sympathetic handling and encouragement. Later experience showed how right Swami Madhavananda was in these matters, for such men did improve, improve much more than anyone had thought possible, thus fully justifying the trust that he had placed in them.

Although Swami Madhavananda stood head and shoulders above those around him, he would sometimes exaggerate his own limitations in such a way while praising the good points of others, that one would have the impression that he was not fit to hold a candle even to the smallest among them. It is not that he believed in false modesty, but that, while he was too great to think that he himself was great, he wished to see others, especially those who were younger than he in age, grow to be better than he in all respects. If anybody ever made complimentary remarks about him in his presence, his reaction would be one of undisguised resentment, as if someone had heaped an unprovoked insult on him. Once a young man, without knowing what he was letting himself in for, happened to praise him in his presence in a speech he had earlier made. He was greatly surprised when Swami Madhavananda reacted sharply to this by saying, ' Do I understand that you have nothing else to do than to flatter others?' On another occasion, his remark was less severe, if also characteristic. He said with a chuckle, 'You see, the fact of the matter is that I am very lucky. I am really not as good as people think I am, but somehow or the other, I seem to have a good "market value" so that people praise me much more than I really deserve'.

In spite of his modesty, he was truly a good speaker who could always hold the attention of his audience. What characterised his speeches most was that he tried to put across his ideas in the fewest possible words, words which were simple as well as elegant. He particularly disliked making long speeches. He used to say, 'It's an outrage to make a long speech. If you are the only speaker at a meeting, speak for 45 minutes at the most; but if there are other speakers, then do not speak for more than 15 minutes and if possible, be even briefer.' He himself always followed this maxim, though naturally this often disappointed his audiences.

Swami Madhavananda belonged to a generation which set much premium on courtesy. Having more than his share of it, he sometimes showed courtesy to others in such a manner that it was an embarrassment to those to whom he showed it. It was a touching sight to see the way he saluted his elders—it was a gesture of profound love and respect, even though some of the elders were intellectually and otherwise far inferior to him. He would similarly show due courtesy and consideration to younger people, though local customs did not make this always obligatory on his part. Once, he was travelling by rail when a young man entered his coach, a cigarette in his mouth. The coach being rather crowded, the young man had nowhere to sit and reconciled himself to having to keep standing, when Swami Madhavananda invited him to come and sit next to him. The young man accepted, but with such an *hauteur* that it looked as if he was doing a singular honour to Swami Madhavananda by consenting to sit next to him. Turning to Swami Madhavananda, he asked stiffly, 'Are you from the Ramakrishna Mission?' Swami Madhavananda replied, 'Yes'. The next thing he asked was, 'What's your name?' 'Madhavananda'. 'Oh, Madhavananda!', the young man ejaculated. While other passengers in the coach felt aghast at this conversation, Swami Madhavananda, more than forty years older than the young man, did not mind a bit and seemed ready to answer more such questions if the young man wished to ask them. On another occasion, Swami Madhavananda happened to scold a young novice for some mistakes he was told he had committed, but as soon as he discovered that he had been wrongly informed, he apologised to the young man, much to the latter's embarrassment.

Another good virtue which he had in common with many of his generation but which by practice had become particularly pronounced in him and which lent a special distinction to his speech and action, was the fact that he tried to follow, in letter as well as spirit, a strict moral code. It was impossible for him to take any step without first being sure that it was morally sound. He believed that the same moral principles could not be prescribed for everybody, that they must vary according to one's station in life and according to what one accepted as one's life's goal, but he was emphatic that for monks the moral standard should be as high as possible. According to him, what could be legitimate and excusable in the case of a householder, but not in the case of a monk? He conceded that sometimes it was difficult to decide what was right and what was wrong, but he would say that if you were not so sure that what you were going to do was right, you had better not do it at all. Because he himself always practised this principle, not merely in his personal life, but also in the conduct of the affairs of the organisation of which he was the executive head; he commanded respect from all, even from those who did not always see eye to eye with him.

Even to the last day, Swami Madhavananda strictly kept up his habit of spending some time daily doing meditation and reading some holy book. There is a fine picture, taken probably within a week before his death, in which he is seen telling his beads lying in bed since illness had incapacitated him from doing even such a small physical exertion as sitting for a length of time. The punctuality he maintained till his last illness in his daily habits, especially in his habits of meditation, etc., used to be much commented upon among his brother-monks and cited as an example for all monks to follow. Many would watch with admiration and wonder, how he would never fail to wake up between 4-00 a.m. and 4-30 a.m. everyday and begin his meditation, despite any special circumstances which might have compelled him to keep late hours the previous night. In the evening, too, he would do his meditation again, starting it almost within minutes of the ending of the evening service at the temple. Sometimes, he would start it so soon after the evening service that if one had to see him on urgent business, one would either forgo attending the service or risk not being able to see him. But Swami Madhavananda did not like that any important work of the Mission should be held up just because he was not available at any given moment, even if it was because he was engaged in meditation. Once, a junior monk belonging to a centre in Calcutta had gone to have his signature affixed to some important papers, but just as he arrived at the Math he saw to his dismay Swami Madhavananda turning off the light of his room, a signal that he was going to begin his meditation. This meant that the monk was not able to see him for the next two hours or so, the time Swami Madhavananda usually spent doing his meditation. When finally he saw Swami Madhavananda at a late hour of the evening, the latter scolded him for not knocking on his door or otherwise calling his attention in order to get his signature earlier, for, he said, in showing the consideration that he had shown towards him, he had caused, maybe unthinkingly, a temporary deadlock in the work of the Mission, which, he thought, was wrong, as in his opinion, nothing should have precedence over the Mission's work. It was not that Swami Madhavananda thought that his meditation was of no importance, but that, being the selfless man that he was, he did not wish that his own interests should come in the way of the interests of the 'Mission'.

As spiritual head of the Sri Ramakrishna Math and Mission, it was his duty to give religious instruction to those who sought it, but he would not like anyone to think that he was a 'teacher'. He would instead have them think that he was only a more experienced man in spiritual matters, so that at the most, he might be able to give them some practical hints likely to be helpful to them. He once expressed great resentment because someone had referred to a young man as being his 'disciple'. He said, 'If anyone, Shri Sri Ramakrishna is the Master and all of us are his disciples.' Similarly, if anyone pressed him for advice, he would say, 'Read the Gospel of Shri Shri Ramakrishna and the speeches and writings of Swami Vivekananda. You have there everything you need to know to strengthen your spiritual life.' Or, 'All that needs to be said about religion has already been said in the books. What's necessary now is to practise it; try to practise whatever you know or understand about religion. The rest will follow automatically.' In some cases, he might also reproduce to you for your benefit, any advice he might have received himself from some direct disciple of Shri Sri Ramakrishna whom he might have approached for guidance in a moment of crisis in his younger days. His reluctance to advise was due to the fact that he did not want anybody to depend upon him, or, in fact, upon anybody else; he wanted him to depend upon himself, for he must have observed, during his long monastic life, how dependence upon others in spiritual matters was often fraught with grave dangers.

What he would prefer was a discussion in which both sides spoke freely, a kind of exchange in which there was a free 'give and take', without any hint of any party trying to dominate over the other. He perhaps believed this was the best way to stimulate in the other man, independent thinking and judging things for himself according to his own lights, a practice so essential in spiritual life, to avoid unnecessary pitfalls. By temperament, he loved to argue and while arguing he would often take a stand just opposite to what he genuinely felt and believed. Perhaps, he did this to provoke the other man into saying whatever he wanted to say, giving free rein to his thoughts and feelings and not keeping back anything, so that the discussion might be really meaningful. On such occasions, Swami Madhavananda would rise to great heights, revealing something of the vast sweep of his mind, the depth of his understanding and scholarship as well as the sharpness of his wit.

Incidentally, it was his wit that was his most formidable weapon. It was like a sabre-thrust that did not exactly hurt you but showed where you were vulnerable. It confused you and the more you tried to cover your confusion, the worse it became. He might enjoy your discomfiture but would never take advantage of it. Indeed, what was remarkable was that in such exchanges, he would forget his age and status and would talk to you as if you were his equal. You might disagree with him, be blunt in your criticism of his standpoint and reject his mature views, saying that they were superstitious; he would not mind a bit; he would, in fact, like you the better if you did it intelligently and with conviction. He always welcomed frank and honest opinions, even if they were most unorthodox and contrary to what he himself believed. You, for instance, might question the validity of what to him was so important and dear. But instead of losing patience, he would try to meet all your objections and with superior reasoning, slowly lead you to a position where you found that you could not but accept those very principles that you had earlier dismissed as worthless. He would do so without throwing into his arguments the weight of his age and position, without even quoting the scriptures, whose authority you might not recognise, but using mostly that kind of logic and commonsense with which you were familiar and which you yourself were using. It was a delightful experience for anybody who ventured to argue with him freely and intelligently. Intelligently it must be, for he had little patience with fools just as he had no patience with people who were vain and ignorant.

Swami Madhavananda's habits were simple and economic, even austere. It was impossible to make him accept what he thought he could do without. When he visited Rangoon as President of the Ramakrishna Mission travelling by air, all he carried with him was a small air bag. When somebody expressed surprise at this, he remarked that there was no reason why he should carry more baggage when all he needed—a change of clothes and one or two other essential items—could be stuffed into that bag. At Rangoon, he was seen using a pair of slippers which were old and worn out. Somebody asked him to let him replace them by a pair of new ones. Swami Madhavananda refused. The man thought he might be able to make him accept new slippers if he removed the old ones and left a pair of new ones in their place. That was what he did, but with the result that Swami Madhavananda was next seen walking barefoot! There was no choice left then for that admirer of his but to restore his old slippers. A monk, due to ill-health, often avoided travelling in public buses. Once, he went to see Swami Madhavananda at Belur Math in a taxi. As he wanted to return to Calcutta immediately, he kept the taxi waiting. When Swami Madhavananda came to know that he had travelled by taxi and had also kept the taxi waiting, he was very much annoyed. Reprimanding the monk, he remarked, 'Is this not a waste? And, whose money are you wasting? Are you not wasting public money? What right have you got to do it?' He was so concerned about public money that he would not like an envelope being used where he thought a postcard could serve the purpose just as well. While returning from his second visit to the West, he discovered that his thick winter clothes added much to his luggage, involving a huge amount by way of surcharge, which the Mission could ill afford to pay. To save the money, he travelled in those heavy clothes though it being summer then, he suffered much discomfort all through the journey!

Mention has already been made of his courtesy and his consideration for others. Since the middle of 1964, he had been very ill and as days passed, he became steadily worse. The illness reached a crisis around the middle of September and he had to be removed to the hospital for better care and treatment. When Durga Puja began on 1 October, his condition was so bad that it was apprehended that the end might come any moment and there was much anxiety felt, lest the Puja programme be upset because of his death. Every moment was a moment of suspense, and when at last the Puja concluded on the 5th of October, much relief was felt. Perhaps, Swami Madhavananda's own relief was greater than the relief that others felt, for every few hours during the Puja he would enquire how the Puja was progressing, and it was clear that he was fighting hard to avert death till the Puja was over. Although the conditions of his illness were such that he might sink into a coma any moment, he remained lucid till the last moment much to the amazement of the physicians. He talked and made witty comments as he always had done, till barely five minutes before his death. When death came on the evening of the second day following Durga Puja, he quietly and gently slipped into it. A happier death could not be imagined. The circumstances surrounding his death were such that not only had the Puja programme been not disturbed, but also none felt the inconvenience. He died just as he had always lived, never causing any inconvenience to others.

The commentator was, therefore, right when he said, 'A gentleman is gone.'

Gandhi, the Great Experimenter

I

WHEN GANDHIJI FELL FROM AN ASSASSIN'S BULLETS, HIS LAST WORDS were '*He Ram!*' It would have been surprising if he had died with some other words on his lips, for all his life he had worshipped God and had acted as he thought God wished him to act. That is to say, God was his constant guide, his source of inspiraton, and whatever he did, he did to please God. This was why he never missed his prayer. He might be in the midst of a hectic political activity, but when the time for prayer came, he would interrupt it and begin his prayer. He never deviated from his time-schedule even if this meant he had to keep a dignitary waiting—a Viceroy, a member of the British Cabinet or somebody else. The dignitary too would gladly accept this eccentricity of the old man, for he knew it was no use protesting. Gandhiji, it will be recalled, died on his way to the prayer meeting. Did he have any premonition about his death? It is difficult to tell, but others—especially the local police—certainly knew that something wicked was brewing. Even the man in the street sensed that something was wrong, for a few days earlier a bomb had exploded at the prayer meeting though no one had been seriously injured. This was a clear warning that some people would stop at nothing. They blamed everything on Gandhiji—the Partition of the country and all the tragedies they suffered in their personal lives. If a man had had his young daughter's modesty outraged or his aged parents killed before his own eyes he held Gandhiji responsible. Had he not promised to lead them to freedom and peace and happiness? They thought he had cheated them. They had so long been impressed by his talk about non-violence, truth and communal harmony, but they now thought it was all humbug. He was a saint to them before but now a villain. They held him and him alone responsible for every misery that they now suffered.

Gandhiji knew the people's mood but he did not worry too much about it. He had never been afraid to tell the truth and he was much less afraid now. He condemned violence in much stronger terms than he had done ever before. Other people might have used moderation considering everything but not Gandhiji. He was blunt and forthright. People were boiling with rage but they did not know what to do. The police knew that though most people would not hurt Gandhiji for old days' sake, there might be cranks or hot-headed young men who would go to any length to punish Gandhiji. If the police could, they would have liked to prevent Gandhiji from holding open-air prayer meetings or at least, to enforce strict security measures. Is it possible that Patel who was Home Minister then, had come to discuss this matter on that fateful day? It will never be known, but if this was what he discussed with Gandhiji, he obviously failed to make any impression on him, for Gandhiji soon walked into the prayer-meeting and into—death. Nothing had yet made him miss his prayer. How could he miss it now because the Home Minister thought there was danger to his life?

II

But if Gandhiji was such a religious man, how could he then join politics? Is not politics contradictory to religion? Can a truly religious man be a politician, too? It is true that Gandhiji spent an entire lifetime fighting for the independence of his country, but it is doubtful if he could be called a politician; at least, he could not be called a politician in the conventional sense of the term. It is true that he was his country's political leader for three decades, but this was a role that his religious beliefs had cast on him. It was his love of God that made him fight against injustice wherever he saw it. It started first in South Africa and then it extended to India—this war against injustice, both political and social. In Africa, he himself had been a victim of racial discrimination. It was his religious feelings that prompted him to protest and launch his Satyagraha movement against it. He suffered much but finally won the battle, thus vindicating his belief that it is possible to change the heart of the enemy. Because he had faith in God he had faith in man too, for he believed that God resides in every heart, and He is constantly telling man to do what is right and avoid what is wrong. His 'still, small voice' can always be heard, if only man will hear it. He himself took all the momentous decisions of his life only after long hours of silent communion with God. He considered himself an instrument in the hands of God and acted as he thought God wanted him to act. This was what gave him the courage to do or say things, he knew for certain, nobody was going to like. It did not matter to him a bit if the whole world went against him so long as he felt certain he was acting according to the will of God. Many people thought he was crazy, impractical and indiscreet. There was good reason to think so, considering how he often behaved. Where there was no reason to give offence he gave offence; similarly when everybody felt it was time to strike at the enemy he would try to appease him. But because Gandhiji believed that God was guiding him, he completely ignored what other people thought about him.

Thus, whatever he did was an act of worship, for he believed he was acting strictly according to the will of God. He always insisted on truth because God and truth were to him synonymous. He calls his auto biography *An experiment With truth* because throughout his life he searched for truth and also applied it to his day-to-day life as he understood it. Even when he launched a political campaign, it was to him an attempt to establish truth, for in the political conditions that prevailed in India then, he felt truth had been trampled on. He bore no ill will against the British, but he fought for the end of the British rule, because that rule was essentially wicked, unjust and evil to him. Anything against man was to him against God, too. This was why he fought against untouchability all his life, for it was, as he saw it, a sin against God. Human misery in any form was to him an evil which fully justified a protest.

But being a religious man he did not hate the people he opposed. He hated the British system but not the British people. He used to claim that he was the best friend the British had in the East. This was perhaps no exaggeration. Again, because he was a man of God, he never adopted dubious means. He did not believe that good ends could be achieved by bad means. However strong the temptation, he insisted that none of his workers adopt wrong means for a right cause. Even when he wanted to break a law (which he did when he thought the law was wrong), he must first warn the rulers. He thought it was wrong to take the enemy by surprise, however powerful or wicked he might be. According to him, he should be duly notified and then only should action be launched against him. Many, of course, thought he was making a fool of himself, but this did not deter him from doing what he thought was right. It only strengthened his purpose further.

The techniques he adopted were entirely new in the history of a subject nation's struggle for independence. People thought he adopted non-violent means in fighting the British, because in the absence of arms and ammunition, he had no other way of fighting them. It was only a matter of expediency. All he was doing was making a virtue of necessity. This is not quite fair to Gandhiji. Non-violence, in his case, sprang from religious conviction; it was the result of his deep love for God. God is love itself and God filled his heart; how could then there be any place for hatred in his heart? Love for all—this was his guiding motto. It is wrong, therefore, to say that he preached non-violence because as the leader of an unarmed people, he had no other way to fight the British. The fact of the matter is that he would not have people use arms even if they had the means to buy arms. He would not mind if they got killed but he would not like that they should kill others. But he warned that he did not want the kind of non-violence that a coward might show; he wanted real non-violence, the non-violence of a bold man who knows he can hit back if he so wishes but he would not, out of his own free choice. He asked people to be violent rather than be a coward.

III

It must not, however, be thought that Gandhiji was a scholar, a mystic or a philosopher. He was a simple man who prayed to God that he might be a willing tool at His hands. He respected all creeds and dogmas but none of them had an absolute claim on his loyalty. He was not interested in theology; he was no great believer in rituals, either. He once remarked that he loved Hinduism to which he was born, but the religion he believed in was bigger than Hinduism or for that matter, any other religion. What he meant by this was that he did not wish to give any particular label to his religion, for it contained in it the elements of all religions and, if possible, even more. He, in fact, did not care so much for institutionalised religion; he preferred a direct approach to God without any intermediary being there. 'My religion is a matter solely between my Maker and myself', he used to say. He was a great believer in religious unity. 'The soul of religion is one, but it is encased in a multitude of forms', he once remarked. He also said that religions were so many roads which converged to the same point. According to Gandhiji, the sum and substance of all religions is truth and non-violence.

He was a practical man who did not bother too much about philosophical niceties. He, instead, preferred to practise whatever he understood of religion. He perhaps argued that just as one could not exhaust God, similarly one could not exhaust the science of religion. Two things were to him most important: morality and restraint. Divorced from morality, there can be no religion. Similarly, no one can be religious without self-restraint.

Gandhiji did not preach religion, but lived it. Because religion was to him more than his life, he took on himself the role of a political leader. He joined politics not in spite of religion but because of religion. He says in his autobiography, 'Such power as I possess for working in the political field is derived from my experiments in the spiritual field.' Religion taught him to love man, God's best creation. This was why he could not keep quiet when he saw millions of Indians suffering due to political bondage. He fought against the British just as he would have fought against his own countrymen if they had held in bondage some other people. In this connection, his fast in protest against India's vacillation over the question of paying Pakistan the money due to her, will be recalled. His action was embarrassing to his close friends and associates and angered his countrymen, but he paid no heed to this because he felt India had no right to hold back the money.

Thus, all his life Gandhiji had fought whenever he thought some wrong was being done to any section of humanity. This was the way he searched for truth (to him, another name for God). He called his life 'an experiment with truth', because in searching for truth, he approached the problems of life entirely in his own way and broke new grounds. Whatever he did was a way of knowing and serving truth as he understood it. He was, indeed, a great experimenter.

Netaji Subhas Bose in the Light of Swami Vivekananda

WE ARE ALL HUMAN BEINGS BUT WE CERTAINLY FIND A DIFFERENT sphere of human character in Netaji Subhas Bose. We do not know from where he comes and departs so suddenly but surely he bears an impressive mark and secures a place in the history which can never be wiped off.

There is a picture of Netaji, I wonder whether you all have noticed it. An imaginary picture where he sacrifices himself. He slays his own head and offers it to Mother India, in an imaginary picture by an unknown painter. This symbol is truly a symbol of patriotism. No one has ever loved one's motherland so intensely and deeply as he did. Certainly, many patriots and many commoners have loved their country, but I doubt if anybody could love one's country so intensely as Netaji did. As Swamiji said, 'Forget not that thou art born as a sacrifice to the Mother's altar.' A strange saying though it is, yet Netaji was an exact instance. He was then a young lad of just, may be, thirteen or fourteen, when he started studying Swamiji. His search for an ideal came to an end only with Swamiji, who was his source of inspiration too.

Netaji was held captive in Mandalay, Burma, for a long time. I can quite well recollect those memories. A meeting was held at Sraddhananda Park, a welcome ceremony to celebrate his comeback.

Netaji stood on the stage of Sraddhananda Park to say a few words. We, the tender-aged, were waiting along with thousands of audience. Tears rolled down Netaji's cheeks, he could not talk, thinking of his motherland. He asked in profound surprise how we could accept this slavery of the British rule, how we could accept this torture, this injustice and insult. And why are we not fighting madly for our freedom? And, we were spellbound listening to his strange and sensational speech. We had never heard such words from anyone else. What a source of inspiration!

In this context, I remember when I once overheard Sarojini Naidu, what she had to say of Netaji. While speaking of Netaji, she said that he was the 'flaming sword of Indian Nationalism'. Truly, he sacrificed himself for his motherland with that sword. His cry was for his motherland. I feel, he still exists and wherever he is, he is weeping for this lazy and weak nation, people who are without any self-respect. He feels ashamed, sad, and deeply insulted seeing such helplessness. This condition could only bring tears to his eyes. A few incidents of Netaji often come to my mind. I was a monk in Belur Math then and Netaji was the Mayor of Calcutta Corporation. On the occasion of Swamiji's birth anniversary, we requested Netaji to accept the presidentship of the programme. So, Netaji came along with Sarat Chattopadhyay, the president of Howrah Congress. The speech given by Netaji still rings in my ears. Just like Swamiji, he spoke about his country, his motherland. And at times, quoting and recalling Swamiji, specified this country as our Mother. A book was published from here written by Netaji on Swamiji. There, Netaji reminds us; do we remember the sayings of Swamiji? Do we remember Swamiji crying out; 'Say, the ignorant Indian, the poor and destitute Indian, the Brahmin Indian, the pariah Indian, is my brother. Say, brother: The soil of India is my highest heaven, the good of India is my good, and repeat and pray day and night, O Thou Lord of Gauri, O Thou Mother of the Universe, vouchsafe manliness unto me! O Thou Mother of Strength, take away my weakness, take away my unmanliness, and make me a Man!' Netaji spoke of Swamiji's thoughts. Swamiji's verses were also Netaji's sayings. Netaji after all represents Swamiji. The same expression, the same ideal, the same flaming strength and the same courage. All this symbolises Swamiji. They are inseparable, we find they are the same entity in different identities.

The other incident that I remember was on the occasion of Saraswati Puja. Saraswati Puja was being organised in the Vidyasagar Hostel. Well! I do not know why or how he was present there. We, a handful of students, were there and Netaji would deliver a lecture. Never before had I heard such a kind of lecture. Netaji, being of an emotional nature, would usually break into tears while delivering lectures but this time he was quite different.

At that time we were in college and so had some knowledge about politics. In that speech he enlightened us about the world of imperialism. And, how it was devouring the whole world, and exploiting the weaker sections, thus crushing the helpless India. I wonder if any professor of Political Science could analyse the factors of poverty and weakness of our country and the spread of imperialism in such a picturesque manner. He was, as if, painting the reality in front of our eyes. And, we listened to him, spellbound. It is ever fresh in my mind. I have never heard such a captivating speech after that. I came across a lot more lectures of Netaji that created sensation but that was an exception. It was like, as if he was painting with the colour of words, speaking slowly with scholarship. He showed us how the Britishers came to India and was continuously exploiting us. He also pointed out our weaknesses. Again, this is Netaji. We, being an ungrateful people, can never repay his debts. I can recall an incident. Swamiji's disciple Miss Macleod used to pay a visit to Belur Math each winter and stay there. We, all college students, went to her. We asked her to say something about Swamiji. She exclaimed, 'Look! If I wish I can say a lot on Swamiji, but you all will not understand that man. You may understand him and his contributions some day perhaps only after India's independence.' Similarly, we do not know or understand Netaji. Only one man could feel the pain, insult, misery, the indignity and the shame of subjugation of thirty-three crore Indians. Often, tears came to his eyes gushing.

You probably know how Netaji, inspired by Swamiji, had taken a resolution to be a sannyasin. He then travelled the length and breadth of Haridwar, met with a lot of saints and sannyasins but nothing could touch his heart. So, along with his other fellow-mates he was returning via Varanasi and they visited Ramakrishna Mission Sevashrama. At that period of time Swami Brahmanandaji, President of Sri Ramakrishna Math and Mission, was there along with his disciple Swami Nirvananandaji. On seeing Netaji, he asked surprisingly, 'Isn't he Janaki Babu's son? Please call him.' And, as Netaji came, Maharaj curiously kept on enquiring, 'What is the matter? Where have you been? And, why are you dressed in this manner?' Then he said, 'Look! Yours is a different path where you have to do something great. So, go back to your place and continue to study until you can decide for yourself what is to be done and what not to be.' As if Netaji was the chosen one. Some people are chosen and marked before time for certain work. They are chosen to work for the country and for the common people. Instead of thinking about his own welfare, social wellbeing would be his ultimate concern. He is no different from others. That is, good for all would be good for him and what is painful for others would be painful for him, too. It is strange that such a personality was born in India. How could this brave heart, this courageous soul and this talented personality be born in India? We know, from time immemorial our country has been blessed with saints and sannyasins and pure souls with great spiritual strengths. But a great soldier like Netaji who seems to know neither fear nor defeat was born for the first time.

We are more astonished as we come to know about his last but mysterious episode of life, how secretly camouflaging he escaped from the enemy captivity. After that a big incident took place. Sometimes, I think about our misfortune. I wonder if you all have seen that place in Manipur. It is certainly unimaginable how Netaji with his army reached that difficult place in Manipur and flew the Indian Independent Flag. His courage, his personality touched the heart of every Indian. He made people spellbound. He waited with a great hope that as soon as he came back, people of his country would accept him and be in a frenzy. They were counting their days for him. With his comeback, people would drive away the Britishers with roaring anger. Nay, that was not the story. He came with a heavy heart and after that when he left India that was for the last time we saw Netaji. What kind of history is ours? We need to change it. Never before in the history of India did we see such a kind of personality. Many have loved their country, many have been hanged until death but a fight without any co-operation, alone, escaping from the hands of the enemy, all alone to a foreign land, which has a common enemy, coming into friendly terms with them and with their assistance planning to make India independent. This understanding and differentiating a friend from an enemy have been practised from time immemorial. From where did he acquire this power of judging a friend from a foe and where did he come across this principle? No body knew these principles of war in our country. So, when and where did he learn these principles? It reminds me of the Congress Party of 1928 where he first explained that we need to fight and defend if required. He put on the uniform of a soldier; he showed us that if necessary we were ready to fight for our Independence. Before this we were only dreaming of Independence but no one knew how to acquire it.

He was born before his time. There was a deep pain inside. He had come to lead this country and to sacrifice himself for this country. In return, apart from applauding, praising and garlanding him, this country could do nothing more. This was the contemporary scenario of the country.

In this regard, if anybody complains that his efforts were in vain, I do not agree. It was because of his efforts the Indian soldiers working under the British imperialism were motivated to acquire Independence. The band of soldiers, who were the pillars of British imperialism, later protested and demanded independence. So, I do not agree that Netaji's efforts were in vain. Indian soldiers under British imperialism, those who had earlier shed blood of their own countrymen, later revolted against the same imperialism. They let all know that Britishers did not leave India willingly but were compelled to do so. This policy was an eye opener for them. Finally, this India that was once thought to be spineless, stood up against the rule of imperialism. And so, the Britishers realised that it would not be possible to stay and rule this country any longer. As there was no proper research done on Netaji, we never had the privilege to study much about his life. And, before knowing about his philosophical thoughts we need to know what a brilliant student Netaji was. He appeared for the Indian Civil Service examination, and was ranked fourth in it. And, what is to be noted is that he secured the first position in English and English composition. After securing such a high position in the ICS, when the British Government offered him the job, he declined it and returned to India. At that time just one person recognised and rewarded his talent. This person, Deshbandhu Chittaranjan Das, made Netaji the Chief Executive Officer in his corporation. Though young in age, Netaji carried on his duties proficiently.

Once, Netaji was invited to Belur Math to deliver a speech. What he said there was nothing but the echo of Swamiji's voice. We also find in a letter to his friend, Netaji writes that Swamiji would have been his mentor if he were alive on that date. Even we heard him repeat the same when he had lectured in Belur Math. It was that time in Singapore where he was the ruling authority. Many people say of Netaji that he had to work under the Japanese but I can never accept such a great lie. While in Singapore, Netaji had arranged for meetings there. And, I heard stories from ladies what kind of respect and love they had for him. The young ladies at that time, at the meeting when Netaji said, 'Help me with whatever you can,' took off their ornaments and gave it to him. And, they accepted humbly whatever he had to say. We had a Ramakrishna Mission orphanage at Singapore. At the time of war in India we were facing financial hardships. Sufficient money was not there to feed the children properly. Everything was in a disorderly state. Netaji came to us with funds that he had collected from grants. Quite often, when Netaji visited there, he meditated in front of Sri Ramakrishna. And, at least for an hour he enclosed himself within the room. As Swamiji told us, to be a man first and we find that man in Netaji. At the time when Swamiji was dreaming of and planning for Belur Math, to many, a question arose. His friends and close ones asked him from where finance would come. Swamiji said quite reluctantly, that he did not think of money since his first priority was of man. Truly, Netaji was that kind of man—a man we should be proud of. And, it would be an unpardonable incapability if we fail to have that pride. Netaji is the national treasure we should be proud of. Let there be a good book on his life. Though we could not collect much information on the last few days of his life, yet let us not forget such a great personality who was born to this country. We do not belong to the warrior class, the race which is quite accustomed to wars but it is strange how Netaji sacrificed himself for his motherland as if since his very birth. Netaji showed this world how one can love one's own motherland and to what extent one can sacrifice for one's motherland.

It would be an unpardonable crime if we cannot reach Netaji's thoughts to the young minds, the students. An instance of how to love one's motherland, how to love one's countrymen and what should be the extent of sacrifice. Our future will never pardon us if this message of Netaji is not spread uniformly among all. So, it is our duty to extend the fire of consciousness, what Sarojini Naidu said 'The flaming sword of Indian nationalism.'

Numerous incidents flash in my mind. I have never missed out on lectures by Netaji. Where is that passionate love for one's country? And, where are those leaders who could, by their lectures, inspire people so that they would sacrifice all for the sake of the country? I offer my prayers to Netaji, so that we all may inherit his strength, power, courage, selflessness, purity and love. Netaji, he is the blessed son of Swamiji. Netaji must have been under the guardianship of Swamiji. Let that purity, sacrifice and love for country find expression within us. This is my earnest prayer to him.

National Education and its Values

- *Crisis in Education*
- *Education: Theories and Practice*
- *Ideals and Methods of National Education*
- *Human Rights and Community Education*
- *Learning Sanskrit*

Crisis in Education

GENERALLY, IN ALL COUNTRIES AROUND THE WORLD, ESPECIALLY in India, there is much unrest among the students at the present moment. This may be part of that ferment now manifest in all sections of the community due to a number of causes, (the chief being maladjustment of relations between one social group and another), or this may be something which relates to the students only, originating from some organisational defect in the field of education. Whatever that may be, the result of this unrest everywhere has been disastrous: a general dislocation of all normal work in educational institutions or a situation approximating to that.

Of all countries India is clearly the worst sufferer in this respect. Apart from the fact that she is still tied down to a system, which is outdated and, therefore, most unsuited to her present needs and future aspirations, conditions in her educational institutions are such that all chances of serious and sustained work have become impossible. In the first place, relations between the teachers and the taught are so poisoned that a large part of their time and energy is necessarily wasted in the attempt to effect an adjustment. That amount of amity and understanding, which is regarded as the *sine qua non* of successful work in the classrooms, is also lacking. Indeed, in many respects, relations between the two present a close parallel to those existing between labour and capital. While students are determined to wrest from their teachers as many rights and privileges as possible, never bothering to give them the love and respect to which they are naturally entitled, teachers, on the other hand, fight bitterly any attempt at reorientation of their existing relations with the students in the light of present-day needs, for this, in their view, involves loss of prestige on their part. Not unoften, this fight for power is marked by resort to strikes by the students, resulting in long breaks in study. There is, indeed, no give and take between the two, no desire even that there should be. Where love and trust should form the basis of treatment, hatred and suspicion exist. Obedience to authority is considered weakness; similarly, leniency to impulsive youth is condemned as cowardice. In any difference of opinion or dispute that may arise, mutual recriminations are freely indulged in and that without any regard for truth and in a language far from edifying. And, what is very deplorable is that the public and the press take sides in the conflict, and so far from trying to bring about an amicable settlement, do everything they can to increase its bitterness. There are instances in which the help of an outside tribunal has to be sought to adjudicate, it being found impossible for the parties concerned to come to a settlement between themselves, and even if this does not end the conflict, the institution (where the dispute takes place) has eventually to be closed down altogether. Very often, there is no settlement, (though both the parties desire it,) because political parties, for their own reasons, make a settlement impossible by clever manoeuvring of things. A well-known trick of their trade is to pounce upon any opportunity that may offer itself to them to exhibit their sympathy for the students and thereby to consolidate their hold on them, so that they can later use them as their tools. No matter how manifestly wrong, they will support almost any demand of the students and egg them on to fight to secure it, even if the students thought it is not worth a fight.

This brings to mind another major factor, apart from that of the strained relations between the teachers and the students, which hampers education in the country equally, if not more, namely, too much preoccupation of the students with politics, not only theoretical, but also practical. In almost every institution may be found groups of students who are active members of different political parties of the country. To them the first concern is to propagate among their fellows the brand of politics by which they swear, and point out to them how the only way they can prevent the world from going to pieces is to seek membership of the party they represent. Study is only a secondary concern to them, if at all.

And as is hardly to be expected, these students are not content with merely doing some propaganda work on behalf of their parties; they are active and ardent participants in any other work which their parties may have chosen for themselves at the moment. In fact, most work of the parties is done by these student-members. The feature of Indian politics is that no party can claim any ardent and really useful following outside the student community. If today, by some suitable legislation it were possible to prevent students joining political parties, most of the flourishing parties of today would then be reduced to ineffectual crowds of do-nothings with only plenty of money—and perhaps, plenty of oratory also, to boast of.

It is, however, remarkable that students who are active members of political parties are not really very large in number. They form, in every institution, a small minority only. But being better organised, better disciplined (in their own way, of course), and above all, being more determined, they easily carry the day with them. Others, though an overwhelming majority, acquiesce in whatever they decide for them, because they lack will, lack organisation. If the determined minority decides something should or should not happen, it hardly lies in the power of the majority to force a change in the decision. Strikes in educational institutions on political grounds are a common enough feature nowadays. Almost any little stir in the political horizon may be deemed a sufficient ground for calling a strike— some incident happening not necessarily within the boundaries of India, but, also, outside, maybe, in Mexico, or Peru or Abyssinia.

In fact, the farther the country, the more important the incident becomes! And, if a strike has been decided upon, the whole body of students has to accept and act up to the decision; else they risk all manner of indignities, not excluding bodily assault. Picketing, that novel and comprehensive method usually employed on these occasions to prevent willing students from joining classes, may cover anything from moral persuasion to physical violence. In the face of the vigorous picketing that is carried on, it becomes impossible for any student (or for any teacher, for that matter) to attend classes.

But not always on political grounds that a strike may be called, though it is on political grounds (and at the behest of political parties) that most strikes are called. There may be a strike on such legitimate grounds because those long-standing grievances have remained unaddressed. But, as is very often the case, there are strikes over such trivial matters as the fixing of a date for an examination, or the stiffness of some question papers, appointment or dismissal of a certain teacher, matters all trivial and all falling, by every accepted standard, within the province of teachers only. Cases have been known of a strike being resorted to over the non-promotion of a student-leader who found politics (and other occupations of life) so absorbing as to find little time to attend to his lessons. In short, a strike is considered, whenever there is any disapproval or dissatisfaction that requires to be vigorously expressed. The method of negotiations is always discountenanced, for there is a suggestion of weakness and lack of heart about it!

A most distressing feature of these agitational activities of students is that, sometimes disgruntled members of the teaching staff (or those who are themselves members of a particular political party and therefore, anxious, from a sense of loyalty, to see that any agitation started under its aegis should succeed) covertly encourage the students or even openly join issue with them in their fight against the authorities. And, what heightens the tragedy is that, most members of the staff, though sincerely concerned about the welfare of the students and, therefore, anxious that the normal work of the institution should go on unhampered, look on helplessly, without knowing what to do in the matter. Thus, as among the students, so also among the staff, it is the minority who always predominate and it is, therefore, no wonder that when a strike is called, without any semblance of justification for it and in utter disregard of the wishes of the majority, it succeeds.

Everywhere, but more so, perhaps, in the field of education, it appears that the forces of good are disorganised, weak, passive and nonassertive, with the result that their sane counsels and sober judgement never recieve the attention to which they are entitled. The forces of evil easily reduce them to nullity by sheer aggressiveness, by the vigour of their organisation and by that new weapon in the armoury of people who know how to use it effectively, propaganda, carried on in the most unashamed mannar.

The question may be asked: why do governments allow this state of things to continue, when it must be clear to them that the primary objects of education are in danger of being defeated? Truly the attitude of the government in this respect is altogether baffling. As a rule, they prefer not to interfere in any dispute where there is every chance they will find themselves up against the students. Only when matters come to a head and there is a general clamour that the government must intervene that some halting and halfway-house measures are taken, even then without making any attempt to eradicate the root cause of the dispute. The fact of the matter is that there is an unusual solicitude on the part of the Government (and on the part of the public, too) to avoid doing anything which might appear unsympathetic to the students. This is often carried so far as to give the impression that the students can do almost anything with impunity. Perhaps, the real reason underlying this attitude is to conciliate youth at any price, so that their support may be available in any future contingency. In other words, the government does not want to lose the support of youth for their own reasons. It is not realised (or perhaps, though realised, the immediate gain seems important, so as to override all future considerations) that this attitude must ultimately prove disastrous to the students and therefore to the nation also.

In India, for generations now, students have been employed, for good or for ill, in political work, and it is largely due to their sacrifices that whatever progress the country has made in recent decades has been possible. For the sake of the country, they have braved incredible hardships by defying the authority of an irresponsible foreign government. This was then commended as an act of the highest patriotism worthy of the country's sincerest gratitude and admiration. Although the context has since changed and it is doubtful if the need for such patriotism exists now, the old mentality of challenging the authority still persists in the students, and they find delight in breaking the law, whenever there is the slightest excuse for it, seeming or real. So it is that indiscipline is rampant today among the youth, and with all their high idealism and noble purpose, nothing of lasting value is being achieved by them. Today, when there is the utmost need for constructive effort, it is most unfortunate that youth, who have always occupied the front rank in all progressive movements of the country, are frittering away their energy in disruptive activities.

All this is because they have long been used to a doctrine of life in which discipline and restraint have not had much place. Habits are hard to die and though in the present altered circumstances indiscipline is admittedly an undesirable factor, it continues to flourish. Strikes on political (as on other) grounds are as frequent as before and respect for the teacher (or for any other authority) is steadily on the decline. And, political activities of the students on party lines still claim most of their time and energy. It was hoped that with the country's attainment of Independence, students would withdraw from active politics but this hope has not been fulfilled. Political parties, without any regard to the future well-being of the country and actuated primarily by party-interests, continue to exploit the patriotic sentiments of the students. Educational institutions, especially those in cities and towns, are used by them as centres of recruitment and training, and scenes witnessed during an election in these institutions are only a replica of those seen when elections to the country's legislatures take place, for each party puts up a candidate of its own, and brisk canvassing and all the other usual accompaniments of a political election (including small skirmishes among the members of different parties) are freely indulged in.

It is not being suggested that students should not take any interest in politics. In a country under foreign rule, as India was until recently, or one which has just regained her political freedom as has India, that would hardly be possible, perhaps much less desirable. But it is one thing to take an intelligent interest in politics, quite another to be engulfed by it. In an hour of national emergency, it is clear students must come forward to play a vital role to preserve national peace and integrity. It would be perfectly justified if students then interrupted their studies or began to pay less attention to them. But when no such emergency is there as of now, to behave otherwise is ridiculous, and extremely harmful. Already, as a result of the overemphasis laid on politics during the last few generations, the country's intellectual level has gone down considerably, as is evidenced by the poor knowledge—with which most graduates of the day leave the university—of subjects studied over a number of years, and as is evidenced by a hundred other things. What would perhaps be regarded as a greater pity is that there has been such a distortion of values, due evidently to the attempt made to meet the demands of politics, that intellectual pursuits, hitherto considered the noblest and most respectable, attract much fewer people now than ever before and certainly not the best. A rich merchant or successful banker, because of the influence he can now exercise, by virtue of his wealth, on the political parties, is now a more respected person in society than a scholar. 'The good student' is now a term of ridicule rather than of respect.

It must be clear that, in more than one sense, the situation is very grave, indeed, and that if India is to attain to the full stature of her nationhood, she cannot afford to ignore the ominous portents which her present educational scene contains. How long can the present spirit of indiscipline be countenanced without gravely imperilling the national cause? How long can the present obsession of politics be allowed to continue when it must be obvious that, like a disease, it is eating into the vitals of the nation? Some action must be taken at once, some method devised, by which things are set right in the field of education. While plans are being evolved in order to organise education on a sound basis suited to the requirements of the present situations, it must be understood that they are bound to remain largely a dead-letter, unless the present chaos is ended. Negatively, the first thing to be done is to discard the present tendency to sacrifice the larger interests of education in order to gain the narrow and immediate objective of pleasing the youth. Positively, the tremendous energy which youth possess and which, for want of a properly controlled expression, has given rise to so much unrest, has to be canalised into constructive channels. In any case, in dealing with problems concerning the youth, the government has to show a great deal of not only sympathy, tact, patience, but also, firmness. Most troubles in educational institutions are attributable to either unimaginative high-handedness on the part of the authorities, or their astonishing lack of courage and lack of purpose.

It is possible to indicate other more concrete remedies, but that is outside the limited scope of the present paper, which is chiefly concerned with the task of focussing the attention of the relevant authorities to the grave problems which threaten education today. It would be sufficient barely to mention that problems of education can best be solved by education itself, and when the problem is bad education, of course, good education is the obvious solution.

Education: Theories and Practice

My first approach to the subject of education will be to view its role in a developing society. When I speak of a developing society, I naturally have the case of India in mind—an agrarian society with a very low per capita income and now in the process of being slowly industrialised. The questions I want to discuss are: What can education contribute towards the progress of such a society? What sort of education does a society like this need to hasten its transition to affluence?

THE ROLE OF EDUCATION IN A DEVELOPING SOCIETY

India is known to be one of the poorest countries in the world; yet, paradoxically enough, the curriculum followed in her educational institutions shows no awareness of this fact. That is to say, there is nothing in the education imparted in the universities which takes into account this crippling problem of the country and shows any sense of urgency to solve it. While famine continues to stalk the country, education follows its solemn course in majestic aloofness. What the students are taught in the classrooms has nothing to do with the problems they face outside. They may know higher mathematics; they may be able to tell the fine difference between one philosophical system and another, they may be familiar with the latest theories of astrophysics, modern poetry may be as clear to them as daylight, yet, believe it or not, they are never taught the simple mechanics of how to earn their daily bread. What can be a sadder commentary on the country's educational system than this?

It is not difficult to explain how education became divorced from life in India, but I will not go into that here. My concern here is to show how this can be rectified. This hiatus between life and education has done much harm already, and my regret is that there is still no serious attempt being made to remove this drawback. The present system of education produces only white-collared workers, but can a country's economy sustain itself on the labour of white-collared workers only? After all, they are people who do not produce wealth but live by others' labour. You cannot afford to have too many of them. It is enough if you have ten percent of your working people doing white-collared jobs, but the remaining ninety percent must do productive jobs. In India, unfortunately, there is a revulsion against manual work. Everyone aspires for a soft and cushy job.

This is not the only misfortune, however. India's greater misfortune is that she has an educational system which teaches nothing useful to the ninety per cent who are supposed to be doing productive jobs. That is to say, they have no opportunity to learn things that really matter to them, things that have any bearing upon the jobs that they will later do. If they go to school which, thank God, many of them do not, they are forced to study subjects in which they are the least interested, subjects for which they have no use at all; for they are taught the same subjects prescribed for the future white-collared workers. That is to say, the system completely ignores the needs of ninety per cent of our working people, people who are the real producers of wealth, and who, by their labour, supply the life-blood of our economy. What can be more atrocious than this? But this is what has been going on for centuries now. It is, unfortunately, going on even now when we have declared from the housetops that ours is a democratic society committed to giving equal opportunities to all. What opportunities have we given to our working people to improve their skills? They are intelligent, ready to pick up new ideas, and they are as patriotic as anybody else. Given the right kind of education, they can compare with the workers of the most advanced countries. But they have been systematically neglected and they are still being neglected. The present educational system has nothing to offer which is specifically meant for them, that is, which will fit them for a particular job. As a result, they swell the ranks of the unskilled workers whom nobody wants. But whose fault is this? And, whose fault is it that so much human material is not put to productive use for the benefit of the economy, but is allowed to languish and become a dead weight hindering its progress?

The only remedy lies in scrapping the present system of education and replacing it by something more logical, that is something that takes due account of the needs of this ninety per cent of the workers of the country. I think we ought to have a system which will be work-oriented, that is, a system which will train a student as a skilled worker. Under this system every child while attending school will be involved in some kind of productive activity. He should study, but he should spend more time over his work, and even the books he reads should be books related to the work in which he is being trained. It may be work in a field or in a factory, but let him be trained in a meaningful way, that is, in a way that he may acquire real skill in it, so that, if he so wishes, he may later earn his bread by doing that work.

THEORY WITHOUT PRACTICE

We must remember that there is a great dearth of skilled workers in this country. Both agriculture and industry need a large body of trained personnel. We have capable planners, supervisors, and administrators, but our workers, though otherwise intelligent and capable, lack the know-how necessary for efficient work. The foundation for this must be laid at school. There are some areas in West Bengal where students miss school for a whole month or more in order to help their parents in the agricultural fields. This should be the pattern for the whole country and it should be made compulsory. When it is time to sow or time to harvest, the whole student-population should be in the field, lending a hand in the operation and, in the process, acquiring invaluable knowledge and experience. It will not do, however, to get the students involved in such work only once or twice a year. This should be a regular feature of their curriculum and it should continue throughout the year in some form or other. Students should divide their time between study and work, but the accent should be on work; it should be productive work and also work chosen intelligently. It should be such that the students have the feeling they are doing something useful, something that will stand them in good stead in later life when they choose a career for themselves.

Attempts are made even now to give the curriculum a vocational bias. But the way this is done is half-hearted and serves no purpose. May be, we make them spend some time every week doing carpentry or tailoring or smithy or agriculture. It is fun to them, and they spend the time idly, learning nothing. We have now what are known as multipurpose schools with diversified courses like agriculture, technology, commerce, and so on. These schools began with much fanfare and raised hopes of providing an answer to the nagging question of saving education from being too generalised. In a few years time, however, the entire multipurpose scheme has proved to be a costly hoax. The idea of involving the students in practical work has been watered down to the extent that it has become merely eye-wash. The students specialise in agriculture or technology without handling machines or tools or doing any practical work. It is enough if they learn some back-dated theories from classroom lectures given by teachers whose own knowledge and experience are of doubtful validity.

We have had ambitious Plans over the last twenty years and have also poured crores of rupees into those Plans. For a poor country like India, this is a tremendous drain on its resources. But the question is: What impact have those Plans made on the economy of the country? Very little, indeed. The reason is that our strategies are entirely wrong. To fight the food shortage we have started a number of agricultural universities. Those universities turn out graduates whose utility is dubious, for they, too, are fit only for white-collared jobs, and for nothing else. At these universities they learn a lot of theory but no practice. The syllabus they study is such that they do not have to do much field-work; it is enough if they learn the theories. And, what sort of theories? Theories that are old and outdated perhaps. Can you solve the problem of food shortage with this kind of agricultural education? The same remark applies in the case of engineering education also. To help carry out industrial expansion programmes, we have started many engineering colleges over the past twenty years. We are turning out thousands of engineering graduates every year. But what sort of graduates are they? A good industry would hesitate to employ them because their knowledge is shoddy and they have no practical experience.

I am not saying that we do not need agricultural or engineering graduates. We certainly need them, but we do not need as many as we are turning out, and also they are not the type of graduates we need. We need people who have direct experience of the work, and not people whose education has remained confined within classrooms. It is not the fault of these young people; it is the fault of the system which gave them no incentive for practical work. What is the result? The result is that while these young men are good at desk-work, they are worthless when it comes to doing things with their own hands. Knowing their shortcomings, they shy away from situations in which they may be required to demonstrate their practical skills. If there is a breakdown of a machine, they would not like to put their hands to it to set it right, lest their ignorance about it be found out. Similarly, if there is something wrong with a crop in a field, our graduates will try to avoid going into the field, for they know people around will then find out how little they know about agriculture.

In contrast, take the case of Dr Norman Borlaug, the man who has created varieties of 'miracle' seed-grains. When the news of his having been awarded the Nobel Prize was broken to him, he was in the midst of an inspection of a wheat-field. The news took him by surprise, but he did not let it interrupt his work. He said, 'Well, that's great. But we've work to do now. We'll celebrate later.' This man is called the 'Maker of the Green Revolution'. He has saved the world from hunger and famine. A great scientist, a great innovator, he thinks nothing of working with his own hands. He is, in fact, always in the field. His sleeves rolled up, he stands surrounded by his research assistants and farmers; all barriers are down between him and the fieldworkers. Such a thing is inconceivable in India. Here, the scientist holds himself aloof, either by choice or by reason of the circumstances in which he has been trained.

Here again, I would blame our education. It is basically so feudal that apart from the fact that it teaches a man nothing worthwhile, it leaves him with a false sense of vanity. For instance, he acquires distaste for manual work and he thinks that those who do manual work are an inferior genre of people. This happens because as a student he was never required to do any manual work. He might have come from a working family himself but, thanks to the pernicious influence of the system, he managed to stay away from manual work and eventually developed distaste for it. What can be more disastrous than this?

We often wonder why our Plans have not succeeded to the extent their authors hoped they would. What is wrong? We ask. One reason is that we have neglected training our workers although they are the kingpin of our production machinery. How can we expect our production curve to go up when our workers know nothing about modern techniques? We have sophisticated training programmes for our engineers, but no programme for bringing the knowledge and skill of our workers up-to-date. This might have been mitigated somewhat if our engineers and scientists had some point of contact with the workers. Unfortunately, the gulf between them remains unbridged. Our set-up is such that they must remain apart.

There is yet another factor: no mechanism has yet been evolved in India by which the fruits of research can be channelled to the workers at grass-roots level. India has made good progress in research, but either her research is too theoretical, that is, without any relation to the real problems of industry and agriculture, or the real producers get no benefit from it. As a result, the production techniques remain as outdated as ever and the workers go on labouring at their jobs frustratingly.

SOME SUGGESTED CHANGES

How can you expect any development in a country when this is the state of its education? Our salvation lies in turning the whole system upside down. Students should be drawn more and more into nation-building work and if this involves progressive withdrawal from the academic field, there is no harm in it. In fact, there is no harm even if students take a year or two off and spend the time doing productive work. When war breaks out, students above eighteen are compulsorily drafted into military service. This is justified in the interests of national security. Why should we not take some such drastic step when the national economy is in danger? To begin with, we should ban higher education except for those who are really brilliant and whose work performance at different levels has been satisfactory. At no time, however, should their number exceed ten per cent of the total student population. They, too, should not be exempted from work, however. They should do their quota of work, though in their case the work should be of the nature of a research programme. For the rest of the students, the terminal point should be at the school level. And, for them education should mean more work than study, for they are the people who would form the bulk of the vast army of skilled workers that the country needs. Among the subjects they should study, top priority should be given to science and technology for, as skilled workers, some knowledge of science and technology is essential for them. Also, the common man in India knows little of science and technology, which is a great drawback from the standpoint of the Plans and their execution. Every child, whether at the primary or secondary level, should be taught science and technology. This should be taught not in abstraction, but as a prerequisite to the work programme in which he is going to be involved.

Finally, I suggest that planning and education be brought closer to each other. That is to say, the nature and content of education at all levels should conform strictly to Plan requirements. If according to the Plan it appears that there are more engineers than the country needs, the annual intake of students in the engineering colleges should immediately be curtailed. Similarly, if it appears that personnel of a particular category are in short supply and their number should be increased, arrangements for an increased turn out of such personnel should immediately be made. At present, admission to various categories of institutions is unplanned and uncontrolled. A system should be introduced which will take into account the personnel requirements of the various development programmes. The students should be directed to appropriate courses of studies so that there is no possibility of any programme suffering from a shortage of technically qualified men, or of anybody being left without a job after completing his course of study. Educators and those who create the Plans should act in concert with each other to ensure this.

Then, a word about the quality of India's human material. Nothing is wrong with her human material, for her people are as good as any in the world. All that needs to be done is to fashion them into a powerful force for growth and development. Because they have been neglected, they have become a dead weight. Planners may have fine ideas, but they do not touch the minds of the people. There is, in fact, no communication between the planners and the people. Education has to fill the gap between the two. The underlying message of the Plans must permeate the entire educational system so that the smallest child at the primary level may feel its impact. People must feel that it is their plan and that their future prosperity is intertwined with it. Then they will not hesitate to make any sacrifice necessary for the success of the Plan. It is education alone that can make the people understand the basic purpose of the Plan and the responsibilities they have to share in its successful execution. Let our education be geared to accept this twofold challenge—first, to make our people understand what a terrible shame this poverty of the country is, and, secondly, to give them the know-how and determination to fight it.

MOTIVATION FOR EDUCATION

Now, we come to the question of the motives behind education. I raise this question because I have noticed that most people are not clear in their minds as to why they send their children to school. If you ask them, they will probably fumble for an answer. The reason is that they have never given any thought to it. They accept it as the norm and if some do not send their children to school, that is something unusual. Some send their children to school because they think that as parents it is their duty to do so. Some also make much sacrifice to do so. I know there are parents who literally starve in order to see that their children receive a good education. What is it that motivates them to do this? What do they expect to gain by sending their children to school? Curiously enough, they are not able to give a cogent answer. At the most they will say, 'Why, I want my child to learn; I want him to have a good education.' The teacher may then say, 'Will you please, be precise? Can you tell me what it is that you want your child to learn? You say you want him to have a good education, but please, explain what exactly is a "good education" according to you?' When pressed like this, they are at a loss to know what to say in reply. Some of them may say, if they say anything at all, 'I want the child to learn everything—everything that is good and useful—everything that the school thinks is good for him to learn. I leave it to the school authorities to decide. They know better than I do. All I know is that I wish to see my child become a real 'man.'

Here again, the parents are vague when they say that they want to see their children become true 'men'. If anyone asks them, 'What do you mean when you say true men? What is your idea of a true man?' Many of them will candidly say they do not know. They want their children to have a good education and be true men, and that is that. Some will probably take umbrage when they are asked such searching questions. The fact remains that most parents just have no idea what in particular they want to see happen to their children when they send them to school. They expect some improvement in the children but they are not able to define that improvement in concrete terms. They have a vague hope that the children will distinguish themselves in many fields. They will probably earn a lot of money, occupy a high social position, and achieve much fame. All this may be quite legitimate for parents to wish for their children, but the question is: Can education guarantee these things or has education anything to do with them? For instance, what connexion is there between education and being rich? There are many people in India and elsewhere who had very little education, and yet became enormously rich. The richest men on earth are not necessarily the most educated; in fact, it is rather the other way round, for they are often the least educated. In any case, to be rich, one need not be very educated. Education brings many advantages but it cannot be said that money is one of them.

The next expectation of the parents may be that their children should be influential members of society and occupy an important position. But there is no guarantee for that, either. An educated man is not necessarily a man prominent in society. As to influence, he may have none except the little he may have on those who are very close to him, and they may be very few. In society today, power means political power. Any other power is of marginal importance and has no practical value. Education does not produce political power, either. It is possible to cite examples of men and women who acquired enormous political power in their countries without the advantage of any worthwhile education. What about Stalin? He wielded more power than any other potentate known to history but he was by no means a highly educated person. There were many around him in Soviet Russia in his time. They were head and shoulders above him regarding education but they were completely overshadowed by him.

THE IMPACT OF EDUCATION

It means, then, that the improvement which, education brings about in a child is unidentifiable? It is not exactly that. It is identifiable, only it often escapes our notice or, at any rate, we tend to ignore it. We are so much enamoured of money, power, social status, and similar such visible signs of worldly success that we tend to underestimate, even completely overlook, the importance of the happy transformation which education brings about or is expected to bring about in the personality of a child. It is like the dew-drop which gives life to the seed while its work remains unnoticed. Education gives new dimensions to a child's life, and it may bring about a complete change in his character and outlook, but it is not likely to be noticed immediately. It may or may not bring about worldly success, but that is not the criterion. Worldly success may be desirable, but it does not necessarily depend upon education. A highly educated man may even spurn what usually passes as worldly success. For instance, he may not care for money at all. If he has the minimum money he needs, he is satisfied. He will not ask for more, for he thinks it a hindrance. Similarly, he may not care for high social status. People may love him, adore him, but he is not interested in that. He prefers to be left to himself as far as possible. He wishes to live his life in peace without any interference from others. As regards power, political or otherwise, he may even think it vulgar, and will of course never have anything to do with it. He does not want to dominate over others, just as he does not want others to dominate over him. He respects others and he wants others to respect him. He loves his own freedom and he wants others to enjoy their freedom.

It is, therefore, not possible to judge an educated man by the usual yardstick of social status or political power. These may completely elude him or he may shun them even if they are at his command, for, in his scale of values they are not at all important. An idea may be more important to him. He may try to build his life around that idea or around a group of ideas. He is happy when he is able to make those ideas a reality. To him, that is the highest achievement.

Then, the question comes, is education scholarship? If scholarship means the collection of facts, that is, information, as it is called in common parlance, then education is not scholarship. A scholar may go on piling up facts, but if he cannot use them for his own good and for the good of others, he is then merely a data recorder, a file, a dossier. There may be people who are well informed, who have read many books, and know many facts. Parrot-like they can quote what different people have said on different subjects. The mass of information they have accumulated in their brains may be amazing but it may be equally amazing that they are not any the wiser or better for having that information. They carry the information as a beast of burden carries a bag of sugar on its back. Such a man has the information all nicely catalogued and docketed in his brain, but does not know how to use it to his advantage or to the advantage of others. It is all lying there in his brain like a huge pile of junk, most of it old and perhaps useless. The facts he has collected in his mind are unrelated to one another and he cannot piece them together to form a system that may have some meaning. What are all these facts for, if they do not carry a warning or a lesson for our guidance? Why do we study history unless we can learn from it how to guide our future course of life? Swami Vivekananda used to decry the tendency to equate information with education. He would say that, if education were information, then the libraries would be the greatest sages in the world, and encyclopedias, the rishis.

THE GOALS OF EDUCATION

What is education, then? What exactly do we want it to do to our children when we send them to school? What particular transformation do we wish to see in our children, as a result of the education they receive? What motivates us to make the sacrifice that we often make in terms of money and in other ways to have them educated?

Education is many things but, first and foremost, it is preparing a child to face the challenge of life. For this, he must first learn a trade so that he may be economically independent. Look at this question from the standpoint of a poor farmer. What does he expect when he sends his boy to school? He may not be able to state clearly and logically what he wants, but there is no doubt that he wants his son to acquire some knowledge and skill so that he will have no difficulty in earning enough money for himself and for the family. It may be, the poor man never went to school himself or, if he did, he did not stay on long enough to learn some trade or something really worth while that would help him earn money. He perhaps laboured under many handicaps, and now he does not wish his son to face those handicaps. He wishes to see him start from a better vantage-ground and with better tools. He wants him to succeed where he himself failed. This, perhaps, gives him vicarious satisfaction, but he wants his son to be miles ahead of him—in skill, in money, in social status, in every respect. This may be a weakness but it is a weakness of which man is not, and need not be, ashamed. There is a Sanskrit saying to the effect that man wants to win everywhere, but where his child or his student is concerned, he wants to lose. This is very true. Man alone among all living beings tries to pass on his knowledge, skill, and experience to his children. The organised attempt to do this is what is called education; but the process is dynamic.

Each generation tries to improve the skill, knowledge, and experience it inherits from the previous one. This is how civilisation has progressed from the cave-man to the space-man. It is the business of education to boost the tempo of this progress. But whatever the role of education is in terms of humanity as a whole, its role in terms of individuals should be clear, specific, and precise. Education in many cases fails because its goals are vague and undefined and aimless. A poor father stakes his all to give his son a good education; the son also spends all his energy trying to learn something useful. In the end, however, it may appear that the boy has learnt nothing that can help him, materially or otherwise.

To stop this aimless drift, courses of studies should be carefully selected so as to fit each child for the career best suited for him. Now that education is being democratised and more and more first-generation students are finding their way into schools and colleges, the utmost care should be taken to make education purposeful in order to avoid undue waste. The farmer, the carpenter, the cobbler, the mason, the blacksmith, or the daily-labourer—whenever such people send their children to school they have every right to expect that their children will acquire some skill and knowledge, that they will be fitted for a particular trade or career, that they will earn money enough for themselves and for their families, and that they will also have social status of some sort. This is a modest but a very legitimate expectation and it will be a pity if education cannot guarantee this. When this has been assured, a child may look for other gains, gains less tangible perhaps, but equally vital and important, perhaps even more so. These are gains relating to the mind and the intellect. The old saying that man cannot live by bread alone still holds good. Education, to be effective, must be all-embracing. It must feed not only the body but also the mind—in fact, the entire human personality.

Education means not only education in skills which are physical but also education in thoughts, ideas, outlook, and attitudes. A child must be taught the right kind of thoughts and atitudes. Here, the question may be raised if this is not interference. Can or should a teacher impose his own ideas and views on a child because he thinks they are good and right? The question of a teacher's role in the education and upbringing of a child has been debated for ages. Some have contended that a child is self-taught and all that a teacher needs to do is to surround him with his protective care. The child is like a plant which grows according to its own potentiality, and the teacher, whose function is like that of a gardener, gives him all the care necessary to help him grow as best he can. He cannot superimpose anything on him; he can only draw out that which is already in him. Perhaps this theory is overstretched. The teacher certainly cannot stand by and watch when the child is struggling; he should play a positive role to help ease his difficulties. The child has both good and bad points. Should not the teacher try to bolster up those good points and help smother the bad ones? One of the ways he can do it—and this is the best—is to expose him to good and noble thoughts. Under the influence of those thoughts, the good points in the child grow stronger and the bad points weaker, till the latter completely wither away. A good teacher does not give his student a list of 'do's' and 'do nots'; quietly and unobtrusively, he helps him choose the right course and reject the wrong one.

Discipline is best when it is self-imposed. A child must increase his inner strength to protect himself from evil. The task of the teacher is to help the child develop this inner strength. He helps him do this by feeding his mind with good and positive thoughts. He never utters a word of discouragement even if the child errs; there is nothing but encouragement from him.

The best example of what a teacher should be like was Sri Ramakrishna who never adopted strait-jacket methods in teaching his disciples. He let each disciple follow his natural bent of mind, for he knew that each individual was unique. If a disciple tried to imitate others, he would discourage. He would much rather have him commit blunders following his natural inclination than be right by imitating others. He knew one could not go against one's own nature for long. The inherent nature of man must assert itself sooner or later.

Another characteristic of Sri Ramakrishna was that he never lectured anybody; gently, with understanding and affection, he would guide the steps of his disciples so that they might grow to their fullness, to the limit of their capacities.

It is said that there is no limit to a child's growth and development. He is born with infinite potentiality and the business of education is to help him realise that potentiality. His growth should be all-embracing, not merely physical or intellectual. He should be a full-fledged man, a man of character, a 'man' in the true sense of the term. Parents may not be able to say what they mean when they say they want to see their children become true 'men', but they are certainly right in expecting that this would be the ultimate consummation of the educative process through which they see their children passing. It may not, of course, happen just at the end of the school period, and school is not the only place where children learn. Children perhaps learn more from family situations, from their contacts with others. Also, the learning process covers the entire life-span of a child. All men and women are, in fact, learners. But what does the school do?

School sharpens the tools by which one is to learn—it sharpens the tools of thinking, reasoning, understanding, moral sense, tools of self-discipline. It also tells the child that his goal is perfection and he should never stop before reaching it. It creates in him the urge to push on through difficulties, to scale heights of moral excellence, to aspire to the best, highest, and noblest.

Parents send their children to school not hoping for an easy miracle, but to see their children equipped to struggle for this fulfillment, not by anybody's mercy, but by their own strength.

THE STRATEGY FOR INTEGRATED EDUCATION

Let us now go deeper into the question of integrated education and the strategy for integrated education.

This subject is important because it is not known to many that education invariably means 'integrated' education, that is, education that cares for the child as a whole. Education is not merely passing an examination or having a degree; education is not even the same as intellectual development though that is a necessary concomitant of education. To be effective education must improve the entire personality of the child; in must help all his components to grow and develop simultaneously. A child needs his brains but he also needs his hands. And, what about his heart? What sort of a man would he be if he did not have any feeling for others? It is, therefore, necessary that head, hands, and heart—all these should develop equally in a child. It is the business of education to ensure this. If it does not, it is incomplete and it may even defeat itself. By integrated education I mean education of the total child.

I have emphasised the importance of teaching trades to children. I said this should be done in order that they might later have no difficulty gaining economic independence. But trades should be taught not for economic reasons only, but also for developing their intelligence. There is a saying that 'intelligence is not only in the brains but also in the hands.' Manual work is now considered an essential part of education in all advanced countries. The child enjoys doing things with his own hands; he especially likes doing creative work. The more he is involved in such work, the more adept he becomes in the use of his hands and his senses. The skill he thus acquires helps to develop his personality and character, apart from the fact that it may prove immensely useful to him in later life.

In Soviet Russia, the school curriculum insists that every child learn how to handle tools and machines. This has been going on for decades. As a result of this, technical education has now attained a much higher level in Russia than anywhere else. The breathtaking advance that Russian technology has made is also attributed to this. In Western countries, every school has a workshop where students spend some time daily working with tools and machines. Even many homes have a workshop for the use of their children. The poorest child wants toys to play with because he wants to feel that he is an adult. Such play is not only a psychological necessity; it is also a physical necessity because it is an outlet for his surplus energy. If he does not get this outlet, he may suffer mentally as well as physically. But a child's manual work may be planned in such a way that while satisfying his physical and psychological needs, it may leave him with a skill which he may later use, for better purposes. In any case, the idea behind manual work is to keep the child busy with activities so planned that his physical growth may proceed unimpeded and his senses and faculties may grow sharper.

In this connection, a word about physical education may not be out of place. It is now universally recognised that games and sports occupy an important place in a child's education. Scientific studies have revealed that they help a child acquire a healthy and well-balanced personality. A good sportsman is socially always a better adjusted person. He has no difficulty getting along with people, but a child who keeps away from sports and games is often suspicious and distrustful of others. He is prone to misunderstand and be misunderstood. Good physical conditions induce self-confidence and courage. A healthy young man is always 'a good sport', a great social success. Some of you will remember the importance Swami Vivekananda attached to good health. He called upon young men to try to acquire 'muscles of iron and nerves of steel'. He even said that heaven might be reached quicker by playing football than by reading the Bhagavad Gita. Quoting the Upanishads he used to say, *Nayamatma balahinena labhyah,* the Self cannot be attained by the weak. He knew that although one might have good brains, unless one is physically strong too, one's chances of success are remote. He also knew that to conceive noble thoughts and ideas, one needed to be bold and strong. That is why he laid so much stress on physical strength. In ancient Sparta, physical fitness was considered the primary object of education. Today, in all advanced countries, physical education forms an essential part of the school programme. Soviet Russia spends huge sums to promote physical education among the youth. Even the Indian government has lately awakened to its importance. Youth welfare is now an important branch of the Ministry of Education. Sports and games are no longer 'extracurricular' activities in India, they now come under the category of co-curricular activities.

THE NEED TO SEE MAN AS PART OF NATURE

As part of his physical education programme, a child should study the environment around him. He should study the sky, the trees and plants, the rivers, forests, hills and fields, the birds, animals, insects, and people that form part of the physical world in which he lives. He should be made to understand that he belongs to this world and anything that happens to this world affects him too. As time passes, it is being increasingly realised that man is greatly influenced by the environment in which he lives. It is, therefore, desirable that he should be thoroughly acquainted with it. This acquaintance should be made not merely through books, but, as far as possible, through first-hand study. Nature study is nowadays an important part of the school curriculum, but it is not carried out in the manner it should be. For instance, the idea behind such study should not merely be the collection of data, as is the case now, but to help the child's senses develop, and train him to study, observe, and appreciate whatever is there around him. He should be able to do so independently, not at others' prompting; there must, in fact, be communion between him and the world around, which is possible when there is no intervention by others.

There is so much beauty around us, there is so much drama going on all the time around us which carries much meaning, but it often does not register with us. This is because we have not been trained to appreciate it. Is it not a shame? Are we not losers because of this? Bird-watching has become a passion with some of us in this generation, but why should we confine our interest to birds? Why not extend it to other objects of nature as well? For instance, how is it that we do not get excited when we see the wind passing through a tree? Does it not strike us as an interesting phenomenon—the way in which the tree, with its leaves, responds to the touch of the wind? Do we not think it a highly rewarding experience to see the first monsoon clouds majestically sailing across the sky? How can we help noticing with a gasp when the first rays of the morning sun kiss the snowy peaks of Kanchanjanga in Darjeeling? There is so much beauty, so much mystery so much purity, and, at the same time, so much meaning in all that we see around us. If we miss all this, we miss much that lends zest to life. Life becomes drudgery if we are not able to feel the thrill of nature or to love and commune with her.

LEARNING TO THINK

I wish to discuss now the real implication of what is called intellectual development. In this country, the hallmark of education is a degree or a certificate. But what has education to do with the degree or the certificate? Some of you may remember that when Maulana Azad was the Education Minister, he proposed that all academic degrees and certificates be abolished. He, probably, felt that if the system of giving certificates and degrees were abolished, people would then be able to concentrate on learning rather than running after degrees and certificates. He did not succeed, of course, for the infatuation for certificates and degrees was such that people rejected the idea. However that may be, the point I want to make here is that even learning is not enough. It is a useful by-product of education, but it is not the same as education, not even the same as intellectual development. That is to say a learned man is not necessarily an intellectual man. He may have read much and amassed a vast amount of knowledge, yet he may be a person with a low intellectual level. Referring to a certain individual, Bernard Shaw once made the comment, 'He is an intellectual fool' by which he meant that, the man was a person who had the appearance of being an intellectual because he had read much and learnt much, but was, nevertheless, only a fool. Book-learning may be a cover behind which lies hidden much intellectual inadequacy. People's weakness for the printed word is proverbial. To underscore this fact, Sri Ramakrishna once made the sarcastic remark that if a man said that he had witnessed the crashing of a house, people would not believe that the house had crashed unless a report about it appeared in the newspaper. This sort of blind faith in the printed word or, for that matter, in book-learning, is evidence of people's confusion about the meaning of what is called intellect.

A really intellectual person may or may not be a scholar, but his judgement is his own. He is an independent person who thinks, argues, weighs the pros and cons, and then decides. He will give a respectful hearing to the opinions of others, but when he decides, he decides according to his own lights. Take the case of Akbar. He was illiterate, but few were his match where intellectual powers were concerned. His sound commonsense, his insight, his shrewdness, his objectivity, his ability to penetrate into the heart of a problem, his courage and self-confidence in the face of a crisis—all these were proof of the extraordinary intellect he possessed. He often had scholars coming to his court to debate philosophical questions. Akbar never had any difficulty in following their polemics. He often joined these scholars and made useful contribution to their discussions. This was possible because, with his intellect, he could immediately go to the heart of the issue, in spite of the verbiage with which the scholars often tended to cloud it. He often made comments which were models of clarity and soundness, and which turned out to be right.

A more recent example of the intellect's superiority over scholarship may be found in Sri Ramakrishna. He, too, was no scholar, yet intellectually he was superior to those who were recognised as scholars in his time. Scholars often visited him and tried to engage him in controversy, but they always come off worst. What was interesting was the way he countered their arguments. He did not have the weight of scholarship behind him, but because his intellects gave him an insight which his rivals lacked he was able to tear their ponderous arguments into shreds. The tribute, Pratap Chandra Majumdar, the Brahmo leader, paid him is significant. He said he had heard great orators like Burke and Disraeli, but none had impressed him as much as Sri Ramakrishna.

What I am trying to stress is that a scholar is not necessarily an intellectual person. I am also trying to point out that the concern of education should be to help a child develop his intellect and not merely make him read a vast number of books. Teach him to think, to argue, to judge; let him use his own talents, let him be himself and not try to be somebody else. We often hear of young people being carried away by some new-fangled thought or ideal or, 'ism'. This so much possesses them that they think nothing of discarding their own cherished heritage. In their enthusiasm for the new credo, they throw to the winds all canons of civilised conduct and act like a mob of gangsters. They destroy life and property; there is no crime at which they will stop. This kind of youth revolt is now a global phenomenon, but if you ask the young people why they behave in the way they do, they do not know. They may want to destroy the present social order which they think is wrong, but they do not know what sort of social order will be a better substitute for it. They act thoughtlessly, without calculating the consequences of what they are doing. One can understand if they revolt knowing why they are revolting, but the wonder of wonders is that they revolt without even knowing why they are doing so.

But why do young people behave in this way? The main reason is that under the present educational system, they are not taught to think. They read much, but they do not think much, in fact, the system is such that they are not required to think much, or even think at all. They are certainly not required to think independently. Because they read much, they often read indiscriminately, that is, they read matter which is not good or healthy. It is not the amount of reading done that is important, but the quality of what is read and how much of it is assimilated. Reading is helpful to the extent that it brings one in touch with new thoughts or ideas, but this is not to say that one should accept them blindly. The basic purpose of education should be to train a young man to think for himself, to think coolly and logically, to think without being hamstrung by any external influence. An ideology may attract him but he must not run after it without examining it in all its aspects. He must not act impulsively; he must act deliberately, after weighing everything. He must have the courage to act independently, even if this means acting against current public opinion or against heavy odds.

Swami Vivekananda once said that if he had his way he would make students practise medication. What did he mean by this? He meant that a student must first be taught to discipline his mind. According to Bhagavad Gita, the mind is as restless as the wind. If the mind is not controlled, then any mental exercise that one may make may lead to frustration, may even bring harm. The amount of mischief uncontrolled minds can do is well illustrated by the so-called youth revolt to which I have already referred.

While talking about the need for mental discipline, I want to refer the important role emotions play in the life of a child. It is now a well-known fact that an emotionally disturbed child is not only unhappy himself he may also be the cause of unhappiness for all around him. A child coming from a broken home tends to become anti-social. It is slowly dawning on the educators that there must be ample provision in the school programme to meet the emotional requirements of the child. Of course, home is the place where the emotional life of the child is best taken care of, but the home situation in industrial societies being what it is today, school has to play its part as best it can. While helping the child to enjoy a sound emotional life, school must also teach him self-restraint. No one can have everything he wants. He has to call a halt to his desires at one point or another. The sooner this is impressed on the child the better. It is natural and legitimate to hope and to aspire, but it is also necessary to know that there is a limit to one's hopes and aspirations. One must not ask for too much. It is also necessary to tell the child that if he is unhappy he may try to remove the cause of his unhappiness but he has no right to inflict unhappiness on others. In trying to give the child a happy emotional life care must be taken that he does not become too demanding, fall into the habit of day-dreaming, or become egocentric. He must learn to feel for others, to share others' sorrow, to be benevolent and compassionate. Intellectualism may be good but if it is not accompanied by the qualities of the heart, it is arid and useless and may even be an instrument of exploitation. The man with a lot of brains but no heart is dangerous.

EDUCATION AND SOCIETY

It must be remembered that education has a social purpose to fulfil. It is not enough if it turns out good individuals, it must make for a good society also. The quality of a community is determined by the quality of its education. The test of good education is how far it makes an individual socially aware. Does it make the individual feel that he owes duties and obligations to society? If he does not feel it, then education has failed in his case. Swami Vivekananda laid much stress on this social awareness. He used to say if an educated man did not care for his uneducated brothers and sisters, then he was a cheat. He wanted every young man to feel that he was committed to the service of others. This applied especially in the case of those who were educated. Because they were educated, they had special duties and obligations to their fellow men. If they shirked those duties, they were guilty of a social crime.

This sense of fellowship is nowadays sought to be fostered in the child by devising special programmes which will make him conscious of his obligations to others. For instance, if there is a calamity in any part of the world, children are asked to contribute to provide relief to the distressed people. It does not matter where the calamity occurs or who are its victims. Children are asked to feel as if they themselves have been hit by the calamity. This always evokes an excellent response from the children. They raise money by going without candies for several days, and they send the money to the children in the affected area. It will be wrong to think that this happens only in the West. I can testify that this happens also in our country. I know of institutions in West Bengal where students go without their only piece of fish each day for several weeks to help their fellow men.

But this sort of fellowship is not to be reserved only for special occasions; it should become a normal feature of the child's nature. It should be the aim of education to widen the mental horizons of the child. His sympathies should include not only his own community but the entire human race. This cannot happen overnight but can happen only after years of training so that it becomes a way of life. The idea that man is essentially one has to be made the basis of all future relationships. Modern societies are mostly multi-racial and the only way to keep them together is by promoting this sense of oneness. Sometimes, parents and teachers inject racial and other prejudices into a child's mind. It is not entirely their fault, because they themselves have had such prejudices injected into their minds by others. The world has seen much human suffering as a result of these prejudices. It is, however, now realised that in most cases these prejudices have no basis in fact, but are due to ignorance and misunderstanding. If children of different racial groups live and work together, they can then see the points of unity that exist between them. They can also see how superficial the differences that divide them from others are. It is not that those differences are to be eliminated. The differences are bound to continue, but the child should be taught to accept those differences as part of life. At home as well as at school, he should see democracy in practice. He should see that give and take is the keynote of life. What he does not give to others he cannot demand for himself. He can have freedom for himself provided he is prepared to give freedom to others. Today, the world needs new elite of men and women who are perfectly at home wherever they may be, people who are the real world citizens. The educational structure should be so oriented as to make this possible.

VALUES

I have so long talked about skills and attitudes. I have tried to show how education should concern itself with the task of imparting useful skills and healthy attitudes. But what about the values? Is it not part of the work of education to see that the child is thoroughly acquainted with the values which man cherishes as his most precious treasure? Suppose, there is no attempt made by teachers and parents to teach the child what is right and what is wrong, is it not likely that he will then go drifting in an uncharted sea? Is it fair to deny him the benefit of the experience of his ancestors over the centuries? The most likely result of such denial will be that while the child will be intelligent and efficient in work, he will perhaps be without any morals. Can any society survive long when most of its members are corrupt? How would we like the idea of an outstanding scientist or philosopher or writer being without morals? Is it not the very contradiction of education that an educated man should be an unscrupulous man, a man without any sense of right or wrong? What is the utility of education if it does not teach the principles of good moral conduct, honesty, love of truth, or self-restraint? If the goal of education is perfection, a child must first be taught to be honest. Honesty should be his first and last lesson. Speaking of evolution, Julian Huxley once said that man's evolution was not biological but psychological, ideological instead of physiological. In the last analysis, a man's success is to be measured not in terms of money, power, social status or the amount of knowledge he has acquired; it should be measured in terms of his moral virtues. Julian Huxley, again, said that man's most comprehensive aim was not mere survival, not mere numerical increase, increased control over the environment but a greater fulfilment, fuller realisation, of more possibilities by the human species collectively and more by its component members, individually. Call it religion or call it ethics or call it by whatever name you like, some sort of device has to be found by which man can learn what, in the words of Einstein, is 'the beauty of holiness', or what Swami Vivekananda described as being 'divine'.

Here, a question may arise: What is the driving force behind the educative process? What is it that will make the child say to himself, 'I want to progress, I want perfection, I want to combine knowledge with compassion, I want efficiency, but I want also moral excellence'? There must be something that will serve as a focal point of all his endeavours that will make him unify all his faculties in order that he may achieve a common purpose. The quest for truth is that common purpose. The ultimate goal of the whole process of education is—Truth.

Ideals and Methods of National Education

IN ANY PLAN OF NATIONAL RECONSTRUCTION, EDUCATION MUST occupy the first place. For, more than anything else, it is education that can solve a nation's problems.

It is clear, India, too, needs some such education: an education that will inspire her people, give them courage and strength, hope and joy, faith in themselves, and a readiness to face life with its many trials. And, it is clear, too, that it is only national education, i.e. education based on national ideals that can do that. At the moment, so many plans are being advocated for her regeneration. Some concern her industries, some her agriculture, some her social life. There are plans concerning her education, too. There is the famous Wardha scheme, for instance. There is the Sargent scheme, also. None of these plans is perhaps completely satisfying. But each represents a new outlook, a new approach; each has many commendable features and marks a definite advance. So far no plan has been finally accepted. Discussions are still going on, on the subject. The moment is, therefore, appropriate for a consideration of what may be regarded as the ideals of national education in India. It is good to be reminded of them again and again, lest in a hurry, in the confusion which controversies often create, we lose sight of those ideals and accept a wrong plan. More than a hundred years ago, Macaulay devised a plan for the education of Indian youth.

It was a plan far removed from the Indian ideals of education. It was a plan conceived in racial arrogance and in complete ignorance of Indian history. It is surprising that the plan was accepted at all. It is still more surprising that the plan has been allowed to continue for all these generations. The consequences that have followed from this have been, generally speaking, most pernicious. It has hindered the country's progress rather than help it. It has created new problems, new difficulties and has not solved the old ones. It has produced a new aristocracy of the educated, and has widened the gulf between them and the uneducated more than ever. The blunder was that the plan was not thoroughly examined before it was accepted. There was too much hurry, too much confusion. That it fell far short of the essential requirement, that it was divorced from the national ideals was not grasped. Such a blunder must not be committed again. No plan shall be accepted which is not in keeping with the national ideals, which is not informed with the best in the national traditions.

What are India's national ideals? From time immemorial, India's national ideals have been not political or commercial but spiritual. It is in spirituality that her genius has excelled most. To her the highest thing has been, and is even now, the attainment of spiritual excellence. To realise God—that is the ambition of every one of her children. Life to them is not for grabbing sense-pleasures. It is for realising God. And, everyone must strive to that end. True, the ideal is very high and not many are able to live up to it. Still it is there. There can be no compromise about it. The ideal must not be lowered. Even for the weak, for the most despicable, that is the ideal. It is for all. And, the surprising fact is no one disowns it. No one says he is not going to attain the ideal. Of course he will take time but ultimately he must attain it. He is not going to stop short of the final goal.

This is the fundamental ideal before India. For good or ill, it is there. It has been her cherished ideal for centuries. She lives for it and for it alone. It is the only thing that matters to her. She has suffered incredibly during the past ages. She has been plundered and robbed. She has been reviled and ridiculed. But through all the vicissitudes of life, she has stuck to the ideal. She has not given it up because she cannot. It is her life-blood. To give it up will be fatal to her. It will be fatal to the rest of the world, too. Was it a mistake for her to choose such an ideal? Maybe, it was. But it is too late now to give it up. It must remain the central thing in her life and all her life must be ordered and governed by it. There is no help for it. But was it a mistake for her to choose this ideal? There are people who will say, 'yes.' They think too much stress on spirituality has been India's undoing. For, according to them, it encourages men to run away from life, to neglect all its duties; and to look upon all mundane affairs of life with contempt. But the ideal, if correctly understood, does not do anything of the kind. It never encourages men to run away from life, for, according to it, life is an opportunity which must be properly utilised for spiritual progress and its duties are the means by which that progress can be attained. To Indians, therefore, the importance of life and its duties is all the greater. There can be no question of neglecting or despising them. In India, in fact, there is nothing one can neglect or despise. One can only transcend. There is, therefore, nothing wrong with the ideal. The wrong is with the Indians themselves, for they have not lived up to it. Let them begin a vigorous practice of the ideal. Then, the apathy which has seized the nation and is responsible for all its miseries, will go and there will be, a happier and rejuvenated India.

It may be asked: Is not this ideal of God-realisation irrelevant in this age? The world is not as it used to be once. It has changed very much during the past one century. And it is daily changing. Now, man has different needs, different aspirations. God-realisation is an ideal of inaction, of idle dreams, of vain pursuits. This cannot suit him any longer. He believes in action now. And, he wants realities—things he can possess and make use of. He cannot be content with dreams only. What use has he, therefore, for this sort of ideal? Is not the ideal altogether out of place in this age?

No, not at all. It is still relevant, still valid. It is more so now than ever before. It may be the world has changed. It may be, too, man has progressed in certain directions. But fundamentally, he remains the same. The real art of life he has not yet learnt. And he is as unhappy as ever. His power, his knowledge and his material possessions—all these have become a mockery to him. He does not know their right use. And, they are often causes of terrific carnages which he cannot stop. He is indeed a very pathetic figure. The fact is spiritually he has not progressed at all. He remains the same brute swayed by passions as centuries ago. To rectify this, he must make his spiritual progress square with his material progress. Here comes the necessity for the ideal of God-realisation. For, it is only by increasing devotion to this ideal that man can evolve into a finer and nobler spiritual being. There can be, therefore, no question but that the ideal is relevant.

II

From the earliest times, India has recognised two kinds of knowledge: *para* and *apara* (spiritual and secular). The former leads to God, to liberation; the latter to earthly enjoyments, to bondage. Obviously, one is higher than the other. All are enjoined to pursue spiritual knowledge, if possible. The qualifying clause—if possible—is to be noted. It is not intended that all must pursue spiritual knowledge, for that is not possible. It is recognised that the vast majority hanker after earthly enjoyments and they must have them. So, arrangements are made that they may have secular knowledge. In India, the most pleasing fact is that there is no attempt to force all to follow one common track. Instead, each man is allowed to have his way according to his inclinations. In fact, he is specifically told to follow his inclinations. It is his dharma and he must not go against it. So, most men and women receive secular knowledge. But they are told that sooner or later they must overcome their hankering after earthly enjoyments and seek God. For that is the ultimate ideal, and they must not lose sight of it. Again and again, they are reminded that earthly enjoyments give no real happiness, no peace. Only God-realisation can do that. So, even in the matter of secular knowledge, the ideal is kept in the forefront. The idea underlying education—in fact, every type of activity—is to lead man step by step towards God-realisation.

But how can secular knowledge be any help towards God-realisation? The answer is, by proper application. In India, the highest use that can be made of anything, material or spiritual, is to employ it in the service of fellow-beings. But service implies renunciation also. So, in India whatever man does, his object should be: service and renunciation. Here life has been from the beginning not competitive but cooperative. Each individual has deemed it his duty to serve his community and to sacrifice for its sake. Here, the king rules not for his own selfish ends but for the good of his subjects. He must use his power, his wealth, his everything in their service. He must not consider these his property. They are the property of his subjects and he is merely a trustee. Similarly, the subjects also should obey the king and respect and support him. Thus, between one man and another, between one social group and another, the relation is one of service and renunciation. The relation is not enforced by law or by the power of guns. It is not enforced at all. It is voluntarily entered into by all, for through such relationship only they are nearer their goal—the goal of God-realisation.

In secular knowledge also the object is: service and renunciation. You learn history, science, literature or whatever else it may be, so that you may be able to serve better, renounce more. If you do not employ your knowledge for the good of your community but for your selfish gains only, then, you are not doing your duty and you are moving away from God. But if you use your knowledge in the service of others and do so selflessly, then you are going nearer towards God.

But the most important thing to know is what education is. The Indian view of it is that it is a training, a discipline: a training which helps to unfold the full man, that brings out 'the perfection that is already in man.' It is, therefore, a training of the whole personality of man—his body, mind and soul. According to this view, nothing is got from outside. Everything is inside and it has got to be brought out. Its contrast with the present-day meaning of education is obvious. Today, education largely means book-learning. It means merely stuffing the mind with some third-rate information. It is a jumble of pickings from all manner of desirable and undesirable sources. There is no assimilation. There is no real change in the character. Almost no part of the human personality is affected by it except the intellect. Today, a so-called educated man may be found to be a knave, a man without any morals. What can be a greater condemnation of present-day education than this? This just shows that it fails to do even what is regarded as the primary function of education, e.g. character-building. We have now more education than ever before. Our depth as well as extent of knowledge is far greater than at any time in the past. Nevertheless, we have more dishonest men among us now than before. And, if statistics are taken, it may turn out that their number is larger among the educated than among the uneducated. It is all because education is lop-sided. Today it is considered enough education if a man has learnt a few things. To know a little bit of everything—that seems the hallmark of education. But mere knowledge is nothing. It must be backed by character. Too much stress on the intellect is a mistake. Of course, it is an important part of man. It must be nourished, must be strengthened. In the process of man's education-surely it plays a vital part. But it is not the whole of man. There are other parts equally important. They must have attention, too. Their neglect has resulted in the paradox of education without character.

In India, however, education has always meant character-building. Scholarship by itself has little value to the Indian mind. Its value comes if only it helps to transform character. Character—that is the first and last thing in Indian education. If education does not evolve a sound and healthy character, then it is no education. Because such a high premium is set on character in India, in the past the rule was that only men of exemplary character should be teachers. For it is through the influence of high characters that character is best formed. Today, however, any one who has obtained a few university degrees is qualified to teach. His character hardly counts. At the most, it is a secondary matter. But in ancient India it was insisted that the teacher must be a man of God-realisation or at least near about that. The rule that 'example is better than precept' was first practised in India. For, most of the teaching in ancient India was done through the personal example of the teacher. His life, his habits—all these moulded the character of the student. The student was constantly with the teacher and his influence was the most decisive factor in shaping him. He learned mostly through living contact with the teacher and not through the mechanical reading of books as at present. Now, there is hardly any contact between the teacher and the taught. And, the little contact that there is, is often marred by lack of sympathy, love and understanding on each side. Previously, the teacher was like father to the student. He would not only look after the intellectual and spiritual needs of the student. He would also feed and clothe him. The student, in his turn, would render personal service to the teacher and love and respect him as a son. The relation between them was absolutely cordial. And it would last to the end of their lives. Education can produce character where there are such teachers and their relation with their students is such.

As has already been said, India does not regard book-learning as education. She knows its limitations too well. Of course, she does not despise it. Surely, it has its use. For instance, it brings the mind in contact with new thoughts, new ideas. And, these thoughts and ideas suggest new lines of development for the character. But they do not avail unless the will is properly trained. The head may be seething with ideas. What good is it if there is no strength of will to translate them into practice? The will must play its part if the ideas are to become action, if they are to be assimilated to the character. So it is important to train the will. And, in India, it is considered the function of education to do that.

In ancient India, great stress was laid on concentration of the mind, for by concentration, the faculties of the mind are strengthened. And, learning becomes easier when that happens. Like concentration, several other practices were enjoined. The idea in each case was to discipline the body and the mind so that they could be used as helpful instruments. India believes there are infinite powers latent in man. These powers have to be awakened and made use of. And, it is the business of education to help in their awakening. But education as it is now does quite the contrary. It definitely thwarts the awakening of a child's latent powers. This is because the system is such that the child is forced to depend upon its teachers and books and to keep its own powers in abeyance. The idea seems to be that the child's education is impossible without their help. But this was not the view in ancient India. Teachers and books were never considered the primary thing. The primary thing was the child and its powers. So, from the beginning, care was taken that the child had plenty of opportunity to use its powers. This made education not only easy but also pleasant to it. And, this gave the child also self-confidence which is the first thing necessary in education as in life itself. The child never felt curbed and thwarted as it does now at every step. Now, there are such fine books and such good teachers. There are such novel appliances also to facilitate education. Nevertheless, the child learns mighty little. And, how it hates to learn! Never did a child feel so bored and tired in learning as it does now. The reason is, emphasis is put on the wrong thing. There is too much attention given to books and appliances whereas the child is almost ignored. This must be stopped. It is the child that should have most of the attention. And, that should be done not by checking it but giving it freedom and opportunity. It should be realised that the ideal condition is that in which the child educates itself, is its own teacher. That is what should be always aimed at. And, that becomes possible where there is not too much interference with the child and it is left free to use its own powers.

Nowadays, there is too much regimentation in education. A child has hardly any choice as to what it should learn or it should not. It is slave to a system which is unreasonable and cruel. It forces the child to learn things it hates to learn and does not allow it to learn what it longs to learn. But this is something foreign to the Indian idea of education. According to it, each individual should be given the option of his own subjects and allowed to concentrate on them. It does not believe in curbing his particular bent of mind. Instead, it believes in encouraging it, giving it full play. According to the Indian view true education must produce *shraddha,* faith in oneself—faith which would know no shaking despite a thousand failures. Such faith can do miracles. It can make a man do almost the impossible. At the root of all great achievements of man lies this faith. Backed by it man can show death-defying courage, superhuman endurance and an indomitable will. England has furnished an example of such faith in this war. Battered by enemy bombs night after night, suffering defeats in every theatre of war; subjected to incredible hardships for lack of amenities of life; distrusted and forsaken by friends and allies, she has stood alone facing the enemy, bold and determined, ready for further reverses of fortune but ready to strike back as well. Even in her darkest hour she did not lose faith in herself, did not doubt that she was going to win.

It is such faith that it should be the concern of education to produce. Judged by this standard, present-day education in India must be considered a failure. Far from producing such faith, it rather kills it, if there is any. Scores of thousands of youth come out of schools and colleges every year with so-called education. And what are they like? They are the poorest specimens of humanity. They are weak both physically and mentally; they are full of pompous ideas borrowed at third-hand, which they do not understand and much less practise; they learn to talk glibly, for to them that is the byword of scholarship and intelligence; they are heroic in their declarations but are nowhere to be seen when action is called for; they are loud in their declamations against old values and old traditions but are the first to cling to them when the time comes for them to choose new ones. They do not dare to look life in the face. Appalled by its difficulties they run away from it and taking shelter under all kinds of high-sounding 'isms' try to conceal their ignominious retreat.

The fact is present-day education, in its methods as well as contents, is too negative. It increases one's doubts and disbeliefs instead of helping to overcome them. Faith is possible when one is convinced of an ultimate which is permanent and unchangeable. And, God is the only such ultimate. But now education is Godless, even anti-God. The result is man does not know what to hold on to. At various stages of his education, he learns many new ideas and arguments. But man cannot be content with mere arguments and ideas. He wants a conviction. And, conviction means a sense of reality, a grasp of the real. God who is the only reality being expelled from present-day education, it cannot give this grasp of the real. The remedy is that God should be restored. Each student should be made conscious that there is a reality at the back of every phenomenon in this world and that reality is God Himself. Then only education will produce faith.

Another thing should be done: its methods should be improved. There is at present too much importance attached to textbooks and examinations. The student dreads them like a nightmare. And, in coping with them he makes himself a physical wreck and a moral coward. By all means this should be stopped. The tyranny of textbooks and examinations must end.

One other thing education should produce according to the Indian meaning of it: that is respect for man and everything concerning him. It will be seen how imperative this respect is for building up peace on sound lines. War and other anti-social activities will cease when there is this respect in every heart. In ancient India pupils were taught that man is essentially divine. This was not meant to be a matter for the mind to dwell upon in idle philosophical moments. This was a matter to be practised by everybody, every social group and in everyday life. But times have changed. Today, the idea has become obscure and few believe in it and fewer still practise it. This is not a little responsible for all the conflicts and clashes that have crowded into the national life today.

It may be asked: can all these ideals of education be practised today? In ancient India they were all right. But now conditions are different. For good or ill, the impact of the West has changed life altogether. Now life is much more complex than ever before. There are new problems, new duties and new demands. Can these be met by the old ideals and old methods of education? Does not the changed environment of the country require new ideals and new methods? Will it not be folly to cling to the old ones merely for the sake of sentiments? Moreover, there are many new ideas of education in the West. They have been tried and found very well. Why not adopt a few of them, too?

These are pertinent questions. But it is not true that the old ideals and methods have become useless. They all still hold good. However much the country may have changed, they still can be and must be applied. Of course, it is conceivable that they will require re-adjustment here and there to be more suitable to modern needs. Perhaps, in some cases, the centre of emphasis will have to be shifted. In others, perhaps, some details will have to be rejected. But that is all. Fundamentally, they remain as good as ever. Further, they are a sort of corollary to the ideals to which the nation stands committed. So, they cannot be changed. Also, their soundness still remains unchallenged. As man's knowledge of psychology is progressing, many new theories and new methods of education are taking shape. Surprisingly enough, many of them bear a close resemblance to these old theories and methods of India. It is possible that with further knowledge of psychology and with more experience, more and more evidence will be available of the soundness of the Indian theories and methods.

But this is not to say that India has nothing to learn from the West or must not learn even if such learning is to her advantage. Whatever else may be her fault, India is not conservative. So, she shall gladly adopt and assimilate whatever good there is in the West. Only she must be sure that it is not repugnant to the ideals for which she stands. At the moment, the great need for her is to learn Western technology. By this her efficiency will increase—efficiency in production, in transport, in everything. A synthesis of Western efficiency and Indian idealism—that is the ideal education for her or for any other country. One gives her prosperity, the other peace. Both are necessary and both must be obtained. Nowadays, the tendency seems to be to overemphasise the second. True, India needs nothing so much now as relief from her poverty. But in the struggle to gain it, let her not forget that peace is a higher and indispensable thing. And, to ensure that, she must stick to her national and educational ideals.

Human Rights and Community Education

MAN HAS ALWAYS DREAMT OF PEACE, BUT SOMEHOW OR OTHER IT has eluded him till now. Almost all Sanskrit texts end up with the cry 'Peace to all.' One text in particular stresses the need for unity of thought, feeling and action among men.

Peace and unity are certainly noble concepts, but how to achieve them? Can discord be simply wished away? In India, it became obvious quite early that peace or unity can sustain itself only on certain conditions being fulfilled. The central theme of the Indian epics is search for peace with social justice. Buddha stressed the more positive aspects of peace by preaching *Maitri* (friendship and goodwill). Social justice is a *sine qua non*, but is not deemed enough; a superior force is needed to efface divisions and to give people a sense of oneness. According to Buddha, Maitri, i.e. friendship is that force. The Gita compares society to a necklace. The pearls do not fall apart because a common thread runs through them. Thus emerges the concept of a common human family. The Upanishads underline the unity of men more pointedly by saying that their forms may vary, but the in-dwelling spirit in them is the same. By implication, it is acknowledged that individuals may and shall differ from one another. They are essentially one, but no two of them need be alike. 'Unity in diversity'—this is the recurrent note in the

Upanishads. Individual liberty is accepted as an essential prerequisite of peace. Unity, not uniformity, is the goal.

Peace is not a mere abstraction or sentiment, but an order of collective existence with some clear and readily identifiable guarantees. Social justice and freedom are among these guarantees.

Peace as a concept is not peculiar to India; it has been a much debated and desired ideal in the West, too. From the time of the Stoicists down to the present day, peace has been one of the West's most vital concerns. To the Romans, their empire was a stage towards a world empire; it was to them a symbol of the unity which bound mankind together. They perpetrated much cruelty in building up their hegemony, but the extenuating factor in their crime was that they wanted to knit together the entire human family. Both Christianity and Islam gave voice to the same urge by preaching 'the Fatherhood of God and the brotherhood of man'. If men are brothers, how can they take up arms against one another?

The quest for peace through giving each individual freedom and a rightful place in society has thus gone on through the centuries in both hemispheres. With the passage of time, the urgency of peace has been felt more and more keenly. It is not enough to have peace within oneself; one has to have a real rapport with others. But more urgent—and more difficult—is peace between groups and races. How to organise community life so that all conflicting interests can be fully reconciled? Not of course by force, for that would be negation of freedom or justice. Peace with freedom and justice for all still remains a far away goal. Though both freedom and justice are man's birthright, there are vast numbers of people who are without them. So, Tagore thought:

> Where the mind is without fear and the head is held high,
> Where knowledge is free,
> Where the world has not been broken up into fragments by narrow domestic walls,

Where words come out from the depth of truth,
Where tireless striving stretches its arms towards perfection,
Where the clear stream of reason has not lost its way in the dreary desert sand of dead habit;
Where the mind is led forward by Thee into ever-widening thought and action,
Into that heaven of freedom, my father, Let my country awake.

Unfortunately, no country in the world today can boast of conditions such as the poet describes here. What lends poignancy to the situation is that conditions are not the same for all people. There are some who enjoy privileges of all kinds, while there are others who are denied even their elementary rights. Freedom and justice are wonderful postulates, but only a few enjoy them. To most people they are empty shibboleths. In Plato's Republic, the question of justice is discussed at length. When Socrates posed the question: What is justice? Some answered, 'Giving everybody his due.' Socrates then pointed out how fallacious it was. He asked, 'Who is going to determine what one's due is?' If law was going to determine it, then, justice would mean, 'an advantage to the strong.' Law, Socrates reminded, was made by the strong who ruled. As is only natural, they always made laws to subserve their own interests.

It is obvious that there can be no peace under such circumstances. If people are quiet and do not protest, it is because they are helpless against the tyranny of the strong.

There are, however, signs that the situation is going to improve. World opinion today is clearly against discrimination of any kind. Just as the United Nations has outlawed war, it has also banned offences against individual freedom or dignity. It has issued a Charter conferring some fundamental rights on every human being. This is the greatest document known to history. This compares well with the edicts of Ashoka. The vague longings for peace which have so long stirred in individual hearts have now crystallised into a Charter with solemn declarations stated in clear and unambiguous words. All member-States are signatories to this Charter. This is a reason to hope that the Charter is going to be a real *Magna Carta* which will guide the States in their dealings with individual citizens.

It will be wrong, however, to expect too much from the government. The community, too,—in fact, every member of it—has a role to play. The Charter binds not only the governments, but also individual citizens. How we behave with one another will reflect the success or failure of the Charter. The government is the overall guardian of our rights, but we have to be each other's guardians. The happiness and security of our neighbours must be our charge. Let us guarantee that they shall not suffer because of us. We must recognise that we need one another, that by helping others we really help ourselves, that our collective well-being is the sumtotal of the happiness, peace and prosperity that we as individuals enjoy. If one section hurts another, the entire community suffers, its progress is retarded; to that extent and maybe, even more, the aggressor too suffers. It is by uniting the energies of our bodies and minds for a common purpose that we can achieve peace, prosperity and progress for the entire community. Peace, prosperity and progress—these are indivisible commodities. Either they are for all or they are for none. All imbalances must go; all disabilities must disappear, so that all sections of the community can contribute their most towards the common well-being of the country. The right kind of climate has to be created so that there is trust and understanding between one another, sympathy and encouragement for all. Help and never hinder—this must be our motto.

It is obvious that this kind of relationship cannot grow overnight. We are used to thinking in terms of groups, communities, or castes. We have to reverse this thinking. We have to learn to think of man as man, completely ignoring his language, religion or race.

An Indian poet once said that 'man is above everything else,' that is, above all his trappings. This should be the basis of our attitude towards each other. But this shift in our attitude can take place only if we orient our education suitably. First of all, we should revise our textbooks so that the students do not get the impression that virtue is the monopoly of a particular community. Anything likely to create a communal bias should be excluded. The purpose of education is to train people to think rationally and objectively. An educated man is expected to judge everything with an open mind, unswayed by any preconceived notions. He must be just, honest and broad-minded; he must place truth above everything else; he must have self-respect, but must not hesitate to show respect to others also. He must fight for his own freedom but must gladly concede freedom to others. According to the Gita, a really wise man is he who sees himself in others and others in himself. That is to say, he knows he is one with others. This may be too much to expect from an ordinary man, but he cannot be excused if he fails to show due consideration to his fellow-men. One of the purposes of education is to make man conscious of his duties and obligations to his fellow-men. Unfortunately, educational institutions do not pay enough attention to this important task.

Apart from this, there are other measures which may be taken to improve relations among the different sections of the people. There is often suspicion, and misunderstanding, because of ignorance. It will be good, therefore, to bring the communities together as often as possible. This may be done by one community inviting another community to its religious and social festivals. If there is exclusiveness, suspicion leading to dislike and hatred is bound to follow. The major truths of all religions are more or less the same. Religious teachers should stress these truths rather than things on which the religions do not agree.

Often, rumours create much misunderstanding. Irresponsible talk, distortion and exaggeration of facts, newspaper articles based on hearsay—these factors do much harm. It is not possible for the government to check them. It is for the public to control them. There should be a small body consisting of representatives of different communities, which should tackle these problems. It will be, as it were, a small replica of the United Nations. It will serve as a local watch-dog for communal peace and harmony. There are men of goodwill everywhere. Such men should be more active than they are when there is a crisis. In times of crisis, often irresponsible elements take the upper hand, because good men are inactive, with the result that where there is only a spark, soon a conflagration arises.

This in brief is the situation that confronts man everywhere today, and the way in which it can be tackled at non-official levels. The solutions suggested may sound amateurish, but there can be no two opinions about the urgency of the problem and the need for some sort of concerted action on the part of men and women of goodwill.

Learning Sanskrit

I RECENTLY MET AN ENGINEER FROM KARNATAKA WHO SPEAKS Sanskrit fluently. He told me he had not studied Sanskrit at school, having been all along a student of science; he, with three other young men, decided to learn Sanskrit after hearing radio news broadcasts in Sanskrit a few times. They thought it was the sweetest of all languages and they learnt it in six months. Not that they mastered the language, but they learnt enough to be able to converse in it amongst themselves. They made it a rule that Sanskrit would be the only language they would use while they talked among themselves and also at home. The result was that their wives and children also picked up the language. I have since learnt that there is a village in Karnataka where everybody speaks Sanskrit. Even Muslims in the village do so.

This is just an illustration to show that Sanskrit is not a difficult language to learn as some people make out. Basic Sanskrit is quite easy to learn. In fact, it is the language that most North Indians speak except for some details. Nobody whose mother tongue is one of the North Indian languages—Hindi, Bengali, Assamese or Oriya should have any difficulty learning Sanskrit. He will find his mother tongue is nothing but a crude form of Sanskrit. The roots are the same, though the derivations are different.

But not only North Indian language, South Indian languages also have a large percentage of Sanskrit words in them. Except Tamil which has always been a well-developed language, both Telegu and Malayalam have drawn freely from Sanskrit and have thus enriched themselves. There was once a move to have Sanskrit declared as the State Language of India. This however, did not happen, which is unfortunate. If Sanskrit had been given the status of the country's State Language, the linguistic chauvinism which now faces a threat to the country's solidarity would not have been there. On the other hand, it would have also greatly enriched out State Language, since they are all off-shoots of Sanskrit. Incidentally, this being an age of technology, we often are at a loss to decide which words would be appropriate to convey the technological concept we have in mind, or the technological product we daily use. Shall we use the exotic word by which we know it, or coin a new word nearer to our mother tongue? Experience has shown that Sanskrit is capable of solving the problem. It can provide us the right word, whether it is just an abstract thought or a tangible object. Sanskrit, with its inexhaustible vocabulary, can meet any demands that modern science and technology can make.

But we need to learn Sanskrit to know ourselves, our culture and civilisation. India is a land with a distinct identity. The identity is marked by certain values which it has nurtured over the centuries. If it has a heritage, that heritage is its values. The highest among the values India has always paid is Truth. The history of India is the history of its pursuit of Truth. This history is in its Sanskrit literature, philosophical or otherwise. This is why no Asian student of Indian history can afford to neglect Sanskrit.

Some people think Sanskrit is a language no one can really master. But is there any language about which one can say that one has mastered? A language is the mirror of a people's mind, carrying in it the whole history of the evolution of that people's thoughts, feelings and emotions. The vicissitudes through which the people can leave their imprint on the language—in its vocabulary, the imageries it uses, its syntactic peculiarities, the nuances of its expressions.

Monastic Order with a New Vision

- *The Sri Ramakrishna Movement*
- *Monasticism with a New Vision*
- *The Ideal of Service: In the Institutions of the Ramakrishna Mission*

The Sri Ramakrishna Movement

RUSKIN BOND ONCE SAID, 'AN IDEA IS MORE POWERFUL THAN AN army'. There must be much truth in this; else it is difficult to explain the influence Sri Ramakrishna had over his contemporaries. He was a humble man without anything to commend him to the sophisticated, English-educated intellectuals of nineteenth-century Bengal, yet we find the best of them falling under his spell. Take first the case of Principal Hastie: a Christian Missionary deeply rooted in Western traditions and an outstanding teacher of Western philosophy, he was among the first from the intellectuals of his time to have met Ramakrishna. He was so fascinated by his personality that he could not help mentioning him and his mystic experiences to his pupils at Scottish Church College. And, what an inscrutable quirk of fate that among those pupils was Narendranath Dutta, who later became famous as Swami Vivekananda and was Ramakrishna's chief disciple! Keshab Sen is another case in point. He was himself a great religious leader; indeed so great that the British press welcomed him as 'the second Christ from the East' when he visited England on a lecture tour. Even Royalty held him in high esteem, for it is said that Queen Victoria herself invited him to dinner and once also attended his lecture. Curiously enough, this great man too was attracted to Ramakrishna from his very first meeting with him and remained one of his ardent admirers to the last day. He was more a Christian than a Hindu, yet it was he who first introduced the idolatrous Kali-worshipping Ramakrishna to the intelligentsia of Calcutta by writing about him in his journals. Incidentally, it is interesting to note that though he himself was a great orator, he was very shy before Ramakrishna and once when pressed by the latter to make a speech, he excused himself by saying that to speak before him would be like carrying coal to Newcastle. All available records show how his religious thoughts under- went a marked change since came in contact with Ramakrishna, how his rigid attitude on religious matters gave way to a spirit of humility, and how he found it possible to see sympathetically many of the current practices in Hinduism (or for that matter, in other religions) he had till then rejected out of hand.

In a remarkable tribute paid to Ramakrishna, we find Pratap Chandra Majumdar, another sophisticated product of English education of the time and also an influential religious leader, asking: 'Why should I sit long hours to attend to him, I who have listened to Disraeli and Fawcett, Stanley and Max Muller and a whole host of European scholars and divines?'[138]

Thus, we watch with amazement Sri Ramakrishna drawing to himself outstanding men of his time, men who were his antitheses in many ways. How can we explain this? The only explanation possible is Sri Ramakrishna himself—Ramakrishna the man and his message. There was something about him which had an irresistible appeal to people. This 'something' was the ideas he preached, ideas which he himself best illustrated in his life. People were thirsting for those ideas and when they came to know of them and what is more, see them exemplified in him, they inevitably flocked to him in spite of their initial dislike for a man who, according to their Westernised tastes, was only a rustic.

---

138. *Sri Ramakrishna in the Eyes of Brahma and Christian Admirers*, by P.C. Majumdar, Ed. By Nanda Mukherjee, Calcutta: Firma K.L.M. Ltd. 1976, p. 3.

What were those ideas? First and foremost, Sri Ramakrishna taught that mere argumentation about God would not serve any purpose but that one ought to concentrate one's efforts on God-realisation. He preached this at a time when scholars were busy trying to decide what God was like—was He a Being or a Thing? Did God have a form? If He had, what was His form like? Was God benevolent and just? If He was, how was it that people suffered so much, often for no fault of theirs? How was it that good people often suffered more than bad people? And, so on and so forth. People quoted different scriptures and different authorities and argued with much heat. In the midst of this verbal clash which often led to much acrimony, Sri Ramakrishna preached that all this attempt to describe God was futile. It was like a salt doll trying to measure the depth of the sea. Can a finite thing say anything about what is infinite? Those who pose they know about God really know nothing about Him. They often talk glibly about Him, but the fact that they do so clearly shows that they are completely ignorant about Him. Either they are suffering from self-delusion, or they are mere pretenders. Anyone having any direct knowledge of God finds his experience so overwhelming that he finds any comment on the subject impossible. As a parallel, Sri Ramakrishna used to refer to the process of an empty vessel being filled with water. So long as the vessel is not full it emits a gurgling sound, but when it is full, it is silent. He would also cite the example of the bee which hums so long as it does not find a flower to sit on. When it finds one and starts sucking honey, it keeps quiet. This, he said, would happen to the person who had found God.

He would also say that only when one has a direct experience of God, one knows what God is like, what it means to be in His presence or what transformation takes place in one's nature. Short of direct experience, one can only guess, and as God is unique, any guess about Him is bound to prove wide off the mark. This is why he used to insist that seekers of God concentrate on their search for God rather than waste time merely talking about Him.

Having declared God-realisation as the supreme goal of life, Sri Ramakrishna said that man should try to reach that goal by whatever means he has at his command. It is wrong to quarrel about the means, for these are bound to vary from individual to individual, seeing that we are different from one another in backgrounds, tastes and capabilities. What is important according to him is sincerity. When a man is sincere and seeks God earnestly, he will succeed even if he chooses a wrong path to begin with. Being sincere, he will soon find out, may be with others' help, the right path and being earnest, he will make quick progress, making good the loss he may have suffered because he had initially chosen a wrong path. According to Sri Ramakrishna, it is not right for others to interfere, for what is good for one may not be good for another. Religion is difficult as it is, but what makes it more difficult is that there are too many people claiming to know more about it than they really know and also trying to impose their ideas upon others. When a blind man tries to lead another blind man, there is a disaster. Similarly, in the religious field, nothing good can come out of a man knowing nothing about God himself but trying to teach others. It was necessary for him to give this caution, for there were too many people in those days as perhaps always, trying to teach religion to others without themselves knowing anything about it. Many equate religion with scholarship, but religion is 'realisation', direct, and first-hand experience of the God.

Another idea Sri Ramakrishna preached was that it was wrong for anyone to claim that the religion he believed in was the only true religion and all other religions were false. According to him, religions are so many paths leading to God, and a seeker can choose from among them the one that he thinks the best. He also stressed the idea that religions looked different on the surface, but underlying all of them was a common truth, which was their core. It was this core which mattered and not the accretions which might have gathered over it. Sri Ramakrishna asked people to fix their minds on this core, ignoring everything else.

The next important idea Sri Ramakrishna preached was that one should treat one's fellow-men with the same respect and affection as one treats God, for, according to him, there is divinity in everybody, be he low or high. Respect for his fellow-men and service to them with humility became a corner-stone of his dealings with others.

What Sri Ramakrishna taught was simple and striking, but it was his personality that gave his ideas the force they carried. He was the best example of what he taught and he was more than what he taught. People loved to hear him because he spoke with the authority which comes from personal experience. If what he said was simple and clear, it was because he did not guess like other people, or depend upon second-hand information. Being in his presence was itself a spiritual experience. Reading anything about Sri Ramakrishna is like walking with God. Mahatma Gandhi describes the experience as to 'see God face-to-face'. No wonder therefore, that people of all creeds flocked to him—Hindus, Muslims, Christians. They found intricate questions about God raised in scholarly books, but Sri Ramakrishna always had the right answers to them. His answers left people wondering about the depth of his scholarship. They found it difficult to believe that he had no formal schooling and had not read many books, either.

What is interesting is that he did not seem to contradict anybody, but only reminded people that the real goal was farther ahead from where they were and they must always keep moving forward. Elsewhere, religion might be merely polemics, but with him religion was 'living', 'being and becoming'. This is why people of all denominations flocked to him for inspiration and guidance. Hindus thought he was the best Hindu that had ever walked the earth; strangely enough, Muslims, Christians and members of other religious groups also thought he was one of them, one who represented the best of their prototype. In this respect, Sri Ramakrishna was indeed a unique person. As Shri Aurobindo said, 'Shri Sri Ramakrishna represents a synthesis, in one person, of all . . .' Thus, Sri Ramakrishna became in his own lifetime the focal point of a new movement which synthesised conflicting viewpoints in religion and also revitalised different religious traditions. Thus, he himself may be said to have initiated what is known as the Sri Ramakrishna Movement.

Sri Ramakrishna was not looking for laurels but for men, who would understand his message and try to live up to it. To the good fortune of future generations, such men arrived headed by Naren, who later became famous as Swami Vivekananda. They were barely a dozen or so, but Sri Ramakrishna selected them out of the big crowd who came to him. Having selected them, he trained them with great care so that they might absorb the great ideas that he represented. Did he visualise that someday those ideas would have a great impact on the religious thought of the world? Perhaps, he did. His conversations such as are recorded in his Gospel are interspersed with hints about such a possibility. The young men he chose for the preservation and transmission of his ideas were apparently very ordinary, but he had great faith in them and later events proved that his faith was not misplaced.

Within seven years of his passing away, his name was known throughout the Western world—first through his disciple, Swami Vivekananda and next through Prof Max Muller. Swami Vivekananda, as we know, created a sensation in the United States as a delegate to the Parliament of Religions held in Chicago in 1893. He literally stormed through America so that the press of that country dubbed him as 'the Cyclonic Hindu'. He preached Sri Ramakrishna's ideas first in America and later in England and the Continent. Churches, Universities and learned societies of all kinds threw open their doors to him and considered themselves honoured if he chose to speak to their audiences. He seldom mentioned his Master's name, but Sri Ramakrishna became known all the same. But if Swami Vivekananda was reluctant to disclose the source of his inspiration, Prof Max Muller had no such inhibition. He wrote an article entitled 'A Real Mahatman' in the Nineteenth Century, August, 1896, dwelling upon Sri Ramakrishna's life and teachings. Coming from the pen of so great a scholar, the article naturally drew the attention of the entire scholastic world, Eastern and Western. Overnight, Sri Ramakrishna became a subject for study and research among scholars. People recognised that a great star had risen in the religious firmament which needed watching.

Meanwhile, significant repercussions had started in India following Swami Vivekananda's success in the West. For the first time, India had become conscious of the great wealth of her philosophical thought. She realised that she had no reason to feel ashamed of herself. She might not possess the military and economic power of the West, but she possessed intellectual and cultural powers which were second to none in the world in their depth and grandeur. This discovery was like a tonic to the dropping spirits of India. There followed a wave of enthusiasm in the country which was unprecedented in scale. This was the beginning of a true renaissance in India, which was later strengthened and brought to fruition by men like Gandhi, Tagore, Aurobindo and Nehru.

One of the first things Swami Vivekananda did on coming back to India was to found the Ramakrishna Mission. It is an organisation specially intended for the study and practice of Sri Ramakrishna's ideas. When it started in 1897, it consisted of a dozen monks or so and had practically no assets. Even now it is small compared with the Christian organisations, but it is a name that commands respect all over India and even outside. Its monks are spread all over the world, either occupied in humanitarian work or in preaching Sri Ramakrishna's message (which happens to be India's message also). They are also working in England, France, Switzerland, the United States, Japan, Malaysia, Fiji, Ceylon, South Africa and Bangladesh. There are other countries wanting to have them, but there is so much to do in India that even though they would like to spread out to as many countries as possible, the Mission has to keep many countries on the waiting list. What is intriguing is that the call always comes from those countries—it is not that the monks go to those countries on their own. What is more, as long as they work in those countries, they are supported by the people there. There is no question of any Indian money being spent on their work.

What exactly do these monks do in India or abroad? It must be made clear at once that the Ramakrishna Mission does not believe in conversion in the sense of the word as understood in common parlance. If anything, these monks try to make 'a Hindu a better Hindu, a Muslim a better Muslim, a Christian a better Christian' and so on. In other words, they ask people to go to the root of religion, which is trying to reach God somehow or other and not merely talking about Him. They quote different prophets and different scriptures to show how in essence they preach the same thing. Their language differs, but their purport is the same. They do not want to replace any system but want to draw attention to the fact that there is much in common between one system and another. In all matters of religion, their approach is one of respect and understanding. Because of this approach, they feel as much at home among non-Hindus as among Hindus. Because of this approach, non-Hindus also feel at home in their company; as a matter of fact they like these monks and often invite them to their services. Today ecumenism has become an active force in the Christian world. It must not be forgotten that long before Pope John gave official blessings to this, Sri Ramakrishna had preached and practised it. His ecumenism was much broader though, for it embraced not some denominations but all denominations of all religions.

Today, the Sri Ramakrishna Movement has become a great power for peace and happiness in this country as well as outside. In India where different religious sects and communities live, the idea of tolerance and brotherly feelings towards each other has great relevance. Another factor which contributes much to its popularity is the rational approach it brings to bear upon every vital problem of life. People who are influenced by Sri Ramakrishna believe religion to be a kind of science open to study and investigation. They do not agree religious truths have to be accepted on trust; they rather declare that nothing need be accepted as final unless it has been tested and found true. Experience, personal and immediate, is the only acceptable proof of religion.

The fact that the Movement lays great store on selfless service as a means of God-realisation also attracts many people. The service it gives is open to all, irrespective of caste or creed or language. Not only the Ramakrishna Mission but hundreds of institutions which have sprung up all over the country today give this kind of service. Since the time of Buddha, this is almost without parallel in India. What is significant is that most of them bear the name of Sri Ramakrishna and draw inspiration from him.

As time passes, the Sri Ramakrishna Movement is growing from strength to strength. People all over the country want the Mission to open more branch centres—schools, colleges, hospitals, orphanages, etc., for they know that the quality of service they will get from the Mission will be better than what they may get elsewhere. Their requests are almost always accompanied by offers of money, land, and buildings, but the Mission proceeds cautiously and avoids proliferation unless there is a compelling reason in its favour. Apart from the fact that it suffers from shortage of manpower, it prefers that people themselves come forward to start such institutions, imbued with the spirit of selfless service. Happily, the present trend clearly shows that this spirit is fast spreading.

As the Movement spreads, the attitude of the common people towards religion is also changing. Previously, religion was equated with rituals, but now people realise that religion is essentially a science of 'being and becoming, something that concerns man's inner nature. The habit of prayer is good but if this is not accompanied by a corresponding improvement in one's nature, it is not worth much. Another change that is noticeable today is respect for religions other than one's own. There was once much arrogance in the attitude of people towards the religions of others, but there is now humility and a spirit of enquiry if not also reverence.

The strength of the Sri Ramakrishna Movement is not in money or men or organisation but in the ideas it tries to present. These ideas are fast spreading, and wherever they are spreading they are producing a great impact. Silently but inevitably, they are changing the minds of the people who come under their influence. They act like a catalytic agent transforming their personalities.

Thus, the ideas that Sri Ramakrishna left are now reaching out to the far corners of the world, not because of any patronage from any quarter, but because of their inherent strength. A new turn has come in the religious outlook of man since the day he was born. It is a turn that makes for unity, peace and blessedness.

Monasticism with a New Vision

SOMETIME IN THE 1980s A MONK OF THE SRI RAMAKRISHNA MISSION had an audience with His Holiness the Pope at the Vatican. In introducing himself the monk said, 'I belong to an order of monks which is the youngest, smallest and poorest. The order is known as the Sri Ramakrishna Mission.' His Holiness smilingly replied, 'I know everything about you.' What he knew about the Sri Ramakrishna Mission he did not, however, disclose. But it is surprising that he knew anything about it at all. The Ramakrishna Mission, formally started as late as the year 1897, with barely 1400 monks now on the roll, and dependent entirely upon charity, is indeed the youngest, smallest and poorest order of monks. Yet, it is today a most prestigious monastic order in the world. It is well known and highly respected for its broadmindedness and the service ('marked by quiet efficiency,' as described by Jawaharlal Nehru) it renders to mankind.

At first, the Sri Ramakrishna Mission faced much opposition in the country of its origin, for it was much too modern to the tastes of the orthodox Hindus. Monasticism had always been known and respected in the country, but there was never any organised monasticism. Individual monks roamed the country, often without roots anywhere. Some of them, outstanding and with a following of sorts, may have had monasteries of their own, but they had no organisation as such. Hinduism itself had, in fact, never been an organised religion. Hinduism is whatever a Hindu thinks it is and no two Hindus may agree about its meaning and contents. It is vast, all-inclusive; it is, in brief, Truth Itself.

Buddhism, an offshoot of Hinduism, is a bit different. Based on the teachings of Buddha, it is easily identifiable. At the height of its influence, Buddhism had monasteries scattered all over South Asia, but they were independent of each other, without owing loyalty to any central authority. Even the monks were independent of each other, though they were courteous enough to observe a common code of conduct when they lived together in a monastery. It was not, however, obligatory that they should live in a monastery. Later, *Buddha, Dharma* and *Sangha* became their Holy Trinity, though it is doubtful if the word *Sangha* here stands for any organised body of monks. The outcome of Buddha's teachings was that many people were drawn to monasticism and many monasteries cropped up. Still, it cannot be said that there was any monastic order as such.

Sankara resurrected Hinduism after it had been in shambles for centuries. He himself was a monk and he gave a new impetus to the monastic institution. He founded four big monasteries in four corners of the country but each one of them was independent. He also founded ten schools of monks but there was no apex body to control them. The monks identify themselves with those schools—that is all. They serve no other purpose.

The Ramakrishna Mission may be the first and only organised body of monks, centrally controlled and with a common discipline, in the history of Hinduism. In many ways, it was a novelty Hindu orthodoxy did not understand, much less approve of. Monasticism was not for everybody, it was only for a chosen few and that too at an advanced age—that is how most Hindus viewed it. The young men who joined the Sri Ramakrishna Mission were mostly below thirty. They were educated and had a middle-class background. People condemned them as escapists because they did not marry and raise families. Some even questioned the authenticity of their monasticism.

Only a properly ordained monk can initiate a disciple into monastic vows. They obviously did not know that Sri Ramakrishna, the Guru of these young people, was himself a monk ordained by one who belonged to one of Sankara's schools. These monks had taken monastic vows strictly according to the scriptural prescriptions. People did not know this and were, therefore, suspicious about their bona fides.

DEVIATIONISTS

What baffled the traditionalists most was these so-called monks engaged in social work. Calcutta was in the grip of a plague epidemic and people found these monks nursing the sick. Next, they heard of the same group of monks working among the famine-stricken people in the district of Murshidabad. As monks, they had withdrawn from the world, how could they then get involved in the affairs of the world? The traditionalists noticed that these monks did not observe caste rules. They did not even mind dining with non-Hindus. Their way of life, their dress, food habits and religious practices—everything suggested a distinct deviation from the accepted norms of Hindu monasticism. They ran two hospitals—one at Kankhal and another at Varanasi. They nursed the patients, even handling their urine and stool. The orthodox monks had always doubted if these Gerua-wearing people were monks at all; now they were convinced that they were not monks; as Hindus they perhaps belonged to the lowest caste.

RECOGNITION

In the face of ridicule and criticism from monks and householders alike, the Mission continued to pursue its twofold ideal of Self-illumination and Service to others. Slowly, the thaw began: People began to recognise the moral and spiritual excellence of the members of the Mission, and the quality of their work. Today, the Mission and the individual monks are both held in the highest esteem. How did this happen?

The change has to be traced to the growing influence of Sri Ramakrishna amongst monks and the laity. Sri Ramakrishna, born a Hindu, accepted every religious faith and practice as valid irrespective of its source; he also respected every religious teacher. To him, God and Truth were synonymous, and religion was an attempt to bridge the gulf that now separated man from God or Truth. Since each religion has produced great saints and sages, one religion is as good as another. This means an individual is free to choose the religion that suits him best. This is why the Sri Ramakrishna Mission is open to all—Hindu, Muslim, Christian, or Buddhist. The majority of the members are, of course Hindus, but there are members of other faiths as well. They do not have to go through any process of conversion to get into the Mission. Having entered the Mission they enjoy the same rights and privileges as others. Incidentally, equal respect for all religions and their teachers is demanded of every member of the Mission. Sri Ramakrishna is worshipped as an embodiment of this attitude of mind. He is deemed to be the meeting point of all faiths. In him and through him, all prophets are honoured, for he honoured them all. He represents the essence of Religion—he is the culmination of religious experience.

SRI RAMAKRISHNA AND HIS DISCIPLES

Sri Ramakrishna had spent most of his life at Dakshineswar, but during his last illness he was removed to Cossipore in Calcutta for better medical care. A group of young men, headed by Naren (later, Swami Vivekananda), began to nurse him. They came of good families and most of them had also received a fair amount of English education. Naren himself was a university graduate. These young men had been hand-picked by the Master, not because of their education or social background, but because of their spiritual potential. He had the rare gift of knowing the past, present and future of each individual who came to him. If he met someone with marked spiritual gifts, he would go out of his way to help him. He would ask, even beg, him to come to him, as if somebody had forced him into the role of a spiritual guide to these people. He concentrated his attention on approximately twenty young men and began to train them for a life of total renunciation. It is these young men who constituted the nucleus of the future Sri Ramakrishna Mission.

From all available records, Sri Ramakrishna was a hard taskmaster. He made each one of them work hard and on the right lines to develop his potential. Sri Ramakrishna taught them to realise God in themselves and in others also. He himself had experienced both the immanent and the transcendental aspects of the Supreme Being. He did not reject the empirical world; in essence it was also divine. He had felt the presence of God everywhere—in plants, animals and humans. If anybody plucked a flower, he felt as if the man was plucking out his heart. When a bullock was beaten by his master, Ramakrishna felt the pain. Two brothers were hitting each other, but he felt as if he himself was being hit. He, in fact, was one with everybody, everything. This, according to the scriptures, is the highest spiritual experience that anyone can aspire to. But Sri Ramakrishna would say that it was not enough to have this experience; one ought to conduct oneself in the light of that experience. Once, his favourite disciple, Naren, came and begged that he help him remain always steeped in God-consciousness. Sri Ramakrishna scolded him for this. According to Sri Ramakrishna, to seek one's salvation regardless of what was happening to others was utter selfishness, and it could never be forgiven. It would be interesting to recall that Sri Ramakrishna himself showed the way one should behave in this regard. The sight of a famine-stricken crowd moved him so much that he would not leave them till they had some relief. He had his spiritual ambitions fulfilled, but he used whatever blessings this brought him only for the good of others. He would never tire of teaching man about his ultimate destiny: being one with God and also being one with the world. He trained his disciples to think and act on these lines. He often met his chief disciple Naren separately to explain to him the implication of this ideal. He urged him to pursue this ideal and see that the other young men also did the same.

Sri Ramakrishna spent the last few days of his life inspiring the young men with the spirit of renunciation. He taught them to think that they were born only to realise God. He gave them Gerua robes and sent them to beg, as if to clinch the issue once for all. He also made them love each other so that they grew into a close-knit group with Naren as their leader. They did not belie Sri Ramakrishna's expectations. Within months of his passing away, they took monastic vows and founded a monastery in an old dilapidated house. Society did not take kindly to them, but they did not care. Their goals had been set and they would pursue them, no matter what came in the way. They lived by begging, which meant they never had a full meal. They felt Sri Ramakrishna was with them, still inspiring. They meditated together or separately, sometimes competing with each other over the time they spent meditating. They sang and danced with the joy of their religious fervour. They studied scriptures, sometimes arguing about their meaning. There was no issue about man or God they did not debate; sometimes they debated for days together. Swami Vivekananda placed intellectual pursuits next to spirituality. Sometimes, they scattered across the country savouring the life of a wandering monk. Wherever they went they attracted notice because of their character, spiritual eminence and progressive views.

Naturally, it was Swami Vivekananda who impressed people most. Peasant or prince, scholar or an illiterate person, old or young, everybody who met him felt he was a Messiah. It so happened that a Parliament of Religions was then in the process of being organised in Chicago, the United States. Some of the princes, a few intellectuals and students urged him to attend this Parliament to represent Hinduism. Some even offered financial assistance. At first, Swami Vivekananda was reluctant but finally he attended the Parliament because he felt this was a call from the Divine. His success in the United States proved that he was right. Not only the West, even India came to know what Hinduism really was. No wonder, when Swami Vivekananda returned, the whole country rose to give him a hero's welcome.

While in the West, Swami Vivekananda had felt the need to have an organisation. At first, he was in two minds about the idea, for he had watched how it could be a blessing and a curse both at the same time. But he finally opted for the organisation, for he realised that in the absence of an organisation, the message Sri Ramakrishna had left behind would be lost with the passing of the first generation. If the message was to have a permanent impact, an organisation was needed. So, the organisation came into being at a meeting of monks and devotees on 1 May 1897. The organisation was named Ramakrishna Mission Association. Its chief aim was 'to preach those truths which Sri Ramakrishna has, for the good of humanity, preached and demonstrated by practical application in his own life, and to help others to put these truths into practice in their temporal, mental and spiritual advancement.

'The duty of the Mission is to conduct in the right spirit the activities of the movement inaugurated by Sri Ramakrishna for the establishment of fellowship among the followers of different religions, knowing them all to be so many forms only of one undying Eternal Religion.'

The Methods of Action are:

(a) To train men so as to make them competent to teach such knowledge or sciences as are conducive to the material and spiritual welfare of the masses;
(b) To provide and encourage arts and industries; and
(c) To introduce and spread among the people in general Vedantic and other religious ideas in the way in which they were elucidated in the life of Sri Ramakrishna.

The Mission was to have two departments: Indian and foreign. The Indian department was to concern itself with the founding of Maths and Ashramas in different parts of India to train both monks and householders to serve others. They would not confine themselves within a particular place, they would travel to other places also. The foreign department would send trained members of the Mission outside India to preach its ideals and thus bring about a closer understanding between India and those countries.

The Association, as initially conceived, did not prove a success. The householders were much too busy to contribute anything in real terms and so the Association had to depend entirely upon the labour of the monks. This was good, for this brought the monks into closer contact with the public, who could now see the birth of a new movement within the Hindu society—monks spearheading this movement. They had their first shock of surprise when they saw Gerua-wearing monks cleaning slums and caring for plague-stricken people. Hindu monasticism negated the world—that was a well-known fact—but relieving its suffering had never been known to be one of its concerns. Earlier, Murshidabad had been hit by famine and here again the same phenomenon was seen—monks caring for the hungry and the sick. This was astonishing not only because monks were doing it but because they were doing it with so much love and care. In Calcutta they handled cases of plague, but in Murshidabad they handled cases of cholera besides distributing food to the starving.

The range of services the monks rendered and the depth of their love and care were something people had never seen the like of. Swami Vivekananda, the leader, felt proud of what his 'boys' were doing. It was the start of a social (and spiritual) revolution, for the monks, drawn mostly from upper castes, served everybody irrespective of caste or religion. Sri Ramakrishna saw God in man. He himself served one who, by profession, cleaned latrines. Swami Vivekananda too, in his turn, later began to see man as 'the living God.' 'God the poor, God the wicked, God the sinner,' were his favourite expressions. 'Man is the great being in the universe,' he would say. He once said, 'Man must love others because those others are he himself.' That is to say, if you serve others you are in fact serving yourself. Herein is the key to the philosophy that inspires whatever the Mission does. 'You' and 'I' are not two separate entities, they are one; one but appearing as 'I' or 'You'. The unity of existence, oneness of things, unity in diversity—these are some of the expressions which emphasise Sri Ramakrishna's rejection of divergence as a reality. This rejection was based on his own experience.

TRAINING OF MONKS

Swami Vivekananda felt he needed a good band of monks who would be physically, intellectually and spiritually strong. He attached great importance to strength. He would often quote the declaration of the Upanishad that 'weak people can never attain Self-knowledge.' Intellectual strength is next to spiritual strength. He wanted the young monks to study the scriptures so that they might know what religion was about. He did not, at any rate, want the monastery to degenerate into a place of idlers. He himself taught the scriptures and invited Swami Turiyananda to do the same. He laid down a strict schedule for everybody to follow and he himself followed it. The schedule, among other things, included prayer, study, physical exercise and community service. The monastery, now shifted to its permanent site at Belur, was always humming with activities. Sometimes, Swami Vivekananda would start a debate over some basic religious issue, in which even the junior monks were free to join. The debate would sometimes go on for days and weeks. He was a great believer in freedom of thought. He had practised it himself all his life and wanted his brother-monks also to do the same. There was nothing they would accept on faith. They would not even mind questioning the existence of God. There was no organised system of belief to which they were required to subscribe. Each was free to believe and act as he thought best, keeping two things in view—his own emancipation and service to mankind. The only thing that the monastery would insist on was to accept Sri Ramakrishna as the model. This was understandable, for if one accepted Sri Ramakrishna as the model, one would never be bigoted, but accept and respect every faith as true, which is what was needed if people with different religious backgrounds were to live and work together.

To Ramakrishna, this kind of openness of mind was cardinal. He would not permit any of his disciples to find fault with any religious belief or practice. He would say, 'You may not like it, but if somebody else finds it satisfying, you have no right to condemn him. Let each individual choose what suits him best.' Since God was Infinite, there were infinite ways of reaching Him. No book, no prophet can exhaust God. Each gives only a glimpse of that mystic Reality we call God. As we grow morally and spiritually, our vision grows clearer. We finally realise that God is someone we can never talk about, we can only feel Him. And, if we feel His presence genuinely, silence is the only possible response. Any group bearing the name of Ramakrishna has to accommodate people of different viewpoints, not only different, maybe even opposite. It is indeed a vast vehicle in which everyone has a place. No wonder the Mission is open to all. All are welcome, all are perfectly at home. They differ from each other, but they have one common meeting point—Sri Ramakrishna. They find in him the culmination of all that a religion has to offer, no matter under what name that religion passes. Sri Ramakrishna was a Hindu, a Muslim, a Christian and a Buddhist, all in one. He embodied the essence of all religions, he was Religion itself. The Ramakrishna Mission does not convert anybody to a new religion, it only makes a Hindu a better Hindu, a Muslim a better Muslim, a Christian a better Christian, a Buddhist a better Buddhist. The ordinary concept of conversion is repugnant to it. The goal of each religion is perfection and there are many paths to that goal. Each path is as good as another, given the will and the effort to reach the goal. What is Ramakrishna's religion? His religion is that which is Islam to a Muslim, Hinduism to a Hindu and Christianity to a Christian.

WORK IS WORSHIP

The Mission runs schools, hospitals, orphanages and ther types of institutions. It also gives relief to people afflicted by natural calamities. Its services are open to all, irrespective of caste or creed. Its work is much appreciated by the State as well as by the public. Where do the funds come from? It comes mainly from the common public, but in some cases, from the State as well. All sections of the public, cutting across their political and religious affiliations, help as much as possible. Similarly, the State also helps, whatever may be the political complexion of the party running it.

Is it social work that the Mission is doing? Far from it. The services are part of its spiritual exercise. If a monk nurses a patient, he is only worshipping God. He is happy that he has the privilege to worship Him this way. Sri Ramakrishna used to say, 'If you can see God when you close your eyes, why cannot you see Him when you open them?' God is indeed everywhere, in every being. You can worship Him in places of worship, but you can also worship Him in hospitals, schools and orphanages. You have only to see God in the man you are serving. Real service is possible when you serve with humility and reverence, for you are serving God Himself. If you serve out of pity, it is not service, it is an insult.

PRACTICAL VEDANTA

Vedanta preaches that the only reality in the world is God (Brahman). What we see around us has no independent identity; it is only God, even though it appears otherwise. Emancipation means being able to recognise the God hiding under the cover of different names and forms. But mere recognition is not enough; it has to be practised also. If one sees God in all beings, should not one behave with those beings with respect and humility? Love and compassion are great qualities, but they can only flow from the knowledge of oneness. God is outside in the world, but He is also inside oneself. That is, God is the Self of all—man, animal, plant, everything. If one serves others, one in fact serves oneself. It is the same Self everywhere—in man, animal and plant, inside and outside. If we are all one, how should we behave with each other? By hurting others, you are hurting yourself; by helping others, you are helping yourself. The recognition of this truth is what produces true love. Our relations with one another should be based on this sense of oneness. This is the only way to achieve peace and harmony in the world.

Sri Ramakrishna stressed the need to *practise* this sense of oneness in one's dealing with others. This, he described as being higher than merely *knowing* of this oneness in theory. Swami Vivekananda made this the corner-stone of the new Mission's philosophy of life. Succinctly, this philosophy is *Atmano moksartham jagad hitdya ca*, i.e. one's own salvation and also the welfare of others. Swami Vivekananda hated selfishness, which he said was immoral. One must share with others whatever one has, even spiritual knowledge. To enjoy spiritual bliss without helping others to enjoy it too was repugnant to him. 'Be and make'—this was his motto. Be perfect yourself and help others also to be perfect—this is what he preached. If one could worship God in images, one could also worship Him in man. The poor, the ignorant, the sick—all were God to Him. He wanted the Mission to worship God in man. This is something distinctive about the Sri Ramakrishna Mission. If the Mission runs a school, or an orphanage, or distributes relief to people hit by a natural calamity, it is only an act of worship, part of its spiritual discipline. It expects nothing in return, it deems it a privilege that it is able to so serve the 'living God.' The services of the Mission are open to all, not to a particular community only. Again, in accepting its services, one need not change one's religious beliefs and practices. One remains the same, perhaps a bit better in the sense that one's religious outlook widens.

Not only are the services of the Mission open to all, the Mission itself is also open to all. There are not only Hindus among the monks, there are also Muslims, Christians and Buddhists; there are also people from different countries. It is a small Mission but it combines both East and West in its representation. All are free and equal here.

IMPACT ON SOCIETY

Besides the monks, there are lay devotees cutting across racial and geographical barriers. The only common tie among them is loyalty to the ideal of renunciation, respect for all religions, and selfless service—ideals Ramakrishna epitomised. Just as Sri Ramakrishna was the meeting point of different sects and communities, so also is the Mission that bears his name. In any branch centre of the Mission, one can see people of different communities living and working together, monks as well as laymen. One can also see much camaraderie among them. The Mission does not just preach but demonstrates in practice the principle of 'Unity in Diversity', how heterogenous people can live and work together with friendship and goodwill towards each other. This is a lesson any multi-racial and multi-religious society can learn to its benefit. 'Live and let live' is rather an axiomatic principle; it can prevent conflicts, but it cannot promote harmony. To have a cohesive society where everybody is free to be himself but without depriving others of the same freedom and always with the consciousness that he is not separate from others, the Ramakrishna Mission provides a model to follow. In any case, it is a worthwhile experiment.

The Ramakrishna Mission is small but highly significant. It gives monasticism a new dimension: it raises life with all its beauty as well as ugliness to the status of worship. It makes everything spiritual, reminds man of his divine potential, elevates service to man into worship of God, rejects all artificial divisions of religion, race and country, and forges unity among all. It symbolises a union between science and religion, and between thought and action. The Ramakrishna Mission is ancient in wisdom but modern in practice.

The Ideal of Service: In the Institutions of the Ramakrishna Mission

ACCORDING TO ITS GENERAL REPORT FOR THE YEAR 1990–91, THE Ramakrishna Mission spent in that year Rs 329.2 million on education and health, and Rs 5.9 million for relief and rehabilitation. It spent similar amounts on its miscellaneous welfare programmes such as adult literacy, tribal welfare, caring for the physically handicapped, looking after orphans, and similar services. All its efforts are directed to the benefit of the disadvantaged. Its services are also open to all, irrespective of race and religion.

The work is modest, but significant. It is significant because of the spirit that stimulates it. The spirit is: work is worship. Everything the Mission does is part of its spiritual discipline. It is a form of prayer. The poor, the ignorant, the sick, even the wicked all are God. Service to man is service to God. It is a privilege to be able to serve God, no matter in what form He accepts it. He accepts it if the service is marked by humility and reverence, if there is no selfish motive behind it. If there is a selfish motive, it is not worship; it is like trade and it defeats its purpose. Selfless service is a way of killing the ego, the source of all trouble. If the ego is gone, the mind is then ready to reveal the Self within. It is the ego that always stands between the Self and Self-knowledge. The whole purpose of religion is to destroy this ego. If there is such a thing as liberation, it is the demolition of the ego.

In founding the Ramakrishna Mission, Swami Vivekananda said its purpose was twofold: First, attainment of salvation by its members; second, service to humanity. The Mission was formally instituted on 1 May 1897. This was the first time a monastic order in India included service as one of its objectives. It was quite a novelty then and even now the significance of the Mission's work is not understood. Many imagine that what the Mission wants to do is social work as is done in the West. That this is practical Vedanta, few people have grasped.

Vedanta says that divinity is everywhere. In his 1896 London lecture 'God in Everything,' Swami Vivekananda said, 'We read at the commencement of one of the oldest of the Upanishads, "Whatever exists in this universe is to be covered by the Lord"'.

This is the first verse of the *Isa Upanisad*. In fact, the whole of Vedanta emphasises that God is the only reality in the world and all that exists is God, though He is not equally manifest in all. This means that there is divinity in everything and in every being. Swami Vivekananda used to say that there was the same divinity everywhere and in everyone, from an amoeba to Buddha. The difference is only in the degree of manifestation.

This is what Sri Ramakrishna called *vijnana*, seeing God everywhere and behaving accordingly. What is important is 'behaving'. It provides a new basis on which human relationship should be structured. High and low, rich and poor, ruler and ruled, all are basically one. The attitude of one individual towards another should be strictly governed by this principle of oneness. This is practical application of the knowledge Vedanta provides. In advocating the use of this knowledge in day-to-day life, Sri Ramakrishna made a distinct contribution for which humanity should remain grateful to him. Sri Ramakrishna experienced this oneness in his own life.

If somebody plucked a flower, he felt as if the man were plucking his heart. If a man beat his bullock, Sri Ramakrishna rolled on the ground with pain. Two boatmen fought and assaulted each other. The assault left its marks on Sri Ramakrishna's body. This personal experience lent his Vedantic views a measure of authenticity not seen elsewhere.

Swami Vivekananda, as Narendra, had been watching Sri Ramakrishna's frequent ecstasies. He did not know what they meant, but it was obvious to him that it was a state of bliss unparalleled in human experience. No wonder he once begged Sri Ramakrishna to help him attain this state. He said that he wanted to stay always in that state except when he wanted to eat to sustain the body. Perhaps Swami Vivekananda thought Sri Ramakrishna would be pleased to hear him make such a request. But far from being pleased, Sri Ramakrishna was annoyed. He said that he never thought Swami Vivekananda was so selfish as to think only of his own peace and happiness when there was so much suffering in the world. Sri Ramakrishna wanted Swami Vivekananda to be like a big banyan tree, giving shade to others and asking nothing in return. This, Sri Ramakrishna said, was an even higher state than liberation. That Swami Vivekananda would think only of his own *moksa* was the last thing he expected of him.

This sharp rebuke gave Swami Vivekananda quite a jolt. His future course of action was not, however, yet clear in his mind. Sri Ramakrishna once made some comments about compassion and this gave Swamiji the light he needed. Sri Ramakrishna condemned the idea of compassion. He said, 'Not compassion—who are you to show compassion? No, serve man knowing him to be God !' Swamiji said that if he had an opportunity, he would spread this message far and wide—this message of serving man as God.

The Ramakrishna Mission that Swami Vivekananda founded marks the fulfilment of that promise. The Mission stands for selfless service as a way of worshipping God. This service is part of its creed. It is as important as any other form of spiritual practice, such as meditation, repeating the name of God, ritualistic worship, etc. If God can be worshipped in stone or wood, why can He not be worshipped in a living human form? Sri Ramakrishna once said, 'You close your eyes and see God within yourself. Why cannot you see Him outside when you open your eyes?' Obviously, he was suggesting that God is present in various forms and under various names everywhere. Sri Ramakrishna himself showed how service to man could be service to God. Once at Deoghar, during his pilgrimage with Mathur Babu, he found famine-stricken people. He was so moved that he begged his guardian cum disciple, Mathur Babu, to give some relief to those people immediately. Mathur Babu expressed his inability on financial grounds. In protest, Sri Ramakrishna went and sat among those famished people. He said he was not going to go to any holy place unless those people got some relief. Mathur Babu finally yielded to his request. The people got some relief and a happy Sri Ramakrishna resumed his pilgrimage.

This is an example of what Sri Ramakrishna described as *vijnana—jnana* applied in everyday life. Swami Vivekananda called it Practical Vedanta. A plague epidemic broke out in Calcutta soon after the land where the Mission headquarters now stands had been acquired. Swamiji had gone to Darjeeling for health reasons, and sent instructions from there to his brother-monks to nurse the sick affected by the plague. Swamiji wanted to see the work done in a big way. He cut short his stay in Darjeeling and hurried back to Calcutta. Some people asked him where from funds would come for the work. He said he would sell the land acquired for Belur Math, if necessary. But Holy Mother objected, saying that this would enable Swamiji to give relief only once. If he wanted to continue serving people, he should not sell the Belur Math land. Swamiji was convinced by her argument and decided not to sell the land.

The future has proved Holy Mother right. The Mission continues to serve mankind whenever and wherever there is large-scale suffering.

The service is distinguished by its philosophy: Service to man is service to God. It is not compassion, it is worship. People are often struck by the efficiency of the Mission: the efficiency arises from the spirit of humility and reverence which the monks bring to bear on whatever they do. The Mission depends entirely upon public charity for its work. The monks make this up by hard work and total selflessness.

A striking feature of the Mission's work is to make no discrimination based on race, creed or caste. It is also free from political affiliation. No wonder it enjoys the trust of all people. The government often invites the Mission to help people hit by natural calamities. Sometimes, private organisations raise funds and hand them over to the Mission to give relief to the suffering. They mention in their appeals to the public that the money will be spent through the Mission. They do this in order to have a better response from the public. And, they often do.

Happily, the Mission's ideals of service are slowly catching on. There are now all over the country small, sometimes even big, centres of service run on the same lines as the Mission by non-monastic groups. Even orthodox monasticism, which once saw a contradiction between renunciation and service, is doing similar work with an increasing zeal.

Meanwhile, the work of the Mission is growing. Of course, it is not growing in proportion to the demand. People everywhere would love to have a school or hospital run by the Mission. They would gladly donate land, money and buildings for the purpose. But the Mission is slow in launching a new project. It will not accept a donation unless it is sure that it can use it well and for the purpose for which it is intended. The Mission is not ambitious: it is humble and knows its limitations. It knows its inadequate manpower is already under great strain, meeting its present commitments. It will not add to its burden, which may affect its efficiency or the spirit of its work. It would much rather do nothing than work only to earn public acclaim. It wants to render true service to man, and also to feel that it is serving God Himself. Service to God is the Mission's real purpose. The purpose is not humanitarian or social work; it is worship, worship of God in man.

Appendix

Appendix

Swami Lokeswarananda: A Life Dedicated to Humanity

SWAMI LOKESWARANANDAJI WAS BORN IN KENRAGACCHI, IN THE DISTRICT of Khulna, East Bengal (now, Bangladesh), the place where Yavana Haridas, a disciple of Chaitanya, was born. Kenragacchi was Lokeswaranandaji's mother's village. His father's home was in Baruipara, at the village Magura in Satkshira. Rani Rasmani's (founder of Dakshineswar Kali temple) son-in-law, Mathur, lived at Sonabere, a village close to Baruipara, and the villages around it were under his jurisdiction. Mathur Babu's guru lived in the village of Tala. Once, there was a dispute among the members of Mathur Babu's guru's family, and to settle it he went there, with Sri Ramakrishna and Hriday accompanying him.

Swami Lokeswaranandaji's mother was Shikharbasini Banerjee, and his father was Basanta Kumar Banerjee. Although he was given the name Shivapada at birth, he was always known by his nickname Kanai. He had three brothers and two sisters. Kanai was the third child.

From his childhood Kanai was handsome, healthy, and energetic. And, he was everyone's favourite in the village. People loved and respected him for his gentle nature and his honesty and righteousness. Kanai did not play childish pranks as other children did, but he had the simplicity of a child. Though he was not mischievous, he was rather obstinate. He would do what he intended to do. Another characteristic of his was that he slept very little. When the whole family took rest in the afternoon, Kanai would be busy with his studies. One day, a neighbour saw him studying and said: 'I cannot believe my eyes. Everyone else is sleeping, and here you are working.'

Kanai was admitted to B. Dey Institution at Talamagura. He studied there up to class nine and always stood first in his class. Kanai loved sports and was good at them. And from his childhood, he was very fond of animals.

From his childhood, Kanai had a strong sense of morality. Once, when he was in class eight or nine, he was taking an exam and could not remember the answer to a particular question. As he was trying hard to remember it, he overheard a boy telling another boy the answer to that same question. Immediately, Kanai decided not to answer that question. He knew he would lose marks. And perhaps, he could have remembered the answer after some time. Still, his conscience did not allow him to answer it—such was his sense of righteousness.

Kenragacchi was famous for its Rama temple. The images of Rama, Sita, Lakshman, and Mahavir are made of wood. The villagers believed that the images were living, and they had reason to believe so. Many miracles happened in connection with them. The following is just one of them: One night, the owner of the temple went to a confectioner's shop to get something to eat for a brahmin guest who had unexpectedly come to his home. The owner had no money, so he offered the confectioner one of the gold bangles that Sita wore in the temple. The confectioner protested that he did not want to accept such a precious thing, but the owner insisted that he take it. At last, he agreed to accept the bangle. The next morning, however, the confectioner went to the owner's house to return the bangle and found that the owner didn't know anything about the incident. There was no brahmin guest in his house. It is believed that Rama himself came to the confectioner, disguised as the temple owner, to prove that he was not just a wooden image. The people who lived at Kenragacchi and the neighbouring villages considered Rama to be their guardian. They felt they were all under his protection. Rama was their king and they were his blessed subjects. They confided everything to him. Before Kanai left home forever to become a monk, he went to Kenragacchi and sought Rama's permission. Then he joined the Mission. After the

Partition of the country, the images were brought to Maslandapur, not far from Calcutta, and they are still there. Swami Lokeswaranandaji used to visit the temple almost every year.

Kanai's parents were liberal and large-hearted. The catholicity that was manifest in Swami Lokeswarananda was indeed, inherited from his parents. Kanai's father, Basanta Kumar, was a contractor, and many roads and bridges were built under his supervision. He earned enough money and he liked to spend it for others. He was tall and had a healthy body. Lokeswaranandaji's mother was very beautiful. She spent most of her time in worship and in reading scriptures. She looked like an ascetic.

Kanai was very close to his mother and was most influenced by her. Even when he was a child she inspired him to become a monk. Later, the headmaster of his school, Shrish Chandra Sanyal, was his main inspiration. Needless to say, his good *samskaras* (the results of his past karma) also helped him a lot.

Shikharbasini knew both Sanskrit and English, and spent long hours in reading. Every day she would read some portion from the *Puranas, Bhagavata, Chaitanya Charitamrita, Ramayana, Mahabharata,* and the *Gita*. In the afternoon she would read out scriptures to the women of the neighbourhood. From his childhood, Kanai listened to religious stories from his mother. Sometimes, Kanai and his mother would lie down with their heads on a pillow and read a book together. If he turned a page too quickly, she would turn it back. And, he would do the same. Swami Lokeswaranandaji often recollected these sweet memories when he was with his intimate friends. His mother urged him to read the *Bhagavata* and the *Chaitanya Charitamrita*, but he deeply regretted that he had not followed her advice fully. He said that he could not read the *Bhagavata* thoroughly.

Shikharbasini was also a good poet and loved to write poems in her leisure time. Sometimes, in the middle of the night, she would get up, light a lamp, and write a poem. If the children asked her why she was not sleeping, she replied: 'I have an idea in my mind. As long as I do not write it down, I cannot sleep. That's why I am writing it immediately.' The next morning his mother would read out the poem over breakfast.

Shikharbasini Devi spent most of her time in prayer and meditation. Shortly after Kanai joined the Mission, she received initiation from Swami Sivananda in a dream, and she wrote to him about it. Mahapurush Maharaj replied, 'Yes, you have got the right mantra.' She came at least once to Belur Math to meet him, but she also sent letters to him frequently, and Mahapurush Maharaj wrote to her in return.

Swami Lokeswaranandaji once said: 'My mother was an extraordinary woman. What exceptional qualities she had! No one was a stranger to her. If I am anything at all today, I owe it to my mother. She inspired me to be a monk. When I left home to join the Ramakrishna Mission, she blessed me from the bottom of her heart, even though she was feeling very sad. After I joined the Mission I received a letter from her in which she said: 'the village women scold me: "How could you let your brightest son run away like this? What sort of mother are you?" My heart breaks when I hear this. But never mind. I want you to be a real sannyasi.' Shikharbasini died when she was about fifty or fifty-five years old. Kanai was then a *brahmachari*, but before her death he went to see her. Touching her tenderly, Kanai asked, 'Mother, are you afraid to die?' She replied: 'Why should I be afraid? When the final hour will come, I shall gladly go leaving you all behind.'

Kanai had his secondary education (from v to ix) at the B. Dey Institution, and he passed his matriculation exam at the Lalmanirhat School in Rangpore. He then came to Calcutta for further studies. From his student days he had identified himself with the ups and downs of the villagers. If anyone in the village was ill, he, along with other boys, would go to help. Once, there was an epidemic of cholera in the locality. No sooner did Kanai hear this than he got ready to go and nurse the sick. His grandmother forbade him, saying: 'Please, do not go there. Cholera is highly contagious.' But Kanai boldly replied: 'We are "Yamadoots" [messengers of Death]. Nothing can harm us.' Saying this, he at once left, and the other boys followed him. They said, 'If our *mej-da* can go, we should go, too.' He was *mej-da* to all—young and old alike. Because of his extraordinary personality and natural qualities of leadership, the older members of the family respected his opinion in all matters.

Kanai studied for the I.A. at Calcutta. At that time India's freedom movement was going on. When Kanai returned to his village, he announced, 'Starting today we must not use refined sugar.' Just at that time, however, preparations were being made in two families for the sacred thread ceremony, and the families had already made sweets with refined sugar. All their arrangements would be in vain, yet no one had the courage to go against his wishes. Finally the senior members of the locality went to him and said: 'Kanai, we have already arranged everything. Please relax your rule just this once.' Kanai reluctantly agreed, but he refused to take even a bite of the sweets himself.

The year 1925 was a turning point in Kanai's life. That year he took the annual examination for class 9, and in December he was waiting for the result. At that time his uncle from Rangpore came and spent a few days with Kanai's family. When he was about to return to Rangpore, he asked Kanai, 'Would you like to go with me?' As his school was then closed, Kanai readily agreed.

His uncle's house was not far from Lalmanirhat. Kanai's cousin Haripada (who later became a monk of the Sri Ramakrishna Mission named Swami Premarupananda) was a student of the Lalmanirhat School. One day, Haripada took Kanai there. Haripada entered the classroom and Kanai followed him. It was the class 10 classroom. Within a few minutes the headmaster, Shrish Chandra Sanyal, who was also the English teacher of that class, entered the room. Seeing a new face, he asked Kanai: 'Who are you? Where are you from?' Kanai answered in English. The headmaster was very pleased, and he asked Kanai to join the school. Kanai replied, 'I will, if you take me as a free student.' The headmaster said, 'Then, you will have to be a good student.' Kanai said: 'I am a good student. In our school the boy that stands first in the class gets free education, and I always stand first.' At this, the headmaster asked Kanai to write an essay on the subject of newspapers, which he did. That was a Saturday. The headmaster then said, 'Please come on Monday and enquire.'

Gradually, Kanai came to know that the headmaster, his wife, and his mother were all disciples of the Holy Mother. Moreover, two of the headmaster's uncles and two other relatives were monks of the

Ramakrishna Mission. The headmaster would take Kanai to his house every day and talk to him about Sri Ramakrishna, Holy Mother, and Swami Vivekananda. Sometimes the headmaster's mother would ask Kanai to read out to her from the *Ramakrishna Punthi*.

Swami Lokeswaranandaji said: 'The headmaster always talked about Sri Ramakrishna, Ma, and Swamiji. That would take me to another world. I would listen to him for hours, completely unaware of the time. Neither of us felt tired—neither the speaker nor the listener. Sometimes, he would lend me some books to read. He also advised me to spend more time in meditation. Back home, I tried to meditate as long as I could. My heart was full of bliss. I didn't care much for study. The other teachers would say: "We expect you to get a scholarship in the exam. You have to be a judge or a magistrate." But the headmaster protested: "Do not pay any attention to them. I want you to be a monk." One day his wife scolded him: "Why are you asking someone else's son to be a monk? How will his parents feel? Why do not you advise your own son to be a monk?" But the headmaster replied: "I would be very happy if my son really becomes a monk. I would deem it a privilege for him as well as for our family."'

Besides Sri Ramakrishna, Ma, and Swamiji, Kanai also came to know from the headmaster about the direct disciples of Sri Ramakrishna such as Raja Maharaj (Swami Brahmananda), Baburam Maharaj (Swami Premananda), and Mahapurush Maharaj (Swami Sivananda). The headmaster said: 'Mahapurush Maharaj is staying at Belur Math now. Please go there soon and ask him for his blessings.' In Lokeswaranandaji's own words: 'I accepted Mahapurush Maharaj as my guru from that very day. I decided to go to Belur Math by any means and take refuge at his feet.

'In Calcutta I stayed at my brother's house at Kidderpore. One day, I took a bicycle and rode all the way to Belur Math, asking for directions along the way. I was determined to reach Belur Math somehow or other, which I finally did. I began my journey from Kidderpore at about 10 o'clock in the morning. When I reached Belur Math it was 4 o'clock in the afternoon.'

At Belur Math, he stopped first in front of Swami Brahmananda's temple and bowed to him. There, he met a monk who told him the location of the shrine. The temple to Sri Ramakrishna had not yet been built, and Sri Ramakrishna was then in the old shrine. As he was about to go up the stairs to the shrine, the windows of the room to his right suddenly opened. The person whom Kanai saw through the open window needed no introduction. Just as the sun is self-luminous, so was he. Swami Lokeswaranandaji wrote: 'I cannot express in words what I saw. What a divine face! How could it be a human figure?' Mahapurushji talked so easily with him. He seemed to have known him for a long time, and it was as if he was very pleased to see him again. Mahapurush Maharaj said again and again: 'You! Where have you come from? Come, come to me!' Lokeswaranandaji often said, 'Even today I get overwhelmed when I go to that spot near the old shrine.'

Seeing Mahapurush Maharaj, Kanai was stunned. Then, Mahapurush Maharaj told him, 'Please go to the shrine first.' After Kanai had visited the shrine, two monks came and took him to Mahapurush Maharaj's room. The Swami asked him some questions about his background, and then he called everyone, saying: 'Look at this boy. He is such a young boy, but he says he has already appeared for the matriculation exam. He has come on a bicycle all the way from Kidderpore.' Then, Mahapurushji asked him many questions, but Kanai was so nervous he could not answer properly. Mahapurush Maharaj understood the situation, and he told one of his attendants, 'Introduce him to Jnan Maharaj and give him some prasad.' After being introduced to Jnan Maharaj and other monks, he went back to his brother's house full of joy. The same day he also met Nalini Maharaj (Swami Saradeswaranandaji), who was a disciple of Holy Mother.

The next day he again came to Belur Math. This time Mahapurush Maharaj said: 'Oh, you have come again? What about your studies?' Kanai replied: 'Maharaj, my exam is over. I am free now.' But the Swami said: 'If you come so frequently, what will your parents think? They will think we have snatched you away from them.' At this, Kanai felt sad. He met Jnan Maharaj and others and then went back to Kidderpore. He visited Belur Math a few more times, however, to pay his respects to Mahapurush Maharaj before going to his village. Returning to his home in the village, he told everyone, 'I went to Belur Math and met Mahapurush Maharaj.'

After the results of the matriculation exams were out, he returned to Calcutta and was admitted in Bangabasi College. He would then regularly visit Belur Math on Sundays and other holidays. In addition to Mahapurush Maharaj, he met four other disciples of Sri Ramakrishna—Swami Akhandanandaji, Swami Vijnananandaji, Swami Subodhanandaji and Swami Abhedanandaji. Kanai was also very close to M, the writer of *The Gospel of Sri Ramakrishna*. And, he had an opportunity to meet Sri Ramakrishna's nephews—Ramlal-da and Shibu-da—and also Holy Mother's 'yogamaya', Radhu.

Entering Mahapurush Maharaj's room, Kanai said, 'Maharaj, I beg you, please bless me', and then burst into tears. He couldn't say anything else. Mahapurush Maharaj smiled softly and said with great compassion: 'You want initiation? But, my son, we are not professional gurus. You want to repeat the name of God? That's wonderful. Please, say it with me.' With these words, Mahapurush Maharaj uttered the mantra. He went on repeating the mantra, his eyes closed, sitting on his bed in meditation posture. By that time the monks had left the room. Sitting in front of him on the floor, Kanai repeated the Mahamantra with him. He didn't know how much time passed like this. He became conscious only when Mahapurush Maharaj stopped. Then Mahapurush Maharaj said, 'Now go to the shrine.'

The next time Kanai went to Belur Math, he received the greatest blessing of his life from Mahapurushji. The conversation started with ordinary questions about *japa* and meditation. Kanai asked, 'Can I do *japa* while walking on the road?' Mahapurush Maharaj replied: 'Of course, you can. Repeating the name is what matters—not where you repeat it. Repeat it as many times as you can and make your life blessed. But beware, my son, do not get run over!' Then suddenly, Mahapurush Maharaj touched Kanai's chest and said some words that were as secret as they were sacred. Swami Lokeswaranandaji later wrote: They sounded strange to me. I didn't understand then what he meant.

Mahapurushji said: 'You will realise the Sacchidananda (God) in this life.' Finally, he told me my relationship with Sri Ramakrishna.

Sometimes, Kanai wanted to be alone with Mahapurush Maharaj, but that was a rare occasion. Mahapurushji was almost always surrounded by monks and devotees, so Kanai would touch his feet and then stand behind the crowd. But he would be filled with a sense of bliss. The amazing thing was that if he had some question in his mind, it would invariably be asked by someone else or Mahapurush Maharaj would answer it on his own. Moreover, Kanai noticed that while answering those questions, he would often look at Kanai meaningfully. Sometimes, when Kanai was standing at the back, Mahapurushji would make a particular gesture, nodding his head at him. Kanai felt that Mahapurush Maharaj was trying to say, 'You will achieve much.' These simple incidents gave him enormous inspiration in later days. As Swami Lokeswaranandaji wrote: 'Maybe, it was all my imagination, but I derived infinite courage from this imagination.'

One day, Mahapurush Maharaj was standing on the verandah, facing the Ganga. Kanai felt an attraction that he had never felt before, and he went and touched his feet. Mahapurush Maharaj was startled. Kanai felt he had made a blunder, but Mahapurushji was pleased and embraced him. Kanai felt he had been blessed. Lokeswaranandaji had another strange experience concerning Mahapurush Maharaj. He said: 'Mahapurushji would be sitting in his own room, but his presence could be felt everywhere in the Math. The moment we stepped in the Math we knew he was there. What a wonderful feeling!'

As he started visiting Belur Math frequently, Kanai was introduced to the disciples of Swamiji, Raja Maharaj, and Holy Mother. Brahmachari Jnan Maharaj was one of them. At the instance of Swamiji, he remained a *brahmachari* all through his life and stayed at the Math, inspiring the young people who came to him. Earlier, Mahapurush Maharaj had asked Kanai to be introduced to Jnan Maharaj. Since then, whenever Kanai went to Belur Math he would meet Jnan Maharaj. Coming to know from Kanai where he lived, Jnan Maharaj gave him the addresses of young devotees who lived near him, and he told Kanai to contact them.

Swami Lokeswaranandaji held Jnan Maharaj in high esteem. He wrote: 'Some people stand out from others as an institution. Jnan Maharaj was one of them. Many people were inspired by him. He hardly talked about anything personal. His discussions mainly revolved around his own country and society. And, there was never a note of despair—only encouragement to go ahead. He encouraged us not to be afraid of danger. Truth alone triumphs in the long run.' We will see later that the main note of Swami Lokeswaranandaji's life was just this—nothing negative, everything positive.

We have already said that Kanai had been admitted to Bangabasi College after his matriculation exam. At that time he rented a room above Shrimani Market. The principal and vice-principal of the college were involved in the freedom movement against the British rule. Kanai also got involved in politics and began to neglect his studies. Finally, after the I.A. exam, he stopped going to classes and gave away his books to others. He decided he wouldn't attend college until India was free. He used to give speeches in different areas, and he attracted many young men to the movement. He openly criticised the police for their brutality and invoked their suspicion.

Kanai had to travel much through the neighbouring areas of his village to inspire people for the freedom movement. But when he returned to Calcutta after about a year, he found the movement in disarray. He became disillusioned and decided to rejoin his college. However, because he had been absent for the whole year, the college authorities wouldn't permit him to appear for the final examination. Fortunately, an English professor, Nripen Banerjee, found out that Kanai had been working for the freedom movement and took him to the vice-principal, Jiten Chakraborty. Finally he got permission to sit for the examination.

By that time Kanai knew many of the monks of the Sri Ramakrishna Mission, and though he had not yet joined the Mission, they would treat him as a *brahmachari*. The monks at Advaita Ashrama, including Swami Nityaswarupanandaji, then asked Kanai to live with them while he was studying for the examination, so he did. There he shared a room with Swami Ashokanandaji, who was preparing to leave for the United States.

During this period, some members of the freedom movement who were advocates of violence, took Kanai to a park and started questioning him about his future plans. When he told them he wanted to be a monk, they said: 'Then you will betray us. You will inform the police about us, so we will shoot you now.' 'Shoot me if you like,' Kanai replied, 'but I am not a traitor. Do I even know your real names? Then how can I betray you?' Kanai said this because everyone in the movement used a fictitious name. This seemed to have a calming effect on them and they let him go.

Kanai passed the B.A. examination from Calcutta University in 1931. After that he went to teach in the Ramakrishna Mission Vidyapith at Deoghar in Bihar, but as a lay teacher—not as a *brahmachari*. He had lost his father a few years earlier, and the economic condition of the family was not very good then. He needed to earn some money for his sister's marriage, so he had to work. His uncle lived at Deoghar and was the station-master there. Kanai lived with him. Now and then, however, he would go to visit Mahapurush Maharaj at Belur Math. By then he had grown taller, so Mahapurush Maharaj would call him 'tall Kanai' or 'Deoghar's Kanai', because there were a few other Kanais at Belur Math then and they were all monks.

Though he was young and not yet a monk, he was appointed a member of the School Executive Committee of the Deoghar Vidyapith, and he was recognised as an expert teacher within a short time. After working as a teacher for a year, Kanai wanted to join the Mission, but a monk of the Vidyapith asked him to continue working another year to help an orphan boy who was a student of the Vidyapith. After supporting the boy for a year, Kanai quietly joined the Mission in 1933. He didn't tell that monk of his plan to join, fearing that he would request him to support the orphan boy for another year. It was impossible for him to wait any longer. After joining the Ramakrishna Mission, he was known as Kanai Maharaj.

For a year after joining the Mission, he remained at Deoghar as a teacher. During that time he studied the Upanishads under Swami Jagadanandaji, a great scholar and sage. Kanai Maharaj didn't sleep much at night, and he often saw Jagadanandaji in the middle of the night, sitting up straight on his bed and reciting verses from the Upanishads. Later, he confided that he learned how to study the Upanishads from Swami Jagadanandaji and Swami Satprakashanandaji. He always remembered Swami Satprakashanandaji's advice: 'Try to study the Upanishads on your own, without the help of any commentary. Get the meaning by yourself. It is more difficult, but only this way can you make the truths of the Upanishads your own.'

Around this time Kanai Maharaj was sent to Bhangamora, near Arambagh, for relief work. This was his first relief work, and he cherished the memory of it even during the last years of his life. Kanai Maharaj used to say that at that time there were three monks of the same age at Belur Math. Two of them had already been sent for relief work, but he was left behind and he was very upset about it. For a long time he wanted to do some relief work, so when the call eventually came, he felt very happy. When he reached the site, he found the area flooded all around. People had taken shelter in the trees along with snakes. A pregnant lady had even given birth to her child on top of a tree. Kanai Maharaj would go out in a boat to bring food to the flood-stricken people. At that time, he lived in a room of a village school and had one meal a day. He stayed there for a year, even after the water had receded; as he was then busy building houses for the rehabilitation of the affected people. He felt very happy to be able to do this relief work at Bhangamora, although it was very hard work.

One day in 1936, Swami Madhavanandaji, who was the General Secretary of the Mission at that time, suddenly called him to his office. He loved Kanai Maharaj very much. Swami Madhavanandaji said: 'We have been requested to do relief work in Burma, where many on the offshore island of Zeduba have lost their lives in a devastating earthquake. We have suggested that you go there.'

The swami went on to say that the residents of that island were descendents of criminals, and many of them were tribal people who had been transported there for life by the British. They carried weapons and would kill a person at the slightest provocation. When government officials went to the island to carry out relief operations, the local people threatened to kill them. They actually beat up some of the officials, took their relief supplies, and chased them back to their steamer. The island was connected to the mainland only by a steamer. But after Kanai Maharaj reached Zeduba, the work was completed in about six months. By that time the crops were ready for harvest, and poultry and other animals were again being raised. The people were in tears when the relief workers left.

After staying at Rangoon for a short time, Kanai Maharaj returned to Belur Math. The moment he arrived at the Math he was put in a car and sent to Serampore, where a meeting was to be held. He had no chance to object. It was then 1936, and many festivals and meetings were taking place as the celebration of the birth centenary of Sri Ramakrishna. At Serampore, the first speaker was Swami Sambuddhanandaji, the Secretary of the Ramakrishna Centenary Committee. Kanai Maharaj was not even a monk then. He was very nervous. His former teacher, Nripen Banerjee, who had helped him get permission to take his final exam in college, was the other speaker. Kanai Maharaj came through the ordeal well. People in the audience thought, 'He will be a great orator in the future.' He was next sent to Dhaka to speak, but while there he received a telegram asking him to return to Belur Math immediately. When he arrived, he was instructed to go with a senior monk to a meeting at Jalpaiguri.

After remaining at Belur Math for a short time, Kanai Maharaj was sent in December 1936 to Cherrapunji, which was then in Assam. A boys' school had been opened there in 1931 by Swami Prabhanandaji (Ketaki Maharaj). It was a branch of the Ramakrishna Mission in Shillong, of which Swami Bhuteshanandaji was Secretary. The Cherrapunji ashrama was then facing great financial difficulties. There were only thirty-one students, all tribals. Neither the government nor the public supported the school in any way. When Kanai Maharaj arrived, he found there was only one teacher who was qualified. The rest were not fit to be teachers. Belur Math had sent him to improve the situation.

Kanai Maharaj learned the Khasi language in three months, well enough to deliver speeches in it. He lived at the school, sleeping on a table at night. Along with a swami who could speak the Khasi language, he went around the area appealing to the public to send their children to the school. In response, they were requested to accept one boy, a school drop-out. As a gesture of good will, they accepted him, and he was given free tuition.

In 1938, Kanai Maharaj went to Belur Math for his *brahmacharya* vows. He received his vows from Revered Swami Vijnanananda, a direct disciple of Sri Ramakrishna, and was given the name Brahmachari Suvrata Chaitanya.

When Kanai Maharaj returned to Belur Math, he was asked to join the Deoghar Vidyapith again—this time as headmaster. After arriving there, he immediately imposed much needed discipline in the school. He was a hard taskmaster, but at the same time he loved his students very much. He was liberal yet firm in his dealings with them. He loved to play football and volleyball with the students and teachers, and was a good volleyball player. But whenever he was with the students, he always tried to instil self-respect, honesty, and a sense of responsibility in them.

Kanai Maharaj was at Deoghar from 1941 to 1944. In 1944, Brahmachari Suvrata Chaitanya received his final monastic vows from Swami Virajananda, President of the Mission, and was thenceforth known as Swami Lokeswarananda. He said: 'Before my final vows, I saw a list of monastic names from an attendant of President Maharaj. But the monastic names had not yet been fixed. I wished I could have the name Lokeswarananda. When I actually got that name I was amazed and happy too.'

Swami Lokeswaranandaji then asked to be relieved of his duties at Deoghar. He was next sent to Mayavati with the idea that gradually he would take charge of the editing of *Prabuddha Bharata*. But this was not to be. He began to have trouble with his health and actually fainted several times.

While he was taking rest at Varanasi, he received a letter from Belur Math saying: 'You are being assigned to Pathuriaghata Students' Home as Secretary. Please, come to Belur Math soon.' He was not happy to receive the message. To understand why, we have to look back at the beginning of the Pathuriaghata ashrama.

In 1943, while the Second World War was going on, Bengal was hit by a severe famine. At that time, a gentleman named Rashbehari Mallik donated two houses to the Ramakrishna Mission. Many poor but intelligent students from rural Bengal had been hit by the famine, and they had to wind up their studies prematurely. The Mission proposed that such students be accomodated in these two houses so that they could continue their studies in their college or university.

The Students' Home was thus started. The students gradually came, but the hostel did not run well. The Secretaries were changed, one after another, but their relationship with the students declined—so much so that one swami-in-charge left after being heckled by the students. Other monks refused to go there as Secretary. Naturally when Lokeswaranandaji received the message about his new assignment, he was far from happy.

Lokeswaranandaji Maharaj took charge of the Pathuriaghata Ashrama in May–June 1946. From Benaras he came in the morning to Belur Math, and the same evening he joined the ashrama. The ashrama had only one boarder left. The other students who had insulted the previous Secretary had already been expelled. As a first step, Lokeswaranandaji informed their guardians that they would not be taken back. Then, an advertisement asking for new boarders was put in the newspaper which read, 'Applications are invited from poor but meritorious students.'

Maharaj himself was then living from hand to mouth. He had practically nothing at his disposal—no chairs, tables, cots, or other pieces of furniture. Still he wanted to keep the students without charge. How could his dream possibly come true? The monthly expense of each student was worked out to be thirty rupees. Fortunately, one day Maharaj met a gentleman on board a train. In course of conversation he explained to him the work of the hostel and told him of its needs. The gentleman was very much impressed and offered to help him. Not only that, he convinced some of his friends to do the same. Thus, in the very first year several poor students were admitted to the Students' Home without charge.

In Swami Lokeswaranandaji's own words: 'Friends and well-wishers grew in number. They were working in different offices. Arrangements were made to collect money from them at the end of the month. And sometimes, they collected the money themselves and brought it to the Students' Home. At that time there was no other monastic to help me. I had to manage everything on my own. Meanwhile, the students were also increasing. But glory to God! Within seven days of my joining the Students' Home, I received a letter from the Indian Red Cross Society. They wrote: 'We have come to know that you are running a free Students' Home for poor and meritorious students. We would like to offer a few things to your Home, such as ice-cream, milk-powder, lozenges, cheese, peanut butter, and other left-over supplies from World War II. We shall be happy if you come and collect these yourself.' I was very surprised to receive the letter. However, I went to the Red Cross Society to fetch the gifts. They gave us so many things indeed! The students were very happy to see the gifts. I still wonder how the Red Cross Society came to know about us. We did not even have a telephone at our disposal so that they could know of us from the directory. People began to say that this incident showed that God's special grace was on me. A few days later, the Indian Red Cross Society again called on us and gave a large number of books, tables, chairs, cupboards, and other such things. The books were all given without charge. As for the furniture, some pieces were donated and others were given at a nominal charge. In addition, they gave us some valuable, good quality clocks. These clocks are now at Narendrapur and are still in working condition.' It is worth mentioning here that the Pathuriaghata Students' Home later became a huge, multi-faceted institution at Narendrapur.

Monetary assistance began to come from different quarters to the ashrama, and the number of students also grew accordingly. Shortly afterwards India gained freedom, and as a result, refugees began pouring in from East Bengal. Swami Lokeswaranandaji wrote: 'Many refugee families took shelter on the platform of Sealdah Station. There were many students from schools, colleges, and universities among them. We accommodated some of the refugee students in our hostel, but there was hardly any room left. We had only two houses at our disposal. However, Harendra Chandra Saha, a childhood friend of mine, donated some money to the ashrama, and with that we added another floor. At this time a committee was formed by the government to look after the needs of the refugee students. The committee referred some of these students to us. As far as I remember, the committee also recommended twenty to twenty-five rupees a month for supporting each student. Besides this, the Bengal Relief Fund was opened during the famine. A gentleman named Bhagirath Kanoria was its treasurer. One day, I went to him and appealed for financial aid. He was sympathetic and sent us some money every month ever since.'

A few years later, the ashrama had grown larger and the number of students had increased substantially. The money required for food each week was two thousand and five hundred rupees. A brahmachari was then the treasurer of the Students' Home. A former resident of the ashrama, he had joined the Mission. His name was Ranjan (Swami Mumukshananda). One day, he informed Lokeswaranandaji that there was no more cash left for the next week's food. Swami Lokeswaranandaji asked him to check the subscriber's list. 'See if any subscription is due', he said. The brahmachari replied, 'One subscriber is yet to pay his contribution, but he gives only sixty rupees a month.' Swami Lokeswaranandaji called him. (By then the ashrama had gotten a telephone.) The gentleman said to Maharaj: 'Swamiji, I was just thinking about you. Could you please, come over for a while? I want to talk to you.' When Swami Lokeswaranandaji reached there, the gentleman said: 'I am leaving for England shortly for four years. I have many expenses ahead, and I regret I shall not be able to pay my contribution to the ashrama during this period.' Swami Lokeswaranandaji replied: 'Please, do not worry about it. When you return you will earn much more, and you can then contribute more.' Although Lokeswaranandaji said this, he was really worried. He thought: 'There goes my last hope. How shall I pay for the next week's food?' The gentleman then continued: 'But if I do not pay anything now, I shall feel very bad.' Saying this, he brought out his cheque-book, wrote a cheque, and handed it over to Swami Lokeswaranandaji. It was for two thousand eight hundred and eighty rupees—the whole sum of money for the next four years at the rate of sixty rupees a month.

The address of the Pathuriaghata ashrama was 18, Jadulal Mallick Road. The house next to it was 20, Jadulal Mallick Road. With the increased number of students, lack of space was a problem. Eventually, news came that the adjacent house was for sale. As it was a residential house, it had been a source of disturbance to the inmates of the ashrama. Swami Lokeswaranandaji decided to buy it by any means. But the price for the house was fixed at 2.5 lakh. How could he possibly get so much money when he himself lived from hand to mouth? Mr D.M. Sen, the then Education Secretary of the Government of West Bengal, was close to Lokeswaranandaji. He was also an admirer of the selfless work of the ashrama as well as of the Ramakrishna Mission as a whole. Swami Lokeswaranandaji sought his assistance. Mr Sen said he could sanction a government grant of one lakh. Another lakh he agreed to give as a loan without interest. The remaining fifty thousand rupees were borrowed from Belur Math and the house was bought. The new house was much better than the old one, and the students were happy. The number of students in the two houses together rose to one hundred and sixty.

Although the Ashrama continued to grow and thrive, the surrounding area was not favourable for an educational institution. Buses ran on the road in front of the ashrama, and the number of shops increased around it. Besides this, there was a plot on the northern side of the newly-acquired house which was used throughout the night as a garage for the repair of defective lorries. As a result, the residents of the Students' Home were having great difficulty with their studies and spiritual practices—not to mention sleep. But what troubled Swami Lokeswaranandaji most was that there was no playground in the neighbourhood for the boys. Lokeswaranandaji informed the Math authorities about these difficulties and proposed to shift the Students' Home to a better and bigger site if they approved. Permission was granted.

Swami Lokeswaranandaji's plan was to build thatched houses on the new plot of land, and he had calculated the expenditure to be twenty-five to thirty thousand rupees. He intended to ask for the whole amount from the Refugee Rehabilitation Department. When he arrived at the Department's Joint Secretary, Mr Chatterjee's office, he explained what kind of work he was doing as well as their need for new accommodation. Mr Chatterjee asked, 'How many students do you eventually want to accommodate?' Swami Lokeswaranandaji replied: 'We now have 165 students. We want to push the number up to 200.' Mr Chatterjee said: 'My God! That's a lot of money. You should have come earlier. Anyway, if you can manage within five lakh, we shall grant the money to you. But we cannot give any more.' Swami Lokeswaranandaji was speechless. From thirty thousand to five lakh! How strange!

The incident that followed was even stranger—if not miraculous. In Swami Lokeswaranandaji's words: 'Just as we were talking, a gentleman with heavy steps entered Mr Chatterjee's room. He had a fine shirt and pyjama on and his feet were bare. I immediately recognised him as Mr Meherchand Khanna, the Hon'ble Minister of Refugee Rehabilitation of the Government of India. I had seen his pictures in the newspapers. Entering the room he addressed Mr Chatterjee: 'Hello, Mr Chatterjee, how are you today?' Mr Chatterjee had been down with asthma for several days and had just returned that day to his office, so the Minister had come to enquire about his health. Later, Mr Chatterjee told me: 'Perhaps, this is the first time a Minister has entered the office of the Joint-Secretary to enquire about his health. This was possible because of you. You, a monk, have been sitting in my office. It is your subtle influence that has worked on the Minister and brought him here.' Anyway, before Mr Chatterjee could answer the Minister's question, his attention fell on me. 'Swamiji, have we not met before?' He asked. I replied, 'No, you have not seen me.' He said, 'I have a feeling you came once to see me in the Governor's house.' Then I said: 'It must have been some other monk of our Mission. Perhaps it was Swami Punyananda. He has started an orphanage at Khardah.' Mr Khanna then asked me what I was doing. I said that I was associated with education. At this point Mr Chatterjee intervened: 'Sir, they are doing wonderful work. Many poor refugee students who are meritorious are getting education under his care. He runs a Students' Home for them. He is helping poor students stand on their own feet, thus saving the whole family. From that point of view he is helping our project of refugee rehabilitation a great deal.' Mr Chatterjee went on and on—even to the point of exaggeration. The Minister was quite satisfied. He said: 'Swamiji, I do not know what my Joint-Secretary and Finance Officer have said to you, but I feel that the government should support your project whole-heartedly. Could you tell me how much you need? How many students do you wish to take care of?' I said: 'We would like to accommodate two hundred students. And, we need four lakh and eighty thousand rupees to carry out our plan.' The Minister expressed his approval: 'Very reasonable, very reasonable.'

Later, I came to know from Mr Chatterjee that the government had its own formula for working out the sum of money that could be granted. And, according to that formula, the amount that could be sanctioned for two hundred students was just four lakh and eighty thousand rupees. Of course, I did not know this at that time. I just mentioned that amount without much thinking. I remembered what Mr Chatterjee had told me—that he could sanction up to five lakh. So I asked for a little less, in case they thought I had claimed that amount because they said so.

A new place called Ukhila Paikpara, near Rajpur, was selected. The government acquired the land and handed it over to the Ramakrishna Mission on 30 March 1956. In all, 26.55 acres of land were taken.

Meanwhile, some students from Pathuriaghata lived there in tents and went to their colleges from the property. The address of the new ashrama was: Ramakrishna Mission Ashrama, Village—Ukhila Paikpara, P.O. Rajpur, Dist. 24 Parganas. The name Narendrapur was given to the place by Swami Madhavananda, the General Secretary of the Ramakrishna Math and Mission. The names of areas nearby had the suffix 'pur'—such as Rajpur, Sonarpur, Mallickpur, and Baruipur. In keeping with that, Swami Madhavanandaji said: 'May this place be known as "Narendrapur" after Swamiji. As a boy Swamiji was known as Narendra. Here, young boys will come to study. So, "Narendrapur" will be a suitable name.' The place was then given that name through proper legal procedures.

At that time Swami Sankarananda was the President of the Ramakrishna Math and Mission. He consecrated the foundation of Brahmananda Bhavan on the auspicious day of Makar-Sankranti, on

14 January 1957. Two days later (16 January) the Refugee Rehabilitation Minister, Mr Meherchand Khanna, laid the foundation stone of the Bhavan. On 5 December 1958, the Union Finance Minister, Mr Morarji Desai, opened the door of Brahmananda Bhavan to the students, and on 23 February 1959, on the auspicious day of Maghi Purnima, Revered Swami Sankarananda installed the picture of Sri Ramakrishna in the shrine of the Bhavan. The students from Pathuriaghata then came to reside at Brahmananda Bhavan. 'Gradually, the whole area surrounding the ashrama complex came to be known as Narendrapur, and a post office, telegraph office, telephone exchange, and banks also came there. Mr Khanna requested us: 'Please, increase the number of students and start your own school and college.' The school was inaugurated in 1958.

The college came into being two years after the school. Then came the Blind Boys' Academy. The story behind the Blind Boys' school is very interesting. One day, when Swami Lokeswaranandaji was at Pathuriaghata, he received a letter which said: 'I am a poor student. Not only poor, I am also helpless in the sense that I am blind. I have come to know from your advertisement in the newspaper that you keep poor and meritorious students free. They study in schools and colleges from there. I do not know if I am meritorious or not, but I passed my matriculation in the first division. I also secured better marks in one subject. I have just taken my intermediate exam, but the result is yet to come out. I want to study for a B.A. If you kindly accommodate me in your hostel I can continue my studies. Without this opportunity it will be impossible for me to continue my studies any longer.'

In reply, Swami Lokeswaranandaji asked to see him, and the boy came with his father. His name was Bhavani Prasad Chanda. Swami Lokeswaranandaji asked him: How can you find your way in the hostel to your room or to the kitchen? Can you get on trams and buses on your own? How will you go to college? He replied: 'If you show me just once where my room or the kitchen or the prayer hall is, I shall be able to find my way out. May someone also help me go to the college on the very first day? Then I shall not need any further help.' Swami Lokeswaranandaji wrote: I was surprised to hear him. Then

Bhavani continued: 'I shall just secure first division in I.A. I do not expect any better result this time.' When the gazette came out, I found he had indeed secured first division. I sent him a telegram to come immediately. He came and got admitted in Presidency College with honours in history. Following Bhavani's example, many blind students contacted us, and quite a number of them got admission in our hostel. Gradually, the need for a separate blind boys' home was obvious. As a result, an institution for blind boys came up at Narendrapur—the Blind Boys' Academy. And Bhavani, who had gotten his M.A. by then, became the first principal of the Academy.'

In course of time, a Commercial Institute, a Junior Technical School, a college, and a training centre for rural workers came up at Narendrapur. When the college was started, Bikas Sanyal, a former student of the Pathuriaghata Students' Home, became its first principal. (Presently, he is a special advisor to the Secretary-General of UNESCO.) He ran the college very efficiently for two years. From the very beginning, the students of the college have been very successful in their university exams. One of the students stood first class first in chemistry honours, the first time Narendrapur College sent students for the honours exam. Today, in the field of education, Narendrapur is a name held in great respect. Former students of Narendrapur are now holding important positions in and outside the country.

The history of Pathuriaghata's evolution to Narendrapur will remain incomplete unless we mention Rambagan. In Swami Lokeswaranandaji's own words: The Duttas of Rambagan were famous. Sir Ramesh Dutta and Taru Dutta were from their family. But in course of time Rambagan turned into an ill-reputed slum whose inhabitants were called 'doms'. But one could hardly see anywhere else people with such artistic talent and intelligence as these inhabitants of Rambagan. They were poor and uneducated. And, it is difficult to imagine how they lived in such unhygienic surroundings. In 1953, a representative of the slum dwellers, Mr Jivan Manik, approached me and asked me to open a school in the slum. Then, the boys of the Students' Home said to me: 'You have done so much for us. Can't we do something for these poor people?' Thus, a night school was started for adult education. A small room was rented for the purpose. The number of students was ten and the teachers twenty. The number of young teachers was twice the number of aged students. A few days later, the aged students said: 'Why waste your time educating us? Our days are numbered. Rather, teach our children and grandchildren.' We said: 'First, you learn. Then, your children will feel inspired to learn, too.' Later, we opened a school for the children also. But soon, we realised that we could not remove the suffering of these people unless we did something to improve their living conditions. They had no fixed income. They played the flute during marriage festivals and other occasions, but otherwise they were unemployed. They were also expert in cane and bamboo handicrafts, but cane was very costly and the price of bamboo was also increasing. In this age, plastic goods have become more popular than cane and bamboo. As a consequence, they could not earn enough for their livelihood in spite of their hard work. So, in addition to giving them education, we also gave them vocational training. Sewing helped women earn well enough. And, some of them became self-sufficient by weaving.

'These days they are being trained in various kinds of handiwork, and their per capita income has also increased. This is not to say that there has been a substantial improvement in their financial state. That needs time. But the young boys and girls are getting an education, and one of them has even become a graduate. In the near future they are expected to excel in intellectual work also. Previously these people suffered a lot from various ailments due to malnutrition, and they could not afford to have proper treatment. The Ramakrishna Mission is now running a charitable dispensary, and arrangements have been made for proper nutrition for the children. There was also a problem in their supply of drinking water, but that has been taken care of.'

Although the ashrama moved from Pathuriaghata to Narendrapur, the work of Rambagan was still going strong. In fact, it was flourishing day by day. All day long the workers do various kinds of social service. The old huts have been torn down, and a new multi-storied housing complex has been built for them. The slum-dwellers themselves took part in the construction work. To make the dwellers aware of their problems and to encourage them to solve them themselves is a unique venture, indeed.

This has been possible only because of Mr Shivsankar Chakraborty, whose inspiration and guide was Swami Lokeswarananda.

In addition to building large institutions like Narendrapur, Swami Lokeswaranandaji was also a maker of men. Many educated youth were inspired to embrace monastic life by Swami Lokeswarananda. Then, there are the householders, like Mr Shivsankar Chakraborty, who have dedicated their lives to the service of human beings. There can be no denying the fact that Swami Lokeswarananda was always successful in kindling the flame of nobility in young hearts.

After the ashrama moved from Pathuriaghata to Narendrapur, Swami Lokeswarananda took up the work of rural development. Mr Shivsankar Chakraborty with the help of dedicated young monks started adult education, and many adult education centres were opened in the neighbouring villages. Swami Lokeswarananda wrote: 'These were not only centres for adult education; they were also involved in over-all rural development. They saw to it that the local young people came forward to help themselves. Different projects were taken up for building roads, supplying drinking water, opening up libraries and health centres, introducing modern methods of cultivation, encouraging small industries, training adults in poultry-keeping, etc. The villages gradually began to wear a new look. At present, Loka-Shiksha Parishad of Narendrapur is looking after these projects. Several hundred of such rural centres [at present, more than eight thousand centres] are working under their supervision. Millions of poor villagers are being benefitted by these projects. The work of Loka-Shiksha Parishad today is not just limited to West Bengal, but it has spread far and wide. Its main characteristic is to bestow responsibility on the local youth. Silently, Loka-Shiksha Parishad is bringing about a revolution that is hard to imagine.'

We do not know how many people in post-independent India have been able to build up as big and as multi-faceted an institution as Narendrapur, but in spite of everything, Swami Lokeswarananda never claimed the glory of making Narendrapur himself. He sincerely believed that Narendrapur came into being through the grace of Sri Ramakrishna, Holy Mother and Swami Vivekananda.

As days passed, Narendrapur continued to grow and thrive. Students from all over India came there, and teachers came from England, Germany, Australia, the United States, and Japan. One crisis after another rolled over the ashram, but each time it was overcome through the grace of Sri Ramakrishna. The most significant incident took place in 1969. A group of workers of Narendrapur formed a union at the instigation of a political party, and they called a strike to paralyse the whole institution. Their demand was that a worker who had been dismissed for stealing should be reinstated. But their real intention was to have complete control over the school. Swami Lokeswarananda called a meeting of the monks and told them: 'This is a challenge. We cannot compromise.'

The students and loyal workers of the ashram did all the work to maintain the institution, and the guardians backed the monks. The mothers of the students met Lokeswarananda and offered to cook and wash utensils if necessary. Lokeswarananda was impressed by the gesture, but he did not need their help. He could somehow manage with the help of the students and loyal workers of the ashram. Police were posted to keep order, but they were sympathetic to the strikers. They requested Swami Lokeswarananda to compromise. Pressure also came from political parties. But Lokeswarananda stood firm. At last, after three months, political leaders withdrew their support for the strikers, and the strike was called off. Swami Lokeswarananda then went to Belur Math. The authorities there praised him highly for his firmness. But his health completely broke down from the extreme mental tension and the sleepless nights he had passed during the strike. He had to be hospitalised for several months for a stomach ulcer.

One day in 1973, the Belur Math authorities told him that he was to take charge of the Institute of Culture at Gol Park immediately. The workers of that centre had been creating trouble for a long time, so Swami Nityaswarupananda had resigned and left for New Delhi. Lokeswarananda sent a telegram to Delhi asking him to return. His reply was: 'I shall think it over.' Within half an hour Nityaswarupananda sent a second telegram saying it was impossible for him to come back. The Math authorities then asked Swami Lokeswarananda to take charge of the Institute without delay. Accordingly, he came straight to the Institute of Culture from Belur Math. Narendrapur, which he had built brick-by-brick, was left behind without a second thought. Later, he said: 'By the grace of Thakur, I didn't feel sad to leave Narendrapur. Not even once did I feel that I had lost anything.'

Swami Lokeswarananda arrived at the Institute of Culture on 20 December 1973. And, for the last twenty-five years (till the end of his life) he remained at the Institute as its Secretary. When he first came, the Institute was in turmoil—just as Narendrapur had been in 1969. The only difference was that the union was formed by the opposite political party from that at Narendrapur. Quite a few workers joined the union. As before, Swami Lokeswarananda was very firm in dealing with the agitators. The top trouble-makers were dismissed, and a group of loyal workers were brought from Narendrapur and placed in important positions of the main departments. But the union continued their agitation, demanding reinstatement of the suspended workers. The Institute's library had to be closed temporarily.

Once peace was restored to the Institute, Swami Lokeswarananda got down to organising the centre. He easily won over the hearts of the workers with his love and sympathy for them. He wanted the workers to consider the Institute as their own place. He made the yearly Foundation Day, on 29 January, a 'get-together' day for the workers. He said: 'This Institute is for the workers, so Foundation Day is especially for them. They will come with the members of their family and stay here all day, eat, and rejoice together.'

Within a year of coming to the Institute, Swami Lokeswarananda started giving weekly classes on the *Sri Ramakrishna Kathamrita (The Gospel of Sri Ramakrishna)*. Before him there had been lectures on Sri Ramakrishna at Vivekananda Hall in the Institute, but nothing on the *Kathamrita*. The class became very popular among the devotees, and gradually the audience increased. At times all 1,000 seats of Vivekananda Hall would be filled, and arrangements had to be made for seats on the portico outside as well as in Sivananda Hall. Previously, the monthly *Bulletin* of the Institute had been coming out irregularly at three to four month intervals, so Swami Lokeswarananda engaged two young brahmacharis to look after its publication as also other works. The *Bulletin* then started coming out regularly, and some research-oriented publications such as *Chintanayak Vivekananda,* as well as small low-priced booklets, were also published.

Processions to celebrate the birth anniversary of Sri Ramakrishna were also started under the guidance of Swami Lokeswarananda. As a result, contact with the people at large gradually increased. Swami Vivekananda laid much emphasis on the study of the Upanishads. Hence, Lokeswarananda started giving weekly classes on the Upanishads in English. A third weekly scripture class was also started by him. To spread the ideals of Swami Vivekananda among the youth (16–30 years of age), the Vivekananda Study Circle was founded by him.

In 1978, there was a flood in Calcutta for several days, due to heavy rain. Swami Lokeswarananda's heart cried out for the flood-affected people around, so relief work began under his supervision. The monks, brahmacharis, and other workers of the Institute worked in unison to save the water-logged people. In the same year, a large portion of South Bengal was under water just before the Puja holidays. As before, Swami Lokeswarananda sent his relief team to work among the distressed people.

In 1980, Belur Math decided to conduct the second Convention of the Ramakrishna Mission, and Swami Lokeswarananda was made the convener. A convention committee was formed under his supervision, and the monks, brahmacharis, and workers of the Institute did their best to make the convention a success. The convention ended in December 1980, but it inspired great enthusiasm and a sense of unity among the followers of Sri Ramakrishna and Vivekananda. Swami Lokeswarananda wanted this enthusiasm to continue, so after the convention he arranged for spiritual retreats at the Institute. These retreats became so popular that the three hundred seats of Sivananda Hall were not enough to accommodate all the devotees and the venue had to be shifted to Vivekananda Hall, which had a thousand seats. Later, in 1993–94, Swami Lokeswarananda was appointed the convener of the centenary celebrations of Swami Vivekananda's addresses at the World's Parliament of Religions in Chicago. Again, in 1997–98, he was the convener for the centenary celebrations of the founding of the Ramakrishna Mission.

All day, Swami Lokeswarananda met innumerable visitors at the Institute and talked to them. Among them were learned scholars as well as lay men and women and youth. He spoke to each person as if he or she was his own. Besides his three weekly classes, he used to preside over lectures given by others at the Institute. He also attended many meetings and learned gatherings outside. Swami Lokeswarananda wrote the Observations for the *Bulletin* every month, as well as numerous articles for newspapers and journals in both English and Bengali. To him the role of the Institute was enormous. It was the meeting point of India with the whole world. Once, at a Foundation Day meeting at the Institute, he observed: 'The Institute represents Truth. It represents India.' Still, he gave the greatest importance to the Institute's library and left no stone unturned to enrich it day by day.

In 1981, Swami Lokeswarananda was invited by the universities of Oxford and Cambridge. At Oxford, he gave lectures on the Bhagavad Gita, comparing the views of Shankaracharya and Ramanuja on the second chapter. He also visited at that time Germany, England, France, Switzerland, and Italy. In addition to his lectures at Oxford, he also spoke at Cambridge University and the Sorbonne University. While he was in Italy, he met Pope John Paul II and gave a talk on 'Jesus Christ in the Eyes of a Hindu Sannyasi', which was broadcast on the Pope's own radio station, 'Vatican Radio'.

In 1984, Swami Lokeswarananda was invited to Sofia, the capital of Bulgaria, to attend an international peace conference. On his way back he stopped at Moscow, and two very influential organisations— the Academy of Sciences and the Writers' Union—gave him a special reception. He became very friendly with the members of these two societies—so much so that the next year an international peace conference was held at the Institute of Culture in collaboration with these two organisations. Swami Lokeswarananda went to Russia seven times. In 1988, a Vedanta Centre was opened in Moscow through his inspiration. Later it was recognised as a branch centre of the Sri Ramakrishna Mission.

Through the years, many countries invited him to come and speak. These include: Bangladesh, Sri Lanka, Thailand, Singapore, Malaysia, England, France, Germany, Switzerland, Italy, the United States, Canada, Japan, Mauritius, Soviet Russia, Lithuania, and Latvia.

During his time, the Institute of Culture was recognised as a truly international centre, as its name spread both in and outside India. The Institute became a meeting place of scholars and research workers from all over the country as well as the world. Moreover, through the youth programme of the Institute—the Vivekananda Study Circle—Swami Lokeswarananda spread the ideals of selfless work to the grass-roots level in the remotest possible corners of the state. For the past 25 years, more than 100 youth conventions a year have been conducted in the main towns as well as the remote rural areas.

Lokeswarananda's continuing endeavour was to instil the highest ideals of truth in the hearts of people of all walks of life. With him as editor, research works such as *Satarupe Sarada*, *Chintanayak Vivekananda*, and *Ramakrishner Priya Sangeet* were published, along with small low-priced booklets such as *Savar Swamiji*, *Yuvanayak Vivekananda*, and *Bharater Nivedita*. He knew that tastes and abilities varied from one person to another, and as a result, people's outer and inner worlds also varied. He realised that people should be encouraged to move forward from where they were, so, with this in mind, he added multifarious dimensions to the work of the Institute.

Several years ago, Lokeswarananda opened a new department in the Institute for the study of and research in Indology, and he engaged for it a number of renowned pandits and scholars of philosophy and Indian scriptures. He encouraged them to have group discussions as well as to translate Vedanta literature. He particularly emphasised the need for learning the Sanskrit language, and supported many foreign scholars in the guest house who were interested in learning Sanskrit and studying Indian scriptures. Another new section of the Institute which he inaugurated was the Vivekananda Archives. There, all material on Sri Ramakrishna and Swami Vivekananda were to be collected and made readily available for research scholars.

In spite of the tremendous work he did, Swami Lokeswarananda was always a support and shelter to countless people—young and old, men and women alike.

Just as Swami Lokeswarananda had tremendous love and compassion, so also he had immense zeal and dynamism. Although he was nearly ninety when he passed away, he was still young in vision and vigour—as if he still had much to offer to the world. He was always full of enthusiasm and had the ability to see the whole ocean in a drop of water. In an ordinary person, he could see extraordinary qualities and thus he could inspire self-confidence in everyone. He respected one and all and showed due regard to everyone, however small and insignificant one might be. Even the postman who delivered letters to the Institute was no exception. After Vijayadasami or some other such occasion, he would go straight to Swami Lokeswarananda's room, and Lokeswarananda would be so eager to feed him that the postman would feel shy and embarrassed. A monk who had never been close to Swami Lokeswarananda as a co-worker said: 'Once, I went to Narendrapur and I saw Lokeswarananda asking a worker, "Do you think such-and-such film could be shown at such-and-such place?" The way he said those words—so soft and sweet—fascinated me.'

Swami Lokeswarananda was always sweet-spoken, an outright gentleman. He could be firm when necessary but never rude. He attached tremendous importance to perfect behaviour. He said, 'You can hurt a person more by rude words than by hitting him.' He always put emphasis on the proper way of speaking—that is, with humility and sweetness.

Another characteristic of Swami Lokeswarananda was his patience and calmness. Even when a situation was very difficult and challenging, he would remain unperturbed. When others felt agitated, he would never lose his composure. He once told a distinguished person, 'Whenever you get excited, you lose ground to your opponent.' He could also endure great physical suffering. Right after his gall bladder operation he caught a cold, and during a bout of coughing the stitches broke open. But he asked his attendant not to disturb the doctors at night. As a result, he suffered from pain the whole night. Swami Lokeswarananda guided his fellow monks and workers not so much by rules as by love. He had faith in them and allowed everyone freedom in his work. He did not like the workers briefing him at every step or consulting him frequently. He wanted everyone to understand his responsibility and to carry on with self-confidence. A monk who grew up under his guidance said, 'If he gave someone the responsibility for something, he would fully back him up. Lokeswarananda would say: "Go ahead. Do not be afraid. I told you to do it, so the responsibility is mine."'

Like a mother to her children, his love was for one and all. Many might have misused his love, but he could not help loving them anyway. It was not that he did not know their shortcomings. But in spite of everything he loved them. He would take on himself the sufferings of so many people, and, like Shiva, he had to absorb much poison. So many people broken in spirit were inspired by him to stand up again. He did this by talking to them or by calling them every day on the phone. Even people who were shallow, who did not care much for religion, were not unworthy of his love. They would later be surprised to see themselves changed. They did not even know when self-confidence and discipline appeared in their lives. They knew they were not the same person any more, and they discovered a deeper meaning to life.

Swami Lokeswarananda felt that a monk must be large-hearted. To him, religion meant Love. Therefore, a heartless person, in spite of possessing all other qualities, was neither a proper monk nor a true devotee in his eyes. He encouraged devotees, including housewives, to study regularly. His idea was that a person should try to remain on an intellectually higher level.

He loved a daring and adventurous spirit. During the centenary celebrations of Swami Vivekananda's Chicago addresses, a worker of the Institute along with three other young men of his locality went around India on bicycles. Swami Lokeswarananda encouraged them to go ahead. He used to say: 'We must encourage them. Swamiji liked this sort of adventurous spirit.' A few days before he passed away, a boy from Uttarpara who planned to tour the world on a bicycle came to see him. Lokeswarananda talked to him for a long time and presented him a bicycle.

He was also fond of sports—especially cricket. Sometimes, in the middle of the night he would come to the television room to find out the score of the match. Those who had stayed up late to watch television would be embarrassed to see him. He particularly wanted to see Sachin Tendulkar. If Sachin went out with a low score, Lokeswarananda would say, 'Oh! He is out. He should have done better.' He would then lose all interest in watching the game any longer. He had a rare ability to study and watch television at the same time. There was no pretension in it. He actually could translate an Upanishad while watching television. He also had a very good sense of humour. He himself could be humorous, and at the same time he enjoyed good humour. But he never indulged in frivolous or cheap fun. And, he was always careful not to hurt anyone even in a joke.

The last few years Lokeswarananda was immersed in the Upanishads. 'I even dream of the Upanishads in my sleep,' he used to say. He had finished translating nine Upanishads into English and was working on the tenth. The characteristic of his Upanishads was their simple presentation of the highest philosophical truths. Swami Vivekananda had said that the truths of the Upanishads should be presented in such a way so that even a child could understand them. Lokeswarananda's Upanishads fulfil this. It is perhaps not possible to present the Upanishads in a simpler manner. He had also completed translating these Upanishads into Bengali, but did not live to see them published. (The Bengali Upanishads were published a week after his passing away by the most renowned publisher of West Bengal.) He used to say, 'The purpose of my translating the Upanishads into Bengali is so that even housewives can understand them.'

In the last year of his life, Swami Lokeswarananda was very busy acquiring the adjoining property, Bedi-bhavan. On 25 October 1998, the Ramakrishna Mission Institute of Culture got possession of one-third of the Bedi-bhavan property. But two days later the people who had occupied the land appealed in court and got a stay order on it, which was not lifted before Lokeswarananda passed away. He had many dreams about how to make the best use of the land. He planned to install a statue of Sister Nivedita in the Corporation Park adjoining the

Bedi-bhavan land, and work on it was almost completed when he left his body. (On 12 January 1999 the statue there was dedicated.)

Swami Lokeswarananda's health was surprisingly good for his age. Immediately after coming to Gol Park from Narendrapur, he had to undergo two consecutive operations—one for his gall bladder and one on his prostate. But for a long time after that he kept fairly well. When he was at Narendrapur, he could walk long distances in that vast property, but in the confined area of Gol Park, he had no such scope. Hence, he put on some weight after coming to the Institute. (His weight was 85 kg and height 6 feet just before he passed away.)

But in the early 1980s he was diagnosed as having 90% blockage in both the carotid arteries which carry blood to the brain, and he went to England and Canada for treatment. There the doctors were divided on whether to operate on him or not, but they finally decided not to. At that time Swami Lokeswarananda was introduced to a well-known neurosurgeon, Dr Ramprasad Sengupta, who later became an ardent admirer of his. As time passed the blockage in the arteries increased to 95%, and he had to take some drugs to keep things under control. But that did not affect his normal busy schedule or his power of thinking.

From August to December 1998, Swami Lokeswarananda was back in his old form. Classes work, meeting visitors—everything went on in full swing. Many of his former students had settled abroad, and whenever they came to India for a visit, they did not miss a chance to see their 'Baro Maharaj'. Seeing him this time, after hearing reports about his illness, they were very happy and went back and informed the other students and devotees of Maharaj that he was keeping well.

In November 1998, Swami Lokeswarananda visited Kamarpukur and Jayrambati for a day, and while paying his homage to Thakur at Kamarpukur, burst into tears. With folded hands he kept staring at Thakur for a long time. He was so anxious to visit the Ramachandra temple at Maslandapur that he visited the temple on 22 November and then again on 17 December.

Monday, 14 December, was the birth anniversary of his guru Swami Sivananda. Each year Swami Lokeswarananda would go to Belur Math in the morning and then to Barasat, the birth place of Swami Sivananda, in the evening.

Every year, on Christmas Eve, Swami Lokeswarananda would preside over the Christmas Eve meeting at Vivekananda Hall. But this year he said he could not do it as he was not feeling well. Someone else presided in his place.

The next day was the annual reunion of former students of Narendrapur and Pathuriaghata. Maharaj was feeling feverish that day, but went all the same. All the former students got together at Brahmananda Bhavan, and their joy knew no bounds seeing their 'Baro Maharaj' with them. Baro Maharaj was also very happy. He said to them: 'I feel proud to see you. You are settled all over India and outside. I do not know how long I shall live. The doctors say I am a miracle. Do you know how much I work at this age of mine? How much I study! You also, please work hard. And do not forget Thakur—Thakur, Ma, Swamiji.'

On the morning of 28 December, Maharaj said, 'I have been feeling some pain in my abdomen all morning.' Immediately, he was admitted to the Kothari Nursing Home. The doctors examined Lokeswarananda and diagnosed the pain to be caused by an obstructed ventral hernia and operated upon him. The pain subsided gradually, but due to the high fever he spoke rather incoherently. At 8 pm other monks came from the Institute and told him, 'Maharaj, the Surendra Paul lecture was a big success.' Swami Lokeswarananda listened to them with a big smile on his face.

Dr Ramprasad Sengupta came at 9:30 pm. He had arrived in Calcutta the previous day, and when he heard about Maharaj's illness he came to visit him. Swami Lokeswarananda was delighted to see him and said, 'O Dr Sengupta, how are you?' He then enquired about his wife, his daughter, and even his pet dog, calling the dog by its name. Then, he asked a monk present to give Dr Sengupta some dinner. This was a special characteristic of Swami Lokeswarananda—he loved to feed people. Nobody could get away from him without having something to eat.

A few minutes after this, Swami Lokeswarananda suddenly had a severe attack of respiratory distress. His face turned blue. Doctors immediately got the nebuliser ready. He said: 'Give me my rosary. Bring me Thakur's photograph.' His face was then covered with the nebuliser mask. There was no way of knowing if he wanted to say something. But the brahmachari attendant standing beside him faintly heard him repeating, 'Ma, Ma, Ma.' Maharaj was then put on an artificial respirator and was sedated to minimize the pain. There was no change in his condition on 29 and 30 December.

Early in the morning of 31 December Maharaj had another attack of respiratory distress followed by a heart attack. As his condition rapidly deteriorated, Belur Math authorities were informed. At 6:30 am, with the consent of attending doctors, Ganga water was poured in his mouth by a monk. The doctors tried to revive him till the last. At 7:25 am they declared, 'Maharaj has left his body.' The message was immediately sent to the Institute and to Belur Math.

By 8 am monks began coming to the Kothari Nursing Home from Belur Math and other nearby centres. Maharaj was brought to the Institute and was kept in the foyer beneath Vivekananda Hall. The news of his departure had already been broadcast over the radio. Innumerable devotees rushed to the Institute in tears to pay their respects to Maharaj. Monks from nearby Ramakrishna Mission centres also arrived.

The President of India sent a condolence message: 'In the passing of Swami Lokeswarananda we have lost a scholar – sage, whose compassion was as great as his vast learning. He was a shining example of the ethos of the Ramakrishna Mission... When I called on him some weeks ago, he was as immersed in programmes for the spread of the Mission work as always, regardless of his debilitated health. His loss will be hard to reconcile to.' The Hon'ble Chief Minister of West Bengal, Sri Jyoti Basu, a personal friend of Swami Lokeswarananda, also sent a condolence message. He wrote: 'He has worked tirelessly in the field of education and service of man... His absence will be strongly felt in this state.'

Others who paid their last tribute were ministers such as Mr Buddhadev Bhattacharya and Mr Ashoke Bhattacharya, the musician Ajoy Chakraborty, Swami Devananda Saraswati of the Gita Prachar Mandali, Bharat Sevashram Sangha, Sahara India, the Asiatic

Society, the Governor of West Bengal, the *Anandabazar* newspaper, and representatives of many other small and large organisations. Representatives of newspapers, television stations, and private television channels came to cover the news.

All day and night, devotees poured in to pay their last tribute to Maharaj. Police took charge to control the crowd, which at times entered in waves. On 1 January 1999, all the newspapers published the message along with Maharaj's picture and obituary on the very first page. At 1:30 pm, Swami Lokeswarananda's body was taken to Narendrapur Ramakrishna Mission with a police escort. All along the way, people lined up along the roads with folded hands to pay their homage. Some threw flowers at the funeral bus. At Narendrapur, the bus was driven around the campus to all the departments. Then his body was taken inside the school building and kept there for some time. The monks, teachers and their families, plus countless villagers from the neighbouring areas paid their homage. Then at 4:30 pm, the funeral convoy left Narendrapur for Belur Math. The scene was the same as before on both sides of the roads in Calcutta through which the convoy passed.

As the convoy reached Belur Math, a large crowd of devotees was seen waiting there. Standing in a long line, controlled by the police, the devotees paid their last respects. After taking prasad at night, the monks and brahmacharis carried the sacred body of Maharaj to Sri Ramakrishna's temple. From there it was taken to Mahapurush Maharaj's temple, Swamiji's room, Raja Maharaj's temple, and finally to Mother's ghat. His sacred body was then bathed in the Ganga. The great *karmayogi* lay there peacefully. His body was kept in front of Mother's temple for a while and then carried to the burning ghat. On the way, Revered President Maharaj, Swami Ranganathananda, came out to see his brother disciple for the last time and paid his tribute.

At the burning ghat, the funeral pyre was ready. The fire was lighted a few minutes to ten, and the monks and brahmacharis began singing bhajans. Defying severe cold, many devotees were still present. The sacred body had gone back to its elemental form.

Swami Lokeswarananda often said: 'I want to die in harness. I refuse to lie crippled.' His wish was fulfilled. Even on 28 December, he had translated a portion of the *Brihadaranyaka Upanishad*, and also gave dictation while leaving for the hospital in a wheelchair. Once, Swami Lokeswarananda told his attendant, who had been with him for 32 years: 'Be fearless. If you are afraid, you will lag behind. Always keep your head high. Do not you know what the soldiers do in the battlefield? They walk on even when fatally wounded. You have to be like them.' Swami Lokeswarananda did just that. He always walked on with unfailing steps towards the goal. 'Maharaj' has gone, but he has left behind an exemplary life dedicated to the ideals of Swami Vivekananda.

* Based on the book *Swami Lokeswarananda: A Life Dedicated to God and Man*, published during his condolence meeting, 1999.